# ABIGAIL and JOHN ADAMS

## The Americanization of Sensibility

G. J. BARKER-BENFIELD

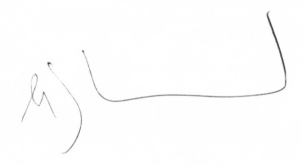

*The University of Chicago Press*  CHICAGO AND LONDON

G. J. BARKER-BENFIELD is professor of history at the State University of New York at Albany. He is the author of several books, including *The Culture of Sensibility: Sex and Society in Eighteenth-Century Britain*.

The University of Chicago Press, Chicago 60637
The University of Chicago Press, Ltd., London
© 2010 by The University of Chicago
All rights reserved. Published 2010

Printed in the United States of America

20 19 18 17 16 15 14 13 12 11 10      1 2 3 4 5

ISBN-13: 978-0-226-03743-1 (cloth)
ISBN-10: 0-226-03743-6 (cloth)

Library of Congress Cataloging-in-Publication Data

Barker-Benfield, G. J.
  Abigail and John Adams : the Americanization of sensibility /
G. J. Barker-Benfield.
    p. cm.
  Includes bibliographical references and index.
  ISBN-13: 978-0-226-03743-1 (cloth : alk. paper)
  ISBN-10: 0-226-03743-6 (cloth : alk. paper)  1. Adams, Abigail,
1744–1818.  2. Adams, John, 1735–1826.  3. Sentimentalism.
4. United States—Social life and customs—To 1775.  5. United
States—Social life and customs—1775–1783.  6. United States—
Social life and customs—1783–1865.  I. Title.
  E322 .B37 2010
  973.4'4092—dc22
  [B]
                                          2010008035

♾ The paper used in this publication meets the minimum requirements of
the American National Standard for Information Sciences—Permanence of
Paper for Printed Library Materials, ANSI Z39.48-1992.

Oh, happy state! when souls each other draw,
When love is liberty, and Nature law:
All other is full, possessing, and possessed,
No craving void left aching in the breast:
Even thought meets thought ere from the lips it parts,
And each warm wish springs aching from the heart.

*Pope, "Eloisa to Abelard" (1717)*

If I could write as well as you my sorrows would be
as eloquent as yours, but upon my Word I cannot.

*John to Abigail (1775)*

I have to combat encourage and Sooth the mind of
my young companion whose passions militate with
acknowledged duty and judgement.

*Abigail to John, referring to their daughter,*
*Abigail Adams Jr. (1784)*

# CONTENTS

# ACKNOWLEDGMENTS

A number of people at my home institution, the State University of New York at Albany, have assisted in the creation of this book. Scott Rummler and Irene Andrea, the staff of the Department of History, helped me in a variety of ways. Aaron Robinson enthusiastically checked quotations. J. Mike Bewsher supplied valuable technical librarianship, and, as always, I have depended on Seung Ill Bae and his staff at our Interlibrary Loan Office. Professor Edelgard Wulfert, dean of the College of Arts and Sciences, gave a generous subvention to the University of Chicago Press, matched in this by Professor Richard Hamm, chair of my department, who has been generous with other very practical aid. University administrators have always granted me vital sabbatical semesters, for which I am always grateful.

Patty Smith of the Adams National Historic Site was generous and prompt in supplying the reproduction of Nabby Adams's portrait. Elaine Grubin, reference librarian at the Massachusetts Historical Society, was very helpful.

Lori Saba typed all the manuscript through its many versions, along with the side manuscripts to which I refer in the notes, devoting years of skill, patience, and thoughtfulness to me and my execrable handwriting. Remaining errors are all mine.

After Lori, the first reader of the whole was Douglas Mitchell, my acquisitions editor at Chicago, with whom I have worked since the 1970s. His observations on an earlier version were salutary, if not traumatic, the more so since his most salient quality is his extraordinary and learned encouragement. He persuaded me to rethink and reorder the whole thing. It was a unique pleasure to deliver the manuscript to him in Chicago because I was able to listen to his masterly drumming at Jimmy's.

Doug found two excellent readers in James Walvin and Andrew

Burstein. Professor Walvin's sympathy with and understanding of the manuscript's purpose, along with his gently expressed criticism, were heartening; he read it anonymously, but I have known and admired his unique range and volume of work for years. Professor Burstein, a historian of Jefferson's sensibility, prompted me to add to the material on Jefferson, and I followed nearly all his other suggestions, to the great benefit of the whole.

Tim McGovern ably directed the transformation of the manuscript, leading a stellar cast for the Press: Joseph Brown combined thoroughness with speed in his superb copyediting; Kate Frentzel was Joe's house liaison; Matt Avery designed the cover; Joe Claude is described by Tim as "the mastermind of the production process"; and Levi Stahl was the result's promotions manager. My great good fortune in having the University of Chicago Press publish *The Culture of Sensibility: Sex and Society in Eighteenth Century Britain* in 1992 has now been doubled.

I hope my notes adequately acknowledge my biggest intellectual debts, although I am pretty sure that I have inadvertently omitted some names, for which I most sincerely apologize.

Beyond this direct reliance, I take great pleasure in acknowledging my lifelong reliance on the hearts and heads of the friends, both within the academy and outside it, who have inspired and sustained me in history since my schooldays in London through my studenthood at Cambridge and Los Angeles and teaching jobs in New York, Washington, DC, Portland, Oregon, and here in Albany. Most immediate are Tony and Tere Axou, John Callahan, Larry Friedman, Michael Hollington, Linda Katz, Warren Roberts, and Larry Wittner. Thor Wickstrom generously permitted the reproduction of his portrait of me. I refrained from inflicting this manuscript on any of them, but, without them, I could not have written it.

To my acknowledgment of their loving influence I wish to add the acknowledgment of my remaining family, chiefly in Austria, there headed by Ingrid and now three generations strong. I wish also to acknowledge the deep impact of my beloved daughter, Chloe. I suspect that my sympathy and admiration for Nabby was influenced by Chloe as she reached the age when Nabby began to break out.

Donald Meyer has been my mentor, inspiration, and friend since I first met him at the University of California, Los Angeles, in 1963 until today. He is the true doyen of historians of gender, all of whom should read his *Sex and Power: The Rise of Women in America, Russia, Sweden, and Italy.*

Linda Layne, my brilliant, beautiful, and loving dance partner, has heard a great deal too much of what follows; her comments on its introduction, the only part I asked her to read, were characteristically and inimitably constructive. Because my own prosaicism cannot do justice to her, the dedication is accompanied by lines from one of Byron's poems, "Stanzas for Music."

# INTRODUCTION

## The Subjects

John Adams (1736–1826) was absent from Abigail Adams (1744–1817) for years at a time, more than any other leader of the American Revolution was away from his wife, except Ben Franklin: hence the sheer number of letters between them. The Adamses wrote frequently about a variety of subjects in several ways, but my interest is in the language they used to express their feelings, most evidently about being apart, and I have concentrated on that period of apartness. The language was that of "sensibility."

To writers and speakers of the Adamses' status and era, the word *sensibility* meant a highly developed capacity for what they called *feeling*. Such a capacity was for particular feelings, by no means the full spectrum of possible emotions or "passions." The feelings registered and aggrandized by cultivators of sensibility were those signifying certain emotional pains or pleasures in oneself or in others: in the former category were feelings of suffering hurts (called *wounds*, *pangs*, or *stings*, e.g.) caused by the actions or behavior of others, especially unfeeling people; grief; nostalgia, and the pangs caused by parting, these latter feelings mixtures of pain and pleasure. On the more evidently pleasurable side were sympathy, compassion, pity, tenderness, and benevolence, although all these still referred to pain, the pain of others.

Men and women of feeling took pleasure in art: in certain kinds of music, for example, and in literature, notably in that poetry and fiction and those sermons that helped propagate knowledge of the value to be placed on these feelings and knowledge of how they were to be spoken or written of. Akin to this artistic category of stimulants to feeling and, therefore, self-consciousness were the acquisition and enjoyment of the proliferating, commercially generated material goods associated with the consumer revolution, to be located most notably in newly domestic interiors, one context for a different kind of childrearing. Persons of feeling spoke positively of "indulgence" in the "luxury" of feeling, although ideally none of these feelings were to be excessively indulged. Of central importance were the feelings generated in oneself by one's "moral sense"—itself a feeling—that is, consciousness of virtue and pleasure in doing good (*complacency* then had a positive connotation), obviously mingled with sympathy, compassion, benevolence, and so forth. An examination of the *Adams Family Correspondence* shows how Abigail and John perpetuated these conventional meanings and put them to their own use. That is the first subject of this book.

The second is the emergence and Americanization of the culture expressed by the language of sensibility. That language was English, being modified in ways beyond the modifications I describe, to become American English. Evidently, both voluntary and involuntary immigrants brought different languages from a range of European and African cultures. As Winthrop D. Jordan wrote, they faced a "voracious dominance of English language, customs, and institutions" sustained by "English numerical superiority." He quotes a Swedish Moravian minister who, in 1745, visited the Delaware River and found that "English did 'swallow up' other peoples."[1] By no means was this process uncontested, as more recent social historians have shown. In a moment, I shall refer to some linguistic variations of class and race, but they were variations in modified English.

While I have focused intensively on Abigail and John, the two of their children who left substantial, written records, that is, Abigail Amelia and John Quincy, and other kin and acquaintances, I have reached out beyond their circle to other people who used this language. I have also pulled back to supply larger geographic and chronological perspectives in order to define the subject.

Describing how proponents of sensibility in Britain drew their terms from religious, scientific, and literary sources, associated them with the material and domestic conditions enhanced by the consumer revolution, implemented them in "manners," in religion, and in reform (most saliently in the attempted reform of sexual relations), and passed them on in a new kind of childrearing, I made the case in *The Culture of Sensibility* (1992) that *sensibility* stood for a culture rather than a mere cult, as many previous writers had suggested.[2] Members of the white, literate, Anglophone elites in Britain's American colonies saw themselves sharing in this culture, but, largely because of the Revolution, they made it American.

Inevitably, such a study casts light on the Adamses' marriage as it was in those years of separation—above all, between 1775 and 1784—that John threw himself into revolutionary activities and then into lengthy negotiations in Europe on behalf of the new nation. In the latter year, Abigail rejoined John and their eldest son, John Quincy, bringing their only daughter with her. Abigail and John were frequently apart, moreover, from before their marriage in 1764 until 1800, when Thomas Jefferson defeated John's wish for a second term as president. Here, I will say something of the historiography of John and Abigail's marriage.

The year after John's death in 1826, a Boston journal wrote of Abigail that she had been "a valuable and critical instrument in critical times, diminishing the political burdens that pressed upon her husband and so far aiding him to promote the general welfare." Readers gained edited access to the couple's correspondence when their grandson, Charles Francis Adams, published *Familiar Letters of John Adams and His Wife, Abigail Adams, during the Revolution* in 1876, the Revolution's centennial year. His text was the basis for *The Book of Abigail and John: Selected Letters of the Adams Family, 1762–1784*; the placement of her name in that selection's title and the editors' removal of the "crust of Victorian propriety" with which Charles Frances Adams had coated his marked the fact that this was a 1975 celebration.[3]

Those editors described the popularization that Charles Francis Adams's selection had initiated: "Within a short time, letters selected from the volume began to appear in popular collections and 'libraries of choice reading'; and down to our own time—the texts as published in 1876 having long since passed into the public domain—compilers of anthologies for school and college use have reprinted selections from the Adams correspondence." So these editors could begin their selection by writing: "John and Abigail, Abigail and John—their names are inseparably linked as those of any human pair in history, or for that matter in legend or literature." They are "the prototypical American couple." Somehow this couple is older than other candidates for prototypicality, perhaps because their Victorian grandson desexualized them, but perhaps because they were not "inseparably linked" until middle age. "Aware of the resonant chords of feeling he was striking" in his nineteenth-century readers (perhaps in deliberate echo of "the mystic chords of memory, stretching every battlefield," which Lincoln had invoked in all Americans in his first inaugural address in 1861, prior to the outbreak of civil war), Charles Francis Adams published the letters recording his grandparents' "fortitude, their sacrifices, their public and private wisdoms—

and yes, their unexpected charm and humour, too"—as they "won their way through the long struggle for independence." This perspective—that of a triumphant safe harbor—has the effect of reducing and justifying their years of suffering, Abigail's especially, as they experienced them at the time.[4] The editors of the *Book of Abigail and John* remarked that, "with astonishingly few exceptions," John and Abigail Adams "read each other's minds as well as they read each other's letters across any extent of land or water."[5]

In his 1962 biography of John, Page Smith suggested that Abigail was able to exercise a powerful influence on John across all that distance, "giv[ing] him, with her love, a gyroscope that brought him safely through the stormiest seas." And, in his widely popularized 2001 biography, David McCullough followed Smith in claiming that Abigail brought "a beneficial, steadying influence" to bear on him.[6] But other students of the Adamses, able to benefit from their own reading of the complete *Adams Family Correspondence* (beginning publication in 1963) and the *Diary and Autobiography of John Adams* (1961), both edited by teams headed by Lyman H. Butterfield, could disagree with Page Smith, even debunk mythology. One of them was Peter Shaw, the author of *The Character of John Adams* (1976), an unflinchingly psychological study concentrating on Adams's public career. Reviewing on their appearance in 1973 volumes 3 and 4 of the *Adams Family Correspondence*, which covered the period April 1778–September 1782, when John and Abigail were entirely apart except for three months in 1779, Shaw noted that the letters reveal the "self-sacrifice" John claimed by his "diplomatic adventures" in France and Holland "involved a temporary but significant estrangement from his wife." He refers to John's neglect of his family and quotes Abigail's outburst in "their quarrel" over it. In sum: "Both partners suffered a loss of feeling during their ordeal of separation." Shaw wrote that Abigail found compensation for the "certain feelings" that John's absence denied her by expressing "emotions" to the Massachusetts congressman James Lovell.[7]

In his 1980 biography of Abigail, Charles W. Akers wrote of "Abigail's agony at the prospect of a new widowhood" in 1778, when John first sailed for France, although, in their first ten years together, "John and Abigail . . . achieved the fullest equality permitted by their society." McCullough would echo this in writing that Abigail "was in all respects his equal." The following year, Lynne Withey's biography asked "why Abigail and John continued to subject themselves to such long separations," which "made them both miserable." Withey supplied each with a different answer. John was driven by "his own ambition and a heightened sense of patriotism." While Abigail also "endured personal misery for the sake of their country's cause," her motives lay in her relationship to him: she "basked in John's glory"; loving John "as deeply as any woman loved any man," she "realized" John's "deep need for political involvement and recognition and could not bring herself to stand in his way." She was in a double bind: "Miserable when he was gone, she would have been equally miserable if he had stayed unwillingly and lived out a life of thwarted ambition." Phyllis Lee Levin's 1987 biography of Abigail gave a bleak picture of the effects of John's absence on her and included a chapter entitled "This Cruel State of Separation," a phrase taken from Abigail's letters. Rosemary Keller took another, "Badges of My Unhappiness"—meaning John's "Honours"—as the title of a chapter of her 1994 book on Abigail. Abigail "experienced severe difficulties in resigning herself to John's continued absence," and Keller refers to Abigail's "resentment" and "anger and fear that his commitment to her was waning." In the first of her two biographies of Abigail, Edith B. Gelles held in 1992 that the Adamses' marriage has been made "legendary" and mythologized as an "ideal."[8]

John Ferling's very thorough *John Adams: A Life*, also published in 1992, paid unidealizing attention to the Adamses' marriage, to John's motives for leaving Abigail aside, to her reaction, and to her life apart from him. Intending to describe "the total man," indeed, interpreting his absenting himself from his wife in pursuit of public recognition as the expression of doubts about his manhood, Ferling declared that John's "absences from his wife were deplorable, his virtual abandonment of some of his children during the long war years . . . unconscionable."[9]

Margaret A. Hogan and C. James Taylor, the editors of the most recent successor to Charles Francis Adams's selection of his grandparents' letters, *My Dearest Friend: Letters of Abigail and John Adams* (2007), again aimed at a more popular audience, write that Abigail's letters "during those wrenching periods of loss are truly pathetic and underscore the great sacrifice she made while her husband served his nation."[10] Evidently hoping to capitalize on the great popularity of Joseph J. Ellis's recent books on founding fathers and founding brothers (which, along with McCullough's, have been called expressions of *founders chic*), the publisher of *My Dearest Friend* asked him for a foreword. Like previous popularizers, Ellis finds a lesson in the marriage of John and Abigail. It tells those "who want to understand how a husband and wife can sustain their love over a lifetime of struggle and tragedy" to read this "splendid story of an emotional and intellectual partnership."[11]

This year (2009), Gelles has published her third book describing Abigail's life, but this time she has combined it with an account of John's as *Abigail and John: Portrait of a Marriage*, "the first double biography of them . . . no one [having] written about Abigail and John in tandem." In the preface, she writes that their "marriage has been mythologized in American history" and that the myth was true: "Just the mention of Abigail and John calls forth an image of an ideal relationship, one founded upon love, loyalty, friendship, and courage, which it was." She describes Abigail's emotional pain (and John's), which she and others have described before, but she now detects in their letters the bases for Abigail and John's "negotiations" and "renogotiation" of their marriage and concludes with their joint entombment, "commemorating a marriage of enduring love and loyalty and duty to the nation." Readers of this book and Gelles's will notice that Gelles and I quote a number of the same passages from the *Adams Family Correspondence* but that, without exception, we put them to different use. We differ fundamentally, not only in our focus, but also in our understanding of the eighteenth century. Quoting a sentence Abigail wrote in 1784 to her sister Mary Smith Cranch about the word *feeling*, Gelles writes: "Abigail was groping for the language to express her emotions in an age that lacked an adequate vocabulary."[12]

## Organization

There are in this book three groups of chapters plus one chapter in conclusion. The first group, chapters 1–5, describes the origins of the vocabulary of feeling, its conventional meanings, and the social circumstances of its gendering. Gender was fundamental to the story of sensibility and is also fundamental to this book's organization.

British Americans, North and South, had drawn on the liberalized Protestantism evolving in England and Scotland after two traumatic revolutions in the mid- and late seventeenth century. It was a religion deeply influenced by Enlightenment science, including the science of human nature, which recognized the value of the passions and broke open questions of gender. The reevaluation of the passions coincided with the beginning rise of women. Chapter 1 first sketches the relevant features of this liberalized Protestantism (in England called *Latitudinarianism*) because those features were absorbed by the Adamses. Second, it describes the Adamses' responses to the most salient of the literature furthering the culture of sensibility. One cannot overestimate the power of reading to eighteenth-century literate minds. In outlining this religious and intellectual heritage, chapter 1 outlines the story of American colonists' adoption of this metropolitan culture.

Chapter 2 describes the conventional meanings the language of sensibility held for the Adamses, their circle, and other Americans. That they drew on words whose meaning and frequency pertained to a time and place makes the Adamses representative, in this broad sense. The language had been clearly gendered: chapter 3 provides an account of the Reverend James Fordyce's theory of sensibility's gendering given in his *Sermons to Young Women* (1766), which was published on both sides of the Atlantic. My immediate reason for paying Fordyce's book the degree of attention that I do is Abigail's great admiration for it; second, it manifests a clear existential explanation for sensibility's gendering in terms with which Abigail largely agreed. Because Mary Wollstonecraft saw such gendering as the most damaging form of the sexism she unraveled in *A Vindication of the Rights of Woman* (1792), she made Fordyce's highly influential *Sermons* (still authoritative in the 1790s) a target second only to Rousseau's *Emile* (1762).

John left Abigail at home because of the superior value he placed on the public stage. The metaphor with which the Adamses explained their respective evaluations of the public and the private was that of concentric circles, expanding from the innermost, the relation of husband and wife, to children, friends, neighbors, town, region, nation, and, the largest circle, "humanity." The meanings of these circles to the Adamses, in the framework supplied by Jürgen Habermas, is the subject of chapter 4. The chapter refers to the fact that women, at first, young urban ladies in Britain, from the late seventeenth century initiated the enjoyment of heterosocial minglings in a wider circle, the new public arenas sponsored by the consumer revolution, which also helped elevate the value of domesticity. Such public self-assertiveness provoked sharp and continuing reactions in those men and women who called themselves *reformers of manners* and whose views Fordyce represents. Women's pleasure seeking coincided with other forms of self-assertion, some of it expressly feminist. Women's thus entering "the world" to face male hostility and predation was emblematized by the contemporary preoccupation with "virtue in distress," the central trope of cultures of sensibility.[13]

Chapter 5 points to the fact that young ladies in British America, cog-

nizant of metropolitan British pleasures, also began to enjoy heterosocial scenes beyond the domestic circle, provoking similar reactions, and
not without ambivalence themselves. The chapter suggests how the Adamses and their kin addressed these circumstances.

The second group of chapters, chapters 6–10, concentrates on the
particular use to which Abigail, and then John, put the language of
sensibility, above all during John's separations from Abigail. (The distinction signified by *definitions* and *applications* in the titles of part I and
part II, respectively, is by no means hard-and-fast.) To luxuriate in the
feeling that was bound up with the pleasures of literacy and consumption was a kind of freedom women could experience; some of them associated it with a moral superiority from which they called on men to
reform by being more responsive to women. Chapter 6 explores Abigail's painful pleasure in her sensibility and her calls on John to show
more of it, and chapter 7 argues that her now well-known March 31,
1776, letter to John, asking him and his fellow delegates to the Continental Congress to "Remember the Ladies," can be seen as an expression
of the call for the reformation of men's manners that had existed for a
century on both sides of the Atlantic, Americanizing it in the revolutionary context. Her potential feminism was inflected by the culture of
sensibility. Chapter 8 shows that the language also supplied Abigail with
the means to protest the suffering John's absence caused her as well as to
attempt to reconcile herself to it.

Manhood's relation to sensibility is the subject of chapters 9 and 10.
John discovered his ambition and the means to pursue it amid the proliferating prospects newly enjoyed by his class. These means included "the
reformation of manners," a disciplinary program he applied to himself
and attempted to apply to the popular male culture focused on the tavern. John's self-conception as "a man of feeling" and his apparent ambivalence over public versus private is complementary to chapter 8, which
describes those subjects in Abigail's terms. It concludes this group by
suggesting that the Adamses themselves, John especially, contributed
to the mythologizing of their marriage that has persisted in popular
representations.

The third group of chapters, chapters 11–13, suggests how sensibility
was implemented in childrearing and helped shape the teenaged Abigail
Adams Jr.'s courtship. John's absence on public business had a serious
impact on the rearing of the Adamses' four surviving children. Abigail
had to rear Abigail Jr., John Quincy, Charles, and Thomas Boylston as a
single parent, drawing on relatives and friends but also on the childrear-

ing text that is the opening subject of chapter 11. The chapter continues by sketching how Abigail, abetted by John, attempted to instill sensibility in her children, along with indicating the degrees of success. The story of young Nabby's courtship by Royall Tyler Jr., and its denouement in her marriage to Colonel William Smith, merits two chapters, chapters 12 and 13, because it offers a clear illustration of the power of tropes of sensibility to affect this most crucial transition in the lives of women of this era.

The concluding chapter, 14, discusses sensibility's "Americanization" in the forming of national identity, including its significance to the debates over race slavery. Here, I combine the evidence left by the Adamses and, in particular, by Jefferson, with recent historical scholarship to suggest how the culture of sensibility was further absorbed and adapted in the new republic and put to political use in the 1780s and 1790s. Concluding pages refer to the perpetuation and popularization of a sharply gendered sensibility into the nineteenth century's "culture of sentiment," although romantic writers and reformers of both sexes drew on the subversive potentials of feeling. It continued to coexist with that masculine popular culture that Constance Rourke identifies with the American "national character."[14]

Scholars of the literature of sensibility, from Herbert Ross Brown through Leslie Fiedler, Cathy Davidson, Julia A. Stern, Elizabeth Barnes, and Julie Ellison, for example, have shown how American writers (defined as such by the fact that they wrote after 1783 or 1789) adapted metropolitan sentimental models to make them American.[15] Garry Wills has shown the same process in describing the Declaration of Independence as a "Sentimental Paper," and Gordon S. Wood extends his definition of the republicanism that the "patriots" adapted from Britain to write that it helped originate "humanitarian sensibility" in America. Andrew Burstein shares this broad focus on documents beyond fiction to illustrate what he calls "the Americanization of sensibility." Sarah Knott uses the same phrase in *Sensibility and the American Revolution*, published as I was completing this manuscript, and I have been fortunate to be able to integrate some of her findings with my own. David Waldstreicher describes that process in his important *In the Midst of Perpetual Fetes*, showing the part played by proponents of sensibility in the book's subtitle, *The Making of American Nationalism, 1776–1820*. He points out the irony of such proponents' invention of "a nationalism that . . . depended upon ideologies and practices truly inherited from England." That these and other predecessors have been able to draw on such different kinds of evidence, as well as such a large amount of it, indicates the sheer salience of sensibility in America.[16]

## Cultural Borders

I have suggested throughout that the Adamses, and cultivators of sensibility generally, defined themselves against other cultures. To adapt what E. P. Thompson said of class, culture "entails a relationship," that is, between itself and other cultures, often within the same nation. Members of a culture have had experiences in common, have felt and articulated their "interests" against those felt and articulated by a contingent culture or cultures. There is always some overlap, even interpenetration— Thompson writes of "fluency" in class relations. He also confines himself to men in representing class consciousness.[17] Men and women of the same culture have had experiences and interests in common, but their common ground can be spasmodic and fluctuate in extent over time. Ubiquitously, women have been second to men (to invoke Simone de Beauvoir's great work); they have had different interests, "against" men of the same class and culture, alongside common ones.[18] Sometimes genders have had common interests across cultural borders. That sensibility brought women closer to men, and had the potential of bringing them even closer, had dynamic effects, a central interpretative theme as we shall see. I conclude this introduction by noting how proponents of sensibility construed three groups who bordered them culturally and whose lives differed from theirs in decisive dimensions: Native Americans, working-class whites, and African Americans.

The long-standing conflict between the European invaders (the New England Puritan ones already including themselves in Foxe's catalog of English "martyrs")[19] and the native inhabitants they called Indians gave rise to an American version of virtue in distress, that trope to which I referred earlier, a figure, usually female, subject to emotional or physical assaults. The first was Mary Rowlandson's account of her capture, captivity, and redemption published on both sides of the Atlantic in 1686, in the early years of the rise of Britons' culture of sensibility. Warfare between Indians and Europeans was continual in the colonial period through the Revolution, sometimes with high proportions of casualties on the European side, let alone the terrible death and enslavement rate among Indians, nearly all of whom were living in subsistence economies, their hard-worked women certainly unable to luxuriate in the sensibility enjoyed or aspired to by increasing numbers of European American, middle-class women from midcentury or before. It was a contrast Margaret Fuller was to make in 1843.[20]

Captivity narratives were "bestsellers everywhere in America" in the colonial period, and the "stories of Indian cruelties . . . slumbered in the minds of those that had been constantly agitated by them, . . . roused . . . to become this fearful topic of the fireside." There were in 1824 few Americans of "middle age who cannot distinctly recollect . . . sitting in a chimney corner when children, all contracted with fear, and there listening to their parents' relating stories of Indian conquests, and murders, that would make their flaxen hair stand erect, and almost destroy the power of motion," wrote the Reverend James Everett Seaver in New York. Stories by "white Indians"—captives—became a "staple" in Southern "folklore," too. According to Bernard Bailyn, the "popular literary idiom" of the narratives drove the fearfulness of captivity by Indians "deep into the American psyche." The experience and dread of Indian attacks and capture (including torture) were among the frontier circumstances that Rourke suggests stimulated that straight-faced, unsentimental, masculine culture of "American humor," against which American sentimentalists came to define themselves. But, as the Adams correspondence illustrates, these American stories coincided with Americans' reading of the archetypal novel, *Clarissa*, and its indigenous descendants. The correspondence also represents this assimilation of both versions of virtue in distress, that is, the white European captured by Indians and the virginal female threatened with rape, to revolutionary purpose and then to one aspect of national character, alongside that described by Rourke.[21]

Second, cultivators of sensibility in America (in this case, as in metropolitan Britain) saw themselves bordered by those historians can call *working-class*. I referred to the largely white, popular male culture based on the tavern: kindred, white, working-class women, domestic servants prominent among them, also having common ground with their middle- and upper-class female employers in the wish to see men's manners reformed, and aspiring to the sensibility of gentility, could not yet afford it. One writer in early-eighteenth-century America remarked: "It is no hard matter to distinguish between the depraved language of common People and the noble refin'd expression of the Gentry." The "common sort are rude or even barbarous." Kenneth Cmiel, who quotes this in his history of the rise of "democratic eloquence," notes that the eighteenth-century "eloquent gentleman or lady was supposed to have the cultivated sensibilities, the *humanitas* needed to check their . . . self-interest."

It was in "Thought, Word, or Deed," in John Adams's phrasing, that a person showed gentility. In his youth Adams reformed his manners: "I have been rash, boastful, prophane, uncivil, Blustering, threatening." He wished to gain respectable people's "warmest Words and assiduous Assistance . . . by using tender and soothing, instead of rough, and reproachful Language."[22]

The principal social arena for the expression of sensibility was among members of the elite and middle ranks, but they depended on the existence of the great mass of human beings still living in age-old misery, unable yet to enjoy enough of the consumer revolution to indulge themselves in the luxury of feeling. The *Spectator* reported in 1712 that in the same London street as people rolling in "luxury" lived "creatures" so miserable, hungry, and naked that one would think them "a different species." The same could be said of American cities later in the century, as their populations increased and diversified.[23] Frequently reprinted, and widely read on both sides of the Atlantic, the *Spectator* described the pleasurable feelings flowing from "the secret comparisons we make between ourselves and the person who suffers." The authors of the *Spectator* asked that their journal be "served up" every morning, "looked upon as part of the tea equipage." Literate, heterosocial circles were knit together in the polite sociability identified with sensibility by such fashionable reading and sugared, caffeinated beverages, produced and served to them by persons who endured contrasting social conditions.[24]

The scholars of American history who rightly insist on the "immense importance" of differences between gentlemen and ladies, on the one hand, and commoners of both sexes, on the other, do so in histories looking ahead in time to further embourgeoisement and even democratization. The spread of the culture of sensibility is implied. As the *Spectator* illustrates throughout, the rise of a culture of sensibility in Britain was interwoven with increasing consumption, which could amplify personal, psychological resources and help subvert the gentry's hegemony from early in the eighteenth century, or at least begin to open it up to the inclusion of more men. The same was true across the Atlantic. Richard L. Bushman describes the process there in *The Refinement of America*—his period being 1700–1850—and he suggests that "sentimental fiction played the most critical part in the extension of refinement to the middle class." Cmiel states that, "in the early nineteenth century, usage of *lady* and *gentleman* broadened to include all adults." Language—languages—manifested the tension between refinement and postrevolutionary egalitarianism, a subject to which Bushman devotes the conclusion of his history. In Cmiel's summary, in "speech there was vulgarity among the few and refinements amid the many."[25]

Of course, Americans lived predominantly in the countryside, including the "backcountry" (significantly not yet called a *frontier*), in the eighteenth and nineteenth centuries. The Reverend Charles Woodmason was an Anglican itinerant and a man of feeling inheriting values articulated by the *Spectator*, but eventually he presented himself as a spokesman for the white, backcountry folk of South Carolina; in 1767, he charged that the governing elite living "midst Scenes of Luxury and Dissipation" in Charleston treated his folk "not as brethren . . . but as if we were of a different Species from themselves," construing them merely as "Hewers of Wood and Drawers of Water." In Wood's summary of Woodmason's view, backcountry folk "had no benevolence and no feeling for one another." Then and later, white farmers lived hardscrabble, often immiserized lives, not conducive to indulgence in feeling.[26]

Christine Leigh Heyrman writes: "Southern whites of humble station were neither incurious about nor unaware of their innermost feelings. Yet most made it their practice neither to dwell daily on those emotions nor to express them often." Her explanation for this "habitual reserve" is that, at the end of the eighteenth century and the beginning of the nineteenth, most white Southerners "often lived on or near the margins of subsistence." They worked their land for domestic consumption, only secondarily growing tobacco and then cotton for commercial sale. Nor had they yet been participants in the demographic revolution, instead producing "large broods of children" for labor, conceiving and rearing them, not under the luxuriating circumstances that the middle class was increasingly able to relish, but "clustered in log cabins with only a few rooms" after exhaustingly laborious days. They "could never forget that death stalked life, as disease, accidents, and natural disasters took their grisly toll." They lived in dread of African Americans' "conspiracies and insurrections" and, in the West, of Indian attacks. Crowded "households set within a world of scarcity and danger did not permit most people the luxury of studying the heart and speaking its impulses." It was not that they did not feel but that "those constraints inclined [them] to . . . repress any emotions that might, if openly expressed, estrange them from relatives and neighbors upon whom their very survival often depended"—and Heyrman refers to the "inner cost" of such repression.[27]

Heyrman contrasts such deprived or repressed inner lives with those fostered by evangelicals—which are comparable to those of the culti-

vators of sensibility—pursued in the big houses of the Southern rich
as well as in cities and towns South and North. Evangelicals explored,
"regularly and relentlessly, the darker recesses of their hearts," adhering
to a "regimen of anxious introspection aimed mainly at inducing and
sustaining certain states of feeling." These may have been oriented to the
question of salvation or damnation, but, in contrast to their Calvinist
predecessors, the evangelicals' god embraced all who felt themselves re-
born. And, always, "the head followed the heart's lead," wherever evangelism took hold. There were other similarities between evangelical culture in the South and the culture of sensibility there and elsewhere, and
intermingling, too, as well as stark differences, but they are subjects that
I must leave aside.[28]

By definition, upward mobility required aspirants to demonstrate the
manners that accompanied the acquisition and use of consumer goods
(among them, books and tea equipment) that signified the possession of
sensibility. Domestic service was an important channel for the transmission of genteel behavior in the eighteenth century. Evidently, female and
male servants were socially ambitious long before the Revolution boosted
their claims to equality.[29] Abigail Adams occasionally found that servants'
positive response to her stimulated her own sensibility and even showed
a natural sensibility akin to hers. She wrote her sister Mary in 1767: "It
gives one a pleasing Sensation my Dear Sister, after haveing been absent
a little while to see one's self gladly received upon a return, even by one's
Servants. I do not know that I was ever more sensibly affected with it,
than I was to Day; I could behold joy Sparkle in the Eyes of every one of
them as I entered the House, whilst they unaffectedly express'd it some
to me and some to my Babe." She implied that being received in this way
by her social peers, let alone superiors, could have moved her still more.
Abigail continued with an account of the servants' other expressions of
joy, perhaps less ambiguous than eye sparkle: "One runs to the Door,
O Mam, I am glad to see you come home again, how do you do? Whilst
an other catches the child, and says Dear creature I was afraid she would
forget me, and a third hovers around and crys Nab, do you know Polly,
and will you come to her?—These little instances shew their regard, and
they endear them to us." The scene Abigail re-created represents her belief in a degree of common ground on the basis of unaffected feeling,
that is, natural and spontaneous, in implicit contrast to its affectation, the
danger of which proponents of sensibility were constantly suspicious.
Of course, servants and other subordinated groups were capable of the

"affecting" responses that power and convention required of them.[30] What Wood construes as "the general well-being and equality" of a relatively large middle class in colonial British North America, "set against the gross inequality and flagrant harshness of both white servitude and . . . black slavery," let alone the increasing gap between rich and poor in the cities, "made many people unusually sensitive to all the various dependencies and subordinations that lurked everywhere in their lives."[31]

Class differences, generating genuine sympathy or providing occasion for its display, were also valuable in elite classes' improvement of their sensibility, as the *Spectator* had suggested to its metropolitan readership. John Adams had found his sensibility improved by a scene to which his public life exposed him. One cold day in March 1767, he and Captain Eben Thayer paid a visit to Robert Peacock and his "poor distressed Family" in Boston, doing so in connection with their duties as recently elected selectmen of Braintree. "We found them, in one Chamber, which serves them for Kitchen, Cellar, dining room, Parlour, and Bedchamber," he recorded in his diary. The division of houses into specialized rooms associated with larger quantities of more comfortable and individualized furniture and furnishings, beginning to be significantly more widespread in the late seventeenth century, has been associated with the spread of individualism, including the intense self-consciousness signified by sensibility.[32] In John's view, that the Peacocks lived in a single room rather than in a house with rooms with discrete functions was itself a sign of their distress, although such cramped and poor conditions were on the increase in American cities, providing a dramatic contrast with the increase in more commodious, cleaner houses, where kitchen work was segregated from the owner's dining. It was in Boston where Abigail found the writing closet in which we shall see she could luxuriate in her feelings and in her writing about them, and, in subsequent years, she would devote herself to enlarging and making more comfortable and specialized the house over which she would preside, able, after her sojourn in roomy French and English mansions, to add more sophisticated, European furnishings.[33]

John's description of that 1767 scene is comparable to William Blake's later drawings of the London poor, typical of illustrations in sentimental literature wherein well-dressed, elite figures were shown charitably visiting distressed and ragged families, usually including children, living in conditions that shocked the visitors and, presumably, the pictures' viewers.[34] Peacock had been lying in one of the two beds for seven weeks, probably sick as well as freezing cold. As John recalled the scene: "He had a little Child in his Arms. Another Bed stood on one side of the Chamber where lay 3 other Children. The Mother only was up, by a fire, made of a few Chips, not larger than my Hand. The Chamber excessive cold and dirty." He expressed his feelings first by way of a series of implicit, ironic contrasts, punctuated by exclamation marks: "These are the Conveniences and ornaments of a Life of Poverty. These the Comforts of the Poor. This is Want. This is Poverty! These the Comforts of the needy. The Bliss of the Necessitous." But Adams and Thayer's job was to reduce Braintree's relief rolls. They found, "upon Enquiry, that the Woman and her two oldest Children had been warned out of Boston. But the Man had not, and 3 Children had been born since." The two Braintree selectmen were, on "this Discovery," able to acquaint "Coll. Jackson, the first Select Man of Boston," with "the facts" and, therefore, demand that Braintree "be excused for any Expense" for the Peacocks' support.[35]

The facts had an impact on Adams, even as they spared the public purse. "When I was in that Chamber of Distress," he reflected in the same diary entry, "I felt the Meltings of Commiseration." Such exposure, following Adams's accepting responsibility for the public good, brought him characterological rewards: "The Office of Overseer of the Poor leads a Man into scenes of Distress, and is a continual Exercise of the benevolent Principles in his Mind. His Compassion is constantly excited, and his Benevolence encreased." Such improving scenes could be staged and entered as Nabby and Abigail were to enter the foundling hospitals in London and Paris or, vicariously (but with the same improving purpose), by audiences' exposure to distressful scenes that novelists, dramatists, painters, and composers intended to stimulate sympathy, in accordance with the process that, as we shall note in chapter 1, was first explained by Descartes and other revolutionaries in the scientific study of human nature.[36] It was to stimulate this process that Jefferson advised his nephew to read Shakespeare and Sterne and Elizabeth Smith Shaw spelled it out to Abigail Adams, her sister.[37]

The combination of sympathetic identification and practical response to the growing gap between rich and poor in Boston that John Adams recorded in 1766 had been illustrated by a group of gentlemen there in 1754. They established the Society for Encouraging Industry and Employing the Poor. As their proposal put it: "Every Man of Sense must see and . . . deplore the Calamities that must arise from increasing Poverty, Idleness and Vice: but every Christian will feel the Miseries of such a State as if they were his own." The remedy they proposed was that poor women and children be put to work manufacturing linen, which would help Massachusetts's balance of trade with Britain and lessen the tax burdens on those supporting the poor as well as teach the poor "to become useful and valuable members of the community."[38] The politics of elected officials in New York in the period 1790–1860 evinced the same combination of sensibility and hardheadedness, as, indeed, these qualities had long been linked in the humanitarianism of British/American, commercial capitalism. In David Hume's phrase, there was a "happy concurrence" between the public good and private gain. The ability to qualify sensibility with such hardheadedness was seen to be more naturally a male strength.[39]

Abigail referred to those she deemed her social inferiors as "the Gaping vulgar," and John's explicit belief in inevitable social hierarchy, while common among republican gentlemen revolutionaries, became a political liability. In Abigail's mind, a distinct female sensibility was a mark of ladyhood. She wrote from aboard a ship in which she had been lucky enough to have shared quarters with gentlemen of delicacy: "Of this I am very sure, that no Lady would ever wish; or a second time [to] try the Sea." Her reason was that, at sea, "the decency and decorum of the most delicate female must in some measure yeald to the necessitys of Nature," that decorum an essential aspect of a lady's self-presentation to a gentleman. Later in the same letter, she referred to the "softness peculiarly characteristick of our sex and which is so pleasing to the Gentlemen," favorably to contrast American ladies with women she had encountered in London, who had laid it aside "for the Masculine attire and Manners of Amazonians."[40]

Abigail's account of her reception by her servants, and, for that matter, of the parting of the Adams family from their French servants at Auteil, resembled the fantasy of social harmony appearing in the British sentimental fiction she read, "a harmony in which hierarchy was fixed and accepted by the lower classes with joy. This fantasy ran counter not only to the widening gulf between rich and poor [in England], . . . but also to the class confusion and anxiety created by the powerful urges to emulation and social mobility." One can say something very similar about the mainland colonies in British North America, but the circumstances of their readers differed in three respects in addition to the history of relations with Native Americans: the significantly larger proportion of a middle class, the scope of slavery, and the social changes eventually opened up by the successful revolution.[41]

African Americans constituted the third cultural group against which white cultivators of sensibility defined themselves. Abigail's vision of her American and French servants' sensibility can be compared to Jefferson's daughter Martha's retrospective description of a scene from her father's life. The scene was one of reunion, its elements, previous loss and present togetherness, reversing those of parting, Jefferson's slaves welcoming him back to Monticello on his return from France in 1789: "The negroes discovered the approach of the carriage . . . and such a scene I had never witnessed in my life. . . . The moment [the carriage] was opened, they received him in their arms and bore him to the house, crowding around and kissing his hands and feet—some blubbering and crying others laughing. . . . They were the first ebullitions of joy for his return, after a long absence, which they would, of course, feel." That "negroes . . . would, of course, feel" illustrates potential in the white definition of sensibility on which antislavery capitalized, but Martha Jefferson Randolph showed that she shared her culture's particular racism in the extremity of terms here. Not only were "the Negroes" obstreperous in their shouting, and not only did they blubber, but it also seemed to her "impossible to satisfy their anxiety to touch and kiss the very earth which bore him." Martha also took the opportunity to comment on her father's slaves' general relationship to him: "It is not out of place here to add they, were at all times devoted in their attachment to him."[42] Jefferson had criticized the Afro-British author of *Letters of the Late Ignatius Sancho: An African* (1782) for his "wild and extravagant imagination," escaping "incessantly from every restraint of reason and taste," in his *Notes on the State of Virginia*, first published in Paris, four years before his slaves welcomed him back to Monticello with those "ebullitions of joy." Both Martha and Thomas illustrate Jan Lewis's characterization of the "sentimental mode" adopted by "the Virginia elite." The "formality required in the expression of feeling acted as a check upon the individual expression of emotion." While this "mannered display" stood in contrast to the emotionalism of lower-class revivalism to which I referred, its bearers also identified it with race.[43]

Jefferson's degrading of Sancho's writings was part of a debate over race slavery stimulated in large part by the elevation of the values of sensibility on both sides of the Atlantic, a subject of my concluding chapter. The relationship between some whites and some blacks in this regard illustrates the existence of cultural fluency and white resistance to it. Sancho, born on a slave ship, had been raised since babyhood in literate, upper-class households in England, wrote in the idiom of sensibility, and became known as "a man of feeling," though "African," though "black." Comparably, when, in 1794, black Philadelphians were excluded from an account of the heroically sympathetic efforts of a "band of brothers" to help the victims of the yellow fever epidemic and, moreover, were accused of exploiting them, the Reverends Richard Allen and Absalom Jones, leaders of the black community, retorted that they had "seen more humanity, more real sensibility from the poor blacks, than from the poor whites." Knott remarks that this "most public exchange . . . turned on sensibility." We can note that, during the eighteenth century, campaigners against slavery adapted the terms that campaigners for the reformation of manners applied to class differences, applying them to perceived racial difference.[44]

Firsthand accounts of the middle passage—the continuous physical violence, the rapes, the deaths of children, and, perhaps most of all, the continual breakup of families by enslavers, traders, and owners—were utterly suited to the language and tropes of the culture of sensibility. That culture had come into existence on other bases, but it coincided with Britain's extension of empire since the revolution of 1688, coupled with the rise of consumerism.

In 1939, Wylie Sypher made the case that the Reverend Francis Hutcheson's *System of Moral Philosophy* (1734–41) forced the "collapse" of all previous arguments that had rationalized slavery, dating back to Aristotle. Hutcheson did so by applying "the ethics of feeling" to enslavement: "men are perhaps akin in reason, but more akin in capacity to suffer wrong." Thirty years later, David Brion Davis insisted that Sypher's case should have been identified with the British religious tradition, in effect originating in the Latitudinarianism that generated "the man of feeling" ideology, which Davis describes as a religious source of antislavery thought.[45] Soon, it would be acted on by women of feeling, too, "a great silent army" of them, in fact, expressing themselves in the same terms of sensibility.[46]

As Abigail Adams recognized, and as her son John Quincy, along with the Jeffersons, illustrated, persons of sensibility could be racists, too, whatever their views of slavery. The contrasting appearances and lives of whites and blacks nourished the self-aggrandizing complacency of sensibility as well as its reformative potentials.[47]

Sancho, Allen, and Jones were exceptional in their relative freedom, their literacy, and their location in leading eighteenth-century commercial entrepôts. The same was true of the poet Phillis Wheatley. Bushman describes the coming into existence of a free "black elite" by the second or third decade of the nineteenth century "in virtually every [American] city, North and South." Subject to vicious caricature by whites, these "families at the top," Bushman believes, "adopted all the forms of respectability that middle-class whites were bringing into their lives at the same period." Ladies adopted "the genteel code," and, as Bushman makes clear, that code included middle-class and feminine sensibility.[48] Brenda E. Stevenson, concentrating on postrevolutionary and antebellum Loudon County, Virginia, suggests that "many slave women" also held notions of behavior resembling white women's but that they were in no position to implement them.[49] If in the eighteenth and nineteenth centuries poor white families did not enjoy the material and psychological luxury on which bourgeois families could capitalize in their cultivation of sensibility, how much more was that the case for the vast majority of enslaved African American families? Philip D. Morgan demonstrates that "eighteenth-century, North American slaves experienced a Spartan material existence." Overwhelmingly, African Americans' part in the consumer revolution was that of producers of addictive, literally consumable items—tobacco, sugar, and coffee—as well as rice and other crops and then, from century's end, of the cotton for mass-produced clothing. The contrast between the pleasure in consuming such items and the knowledge of the misery of the slaves who produced them helped animate humanitarianism.[50] "The ironic images of slavery were there for all to see," writes James Walvin of those households that owned slaves or hired Africans. Black servants, like Sancho or Jefferson's domestic slaves in Virginia (drawn from his Hemings relatives), "carried the tea services, including the sugar bowls, and fetched their masters' pipes, just as their contemporaries toiled in the fields to bring forth those same natural products."[51]

The contrast in marital lives was as stark. If eventually the evening out of the sex ratio and the creolization of the population mitigated the destructive effects of the first phases of British-American mainland settlement, protracted for over a century through the Chesapeake colonies, the Carolinas, and Georgia, African American family relations were always subject to destruction by sale, let alone sexual violation. Hector St. John Crèvecoeur, a sentimental "American farmer" deeply influenced by the Scottish psychology that promulgated sentimental childrearing, wrote in 1782 that slaves "have no time, like us, tenderly to rear their helpless offspring, to nurse them on their knees, to enjoy the delight of being parents. Their paternal fondness is embittered by considering, that if their children live, they must live to be slaves like themselves."

"Slave couples committed to monogamous marriages," Stevenson concludes, "may have been devoted to one another and able to sustain mutual feelings of love and respect, but many did not have the opportunity
to express such sentiments for more than a few years while enslaved."[52]
The conditions of frontier settlement would be extended with a vengeance in postrevolutionary expansion west and the corresponding internal slave trade. In the upper South during the antebellum period,
"one marriage in three was broken by forced separation," writes Peter
Kolchin, and "the forced separation of men, women and children from
their relatives and friends constituted the most devastating experience of
bondage for the slaves." And he reminds us that the family was the site
where slaves could express the negative effects of their daily exploitation
and that folk culture points to that expression in "violence, jealousy, deceit, wife-beating, and child-abuse."[53]

This is not to say that relations even within more prosperous white
families were not often fraught with parallel conflict and abuse, to which
sentimental literature and the goals of reformers testify. A major source
of the popularization of cultures of sensibility was the wish to reform
men's treatment of wives, mothers, and women in general: "Behind the
manifold indictments of the slave system, there flickered, dim, fascinating and horrifying, the fact of the slavery of [all] women." But the
family bonds of enslaved African Americans were incomparably more
frequently and indiscriminately broken, to the horror of white sentimentalists, let alone African Americans themselves.[54]

The evangelization of African Americans in the latter part of the
eighteenth century indicates the possibility of more common ground
with whites, insofar as evangelical Christianity could be an important reinforcement of sentimental tendencies in Protestantism. Sancho, Wheatley, and the Reverends Allen and Jones illustrate this possibility. But, in
religion, reciprocal "influence across the racial divide should not be exaggerated." Even where one can hypothesize some sentimental common-
ality in eighteenth-century, evangelized congregants, "blacks so often
exceeded whites in the expression of their evangelism that the question
of distinctiveness cannot be . . . easily dismissed." Morgan quotes contemporary observations of *"divine ecstasies"* of black people at evangelical gatherings and of "Hundreds of Negroes . . . , with Tears streaming
down their faces," and he demonstrates that the result of late-century
evangelization was a fusion of Christianity with the then more deeply
rooted African traditions. Heyrman writes that, when "black worshippers wept and screamed, collapsed and sank into trancelike states, . . .

such behavior meant something other to them than what it did to white evangelicals" and that, "even as blacks exhibited outward forms of religious engagement similar to those displayed by whites, . . . such responses arose from inward states of feeling and belief different from those of whites, expressing spiritual truths of their own devising."[55]

So, while black abolitionists, members of the African American urban elite, and those slave and free blacks with particularly ongoing and intimate relations with white cultivators of sensibility could write and speak its language, most others habitually spoke differently. Morgan has provided us with the clearest account of the formation of the language and dialects that the vast majority of eighteenth-century African Americans spoke, focusing on the South Carolina Lowcountry, where the Creole language of Gullah emerged, and on the Chesapeake, where slaves eventually came to speak "a dialectical form of Standard English."[56] These were the words with which, of course, the enslaved raised their children. Recent scholarship has begun to describe the childhoods of African American slaves and to show that they were quite distinct from those of free European Americans,[57] even though there was a degree of exchange between black and white. Common country white folk might "talk very much like Negroes," and white children who were suckled by black nurses "contracted a negroish kind of accent, pronunciation, and dialect," according to the younger Josiah Quincy, who traveled through the South in 1773, writing a sentimental record of his "journey," referring to Laurence Sterne, perhaps the most influential writer of sentimental prose in English in the last four decades of the century.[58]

In her *Incidents in the Life of a Slave Girl*, Harriet Jacobs, born to slavery in 1818, manifested a comparable contrast. She recorded the diction of African Americans of early-nineteenth-century Edenton, North Carolina, and its backcountry plantations, where those she called "lower class" slaves lived. She represents it to have been distinct from her own, which "used the style of a sentimental novel," harnessing that style to what B. A. Botkin called the "autobiographical propaganda" of the slave narrative. Jacobs aimed to move her white, Northern, female readers according to virtually the same psychology the Latitudinarians had described so long ago, or, as Harriet Beecher Stowe said in the preface to *Uncle Tom's Cabin*, "to awaken sympathy and feeling," in her audience.[59]

I will refer further to these borders of the Americanizing culture of sensibility as we go along, but first I turn to the religious and intellectual origins of the culture and its gendering in England.

# PART I

# Origins, Definitions, and Social Circumstances

## CHAPTER I

# The Metropolitan Sources of the Adamses' Views of Sensibility

## Heritage

The Adamses shared in the particular tradition of moral thought that fed cultures of sensibility on both sides of the Atlantic. Norman Fiering's intellectual history of this tradition and its relation to sensibility is invaluable.[1] Fiering writes that "the most significant development in the history of ethics between 1675 and 1725" was the rise of the view that "the source of moral judgment and moral conduct is special feelings or affections rather than in reason or intellect, which at best play a complementary role, and that man is naturally endowed with moral affections."[2]

The belief in the power of feeling (and ambivalence over its relation to reason), and other characteristics of the culture of sensibility, had ancient intellectual roots. In referring to such precedents, Fiering quotes Geoffrey Atkinson, a historian of "the sentimental revolution" in France in the years 1690–1740: "What is important in the history of ideas is always their expression and frequency of expression by different authors, for the date of the onset of ideas is impossible to find." It was the frequency of sentimental terms (beginning around 1675 in Fiering's view) that made for a historical development different from their previous occurrence: it coincided with the emergence of women.[3]

Fiering's subject is the absorption and adaptation of seventeenth-century European moral thought in New England, sponsoring the rise of sentimental ethics. While his focus in the first of his books on the seventeenth-century Harvard curriculum might seem limited, Fiering quotes Samuel Eliot Morison to emphasize that Harvard "was a narrow gorge through which a stream of learning, the Arts and Sciences, Philosophies, and Humane Letters poured from the Old World into New England."[4] There were other channels. Ministers of the many Anglican colonial establishments preached benevolent feelings.[5] The Quakers, penetrating the American colonies beyond Pennsylvania, generated

humanitarian sympathy, and, as Christine Leigh Heyrman's history of
the rise of evangelicals in the South from the later eighteenth century
through the 1840s indicates, they, too, fostered belief and behavior akin
to that of their contemporary cultivators of sensibility. The influence of
popular sentimental literature became pervasive from early in the eighteenth century.[6]

Fiering recognizes that "the great strides in the modern interpretation of the passions did not begin until Descartes' treatise on the passions
[*The Passions of the Soul*] was published" in French in 1649 and then in English translation in 1650.[7] There, Descartes wrote: "the use of the passions consists in this alone: they dispose the soul to will the things nature
tells us are useful and to persist in this volition, just as the same motion
of the spirits that usually courses through them disposes the body to the
movements conducive to the execution of those things." (This sentence
reflects his division between passions that originate in the soul/mind
and those that originate in the body, although he theorized that both
are inevitably bound up with each other.) Elsewhere, he declared that
passions "are in their nature good and we have nothing to avoid but
misuse or excesses of them."[8] Descartes contributed decisively to the
rehabilitation of the passions in the context of others who were also re-
assessing them and demonstrating their central importance to the operation of human psychology.[9] That psychology included Descartes's psychophysiological model wherein impressions were transmitted by spirits
through the nerves to the brain; it was very widely popularized. Heavily influenced in his youth by Descartes, Locke assumed it. In this he
had common ground with his predecessors in English efforts to scien-
tize psychology, the Cambridge Platonists, a group of reformers within
the Anglican church.[10]

Henry More (who corresponded with Descartes, their correspondence subsequently being published)[11] was preeminent among this group
in his championing of Descartes, although others (including Ralph Cudworth, their leading theologian) adapted Cartesianism to their purposes
and illustrate its being linked to ancient precedents. More "must be credited with being one of the first to bring Descartes' work on the passions
into the mainstream of British and American thought." Thereafter, his
own work "laid the basis for sentimentalist ethics and the romantic view
of the passions." His *Enchiridion ethicum* (1667) was adopted at Harvard
"in the 1680s . . . as the principal text for moral philosophy there" and
"used continuously there until about 1730."[12] (It was translated into English in 1690.) According to Fiering, More was "the leading intellectual

force in American philosophy" in that period, and some of his ideas found other routes to a popular audience, including the *Spectator*.[13]

More, other Cambridge Platonists, and their Latitudinarian successors grew disillusioned with Descartes, coming to identify him with mere materialism and atheism. They replaced him with the more orthodox-seeming Newton. Latitudinarians were Anglicans who saw themselves forging a compromise position within a church riven to the point of civil war between Puritans and neo-Catholic, high Anglicans. While they conferred authority on natural philosophy (the new science), of which at first Descartes was the most prominent theorist, they had been avid to absorb its power into their theology.[14] It depended on "the two Books" wherein God's plan could be read: the Bible, of course, but the book of nature, too, represented by Descartes and then by Newton, who published his own view of the operation of the nerves, both men believing that everything from the human body to the stars was governed by the same laws. The scientific reassessment of the passions and its populariza-tion was fundamental to the rise of a culture of sensibility.[15]

The Cambridge Platonists and their Latitudinarian followers were the subject of R. S. Crane's still highly influential and valuable account of "the propaganda of benevolence and tender feeling preached by nu-merous divines of the Latitudinarian school," along with lay publicists (in Fiering's 1675–1725 period).[16] Crane's divines rejected the Stoicism that from early in the seventeenth century had been reconciled with Christi-anity as "neo-Stoicism" and become fashionable in European courts. By 1650, however, "the Stoic negative attitude toward the passions . . . had become mainly a foil for arguments in defense of the passions." Crane's subjects consciously revolted "against the distrust of the passions and the exaggerated assumptions concerning man's rationality which they attrib-uted to the Stoics." This coincided with the Latitudinarian repudiation of the grimmer view of human nature professed by the English Puritans, whom they condemned, not only because they saw them as fomenters of civil conflict, but also because they saw that the hopelessness of predes-tination drove people to atheism and rakery.[17] Cambridge Platonists and Latitudinarians wished to have the opposite effect, bending their theol-ogy and their view of human nature to their own campaigns for "the reformation of manners."[18]

The Latitudinarians insisted that Thomas Hobbes encouraged, in the words of Margaret Jacob, "rapacious self-interest, the pursuit of profit and status by ungodly men whose success galls and even imperils men of virtue." The corollary was competition unchecked by inner morality. This vision reflected the coming into existence of commercial capitalism: Hobbes had "addressed himself to the market society and therefore self-interest," and so, too, did the Latitudinarians. Their leading divines, including Crane's subjects, themselves had middle-class, commercial roots and "rose in the Church through dint of hard effort." At first establishment targets, after the Glorious Revolution of 1688 they came to dominate the Anglican establishment; in 1692, one of their best-known preachers, John Tillotson, became archbishop of Canterbury, the Anglican primate.[19]

The Latitudinarians endorsed self-interest, but they did not wish to see "the forces of greed and disorder . . . get out of hand entirely, destroy Anglican and moral and social leadership and defy the providential plan." They defended capitalism and "encouraged social inequality," sometimes justifying it as "the natural order of society." By "diligence in one's calling, calculated charity toward inferiors, . . . the Latitudinarians would bend private interest to serve the public good." They were more unambiguously proponents of what Max Weber named *the Protestant ethic* than their Puritan predecessors. Modifying Weber, Colin Campbell also locates the psychology of consumerism in the Latitudinarian elevation of feeling. A 1733 statement of the rationale that Latitudinarians popularized was Pope's lines at the end of *An Essay on Man*:

> Whatever is, is Right;
> That Reason, Passion, answer one great aim;
> That true self-love and social are the same.

One could say that that third line was the wish that preoccupied the Adamses and their literary contemporaries and is still with us.[20]

The Adamses also subscribed to the reformation of manners, a formal and informal campaign against certain kinds of behavior, particularly sexual behavior, and the promotion of a politeness that included sensibility, a campaign ebbing and flowing from the Reformation through the Victorian era. Following the death of Charles II and the chasing of his Catholic brother, James II, from the throne in 1688, the new monarchs, William and Mary, backed the churchmen who, horrified by the exuberantly sexual and intellectual license associated with the Stuart court, institutionalized societies for the reformation of manners.[21] The author of a history of "erotica of the Enlightenment" remarks that these societies "fought a losing battle against man's carnal lust."[22]

The theater was one of the reformers' very public targets. The two London theater companies had been King Charles's and his brother's, and

Charles had taken his sexual picks from the pool of actresses. Women played on the stage for the first time, which can be seen as emblematic of their emergence in other ways, not the least in publishing books in their own names, some of them including feminist arguments.[23] Notoriously bawdy Restoration plays, incorporating depictions of women's sexual appetite, along with feminist assertions about women's lack of education, their seduction and abandonment, their being bought and sold on the marriage market, and the horrors of victimization in a bad marriage, supplied archetypal characters and plots for subsequent sentimental fiction, including Richardson's.[24] Some seventeenth-century English feminists, saliently Mary Astell, were reformers of manners, antisexual, or at least opposed to the sexuality of "libertine" men.[25]

The leading cleric on the theatrical front of the campaign for the reformation of manners was the Reverend Jeremy Collier, who first published *A Short View of the Immorality and Profaneness of the English Stage* in 1698. It must be noted that Collier shared the worldview of the divines Crane described, prizing "benevolence and good nature." He carefully analyzed plays by several writers, but his chief target was John Dryden, the greatest writer of the Restoration and an opponent of the Glorious Revolution.[26] Dryden had absorbed the new science of human nature and argued on behalf of the representation of a greater range of passions on the stage than Aristotle's pity and terror. Above all, he wrote of heterosexual passions, including sexual love. He was keenly attuned to the presence, the interests, and the wishes of the women in his audiences. One feminist playwright who shared Dryden's views and openly represented sexuality, including women's sexuality, was Aphra Behn, but she had immediately faced criticism for indecency on account of her gender, that is, long before Collier's full-scale assault on male dramatists, and she was only the most prominent of several women writing Restoration comedy and drama.[27]

Like Dryden, Collier assumed the mechanical operation of the passions, specifically in response to art, and he urged playwrights to use their words to incline audiences to virtue, rather than vice. He singled out women; in ordinary "Conversation," Collier wrote, women found "Obscenity" "particularly rude." It could not be "endur'd" by any "Lady of Reputation." Collier asked: "Do the Women Leave all regards to Decency and Conscience behind them, when they come to the *Play-House*?" No, he answered, resting his reassuring assertion on the ascendant, gendered, scientific psychology: "Modesty is the distinguishing Vertue of that Sex, and serves for both Ornament and Defence: Modesty was design'd by Providence as a Guard to Virtue; And that it might be always at Hand, 'tis wrought into the Mechanism of the Body."[28]

This mechanism was the Cartesian one that Nicolas Malebranche had gendered in *De la recherche de la verité* (1674–75), translated into English by the Reverend Thomas Taylor as *Father Malebranche, His Treatise concerning the Search after Truth* in 1694, four years before Collier launched his attack. Malebranche's psychology, writes Fiering, "had a major influence on British and American theories of the passions."[29] (John Adams had both French and English versions in his library.)[30] Malebranche gendered Cartesian psychology apparently in reaction to Poulain de la Barre's application of it in the radically feminist *De l'égalité des deux sexes* (1673), which appeared in translation in England in 1677, where it met an English feminism already capitalizing on Descartes's nongendered account of the operation of mind and passions.[31] According to Malebranche, the greater delicacy of women's brain fibers gave them "great understanding of everything that strikes the senses" and had "more knowledge, skill, and finesse" in fashions and good manners, in fact everything depending on "taste," but "normally they are incapable of penetrating to truths that are slightly difficult to discover." Women "consider only the surface of things, and their imagination has insufficient strength and insight to pierce it to the heart, comparing all the parts without being distracted." Their greater responsiveness to sensations explained why a "trifle is enough to distract them": "the least motion fascinates them . . . because insignificant things produce great motions in the delicate fibers of the brains, these things necessarily excite great and vivid feelings in their soul completely occupying it." Malebranche, in short, supplied apparently scientific authority for the sharp reaction to the public emergence of women, part of the revival of the campaign for the reformation of manners being formalized in the 1690s.[32]

Reformers of manners aimed at men, too, and not only libertines. Malebranche, like Dryden, had criticized the Stoicism identified with the warrior ideals of knighthood and the ancients. Dryden and his contemporaries elevated male characters who were responsive to women. Antony, in Dryden's reworking of Shakespeare's *Antony and Cleopatra*, having shown his crippling ambivalence over military values, gave them up, choosing "all for love," as Dryden renamed his version. His Cleopatra was very clear in her expression of the joys of sex with Antony. Dryden, "always aware of his audience," wrote in *An Evening's Love* of his "love" for it, comparing his approach to that of "a young Bridegroom on his Wedding-night," but in the same place he complained to his audience of being bound "To strain himself, in complaisance to you."[33]

Whether or not Collier had read Malebranche (and it seems likely that he had), his own account of women's psychology is essentially gendered Cartesianism. He explained that the "Guard to Virtue" worked instinctively in women, its power reflexively manifested in the blush of modesty: "The Enemy no sooner approaches but the Blood rises in Opposition, and looks Defiance to an Indecency It supplys the room of Reasoning, And Collection: Intuitive Knowledge Can scarcely make a quicker Impression. . . . It teaches by sudden Instinct and Aversion." Ladies in the audience were, he said, affronted, offended, and disgusted by swearing and smut, "Libertinism and Profaneness."[34]

Poets, Collier urged, should be admired for teaching religion and political deference, "for refining the Manners, tempering the Passions, and improving the Understanding of Mankind." (Notice that the passions were not to be entirely repressed. In fact, according to the scientific model on which poets depended for their power, they could not be.) Ostensibly taking ladies' interests into account, Collier added to this list of goals making "Understandings" "more useful in Domestick Relations, and the publick Capacities of Life."[35]

The insistence that women were naturally more susceptible even than men of feeling reasserted sexual binaryism and male superiority. Women's passions were to be confined to the "feeling" that signified compassion, sympathy, pity, and so forth, listed in my introduction. Reformed men—men of feeling—were to have such feelings, too, but modified naturally by the virtuous power of the mind. The popularization of gendered sensibility coincided with the reactionaryism represented by Collier, but it seems accurately to have expressed the wishes of some of the women in the theater's audiences, their views coinciding with Astell's, who demanded an end to the direct expression of sexual passion, especially by rakes and libertines, and a turn toward the more sentimental and puritanically inclined plays that began to appear toward the end of the century.[36]

Sentimentalization and Collier's view of the theater were propagated by the *Spectator*, a journal whose authors (notably Richard Steele) themselves wrote plays as vehicles for the desexualized domestic virtue espoused by Collier. It seems to have been Collier's view of women's modesty that Joseph Addison, the other principal author of the *Spectator*, had in mind when, in no. 231, he made gendered sensibility synonymous with it: "Modesty is not only an Ornament, but also a Guard to Vertue.

It is a kind of quick and delicate *feeling* in the Soul, which makes her shrink and withdraw her self from every thing that has Danger in it. It is such an exquisite Sensibility, as warns her to shun the first appearance of every thing which is hurtful." As the modern editor of the *Spectator* notes, the *Oxford English Dictionary* given this as the first historical example of the meaning of *sensibility* ("quickness and acuteness of apprehension or feeling: the quality of being easily and strongly affected by emotional influences"). There were two earlier uses, one in 1698, with the same meaning as this, the other in the 1690 translation of More's *Enchiridion ethicum*, which, while nongendered, illustrated the transition from passions to feeling: "Thus by subjecting our Passions, and the purifying of our Bodies and Souls, there springs up to us, as it were, a new *Sensibility* in the Mind or Spirit, which is the only portion of the prudent Man." More finds a precedent for this quality, "a Sense and Feeling," in what "the Pythagoreans . . . called a quick and perfect Sensation . . . a sort of feeling in our practical Intellect." But it was the frequently reprinted and exemplary *Spectator*'s definition that was to be even more influential, meeting as it did the wishes and values of Anglophone, Protestant embourgeoisement.[37]

## The Adamses' Liberal Protestantism

The Adamses' religious and moral beliefs are consistent with those described by Fiering, Crane, and Jacob and illustrated by Collier. Abigail's father, the Reverend William Smith, learned the importance of moral affections at Harvard and preached "liberal congregationalism," opposed to Jonathan Edwards's attempt to restore Calvinism. Like other literate women of her class, especially the womenfolk of clergymen, Abigail had access to her father's library, where she and her two sisters "spent hours, . . . learning from him how to read seriously . . . and gaining from him an appreciation of literature, history and theology." Abigail "wholeheartedly embraced" her father's "intense faith, . . . the only sure comfort to the afflicted," when she became a full-fledged member of his Weymouth church in 1759, shortly before she met John Adams, another Harvard graduate. Her sisters, Elizabeth and Mary, married Harvard graduates, too, respectively, John Shaw and Richard Cranch.[38]

Abigail wrote John in 1775 of the preacher "Mr. Taft," "a good man" who was "earnest and pathetick": "I could forgive his weakness for the sake of his sincerity—but . . . I want a person who has feeling and sensibility." In 1776, she rejoiced "in a preacher who has some warmth, some

energy, some feeling. Deliver me from your cold phlegmatick Preachers."[39] At the beginning of the Revolution, in Philadelphia, John had in
his diary praised a preacher for his "Benevolence and Humanity" and
written Abigail of the substance and effects of a sermon by the Reverend
George Duffield: "He fill'd and swell'd the Bosom of every Hearer."[40]
Both John and Abigail admired the kind of preaching that, in John's 1774
words, "reaches the Imagination and touches the Passions," although
doing so "with great Propriety." God gave the passions moral value, as
Descartes and his successors had argued: God "has annexed pain to vice
and pleasure to virtue." John had intended to become a minister when
he entered Harvard but quit divinity in favor of the law, which, he said,
did not "dissolve the obligations of morality or of Religion." Indeed, he
saw the law that he inherited from England as an instrument of "Benignity and Humanity," the word *humanity* being another significant feature of the Protestantism that Crane defined and one used with remarkable frequency by Adams in all his writings.[41]

He read and copied out "large extracts from the works of Tillotson,"
and he raised the question, "Will it not be worth while for a candidate
for the ministry to transcribe Dr. Tillotson's Works?" At the time he
was himself such a candidate. Nine years later he introduced his *Dissertation on the Canon and Feudal Law* with a sentence of Tillotson's. John
owned a multivolume set of Tillotson's works, each one of which he autographed. In a 1777 letter to John, Abigail quoted a passage from "Our
favorite Dr. Tillotson." Fiering notes that possibly "no other Anglican
writer was more widely read in America, North and South."[42] Like his
father-in-law, John was contemptuous of the "New Lights," eighteenth-
century evangelicals. He described a landlady with whom he stayed in
1771, a descendant of Governor Endicott, as "a new Light—continually
canting and whining in a religious Strain." He interpreted her religious
style as the attempt to keep up the honor of her Puritan forebears; he
quoted her "canting": "'Terrible Things, Sin causes.' Sighs and Groans.
'The pangs of the new Birth.'" Abigail's much admired James Fordyce
pictured Christ "as the perfect model of meekness and sensibility" and
said that for "unintelligible impressions, or wild enthusiasms"—the latter a term carrying a powerful negative charge in reaction to the English
Civil War—"I am not an advocate."[43]

Yet, while Fordyce and the Adamses were clear on the distinction between the "canting" "signs of new birth" and adherence to preaching
warmed by sensibility, the trend toward the legitimization of the passions helped open the door to such popular religious forms. The Great

Awakening intensified the emotionality of religious expression and, it
has been argued, provided still more of a basis for women's claim on religious power.[44] Neither the third Earl of Shaftesbury, "the father of sentimental ethics," who also condemned enthusiasm, nor the Latitudinarians had intended the large unleashing of feelings. The process for which
the Adamses and Governor Endicott's descendant stood was, perhaps,
analogous to the transition that American republican revolutionaries
unintentionally brought about from "Monarchy" to "Democracy."[45]

John owned books by Ralph Cudworth, at the headwaters of that
propagandizing of benevolence Crane outlines, and recommended Cudworth to his son John Quincy (another Harvard graduate) along with
Isaac Barrow, Tillotson, the Latitudinarian William Wollaston, and the
Reverend Francis Hutcheson, the nominally Presbyterian Scot and theorist of the moral sense, a list representing the early phase of the intellectual history of sensibility in Britain.[46] Barrow's sermons (which John
owned in an edition published by Tillotson) "were a model for . . . ministers in Britain and America," and Wollaston's *Religion of Nature Delin-
eated* had "a remarkable vogue in early America."[47]

Hutcheson was a disciple of Shaftesbury and himself became a chief
progenitor of the Scottish school of moral sense, "the moral sense" being a key tenet of sensibility. Like other senses, it was innate, and it
was a feeling. The second entry of John's diary (January 16, 1756) was,
"Reading Hutcheson's *Introduction to Moral Philosophy*," a book he may
well have first encountered at Harvard, where it was a standard text. He
owned a copy of this, in an edition published in 1755, of Hutcheson's *Essay on the Nature and Conduct of the Passions and Affections with Illustrations of
the Moral Sense*, in an edition published in 1756, and of Hutcheson's *Inquiry into the Origin of Our Idea of Beauty and Virtue* (1726). Fiering writes
of the latter that it was "in many ways the culmination of the trend that
made compassion and pity authoritative in human nature." Hutcheson
had absorbed Descartes's view of the passions by way of Malebranche,
although he had also read Henry More on the passions. He overtook
More to become "the most influential and respected moral philosopher
in eighteenth-century America." The central idea of the second of his
three books, the existence of an innate moral sense, appeared and re-
appeared in the letters of Abigail and John. Subsequent writers in the
school of moral sense stemming from Hutcheson whose works John
owned included Lord Kames, David Hume, William Robertson, Adam
Smith, and Dugald Stewart.[48]

Abigail also asked her daughter Nabby to send her a copy of "Blair." Her wish to read the Reverend Hugh Blair's writings—most likely one of the collections of sermons he published in 1777 or 1780—might have reflected the glow of admiration she felt for the sermons of his fellow Scot James Fordyce, although, according to the historian John Dwyer, Blair's sermons were, "next to the *Spectator*, the best-selling work in the English language written in the eighteenth century." (He was Nancy Shippen's "favorite author.") With Fordyce, Blair was one of a group of the "Moderate" clergy in Scotland, popularizing ideas nowadays more usually associated with Adam Smith (to whom Blair was extremely "close") and David Hume. Dwyer emphasizes Blair's orientation toward moral reform, an orientation that was rooted in the development of sensibility and that Blair shared with all these fellow Scots. The powerful impact of the Scottish Enlightenment on white, literate, male, eighteenth-century British North America is well-known.[49]

The Adamses combined belief in an innate moral sense with the open-ended, blank-slate psychology associated with Locke, an apparently contradictory combination characteristic of cultivators of sensibility and generally widespread among the literate. In his *Dissertation on the Feudal and Common Law*, John expressed his opposition to the idea of "indelible characters," arguing instead on the basis of "a knowledge of human nature, derived from history and [people's] own experience."[50] At the same time, and like the Cambridge Platonists, the Latitudinarians, and the subsequent upholders of the belief in a moral sense, John believed that "nature had implanted in the human heart a disposition to resent an injury when offered"; such a passion could be followed by another, that is, the wish for revenge, "and the man feels the sweetest, highest gratification, when he inflicts the punishment himself."[51] In his diary, Adams noted that God had made provision "for the Gratification of our senses." There was also in human nature "a love of truth and a veneration for virtue." Adams's terms extended to a "sense" of "feeling the difference between true and false, right and wrong, virtue and vice," a virtual quotation of More's *Enchiridion ethicum*, and he asked, "To what better principle can the friends of mankind apply?" He named this the "moral Sense" in an 1777 letter to Abigail.[52]

His phrase "friends of mankind" also connoted sensibility. A. R. Humphreys explains that it expressed the social psychology developed by that line of thinkers from the Cambridge Platonists though Shaftesbury, Hutcheson, and the Scottish moralists as well as the later associationist philosophers David Hartley and Joseph Priestley. The "friend of mankind" appeared throughout the eighteenth century, from characters in Steele's *The Christian Hero* in 1701 through the self-styled "Friends of Humanity" at century's end. In Humphreys's definition, the friend of mankind was "humane, charitable, opening at a hint the sacred source of sympathetic tears": "he enlivens many a chapter of the century's literature, and inspires that glow of benign sentiment which warms the pages of sensibility." Humphreys's epigraph is a quotation from Richardson's *Sir Charles Grandison* (1753–54), whose eponymous hero exemplified these qualities: "How much more glorious a character is that of the friend of mankind than that of the conqueror of nations." The exclamation reflected the transition from previous martial ideals. Perhaps John used the phrase *friend of liberty* more often than he did *friend of mankind*, but the two were closely associated, especially by those of the republican persuasion. Abigail used the phrase *Friends of Liberty* for American colonists threatened with becoming British "Slaves." In that same place where John Adams listed the several "senses" implanted in human nature, he said that "a latent spark in the breasts of the people" was the "love of liberty," and there seems to have been a close kinship in his mind between friends of liberty and friends of mankind. Liberty, liberalism, humanity, and humanitarianism had a common denominator in sensibility.[53]

In that 1777 letter to Abigail, John revealingly adapted the conventional tenet of an existence of a moral sense to his own often vengeful, or, at least, self-righteous and easily aroused, temperament, here in response to Howe's occupation of Boston. Feeling himself "so much injured by these barbarean Britains," John wished to do battle with them, not out of "Revenge," he said, but, still, there was "something sweet and delicious in the Contemplation of it." This relish was the manifestation of a heartfelt righteousness, comparable to the active humanitarianism already being expressed by opponents of the slave trade: "There is in our Hearts, an Indignation against Wrong, that is righteous and benevolent, and he who is destitute of it, is defective in the Balance of his Affections and in his moral Character." Then John illustrated how the moral sense could shade into self-righteousness and even schadenfreude: "As long as there is a Conscience in our Breasts, a moral sense which distinguishes between Right and Wrong, approving, esteeming, loving the former, and condemning and detesting the other, We must feel a Pleasure in the Punishment, of so eminent a Contemner of all that is Right and good and just, as Howe is. They are virtuous and pious Passions that prompt Us to desire his Destruction, and to lament and deplore his success and Prosperity."[54] John's insistence that such passions "are virtuous and pious" was an inheritance from the seventeenth-century reassessment of the value of the passions. That "we must feel a Pleasure" in punishment is the obverse of what Fiering describes as "irresistible compassion." John's statement of the existence of a moral sense in connection with Howe had been preceded by a paragraph in which he confessed a degree of self-indulgence in expressing an inclination to fight. Madison gave the same explanation in describing Jefferson's anger at his treatment by the Virginia General Assembly in 1782: "the note in which he seems determined to revenge the wrong received from his Country [Virginia], does not appear to me to be dictated either by philosophy or patriotism. It argues indeed a keen sensibility and a strong consciousness of rectitude."[55]

John's self-consciousness on the subject is illustrated by his response to reading Burke's *A Philosophical Enquiry into the Origin of Our Ideas of the Sublime and Beautiful* (1757), another contribution to the intellectual development of sensibility influenced by Hutcheson. John's diary illustrates that American colonists, in his circle at least, discussed this book quite soon after its publication. Recording several readers' responses, John wrote in 1763: "the Chapter upon Sympathy, they all disapprove. The Author says we have a real Pleasure in the Distresses and Misfortunes of others. Mem. To write a Letter to Sewal or Quincy, or Lowell on the subject of that Chapter." One can see how such a view might have developed from the Cartesian one Tillotson expressed, that there was "no sensual Pleasure in the world that is comparable to the delight of doing good."[56] Accusations of schadenfreude made by contemporaries against advocates of sensibility have been revived by some modern scholars, especially in relation to opponents of slavery.[57] John's admission of taking pleasure in the just punishment of others indicates, perhaps, some long Calvinist root to what became enhanced as this characteristic issue in cultures of sensibility. In this instance, his response to Burke, John had continued, with notably scientific self-consciousness: "Q. Do we take pleasure in the real distress of others? What is my sensation when I see Captain Cunningham laid up with the gout, and hear his plaintive groans? tlineWhat are the feelings of the women at groanings? What is my feeling when I hear of an honest man's losing a ship at sea?" *Groanings* referred to parturitions, and John is asking about the feelings of female attendants at a scene of childbirth, comparable to, but distinct from, men's pains.

In the aftermath of the Revolution, John consistently fell back on a far bleaker, even Hobbesian view of human nature (as Wood has remarked) in contrast to the more positive, optimistic, Latitudinarian-influenced psychology that he believed had to counter it.[58] Fresh out of Harvard in 1755, he was capable of writing in response to Bolingbroke (whom Zoltán Haraszti calls "the Ishmael of his age"): "Life on the whole seems to be a blessing."[59] Abigail expressed a Hobbesian view when still a newlywed and depressed by the distance between herself and Mary, the second of her sisters. Mary's Salem acquaintances were, Abigail said, pupils of Iago's dictum "Put money in thy purse": "This is a selfish world you know. Interest governs it, there are but very few, who are moved by any other Spring."[60] Proponents of sensibility may have hypostasized the goodness of people of feeling, but they always set them in, or rather against, a "world" of selfishness and intrigue, a vision shared by republicanism. In 1775, Abigail raised questions about the new "form of Government to be established in Massachusetts" and wrote John that she was "more and more convinced that Man is a dangerous creature, and that power whether vested in many or a few is ever grasping, and like the grave cries give, give." She disagreed with the view John had expressed "of degrees of perfection to which Humane Nature is capable of arriving."[61]

John made clear his acceptance of the compatibility of "the two books," the Bible and nature, propounded by the Latitudinarians. He recorded reading "Bentleys Sermon at the Boilean Lectures," Richard Bentley (1662–1742) being yet another Latitudinarian. His were the first of those annual series of lectures established in 1693 by Richard Boyle and attempting to reconcile the Bible and nature. (Bentley's were on *The Folly and Unreasonableness of Atheism.*) John wrote Benjamin Rush that the "Bible contains the most profound philosophy, the most perfect morality, the most refined policy, that ever was conceived on earth." In addition to stimulating what we can call *the Protestant ethic* in every inhabitant and fulfilling the goals of the campaign for the reformation of manners, the Bible was, in John's view, the source of the more humane characteristics elevated by the softened Protestantism of the eighteenth century.[62] But he also read "Leibnitz, Descartes, Malbranch, and Lock," and he placed Newton and Locke at the pinnacle of human intellectual development. Unsurprisingly, then, he believed that God was "the Author of Nature," a realm including those invaluable passions. He wrote Abigail that "Nature is a Machine whose Author and Conductor is wise kind and almighty," a view of nature decisively established in the seventeenth century, above all by Descartes, and very generally held in the eighteenth. It was fundamental to Pope's *An Essay on Man*, and it underpinned the conception of sensibility.[63]

John and Abigail both shared in the reaction to Stoicism that Crane suggests was a characteristic of the theology that contributed to "the genealogy of the man of feeling," which had been further popularized later in the century, notably in Pope's poetry. So, for example, Joseph Shippen of Pennsylvania wrote in his commonplace book: "All passions in general are planted in us for excellent Purposes in human life. Stoical Apathy is not a human Virtue. Agreeable to this Mr. Pope speaks in his Essay on Man [1733], Epist. 2—v. 2." And he copied out ten lines, including:

> In lazy apathy let stoics boast,
> Their virtue fixed, 'tis fixed in a frost.

In 1763, John Adams urged his fiancée: "Learn to conquer your Appetites and Passions." He then went on to ask her: "Did you ever read Epictetus? He was a sensible Man. I advise you to read him." This might seem an endorsement of Stoicism, but John's phrasing in that adjuration referred to the highly modified version of Epictetus that Abigail was to read, the bluestocking Elizabeth Carter's translation *All of the Works of Epictetus* (1759), the only English translation that John had in his library. It had been "an immediate critical success," said to have "made a great noise all over Europe." Carter's view of Epictetus, however, was one already adopted and publicized by the *Spectator*. Carter's predecessor in translating this Roman Stoic had been George Stanhope, another of Crane's divines, who made clear his disagreement with the thinker he translated. It was Stanhope's 1694 translation to which Addison referred in no. 397 of the *Spectator*: "If thou seest thy friend in trouble, says Epictetus, thou may'st put on a look of sorrow, and condole with him, but take care that this sorrow be not real." Addison commented: "for my own part, I am of the Opinion Compassion does not only refine and civilize Human Nature, but has something in it more pleasing and agreeable that what can be met with in such indolent Happiness"—indolent because not prompted by passion—"such an Indifference to Mankind as that in which Stoicks place their Wisdom."[64]

Carter's translation was prefaced by "An Irregular Ode" by "M.B."
(actually Hester Chapone) addressed to Carter. At first it parodied
Stoicism:

> Oh teach my trembling Heart
> To Scorn Afflictious Dart;
>
> . . . . . . . . . . . . . . . . . . .
>
> Oh! Seal my Ears against the Piteous Cry
> Of innocence distrest,

But then it depicted Christ the same way that Carter's contemporary
Fordyce did in his *Sermons to Young Women*. It asked the reader to

> behold his Aspect meek
> The tear of Pity on his Cheek.

Christ shows feeling. His "spotless Bosom heaves with tender Sighs" for
the "heart felt Wound."[65]

In her own introduction, Carter outlined Epictetus's failings in order
to contrast them with Christianity's truths. "Moral Goodness," tantamount to the moral sense, was "the Ornament and Perfection of all rational Beings," resulting in a feeling contrary to what the Stoics taught,
one that Descartes had described: that, until "Conscience is stifled by
repeated Guilt, we feel an Obligation to prefer and follow . . . and find
an inward Satisfaction [in], and generally receive outward Advantages
from so doing." Carter wrote, too, that life's misfortunes afflicted even
the innocent: "The natural Consequences of Virtue in some, may be interrupted by the Vices of others." And, here, Carter invokes the figure
of virtue in distress: the vices from which "the best Persons" are "liable
to suffer" are "the Scorn of the Malevolent," and "the cold and penu-
rious Hard-heartedness of the Unfeeling," and "an innumerable Train
of other Evils, to which the most amiable Dispositions are usually the
most sensible."[66]

The Stoics had generated, Carter wrote, "excellent Rules of Self
Government," the aspect of Stoicism that John had in mind in recommending Epictetus to Abigail. But the "natural Consequences of Virtue are interrupted by the Struggles of our own Passion, which we may
overcome, though very imperfectly." In 1785, Abigail referred to the
difficulty French Catholic religious orders had in conquering "those passions, which nature has implanted in Man," a phrase embodying the
findings of seventeenth-century writers on human nature and popularized in the eighteenth century as Joseph Shippen illustrates.[67] Vir-

tue, Carter wrote, was interrupted, too, "by what we feel from the Death, or the Sufferings of those, with whom we are most nearly connected." She allows that we "are often indeed afflicted by many of these Things, more than we ought to be." This flowed from dutiful, virtuous sympathy. "But Concern for some, at least our own failings, for Instance, is directly a Duty; for others, it is visibly the Instrument of moral improvement."[68]

Carter invoked the egalitarian standard of the person who found inward satisfaction in the moral sense to elevate the value of non-Stoical feeling: "Take any Person of plain Understanding, with all the Feelings of Humanity about Him, and see whether the subtlest Stoic will ever be able to convince him, that if he is insulted, oppressed and tortured, he doth not *suffer*." The Stoics had attempted to establish virtue on principles "inconsistent with the Nature of Man" and, thus, "often were seduced into Pride, Hard-heartedness and Self-murder." Crane could have included Carter in his list of Latitudinarian propagandists on behalf of feeling.[69]

Carter's view of human nature can be linked to her wish to amplify education for women, giving them access to the classics, which for so long had been the privilege of elite men. (Linda Kerber observes that the "disparities in literacy"—"from the basic ability to sign one's name . . . to the sophisticated ability to read . . . the classics"—had "enormous implications for the relations between the sexes.") The Stoics, Carter wrote, "seemed to consider All (except the few, who were Students in the Intricacies of a philosophic System) as very little superior to Beasts: and with great Tranquility left them to follow . . . their own ungoverned Appetites and Passions."[70] A linguistic prodigy as a child, to her learning Portuguese and Arabic as an adult Carter added musicianship and became "a student of astronomy, history, and geography." Recognizing that other women shared her appetite, she translated *Sir Isaac Newton's Philosophy Explain'd for the Use of the Ladies* (1739) from the Italian. She added her translation of Fontenelle's *Plurality of Worlds*, an exposition of Galileo's and Descartes's cosmologies likewise addressed to female readers. Carter had been preceded in her translation of Fontenelle by others, most notably the Latitudinarian Joseph Glanville and the feminist poet and playwright Aphra Behn.[71] In 1684, Behn had praised Henry Creech for his "Excellent Translation of Lucretius," that is, the great Roman poet's Latin exposition in *De rerum natura* of Epicurean atomism, an ancient vision of nature that had an enormous influence on the seventeenth-century scientific revolution. (John Adams's reading ranged to Lucretius.) Behn's praise, her poem explained, was particular because she gave it as a woman denied the classical university education privileging men.[72]

Dryden's translation of the *Aeneid* and then Pope's of the *Iliad* and the *Odyssey* (i.e., of works seen to be foundations of Western literature) were aimed at reaching an increasingly heterosexual, heterogeneous readership, in the context of the other poems, plays, and novels tributary to the rise of sentimentalism.[73] Pope's translation of Homer was a softened, sentimentalized version, and Pope addressed women's interest in his footnotes too.[74] In 1782, reminding John that "Eight years have already past, since you could call yourself an Inhabitant of this State," Abigail quoted Pope's *Odyssey* in comparing herself to Penelope's awaiting Ulysses' return. It was because of Pope's translation that Phillis Wheatley shaped her representation of revolutionary warfare the way she did and that Hannah Quincy was able to make "Observations on Actions, Characters, Events, in Popes Homer" among her other reading and to ask: "Questions about them in Company. What do you think of Helen? What do you think of Hector &c." To her suitor, John Adams, these questions proved "a thinking Mind."[75]

While some seventeenth-century feminists had concentrated on the rational side of Descartes's philosophy (because it protected them against the customarily invidious association of women's voices with sexual passion), there was a striking coincidence between the rise of women as readers and writers and the rise of an ethic based on feeling. Fiering hypothesized that "there is probably a connection between the emergence of women into the intellectual world at this time—a world that had formerly been the exclusive preserve of men trained in Latin—and the rise [of humanitarian sympathy]." (At the same place he quotes Adam Smith's *Theory of Moral Sentiments* [1759] on the concurrent modification of manly ideals: "Our sensibility to the feelings of others, so far from being inconsistent with the manhood of self-command, is the very principle upon which that manhood is founded.") Carter's publications embodied the connection that Fiering notes. We should add that Carter's public success as a poet and translator made her vulnerable to accusations of sexual misconduct, and to refute them she had herself painted as Minerva, the goddess emblematic of "the best Accomplishments of the Mind, together with all Virtues, but most especially that of Chastity." That Epictetus was the philosopher being read by a character in "Copy of a Letter from M. Morris" (1765), an apparently American "burlesque of the battle of the sexes," was because he had been translated by the bluestocking Carter.[76]

## Addison, Pope, and the Adamses

Abigail's parents subscribed to the *Spectator*, and she quoted it in her correspondence, apparently by heart. Her grandson Charles Francies Adams found "most remarkable" the influence the *Spectator* ("and the poets") had on the youthful Abigail and her literary circle.[77] John read the *Spectator* on several occasions, copying out issues, or picking it up casually for pleasure ("by Reason of my Inattention my mind is liable to be called off from Law, by a Girl, a Pipe, a Poem, a Love Letter, a Spectator, a Play, &c."), but recommending Addison's essays as models for essay writing. Published from March 1711 through December 1712 and again in 1714, the *Spectator* was "widely circulated throughout England and America in pamphlet form," popularizing the new philosophy in combination with the Protestantism described by Crane and Jacob: "It is likely that no single collection of eighteenth-century prose had been oftener reprinted than the *Spectator*, at least during its own century and the nineteenth." Its intended audience included middle-class women, whose appetite for reading could not be stanched. American ladies read it in the Southern colonies as well as in New England. The *Spectator*, advocating the reformation of manners, coupled its appeal for the improvement of women's education with that emphasis on Malebranchian gendered sensibility described above.[78]

The *Spectator*'s influence on Abigail's view of gender is suggested by her calling John "Lysander" and by her writing to him as "Diana." The original Lysander was Diana's Spartan general, but it was the *Spectator*'s representation of a hypothetical Lysander in no. 522, in which Steele advised his female readers how to go about "their Choice in Marriage," to which Abigail referred. This Lysander would look on "his Partner with the Eye of Reason and Honour," though "the well-chosen Love" would be "moved by Passion on Both Sides." While evidently the wife was still to be secondary, Lysander, a man of feeling as well as "sense," would treat her with respect, and she would find "her Mind . . . improved and her Heart more Glad." They were modern, bourgeois, sentimental, but reasonable, most obviously a couple.[79]

The *Spectator*'s principal authors, Addison and Steele, advocated the reformation of manners and gendered sensibility in other forms, too. As

noted earlier, Steele was a major factor in desexualizing and sentimen-
talizing English plays, following the sexually explicit and protofemi-
nist (and libertine) Restoration theater.[80] Addison's *Cato: A Tragedy* (1713)
promulgated the same gender values as the *Spectator*. Its prologue, written by Pope (also a contributor to the *Spectator*), illustrates the wish to
use sentimental means to instill the virtue of patriotism in the audience, claiming (as Shaftesbury recently had done) that these had been the
means and ends of Greek and Roman poets:

> To wake the soul by tender strokes of art,
> To raise the genius and to mend the heart,
> To make mankind in conscious virtue bold,
> Live o'er each scene, and be what they behold;—
> For thus the tragic muse first trod the state,
> Commanding tears to stream through every age.

*Cato* is distinct from its predecessors and contemporaries, Pope declares,
in not using such means to move its audience's response to the "hero's
glory or the virgin's love." This was disingenuous because, not wishing to lose any of his audience, Addison included both subjects. Instead,
Pope's prologue promised:

> Here tears shall flow from a more generous cause,
> Such tears as patriots shed for dying laws:
> He bids your breasts with ancient ardor rise,
> And calls forth Roman drops from British eyes.

And it adjured his audience:

> Britons attend: be worth like this approved,
> And show you have the virtue to be moved.[81]

American revolutionaries, "patriots," were to claim that the "ancient
ardor" of patriotic virtue had been corrupted in Britain but sustained
in the American colonies, and the adaptation of *Cato* was an element in
the Americanization of sensibility. Pope's prologue to *Cato* was widely
distributed in America, printed separately in cheap editions and in patriotic collections. (Abigail quoted a line from it by heart in a letter she
wrote her niece in 1785.) Prologue and play illustrate that sensibility and
republicanism went hand in hand.[82]

The historical Cato (of whom Abigail also read in Plutarch's *Lives*)
had a daughter named Portia, not Marcia as in the play: Mercy Otis Warren adopted the latter and Abigail the former as pen names when Ameri-

can opposition to the British Empire broke into full-fledged revolution, and it is likely that Abigail had Shakespeare's depiction of Portia (in *Julius Caesar*) in mind, conforming as closely as that character did to her ideal of wifehood.[83] She quoted some of Addison's Marcia's lines to John in 1764, amending them to better fit his circumstances in Boston, where he was about to undergo a smallpox inoculation, and, in 1773, she anticipated Nathan Hale in quoting Cato's speech on the suicide of his son, writing to the playwright, historian, and True Whig Warren, that is, Marcia: "Such is the present Spirit that prevails, that if once they are made desperate Many, very Many of our Heroes will spend their lives in the cause, With the Speach of Cato in their Mouths, 'What pitty, it is, that we can dye but once to save our Country.'"[84] John, too, wrote Portia his version of lines from *Cato*: "The Events of War are uncertain: We cannot insure Success, but We can deserve it."[85]

Pope was the dominant figure of English literature in the first half of the eighteenth century, as popular and influential among literate Anglophones in the American colonies as he was in England. His most popular poem in America was *An Essay on Man*: the second of the four "epistles" into which it is divided incorporates a summa of ideas about the passions to 1733 and a virtually unarguable demonstration of their value; although a few seem to have been deeply shocked when they first came across his argument, it was already widely known and generally accepted.[86]

While Pope was notoriously a satirist, very significantly for the history of sensibility (in Britain and its colonies) he was a man of feeling, too: Jean Hagstrum calls his 1717 poem "Eloisa to Abelard" "a high point in the development of sensibility and the best expression by Pope of his own 'Romantick spirit.'"[87] Such a spirit can be found in much of his poetry. The meaning he gave the word *sensibility* in his correspondence is one with which the Adamses could agree. (Her adoption of "the words of Mr. Blount in a Letter to Pope" on politics illustrated that Abigail read those letters published in a volume of Pope's *Works* in John's library. John recorded his friend Colonel Quincy's modeling his letters on those of Pope and Pope's friend Swift.)[88] This sentimental aspect of Pope's writing, like his translation of Homer, must be linked like that of his predecessor Dryden's to his consciousness of the wishes of the increasingly female part of his audience, but it was also apparent in his ideals of masculinity. Indeed, he contributed to feminism, as contemporary female writers acknowledged, along with degrees of sexism, notably in his satires of the trivialization of ladies' minds and manners, which he attributed in part to men's "tyranny." One place he did so was in his "Epistle to a Lady, of the Characters of Women," one of two poems deliberately specifying gender differences after the generalizations of *An Essay on Man* and a poem imitated by John Quincy Adams.[89]

John Quincy's parents were deeply familiar with Pope's poetry, which they often quoted. John's library included Pope's *Works* and his translations of the *Iliad* and the *Odyssey* as well as Greek and Latin versions. He recorded reading "Pope's Homer" in a week's time in 1760, calculating therefore he could "conquer him in Greek" in six months and "make [himself] able to translate every line in him elegantly." In addition to Pope's *Homer*, Abigail read Joseph Warton's *An Essay on the Genius and Writings of Pope* (1782).[90] When in England in 1783, John met Lord Mansfield: he recalled for an autobiographical piece in the *Boston Patriots*: "Pope had given me, when a boy, an affection for Murray [i.e., Mansfield before he was ennobled]." Of his visit to Windsor Castle during the same trip, he confessed: "all the pomps and pride of Windsor did not occupy my thoughts so much as the forest, and comparing it with what I remembered of Pope's Windsor forest." That early poem (which Abigail also read) and the contrast John made here can also be seen as emblematic of the pastoral, nostalgic values aggrandized by cultivators of sensibility. John did not then have time to visit Pope's house down the river at Twickenham, but, when the following year Abigail joined him in London, they made a pilgrimage there and to "Popes Grotto" adjoining, which Abigail called "the most delightfull Spot my Eyes ever beheld."[91]

Two quotations from Pope and their applications by Abigail and John illustrate their gendered notion of sensibility. In 1780, Abigail quoted the poem of his best known to Americans in a letter of advice to John Quincy, asserting its relation to what she called Christ's expression of "universal Benevolence 'Thou shalt Love thy Neighbour as thyself.'" This, she wrote,

is elegantly defined by Mr. Pope in his Essay on Man.

> Remember, Man, the universal cause
> Acts not by partial, but by general laws
> And makes what happiness we justly call
> Subsist not in the good of one but all
> Theres not a Blessing individuals find
> But some way leans and hearkens to the kind.

This was to emphasize the social side of the harmony that, as we have seen, Pope expressed at the conclusion of his poem (illustrating congruence with Latitudinarian tenets):

> Reason, Passion answer one great aim;
> That true Self-Love and Social are the same.

Abigail was warning her eldest son against unchecked individualism. She insisted: "Thus has the Supreme Being made the good will of Man towards his fellow creatures an Evidence of his regard to him, . . . has constituted him a Dependent Being, and made his happiness to consist in Society. Man early discovered this propensity of his Nature and found 'Eden was tasteless till an Eve was there.'" God made woman the force for social feeling (parallel to Abigail's imparting social love to her son). Malebranche had identified taste with woman, too.[92]

John took up the self-love dimension of *An Essay on Man* in his *Discourses on Davila*, published semiweekly in 1790 in the *Federalist Gazette of the United States* (New York), and reprinted as a book in 1805. It was written in response to the passage of the American Constitution and the onset of the Revolution in France. Adams took brief epigraphs from Pope for six of the individual papers comprising *Discourses on Davila*, and he took fourteen of the sixteen lines of his epigraph for the whole work from *An Essay on Man*, the first two of which refer to the "friend of human kind" (by implication, the writer of the *Discourses*) who

> Taught Power's use to people and to kings,
> Taught not to slack nor strain its tender strings,
> The less or greater set so justly true,
> That touching one must strike the other too;
> Till jarring interests, of themselves create
> Th'according music of a well-mix'd state,
> Such is the world's great harmony, that springs
> From order, union, full consent of things;
> Where small and great, where weak and mighty made
> To serve, not suffer, strengthen, not invade;
> More powerful each, as needful as the rest,
> And in proposition, as it blesses, blest.

Thus was the political dimension of Pope's general argument Americanized as Addison's Anglicized *Cato*'s republicanism had been.[93]

We should note that Adams's major resource for the parts of the *Dis-*

*courses* that are not translations of Enrico Caterino Davila's *Historia della querre civili di Francia* (1630) was Adam Smith's *The Theory of Moral Sentiment* (1759), specifically, chapter 2, section 3, of a book that was an extended, highly influential exposition of the natural philosophy underlying sensibility at that date. Haraszti writes that these words of Adams were his "most sustained effort as a 'moral writer.'"[94]

In the sixth of the papers, John wrote that nature "has wrought the passions into the texture and essence of the soul" and that to "regulate and not to eradicate them is the promise of policy," in entire keeping with Descartes as well as with Pope. He laid out his view of the passions in the fifth paper of the *Discourses*, although he refers to "the constitution of the human mind" throughout. It opens with a catalog of passions that echoed Pope's list in *An Essay on Man*—avarice, ambition, vanity, pride, jealousy, envy, hatred, and revenge and the positive "love of knowledge" and desire of "fame," all of which, in John's view, were manifestations of the same fundamental passion, "that desire of the attention, consideration, and congratulation of our fellow men, which is the great spring of activity."[95]

This desire, a central theme in the chapter from Smith's *Theory of Moral Sentiments* that John quotes, was, in fact, Pope's notion of the "ruling passion." Pope had summarized its development in an individual man in *An Essay on Man*, but he elaborated it at much greater length in the first of that poem's sequels, the "Epistle to Cobham . . . of the Knowledge and Characters of Men," a companion to "Epistle to a Lady, of the Characters of Women." (John referred to Pope's "Argument" for this latter poem in a letter to Jefferson, predicting that future historians would write of his [Adams's] cabinet that it, "like Pope's Woman, will have no Character at all.") Having described the sheer complexity and variability of the motives and characters of men, Pope advised, "Search then the Ruling Passion," the essential spring in a man. "This clue once found, unravels all the rest." His most extended illustration is the character of Philip, Duke of Wharton,

> the scorn and wonder of our days,
> Whose ruling Passion was the Lust of Praise,

more or less identifiable with John Adams's "desire of the . . . congratulation of our fellow men." Wharton had given in to his ruling passion entirely, and it had sustained him in vice to the end of his life. It was, nonetheless, the expression of "honest Nature."[96] This is consistent with a powerful theme in epistle 2 of *An Essay on Man*:

Passions, though selfish if their means be fair,
List under reason, and deserve her care;
Those that imparted court a noble aim,
Exalt their kind, and take some virtue's name.

Passion can lead to vice, but, in the lines Joseph Shippen copied,

In lazy apathy let Stoics boast
Their virtue fix'd; tis fix'd as in a frost,

leading to one of Pope's most famous lines, their metaphor to be found in Henry More and John Locke and echoing one in Descartes's *The Passions of the Soul*, in turn derived from Aristotle:

On life's vast ocean diversely we sail
Reason the card, but passion is the gale.[97]

Later, Pope continues:

The surest virtues thus from passions shoot,
Wild Natures vigor working at the root.[98]

In accordance with this central thrust of the poem with which he has introduced his *Discourses*, John emphasized the fundamental value of passion, a given of nature created by its "Author," God, a view widely shared by Pope's contemporaries and predecessors: "Nature has ordained it as a constant incentive to activity and industry, that, to acquire the attention and complacency, the approbation and admiration of their fellow, men might be urged to constant exertions of beneficence."[99]

Nature, then, elicits good out of passion, in spite of individual selfishness: "By this destination of their natures, men of all sorts, even those who have least of reason, virtue or benevolence, are chained down to an incessant servitude to their fellow creatures." This was intensely personal because Adams, who by no means thought himself least gifted with reason, virtue, or benevolence, complained frequently of the demands and damage inflicted on him and his fortune by his dedication to the public good, but who also revealed, one way or another, that at that dedication's root was his passion for fame, intermixed with a vanity uncomfortably close to Wharton's ruling passion.[100]

In the final paragraph of this *Davila* paper, Adams turns to the pleasures gained by such labors, first rephrasing his ruling passion: "When the love of glory enkindles the heart and influences the whole soul then and only then, may we depend on a rapid progression of the intellectual faculties." He returns to the negative effects before describing his relish in "complacency and satisfaction," "so sweet and delightful to the human heart," a value central to the culture of sensibility, stemming (via the Cambridge Platonists and those Latitudinarian generators of feeling) from Descartes's evaluation of "self-satisfaction," which he had called "the sweetest of all the passions," the result of "the good done by ourselves." In John's account, that good is done via "public office." He continues in the language of feeling: a "mind must be sunk below the feelings of humanity, or exalted by religion or philosophy far above the common character of men, to be insensible, or to conquer its insensibility." Conversely, he doubts the "sincerity" of "pretenders" to such exalted dispassion. The conversation, conduct, and countenances of such men arouse suspicion in "the people," who are "sensible," presumably sharing in "the common character of men." Joined by "feelings of humanity," however, they have compassion for the man pretending to be stoic over his loss of office: they "console him in his afflictions."

Pope, then, provided John a naturalized, psychological rationale for his passion for the glory of public office, which John identifies with the values of sensibility. Pope had held that a ruling passion was central to the character of men, and John saw its virtuous culmination in public office, which only men could hold. Abigail elicited the "social" side of *An Essay on Man*, identifying it with women, and articulating it as maternal advice to restrain the manly individualism of her son. These contrasting emphases characterized Abigail's and John's respective evaluations of the public and the private coursing through a correspondence that resulted from John's absence from Abigail on behalf of the public good.

## Richardson and Sterne and the Adamses

Novels were also a primary vehicle for the promulgation of cultures of sensibility, Richardson's perhaps most of all. Richardson's influence was to extend not only to Rousseau and Goethe but also across the Atlantic, where it suffused early American fiction as well as the fiction that continued to be imported from Britain in quantity, from Walter Scott's to Dickens's, and Little Nell would contribute to Stowe's description of the effects of Little Eva's sentimentalism in *Uncle Tom's Cabin*.[101] According to Bushman, Richardson's novels were "handbooks of refinement" for eighteenth-century American readers. In 1784, Nabby Adams defined the meaning of Sir Charles Grandison's politeness as well as her father's ready application of it. She declared a "Mr. Jackson . . . the most polite man I have ever seen; by politeness I mean not just that light superficial frothiness which we often meet with, and which sometimes conceals a great deal of rudeness, but a certain something in his manners and appearance that cannot fail to please every one who is acquainted with him; my papa calls him the Sir Charles Grandison of his age." John drew on *Clarissa* to characterize his reaction to American political and social change in the early nineteenth century, to declare, "Democracy is Lovelace and the people are Clarissa," and developed the metaphor in a way that demonstrated his familiarity with Richardson's greatest novel.[102]

Abigail "admitted her passion for all" Richardson's three novels, *Pamela, Clarissa,* and *Sir Charles Grandison,* and the third's eponymous hero was her ideal of manhood. Six months before their marriage, she playfully berated John and told him how he fell short of the standard epitomized by Sir Charles. Her letter was typical of literary and sentimental flirtatiousness. She had begun by describing a meeting she had just witnessed between "a Gentleman and his Lady," their "Cloathe[s] all shifted no danger—and no fear. A how do ye, and a how do ye, was exchanged between them, a Smile, and a good naturd look. Upon my word I believe they were glad to see each other. A tender meeting. I was affected by it." Their tenderness made an impression on her because of her own tenderness, her sensibility. It also stimulated a thought about her own gentleman fiancé: "And thought whether Lysander, under like circumstances could thus coldly meet his Diana, and whether Diana could with no more Emotion receive Lysander. What think you. I dare not answer for a different meeting on her part were She under no restraint." But then she quoted this charge against him: "'An intolerable forbidding expecting Silence, which lays such a restraint upon but moderate Modesty that tis impossible for a Stranger to be tranquil in your presence.' What say you to that charge? Deny it not, for by experience I know it to be true." He was the cause of her feeling "under restraint": "Yes to this day I feel a greater restraint in your Company, than in that of allmost any other person on Earth, but thought I had reasons by myself to account for it, and knew not that others were affected in the same manner till a late complaint was entered against you."[103] One of her reasons was, perhaps, the "Modesty" she felt in view of their forthcoming nuptials or her belief that she had a greater degree of sensibility than other women.

She tried to read his remembered face for an explanation of his inhibiting her: "Is there any thing austere in your countenance? Indeed I cannot recollect any thing. Yet when I have been most pained I have thoroughly studied it, but never could discover one trace of the severe. Must it not then be something in Behaviour, (ask Sylvia . . . what it is) else why should not I feel as great a restraint when I write." ("Sylvia," their mutual friend, was apparently the source of the quotation about John's "forbidding . . . Silence" and similar "complaints.") She can tell John about this in a letter, when she is not affected by his visible "Behaviour." "But to go on"—and here Abigail again quotes "Sylvia" on John's inhibiting effects—"'Why did he read Grandison, the very reverse in practice. Sir Charles call'd forth every one's excellencies, but never was a thought born in Lysander's presence.'" Abigail had not done with John's faults. "Unsociable Being is another charge, consistent with that emphasis on social" as opposed to selfish love she would draw from Pope. Abigail wanted to enjoy mutual warmth with her lover, to feel her excellences "call'd forth" by the supportive responsiveness comparable to Sir Charles Grandison's, both indications of the social affections aggrandized by the culture of sensibility.[104]

Richardson's hero had continued to be Abigail's ideal, one she shared with her niece, Betsy Cranch. She wrote her from Paris in May 1785, opening with: "Did you ever my dear Betsy see a person in real Life such as your imagination form'd of Sir Charles Grandison? The Baron de Stael the Sweedish Ambassador comes nearest to that Character in his Manner and personal appearance of any Gentleman I ever saw." Reading his face aroused Abigail's image of Grandison, "for his countanance Commands your good opinion, it is animated intelligent sensible affable, and without being perfectly Beautifull, is most perfectly agreeable." The letters from Betsy and her mother, Abigail's sister Mary, illustrate their familiarity with *Sir Charles Grandison*, too. The thirteen-year-old Nabby copied out some "paragafts" from "Grandison" for which Betsy had asked and sent them to her.[105] In 1785, John Quincy described to Nabby a couple he had met in Cambridge, Massachusetts, drawing on their shared familiarity with *Clarissa*: "[They] called to my mind Mr. Hickman and Miss Howe, but I don't know that Miss Howe, is any where represented as a Coquet."[106]

From London that same year (1785), Abigail wrote her most extensive assessment of Richardson, in a letter to Betsy's sister Lucy Cranch, the first part of which made a sustained analogy between letters and the courses of a meal. She hoped that her letters could be compared to the "solid food" of the first course. She then supplied the standard for this favorable comparison: "it is not the studied sentence, nor the elaborate period, which pleases, but the genuine sentiments of the heart expressed with simplicity." This standard, in which morality was conflated with taste, was central to sensibility. Richardson developed the form of the epistolary novel to high art but had begun *Pamela* with the intention of supplying the growing number of literate women with models of letters. Abigail here referred to such models as her introduction to her view of Richardson: "All the specimens, which have been handed down to us as models for letter-writing, teach us that natural ease is the greatest beauty of it." A second quality, simplicity, was not limited to writing: "It is that native simplicity too, which gives to the Scotch songs a merit superior to all others. My favorite Scotch song, 'There's na luck about the house,' will naturally occur to your mind."[107]

Abigail implied that Richardson's novels had provided her own model for writing letters: "I believe that Richardson has done more towards embellishing the present age, and teaching them [women] the talent of letter writing, than any other modern I can name." Women were denied the education that would have allowed them to model their literacy on the ancients, as men could. Richardson probably had had this in mind. Perhaps the rise of simplicity as an aesthetic imperative had the same cause. Cartesians had celebrated minds free of archaic, scholastic obscurities. Abigail continued in her assessment of Richardson: "You know I am passionately fond of all his works, even to his 'Pamela.' In the simplicity of our manners, we judge that many of his descriptions and some of his characters are beyond real life; but those, who have been conversant in these old corrupted countries, will be soon convinced that Richardson painted only the truth in his abandoned characters; and nothing beyond what human nature is capable of attaining, and frequently has risen to, in his amiable portraits." The "we" here are Americans—New Englanders, at least—and Abigail's contrast with the effects on the inhabitants of the "old corrupted countries," two of which, France and England, she has now experienced firsthand (albeit for little more than a year), represents another adaptation of a central contrast of the British culture of sensibility (emblematized by Richardson) between the country and the city. Eliza Lucas had also written a critical assessment of *Pamela*, assuming its applicability to "our sex" in South Carolina in 1742.[108]

Abigail's point, however, was Richardson's universality, more precisely, his representation of the humanity that was identified with sensibility: "Richardson was master of the human heart; he studied and copied nature; he has shown the odiousness of vice, and the fatal consequences which result from the practice of it; he has painted virtue in all her amiable attitudes; he never loses sight of religion, but points his characters to a future state of restitution as the sure ground of safety to the virtuous, and excludes not hope from the wretched peni-tent." This was the liberal Christianity that her father preached and a version of the faith that, with Quakerism, Methodism, and Latitudi-narian Anglicanism, helped promulgate English and American cultures of sensibility.[109]

Abigail's own beliefs had been improved by her immersion in Rich-ardson's novels: "The oftener I have read his books, and the more I re-flect upon his great variety of characters, perfectly well supported, the more I am led to love and admire the author. He must have an aban-doned, wicked, and depraved heart, who can be tempted to vice by a perusal of Richardson's works." This was to defend Richardson against those who condemned fiction, especially sentimental fiction, for its pu-tative effects on female readers, a concern that accompanied their ris-ing literacy and appetite for the novels that appealed to the potentially arousing connotations of sensibility. Reading sentimental novels, it was argued, could lead women to fantasy, masturbation, being seduced, or adultery. Women could also be led to seduce men. Henry Fielding paro-died *Pamela* as *Shamela*, depicting the eponymous heroine as a "calculat-ing hussy," using her sensibility to stimulate her suitor, Parson Tickle-text. John illustrated that women should be forbidden other kinds of books, too, in warning Abigail off the libertine Chesterfield, as we shall see in a moment. Recognizing this boundary, sentimental novelists de-clared their object the reformation of their readers' manners, even as they titillated them.[110]

Abigail gave Lucy Cranch her assessment of "Richardson's works": "I know not how a person can read them without being made better by them, as they dispose the mind to receive and relish every good and be-nevolent principle." They improved the reader's sensibility. Eliza Lucas discussed the defects in Pamela's character but then praised Richardson for his "truth to nature," esteeming him "much for the regard he pays to virtue and religion throughout the whole piece."[111]

In reply to Abigail on Richardson, Lucy Cranch declared that she too, had been able to enjoy the consumption of novels and was "flattered by" Abigail's "encomiums upon Richardsons works as it is what I have often thought. He was always a favourite author of mine. I think I never read any Romances, that taken alltogether were equal to his." In pur-suing the pleasures of reading "Romances"—and we can assume that they were sentimental novels—Lucy knew that she had run the risks of which she knew her aunt was aware. "Too many of them," she continued, "if they do not lead directly to Vice, tend to enervate the mind and robs it of the strength which is necessary to make it stem with resolution the torrent of folly, which too often prevails."[112]

Laurence Sterne increased the pleasurable risks in the literature of sensibility. The publication of the first two volumes of *Tristram Shandy*, five years after Richardson's *Sir Charles Grandison*, opened a new phase in the evolution of the literary side of cultures of sensibility. His work was widely read and, because of its sexual double entendres, provoked sharp reaction in the American colonies, as it did in Britain.[113] John read Sterne's *The Sermons of Mr. Yorick* in 1761, the year after it was published, and he alluded familiarly both to *Tristram Shandy* and to Sterne's second novel in 1776 ("I have had a very unsentimental Journey").[114] In 1780, Abigail wrote James Lovell: "I have read Sterns Sermons and Yoricks Sentimental journey, [and] his Letters to Eliza [and found his writings] a rich Stream of Benevolence flowing like milk and Honey, that in an insensible heart, he creates the sensation he describes—in a feeling one, he softens, he melts, he moulds it into all his own." She quoted *A Sentimental Journey* to her sister Mary in 1788 in response to the news of their uncle's death. Sterne had forecast that those "who had read *Tristram* in the bedroom, would read his *Journey* . . . in the parlour," and, like many of his readers, Abigail distinguished between "the purest of his works," which she admired, and the "risqué" *Tristram Shandy*, which she "absolutely refused to open." Or at least that is what she told Lovell, who engaged her in a flirtatious, Sternean correspondence. She had begun the same letter by telling Lovell: "I must I will call you—wicked Man. I told you that I had discovered in your character, a similitude to that of Sterns and Yorick, but I never was before tempted to add that of Shandy." She added: "From your own Authority I quote him as a wicked creature—what demon prompted you to carry the character through." John had written to Abigail from Philadelphia in 1777, telling her that one of his fellow lodgers was "as droll and funny as Tristram Shandy," assuming that she knew those characteristics of Sterne's novel and responded positively to them. But John, too, had comparable reservations, as he illustrated in a letter to Jefferson (who revered Sterne) in which he praised the Psalms of David for their "sublimity, beauty, pathos and Originality": "[Their] Morality, however, often shocks me, like Tristam Shandy's execrations."[115]

Abigail also referred to Sterne in her correspondence with Jefferson; it seems likely that they had discussed Sterne during the intimate times they spent together at the Auteuil house the Adamses rented when Adams and Jefferson were fellow diplomats in Paris. After leaving that house for John's embassy in London, Abigail had written her first letter to Jefferson, telling him that she had "to resign her pet," a "little bird," to "[her] Parisian chambermaid, or the poor thing would have fluttered itself to Death": "I mourned the loss." But a "young Gentleman" on the Dover packet gave her two others, "in gratitude" for her letting him share the Adamses' cabin because he was "excessively" seasick. This was an episode she cast in Sterne-like terms for Jefferson. Eight months after telling him about mourning her bird, Abigail wrote Jefferson of her homesickness, saying that at "present we are in the situation of Sterne's starling," knowing Jefferson's familiarity with *A Sentimental Journey*. John referred to the same episode in a letter to Rush. Abigail assumed that her sister Elizabeth knew *A Sentimental Journey*, too, and, in an 1800 letter to Mary, Abigail referred to the "sparrow as Sterne commented upon, in his Sentimental Journey." The association of Sternean sensibility with sympathy for a bird would be politicized with a vengeance at the turn of the century.[116]

Nabby showed her familiarity with Sterne's posthumous *Journal to Eliza* in one of her letters to Betsy Cranch and then with *A Sentimental Journey* when she crossed the English Channel. (She and her mother had first landed in London, and John had rejoined them there, the three then traveling together to Paris.) Nabby recorded that they "came to Monsieur Destaing's Hotel the very place made famous by Yorick; in this yard he wrote his preface to his journey, and perhaps in one of these disobligeants [a carriage], he met Madame De——," and she continued by imagining that "the Monk" they next saw was the very one "that gave his benediction to our writer and who has just passed my window to present himself to papa." Then they "passed through Montrieul; this place is made famous by every one who has read Yorick's Journey. I regret that I have it not with me—I should read it with more pleasure now than ever before, as we are to pass through every place which he describes." Quite soon thereafter, when Nabby was back in London, she referred to the opening of *A Sentimental Journey* in a letter to John Quincy, who also knew Sterne's writings. After he married Nabby, in June 1786, Colonel Smith, traveling through France, wrote her with similar allusions.[117]

## Chesterfield versus Rousseau

Rousseau came to be categorized on one side of the century's long-standing debate over nature and artificiality. Adherents of sensibility identified themselves with the former, and the latter came to be identified with Chesterfield, that is, *Letters to His Son and Others*, by Philip Dormer Stanhope, Lord Chesterfield, published posthumously in 1774. In 1776, Abigail asked John, then in Philadelphia, to "purchase Lord Chesterfields Letters—I have lately heard them very highly spoken of." But John replied: "Chesterfields Letters are a chequered sett. You would not choose to have them in your Library, they are like Congreves Plays, stained with libertine Morals and base Principles." This, incidentally, illustrated John's agreement with Collier, who had criticized Congreve and other Restoration playwrights for their libertinism.[118] John also shared in the reaction that made Chesterfield the byword for artificial manners aimed at seduction. Dr. Johnson said of Chesterfield's *Letters*: "[They] teach the morals of a whore and the manners of a dancing master." In fact, Chesterfield's advice can now be seen as a further contribution to what Norbert Elias describes as "the civilizing process," advising how to drink coffee and tea and use a fork, among other things, but quite frank in its embrace of a man's pursuit of less reputable pleasures.[119]

Abigail replied to John's rejection of her request: "I give up my Request for Chesterfields Letters submitting intirely to your judgment, as I have found you ready to oblige me in this way whenever you thought it would contribute either to my entertainment or improvement." This was telling deference, but one wonders if she meant that she would have been less submissive had John been less obliging. John did want Abigail to benefit from the expansion of her reading, even if he assumed his right to direct it. He read Chesterfield's *Letters* himself, and he would continue to refer to them without disapproval when he found them useful.[120]

In fact, as Abigail wrote disingenuously to Mercy Otis Warren in February 1780, a "collection of his Lordships [Chesterfield's] Letters came into my Hands this winter which I read." In spite of her defiance of John's refusal to sanction her reading Chesterfield, Abigail was led to share his opinion, although she qualified it. She continued: "I found enough to satisfy me, that his Lordship with all his Elegance and graces, was a Hypocritical, polished Libertine, a mere Lovelace, but . . . Lovelace was the most generous Man of the two, since he had justice sufficient to acknowledge the merit he was distroying, and died penitently

warning others, whilst his Lordship not content himself with practise-
ing, but is . . . inculcating the most immoral, pernicious and Libertine
principals into the mind of a youth whose natural Guardian he was, and
at the same time calling upon him to wear the outward Garb of virtue."
This was a masking of villains with which sentimentalists and republicans were obsessed. But, while she despised him, Abigail told Warren:
"I am not so blinded by his abuse upon our sex, as not to allow his Lordship the merit of an Elegant pen, a knowledge of *Mankind* and a com-
piler of many Excellent maxims and rules for the conduct of youth, but
they are so poisoned with a mixture of Libertinism that I believe they
will do more injury than benefit to Mankind."[121] This combination of
responses—the expression of her own wishes regarding the book, her
following John's willfulness, her continuing attraction to an elegant literary man, and her vulnerability to being deceived by him—resembled
not only Clarissa's response to Lovelace (and women's responsiveness to
fictional and real rakes) but also the course of her subsequent relations
with Royall Tyler.[122]

Five months later, she again referred to Chesterfield in a letter to John
Thaxter, her cousin, then in Paris as John's secretary. She had flattered
Thaxter, a bachelor, by contrasting his style of manhood with Chesterfield's. American ladies, she wrote, feared "that the Parissian Ladies
will rob them of their favorite American," that is, Thaxter. In America
of 1780, she continued, "we have so few Gentlemen . . . whose morals
and principals are so pure and unimpeachable," like Thaxter's, who possessed, "a Heart unhacknyed in Gallantries": "It is a *rara avis* in these days
of Modern refinement and Chesterfieldian politeness, but the Devotees
to his Lordships sentiments, must excuse me if I observe, that with all
his Graces and politeness he has exhibited a peculiar Asperity against the
Sex, inconsistent with that boasted refinement of sentiment upon which
he lays so great stress, and Marks him in my mind a wretched votarie of
vice, a voluptuary whose soul was debased by his dissolute connexions,
a habit which vitiates the purest taste." Abigail's words illustrate that
Chesterfield, too, had been a writer of sensibility but that it had been
a false sensibility, used against women. Her indignation here may well
have been animated by her anger against the Parisian ladies whom her
letters show she feared were attempting to rob her of her favorite American (who had blithely revealed his attraction), that is to say, John. And,
here, Abigail continued in terms with which she habitually idealized her
relationship with him, in further contrast to the false and misogynistic
Chesterfield: "and excludes all that refined and tender Friendship, that

sweet consent of souls in unison, that Harmony of minds congenial to each other." She then quoted two lines from Pope's "Eloisa and Abelard," that poem of sensibility, written in the voice of a woman attempting to transform her sensual, earthly love into a sublimated kind:

"Where thought meets thought e'er from lips it part
And each pure wish springs mutual from the Heart"

and without which it is vain to look for happiness in that indissoluble union which Naught but death dissolves.[123]

In the same letter, Abigail contrasted the kind of sex enjoyed by Chesterfieldian gentlemen as they capitalized on sensibility merely for that purpose with the kind that, implicitly, she had with John: "The Heart must be engaged to reap the genuine fruits of tenderness; contemptibly low must that commerce be in which the mind has no share. Love is an intellectual pleasure, and even the senses will be weakly affected where the Heart does not participate." Abigail explained that she urged this point to persuade Thaxter not to become Chesterfieldian in his sexuality but instead "to find a soft and tender Friendship, enlivened by taste, refined by sentiment"—genuine sentiment, that is—in a relationship like the one she believed she had and would share again with the absent John, "which time instead of destroying, will render every hour more dear and interesting."

Then she described a forthcoming marriage in Boston that embodied this same contrast in morals and sensibility and demonstrated that Chesterfieldian rakery was by no means absent from America. She could not close, she wrote Thaxter, without mentioning "a connexion soon to take place between a Brother of your profession and a celebrated Lady who resides some times here and some times at B[osto]n." She knew that Thaxter would know the future bridegroom and bride: "You know who publickly affronted the whole Sex, and you know what Lady had refused such a Gentleman and such a Gentleman—for a Gambling Rake." The "Lady" here Abigail mentioned to Thaxter was celebrated, in part at least, she suggested, for the notably higher degree of refinement shown by her refusal of immoral men, one of them known for his seduction and abandonment of women. She asked Thaxter, "Can a Bosom of Sensibility and Innocence, accept a Heart hardened by a commerce with the most profligate of the Sex? [i.e., prostitutes] a Constitution enfeabled, the fine feelings of the soul obliterated?"

The hardening of the heart was synonymous with the obliteration of

fine feelings and both with the loss of that sensibility that made a gentleman such as Thaxter, if he persevered in "purity of sentiment," capable of "a soft and tender friendship" with a lady. The contrary outcome of the forthcoming marriage Abigail predicted with this rhetorical
question: "What but disgust, suspicion, coldness, and depravity of taste,
can be the consequence?" This, of course, also alluded to sex. The yok-
ing of a lady of sensibility to a man without it, caused either by a willful but naive daughter's choosing a husband for herself or by an archai-
cally arbitrary father who arranged his daughter's marriage against her
wishes, was a frequent theme in sentimental culture, signifying the rise
of the former and the decline of the latter. Again, the best-known example was that in *Clarissa*, where the heroine faced her father's choice for
her in the crude, ill-educated, and insensitive Solmes; Richardson here,
as elsewhere, suggests the influence of the feminist Mary Astell.[124] The
actual mésalliance that Abigail forecast to Thaxter may have been the
anonymous marriage that gave rise to the first post-Constitution, but
still Richardson- and Rousseau-inspired, American sentimental novel,
William Hill Brown's *The Power of Sympathy; or, The Triumph of Nature:
Founded in Truth* (1789).[125]

Thaxter defended himself to Abigail as a man of feeling, despite some
degree of slowness in its expression. He wrote her from Paris in 1783 that
he had been reading a life of Eloise and Abelard, his interest probably
"sparked" by Pope's poem, to which Thaxter referred in another letter
and from which Abigail had quoted to him. While he ascribed his ability
to "read the History of the unfortunate Pair without the ordinary Marks
of Sensibility" to the extinction of the "Sentiment" of love and his loss
of an "Inclination" for matrimony, he also remarked: "No one is to be
deemed callous whose Sensibility does not instantly melt into Tears on
reading or hearing an affecting History or Anecdote. Passions operate
differently on different Subjects—more or less violently." He asked:
"Who knows the Sufferings and convulsive Agitations of one who shews
few external Marks of them? A Tear is often an equivocal proof of Sensibility." This was Sternean: Thaxter wanted Abigail to know that he was
still a man of feeling.[126]

John posed Rousseau against Chesterfield in writing Abigail from
prerevolutionary Paris: "Have you ever read J. J. Rousseau. If not read
him—your Cousin Smith has him. What a difference between him and
Chesterfield, and even Voltaire? But he was too virtuous for the Age,
and for Europe—I wish I could not say for another Country." John's
library contained Rousseau's collected works and a separate edition of

*La nouvelle Heloïse* (to which John added his own marginalia), its heroine's name charged with Pope's sentimental rendering of the medieval
lover. Kerber has noted "the widespread popularity of Rousseau's less
theoretical works in America, particularly of *Emile* and *Heloïse*," a popularity that she links to what these books said of women's education.
*Heloïse* "prompted an . . . intense debate on the nature of women's emotions."[127] In Rousseau, Abigail found a resource when writing to John
of her greatest emotional pain: "Most feelingly do I experience that sentiment of Rousseau's 'that one of the greatest evils of absence, and the
only one which reason cannot alleviate, is the inquietude we are under
concerning the actual state of those we love, their health, their life, their
repose, their affections. Nothing escapes the apprehension of those who
have everything to lose.'" She added some sentimental exclamations of
her own, including: "How tormenting is absence!"[128]

But John later reversed his opinion of Rousseau, calling him, in response to the *Confessions* (1782), "a coxcomb and . . . satyr."[129] He read
the *Discourse sur l'inégalité* in 1794, "during the worst period of the Terror," and, like English anti-Jacobins (who followed Burke's attribution
to Rousseau of "a systematic scheme . . . to destroy all social and family
relationships, thus enabling the French revolutionaries to take power"),
he grouped Rousseau with other Enlightenment writers, Voltaire notably among them, who were accused of causing the French Revolution.[130] The Revolution appalled him—he read Burke's *Reflections on the
Revolution in France*, and he bought the English anti-Jacobin *Pursuits of
Literature* by Thomas James Mathias (1798), which targeted those same
writers. His reversal of his view of Rousseau can stand for the more general postrevolutionary reevaluation of sentimentalism, the excesses of
which were held to lead to sexual and political anarchy.[131] Abigail, however, drew on John's now detested Rousseau in 1799 to make a bitterly
ironic comment on the effects of John's absence on her happiness. She
had just received a letter of his, "with a Heart filled with Gratitude, for
the many Blessings I have enjoyed through the 35 years of our union."
For many of them he had left her on public business. "I would not," she
continued, "look upon a single shade in the picture; for it according to
Rousseau's philosophy, abstinence of what we delight in, is the Epicurism of Reason; I have had my full proportions of enjoyment."[132]

CHAPTER 2

# The Meanings of Sensibility

## The Effects of Reading and Writing on Persons of Sensibility

The Adamses' conception of the effects of reading and writing on persons of sensibility reflected the hypostasis of the nervous system denoted by the word *sensibility*. An "Ode to Sensibility," published in the *Carlisle (PA) Gazette* in 1786, saw it implemented by reading:

> From thee proceed those joys refin'd,
> That luxury of the exalted mind,
> Which reading gives—that bliss divine,
> The soul receives from every line.

It operated by the Cartesian psychophysiology that Latitudinarians and others had begun to popularize long before:

> let my heart, like wax, receive
> Each soft impression thou can give!

The Adamses described the effects of books on them, but handwritten words made the same kinds of impressions and were the constant subjects of sentimental correspondence. John wrote Abigail in 1775: "Your two last Letters had very different Effects. The long one gave me vast Satisfaction. It was full of usefull Information, and of excellent Sentiments. The other relating to the ill Usage you have received . . . gave me great Pain and the utmost Indignation." A letter about her mother's illness "renewed" John's "Grief and Anxiety." These letters stimulated his emotions directly.[1]

Abigail made it clear that she believed that words could affect readers involuntarily, or "irresistibly," to invoke Norman Fiering. The "news" of Francis Dana's return from Europe without John (whose secretary Dana had been) reached Abigail's "Ears" and then, via her nervous system and her brain, stimulated her eyes: "how was I affected? The Tears involuntary flowed from my eyes . . . my Heart swelled with Grief, and the Idea that I, I only, was left alone, recall'd all the tender Scenes of seperation, and overcame all my fortitude."[2] Mary Cranch wrote Abigail in 1784: "Your Letters excited a variety of immotions in my Breast as I read them." She explained the process, culminating in tears: "Your tender and affectionate expressions for me and mine soften me to a Baby, and your sufferings wounded my Heart. In short when I had finish'd I set down and weep'd heartily." Similarly, John Quincy Adams wrote Nabby in 1785 that he had kept her "letter for the last" to read: "I will not attempt to express my sensations in reading it, were I to tell you that a tear involuntarily started from my eye, you would think I carry sentiment too far, and that I am weak—that circumstance I will keep to myself." Evidently, he did not. To these private illustrations can be added Tom Paine's published wish that the readers of his *Crisis Papers* "look on this [verbal] picture and weep."[3]

Nabby received a letter from Betsy very soon after she and Abigail arrived in London in 1784. Abigail described her response to it in a letter to her niece Betsy's other aunt, Abigail's sister Elizabeth Shaw: "Dear Romantick Girl, her little narative of her visit to the deserted cottage made me weep." Her weeping indicated the extent of her affection for her home as well as the pain of being apart from it, the word *deserted*, of course, connoting the presence of her family there as well as their absence. Nostalgia was another expression of the juxtaposition of pleasure and pain, which enhanced each other and, along with other such contrasts, were aggrandized by cultures of sensibility. *Romantick* was a word that Mercy Otis Warren, too, associated with the sentimental.[4]

The absence of Nabby and her parents in Europe made Betsy susceptible in the same way: "I have felt an unusual tenderness [for the two youngest Adams children, Charles and Thomas, left with the Shaws], a tenderness, bordering upon (if not really, a weakness) fills my heart, whenever I look upon them." This was because they had been "left behind" and because they therefore reminded her of Nabby's absence: "One Clause in my Uncles Letter to Papa [i.e., John's letter to Richard Cranch] affected me more than I have been in reading a deep tragedy. I know not why, but I instantly burst into tears, as I read it, nor can I recollect it without feeling the same emotions. . . . I cannot tell you *why* it had this effect, but it touched the tenderest string in my heart."[5]

In 1782 Nabby wrote her cousin Betsy of "your susceptible heart, the seat of goodness, of benivolence and every worthy sentiment." Persons of sensibility believed that feelings could be generated by the heart,

which operated mechanically. While Descartes thought that "the seat
of the passions is not the heart"—the traditional belief that continued
to be held—he allowed that the passions could not be readily altered or
checked by the soul because "they are almost all accompanied by some
excitation taking place in the heart, and consequently also throughout
the blood and the spirits."[6] Passions were moved by the heat generated
by the pumping of the heart. According to Jefferson's "Heart," one side
of the dialogue he created between "Heart" and "Head" in 1786, "Nature" allotted the field of morals to the heart, "the feelings of sympathy,
of benevolence, of gratitude, of justice, of love, of friendship." Jefferson explained that nature had adapted "the mechanism of the heart" to
these feelings: "[Morals] were too essential to the happiness of man to
be risked in the uncertain combinations of the head. [Nature] laid their
foundation therefore in sentiment, not in science. This she gave to all,
as necessary to all." By *science* here, Jefferson referred to architecture, astronomy, and physics.[7]

According to the mechanical system connoted by *sensibility*, the nerves'
signals triggered an idea or a thought or a recollection in the brain, a
kind of relay station that stimulated return signals, emotion first, then
tears or sighs, trembling or blushes, or silences, the dropping of a pen, or
words, all of which had to be recorded when the purposed recipient was
at a distance. Pinckney wrote to Lady Nicholas Carew in 1755: "I took
up my penn [the day after receiving your last letter] in order to write
[you] but really was so affected when I began upon recolecting the many
repeated trials you have had for the last 2 years . . . that I was lost in the
gloomy contemplation and threw aside my penn as utterly uncapable of
giving the least consolation to my afflicted friend." We saw that Abigail
thought of "Idea" in this way and that Betsy Cranch was moved at the
recollection of a line in John Adams's letter. Similarly Abigail wrote,
"I had many disagreeable Sensations at the Thoughts," etc., and, "Aya
why drops the tear as I write? Why these tender emotions of a Mothers Breast, is it not folly to be thus agitated with a thought?—Nature
all powerfull Nature!" Descartes had explained that, once the passions
have been excited, "they remain present to our thought in the same way
as objects capable of being sensed are present to it while they are acting
upon our sense organs." He noted that "some remnants of love or pity,
presented to [a man's] imagination draw genuine tears from his eyes."[8]

Abigail wrote to John in October 1774, imagining having him to herself for twelve hours straight. "The Idea plays about my Heart, unnerves
my hand whilst I write, awakens all the tender sentiments that years have

encreased and matured, and which when with me were every day dispensing to you." (*Unnerve* here is an older usage, meaning "weaken," as today *having nerve* means "bold.") Evidently also having absorbed Locke's development of Descartes's conception of the association of ideas and conveying it with mixed metaphors, Abigail wrote her uncle, Cotton Tufts: "You blew up a train of Ideas—not very delicate ones I assure you. What a Scene did you paint? The thought of it makes me Squemish." *Train of ideas*, *scene*, and *thought* all operated as such relay points.[9]

Words could have the same effect as music. Musical metaphors were prominent in sentimental language, linked to the word *strings*, and indebted to Newton as well as to Henry More and their literary descendants. One of Newton's followers, Dr. George Cheyne, some of whose work John had in his library and whose fashionable regime of purgative vomits he and Abigail followed, further popularized the metaphor, writing in 1705 that the "Intelligent Principle, or *Soul*, resides somewhere in the Brain, where all the Nerves, or instruments of sensation terminate, like a *Musician* in a finely fram'd and well tun'd Organ-Case; theses Nerves are the Keys which, being struck on or touch'd, convey the Sound and Harmony to this Sentient Principle, or *Musician*." In describing the "fibres" of the nerves, Cheyne suggested that the compactness and closer union of parts "seems to be the Reason for the greater Degree of Sensibility." Abigail wrote John in 1781, during his mission in Europe, that she had received a letter from Jean de Neufville: "How did this Man discover, that extolling my Husband was the sweetest Musick in my ears? He has certainly touched the key which vibrates Harmony to me!" John, too, found the effect of words on his nervous system comparable to that of music. In 1783, he wrote Abigail: "A Packet [of letters] from you is always more than I can bear. It gives me a great Pleasure, the highest Pleasure, and therefore makes me and Leaves me Melancholly, like the highest Strains in Music." The second sentence explains the unbearability of the first. The extreme pitch of the pleasure in his receipt and reading of Abigail's words touched him as emotionally as the highest of musical strains, but, implicitly, the transmittal of the letters was a limited substitute for the presence of the writer—they represent absence and distance as well as limitation. The pleasure they brought must be soon over, like that part of the music. That was another combination of pleasure and pain. Responsiveness both to musical notes and to words was believed to operate in the same way.[10]

We saw in chapter 1 that Abigail praised "the Scotch songs" for their simplicity: she described their effect in another letter, introducing her

description with a quotation asserting the perfect harmony of her relationship with John:

> "For in one fate, our Hearts our fortunes
>   And our Beings blend."

> I cannot discribe to you How much I was affected the other day with a
> Scotch song which was sung to me by a young Lady in order to divert
> a Melancholy hour, but it had a quite different Effect, and the Native
> Simplicity of it, had all the power of a well-wrought Tradidy. When I
> could conquer my Sensibility I beg'd the song, and Master Charles has
> learnt it and consoles his Mamma by singing it to her. I will enclose it
> to you. It has Beauties in it to me, which an indifferent person would
> not feel perhaps.

Abigail's having had to conquer her sensibility in this case was by no
means because it was bad but because doing so was necessary in order
to be able to speak words. The song's attraction lay in this effect, arousing her sensibility to something like awe or wonder by way of pain (the
power of tragedy) combined with the aesthetic pleasure in simplicity.
Having it repeated to her (the pleasure perhaps strengthened by the natural simplicity of her eight-year-old's soprano voice) either had the same
effect or one she was able to temper by familiarity. Finally, she represents her responsiveness here as a mark of superiority to a person without such a refined capacity. Those "who feel," a phrase marking adherents of the culture of sensibility, were synonymous with those with
sensibility. She next quoted the words of the song, clearly applicable to
her re-creation of her feelings about John's absence and her apprehensions that he would not return:

> His very foot has Musick in't,
>   As he comes up the stairs.

> How oft has my Heart danced to the sound of that Musick?

> And shall I see his face again?
>   And shall I hear him speak?[11]

So music affected Abigail with prospective pain, too, heightening her
sensibility to a pitch comparable to John's.

The value that Abigail placed on the emotional effects of this song was
an adaptation of convention. Franklin had praised Scottish folk ballads
as "simple tunes sung by a single voice" because of their harmonizing of

the individual note with each one proceeding. This was in 1762, shortly after James MacPherson's supposed discovery of the ancient Gaelic of Ossian, with whom proponents of an "elocutionary revolution" associated Homer. Both poets had articulated a "natural spoken language akin to music." Jefferson spelled out the musical characteristics of Homer's Greek and, with others, believed that Ossian's verse originally had been sung. Both were identifiable with the "natural language" (defined by the Scottish moralist Thomas Reid), which Jay Fliegelman suggests inspired sentimental writers' attempts to make words correspond to feelings. According to the Adamses' beloved Pope, Homer's poetry was "nature."[12] John Wesley, too, associated Gaelic melody with ancient Greek in his "Thoughts on the Power of Music" (1779), and he also believed that the music of Celtic peasants was "composed not according to art, but nature—they are simple to the highest degree." Hence, listeners were "much affected." He put this power to use, setting many of his hymns to "Scotch and Irish airs." The New England composer William Billings said in *The New England Psalm Singer* (1770) that the solo human voice was capable of "awakening every passion of which the heart is capable."[13]

John replied to Abigail's gift: "Dr. J is transcribing your scotch song, which is a charming one. Oh my leaping Heart." The adjective perhaps referred to the movement of the music as well as of his foot up Abigail's stair. In this subject as in others, the Adams correspondence illustrates direct and indirect ways in which the ideas of preceding originators and popularizers were absorbed and put to individual use.[14]

Music could invoke a combination of pleasure and pain, a combination prized as a mark of heightened sensibility. Describing the virtues of her dead husband, Eliza Lucas Pinckney told her mother: "This pleases while it pains and may be called the luxury of grief." Abigail recorded that the tears one of her sons shed at parting "melted [her] Heart a thousand times"—another's tears could act on the system in the same way that words did. Then she asked with the intensity of self-examination so essential to cultures of sensibility: "Why does the mind Love to turn to these painfull scenes and to recollect them with pleasure." Abigail had written three years earlier that she often sat

> myself down alone to think of my absent Friend, to ruminate over past scenes, to read over Letters, Journals, &c.
>
> 'Tis a melancholy kind of pleasure I find in this amusement, whilst the weighty cares of state scarcly leave room for a tender recollection or sentiment to steal into the Bosome of my Friend.

Part of her pain was caused by the thought that John's thoughts were not commensurately devoted to her.[15]

Such passages recall that *scene* was another frequently employed term for the conscious renewal of painful/pleasurable sensations and, like music, a metaphor that connoted performance. The Adamses often represented John's public life with theatrical metaphors, reflecting that psychology that Abigail's sister, Elizabeth Smith Shaw, laid out in response to a letter Abigail wrote her from France in 1785, introducing it with: "Knowing your Taste for Literature, I am not at all surprized that you should prefer Theatrical Amusements to any-other." "To find the Soul alive to all the finer feelings," she continued, "can be no unpleasing Sensation to the humane Breast, and the frequent Exercise must give them strength and greatly conduce to refine the moral Taste, and strengthen the virtuous Temper, for a very slight inspection into human Nature must convince us, that no Objects have so powerful an impression on us, as those which are immediately impressed on our Senses—and therefore those things which have not a tendency to mend the Heart, and improve the Genius, ought never to be exhibited." John had been improved in this way by his visit to the Peacocks. In discussing the history of sensibility in eighteenth-century metropolitan Britain, Jessie Van Sant argues that experts on sensation emphasized "the significance of sight in moving the passions," even though she contends that touch "is the central sense of sensibility." This is "crucial to an understanding of the pathetic presentations" of characters in fiction, in poetry, and on the stage and of inmates at various charitable institutions in London and other cities. Such institutions' audiences were composed of middle- and upper-class visitors, preached to by resident ministers. In London, Abigail visited "the foundling hospital," where she "attended divine service on sunday morning," and "the Magdeline in the afternoon," the latter a "publick Building" erected to house reformed prostitutes. (In the South Carolina backcountry, Charles Woodmason recalled listening to the singing of "the Girls at the Magdalene Chapel.") In Paris, she and Nabby visited the Hospital des Enfants Trouves. John went too.[16] Van Sant argues that the inmates of such philanthropic institutions were "instruments," both for the creation of pity and for scientific demonstration.[17]

This kind of exposure could be imagined, of course, most obviously in reading novels, but John was capable of depicting an interior scene to Abigail resembling those in which she set herself in her letters to him, a scene within which he described his creating another one: "Sitting down to write to you, is a Scene almost too tender for my State of

Nerves. It calls up to my View the anxious, distress'd State you must be in, amidst the Confusions and Dangers, which surround you."[18]

Like other persons of sensibility—Pinckney, for example—Abigail and John told each other of the pleasure that reading letters brought them. John told Abigail during their courtship: "next to Conversation, Correspondence with you is the greatest Pleasure in the World to yr. John Adams." In later years, when all they had was correspondence, he wrote: "Your Letters never failed to give me Pleasure—the greatest Pleasure that I take, is in receiving them." Abigail wrote him: "My Heart is as light as a feather and my Spirits are dancing. I received this afternoon a fine parcel of Letters."[19]

That words could wound as well as bring pleasure was conventionally represented by metaphors derived from literal torture, a practice that was then the object of humanitarian reform, in part prompted by the spread of sensibility. As in other cases, this was a literary trope that had existed since classical times but was now reiterated to the extent of being a mark of the culture of sensibility. John wrote Abigail in 1774, "I have suffered such Torments in my Mind," in order to invoke the kind of sympathy that Adam Smith had illustrated by asking his readers to imagine "our brother . . . upon the rack." (Mary Cranch wrote her sister in 1774: "I have been so long in an uncertainty what we ought to do; and one Friend advising one way and one another that I feel rack'd.")[20] Abigail's letters were more marked than John's by this convention, above all because of the suffering that separation from John caused her. She wrote at one point: "my Soul is wounded at a Seperation from you." And elsewhere she referred to "the cruel torture of Seperation," *separation* being a word that emphasized the literal possibilities in being "Bereft of my better Half."[21] When her grown and ne'er-do-well son Charles died in 1800, Abigail wrote her sister Mary: "Weep with me over the Grave of a poor unhappy child who cannot add an other pang to those which have pierced my Heart for several years past."[22]

It was because of the power of words to wound persons of feeling that Abigail warned John not to mention the tribulations of one of their sons to the Warrens, "not even to them by the slightest hint. Tis a wound which cannot be touched." Early in their relationship, she had told John that his words could hurt her. She wrote him that she had been "discomposed" when his words had applied a "corrosive . . . when a Lenitive would have answered the same good purpose." In stating the "lesson" that she had learned from this, she emphasized how susceptible she was because of her possession of "a feeling heart": "But I hope I have drawn a lesson from that which will be useful to me in futurity, viz. never to say a severe thing because to a feeling heart they wound to deeply to be easily cured." The feeling heart held the same positive value as the phrase characterizing her responsiveness to that Scotch song, "an indifferent person would not feel, perhaps," aggrandizing her sensibility. Here, typically, she muffled her apparent criticism: "Pardon me this is not said to recriminate, and I have only mentiond it, that whenever there is occasion a different method may be taken."[23]

The absence of words, too, could do emotional harm. Later in 1778, she wrote John, now having been in Europe for the best part of a year: "My Heart so wounded by the Idea of inattention that the very Name of my Dearest Friend [uttered by another] would draw tears from me." It is difficult to exaggerate how persistent were Abigail's complaints about John's not writing or not writing often enough. "What can be the reason I have not heard from you since the 20 of April, and now tis the 27 of May. My anxious foreboding Heart fears every Evil, and my Nightly Slumbers are tortured," she wrote him in Philadelphia.[24]

The right words could have the opposite effect to wounding; they could soothe, heal, or restore. On the receipt of letters from John, Abigail reported: "[They] calmd my Soul to peace. I cannot discribe the Effect they had upon me, cheerfulness and tranquility took place of grief and anxiety." The paper that John had touched in writing to her could substitute for his body or, one could say, was a substance both of them could invest with feeling: "I placed them Next my Heart and soothed myself to rest with the tender assurances of a Heart all my own." This may be compared to the actions and words of a male reader, described in a 1785 issue of the *Liberal American*, who had opened a book to a page still "wet with tears." Looking at the woman who had left this evidence of her responsiveness to the book's words, and "pressing the page to his lips, he exclaimed: 'Gracious Heaven! What enchanting sensibility.'"[25] John conveyed a similar response: his mind, he wrote Abigail in 1776, had been supported by "the choice Blessing of a Wife." When remote from her, he was "deprived in great Measure of this Comfort": "Yet I read, and read again your charming Letters, and they serve me, in some faint degree as a substitute for the Company and Conversation of the Writer."[26] Other intimately associated items moved Abigail's sensibility: "even the sight of a Garment (worn) belonging to him [John] will raise a mixture both of pleasure and pain in my Bosome." Abigail deleted the word *worn* evidently because of its sheer, intimate tactility of arousal, a measure of sexual self-consciousness and repression.[27]

The Adamses and their correspondents used medicinal metaphors to describe the effects of reading letters. John wrote Richard Cranch, his close friend and brother-in-law: "Every Line from Boston is a Cordial, and of great Use to us in our Business." Eunice Paine wrote Abigail that a letter from her, "as a token of your Love . . . revived my drooping Spirits." Warren, having heard, she wrote her, that Abigail and "the Little flock about you were very Ill," wrote her: "it is a great relief to my mind to be informed that so many of them are in better Health." She hoped Abigail would have her "Drooping spirits Revived Ere Long by a Letter from a Gentleman," that is, John. "Your Letters administer comfort to my wounded Heart."[28]

Writing letters as well as reading them had positive, self-medicating effects on persons of feeling. That John wrote to Richard Cranch, "It is a grief to my Heart that I cannot write to my Friends so often and particularly as I wish," is similar in its psychotherapeutic meaning to Abigail's telling John, "I do not feel easy more than two days together without writing to you." To John she wrote in 1778, "I have taken up my pen again to relieve the anxiety of a Heart too susceptable for its own repose," and, after hearing of Joseph Warren's death at Bunker Hill, "My bursting Heart must find vent at my pen." Such a view was analogous to the contemporary "heroic" medicine of bleeding, blistering, and purging; the notion that getting feelings out is psychologically beneficial contributed to that convention in twentieth- and twenty-first-century psychotherapy but is now at last under challenge.[29] Writing words for relief was a substitute for speaking them to a trusted, sympathetic bosom. Abigail wrote John in 1775, asking him: "Forgive me then, for thus dwelling upon a subject sweet to me, but I fear painfull to you. O how I have long'd for your Bosom to pour forth my sorrows there, and find a healing Balm." So relief was interactive, one's writing or speaking stimulating the other's production of balm.[30]

But here, as on other occasions, John's absence drove Abigail back to God, in effect, closer to her own psychological resources: "But perhaps that has been denied me that I might be led to a higher and more permanent consolater who has bid us call upon him in the day of trouble." Writing of New England women's greater predilection for religion, Nancy Cott has suggested: "Religious identity . . . allowed women to assert themselves. . . . It enabled them to rely on an authority beyond the world of men." Extending the notion to women from Anne Hutchinson to Sarah Grimké, she writes: "Religious faith allowed women a sort of holy selfishness or self-absorption, the result of self-examination intrinsic to the Calvinist tradition." Of course, it was intrinsic to Protestantism as a whole and central to male Protestant identities, too. Be that as it may, Cott's elaboration of her point reminds us of the connections between those seventeenth- and eighteenth-century developments in American and English Protestantism that supplied a genealogy to the rise of sensibility: "In contrast to the self-abnegation required of women in their domestic vocation, religious commitment required attention to one's own thoughts, actions, and prospects. By recording their religious meditations women expressed their literary and rising self-consciousness in a sanctioned mode." That mode—with the particular impress of Cartesianism and its successors, notably Lockeanism—pointed to modern psychology. But, while evidently holding the subversive potential to which Cott here refers, religion sought purely "as compensation," Donald Meyer points out, "could compound, not ameliorate women's lack of power," in such ambiguities mirroring the culture of sensibility with which it was intermixed.[31]

## Sensibility

I now turn to the meanings that the Adamses gave to individual terms signifying the culture of sensibility, members of a group that R. F. Brissenden, following William Empson, calls a "family of words."[32]

John's first written use of the word *sensibility* in a letter to Abigail was in an ironic premarital (May 1764) catalog of her "Faults," attributing to her "Country Life and Education" her "Modesty, sensibility, Bashfulness, call it by which of these Names you will, that enkindles Blushes forsooth at every Violation of Decency, in Company, and lays a most insupportable Constraint on the freedom of Behaviour." Here, and in the sentence following, he showed the value he placed on Abigail's sensibility insofar as it embodied propriety. Earlier, when Abigail was eighteen, John had made these notes about her: "Di. [Diana] was a constant feast. Tender feelings, sensible, friendly. A friend. Not an imprudent, not an indelicate, not a disagreeable Word or Action. Prudent, modest, delicate, soft, sensible, obliging, active." That *sensible* followed the words, *tender feelings*, *delicate*, and *soft* links it to sensibility, and, again in keeping with the *Spectator's* definition, John also linked the notion with modesty.[33]

Sensibility was identifiable with a high degree of receptivity, that is to say, the "softness" capable of registering delicate impressions, so it was with a matching irony that Abigail had answered his letter: "I was so hardned as to read over most of my Faults with as much pleasure, as an other person would have read their perfections. And Lysander must excuse me if I still persist in some of them at least till I am convinced that an alteration would contribute to his happiness." Abigail specified modesty, declaring: "there is such a thing as Modesty without either Hypocrisy or Formality." She accepted John's identification of modesty with sensibility, specifically, that a woman signaled her inner sense of propriety by the immediate, physiological responsiveness of blushing. This signal marked a boundary of politeness that should, she and John believed, be observed by both the blusher and by those who had it in their power to stimulate such signs. This, too, was consistent with the *Spectator*'s definition of modesty, signifying feminine sensibility.[34]

Later, in his diary, John made still more explicit the relation between nerve quality and sensibility. Describing himself (in the third person) and his cousin Sam Adams in relation to the "malice" of Governor Thomas Hutchinson, John wrote that the "Maker has given them Nerves that are delicate; and of Consequence; their Feelings are exquisite, and their Constitutions tender, and their Health . . . very infirm." In this, so far, they shared the value that women found in the finer sensibility that their supposedly distinctive nervous system gave them. It could be the basis of moral superiority. When, in 1776, it was rumored that John was dead, Abigail exclaimed: "How unfealing are the world! They tell me they Heard you was dead with as little sensibility as a stock or a stone." This ungendered sensibility, as it were, synonymous with "unfealing," conventionally adopted a stance at odds with *the world*, a phrase with evident Christian connotations ("My kingdom is not of this world" [John 18:36]), but one also connoting falsity of several kinds—fashionable display, political and courtly intrigue—as well as materialism, even though feeling could be feigned and sensibility itself had become a fashion. Abigail had read the Reverend James Fordyce's use of the word, for example, in his quoting "that great maxim of the apostle, 'Be not conformed to this world but be ye transformed,'" and in his referring to those, "unacquainted with the falsehood of the world, and warmed by affections which its selfishness has not yet chilled." Such a stance was synonymous with being a figure of "virtue in distress."[35]

This figure tended to be a female one: following Malebranche's redefinition and its popularization by the *Spectator*, women's nerves were deemed naturally more tender than men's, orienting them to greater mental weakness and physical inferiority, even susceptibility to nervous disorders. Because he and his cousin were male, John hastened to make clear in that passage referring to Hutchinson's malice that, not only had their "Maker" left them with their vulnerable delicacy of nerve, "But, as a Compensation for this He had been pleased to bestow upon them Spirits that are unconquerable by all the Art and all the power of Governor Hutchinson and his Political Creators and Creatures on both Sides of the Atlantic."[36] Earlier in his diary, John had described Sam Adams as "zealous, ardent, and keen in the cause, is always for Softness, and Delicacy, and Prudence where they will do, but is staunch and stiff and strict and rigid and inflexible, in the Cause." Colonel Sparhawk observed that Sam Adams was "a man . . . of great Sensibility, of tender Nerves, and harassed, dependent, in their Power." Sensibility, a physiological as well as a moral/psychological quality, was fine, but too much could incapacitate a man, unless he exercised his will, as Sparhawk immediately said Sam Adams had done: "Yet he had born up against all—it must have penetrated him very deeply." The latter reiterated the effects on his sensibility and underlined Sparhawk's admiration for Sam's endurance.[37]

Abigail usually held to the belief that nervous systems were gendered, but what this implied for character and what value she should place on it were long at issue for her. One could interpret her ambivalence as her not being able to attain the central insight of her younger contemporary Mary Wollstonecraft that a gendered sensibility was disabling for women, although her ambivalence was typical. Even Wollstonecraft could be ambivalent.[38] Abigail wrote John during their courtship that she was "often tempted to believe" that their hearts—operating as symbols for cognition—"were both cast in the same mould, only with this difference, that yours was made, with a harder mettle, and therefore is less liable to an impression." Liability to impression referred to degrees of sensibility, but Abigail implied that difference in mettle did not mean that they did not both have "an eaquil quantity of steel." Evidently, there could be significant common ground between women and men of sensibility—both had nerves more refined than those of persons without it—but sensibility was still gendered, a belief that Abigail consistently expressed. The definition supplied by the *Spectator* had become conventional in America as well as Britain. Franklin—a conscious imitator of the *Spectator* (he also printed extracts from it in his newspaper), and would-be improver of American manners, and yet another writer who demonstrated his absorption of Cartesian psychology—had written in 1745 that, while a woman lacked a man's "force of Body and

Strength of Reason," a man lacked a woman's "Softness, Sensibility and acute Discernment."[39]

Another expression of the value placed on women's naturally more responsive sensibility was in an unattributed poem written sometime after midcentury (it quotes Gray's sentimental "Elegy in a Country Churchyard" of 1751). The Pennsylvanian Milcah Martha Moore copied it into her *Commonplace Book*. A male speaker prayed to be

> Blest with a Wife the Mistress of my breast
> In whose fond Bosom all my Cares may rest,
> Let her possess a tender feeling Mind
> By sweetest Sensibility refin'd,
> A Heart that can with sympathetic Glow
> Partake a Brother's Joy, a Brother's Woe.

James Blair Linn reiterated this belief in 1795, when it was being strenuously reasserted: "female sensibility [is] naturally more refined than the male."[40]

## Sentimental, Sentiment, Sense, Sensible, Insensibility, and Sensation

Abigail wrote John on July 25, 1775, and told him that his letter of July 7 "was the longest and best Letter I have had, the most Leasurely and therefore the most Sentimental." Abigail had continued by rewarding him for this sentimentality by promising that she would take back the "complaints of you" she had made in her previous letter, provided, she warned, "only continue your obliging favours whenever your time will allow you to devote one moment to your absent Portia." In her view, his being sentimental was his paying attention to what was important to her. Conversely, she told him how wounded she was by his "inattention."[41]

The following items were the contents of the letter Abigail praised because it was sentimental. First, John referred to hers of June 22 and 23 as "very agreable Favours." He then used words connoting emotional and physical painfulness—"wanton, cruel, and infamous"—to describe the British burning of Charlestown, which had special meaning to Abigail, he acknowledged, as "the Place of your Fathers Nativity." John showed his awareness of how that would "afflict him." The "melancholly Event" was evidence that the British were "disreputable among civilized Nations," indeed, worse in their "Cruelties" than "the Savage

Indians," a comparison indicating the potential of applying the captivity narrative to the Revolution. His outrage was a sign of the patriot's
contrasting civility.[42]

That Abigail's account of Massachusetts casualties was "affecting to
Humanity," in John's judgment, demonstrated her literary power, as
did her "Description of the Distresses of the worthy Inhabitants of Boston." It was, John wrote, "enough to melt an Heart of stone." If the
her father's birthplace had been destroyed, the "Loss of Mr. Mathers Library, . . . a Collection, of Books and Manuscripts made by himself, his
Father, his Grandfather, and Great grandfather . . . is irreparable." The
pain this caused John he then contrasted with Abigail's affecting words
on their immediate family: "The Family picture you draw is charming indeed. My dear Nabby, Johnny, Charly, and Tommy, I long to see
you, and to share with your Mamma the Pleasures of your Conversation." This is a brief indication of a more egalitarian, more sentimental
view of the relations between parents and children, the subject of chapter 11 below.

John asks her to tell the Reverend Wibird that the Philadelphia clergy
"seems to feel as if they were among you," but then, in answer to her
particular question about the responses of his fellow delegates to the
sufferings of Boston Massachusetts, he notes: "You ask, can they realize what We suffer? I answer No. They cant, they dont—and to excuse
them as well as I can, I must confess I should not be able to do it, myself,
if I was not more acquainted with it by Experience than they are." Here,
he assumed the Hutchesonian scale of sympathy, the less likely the more
remote from direct experience, although he elsewhere described delegates strongly moved by accounts of the sufferings of people in Boston.
*Degree* was the usual method of gauging feelings, for instance, "social
Affection" ("which extends to our whole Species. Faintly indeed, but in
some degree"), and, while widely used synonymously with *social rank*,
was derived from trigonometrical calculations, in this case, measuring
the radii of circles, but applicable to the relative heat of affections.

The next paragraph Abigail may have found most pleasingly sentimental, describing his feelings beholding her as virtue in distress: "It
gives me more Pleasure than I express to learn that you sustain with so
much Fortitude, the Shocks and Terrors of the Times. You really are
brave, my dear, you are an Heroine. And you have Reason to be." The
reason is that her Christian virtues assured her of heaven, even if she
was to be killed by the British, the terms of his praise representing his
era and his class's conventional feminine ideals, notably here all linked to

the sentimental. "For the worst that can happen, can do you no Harm. A soul, as pure, as benevolent, as virtuous and pious as yours has nothing to fear, but every Thing to hope and expect from the last of human Evils."

Praising her for such moral qualities and reinforcing such praise by telling her of the inexpressible pleasure she thus brings him was not incompatible with the kind of family banter with which he continued this same, sentimental letter and that he and Abigail had expressed to each other in their courtship. He refers to Abigail's youngest sister, Elizabeth—"Betsy"—Smith, born in 1750, whom John called "an amiable, ingenious Hussy," and he asks Abigail to be "pleased to make my Love acceptable to her" and to tell her that "her elegant Pen cannot be more usefully employed" than in writing him in Philadelphia, "tho it may more agreeably in writing such Billet doux to young Gentlemen." This was to perpetuate a familial theme, Abigail having told John during their courtship, for example, that "Betsy sends her Love to you, says she designd to have kissed you before you went away, but you made no advances, and she never haveing been guilty of such an action, knew not how to attempt it."[43] The rest of John's "sentimental" letter continued to address personal matters, including his eye trouble. He concluded all this with: "Have received two kind letters from your Unkle Smith—do thank him for them—I shall forever love him for them. I love every Body that writes to me. I am forever yours?"

Abigail once wrote her niece Betsy in praise of "a Mr. Murray, a Friend of your cousin Jacks," that is, John Quincy, "an American who bears a very good Character is a young Gentleman of polite Manners easy address and real good sense, very chatty and Sentimental, writes handsomely and is really an accomplished youth." We can imagine that his chattiness included characteristics comparable to those of John's sentimental letter.[44] But the Adamses did not use *sentimental* as often as its cognates and other members of the culture's "family of words," and the word still held the positive connotations illustrated by Fordyce's 1766 *Sermons*.

A 1785 letter of John Quincy's to Abigail points toward the ambiguous values that the word *sentimental* began to take on later in the century. John Quincy had just returned to Braintree after a long absence in Europe: referring to his first dinner at Uncle Cranch's with his cousins Lucy and Betsy, he wrote: "We sat, and looked at one another; I could not speak, and they could only ask now and then a Question concerning you. How much more expressive this Silence, than any thing we

could have said . . . may I always find a silent reception from my real
friends. Don't think I am grown too sentimental." John Quincy's sensibility had been stimulated by particular contrasts: the pain of absence
relieved by the pleasure of reunion and the tension between silence and
speech. Contrasts in certain feelings, above all, pleasure and pain, were
the very grist of sensibility. His concluding request, by no means dis-
counting the strength of his feelings, nonetheless did express a mild embarrassment over his being too sentimental, perhaps analogous to his
mother's ambivalent efforts to conquer too much sensibility, or perhaps
on account of the particular limitations men of feeling were expected to
place on their sensibility.[45]

The passage sharpens our understanding of the meaning of *inexpressible*, when feelings were too powerful, presumably, to find articulation,
as Abigail's could be before she composed or recovered herself. The "figure of incapacity" or the "topos of inexpressibility" were very salient
features of the culture of sensibility, even if they had been used since
Homer. (Barbara Hardy suggests that the figure was characteristic of
novels "of feeling" from Defoe to Henry James.) Eliza Lucas Pinckney
had written Lady Carew in 1759 on the death of her husband: "Tis not
in the power of words to paint my distress." Nabby wrote Betsy Cranch
in 1784 to convey "the idea of a fathers haveing been dangerously ill" but
failed: "Oh my friend the picture is too painfull, my imagination paints
the scene far more distressing than words can express." And, in her reply to Abigail's detailed account of her family's reunion in London after
so many years' absence, Betsy wrote that her aunt's words enabled her to
be present virtually "through every stage" and, finally, to have "enjoyed
the transports of that happy moment, when your maternal Arms embraced a dear and long absent Son. I have seen him, you and my Nabby
dissolvd in the softest tears of fond Affection, when Silence only could
express your joy." She then exclaimed: "Ah! I felt this moment." A little
later in this letter she exclaims, too: "How descriptive is your Pen! How
tender, how feeling the Heart which dictates it!" Feelings, then, not
only preceded their expression in words but were also superior to it.[46]

The word *sentiment* was synonymous with a view or an opinion. John
described John Dickinson's speaking of his "System" at the Continental Congress in 1775, when "his Sentiments were clear and pertinent,
and neatly expressed." Or as he wrote Rush in 1811: "I agree with you
in sentiment that religion and virtue are the only foundation of republicanism." Paine introduced *Common Sense* (1776) by referring to "the
sentiments contained in the following pages."[47] The word could mean

a formal toast: "A sentiment was given: 'May the Sword of the Parent never be Stain'd with the Blood of her Children.'" Sometimes it clearly meant feeling, of awe and veneration, say, or simply the capacity for appropriate feeling. In 1740, Eliza Lucas had written to her father of one of the suitors he proposed for her: "I am sorry I cant have Sentiments favourable enough of him to take time to think on the subject." In its singular form, the word's content need not be specified, any more than the duplicative *feeling* had to—to have or be "of feeling" and to show sentiment were synonymous with having sensibility, that is, being capable of moral responsiveness or of sympathy. Jefferson's "Heart" identified the feelings of sympathy, benevolence, gratitude, justice, love, and friendship with "sentiment."[48]

On hearing in 1804 of the premature death of Jefferson's daughter Polly, whom Abigail had met as a child, she wrote him a letter of condolence, despite the hostile silence that had prevailed between him and the Adamses for several years. It was an entirely sentimental letter, Abigail explaining from the beginning that she was prompted to write "by that sympathy which a recent event has awakened in my Bosom."[49] While Jefferson's reply began by saying that "the affectionate sentiments which you have had the goodness to express in your letter . . . towards my dear departed daughter have awakened in me sensibilities natural to the occasion," he then took the opportunity to range beyond the sentimental subject, reminding Abigail of John's causing the breach in part by his "last appointments to office . . . from among my most ardent political enemies," which he considered "personally unkind," although he then entreated Abigail's "forgiveness for this transition from a subject of domestic affliction to one which seems of a different aspect." In this case, "political events" bore on "private friendships."[50]

The exchange of sentiments, then, was understood to have formal, conventional limits. Ignoring Jefferson's explanation, Abigail replied that, if his letter "had contained no other sentiments and opinions than that which my Letter of condolence could have excited, and which are expressed in the first page of your reply, our correspondence would have terminated there." Jefferson's transgression enable her to open up, too: "you have been pleased to enter upon some subjects which call for a reply: and as you have wished for an opportunity to express your sentiments. I have given them every weight they claim." Here, *sentiments* means views, predominantly at least.[51]

Sometimes it is not clear whether *sentiment* meant view or feeling, as in Jefferson's phrase "affectionate sentiments" or in "the doctrines and sentiments of religious liberty," and, in fact, here and elsewhere, it seems to have meant views charged with feeling: "They know that all America is united in sentiment and in the plan of opposition to the claims of parliament."[52] John Quincy's letters to Nabby are a clear illustration of this double denotation. In March 1786, he wrote: "to you, I can venture to give my real sentiments, such as arise spontaneously in my mind, and that I cannot restrain." Another of John Quincy's letters to Nabby referred to his Harvard tutors: "you will have my real sentiments, unterrified by authority, and unabridged by prejudice." The exaggeration told her his tongue was in his cheek: still, he does reveal how his sense of others inhibited him and even made it necessary for him sometimes to express false sentiments, becoming views drained of feeling.[53]

Abigail's December 27, 1778, letter to John illustrates the identifications of *sentiment* with *sentimental*:

> I love to amuse myself with my pen, and pour out some of the tender sentiments of a Heart over flowing with affection, not for the Eye of a cruel Enemy who no doubt would ridicule every Humane and Social Sentiment long ago grown Callous to the finer sensibilities—but for the sympathetick Heart that Beats in unison with
>
> *Portias*

Evidently, she has the time here ("I love to amuse myself"), thus to give herself pleasure, to indulge herself. Every "Humane and Social Sentiment" was synonymous with, or subsumed by, "the finer sensibilities"; the plural form was less frequently used than the singular, at least until late in the century. She identified, too, her heart's "overflowing with affection" (the latter including said sentiments) with her reader John's "sympathetick Heart" harmonizing perfectly with her own, her terms here charged with the systemic meanings laid out by the divines and philosophers described in chapter 1 above. Abigail's private self-pleasuring for John's sympathetic reading was in conscious contrast to her hypothesized vulnerability to those with hostile, cruel eyes, against the hardness of whom persons of sensibility defined themselves.[54]

Then there was the word *sense*. John used it in the same way we use it today, denoting the body's qualities of sight, smell, touch, taste, and hearing. As we saw, he also used the term *moral sense* in the way Hutcheson used it. His phrase "the sense of this difference" subsumed the "understanding, seeing, and feeling the difference between . . . right and wrong." His phrases "the Sense of the Nation, and our Predecessors," and "the Sense of the People and of the Government" carried the same meaning.[55] The extension of *sense* in the word *sensible* meant conscious, with a slightly more acute connotation, as in John's "I was sensible of the honor done me by the Governor"; that same connotation is evident, too, I think, in John's saying that the "most sensible and jealous people are so little attentive to government, that there are no instances of resistance until repeated, multiplied oppressions cause them to resist tyranny." In 1761, he wrote to Samuel Quincy that it was "not improbable . . . that some [men] may be, by the constitution of their bodies more sensible than others"; he assumed as much in his account of his own nerves and those of Sam Adams. The relation between *sensible* and *sensibility* is particularly obvious in Lucas Pinckney's sentence explaining why she felt what she did on her husband's death: "I was for more than 14 years the happiest of mortals. I was truely sensible of it and therefore as truely felt the sad reverse." Again, this illustrates the characteristic contrast of the culture of sensibility. Franklin's 1781 use of *sensibly* connotes, perhaps, emotional pain as well as the keenest of consciousnesses: "I find myself incorrigible with respects to *Order*; and now that I am grown old and my memory bad, I feel very sensibly the want of it."[56]

We can see from the relation between the extent of happiness and the truth of its reversal that Pinckney described, as well John's guess to Samuel Quincy, that people believed that there were degrees of being sensible, a belief also illustrated by Abigail's writing Mary of her grandsons in 1797: "I was fully sensible that the Boys must be taken from all their connections to break them of habits which they had imbibed." Being thus conscious could be a quality that developed as a child grew up. Writing of her young niece's awareness of her father's death, Abigail told John: "I feel a tenderer affection for her as she has lost a kind parent. Though too young to be sensible of her own loss, I can pitty her."[57] While Hutcheson had used the word *sensitive*, a rare word in the eighteenth century, he meant beings with senses rather than acutely aware of subtleties, say, and eighteenth-century writers tended to use *sensible* in context to convey that idea.[58] Or *sensible* and *sensibly* could more evidently denote showing or having sensibility. John wrote Abigail: "My Mother's Indisposition continues to affect me most sensibly." And Abigail wrote John of her father's death: "I know my dear Friend, you will most sensibly feel this bereavement." Or, in response to the British navy's defeat in 1782 of the French in the West Indies, Abigail wrote: "[The] Count de Grasse misfortune in the West Indies we sensibly feel."

As *sentiment* could mean "opinion," or "feeling," or "opinion charged with feeling," so *sensible* could mean "conscious " or "consciousness charged with feeling."[59]

In 1775, Abigail wrote Warren a letter in which a passage of sensibility (referring to Warren's "benevolent sympathy of her Heart") preceded her use of *sensible* to mean simply "conscious": "You will be sensible no doubt . . . that [their menfolk] have to combat [political obstacles]." Similarly, John Adams wrote Rush telling him of Frederick Muhlenburg's "beseeching" Adams, then president, to give him the office of treasurer of the Mint: "I was desirous of obliging him, I pitied his situation, and I was very sensible of the policy of attaching the [Pennsylvania] Germans to the national government."[60]

That same 1775 letter of Abigail's to Warren illustrates the meaning of *insensibility*: "I sometimes wonder at my-self, and fear least a degree of stupidity or insensibility should possess my mind in these calamitous times or I could not feel so tranquil amidst such scenes, and yet I cannot charge myself with an unfealing Heart. I pitty, commisirate and as far as my ability reaches feel ready and desirous to releave my fellow creatures under their distresses. But I am not naturally (tis no virtue acquired in me) of that restless, anxious disposition."[61] Abigail considers whether the degree of feeling she experiences could be judged negatively: *insensibility* was being not merely oblivious but immorally so, the sign of an "unfealing Heart," according to the standards of the culture of sensibility. In London in 1785, Nabby criticized the performance of Mrs. Abington, playing "the part of Mis Rusport," in the sentimental comedy *The West Indian* (1771) by Richard Cumberland and first produced by David Garrick (Abigail's cousin Isaac Smith Jr. had sent its printed version to her from London in the year of its first performance): "wretchedly performed. Stiff aukord insensible and unfeeling, void of that engaging delicacy which the character merited." Nabby described her response to the mock death of novitiates in Paris, young women she called "victims" as they prostrated themselves during their final renunciation of the world: "This was an affecting sight; I could not refrain from tears; every one seemed affected . . . particularly the French. One of the priests seemed affected; the others appeared as insensible as statues of lead or wood." We saw that Abigail divided those with sensibility from "the world" in the same terms.[62]

In that 1775 letter to Warren, Abigail had amplified the meanings of having a feeling heart, having feelings (pity, commiseration) for and actions ("releave") toward distressed others. She experienced *tranquility*, not *insensibility*, which latter term was, she suggested, synonymous with *stupidity*—that is, *stupefaction*, without the moral connotation of insensibility. In fact, were she to have a higher degree of feeling, it would manifest a "rastless anxious disposition." Abigail then quickly expressed her modesty in making the final distinction in the passage, illustrating her belief that one's will could play a part in exercising various degrees of sensibility. Writing to Catherine Macaulay the previous year and referring to "the late inhumane acts of the British parliament," she illustrates further the closeness in meaning of *unfeeling* and *insensible*: "Tho there are but few who are unfealing or insensible to the general calamity, by far the greater part support it with that firmness, that fortitude, that undaunted resolution which ever attends these who are conscious that they are the injured not the *injurer*." Here, the consciousness of suffering is joined by consciousness of self-righteousness, in contrast to those who were unsympathetic and/or oblivious. John's letter of the same time illustrates that the use of *insensibility* could be neutral. He was describing the policy of the Massachusetts delegation to the Continental Congress: "We have a delicate Course to steer, between too much Activity and too much Insensibility, in our critical interested situation." His qualifying "Insensibility" by "too much" conveys the same notion of the need to calibrate it as Abigail had with her phrase "a degree of . . . insensibility." A person of feeling had to gauge when not to be too responsive.[63]

That is evident, too, in a 1785 passage from Nabby's London journal, in which she described a discussion between Horne Tooke, the radical politician and philologist, and a "gentleman lately robbed by a young man in whom he had placed some confidence." Nabby described Tooke as "about fifty years old": "his countenance is open and amiable, expressive of benevolence, charity, and liberality." This appearance "pleased [her] much," and all her terms show that she thought him a man of feeling; for example, that he had an open countenance meant that his feelings could be read from it. She characterized the robbed gentleman, on the other hand, as boastful, relentless, and vengeful in his efforts "to bring the unhappy youth to the gallows." (One of the first of her mother's observations in England the previous year had been that of the shock at the casualness with which a group of English people consigned a young highwayman to the gallows, in contrast to what she saw as the sympathy of Americans.) Said gentleman "did not seem to be satisfied that any one should use their endeavors to alleviate his situation by a proposal of transportation." The liberal Tooke appealed to head and heart: "Mr. Tooke reasoned with him, and endeavored to appeal to his heart for some lenitive consideration." His opponent, who had already represented his preferred course of action as a "duty" and now said he "owed it to society," was impenetrable. He "openly avowed that he should feel no remorse in bringing the youth to the severest punishment." Then Nabby—the only lady present, she noted—recorded her own feelings. She was "not so gratified" with the gentleman's reasons, including what he "owed to society, . . . as with Mr. Tooke's interposition on his behalf": "There was so much benevolence and mercy in the latter, with so much insensibility in the former, that clemency never appeared to me in more amiable point of view."[64] Nabby was witnessing an emblematic debate over penal reform that Paul Langford describes (including the publications and parliamentary appearances of the prison reformer John Howard) as the expression of "the sentimental revolution" in England. John Adams, Jefferson, and, above all, their fellow revolutionary Benjamin Rush, each of them influenced by Cesar Beccaria, as were the English reformers, were participants in the American version of this branch of humanitarianism. Like Tooke, those men all regarded themselves as men of feeling, although analysis illustrates the extent and occasion on which they might open and close their countenances.[65]

The Adamses used the word *sensation* in addition to the words *sentimental, sentiment, sense, sensible,* and *insensibility.* It was a word most evidently referring to nerve physiology. Both Adamses knew Descartes's model as well as Locke's work. John seems to have Locke's explanation of human understanding in mind when he declared in his 1759 diary entry: "[As] all our knowledge is acquired by Experience, i.e. by sensation or Reflection, this faculty is necessary to retain the Ideas we receive and the observations we make, and to recall them, for our Use, as Occasion requires."[66] In one passage in his diary, where he laid out God's authorship of nature, including giving "us . . . a nature . . . capable of enjoying Happiness and of suffering Misery . . . [and] several senses and has furnished the World around us with a Variety of Objects proper to delight and entertain them," and described the pleasures of sight, smell, and imagination (the latter a Hutchesonian sense), he specified the operation of these senses: "[God] has So wonderfully constituted the Air that by giving it a particular Kind of Vibration, it produces in us as intense sensation of pleasure as the organs of our Bodies can bear, in all the Varieties of Harmony and Concord." *Vibration* reflected the influence of Newton's notion of the transmission of signals through the nerves (whereas references to heat-driven *spirits* refer to Descartes). We should note, however, that having celebrated this sensational aspect of human nature in relation to the external world, including "the Heavens over our Heads," John then emphasized its subordination to other, God-given capacities: "all the Provision[s] that He has [made] for the Gratification of our senses, tho very engaging and unmerited Instances of goodness, are much inferior to the Provision, the wonderful Provision that He has made for the gratification of our nobler Powers of Intelligence and Reason." Significantly, the exercise of these powers, John says, consistent with the psychology described by Descartes, Shaftesbury, and Hutcheson, and propounded by Crane's generators of sensibility, is "attended with a conscious pleasure and Complacency," and he immediately explained this feeling as one side of the moral sense: "On the Contrary, he has made a different Course of Life, a Course of Impiety and Injustice, of Malevolence and Intemperance, appear Shocking and deformed to our first Reflections."[67]

This celebration of the gratification of the senses, on the one hand, and the exercise of the nobler powers of the mind, on the other, was more or less equivalent to the very frequent combination/bifurcation of heart and head, usually in the order representing their relative values. John wrote on March 30, 1774: "My Head is empty, but my Heart is full." Or Rush wrote to him on May 12, 1807, that a recently discovered letter written by Adams "does great honor to your head and heart." The best known of this combination to historians is Jefferson's "Head vs. Heart" letter.[68]

Nancy Shippen's exclamation (possibly in imitation of Sterne's in *A Sentimental Journey*), "Sweet sensibility, source of a thousand heaven born sensations for all of the wealth of the Indies I would not be without," illustrates one reason why having a refined sensibility was valued, although Elizabeth Sherman's 1786 statement that "the sensations of the heart are not controllable" implied a danger. A 1780 New England man confessed to his journal: "even a Man of Sense is unable to command himself when his heart is affected by this passion."[69] Jefferson's "Head vs. Heart" letter wished to suggest this to Maria Cosway, although evidently its form demonstrated Jefferson's characteristic self-control. That letter of condolence that Abigail sent him in 1804 had declared: "Reasons of various kinds withheld my pen until the powerful feelings of my heart, have burst through restraint and called upon me to shed a tear of sorrow over the remains of your beloved and deserving daughter, an event which I most sincerely mourn." But that expression of mourning was confined to exciting only the appropriate, reciprocal feelings in her correspondent. Here, we can refer to R. H. Brissenden's

remark that which of the two, "the head and the heart," representing
"the supposed division within the psyche," "either is or ought to be the
dominant element in man provided the ground for continuous contro-
versy . . . throughout the century." Abigail was intensely ambivalent, as
we shall see in the next chapter.[70]

John Quincy's letters further illustrate the usage of *sensations*. He
wrote his mother in May 1786, first describing the "anxiety" and "impa-
tience" caused by a recent letter hinting at Nabby's engagement to Colonel William Smith, then remarking: "nor did I ever feel such strange
Sensations, as at reading the first page of my Sister's Letter, where in the
most delicate manner possible, she inform'd me of the Connection."
The previous August he had written his sister about the effects on him
of his return to their Braintree home: "This afternoon I went down, and
view'd the well-known habitation. My Sensations on this occasion cannot be described, but they were such that I did not stay two minutes in
the House, nor would it give me the least pain, was I forbidden to enter it again, before your return." Despite telling Nabby that his "Sensations" were inexpressible, he conveyed that they were painful.[71]

John Quincy also wrote his mother about visiting the old family
home: "I felt the strangest sensations, of pleasure and pain mingled together, that I ever knew of." In fact, he initially felt pleasure: "The first
sight of it, brought to my mind the years I had past in it, and many little
circumstances which I had entirely forgot but which then were peculiarly pleasing. When I entered in it, my feelings were very different.
Bereft of its former inhabitants, it appeared to me, in a gloomy, un-
pleasant light." This latter stimulated a symptom of pain: "Every time I
go into it, the involuntary sigh, rises in my breast, and ever must untill
the return of those, who will renew its attractions." He shows that his
account of such sensations was properly termed *sentimental*: "I believe
I have heard you say, you don't want Sentiment in your Letters from
America, but surely on this occasion it is excusable in me. And I know
not that I am apt to be over-Sentimental." This apology is very similar to the cover he gave his being sentimental when having dinner with
the Cranches.[72]

The following year, John Quincy had used the word *sensations* in
his description of feelings almost identical to those he had called *sentimental* a few months earlier. Again he was dining with their cousins:
"every now and then, the rising sigh would betray, that something yet
was wanting; I assure you I was not the only person present who recollected you, with painful pleasing sensations."[73] Nostalgia was one of

those mixtures of pleasure and pain, like parting, with which evidently it was connected since both past and present were felt as being left. In addition to its being another juxtaposition, this occasion for nostalgia was enhanced, perhaps, by the elevation of childhood. The contrast of an idealized childhood with an adulthood that had inevitably suffered its loss was dramatized still further when that between life and death overlaid it.[74]

## Impressions and Nonverbal Signs of Sensibility

The word *impressions* was a sign of the same system as that indicated by *sense* and *sensation*. Descartes's psychophysiology employed the term. John had recorded a summary of Lockean psychology in the early years of his diary. He was considering "the surprizing Faculties and Opperations of the Mind": "Our minds are capable of receiving an infinite Variety of Ideas from those numerous material objects with which we are surrounded. And the vigourous Impressions which we receive from these, our minds are capable of retaining, compounding, and arranging into all the Varieties of Picture and of Figure." The proliferation of material objects by way of the consumer revolution accompanied the rise of such psychology, although, here, John had in mind the whole sublunary world.[75]

Abigail pleasured herself with the idea of possessing John's heart, "Eaqually warm with my own, and full as Susceptable of the Tenderest impressions." This assumed that impressions varied in quality, as did John's use of the phrase *indelible impressions*, but, more important to the value scale assumed by persons of sensibility, the capacity to register impressions varied. The highest level was the heart that was tender enough—"Susceptable" (in Abigail's spelling), another of the family of words—to register the tenderest, most delicate or refined impressions. At the bottom of the scale, in fact, right off it, was the "insensible" or "unfealing Heart."[76]

Revolutionary and counterrevolutionary propaganda (like sermons) was promulgated in order to affect minds and hearts. Tory papers, well "conducted with a Subtlety of Art and Address, wonderfully calculated to keep Up the Spirits of their Party, [and] to depress ours, . . . made a very visible impression on many Mind[s]." John wrote his *Novanglus* papers similarly to make an impression. That he tells us the last one could not be printed using the same terms—it was "prevented from impression"—reminds us of the associations between the widespread acceptance of environmental psychology and the rise of print literacy, although the origins of the usage lay further back in time, with the impressing of signet rings on wax and emblems on coinage. John described the effects of spoken words in the same way, saying of his 1775 speech to the Congress, which advanced neutrality for the independent colonies: "I never saw a greater Impression made upon that Assembly or any other." The impressions of his words reached the delegates' brains through their senses, in turn sending out signals to their faces: "Attention and Approbation was marked on every Countenance."[77]

A central quality of the possession of sensibility was acute consciousness of others as well as of self. Nabby interpreted Horne Tooke's open countenance as a sign of his sensibility. The ability to read as well as show feelings on faces was another quality valued by persons of sensibility. Of course, this was a skill long practiced and recorded, but it had been "on the basis of the theory of the passion found in Descartes's treatise" that Charles Le Brun had in 1696 published scientific drawings of the various facial expressions and had taught "a generation of French artists to do the same." The development of passionate psychology and the fashionability of sensibility was the context for the popularity of the "Swiss Cartesian," the pastor Johann Caspar Lavater's doctrine that "the human face is the 'magic mirror' of the soul."[78] Describing Franklin as "grave, yet pleasant, and affable," Abigail had continued: "You know I make some pretensions to physiognomy and I thought I could read in his countenance the Virtues of his Heart, among which patriotism shined in its full Lustre—and with that is blended every virtue of a christian, for a true patriot must be a religious man." In the aftermath of the 1796 election, Abigail wrote of Hamilton: "O I have read his Heart in his wicked eyes many a time. The very devil is in them, they are lasciviousness it self, or I have no skill in physiognomy."[79]

As a young man, John recorded in his diary the effect on younger siblings of their registering their parent's angry feelings, putting the "whole Family into a Broil by a Trifle": "My P and M [pater and mater] disagreed . . . that Difference occasioned passionate Expressions, those Expressions made Dolly and Judah snivell, Peter observed and mentioned it, I faulted him for it, which made him mad and all was breaking into a flame, when I quitted the room and took up Tully to compose myself." He then faulted himself for not putting the event to more scientific—more Cartesian—purpose: "I might have made more critical observations on the Course and Progress of human Passions if I had steadily observed the faces, Eyes, Actions and Expressions of both Husband and Wife this morning." In his political career he recommended George Washington for commander of the revolutionary army. John Hancock had shown "visible pleasure" when Adams had been speaking of other, related subjects leading up to this recommendation. "But," Adams wrote, "when I came to describe Washington for the Commander, I never remarked a more sudden and sinking Change of Countenance." Adams was primed for such remarking because he knew Hancock lusted after the job: "Mortification and resentment were expressed as forcibly as his Face could exhibit them. Mr. Samuel Adams seconded the Motion, and that did not soften the Presidents Physiognomy at all." Elsewhere, Adams noted that, in response to his "public Harangues" on behalf of independence, he had seen "horror, terror, and detestation, strongly marked on the Countenances of some of the Members." Implicitly, some men did not show what they felt in public, and those who did, did not do so regularly.[80]

Public life required one to put on a face, but, according to the ostensible—and deeply felt—values of the sensibility that such familial developments also nourished, such masking was a contradiction of the true self. Republican as well as sentimental ideology represented a false and corrupt world as a masquerade. "Our country is in masquerade!" wrote a disillusioned John Adams to Rush in 1808. "No party, no man, dares to avow his real sentiments. All is disguise, visard, cloak." In private, or in certain letters, or on certain subjects, to certain people, a man or a woman of sensibility could freely express himself or herself. That reply to Abigail's letter initiating a renewal of correspondence after his daughter's death wherein he had seized the chance to review the difference that had come to divide him from John Adams, Jefferson concluded: "I have thus, my dear Madam, opened myself to you without reserve . . . and, without knowing how it will be received. I feel relief from being unbosomed." Fordyce's recommendation for the reform of women's education included their reading for more than just "a little transient amusement," but in the end women were armed to shape them to an extreme of gendered sensibility, reflexive of the needs of men: "Your chief business is to read Men, [not books,] in order to make yourselves agreeable and useful. It is not the argumentative but the sentimental talents [sentimental because such reading was of others' feelings], which give you that insight and those openings into the human heart, that lead to your proper end as Women."[81]

Abigail wrote John in 1775, imagining his return: "I know (I think of, for am not I your Bosome Friend?) your feelings, your anxieties, your

exertions, &c. more than those before whom you are obliged to wear
the face of chearfulness."[82] In England in 1785, "the Etiquette of [her]
Country," she wrote her sister Mary, extracted from her the "penalty"
of being "in publick Character," to enter the "Court" as the U.S. minister's lady. She first thanked Mary "for the particular manner in which
you write": "I . . . take an interest in every transaction which concerns
those I love. And I enjoy more pleasure from those imaginary Scenes,
than I do from the drawing room at St. James." There was a political
dimension to this contrast. In the "Scenes" back home, with those she
loved, Abigail wrote, "I feel my self your Friend and equal, in the other
I know I am looked down upon with a sovereign pride, and the Smile of
Royalty is bestowed as a mighty Boon." But she could not receive it as
condescension because her appearance in the Court of St. James on behalf of the United States was equal in "complimenting" to that which
British monarchical "Power" was bestowing by way of its smile. "With
these Ideas," Abigail remarked, "you may be sure my countanance will
never wear that supplicant appearence which begs for notice."[83]

John implied a wish that women wear only a certain kind of mask:
a diary entry written in 1759, when he was twenty-three, recorded that
"O" (Hannah Quincy) "knows and can practise the Art of pleasing,
yet she fails, sometimes. she lets us see a face of Ridicule, and Spying
sometimes, inadvertently, tho she looks familiarly, and pleasantly for
the most part." This seems to be critical of both her failure to wear the
proper mask and her real feelings (ridicule and spying), which, therefore, she had revealed. John continued: "She is apparently frank, but
really reserved, seemingly pleased, and almost charmed, when she is
really laughing with Contempt. Her face and Heart have no Correspondence." We can infer that John wished she would successfully represent
the feelings she genuinely had.[84]

The most frequent nonverbal signs of sensibility were tears. To previous illustrations of this point may be added Abigail's account of her
response to Dana's return to Braintree from Russia, but without John:
"I have not time to Say what my Sensations were. A flood of tears un-
bidden flowed from my Eyes. Yet I am sure I sincerely rejoiced in his return." Her words about tears she knew would signify to John the sensations she would need more time to analyze, although, here, she does
manage to indicate that, if tears usually meant pain, they could express
conflict, joy, or a combination of both.[85]

Blushes were, along with pulse, according to the phrase of Markman
Ellis, "the sanguinary indices" of sensibility. The blush, or the flush, had

been one of the external signs of the passions that Descartes had considered, not that his predecessors among the poets and other writers had not recorded those and related signs. Again, however, Descartes and his successors explained them in the neuropsychological and psychophysiological terms that would undergird ensuing cultures of sensibility.[86] As we saw, John read Abigail's blushes in company as a sign of her modesty and her sensibility. The Pennsylvania poet Hannah Griffitts illustrated the value of blushing, doing so in a sentimental poem that posed "native Innocence / The Female Glory & our best Defence" against Chesterfieldian "satyr." She asked where that innocence had fled and

> Where now that conscious Dignity refin'd
> That checks the rude & awes the darkest Mind?
> The Just Resentment & the Blush sincere
> The Eye corrective, & the Heart severe?

the signs that women of sensibility were urged to show to men who threatened, one way or another, to impugn their innocence.[87]

In Paris with her mother and two male friends, Nabby and one of the latter, "Mr. R." "had a learned discussion upon blushing while Mr. Jarvis was in a shop making some purchases." It was prompted "by a girl passing by the carriage with a veil on, which are very common in the streets here." Mr. R. "observed that the blush of innocence was a better veil," a notion more or less identical with the one expressed by Griffitts. Nabby perpetuated Griffitts's view, too, that innocence was being lost: "I said there were few of these known in Paris." This American derogation of French ladies was charged at some level with a reference to sex that was simultaneously veiled by the young man and woman themselves: "He inquired if they had any word in the French language for innocence? There is not any other word but innocence, and it is almost without a use here." Nabby got back to the subject of blushing: "I said, it was a very painful sensation—I thought it a great advantage to be exempt from it; he was not of this opinion." Presumably, she did not want so easily to reveal consciousness of sex; Mr. R., with Nabby's blushing in mind, conveyed to her that, despite (or because of) her pain, he found it attractive as a color and a sign of sensibility (as did John Adams). Then Mr. J. came out of the shop: "Mr. R. told him of our conversation, upon which commenced the dissertation; Mr. J. decided not agreeably to my opinion or belief, that we never blushed but from the consciousness of something wrong in what was said or done, that caused the blush." In this view, Nabby could not be innocent. "I do not believe it," she wrote, and perhaps told the men that "a person so subject to blush as myself, should be interested in removing every idea of evil from it."[88]

Declaring in his *Notes on the State of Virginia* that color was "fixed in nature," and asking rhetorically, "Is it not the foundation of a greater or less share of beauty in the two races?" Jefferson then asked: "Are not the fine mixtures of red and white, the expressions of every passion by greater or less suffusions of color on the one, preferable to that eternal monotony, which reigns in the countenances, the immovable veil of black which covers the emotions of the other race?" He associated this "fine" mixture of expressivity of passion with the sexual attraction that all blacks—implicitly male—felt for white women, a passion analogous with "the preference of the Oranootan for the black woman over those of his own species." Ignatius Sancho, that "African" whose *Letters* Jefferson criticized in the same passage denying that blacks could blush, had given the lie to that notion in his book.[89]

Some men of feeling blushed, too. To Rush in 1813, John Adams quoted this line from Pope's *Essay on Man*: "Sons will blush, their fathers were your foes." To say that one blushed, as John did in a diary entry of 1760, had become a conventional sign of sensibility. "I blush even to think what he said to me," John had noted, referring to the Tory judge Peter Oliver's insulting language. Perhaps, too, John was ashamed that he could be bullied in this way or that such things could be thought of him. The reason Eliza Lucas wrote that she accepted "with blushes" Miss Livingston's offer to assist her as she had asked, in 1743, was that she was "really ashamed of being so troublesome."[90]

So blushing was also a characteristic that women and men of feeling could hold in common. That "the Horrours of a civil war" threatened Americans, "on one hand," and "the chains of slavery," "on the other," led Abigail to write to Catherine Macaulay in 1774: "We Blush when we recollect from whence these woes arise, and must ever execrate the infamous memory of those Men whether they are Americans or Brittons, whose contagious Ambition first opened the pandorean Box." She and those who shared her blush in that way thereby revealed their moral superiority. The following year, Abigail linked blushing to tears, both signs of virtuous feeling: "Blush o! Americans that ever thou derivest thy origins from such a race." Already Abigail believed that Americans could distinguish themselves from metropolitan Britons by that quality of sensibility. One British crime was the treatment of James Warren's body after he had been killed at Bunker Hill, his head reportedly being severed and carried in triumph to General Gage, who, Abigail fancied, responded by "grin'd horrible a ghastly smile" instead of, as in the case of Caesar when shown Pompey's head, turning away with disgust and giving "vent to his pitty in a flood of tears." Thus "pagan tenderness put christian Benevolence to shame." (This referred to an incident at the conclusion of Plutarch's "Pompey," which in all likelihood Abigail had read in Dryden's popular translation of Plutarch's *Lives*.) Subsequent usage in the phrases *at first blush* and *put to the blush*, for example, were still more self-evidently conventional.[91]

Trembling and shuddering were other external signs of the passions that Descartes had considered along with blushes; cultivators of sensibility were to aggrandize them. In his 1765 "Instructions of the Town of Braintree" to Ebenezer Thayer, the town's representative to the General Court, John presented the townspeople as persons of sensibility: "Such is our loyalty to the King, our veneration for both houses of Parliament, and our affection for our fellow-subjects in Britain, that measures which discover any unkindness in that country towards us are the more sensibly and visibly felt." What, in light of "the scarcity of money" (which would reduce "whole multitudes to beggary"), "the consequence" of the implementation of the Stamp Act would be to "the whole peace of the province, from so sudden a shock and such a convulsive change in the whole course of our business and subsistence, we tremble to consider." Having further given "our sentiments of this act," the Braintree townspeople resolved to oppose it "till we can hear the success of the cries and petitions of America for relief." In short, America was personified as a suppliant, "under many uncommon difficulties and distresses," anticipating that its voice would make an impression on a Britain still personified as a sympathizer of sensibility.[92]

This generalized from the kind of individual trembling illustrated by the Adams family correspondence. In 1773, Abigail wrote Warren: "[such] is the present Situation of affairs that I tremble when I think what may be the direfull consequences—and in this Town must the Scene of action lay." Warren demonstrated her own sensibility in a January 1775 letter to Abigail, by telling Abigail that she had perceived her unarticulated, inner feelings, representing them as a metaphoric trembling: "Your Last I perceive was wrote with a heart trembling with the Laudable feelings of Humanity Least your suffering Country should be driven to Extreemities, and its Inocent inhabitants be made the sacrifices to Disappointed Ambition and Avarice." There are many such expressions of the Adamses' and others' elevation of patriotic Americans' superior sensibility, figures of virtue in distress, in contrast to

the now barbarous British and their allies.[93] At the end of 1775, Warren wrote to Abigail of her own near trembling: "When I Look forward I almost tremble at the prospect. So Many Internal Difficulties
to struggle Through, as well as A [violent] Foe without." Abigail predicted: "my Hand and heart will tremble, at this domestick fury, and
firce civil Strife."[94]

John Adams's diary illustrates the meaning of *tremor* and the international dimensions of cultures of sensibility among the genteel (as Pinckney's correspondence with Lady Mary Drayton does, too).[95] John's first
interview with George III as the U.S. minister to Great Britain—the
first postrevolutionary meeting between an erstwhile subject, now independent American, and the king—was fraught with particular emotions,
couched in particular language, because they were both eighteenth-
century gentlemen, that is to say, men of feeling. Adams wrote John
Jay: "The King listened to every word I said, with dignity but with apparent emotion." That emotion was apparent, for one thing, because
of his "tremor," a word that suggested his effort to maintain his dignity despite his feelings, although to signify emotions in that way was
a quality on which both men seemed to place high value. Adams continued: "Whether it was in the nature of the interview, or whether it
was my visible agitation, for I felt more than I did or could express, that
touched him I cannot say. But he was much affected, and answered me
with more tremor than I had spoken with." Adams had himself made his
feelings visible, showing a similar tension between dignity and emotion
to that which he reported of George. The king, in turn, had read Adams's feelings and was, as a result, "touched," like a musical instrument,
and "much affected"; that is, his social affections were stimulated to the
extent that he matched John's visible and even invisible feelings with a
sign (a "tremor") of his own. Adams quoted what the king had said to
him, including this: "the language you have now held is so extremely
proper, and the feelings you have discovered so justly adapted to the occasion . . . that I am very glad the choice has fallen upon you to be [the
U.S.] minister."[96]

The king limited his observation to Adams's "discovered," visible
feelings, at least apparently, and his stylized reply assumed that Adams's
own expression of them had been as controlled and stylized. That very
stylization testifies to the formal establishment of an international dimension to cultures of sensibility, among elites first. Adams placed it in
a context of more invisible feelings in his letter to Jay. His aside ("for I
felt more than I did or could express") was ambiguous, insofar as could

meant either his power to express or what formal court etiquette allowed, along with the expression of what was "justly adapted to the occasion." If it was the former, then it expressed another level of convention, the figure of incapacity.

A comparable symptom, manifesting pleasure, was a "shudder." Writing from London in 1785, Abigail asserted that, to "those who have a taste and ear for it," "Musick must be one of the most agreeable of Amusements." It tends to "soften and harmonize the passions" and "elevate the mind" (all this signifying the existence of sensibility). She then declared: "the most powerfull effects of Musick which I ever experienced, was at Westminister Abbey." The piece was Handel's *Messiah*, the particular part of it the Hallelujah chorus. "I was one continued shudder from the beginning to the end of the performance." That shudder is comparable to the shiver with which she responded to Trumbull's painting *The Death of General Warren at the Battle of Bunker Hill* in London: "my whole frame contracted, my Blood Shiverd and I felt a faintness at my Heart."[97]

## The Limits of Sentimental Language

Abigail believed that John was able to combine the "tenderest" of sensibility with the "stern virtue" she attributed to Cato's style of manhood. The combination represented the versatility that the world required of men. But, if the identification of women with, and their own aggrandizing of, feminine sensibility reflected the limitations they had to face, they, too, showed signs of versatility. On reading "the first volume of Virgil," Eliza Lucas wrote Mary Bartlett that "the calm and pleasing diction of pastoral and gardening agreeably presented themselves, not unsuitably to this charming season of the year"—we can assume that she was reading Virgil's *Eclogues* rather than "the battles, storm and tempests" she had imagined thinking of the *Aeneid*, also perhaps in Dryden's translation—which "puts one in a maze and makes one shudder when one reads." "I am so much delighted [with that aforementioned season]," she continued, "that had I but the fine soft language of our poet to paint it properly, I should give you but little respite till you came into the country and attended the beauties of pure nature unassisted by art." And then she went ahead to paint the picture ("the majestick pine imperceptibly puts on a fresher green; the young mirtle joyning its fragance to that of the Jesamin of golden line," and so on), just as she had had the "presumption" to criticize Richardson.[98]

Similarity, Lucas described the "Gentlemens Seat" of "Crow-field" in the pastoral vein, referring to the birds there as "Airry Choristers." Crowfield was a plantation, its laborers enslaved African Americans working Ceres' fields to supply the hospitable board on which they also waited as they implemented the growing of rice and indigo on Lucas's plantation, indeed, as their forced labor sustained the other material and literary delights of South Carolina's elite. Lucas's sylvan scene did not include them. Others of Lucas's letters refer to "Negroes" frequently, but in another vein. She noted to herself that she had informed her father "of some Negroes," that is, among the gangs the Lucases owned, who had been "detected going to Augustine": "They accused Mol[att]o Quash. I was at his tryal when he proved him self quite Innocent. The ring leader is to be hanged and one Whyped."[99]

Abigail, too, wrote in styles other than the sentimental. She had followed that sentence in which she fantasized John's combination of sensibility and stern virtue with this: "I must leave my pen to recover myself and write in an other strain." This was another kind of freedom, one that Abigail was to develop in relation to the practical challenges she faced in running the farm while John was away and in relation to his immersion in politics. In this case, her turning to another "strain" defined the emotional episode she had just presented to her correspondent in its appropriate language of sensibility. That writing of practical matters was not so charged with the feelings associated with sensibility is evident. She wrote John in 1775, first describing "the impudence of a tenant," next explaining, "It moved me so much that I had hard Work to suppress my temper," and then continuing: "I feel too angry to make this any thing further than a Letter of Business."[100] By the same token, in May 1776, Abigail began a detailed accounting of farm labor with: "I set down to write you a Letter wholly Domestick without one word of politicks or any thing of the Kind." Later in the letter, she described the pleasure that coping with farm finances brought her, although this was, she said, because she knew "it will be an Ease to your mind." Mary Beth Norton has suggested that the fact of practical farming and business demands falling so widely on women's shoulders in the Revolution increased their range of activities and elevated their self-esteem, along with men's acknowledgment of their value in this regard.[101]

During his and Abigail's courtship, John had shown his capacity for writing in several strains. These strains corresponded to his greater range of experience. Living in 1764 with other men in Boston in preparation for their smallpox inoculation, John described their room as "a Den of

Thieves, and a Scene of Money Changers," and mentioned his "hopes to be bound to your Ladyship in the soft Ligaments of Matrimony." This would be a reformative restraint. Then he commented: "Hitherto I have written with the Air and in the style of Rattle and Frolic; but now I am about to shift to the sober and the Grave." A little later he told her: "I have Thoughts of sending you a Nest of Letters like a Nest of Basketts; tho I suspect the latter would be a more genteel and acceptable Present to a Lady." He told her he could "furnish a Cabinet of Letters" on medical scenes, which would "be exceeded in Curiosity, by a set describing the Characters, Diversions, Meals, Wit, Drollery, Jokes, Smutt, and Stories of the Guests at a Tavern in Plymouth," taverns being central foci of male countercultures and their corresponding languages, against which genteel American and British cultures of sensibilities defined themselves. Such a set of letters, John continued, "could be equalled by nothing excepting a minute History of Close Stools and Chamber Potts, and of the Operation of Pills, Potions and Powders, in the Preparation for the small Pox." Peter Wagner holds that scatological folklore and literature constituted "an essential part of eighteenth-century humor" under the "stercoraceous" conditions of English and American cities. John expressed himself in the way he did because of its unacceptability to a genteel "Lady." His playfulness in a letter is marked with the perspective on sex and gender furthered by Jeremy Collier and absorbed by the culture of sensibility: "Heaven forgive me for suffering my imagination to struggle into a Region of Ideas so nauseous And abominable."[102]

In fact, Abigail told John that she found his "minute description of persons . . . very entertaining." She hoped he would continue "writing to a Lady" of his "amusement." The only reason not to would be if it damaged his health. Replying to his teasing confession to her that he longed for a "game of Romps" with another "lady" "because she is a Buxom Lass," Abigail said: "all I insist upon is that you follow that amusement that is most agreeable to you whether it be Cards, Chequers, Musick, Writing, or Romping." While romping was by no means always sexual (Abigail wrote Royall Tyler from France that Nabby—then nineteen—"plays with her Brother," two years younger, "which they can do together in a game of Romps very well"), evidently there could be a degree of sexual pleasure in their bantering over sensibility and modesty.[103]

In 1774, the American writer "Mira" would reiterate what Richardson's Lovelace had so richly expressed. "Modesty, while it is a shield to the social virtues, . . . is likewise an incentive to desire," to be maintained even when the hymen was first pierced: modesty "heightens the merit of a Lady's favours . . . essential to the whole course of pleasures, that it must be preserved, even in the very moment appointed for its loss; it is . . . an exquisite kind of coquetry."[104] It was fundamental to Abigail herself not to bring such possibilities to the surface, although the potentials in the pleasures of sensibility were long at issue, as American and English reactions to Sterne illustrate. From London on Christmas Day, 1786, John teased Abigail, Gelles writes, "as he had teased her during their courtship," telling her not to worry: "If I am cold in the night . . . I will take a Virgin to bed with me." "Ay a Virgin—What? Oh Awful!" he imagined Abigail exclaiming, before telling her a virgin in England "was a Stone Bottle, . . . filled with Boiling Water, covered over and wrapped up in a flannel and laid at Mans feet in Bed." He referred to one of Abigail's propensities: "An Old Man you see may comfort himself with Such a Virgin . . . and not give the least jealousy to his Wife." Such double entendres, far more graphic in Sterne's novels, for example, were also made direct in works combining sex with sensibility, part of "the vast and varied field of erotica . . . read in both England and America." Sterne was a collector. The cartoonist Thomas Rowlandson parodied Henry McKenzie's sentimental novel *The Man of Feeling* (1771), a less titillating and highly popular imitation of Sterne's *A Sentimental Journey*, in two prints with the same title as the novel, showing a man groping, respectively, one woman's vagina and another's breasts. Wagner remarks of these pictures that "'feeling' is given a secondary obscene meaning." John Ferling suggests that, after Abigail and John's wedding, their reception followed the convention where "the men gathered in one room to drink, smoke, and swap stories—frequently ribald wedding night tales" (and, by his own admission, John was amorous in temperament)—"while the ladies adjourned to another portion of the house to gossip and advise the bride," that is, about sex.[105]

Later in 1764, John wrote to Abigail of the "stories, Squibbs, Gibes, and Compliments" he knew he would hear in the world to which his legal business took him, including the circle of worldly wittiness described by the literary historian David S. Shields. John referred in general terms to a particular gentleman's conversation, which mingled the characteristics of unreformed, unsentimental manners with those associated with sensibility. He could write her in the same mode but would, he said, refrain, implicitly as an expression of her own standards and/or his sense of what was fit for ladies' ears, thus telling her, too, of his own versatility: "If I should I could entertain you with as much Wit, Humour, smut, filth, Delicacy, Modesty and Decency, tho not with so exact Mimickry, as a certain Gentleman did the other Evening." It was his playfulness in language that explained "why that Gentleman does not succeed in Business"—he needed to control it in the way that John was illustrating he could. Instead, the gentleman's "whole study and Attention has been so manifestly engaged in the noble Arts of smutt, Double Ententre, and Mimickry of Dutchmen and Negroes." Here, John attributed the negative judgment of such mimicry to one side of an aesthetic debate to which he had also been exposed: "I have heard that Imitators, tho they imitate well, Master Pieces in elegant and valuable Arts, are a servile Cattle. And that Mimicks are the lowest Species of Imitators, and I should think that Mimicks of Dutchmen and Negroes were the most sordid, of Mimicks." But this was only a hypothetical judgment: "If so, to what a Depth of the Profound have we plunged that Gentleman's character."[106]

John had concluded this with an ironic and unambivalently negative judgment of "all the Ladies who are now entertained with that Gents Conversation"—acknowledging that there were ladies so entertained—and asked Abigail to pardon his "Candour" as one of his characteristics. She told him in response to his earlier letter that she had been entertained by it, and one can detect some sexual playfulness in her prenuptial rebuke to his faulting her (in the same letter effectively praising her for her "decency" and "sensibility") for "sitting with the Leggs crossed": "[You] know I think that a gentleman has no business to concern himself about the Leggs of a Lady, for my part I do not apprehend any bad effects from the practice, yet since you desire it, and that you may not for the future trouble Yourself so much about it, will reform."[107] Much later in their marriage, they still mildly titillated each other: John sighed off a 1794 letter with, "I am, impatiently yours," and Abigail concluded her reply, "I understand the *Term impatiently yours* but I had a good mind to be a little Roguish and ask a Question," before typically backing off, "but I think I will only say that I am most Patiently Your ever constant and affectionate A Adams."[108]

Not only was this euphemistically mild; it was between a married couple. Consciously and explicitly, Abigail and John generally placed the highest value on the modesty associated with female sensibility, despite its sexual potentials. In 1779, referring to the case John had made for refusing to bring her with him to France, Abigail said she would "not wish" herself with him on the voyage when he brought their sons John Quincy and Charles with him, despite the terrible emotional pain of

parting with them, "because you say a Lady cannot help being an odious creature at sea, and I will not wish myself in any situation that should
make me so to you." Five years later, and on board ship without John,
Abigail shared a cabin with Nabby, but the door opened, she wrote to
Mary, "into the Cabbin where the Gentlemen all Sleep: and wh[ere] we
sit dine &c. We can only live with our door Shut, whilst we dress and
undress." She asks: "what should I have thought on shore; have layed
myself down to sleep, in common with half a dozen Gentlemen? We
have curtains it is true, and we only in part undress . . . but we have the
satisfaction of falling in, with a set of well behaved, decent Gentlemen,
whose whole deportment is agreeable to the strickest delicacy, both in
words and action." Consciously, at least, the Adamses and other cultivators of sensibility made the distinction that Rousseau articulated in
explaining his beloved Mme de Warens's taking him as a lover as well
as her willingness to have sex with another man alternately: "Her feelings were the result of error, never passion." Both Adamses believed
that passions were naturally implanted in man, and, with Pope, they believed that they could animate people to the good; at the same time, they
shared the view that reputable, nominally nonsexual feeling could be
distinguished from the passions. The distinction was fragile, especially
in view of women's psychology. Toward the end of her life, and despite
her insistence on her special susceptibility to feeling, Abigail insisted:
"in no period of my life have the vile passions had control over me." As
she aged, Withey has observed, she "became more and more obsessed
with 'delicacy' and moral purity in women." But, all along, her views on
these subjects had been close to those expressed by Fordyce.[109]

## CHAPTER 3

# The Theory of Gendered Sensibility

In 1767, the twenty-three year old Abigail was so impressed by Fordyce's *Sermons to Young Women* that she sent its two volumes, published that year in Philadelphia, to her twenty-six-year-old sister Mary, enthusing: "I cannot say how much I admire them, and should I attempt to say how justly worthy they are of admiration I fear I should not do justice to this most excellent performance." Fifteen years later, in a letter to her young unmarried cousin John Thaxter, she did articulate one reason for her admiration for the *Sermons*. The context was her observation of a decline in manners in Braintree. Explaining why "Matrimony is not in vogue here," Abigail wrote that men were not genteel any more: "We have Ladies but not a gentleman in the whole Town, and the young Gentlemen of the present day, are not intirely to the taste of those Ladies who value a virtuous Character. Licentiousness and freedom of Manners are predominate." The first authority she cited was Rousseau: "Rosseau observes, that the manner of thinking among Men in a great extent depends upon the taste of the Ladies." In this, as in some of his other views of women, Rousseau followed in the footsteps of Malebranche. "If this is true," Abigail went on, suggesting that she believed it was, "the manners of the present day are no complement upon the fair Sex." The fair sex were largely responsible for making men into gentlemen, that is, it seems, first reforming their manners, although, then, the "Manners of the two Sexes, I believe keep pace with each other; and in proportion as the Men grow regardless of Character, the women neglect the Duties of their Sex."[1]

The general cause for this decline in manners was the consumer revolution: "Tis Luxury my dear Sir which ruins and depraves our Manners." According to her logic, ladies' "taste," that is, their response to luxury, drew them away from their proper focus, the reforming of men's manners. The result had serious implications for the national character: "We are ready imitators of the Nations with which we are connected, and it is much to be feared if the days of American simplicity and virtue are not already passed." Here, Abigail brought in Fordyce, her second authority: "Fordyce, to whom our Sex are much indebted for the justice he had done them, observes that the company of virtuous and well bred women is the best School for Learning the most proper demeanor, the easiest turn of thought and expression and the right habits of the best kind, that the most honorable, the most Moral the most conscientious Men, are in general those who have the greatest regard for women of reputation and talents."

Fordyce's *Sermons to Young Women* was first published in 1766 in London. Fordyce had become a doctor of divinity at the University of Glasgow and "made his reputation" by his sermons to the General Assembly of the Church of Scotland, entitled *The Folly, Infamy, and Misery of Unlawful Pleasure.* (They were published in Boston in 1761.) He had moved to London early in the 1760s, and his *Sermons* addressed "ye fair daughters of Britain" as "my fair country women," who were hurting their country by "flaunting French attire." By 1814, fourteen editions of the *Sermons* had appeared. In challenging that book in her *Vindication of the Rights of Woman* (1792), Wollstonecraft wrote: "Dr. Fordyce's sermons have long made part of a young woman's library; nay, girls at school are allowed to read him." She, in turn, would be challenged by contemporaries, notably the bluestocking evangelical Hannah More in 1799, after Godwin's vindicating revelations about Wollstonecraft's sexual freedom and religious practices; More reiterated the view of feminized sensibility that Fordyce had popularized. It was the same as that held generally by the Scottish school of moral sense. These writers had described men of sensibility as the product of the most developed level of civilization, identifiable with British commerce and cities, and, like the *Spectator* and *Cato*, they argued that women had a still higher level of sensibility than men.[2]

Rosemary Keller writes that Abigail "affirmed" Fordyce's views of women, views shared, she notes, by the *Spectator* and Franklin's writings. While two of her other biographers suggest that what she read in Fordyce's *Sermons* helped strengthen her self-conception (and Wollstonecraft conceded that "they must be allowed to contain many sensible observations"), when we face the value that Abigail placed on the power of her sensibility and the severe conflict she said it caused her, we might bear in mind that Wollstonecraft also wrote of Fordyce's *Sermons*: "I should instantly dismiss them from my pupil's [reading], if I wished to strengthen her understanding, by leading her to form sound principles on a broad basis." Fordyce's book was second only to Rousseau's *Emile* on Wollstonecrafts's list of "Some of the Writers Who Have Rendered Women Objects of Pity, Bordering on Contempt." Wollstonecraft focused on women's internalization of such renderings as well as on the motives of the men who propounded them. Fordyce, she wrote, in "declamatory periods . . . spins out Rousseau's eloquence, and in most sentimental rant, details his opinion respecting the female character, and the behavior which woman ought to assume to render her lovely."[3]

For Wollstonecraft, writing in 1792, *sentimental* had negative connotations, and, for Fordyce, writing in 1766, it did not, but he confined its use to his description of women's behavior. It meant "susceptible to impression" (some women, those "more sentimental spirits . . . might be dazzled in the beginning" by men who pursued them) or "openly emotional" (with "congenial minds" a better but properly educated woman will find her "attachment . . . increased . . . she will enjoy . . . sentimental and friendly delight"). Fordyce gave a second illustration of this latter meaning in his concluding praise for women: in contrast to "the other sex," they were "by far the devoutest worshippers, the warmest friends, and the most sentimental as well as the warmest companions." These different evaluations of *sentimental*, Fordyce's versus Wollstonecraft's, can stand for changes over time within and toward cultures of sensibility on both sides of the Atlantic. It was the word's association with women that potentiated its negative value.[4]

Fordyce appealed to the authority of the "two books," the Bible and nature, for his asseveration that sensibility was gendered. The New Testament's Peter called women "the weaker vessel" (1 Pet. 3:7), and Fordyce explained that he had styled them thus because such vessels, "being of finer materials, or more delicate construction, and therefore easily broken or hurt, are for that reason, and for the regard also that people have for them, used with particular tenderness." Moving on from chinaware to the Malebranchian psychophysiology that the *Spectator* and its ideological successors (in all literary forms) had propagated, Fordyce declares: "Nature has endowed the greater part of the sex with a constitutional Softness." He continued: "God's revelations coincided with the dispositions to modesty, sympathy, generosity, the desire of pleasing, the dread of violence, the horror of barbarity, the promptness to cherish tender sentiments, and form endearing connexions, which are all so natural to the worthiest part of your sex." He gave his audience a mor-

phology of the development of the sensibility of "your sex," switch-
ing pronouns to declare: "Their earliest days are marked by a mixture
of sprightliness and simplicity. They run, they laugh, they prattle; and
then they often blush, for fear of having offended."[5]

Abigail may have had the next idea in mind when she showed her
concern over her teenage daughter's unawakened sensibility, a concern that Nabby herself internalized.[6] "As they grow up," Fordyce
went on, "[women's] sensibilities become more enlightened and more
awake. They blush oftener. It is the colouring of virtue." John admired
such evidence in Abigail when he courted her. In keeping with Malebranche, Collier, and the *Spectator*, Fordyce asserted: "[Women] contract
a quicker perception of what is decent, and of what is wise. A sweet timidity was given them to guard their innocence, by inclining them to
shrink from whatever might threaten to injure it." The "nature and situation of the men is very different." Differences were the result of nature and nurture: "[Men's] constitution of mind, no less than of body, is
for the most part, hardy and rough. By means of both, by the demands
of life, and by the impulse of passion they are engaged in a vast diversity of pursuits, from which your sex are precluded by decorum, by
softness, and by fear." Norton opens her account of the lives of white
eighteenth-century American women by contrasting their experience of
"the invariable daily and weekly routines of housewifery" with "their
husbands' diverse experiences," particularly in travel and "a variety of
business activities that took them on numerous errands."[7]

Fordyce considered one advantage that men had: "their diversity of
daily pursuits, joined with the multiplicity of female objects that freer
modes of living present to their imagination, and the power they have of
unlimited choice whenever they are disposed to make it (a power which
Nature probably and Custom certainly; have denied to the others) . . .
must . . . be productive of very different effects." In his allowance for
custom's certain contribution to sexism, he reflected the view of feminist predecessors from Poulain de la Barre to Pope and many women
writers, too. Fordyce had earlier suggested that "the circumscribed situation of the sex" increased women's dangerous "taste for amusement."
He considered the effects on "the faculties" of men's freedom to range,
again suggesting that nurture reinforced nature: "Nature appears to have
formed the faculties of your sex for the most part with less vigour than
those of ours; observing the same distinction here, as in the more delicate frame of your bodies." He admitted that there were exceptions (as
Hume admitted of Queen Elizabeth): "But you yourselves . . . will al-

low that war, commerce, politics, exercise of strength and dexterity, abstract philosophy, and all the abstruse sciences, are most properly the province of men." Women who pleaded to share "any part of this province equally with us" were "masculine," and he told them: "you do not understand your true interests." He aggrandized the territory that did belong to circumscribed women by calling it "an empire," "that which has the heart for its object, and is secured by meekness and modesty, by soft attractions and virtuous love."[8]

Fordyce's assertion that "there is a sex in minds" expressed one side of a long debate, the *querelle des femmes*, galvanized and popularized since the later seventeenth century, notably in England by the feminists described by Hilda Smith.[9] Fordyce allowed that women "were capable of writing Novels and Romances," "admirable productions of the present century," because their literary forms were, "in a particular degree, proportioned to the scope of [their] capacities." Elsewhere in the same book, he scorned most novels. In fact, women had emerged in Fordyce's era as highly popular novelists, much to the chagrin of several male competitors.[10] Here, Fordyce had continued by saying: "Amongst women of sense I have discovered an uncommon penetration in what relates to characters, . . . hitting them off through their several specific distinctions . . . with a fund of what may strictly be termed Sentiment, or a pathetic manner of thinking, which I have not so frequently met with in men." He wrote of an exemplary woman of sensibility that "her pen flowed in a stream of sentiment alike tender and exalted; it was the interpreter of her heart."[11] Perhaps this was derived from Richardson, whose novels (especially *Clarissa*) Fordyce praised enthusiastically in his *Sermons to Young Women*. In the view he ascribed to Clarissa, Richardson wrote: "those women who take delight in writing, excel the men in all the graces of the familiar style. The gentleness of their minds, the delicacy of their sentiments (improved by the manner of their education) and the liveliness of their imaginations qualify them . . . while the men of *mere* learning, aiming to get above that natural ease and freedom which distinguish this (and indeed every other kind of writing) when they have best succeeded, are got above, or rather beneath all natural manners."[12] Fordyce also suggested that women's ability to read aloud so well was, "in some measure, owing to that fine feeling of nature and sentiment, which may be supposed to result from the delicacy of their organs." Because of this, however, they were "often deficient where force and vehemence are requisite."[13]

There were other corollaries of such deficient psychology. Fordyce told his readers: "The Almighty has thrown you upon the protection of our sex." This, however, was a source of entitlement: "Nothing can be more certain than that your sex is, on every account, entitled to the shelter of ours." But no sure power inhered in the possession Fordyce allowed women: "Your softness, weakness, timidity and tender reliance on man; your helpless condition in yourselves, and his superior strength for labor, ability for defense, and fortitude in trial; your tacit acknowledgement of these; and frequent application for his aid in so many winning ways, concur to form a plea, which nothing can disallow or withstand but brutality." But men could be brutal, even men of sensibility, men who "in a sober mood were open to the tenderest feelings of humanity" but who, giving rein to "lawless desire" by "the rebellion of their blood, were as ungovernable and fierce as any beast of the forest," posing a danger to women to which Fordyce repeatedly returned.[14]

Women's resources lay in their own behavior—to stay as circumscribed as they could and not pursue "public" pleasures, but also to place themselves "in the Guardianship of Omnipotence." Their gendered sensibility meant that women were naturally pious, a characterization disputed by Wollstonecraft and reasserted by Hannah More.[15] Women may have been reproached, Fordyce argued, because they were "in a particular degree, susceptible of all the tender affections." In his view, however, "the warmth of their attachments, and their aptitude to be affected with whatever has a tendency to touch the heart," did women "honour." Moreover, these traits coincided with that emotional element in various Protestant denominations that was fundamental to the rise of sensibility: "I have always thought that the spirit of devotion depends on sentiment, rather than ratiocination; on the feelings of gratitude and wonder, joy and sorrow, triumph and contrition, hope and fear, rather than on theological disquisition however profound, or pious speculation, however exalted." Religion was "kept alive" by such feelings when "lost in the labyrinth of school-divinity."[16]

The language Fordyce employed in reiterating this apparent elevation of his female readers was the Rousseauistic, "sentimental rant" with which, Wollstonecraft was to say, he "details his opinions respecting the female character and the behavior which women ought to assume to render her lovely." This is what he wrote in his sermon 5: "With the character of the Christian Woman nothing, methinks, can better correspond than a propensity to melt into affectionate sorrow. It becomes alike her religion and her sex." His pleasure that a woman's emotional pain brought him is comparable to that which Lovelace or Yorick took in a woman's tears,: "Never, my fair auditory, never do your eyes shine with a more delightful effulgence, than when suffused with all the trembling softness of grief, for virtue in distress or solicitude for friendship in danger."[17]

Brissenden took the emblematic phrase *virtue in distress* for the title of his study of the European novel of sentiment from Richardson to Sade. Fordyce wished to persuade women to "assume" this nominally religious "behavior" by continuing here to argue that it will make them more attractive to men, men, that is, of sensibility: "Believe me, if the gaiety of conversation gave place somewhat oftener to the tender tale of woe, you would not, to such at least as have hearts, appear as the less lovely. The sigh of compassion stealing from a female breast, on the mention of calamity, would be rather more musical in their ears, than the loud bursts of unmeaning laughter, with which they are often entertained." Salient is that the tale is one of pain and that it is merely a "mention" that stimulates the woman's response, signaling the refinement of her sensibility. He adds that "the charms of innocence and sympathy appearing in your discourse will, to every discerning man," a man with a "heart," that is, of a sensibility capable of registering and appreciating such female sensibility, "spread around you a lustre which all the jewels in the world cannot bestow." And he apostrophized this quality: "Merciful Redeemer, how edifying to the soul is this generous sensibility!" The eighteenth-century argument that "women are happily formed for religion" by means of their "natural endowment" of sensibility, delicacy, imagination, and sympathy was to be perpetuated by early-nineteenth-century New England ministers (e.g., the Reverend David Chaplin) and peripatetic evangelists as well as their congregations. It was an ideology absorbed by white women in the American South, too.[18]

Fordyce's conception of God matched women's special capacities to reach him. If he was "infinitely removed from every painful impression," the Bible "ascribes to him all the guiltless emotions of humanity." In heaven, Christ was "touched with the feeling of our infirmities." His history on earth is "unspeakably affecting," which "carries with it a vital, home-felt, and heart-awakening influence." Christ, the "Friend of Man," was "the perfect model of kindness and courtesy . . . he conversed with those whom the world despised; he stood still to hear the cries, and relieve the miseries of the wretched . . . the beauty of compassion, he exemplified in all occasion." In short, he was the original man of feeling. His exemplification of such manhood should replace warrior ideals, an argument being made since the Restoration and coinciding with the attack on Stoicism. Christ's "weeping over . . . Lazarus, con-

soling his mournful sisters," was infinitely "more interesting and glorious, than all the conquerors of the earth crowned with laurels . . . with
numberless captives riding in their train."[19]

There was an evident relation between this reconceptualization of
God (as evident in the American colonies as in metropolitan Britain) and
the changes in some men's behavior, changes wished for by women. It
was to such changed men that Fordyce urged women to shape themselves, that is, to become "pleasing to men of sentiment." Fordyce represented himself throughout as a man of feeling, essentially sympathetic
to women, wishing "to engage the heart" of his readers, but women
themselves needed reform, and his intention was "to mend" women's
hearts, "to engage" them "to goodness . . . by sentimental persuasion
and the native influence of fraternal counsel." He was, he said, a man
capable of reading women's emotions from their faces. In the "countenances, words and gestures" of those woman described in the Gospels as
going to Christ's tomb, he told his audience, "I think I read the painful,
yet amiable emotions, that wrought in their tender throbbing hearts."
He was "particularly charmed with the eager anxiety, and beautiful distress of Mary Magdalene." Conversely, he felt "abhorrence . . . caused
by the bare idea" of an "impudent woman."[20]

Fordyce advised women how they could please such men of feeling. Women were "intended" "to be a kind of softer companion, who,
by nameless delightful sympathies and endearments, might improve our
pleasures and soothe our pains; to lighten the load of domestic cares, and
thereby leave us more at leisure for rougher labours or severer studies;
and finally, to spread a certain grace and embellishment over human life."
Wives who were left alone by their husbands had themselves to blame,
he told them, for not "studying their humours, overlooking their mistakes, submitting to their opinions in matters indifferent, . . . giving soft
answers to hasty words, complaining as seldom as possible, and making
it your daily care to relieve their anxieties, . . . to enliven the hour of
dullness, and call up the ideas of felicity." To do these things would be to
increase husbands' "esteem," he said, and "to have secured every degree
of influence that could conduce to their virtue, or your mutual satisfaction," making your house "the abode of domestic bliss."[21]

Not only should women devote themselves to reading men's pleasures and pains in order to enhance and soothe them; they had to restrain any qualities of their own that might jar. For example: "Men of
the best sense have been usually averse to the thought of marrying a
witty female." Male "wits" had been targets of reformers of manners,

too, associated as they were with Restoration libertinism. Fordyce insisted throughout that it was the best kind of men—men of sense and sensibility—that women would lose should they reject his recommendation for feminine behavior. They were modern men, men like himself, like the *Spectator*'s Lysander, sympathetic to women, and interested in a happy marriage: "Men who understand the science of domestic happiness, know that its very first principle is ease." Then, in a dead giveaway, he explained: "But we cannot be easy, when we are not safe. We are never safe in the company of a critic; and almost every wit is a critic by profession. In such company we are not at liberty to unbend ourselves." In effect, husbands married to witty wives found themselves having to read them when, properly and naturally, wives were supposed to read husbands: "All must be the straining of study, or the anxiety of apprehensions how painful!" Men wanted to experience home life with a freedom (as well as ease and safety) that depended on women's restraint,: "Where the heart may not expand and open itself with freedom, farewell to real friendship, farewell to convivial delight! But to suffer such restraint at home, what misery!" Wit was a "weapon pointed at a husband," and Fordyce said that he had seen such a man "in continual fear on his own account, and that of his friends."[22]

Similarly, Fordyce urged women to improve their education in order to be more pleasing companions to their husbands. "Mental Acquisitions" were to give women better "powers of pleasing," but they should not "push their applications so far as to hurt their more tender health, to hinder those family duties for which the sex are chiefly intended, or to impair those softer graces that give them their higher luster"; that would be to "relinquish their just sphere." He mentioned that "all the most sensible and worthy of [your sex] have ever professed a particular relish for the conversation of men of sense and worth." Women who followed his prescription could be assured that such "men . . . are attached to the society of such women beyond every thing else in the world." Hume had listed mutually beneficial heterosociality as one of the signs of increased "humanity," the fruit of economic progress, a view generally shared by the Scottish school of moral sense. Fordyce continued: "Both sexes meet in an easy and sociable manner; and the tempers of men, as well as their behavior, refine apace . . . they must feel an increase of humanity from the very habit of conversing together, and contribute to each other's pleasure and entertainment."[23]

The year before Fordyce's remarks, the *Scots Magazine* printed "A Picture of True Conjugal Felicity," in which the wife, Amanda, exemplifying precisely the behavior Fordyce described, had married "Manly," "an individual 'firm from principle' but with that 'quick sensibility' that often accompanied a 'good heart.'" Amanda's job was to enhance his sensibility, play on his feelings to make "the truest harmony in souls," so that the "force of the manly mind and heart when mingled with the sweetness of the female" resulted in "mutual felicity." To insist on the manliness of men thus softened to a significant degree of sensibility was a feature of sentimental literature, warding off apprehensions of their effeminacy. Fordyce declared that "this mutual tendency," that is, of the conversation and society of men and women of sense, "cannot fail to be a rich source of mutual improvement." While "humanity" indicated common ground, that very convergence required the difference that Fordyce emphasized: "Was not such reciprocal aid a great part of Nature's intention in that mental and moral difference of sex, which she has marked by characters no less distinguishable than those that diversify her outward forms."[24]

There were men who did not appreciate or want women of sensibility who were oriented to please them. Thereby, they indicated "a mixture of ignorance, grossness, and barbarity." The latter term subsumed the same Scottish scale of values at the opposite end of which stood humanity and sympathy, the signs of the highest point that civilization had reached. Insensible men missed out on enjoying "the tenderest sentiments and most delicious feelings of the human heart." It was, therefore, in men's own interest to "cherish the kindest opinion of the female destination." Fordyce has concluded here by identifying men's self-interest with women's.[25]

But, despite his urging women to prepare themselves to catch a man of sensibility, Fordyce admitted that "an attachment without tenderness, or at most an affection without delicacy, is as much to be hoped from the ordinary run of husbands." There were only a "few men to join sentiment to knowledge." And there were some men "so grossly insensible, as to be for the most part little or nothing affected by the temper or behaviour of their wives; provided only they do not ruin their affairs." Were a woman of sensibility, anticipating a reciprocity of feeling or at least that she might "influence" him in that direction, to marry such an "insensible" man, she would become a figure of virtue in severe distress. Of women in these circumstances Fordyce exclaimed, displaying his own sympathy: "How much are they themselves objects of compassion, thus condemned to drag a wretched life with beings, on whom all their endeavors to delight are lost! How sensibly must such a situation pain a delicate and ingenious mind!" It was Clarissa's refusal of such an insensible man in Solmes, her father's choice, that had initiated her tragedy.[26]

Clarissa went on to reform one rake (Belford), and she came close to reforming Lovelace himself. Her predecessor, Pamela, had succeeded in reforming a rake and then marrying him. Fordyce illustrated the convergence between Richardson and his contemporary Scots, agreeing on the need for the reformation of manners. Women's sexual difference gave them a power over men, Fordyce told them, "a very great and extensive influence which you, in general have over Our sex. There is in female youth an attraction, which every man of the least sensibility must perceive. If assisted by beauty it becomes in the first impression irresistible." By making themselves "agreeable companions in a relation of which of all others is the most intimate," women conferred felicity and showed themselves worthy of a virtuous tenderness from men. And, Fordyce asked, what "can be conceived so properly female as inspiring, improving, and continuing such a tenderness, in all its charming extent"? Women should show their preference for men who are "sober, sedate, and sentimental" and begin to reform those men who "dare to speak a language unfit" for their company "by letting loose on them" "a spirit of indignant virtue." They could work on men's sensibility: "Should not your eyes at least make them sensible of the affront offered to your ears?" What if such men were insensible? "And if they are hardened enough not to be ashamed, does it not become your duty ever after to shun their sight, as you would shun a bear or a satyr?" Evidently, men were in need of reform, particularly in their attitude toward women: "Hardly can one go into a company of men, where, licentiousness of tongue passes for freedom of conversation, without hearing the poor women abused for their worthlessness, or weakness, or both."[27]

Here, then, Fordyce suggested, women could construe their gendered sensibility as power: "To form the manners of men various causes contribute; but nothing, I apprehend, so much as the turn of the women with whom they converse . . . such society, beyond every thing else, rubs off the corners that give many of our sex an ungracious roughness." The "more perfect polish" the society of refined women gives men, in contrast with the polish they can obtain from "general commerce with the world," was rooted in a change of heart, which "is the result of gentler feelings, and more elegant humanity; the heart itself is moulded; habits of undissembled courtesy are formed; a certain urbanity is acquired." Men lose their taste for the features of the same, all-male society that abused women behind their backs: "violent passions, rash oaths, coarse jests, indelicate language of every kind, are precluded and disrelished."[28] This was the argument for which all women were indebted to Fordyce, Abigail would write to Thaxter in 1787, and one that Wollstonecraft would scorn in the *Vindication of the Rights of Woman* five years later, referring to "the fair defects in Nature; the women who appear to be created not to enjoy the fellowship of man, but save him from sinking into absolute brutality, by rubbing off the rough angles of his character."[29]

The reformation that he urged would bring men closer to women in manners and in sensibility, so Fordyce, like his fellow Scots, like Richardson, and like other would-be reformers of men's manners, added: "I do not mean that the men I speak of will become feminine. . . . Their principles will have nothing ferocious or forbidding; their affections will be chaste and soothing at the same instant." Perhaps they would be less prone in their nonsober moods to "lawless desire." Thus chastened, "the Gentleman, the Man of worth, the Christian, will all melt insensibly and sweetly into one another. How agreeable the composition!" Richardson had composed such a man in Sir Charles Grandison, Abigail's ideal. Fordyce suggested that the power exercised by women in the way he has specified would lead to the taming of men in "Honourable love! that great preservative of purity, that powerful softener of the fiercest spirit, that mighty improver of the rudest carriage, that all-subduing, yet all-exalting principle of the human breast, which humbles the proud, and bends the stubborn . . . which converts the savage into a man and lifts the man into the hero!" Such a conversion was a central objective of the culture of sensibility, the climax of sentimental novels.[30]

That apprehension over effeminacy was characteristic of cultures of sensibility as it was of republicanism because of the closer convergence of the sexes in the value both placed on feeling, but also because of the growing assertiveness of women as participants in public, heterosocial minglings (a feature of consumer cultures) and in religion and as writers and readers. In fact, Fordyce and others with his views were responding to emergent feminism. But women, too, were apprehensive over effeminacy. Abigail compared the present state of Britain "to Rome when it fell from its ancient Virtue" as a "commonwealth" to an empire, the "Nobility" abandoning "themselves to their Lusts." Neither "the Eloquence of *Cicero*, the stern virtue of Cato, nor the poignard of Brutus and Cassius, could stem the Torrent of vice nor save a people who were sunk into every excess of debauchery grown wicked and Effamanate." This was an aspect of republican ideology that Wollstonecraft turned to feminist purpose, wishing neither sex to be effeminate. John wrote Abigail from Paris in 1778 to declare that "Luxury, dissipation, and Effeminacy, are all pretty nearly at the same degree of Excess here and in every other Part of Europe." Implicitly, republican, middle-class America virtuously had avoided what Crèvecoeur called the "great refinements of luxury," and, if the European wretch was regenerated into an American man of feeling, he was a manly one.[31]

## CHAPTER 4

# Social Circles and the Reformation of Female Manners

## Public and Private

The apparent polarity of private and public was central to cultures of sensibility. It reflected the simultaneous development of both spheres during the seventeenth and eighteenth centuries.[1] The private evolved from the ancient ideal and reality of the *oeconomos* or "household," in the context of the change that Norbert Elias describes when the "national economy developed from the 'private economy' of feudal ruling homes. More precisely, there [was] at first, no distinction between what are later opposed as 'public' and 'private' income and expenditure."[2] Such household fiefdoms were what eighteenth-century republican idealists had in mind when elevating their commitment to the public good above personal interest. The public was to evolve from its ancient identification with "the court scene," amplified in the creation of a variety of formal "and informal institutions, facilitating the expression of public opinions, . . . coffee houses, salons, literary societies, libraries, concert halls, opera houses, and above all, journals and a commercial press." Gurpreet Mahajan, following Jürgen Habermas, emphasizes the emergence and coexistence of the private and the public as "complementary entities." Habermas challenged the belief that "the market"—the public—was "independent" of "the sphere of the family . . . the core of the private sphere." In fact, the family "was profoundly caught up in the requirements of the market."[3]

In the "small-scale society" of the earlier eighteenth century mainland American colonies, writes Gordon S. Wood, "privacy as we know it did not exist, and our sharp distinction between public and private was scarcely visible." While the emergence of public space provided some heterosocial opportunities, especially for elite urban women (and the importance to them of public entertainments has, I think, been underestimated), they and the mass of women below them began only in that century to be able to construe where they lived and worked as domestic, as Carole Shammas has argued in addressing the effects of commercial consumption on Massachusetts and old England.[4]

Habermas, like Elias, conceived of a relation between the psychology associated with the emergence of domesticity and the material transformation of houses. The value to women of houses' becoming primary "sites for consumption" seems indisputable, and Shammas suggests that women were "a major force in promoting enhancements to the domestic environment": "The evolution of a house into a home made social interaction more accessible to women and put more under their control." These new, more abundant interiors promised to be "a source of power and influence for the physically vulnerable and legally unequal women of the early modern period."[5] It has been argued, too, that middle-class wives' subordination to their husbands' patriarchalism was modified during the seventeenth century, en route to the more "companionate" marriage of the eighteenth. But Habermas refers to the "patriarchal authority" that still dominated both private and public, and one can infer from the *Spectator* and the literature that followed it that men could and did operate unchecked within the private sphere, although there is evidence that many men increasingly checked themselves and became more responsive to women and children. This was the major reform goal of proponents of sensibility. Evidently, mothers played a key role in this, a subject to which I turn in chapter 11 below. Here, however, we can note that, in Habermas's view, family members were "bound together" by a "human closeness." Ideas "of freedom, love, and cultivation of the person . . . grew out of the conjugal family's private sphere." That human closeness generated "humanity."[6]

## Humanity

The religious tradition that elevated the feelings of human nature charged the notion of humanity with the scientized responsiveness of the nervous system. The word *humanity* became very closely associated with *sensibility*. At Harvard, John may as well have read the Cambridge Platonist Henry More's definition of *humanity*, a "Virtue which, from the sense of that Excellency that is in human Nature and the common Affinity we have with all Mankind, leads us to be officious and benevolent to every one."[7] John and Abigail admired Tillotson, who identified humanity with benevolence. The same scientific and religious line of thought informed Shaftesbury, of whom Fiering writes: "No one before him had argued so eloquently for the identification of fellow-feeling with the essence of true human nature."[8]

In 1711, the year Shaftesbury's *Characteristics of Men, Manners, Times* was published, the *Spectator* also made clear that the word *humanity* connoted the scientific definition of human nature. "Man is subject to innumerable Pains and Sorrows by the very condition of Humanity," but "we" aggravate "this common Calamity by our cruel Treatment of one another." Unnatural suffering could be avoided, and the *Spectator*'s definition was oriented toward the reformation of manners: "Half the Misery of Human Life might be extinguished, would Man alleviate the general Curse they lye under by mutual Offices of Compassion, Benevolence, and Humanity." One can discern here that reaction to Calvinistic Puritanism informing Crane's men of feeling. The sentence implies a second definition of *humanity*, denoting sympathy and sympathetic action, that the *Spectator* expressly wished to foster in its readers: "There is nothing therefore which we ought more to encourage in our selves and others, than that Disposition of Mind which in our Language goes under the Title of Good-nature [the subject of this number]." Humanity thus modified assumed consciousness of other people's suffering. The *Spectator* further defined good nature as "an overflowing of Humanity . . . an exuberant Love of Mankind . . . and a general Benevolence to Mankind."[9]

Because society could not exist "without Good-nature," mankind has had "to invent a kind of artificial Humanity," which the *Spectator* identified with class, "Good-breeding," the aristocracy previously having associated itself with the "humanism" of the Renaissance, a heritage now modified with that critique of Stoicism that the *Spectator* also helped pass on to its bourgeois audience. It said that "Good-breeding" was manifested in "affability Complaisance and Easiness of Temper reduced into an Art." The reformation of manners was essentially condescending, although reformers also attacked libertine aristocrats.

Yet again, "Good-nature is generally born with us," a statement referring to the definition of humanity that Latitudinarian Anglicanism had strengthened by coupling it with scientific psychology. Class came in because of good nature's dependence on "Health, Prosperity and kind Treatment from the World," although, as usual, the *Spectator* twists and turns: "nothing is capable of forcing it up, where it does not grow of it self. It is one of the Blessings of a happy Constitution which Education may improve but not produce."

Finally, the *Spectator* bore witness to the fact that a man (and from common humanity the subject evolved into a discussion of men's manners) who displays humanity was vulnerable to being mocked, a measure, perhaps, of the novelty of such behavior but certainly of the "World" the *Spectator* wished to reform. Ordinary observers were accustomed to enjoying spiteful sallies, so they assume that "Good-natured Men are not always Men of the most Wit." As the author insisted, however: "[The] greatest Wits I have conversed with are Men eminent for their Humanity." This was a live question that John Adams had debated when considering how he should present himself to the "World," obviously in conjunction with his reading the *Spectator*, perhaps during one of those times when he just picked it up for a spot of pleasurable self-indulgence: "Quaere, was there ever a Witt, who had much Humanity and Compassion, much Tenderness of Nature?"[10] A second reason the *Spectator* gave why the good-natured man was sometimes thought naive or a bit dim was because "he is apt to be moved with Compassion for those Misfortunes or Infirmities which another would turn into Ridicule, and by that means gain the Reputation of a Wit."

Like Descartes, Locke, Shaftesbury, the Latitudinarians, and the authors of the *Spectator*, the widely influential Hutcheson also took human nature as his subject, wrote positively of what was in the "human Heart," and assumed the synonymity of goodness and humanity in asking rhetorically: "How great a Part of Human Actions flow directly from *Humanity* and *Kind Affection*?" This indicates that humanity was held to be an interior, moral virtue, as Hutcheson's disciples in the Scottish moral sense school, including Fordyce, would explain. The notion was further disseminated by the sentimental fiction and poetry I have mentioned as well as by American preachers of a variety of stripes.[11]

By the mid-eighteenth century, *humanity* was in frequent use among the literate, English-speaking population of the American colonies. In 1742, Eliza Lucas wrote to Mary Bartlett, staying at the Pinckney house in Charleston, and described a visit she had just paid to "my poor friend, Mrs. Chardon, whom I found quite out of her Sences, an object that must greatly move a stranger that had not lost every spark of humanity." She asserted in a later letter to Lady Carew: "I can by no means consent to your silence least you give me pain by what you suffer." This was to attribute sensibility to the lady. "Tis a faulty tenderness, my dear madam, for though they must be void of tenderness and humanity as well as friendship that dont feel for those in affliction, there are advantages to be reaped from it." Letters written in the 1760s, and cited by the historian Kathleen M. Brown, indicated the penetration of notions of humanity into the Anglican elite of Virginia, too, and Nicole Eustace has described its ubiquity in an array of Pennsylvania sources generated soon after, reflecting Quaker but also wider influences.[12]

The Adamses' writings are peppered with the word *humanity*. Prior to their marriage, Abigail defined it in a letter to John in terms synonymous with *irresistible compassion*: "Humanity obliges us to be affected with the distresses and Miserys of our fellow creatures." John's *Autobiography* illustrated the term's conventional grouping with related qualities: having written, "my heart bled for the poor people of Boston" under siege in 1775, he recorded his recommendation that all British officers should be seized but held "with civility, humanity, and generosity."[13] The obituary of Abigail's mother (published in Hall's *New England Chronicle, or Essex Gazette*, October 19, 1775) indicates that the word *humane* was in conventional use long before, together with the word *humanity*: "She was kind, tender and humane." We have seen *humanity* associated with tenderness before, assuming that fundamental link to the nervous system and its sensibility that John Quincy spelled out to Abigail. Other cognates were *inhumanity* and *inhumane*. John wrote in his diary in 1771 of an acquaintance's telling him "of an Instance of Cruelty and Inhumanity" in the Boston wharfkeeper, named Hall, "in ordering a poor Widow to be taken with a single Writ, when her Daughter was dying."[14]

## The Outer Circle of Humanity

That passage in which Abigail had written that humanity obliged one to be affected with the distresses of "our fellow creatures" illustrates the Hutchesonian assumptions back of the term's conventional usage. She had continued by attributing still greater power to friendship: "Friendship is a band yet stronger [than humanity], which causes us to [feel] with greater tenderness the afflictions of our Friends." Pinckney once wrote Lady Carew: "I wont lengthen my letter by apoligizing to your Ladyship for troubleing you with my own little concerns; it might be necessary to a Lady of more ceremony and less tender sentiments than yours. But I have been too long acquainted with the goodness of your heart to imagine you prefer the form and distance (with your friends) to which your station entitles you (if you chose it) to the friendly simpathy and tender feelings of humanity." This is yet one more charged contrast, a literally social one, so characteristic of the culture of sensibility. We noted that *friend* held a far more powerful, intimate, literally familial significance in the eighteenth century, in that case extending to humanity. Abigail's letter illustrated the notion that intensity of feeling corresponded with degrees of closeness, in a series of concentric circles, *humanity* the furthest out, embracing all "our fellow creatures," as the term still does. She continued: "And there is a tye more binding than Humanity, and stronger than Friendship, which makes us anxious for the happiness and welfare of those to whom it binds us. It makes their Misfortunes, Sorrows and afflictions our own." All the degrees, humanity, friendship, and love, were of social affection, including having the capacity of being affected by distress.[15]

These degrees had been laid out in schemes to be found in Shaftesbury's writings and in Hutcheson's as well as in their popularizers'. Hutcheson's *Moral Sense* describes one class of "Publick Desires." (His general purpose was to refute the idea, especially as expressed by Mandeville, that human nature was essentially selfish, in favor of the idea that people naturally desire the happiness of others.) This third class "contains many different sorts of Affections, all of which tend toward the *Happiness of others*, or the removal of Misery; such as those of *Gratitude, Compassion, Natural Affection, Friendship*, or the more extensive calm *Desire of the universal Good of all* sensitive Natures, which our moral sense approves of as the Perfection of Virtue, even when it limits and counteracts the narrower Attachments of Love." Subsequently, Hutcheson restated the idea but with still more direct emphasis on the value of counteracting "the narrower" feelings in favor of the "more extensive" one: "Our *moral Sense*, tho it approves all particular *kind Affection* or *Passion*, as well as *calm particular Benevolence* abstractedly considered; yet it approves the *Restraint* or *Limitation* of all particular Affections or Passions, by *the calm universal Benevolence*. To make this Desire prevalent above all *particular Affections*, is the only sure way to obtain constraint *Self-Approbation*." In her letter, however, Abigail ignored the devaluation of the closest tie of social affection. Elsewhere she acknowledged the supervening value of public affections, although not without very significant conflict and emotional pain.[16]

John wrote Abigail in 1775 that her "account of Number slain in the side of our Enemies is affecting to Humanity, altho it is a glorious Proof of the Bravery of our Worthy Countrymen." Abigail's ranking explains this; humanity extended to all persons, including enemies. Nabby expressed the same value in order to highlight the perfunctoriness of British court mourning, in which, she wrote in the journal she kept in London, "one only follows the fashion, and not supposed to feel the least interested, than as we feel a kind of connection with all the world as when we consider the whole human race one family." Yet she could also assume that a value higher than the immediate, personal one should be

placed on "humanity and the interest of [one's] country."[17] One of her
English contemporaries, more widely traveled than she was, illustrates
how such experience provided the distinction between the generic sense
of *humanity* and more specific cultural qualities. He was James King,
a lieutenant on James Cook's last voyage (in 1778), who exclaimed on
meeting Russians in Alaska, not just the native Aleutians: "To see people
in so strange a part of the World who had other ties than that of common humanity was such a novelty, & pleasure, & gave such a turn to our
Ideas & feelings as may very easily be imagined." He, too, assumed that
his readers had the sensibility to put themselves in his shoes.[18]

Miffed by her failure to write, Mercy Otis Warren had rebuked Abigail in accordance with the Hutchesonian hierarchy of values. She hypothesized that her friend "is so wholly Engrossed with the Ideas of
her own Happiness as to think Little of the absent." Her irony was self-
pitying, if not sarcastic: "Why should I interrupt for a moment . . . the
Vivacity and Cheerfulness of Portia Encircled by her Children in full
health . . . to look upon her Friend in this hour of solitude, my Husband
at Boston, my Eldest son abscent, my other four at our Hospitall Ill with
the small pox, my Father in a bed of pain Verging fast towards the Clos-
ing scene, no sisters at hand nor Even a Friend to step in and shorten the
tedious hour."[19]

Similarly, her Aunt Shaw wrote Nabby in London, having heard she
was engaged, in order to get her to write. The letter was dated June 12,
1786, Nabby's wedding day, not that Aunt Shaw knew that precisely. It
was a premarital letter, however, as Abigail's had been when she had written her fiancée that "there is a tye more binding than Humanity," namely,
marital love. Aunt Shaw's letter reported a conversation she had had with
John Quincy in which he expressed the same, Hutchesonian view of sexual love and marriage to which his father subscribed. She asked Nabby:
"Is *Love really a narrower of the Heart*? Does it as Mr. J.Q.A. asserts, '*diminish
general benevolence particular Friendships*'?" That is, does it affect two outer
degrees of affection? "Does it like a Vortex draw all in into one point and
absorb every stream of social Affection?" (Her simile was derived, ultimately, from Descartes's cosmology, which, while discredited, was perpetuated as a social metaphor.) Mary Smith Cranch had written Abigail
two weeks earlier to ask: "Why has She [Nabby] not written to any of us?
Her amiable Partner must not ingross all of her time. He must spare her a
little for her Freinds." And the protagonist of Foster's *The Coquette*, Eliza
Wharton, gave as one reason for her not marrying: "Marriage is the tomb
of friendship. It appears to me a very selfish state. Why do people, in gen-

eral, as soon as they are married, center all their cares, their concerns, and pleasures in their own families? . . . The tenderest ties between friends are weakened, or dissolved, and benevolence itself moves in a very limited sphere." The friend to whom she made this complaint explained the "circumscribing of our enjoyments," "the glory of our marriage state," by the wish that "we" women had to "repose in safety." Eliza, pursuing individual happiness, would be seduced and die alone.[20]

In any case, Aunt Shaw had continued by giving Nabby her own response to the question of whether marriage had absorbed all her social affections: "If so—Why then I have been a long while mistaken—For I have ever considered it as an Emmanation from the almighty Mind." She allowed for variations among individuals but evidently thought that, in respect of its relation to "general benevolence and particular friendships," the effects of being in love were the same for everyone, male as well as female: "Though, like a variety of other Passions, it may operate differently upon different Characters; yet when this divine Spark is lighted up in a Virtuous Bosom, and directed to a worthy Object, how is it productive of every generous and noble deed." This was to downplay sexuality, distinguishing between the love in virtuous and vicious bosoms and between worthy and unworthy objects. The spark glowed outward: "How does it enlarge the Heart, give elegance to Thought, and refine the Taste, and from believing *one* Object deserving of the best affections, find ourselves drawn out in universal benevolence, and Complacency towards the whole human Race."[21]

The young John Adams's expression of feeling to Abigail Smith ("I begin to find an increasing Affection for a certain Lady . . . quickens my Affection for every Body Else," perhaps to the extent of igniting "the fires of Patriotism"), though brief and jocular, was consistent with the view that Aunt Shaw expressed, though her version can be seen to place more value on the domestic center, the circle to which women were theoretically more confined and more suited, as had Abigail's. It was, apparently, a variation of Hutcheson's approval of the moral sense "even when it limits and counteracts the narrower Attachments of Love" because it made "the Desire of the universal Good" extend to "universal Benevolence."[22]

One of Hutcheson's Scottish disciples was Fordyce, who, in his sermon on good works, explained how a woman's immediate circle of affection should be extended to humanity. His ideal ran counter to those "narrow-souled women" "who no sooner step into a house of their own, than they seem to have all their affections and ideas absorbed in their new condition . . . and shrinking up into a little circle of anxieties that exclude every liberal sentiment, and every enlarged connexion." Against such a contraction, Fordyce posed a "lady" he had known who "became a mother to . . . helpless orphans, superintended their education, . . . and sympathized with them in all their distresses." When they "spread out into families, she acted like a parent to their children," exemplifying a "maternal complacence and mildness . . . almost irresistible." There were "many other families who shared in her labours of love, and among the rest a very large one, the Poor." "Good Works," Fordyce declared, "proceed from kindness and compassion." He preached: "Next to religion, those in reality contribute to it most largely, who give the greatest consolation by their sympathy, and the greatest pleasure by their friendship. Friendship and sympathy, when thoroughly awake [*awakening* being cognate with *sensibility*], are constantly employed in numberless pleasing services . . . which the heart of the person obliged feels, and which rebounds with delight on the heart of the person obliging."[23] This was to anticipate the course of Protestant humanitarianism in which women who identified themselves with gendered sensibility were to be so prominent. But Fordyce's other point was that women were failing to recognize and exercise such power: "Why, ye daughters of Britain are so many of you insensible to those brightest glories of your sex? Where is your love for your native country, which by thus excelling, you might so nobly serve?" Instead, women were "ambitious of flaunting in French attire, of fluttering about with the levity of that fantastic people." While mothers "were intended to be . . . the formers of rational and immortal offspring," they were modeling those modern manners that Fordyce, like other Scots, saw as needing reformation. It was a vision to be adapted to postrevolutionary American nationalism.[24]

Aunt Shaw had been pressed to her evaluation of the domestic circle by John Quincy's more orthodox Hutchesonianism. She presented their debate to Nabby, suggesting that John Quincy had taken the line that love was mere selfishness, even mere animal passion (Hutcheson had identified it with the "Desire for sensual Pleasure"): "I would never allow, it was so *base, and sordid, a Passion* as *he* thought it. I told him however wise he was in other things, yet he was but a novice in this—that he was no judge and in a few years, I should hear quite another Language from him." Her own experience of having fallen in love, consummating it in marriage, of age, and perhaps, of having the relational specialization of gender in the matter of love outstripped her nephew's experience and his learning. It even qualified her to modify an authoritative psychosociological theory that reflected men's formal monopoly of public life, although she did not develop such a potential. She explained that John Quincy's argument merely reflected the "time and circumstances" of his being a student. So far, then, in this wedding letter Aunt Shaw has insisted on the significance of love and marriage.[25]

She then turned to the cautionary story of Nancy Hazen, after whom Nabby had inquired, and whom Shaw had taken into her home, placing her under her "fostering hand of Education." But she had to throw her out because she had "found it utterly impossible to establish those Sentiments of Sincerity, Delicacy, and Dignity of manners which I consider as so essential to the female Character." This was further background to her letter's chief emotional purpose, at which her opposition to the idea that love was "like a vortex" absorbing "every stream of social affection" was also aimed: "And now, my dear niece, I will plainly tell you that I feel hurt that so many vessels have arrived without one line to your aunt Shaw, who loves you so tenderly, and feels as interested in every thing that befalls, or can happen to my dear friend, as any one in America." Her hurt was commensurate with this extent of love and "interest." She hypothesized a reason for Nabby's not writing, first explaining why she has just written such a sentence, typically showing sensibility to her correspondent's feelings: "I am sorry if you want assurances of this." She then made explicit the connection between the two main subjects of the foregoing, the story of Miss Hazen and her disagreement with John Quincy: "I cannot believe my niece so wholly devoted to scenes of dissipation as to forget her friend; nor will I believe that her new connection has engrossed all her time and attention."

If Aunt Shaw really thought the latter "to be the case," she would appeal to Colonel Smith, the monopolizer of her niece's affection, to permit Nabby "to appropriate a certain portion" to her aunt. Consistent with her earlier application of the model, she would explain to him that this was "really an act of benevolence" insofar as Nabby's "descriptions . . . sentiments . . . reflections, constituted a great part" of her aunt's "pleasure and happiness." But it was also an act of benevolence to him, making her "a more obliging wife." Her benevolence benefited her husband's interest: "the mind gained strength by exercise; that every benevolent act sweetened the temper, gave smiles and complacency to the countenance, and rendered you more fit and disposed for the kind and tender offices of that new relation which, I presume, ere this, you have entered into." In her dispute with John Quincy over the importance of the inner, marital circle relative to the outer one that embraced the public good, Aunt Shaw was asserting the particular interests of women, but she also demonstrated that, at the heart, interest was subordinate to her husband. A mark of gentility for both sexes was pleasingness to others, but, for women, this meant a sharply gendered sensibility along the lines Fordyce had laid out and Aunt Shaw here recommended.[26]

## John's Ambivalent Humanity

In October 1775, John had written Abigail his version of that concentric scheme of social affections in which one can trace the influence of Shaftesbury as Hutcheson had developed it, beginning with the generic: "There is in the human Breast, a social Affection, which extends to one whole Species. Faintly indeed; but in some degree. The Nation, Kingdom, or Community to which We belong, is embraced by it more vigorously. It is stronger still towards the Province to which we belong, and in which we had our Birth. It is stronger and stronger, as We descend to the County, Town, Parish, Neighborhood, and Family, which we call our own." But, in contrast to Abigail, he added the Hutchesonian judgment of the latter degree, most remote from the sublime, universal social affection. This was consistent with his placing public interest ahead of private. He continued, referring to "our own" families: "We find it ['social Affection'] often so powerful as to become partial, to blind our Eyes to darken our Understandings and pervert our Wills." Again in keeping with the account of preceding schematizers, that degree of social affection was inflected by love, subsuming sex, although another form was nepotism or any personal, familial interest. The worst, tightest circle was indrawn entirely to self, in accordance with the vision of human nature presented by Hobbes and celebrated by Mandeville in opposition to Shaftesbury, Mandeville arguing that private vice was public virtue.[27]

As we have seen, however, the liberal Protestantism advancing sensibility and good nature also reconciled itself to market-oriented "self-love" or individualism. A diary entry of June 30, 1772, illustrates that John was by no means opposed to self-interest *tout court*: to the contrary. It was introduced by his reference to "my Business" as a lawyer, which brought him into contact with a number of rich men who had acquired their wealth either "by their own Industry," or "by Succession, Descent, or Devise," or, in one case, "by Marriage": "There is not one of all these who derives more Pleasure from his Property than I do from mine. My little Farm, and Stock, and Cash affords me as much Satisfaction as all their immense Tracts, extensive Navigation, sumptuous Buildings, their

vast Sums at Interest, and Stocks in Trade yield to them." He was about
to elaborate that idea of pleasure derived from ownership that we can
connect with the psychology of consumption. He frequently expressed
his chagrin, if not envy, over his lesser wealth, in contrast to what he
could have had had he not devoted himself to the public good. His point
here was to justify the latter, although it bears on consumer psychology: "The Pleasures of Property, arise from the Acquis[it]ion more than
Possession, from what is to come rather than from what is." His subjects are the feelings that exist between men and property: "These Men
feel their Fortunes; they feel the Strength and Importance which their
Riches give them in the World. Their Courage and Spirits are buoyed
up, their imaginations are inflated by them." Later commentators, notably Tocqueville, would celebrate such buoyancy and imagination as
characteristic of American men.[28]

John frequently invoked the quality of humanity in his public documents, too. For example, his 1765 *Dissertation on the Feudal and Canon
Law* aligned "integrity and humanity" with "public interest, liberty,
and happiness," in opposition to avarice and ambition, but he then presented humanity as one explanation for the "timidity" of the American
colonists as well as "nine tenths of the species . . . groaning in misery and
servitude." He had described various habitual manners Americans had
brought with them from England "and transmitted down to us," along
with "the great affection and veneration Americans always entertained"
for their mother country: "These peculiar causes might operate upon
them; but without these, we all know that human nature itself, from indolence, modesty, humanity, or fear, has always too much reluctance to
a manly assertion of its rights." Adam Smith's *Theory of Moral Sentiments*,
published six years earlier, had associated humanity still more strikingly
with unmanliness, in distinguishing it from generosity. These two psychological characteristics seemed, Smith wrote, "so nearly allied, [but]
do not always belong to the same person. Humanity is the virtue of a
woman, generosity of a man. The fair-sex, who have commonly much
more tenderness than ours, have seldom so much generosity. . . . Humanity consists merely in the exquisite fellow-feeling which the spectator entertains with the sentiments of the person principally concerned,
so as to grieve for their sufferings, to resent their injuries, and to rejoice
at their good fortunes." Humanity was a virtue, but it did not require
any exertion of will, of reason, which marked the usual gender difference for Smith and for other Scottish moralists: "The most humane actions require no self-denial, no self-command, no great exertion of the

sense of propriety. They consist only in doing what this exquisite sympathy would of its own accord prompt us to do." There is an echo here of Malebranche's view of women.[29]

John's apprehension that humanity might inhibit manly assertiveness and Smith's assertion that it was literally "the virtue of a woman" reflected a problem stemming from what purported to be scientific definitions of *human nature*. Above all, this lay in their acceptance of the passions and then, more narrowly, of the validity of those feelings that established fundamental common ground among men and women, indeed, all humanity, to which Malebranche had reacted. The word was widely used in this gender-neutral sense. We have seen Abigail use it in this way. Her son, moreover, wrote on her death in 1818: "Her life gave the lie to every libel on her sex that ever was written. It was a continual refutation of all satirists upon human nature, frailties and infirmities."[30] I have described the social circumstances that accompanied the potentially gender-neutral, scientific view, which brought men and women closer together in certain respects. The widespread preoccupation with effeminacy can be put in the same category with John's association of humanity with a lack of manliness and Smith's defining humanity as a woman's virtue.[31]

Still, John and Abigail both believed that men were fully capable of humanity (even that Smith passage can be read to allow that, faintly), and, in other contexts, John placed a high value on it. His letters to Rush illustrate the meanings most familiar to students of humanitarianism. In 1810, he praised his own and Rush's employment because it was superior to reading and writing political pamphlets: "You are employed in healing the sick and extending the empire of science and humanity; I in reading romances in which I take incredible delight." Of course, *humanity* assumed the scientific view of human nature, which was assumed, too, by the romances—sentimental literature—which stimulated the great pleasure Adams felt. Rush was in the forefront of American humanitarianism.[32] Like Jefferson in the case of Virginia, Rush wished to reform what he called "the old sanguinary criminal law of our state," Pennsylvania. This was a subject that Nabby had encountered in London in the dispute between the liberal Horne Tooke and the gentleman of insensibility.[33]

## The Reformation of Female Manners

The pleasure-seeking behavior of young ladies in London was the primary provocation prompting Fordyce's advocacy of a sharply feminized sensibility. Fordyce made out that "ladies" in the past had been "simple enough to be in love with their home, and seek their happiness in their duty," although he also recognized that such a choice depended on "leisure" and, therefore, carefully designated their rank. He characterized the behavior that had provoked him to preach and publish his sermons as an aspect of modern manners. Modern manners had so "warped" his readers' minds that "the simplicity of ancient virtue"—and by *ancient* Fordyce meant biblical times—"instead of appearing to you an object of veneration, looks romantic and ridiculous."[34]

"Now," Fordyce stated, "there are many young ladies, whose situation does not supply a sphere of domestic exercises sufficient to fill up that part of their time which is not necessarily appropriate to female occupation and innocent amusements." They were "young persons in genteel life," exhibiting "manners . . . fashionable amongst the young and the Gay of this metropolis." Their work had been replaced by purchased goods and by more servants. (Fordyce recommended an "unaffected propension to use" servants with "Humanity" and "Christianity.") In "the Country," Fordyce observed, "the contagion of vice and folly . . . is not so epidemical," although certainly the eighteenth century saw the rapid, if uneven, dissemination of London fashions throughout England and across the Atlantic. Implicitly, "the young and the Gay" were the daughters of the urban elite, pioneering bourgeois leisure culture. They shopped, had their hair dressed, visited, walked in pleasure gardens, attended plays, concerts, operas, and assemblies, and danced at balls and masquerades. The public venues for these activities should be seen as more of the sites Habermas lists in his account of the new public space coming into existence in relation to the new domesticity. Historians have differed on whether women were included in Habermas's notion of public space. It is clear, however, that their entrance into what contemporaries called both *the world* and *public entertainments* held promise for women as an important beginning for their wider participation in public life.[35]

Such activities, fostering modern manners, were not limited to the very wealthy. They were fueled by the proliferating wishes (whether for more varied self-expression, for upward mobility, or in the service of the marriage market) generating the consumer revolution. Fordyce sneered that parents "now a days almost universally, down to the lowest tradesmen, or mechanic, who ape their superiors, strains himself beyond his circumstances, send their daughters to Boarding-schools."[36] Boarding schools were targets of sentimental novels read on both sides of the Atlantic. One major line of criticism can be illustrated by an English writer who charged that religious instruction was compromised by "all the end-less pursuits of personal accomplishments," leaving pupils' minds "with-out one ornament." They were also said to teach "an aversion to work." Paradoxically, perhaps, one of the sins of boarding school education was its encouragement of reading sentimental novels. The sentimental novel–reading, boarding school, young lady type could be as sexually inflam-mable as Aunt Shaw would hint that her lodger, Nancy Hazen, had become.[37] But boarding schools were just one of the sources of corrup-tion that Fordyce listed in "that whirl of dissipation, which, like some mighty vortex, has swallowed up in a manner all conditions and charac-ters." It was this same vision that Lucy Cranch had in mind in referring to a "torrent of folly" (see chapter 1) or Abigail in referring to a "Torrent of vice" (see chapter 3). British writers, including Fielding and Smollett (also familiar to the Adamses), saw the pursuit of consumer pleasures in very similar terms, that is, unleashing a social flux that threatened to dissolve all ranks, although Fordyce concentrated on the dissolution of gender hierarchy at the instigation of women: "to this nation there can accrue no good from the spirit of luxury, of levity, and of vice, so prev-alent, and so spreading, in a sex that leads the world."[38]

According to Fordyce, young women displayed themselves and their wishes for pleasure in "public," "those places of public entertainment now so fondly frequented by so many women" that he saw as "catering" to "temptation." He referred to "the passion for idleness and sauntering" and may well have had the gardens at Ranelagh and Vauxhall in mind, sites incorporating a variety of delights where men and women could observe one another, in the words of a more pleasure-oriented contem-porary, "with mirth, freedom, and good humor." "[Your] mornings," Fordyce continued, "are spent in rambling and dressing, your evenings in visits and cards, or public entertainments."[39]

Women, Fordyce insisted, had an "astonishing prepossession in fa-vour of public places, greatly owing to their want of something ratio-nal and agreeable to employ them at home." Given the opportunity, young women preferred to leave home for "public entertainment." Eve-ning pleasures included "gay assemblies" preceded by formal tea parties, where women presided over the proper making and dispensing of one of the most prominent of the new, addictive substances, sweetened by another, and Fordyce's characterization of women on the "sweetner" of men's lives well may have referred to their role in this dispensation. Other scholars have described in detail the significance of tea in the consumer revolution on both sides of the Atlantic, to be formally politicized in the American Revolution.[40]

Women enjoyed other consumer goods in preparing themselves for teas, assemblies, and the other entertainments Fordyce excoriated, "the placing of a ribbon, or adjusting an head-dress, the glittering in an assembly room, or prattling at tea-table." Young women's appetite for the purchase and display of fashionable clothing was, perhaps, the feature of their lives that irked Fordyce most. The young woman sacrificed "her improvement, her salvation, her prospects of usefulness and dignity in life, . . . to the idol Dress." It was her absorption in her own wishes, which contradicted what Fordyce on behalf of the true God designated her natural absorption in the wishes of men, that he found outrageous. This "miserable idol is suffered to swallow up the consideration of all that is solid, rational, and praiseworthy." The consumer was consumed: "to consume those precious hours that were allotted for the most valuable of purposes [i.e., preparing in this world for the next] . . . to pervert the capacities of nature, the acquirements of education, and the bounties of providence—to pervert them to the low design of being admired for the embellishments that imply no merit in the wearer, and can confer no honour in the eye of any but the worthless and the vain." He asked rhetorically, "Can such a conduct be thought innocent?" implying that women who did this were guilty of sexual transgression or, at least, of giving themselves the reputation of it. Fordyce was one among those male authors increasingly resentful at midcentury of "the attempt of women to show their newly acquired sexual liberty in daring manners of dressing." One of them, using the nom de plume "Adam Eden, Esq.," because he saw women on the road "to appearing in Publick quite Naked," in 1755 gave his ironic support to "the reformation among ladies to abolish modesty and chastity."[41]

Another target was ladies' passion for cards. It "so strangely predominated," Fordyce said, in terms suggesting the power of an addiction, "so as to take the lead of every thing else in almost every company of every rank." People pursued it "in the country with the same unabating ardour as in town," oblivious "to all the beauty and sweetness of rural scenes," crowding "round the card table for hours together." And even if "the desire of winning should in you [ladies] never rise to that rage, which agitates the breast of many a fine lady, discomposes those features, and inflames those eyes, where nothing should be seen but soft illumination"—again, his point was that women were, thus, behaving unnaturally—"are there not lower degrees in the thirst for gain, which a liberal mind would ever carefully avoid?" He asked rhetorically, "Is this the spirit of . . . humanity?"[42]

Playing cards was yet another modern way in which sentimental relations between the sexes were vitiated, according to Fordyce: "the sweet emotions of love and tenderness between the sexes are often swallowed up by this all devouring appetite . . . which . . . tends to harden and contract the heart." And he continued to condemn card playing in accordance with the values of sensibility. The "unmoderate indulgences" in it "excludes a thousand little reciprocations of sentiment and joy, which . . . serve to kindle and feed the flame of virtuous affection." Some women preferred cards to men. The "passion for play" forces "you," Fordyce told his lady listeners and readers, "on the alternative of preying either on the reputation or the property of others." But, as in the case of dress, he made a concession to the inevitable. There were "many general companies" where, in conforming to the wish of "ease" and "propriety," a young lady had to lend "assistance at the card-table." But still he asks, "Are these the scenes of true enjoyment? What, where the heart cannot be unfolded . . . where the smile of complaisance is frequently put on to deceive." And he launched into further extremes of condemnation of "the fatal passion for play," listing among its mischiefs its tendency "to destroy all distinctions both of rank and sex."[43] Peter Borsay suggests of gambling women in England, particularly visible in the new pleasure resorts associated with spas: "Disadvantaged by their sexual position, this pastime allowed them to enjoy the unfeminine thrill of competition, . . . and compete on equal term with men." Steele had remarked serious play's effect in defeminizing women's faces and gestures or, one might say, freeing them to be utterly unself-conscious, playing as intently as men could on larger and more varied stages. Fordyce did not want to see that kind of emotional engagement.[44]

Women's appetite for consumer pleasures held even graver dangers: "Consider, my dear sisters, how many women are, in a discerning eye, lessened by their extravagant attachment to dress and toys, to equipage and ostentation, in a word to all the gaudy apparatus of female vanity, together with the endlessly ridiculous, no less than frequently fatal consequences, which these draw after them." It might seem that this pointed to women's being seduced by men, a subject Fordyce took up elsewhere in his *Sermons*. But, here, he has the reverse in mind: "Consider how trite and childish, men of sense must necessarily deem those arts, that are daily practiced on our sex by a multitude of yours; not to speak of worse enticements." Fordyce may have been concerned with the dangers posed to "youth" generally; here, he expressed his sense of men's vulnerability to young women. Men had a propensity to "a restless attachment to the other sex." In any case, one result of these potentially corrupting heterosocial, fashionable minglings was "emptiness, insipidity, and inelegance of conversation." Fordyce's educational proposals were intended, in part at least, to fix this.[45]

By no means did Fordyce reject fashionability altogether, any more than did other reformers of manners, including his more famous fellow Scots. Like Adam Smith, say, who combined the case for consumerism made by Mandeville (private vice served public good) with traditional suspicions of luxury and materialism, Fordyce allowed that a degree of consumption was not only permissible but also of important value to the national economy. (Adams and Jefferson assumed the same in their postrevolutionary negotiations with European powers.) Women, Fordyce told his readers, should join "frugality and simplicity together." They should reject "finery" and distinguish "between what is glaring and what is genteel, in preserving elegance with the plainest habit; in wearing costly array but seldom, and always at ease." Such a balance could be reached by a woman "who has not learnt to think more highly of herself for the richest raiment she can put on." Historians agree with Fordyce to the extent that women's choices were vital to the consumer revolution in Britain.[46] "What sums would be kept at home," he exclaimed, "that now go abroad to enrich our most dangerous rivals! French gewgaws would give place to British manufactures." French influence in other novel forms of fashionable consumption, literally in cuisine, had bothered the Scottish Dr. Cheyne earlier in the century. Fordyce imagined: "the ladies of this island, inferior to none in beauty, would be the apes of none in dress. They would practice that species of patriotism, which is the most proper for their sex; they would serve their country in their own way."[47]

Women's discriminating frugality in consumption would also ease tension in the smaller domestic circle. Fordyce reported that he had talked to many young men on the subject of women's extravagance: "Some, I find, would like a sprightly companion in marriage, but none a dissipated one, and all of them, to a man, dread a woman of expence." Certainly, this was a fear that John expressed in contemplating the effects on his purse of Abigail and Nabby's being directly exposed to European fashions. Fordyce, who played constantly on what he saw as his audience's chief interest, getting married, suggested that women's level of consumption was "a principal cause" of men's becoming "more backward than for-

mally to enter into the holy bands of wedlock." He rationalized his concession to women's dressing fashionably by linking it to rank ("there are
stations and circumstances, in which splendor of dress is perfectly al-
lowable, nay extremely proper") but intimated that women of inferior
rank were challenging such class limitations, causing the social disarray
that so bothered him and his contemporaries: "In Truth, splendor without gentility . . . will ever seem poor and insipid to all but untaught and
vulgar spirits." He preached, nonetheless, that the genteel should aim at
"Elegant Simplicity," illustrating the identification of taste with virtue
as well as sensibility.[48]

Fordyce made other concessions to the consumer-related appetite
that he could not stem. Dancing was all right, provided young women
did not do it "often in public assemblies." So, too, young women could
learn music, provided they admitted their limitations and studied it seriously. He allowed that women might read certain novels, Richardson's
above all, and others that embodied similar aesthetic qualities. Richardson touched the heart. And, just as Fordyce recommended "Simplicity
of Dress" and appreciated simplicity in music, so he asserted: "In all the
sciences, in every valuable profession, in all the common intercourses
of life, and . . . in the sublimest subjects, Simplicity is that which above
every thing else touches and delights . . . all else is feeble and unaffect-
ing." In short, Fordyce, like Hume and Smith, accepted consumption,
provided it was controlled by taste, a taste identifiable with the culture
of sensibility.[49]

According to Fordyce, the "laws of good sense," that is, the discov-
eries of the Hutchesonian school, capitalizing on the precedents I have
mentioned, were "just to allow to woman a degree of curiosity and care"
in matters of dress and ornament, but "sound philosophy and masculine virtue" refused such concerns "to men." Tastefulness in association
with sensibility was liable to gendering, as Hume had illustrated. Some
men, however, had been captivated to a similar degree as women by the
possibilities for display on those new public, heterosocial occasions. In
Fordyce's view, men who "display a particular solicitude in adorning
their persons beyond cleanliness and a certain graceful care, seldom fail
to make themselves little, in the eyes of every man who is not effeminate, and every woman too who is not a slave to fashion." Their seizing
on such possibilities goes some way toward explain the preoccupation
with "fops" and "effeminacy," along with the other explanation I suggested earlier, that is, men's greater approximation to female stereotype
with the recognition of feeling as a valuable human characteristic. That

the same eighteenth-century circumstances also affected expressions of male homosexuality is a subject that other historians address.[50]

Fordyce said that he "despaired" of seeing such fashion hounds become "truly Men" because women gave "so visible preference to embroidery, finery, and foppish manners, above a plain coat, and a manly deportment." Women, then, were responsible for effeminizing men. To get them to stop and "to acquire a taste for plainness, sobriety, and wisdom," that is to say, to reform men's manners, too, was a significant motive in publishing the *Sermons to Young Women*. One can see the relation between this and the book's accompanying message, that women should effeminize themselves more, particularly in relation to men who showed feeling. Either way, the kind of gender line on which Fordyce's moral system depended would be clarified and, from his point of view, restored.[51]

## Self-Assertion, Feminism

In a book subtitled *The American Revolution against Patriarchal Authority, 1750–1800*, Jay Fliegelman draws on many metropolitan sources, reprinted and read in the colonies, including Richardson's *Clarissa*, the eponymous heroine of which blamed herself for resisting her father's will. Fordyce's *Sermons to Young Women* indicated the existence in Britain of what was to him a troublesome degree of resistance to patriarchy. It may be, he told his young women readers, that "your parents lacked religious principle" or exercised "willful authority" over you, but that still did "not dissolve the ties of duty, however it may affect the sentiments of esteem." In fact, "if you think rightly," such "faults" would "only excite your endeavors in every winning respectful way." Fordyce believed that "such conduct in a child" was most likely "to draw down the grace of conversion on a parent." And of this behavior he exclaimed: "What a noble superiority to these unfeeling creatures of your sex, who show no solicitude . . . to their parents, but how to obtain from them some new article of dress, or other gratification on which they have fixed their foolish fancies!" "But some of you complain," he continued, "that your parents are cruel and tyrannical." Such daughterly challenges merely signified that "your parents . . . will not indulge your extravagant vanity, or that they choose to restrain you from pursuits that would be hurtful." Implicitly, daughters could not trust their own judgment.[52]

At least some women wanted independence in choosing husbands. Marital choice was the subject to which the opening of the subject of daughters' conflict with parents led Fordyce: "But they would force you to sacrifice your happiness to a man whom you cannot love." He imagined how those of his readers who accused their parents of being "cruel and tyrannical" would respond to his preceding advice to bear their treatment even if it was "really hard hearted": "You are called forth to the conflict, as to a field of battle, where even your sex may reap immortal laurels." He did draw the line at "hard hearted" parents' forcing daughters to marry without love. Such parents forced their daughters to contravene a central value of the culture of sensibility, even as they made them figures of virtue in distress. He asserted, however, that "such compulsion was used but seldom" and that the "greatest danger" was not parental tyranny but, as he told his readers, that "you, my unexperienced friends, should be tempted to form the most important of all connexions, without the approbation of your parents." Again he wished to beat back young women's assertion of independence. He threw doubt on the validity of their feelings, on passionate love: "We would address you while in your sober senses, before your imagination is perverted and inflamed. . . . The passion that guided and hurried the parties is quickly abated." After marriage, "our romantic adventures" are "disenchanted," and the result was "perpetual unhappiness," not "lessened by being devoured in secret, and in public disguised." In his view, the perpetuation of the terrible outcome he warns against lay in the wife's persistence in insubordination. A daughter's "tender and respectful" "behaviour to her parents . . . being transferred to the married state, will not fail to render her a mild and obliging companion."[53]

Tellingly, Fordyce's model for this transferred dyad was a daughter's responsiveness to her "honoured father." It was her gender that kept a daughter "more at home than sons," nature here reinforced by education, resulting in "the softness of your frame, that fits you for a thousand little soothing offices, as well as domestic services, which they [sons] cannot properly perform, [and] seem to point out to you a peculiar sphere of filial excellence." Women, Fordyce fancied, had it in them to take pleasure in such subordination, especially when a parent was "sick . . . or aged." This convention was to be another provocation to Wollstonecraft's feminism, after she, not her brothers, was called on to nurse her dying mother.[54]

Fordyce described his feelings toward the vision of subordination he conjured up: "And here I please myself with the thought, that some of your bosoms are at this moment throbbing with tenderness towards a sick or aging parent whom heaven, willing to furnish a field for the exercise of all your gratitude and zeal, has at last thrown upon your care." It is not irrelevant to mention that Fordyce suffered from "longstanding asthma," chronically sick like Shaftesbury, another ideologue of sharply gendered sensibility.[55] In any case, speaking to an exemplary female reader, Fordyce imagined her, "my charming friend, like some guardian angel, tending day and night, the bed of an honoured father, who has lost your mother, and is worn out with toil, and years, and pain." This was where her sensibility could show its utmost responsiveness: "I see you listening in deepest silence, to catch the least intimation of his wishes . . . watching eagerly every look; to learn his wants before he speaks them." Here, she can respond like a mother to her inarticulate baby. "His groans are answered by sighs stealing from you, but suddenly suppressed, for fear of adding to his anxiety on your account." Such virtuous behavior brought this good daughter extreme pleasure, in accordance with the psychology that was central to the religious tradition that fed the culture of sensibility: "To be the instrument of imparting to him a minute's comfort . . . is rapture."[56]

Fordyce's culminating tableau here was meant, perhaps, to stir virtual rapture in his female readers, but certainly to persuade them to subordinate themselves to their fathers and to manifest to them the extreme of feminine sensibility, somehow incorporating the sense (or illusion) of an acceptable exercise of power over men: "Mean while, the good old man's eyes are now turned to you, with all the unutterable fondness of paternal love, melted by those marks of duty; anon they are lifted to heaven in thanksgiving for such a child, and supplication for everlasting blessings on your head! Good God! what must a mind like yours experience in this conjuncture?" Fordyce, a constructor of the concept of adolescence, according to John Dwyer, recognized that daughters' search for pleasure was rebellion. His point here was to claim that obedience to others brought superior pleasure. In the case of caring for a sick and aged father, it promised power, too: "Where is the daughter of Disobedience or folly, that ever felt in the gayest hour satisfaction, a transport to be compared with that, which conscious piety diffuses through your bleeding heart?" The latter suggested that one reason for these "exalted sensations" was that the pleasure was mixed with pain, in the emotional cocktail prized by superconscious, moralistic beings of refined sensibility. We should recall that this passage elaborated the behavior that Fordyce regarded as appropriate to parents but applicable in wives' behavior to husbands.[57]

The context for all this was the growing self-assertiveness of daughters in their marriage choice, accompanied by its rationale in love. That

women still "often solicited their parents' advice" regarding a husband
is emblematic of the fact that this was a point of historical transition,
marked above all by *Clarissa*. On what resources of their own could
young women draw to avoid the dire consequences they knew followed a
mistake? Linda Kerber and Cathy N. Davidson suggest that one of them
was the sentimental novel. The prospects of more independent marital
choice accompanied the rise of the demand that men become men of
feeling, responsive to women's wishes.[58]

Women, then, wished to assert themselves by dressing to their own
taste, entering a heterosocial world of public entertainments, and there
choosing a husband. In Fordyce's view, however, a woman's "unaffected
bashfulness" was "the flower of female chastity, of a nature so delicate
and tender, as always to thrive in places least frequented." Presumably,
that was in private, at home: "What pity, then, instead of being sheltered and cherished with care, it is heedlessly exposed to the wanton
gaze of every wandering eye, to the cruel hand of every rude, or every
sly invader." Leaving the shelter of home at all was to be a figure of virtue in distress. But women, young ones in particular, wanted out. So
Fordyce told them, since they insisted on entering the world, to show
"Modesty of Apparel." They were to remember "how tender a thing a
woman's reputation is." He advised his readers "to preserve the ornament of Sobriety" by the "unremitted exercise of prudence, vigilance,
and severe circumspection," for which they should depend on him, "a
brother . . . to show you . . . those things you ought to shun," as well as
the kind of femininity that would best serve them.[59]

Above all, a woman must avoid "Dangerous Connexions," and, here,
Fordyce stressed how difficult a challenge this was: "in real life . . . it is a
question sometimes of very nice decisions." His catalog of the behavior
of male predators is the same as that so insistently reiterated in the sentimental novels to which young women were addicted. One of many such
warnings he preached was of "artful men": "[Their] Approaches will
be silent and slow; all will be soft insinuation; or else they will put on
a blunt face of seeming good humour, the appearance of honest frankness, drawing you to every scene of dissipation with a kind of obliging
violence, should any violence be necessary. If they be also agreeable in
their persons, or lively in their conversation; above all, if they wear the
air of gentlemen, which, unfortunately for your sex, is too often the
case; then indeed your danger is extreme." But Fordyce warned women
against their own "dissembling," too, accusing them of misrepresenting
themselves in order to take "profligate and foolish men in their toils."

That is, they were diabolical: "There are [some] who, with hearts of adamant to the best impressions, and without any remains of natural modesty, yet practice the art of feigning its decent demeanor." Again, this was a foil for the aggrandization of feminine sensibility. But, recognizing its power, women could feign that, too; they were capable of "that transient flow of mechanical grief, so easily furnished by too many eyes, where the heart has little or no share in the soft effusion."[60]

*Sensibility* denoted "mechanical" operation anyway, and its rise was accompanied by various efforts to give it moral and spiritual meaning. But it was accompanied, too, by the rise of the figure of false sensibility, female as well as male, testifying to its power, including the power of the natural in the face of the growth of commerce, of urbanity, and of fashion. Fordyce declared in almost oxymoronic terms, insisting on the depth to which he expected women to internalize their pleasing, self-subordinating sensibility: "A meek deportment is the natural and spontaneous growth of a lowly mind. Politeness in you will be the offspring of the heart." Somehow women had to learn the distinction between behavior manifesting heart and the same behavior manifesting head, that is, calculation, even as they were to be persuaded that showing a natural, feminine sensibility was more likely to catch them a good husband. Fordyce exclaimed: "How much preferable to that specious, but hollow compliance, studied by the fashionable and the false; which consists of the artful disguising of their own passions [the selfish kind, aiming at catching a wealthy and naive husband, rather than sympathy, say] and a flattering application to those of others [i.e., evidently a man's sexual feelings], in a framing of the face to all occasions, in professing the greatest respect without feeling the least, and in hiding very often the worst designs under the smile of familiarity and the show of friendship." The difficulty, perhaps the impossibility, of distinguishing genuine from assumed sensibility (in winning a husband, say) was epitomized by Fielding's retelling the story of Richardson's *Pamela* as *Shamela*.[61]

Moralists asserted that women had greater difficulty in controlling their feelings than men but associated such an assertion with the value they placed on sincerity. Upholders of these conventions of sensibility defined themselves against a world that was essentially duplicitous. This was on orientation widely held not just by republican men but by all those writers more widely liable to the conspiratorial interpretations of politics that Wood suggests were the applications of newly assured, scientific-psychological understanding to vastly more complex demographic and political circumstances. Fordyce was a member of a group that is one of Wood's subjects. He compared "the world" to a masquerade in describing a previously deceitful rake's taking off his "visor." Women, then, were to draw on the same psychology to face new kinds of men, enjoying new possibilities of self-representation, and capable of putting them to use in sexual predation.[62]

"Thus far," Fordyce had continued in his account of the men whom naive young women would encounter in pleasure-focused, heterosocial scenes, "the trap is concealed. You apprehend nothing; your unsuspecting hearts begin to slide: they are gone before you are aware." Fordyce suggests the weakness of women's defenses: "A sense of reputation? A dread of ruin?" The best defense was "religious principle": "The experiment, however, is hazardous. Multitudes have trusted and been undone." Moreover, even women who are not "in the world's sense . . . undone [i.e., seduced or raped] were hurt in their health and spirits, in their serenity and self-enjoyment, in their sobriety of mind and habits of self-control." Why? Precisely because of that characteristic that Fordyce devotes so much of his book to proving is essentially feminine: "Very seldom at least can you suppose, that, where there is much sensibility of temper, an ill-placed passion shall not leave behind it, in a youthful breast, great disorder and deep disquietude."[63]

That young women wished to assert themselves in choosing a husband where they lacked resources and where unreformed men regarded independently minded and even sexually oriented women as fair game was the context for the question posed throughout eighteenth-century literature, especially after Pamela's successful conversion of Mr. B., and presumably asked by women tempted by rakish men or aware, perhaps, of how commonplace rakery was among marital prospects: "One thinks I hear some of you ask, with an air of earnest curiosity, Do not reformed libertines make the best husbands? I am sorry for the question." In answering it, Fordyce claimed to appeal to individualistic, sentimental morality, desiring his female readers "to ask [their] own hearts, without any regard to the opinions of the world," which was more desirable, a reformed rake or "the pure unexhausted affection of a man who has not" irreparably damaged his own health and who has not "betrayed the innocent that trusted him, never abandoned any fond creature to want and despair." Bishop Burnet's figure of Rochester, the most notorious Restoration rake, loomed behind this. Fordyce lists other forms of the abuse of women that the good man has not engaged in. He did not dispute that "he who has been formerly a rake may after all prove a tolerable husband, as the world goes," but he suggested very strongly that he was likely to return "to his old ways" or that "the insatiable love of variety which he has indulged in so freely, will . . . lead him astray from the finest woman in the world." Typically, rakes (and here Lovelace was emblematic) were seen to apply that element of consumer psychology— "the insatiable love of variety"—to their view and treatment of women. They were, moreover, depicted as extravagant spenders.[64]

In Fordyce's reaction to young women's worldly self-assertion, including his warning them of the virtually fatal dangers they faced by such a course of behavior, we can see another major explanation, a representative one, for his insistence on the sharply distinct psychology of a gendered sensibility. That she was naturally susceptible to impressions, weak, and, therefore, dependent meant that a young woman had to give up her wishes for a wider world. Wollstonecraft, challenging Fordyce and the views of authorities like him, would see this view and women's internalization of it as the major obstacle to their freedom. Fordyce could not help registering the existence of feminist stirrings in his time, which can be aligned with his apprehension of Amazons. Those seventeenth-century feminists had successors (including Mandeville in the 1720s), their context the increasing literacy capitalized on by the *Spectator*, by successor journals, and of course, by sentimental literature of all kinds. In 1740, "Sophia" published *Vindication of the Natural Right of the Fair Sex to a Perfect Equality of Power, Dignity, and Esteem, with Men*, and then, in 1758 (shortly before Fordyce began his *Sermons*), a "Lady" published *Female Rights Vindicated; or, The Equality of the Sexes Morally and Physically Proved*. By the 1770s, writes Langford, three decades' worth of "feminist tendencies" in Britain appeared, in the eyes of contemporaries, "to have developed into a full blown revolution," provoking a "cultural crisis." Such tendencies were accompanied by the rise of an ideology of gendered sensibility, mingled with the concession of calls for limited reform of women's education and of husbands' treatment of wives. A "torrent" of reactionary "sermons and addresses" poured down on women in the 1760s and 1770s, including Fordyce's as well as Hannah More's *Essays to Young Ladies* (1777). Fordyce said to his readers: "I hear you exclaiming that though God has given you the capacities of intellectual improvement, men have denied you the Opportunities of it." His further consideration included men's reason for keeping women down. "If the men, jealous of dominion, do really seek to depress the women by keeping them in a state of ignorance," it made them "guilty of equal cruelty and meanness." Fordyce noted that "this complaint" was "a very common one, and very popular with your sex." "But," he continued, "it appears to me without any foundation adequate to the bitterness with which it has been made, or to the keenness with which it has been propagated."[65]

Fordyce's counterargument included the fact of women's access to books, fundamental to the origins of feminism. But women, he suggested, preferred to decorate their bodies rather than read, here in agreement with feminists, including Wollstonecraft: "this price of one expensive gown, or of one shining toy, will . . . furnish a little library of the best authors." "Nor does it appear," he added sarcastically, "that you are at a loss to find as many plays and novels as the most insatiable avidity can devour." He again refers to that demographic feature, the existence of a class of young ladies "not under the necessary of earning their bread," with the leisure as well as the opportunity to read. Women's appetite for public entertainments and related consumer pleasures (including reading the wrong books or reading too much) represented self-assertion and was, Fordyce suggests, linked to feminism.[66]

In refuting women's complaint that men wished to keep women down by keeping them in a state of ignorance, Fordyce revealed another way in which women's self-assertion was the issue. He attributed to the woman who baulked at reading the "proper" books that imparted "Truth and Virtue" the fear "that the men should suspect her of being what the world styles in derision a Learned Lady." His context was the rise to prominence of the Bluestocking Circle in London, which, while including some men, was perceived to be a formidable group of intellectual, socially well-connected ladies producing a "voluminous" "cultural output," including "poetry, educational tracts, history, philosophy, political pamphlets, classical translations"—most famously, Elizabeth Carter's— "drama, novels and criticism." Female "artists worked in a wide range of genres, from portraits and decorative work to ambitious history paintings." Such challenges to stereotypes of women provoked continuous reaction.[67]

Fordyce said that he had never seen a "Learned Lady" and that what was really meant by the phrase was "a smatterer in learning." In such a figure he found "nothing to excite terror." But that "men are frightened at Female pedantry, is very certain." Men, including Fordyce, were frightened by an educated woman who showed her learning in company by her "boundless intemperance of tongue." We can add this fear to the "dread" that Fordyce said men had of "a woman of expence," the sense of threat they felt when facing wit in a woman, and his criticism of and women's cunning exploitation of young men's sexual attraction to them. Elsewhere, he described women who had freed themselves from religious orthodoxy and reminded them that "the daring and disputatious spirit of unbelief is utterly repugnant to female softness, and to sweet docility which, in their sex, is so peculiarly pleasing to ours"; not only was it bad for women, but, from such "an infidel partner, a man can have no prospect of consolation in those hours of distress, when the hopes of futurity can alone administer relief." This could reinforce the implication of Fordyce's argument that a feeling man's sense of himself was dependent on the sharper gendering of women.[68]

## CHAPTER 5

# Young American Women
# Enter the World

## Public Pleasures for American Women

In the eighteenth century, the British North American mainland colonies became more densely settled, some of their towns became cities, and the composition of white immigration shifted to "the more skilled, more sophisticated, more respectable," matching "the great range of service trades necessary for the increasingly affluent colonial communities," leaving "brute labor" more exclusively to slaves.[1] The "impressive aspect of the free population of Britain's American colonies was the extraordinarily large number of families of independent middling status, which was proportionately substantially more numerous than in any other contemporary Western society."[2] This was the context for the creation of heterosocial leisure occasions, places, and institutions very similar to those in metropolitan Britain.

Married women enjoyed—or wished to enjoy—such socializing. John recorded in a 1770 diary entry a Mrs. Webb's longing "to be genteel to go to dances, assemblies, dinner suppers &c., but cannot make it" because of her husband's economic insufficiencies. Sensibility was essential to the gentility for which Mrs. Webb longed, as Bushman has shown. Unmarried young ladies more easily participated in eighteenth-century public pleasures. "City daughters from well-to-do homes were the only eighteenth-century American women who can accurately be described as leisured" because of the less work required of them in a city and the availability of servants and of purchasable cloth: "Accordingly, they could live at a relaxed pace, sleeping late, learning music and dancing, spending hours with male and female friends, and reading the latest novels." The latter consumer items promoted the gendered sensibility that I have described; that young women prized "the latest" is synonymous with their fashionability. Linda K. Kerber suggests that fairly well-off young women still had "to rearrange their priorities" and make "time to read" because of a continuing burden of domestic responsibilities, but, even if that was so, it is testimony to the appetite that Kerber also emphasizes. It was the same one that had provoked the Reverend James Fordyce to adjure metropolitan British young women to become creatures of sharply gendered sensibility, even as he was forced to compromise with it.[3]

Mary Sumner Benson listed the following as activities in which young New York women largely but not exclusively bourgeois engaged from the eighteenth century: making calls, playing cards, attending concerts, plays, and balls, taking sightseeing excursions to Long Island, sailing on the East River, or simply walking on Broadway or strolling on the Battery as well as eventually in a New York version of London's Vauxhall Gardens, established there in 1798. They rode in carriages and chairs. They dressed appropriately and elaborately for these activities, as they had long done for church. Benson included a chapter on the fiction they read, and, recently, Fredrika J. Teute has added to this picture, describing a "sociable world of elite young men and women, reading books, discussing intellectual topics, and conversing together" in "numerous learned societies" in New York. Working-class women walked on the Battery in the late eighteenth century, too, but the flourishing of a heterosocial, working-class public leisure culture awaited the 1830s, by when the "streets offered a panoply of places for the sexes to mingle." In 1840, P. T. Barnum converted Vauxhall Gardens to a center for more popular entertainments, "skits, dancing, singing, and comedy," and, by then, the working class could enjoy balls, too. The literary magazine the *Lowell Offering* stands for the extensions of sentimental taste to some working-class women, along with literacy and self-assertion.[4]

Benson found the same of eighteenth-century elite and bourgeois Philadelphia as she did of New York (Philadelphians also took trips to New York) and of Boston, which held mixed dances from the 1740s. Bushman, who describes the importance of sentimental literature in the creation of genteel sensibility, has written: "[Dancing] masters organized assemblies in the larger cities in the 1720s and 1740s, and . . . organized groups of citizens sponsored still more ambitious gatherings. Philadelphia had an assembly in operation by 1749, New York by 1745, Boston by 1744, and lesser cities like Cambridge, Massachusetts, and Alexandria, Virginia, in the 1760s." There, large groups of men and women "danced, played cards, talked, and enjoyed refreshments." In Boston, Benson wrote, "it seemed to some" that ladies "attended church as much from a desire of self-display as for motives of piety." Anna Green Winslow frequently went to church while living in Boston in 1771–73 and read the Bible every day, but her diary also indicates the range of more modern pleasures in which an upper-class young woman could enjoy, even in her early teens.[5]

Young Eliza Lucas referred to the "gay world" of Charleston, South Carolina, where, in the 1740s, she was one of the white elite who read sentimental literature, went to balls, played cards, and made formal social visits. The young, novel-reading Jefferson and his peers joined young ladies in similar rounds of pleasure in Williamsburg, Virginia. Other Southern cities can be included on this roster, and Rhys Isaac, Kathleen M. Brown, and David Shields have added to what Benson had also suggested of eighteenth-century elite white women on Southern plantations when not staying in, say, Williamsburg, Charleston, or Baltimore. They took pleasure there in novels, dancing, music, tea parties, and cards as well as in riding parties: white Southern daughters, moreover, especially after the Revolution, traveled to Northern cities for education in the burgeoning academies, where they could join in urban equivalents. Catherine Clinton and Brenda L. Stevenson describe the extension of these entertainments into the antebellum period. Southern elite women, but women of lower status, too, displayed their "new finery" at church as well as at balls, plays, raffles, parties, and card games. Other parts of the colonies, rural and small town, reflected the influence of cities and of metropolitan Britain in these respects as they absorbed and disseminated consumer fashions. This is evidence of women's "pursuits of happiness," to refer to Jack P. Greene's application of the Declaration's phrase to his interpretation of the British colonial economic takeoff, very largely on the backs of indentured servants and slaves, the context for the "conception of a place where free people could pursue their own, individual happiness."[6]

The rise of such pleasures was accompanied by apprehension and reaction from the beginning. Puritan jeremiads coincided with the onset of the consumer revolution in late-seventeenth-century New England. The Reverend Joseph Rowlandson had preached them, and Mary Rowlandson's captivity narrative was construed and published from the same perspective, expressing her own guilt over consumption, the latter more modest in scope because she wrote at the very beginning of the consumer revolution.[7] Material developments half a century later provoked Jonathan Edwards and the itinerant George Whitefield, among others. Whitefield preached that "the people of Charlestown seemed wholly devoted to pleasure, polite entertainment . . . dancing masters . . . and the sin of wearing jewels," according to the criticism made of him by South

Carolina's commissary, the Reverend Alexander Garden, whose son ru-
inously devoted himself to fashion in London. In 1742, Lucas replied to a
married woman's "importunity" for Lucas's "sentiments on those divertions commonly called innocent ones and which under proper restrictions are so." We can infer that this was Garden's position in criticizing
Whitefield's condemnation of white Charlestonians' pleasure seeking.
Lucas specified the "divertions" they pursued: "That there is any real
hurt in a pack of Cards or going on a suet figure round a room [i.e., danc-
ing], etc., no body I believe are obsurd enough to think." But then she
explained "the proper restrictions": "The danger arises from the too frequent indulging our selves in them which tends to effeminate the mind as
it takes it of[f] of pleasures of a superior and more exalted Nature as well
as waists our time; and may at length give it a disrelish for them." This
was the same dangerous process the Adamses would attribute to indulgence in luxury generally, identifying it particularly with its European,
courtly headwaters. Lucas assumed that those able to choose card playing, dancing, or superior alternatives had the time and means to do so,
circumstances explaining the eighteenth century's preoccupation with
taste, as increasing numbers of people, further down the social scale, were
able to consume on a revolutionary scale. Taste was identified with morality as well as class.[8]

One of Lucas's defenses against those "airry pleasures" was that
high degree of self-consciousness back of the self-discipline that post-
Cartesian, post-Lockean preachers had recommended in controlling the
passions. Card playing and dancing, she continued, "should be matters
quite indeferent, and we should very carefully observe the effect they
have upon our own temper if that is not ruffled or too much pleased with
them."[9] I have referred to her careful weighing of the literary merits of
Richardson's *Pamela*. She thought that she could square pleasure seeking
with "those dutys which we are indispensably bound to as rational creatures related to God and to one another," and so she was able to indulge
herself "immoderately" in playing the harpsichord because it did not "in-
dispose" her to her duties: "[Music is] my own darling amusement . . .
and which I indulge in more than in any other. This, methinks, has something of a devine original and will, as Mr. Addison observes, doubtless
be one of the imployments of Eternity, and oh! How ravishing must
those strains of music be in which exerted the whole power of harmony." She ended with some lines from *Paradise Lost* describing angels
in heaven playing their golden harps. Here, she was quoting from Addison's *Spectator*, no. 580, which, after the word *harmony*, had continued:

"The Senses are faculties of the Human Soul, though they cannot be employed, during this our vital Union [i.e., while we are on earth], without proper Instruments in the Body. Why thereafter should we exclude the Satisfaction of these faculties, which we find by Experience are Inlets of great Pleasure to the Soul, from those Entertainments which are to make our Happiness hereafter?" Lucas's and Addison's justification of indulgence in music also point to the "autonomous hedonism" that Colin Campbell roots in their religious tradition, which had absorbed the Cartesian view of the relation between the passions of the body and those of the soul.[10]

Winslow recorded the pleasures she took in Boston in the early 1770s. Among the books she read were sentimental anthologies addressed to women, *The Mother's Gift* and *The Female Orator*, but also *Pilgrim's Progress*, *Gulliver's Travels*, and Pope's *Dunciad*. The *Boston Gazette and Country Journal* of January 20, 1772, supplies "a very exact notion of the books imported and printed for and read by children," according to Winslow's editor, Alice Morse Earle, who printed the list. Notable for the history of sensibility in America were two books advocating the reformation of manners and related to *The Mother's Gift: The Brother's Gift; or, The Naughty Boy Reformed* and *The Sister's Gift; or, The Naughty Girl Reformed*. The list included abridged versions of Fielding's *Tom Jones* and *Joseph Andrews*, both of which were fundamentally sentimental, as well as all three of Richardson's novels.[11]

Winslow was in Boston for schooling, and she associated with other girls sent there for the same purpose, some of whom lodged with her aunt, Sarah Pierce Deming.[12] While living there, Anna recorded learning some traditional household tasks—spinning flax, making cloth, knitting lace—but she usually purchased her own clothes and was in Boston for other, now characteristically elite purposes. She lived in a well-furnished house, her enjoyment of it recalling young Abigail's pleasure in her Boston aunt's chamber. She described it as "very warm, always, with a nice fire, a stove, sitting in Aunt's easy chair, with a tall, three leav'd screen at my back, I am very comfortable." Another memoir specified still more luxury in the same house, including a Persian carpet, green damask curtains and window-seat cushions, a tea set of rich china, and a library, let alone crayon portraits by Copley.[13] Winslow attended teas regularly, and her other pleasures, more homosocial than heterosocial because of her youth, included assemblies, dances, a "rout," skating, playing cards and other games, attending a musical entertainment, and visiting an exhibition.[14] Very striking is her detailed knowledge of and enthusiasm for the lavishly decorated fashionable dress, typical of her era and class.[15] She also described her elaborate hairstyle, including a "HEDDUS," a roll of false hair, fashionable at the time.[16]

It is not surprising that one of the sermons she recorded the Reverend John Bacon giving at the Old South Church was on the text of a Psalm that included the phrase "the Lord . . . will beautify the meek with salvation." Her aunt quizzed her about it at tea afterward. Young Anna said that "he would lastly address himself to young people," and she then quoted his words from memory: "Let me tell ye, you'l never be truly beautiful till you are like the king's daughter, all glorious within, all the ornaments you can put on while your souls are unholy make you the more like white sepulchers garnish'd without, but full of deformyty within." Bacon thought he knew how his congregants would respond to his words: "You think me very unpolite no doubt to address you in this manner, but I must go a little further and tell you, how cource so ever it may sound to your delicacy, that while you are without holiness, your beauty is deformity—you are all over black & defiled, ugly and loathsome to all holy beings, the wrath of th' great God her upon you, & if you die in this condition, you will be turn'd into hell, with ugly devils to eternity." His reference to his young, fashionable dressed female congregants' *delicacy*, a word signifying proper sensibility's innate taste and self-control, was ironic. He implied that it, like their ornamental apparel, was worldly fashionability: to call his judgmental words "cource" and "very unpolite" would be false delicacy. One can infer that his view was the same as Fordyce's: that young women had made an idol of dress and that they should replace it with simplicity, manifesting not only true holiness but also sincere female sensibility. Bacon perpetuated the disgust at the world repristinated by Luther, further stimulated by the consumer appetites that had inspired the Reverends Collier, Whitefield, and Fordyce, among hundreds, indeed, over time, thousands of others, to call for the reformation of women's manners. Heyrman illustrates the resistance of turn-of-the-century Southern women to puritanical evangelists by quoting "Madame Depew, a Kentucky Lady," described by a preacher as being of "a gay turn." She irked him by "encouraging balls . . . which had grown to such a hight . . . that the chief of the youth of the neighborhood had become distracted." While Depew attended Baptist meetings, where she also heard the same views Winslow and her fellow young ladies heard in Boston in 1771, she attempted to reinforce "her female disciples" resistance "by saying to them," as the preacher, John Taylor, recorded: "Girls we shall hear enough of our dancing to day, but let us not mind what Mr. Taylor says, we are at liberty and we shall do as we please, let [him] say what he will." Eliza Wharton, the "coquette" of Foster's 1797 Richardsonian novel of that name, had resisted the Reverend J. Boyer's preachments on the same, self-liberating grounds. Christine Stansell describes such self-assertion among postrevolutionary New York City women, too, and notes that they extended it so far as sexual self-expression in the face of patriarchal authority attempting to maintain its hold on immigrant families, a challenge corresponding to other such challenges enhanced by the revolutionary inheritance, despite the efforts of evangelical reformers.[17]

## The Adams Family and Public Heterosociality

Young John Adams had courted Abigail Smith against the pull of the new heterosocial pleasures, in 1764, for example, registering his feelings about card playing's fashionability in Boston. His "Catalogue of your faults," ostensibly aimed at the "Reformation" of the twenty-year-old Abigail, had dripped irony—"you have been so extreamly negligent, in attending so little to Cards"—in order to praise her. Three years later, Abigail read Fordyce's views on card playing, and, when she went to Europe with Nabby, she experienced the full force of its fashionability. In 1774, she attempted to draw her young sister, Betsy, away from John Shaw, writing her (according to Betsy's summary of the now lost letter): "You say you hope to see me in Town soon, and as an Inducement, tell me of killing Eyes, fascinating Tongues, inward greatness, and unaffected Manners." She pointed out the obvious contradiction: "But ought these to allure, or have an effect on One, who is enjoined"—and here she quoted Abigail's letter—"not to seek Temptation, which to avoid were better." The "Town" was Braintree's metropolis: "Boston you inform me, is an excellent place to quench old Flames and kindle new ones."[18]

Ten years later, Betsy, now a respectable matron married to John Shaw despite Abigail's efforts, wrote Nabby about that young woman we met in the last chapter. Nancy Hazen, after whom Nabby had inquired, "left our family last February." She had been a boarder at the Shaws after losing her parents; Aunt Shaw explained that the seventeen-year old Nancy's "frequent Assemblys occasioned her being out at so late hours as made it very inconvenient." She suggested that her twenty-one-year-old niece, abroad now for two years, may not have kept in mind the traditional standards Aunt Shaw upheld: "You may possibly recollect that *in America*, late Hours were considered as greatly prejudicial to Health and as incompatible with the Peace and good Order of Families. And any deviation from these good and wholesome Rules would be viewed as more criminal in our Family than in Others." As we saw, the letter's purpose was to correct Nabby's own forgetfulness of America—even American moral standards, distracted as she might be by old Europe—in not writing to her aunt. In any case, the latter shows that Nancy's breach of the family curfew had a tangible effect on the Shaw household but that it manifested flaws of appearance and style that bothered the older woman much more.[19]

For a start, "Nature" had "lavished her Favours (I had almost said) with too liberal a hand." Aunt Shaw quoted a line of Lord Lyttleton's: Nancy "appears at first Acquaintance, 'Made to engage all Hearts, and charm all Eyes.'" Shaw wished that she could continue with the quotation, but "with grief" found herself "necessitated to forbear." She sustained the theme of Nancy's misleading appearance, combined with the note of her own regret: "At the first interviews my Neice would have thought her a precious Vine, that would have yielded the choicest Fruit, under the kind, fostering hand of Education." This praiseworthy hand might have been Aunt Shaw's. "Unhappy girl! she lost a Parent in Infancy, feign would I, have endeavoured to supply the place—but, alas!" These exclamations were conscious signs to Nabby of her aunt's grief over Nancy's fall. "Her opinions were formed and her Mind had received a Bias entirely inconsistent with my Ideas of a wife, amiable Woman, before she came into Haverhill."

So, when she entered the Shaw household, Nancy had already been formed without the moral ability to resist the heterosocial attractions now widely available to young women of her class: "Gay company, Scenes of dissapation, and the adulation payed by other Sex, had called her attention from things of real importance and every worthy pursuit." She had been exposed to the influence of other young ladies at one particular fashionable urban site; "two years at a boarding school"—"Mrs. Sheaffe's in Boston," we learn from John Quincy[20]—had "induced her to think that to dress, to dance, to Sing, to roll the Eye, and to troll the Tongue"—such details invaluable to the historian of manners—"were the only essential and the highest Qualifications of a Lady." Shaw conceded that Nancy had "quik Wit, a fine flow of Spirits, good humour, a lively imagination, and an excellent natural Capacity," qualities that Nabby admired. Her aunt intimated, however, that they had been a source of conflict before she decided to throw her out. Nancy being "too lovely and too charming to be given up, and lost," Shaw had tried on a weakened foundation to build her lodger into her ideal, her terms emphasizing the proper degree of sensibility: "Yet, with all these Endowments I found it utterly impossible to establish those Sentiments of Sincerity, Delicacy, and Dignity of manners, which I consider as so essential to the female Character." Nancy's inheritance dictated goal and means: "As she was a Lady of leisure, I wished her to appropriate certain portions of time, to particular Employments. To read with attention and methodically." But young Nancy would not follow directions. Aunt Shaw could not persuade her to write, read, or work methodically. She would do so "only as her volatile Spirit, and inclination prompted her. Words which would turn a double Construction, a double entendre, that subtle and base corruptor of the human Heart she was in no ways averse to." *Tristram Shandy* was the novel of sensibility most notoriously full of such words, albeit a cut above the erotica characterized by them.

Nancy, continued Aunt Shaw, "did not fully consider that an ungaurded look, or gesture would excite familiarities from the Libertine, and in the Eyes of a sensible, delicate Youth, forever tarnish her Reputation." Aunt Shaw's terms were those supplied by sentimental literature. She said that she might as well "have turned the Course of the Merrimac . . . as persuaded her," that is, to dissuade "Libertines," and the result of her effort was the kind of conflict she had represented earlier, between the good and the wholesome, on one hand, and the near criminal, on the other, a conflict overlapping, in this case, with that between reality and fantasy: "Accustomed to the voice of adulation, the Language of sober Truth was too bitter an ingredient for her to relish, and was never received without many Tears, which always grieved me, for it is much more agreeable to my feelings to commend rather than reprove." Susceptibility to fantasy was one of the symptoms of excessive, unregulated sensibility stimulated by the wrong kind of novel reading. But, even if Nancy's tears were shed in the expression of the wrong feelings (perhaps they, too, were tears of sensibility—we can imagine how Nancy represented Mrs. Shaw's authoritarian moralism to her tender self), they still affected Shaw's feelings, revealing the degree of sensibility she had already exhibited to Nabby by her earlier "grief" and exclamations. I referred above to Aunt Shaw's concluding subject in this letter, her feeling "hurt" over Nabby's not writing, but she had demonstrated throughout that her sensibility was combined with morality and self-control.

The eighteen-year-old John Quincy Adams also sent Nabby his opinion of Nancy Hazen and her orientation toward public entertainments. On his return to Massachusetts from Europe, he mingled in scenes of heterosocial pleasure equivalent to, if more modest than, those that his sister and their parents were then ambivalently experiencing in Europe. He enjoyed a "continuous round of tea-drinking," attended an assembly in Boston, where he also went for evening walks on its "mall," on one occasion encountering a "streetwalker," Robert East suggests. John Quincy had also walked with a respectable young lady on New York's mall. He enjoyed "sleighing parties" and local assemblies for dancing as well as a ball at Newburyport. He went to concerts, took up the flute, and played cards, although he said of the latter: "it is not the first Time since I arrived: it is not the most agreeable way of spending time, to me." He explained: "We must endeavour in matters of little Consequence, to conform, to the customs of the world, enough to preserve us from the reproach of singularity."[21]

John Quincy introduced the subject of Nancy Hazen by way of answering his supposition that "you will be curious to know my opinion of the young Lady who boards here." He was himself boarding with the Shaws at Haverhill while he prepared "to gain admittance with honour, next Spring in the junior Class at the University [i.e., Harvard]." (He would be learning Greek, reading the *Iliad*—he read Pope's translation, too—Horace in Latin, and "Locke, on the human understanding," among other subjects.) He told Nabby that Nancy was "rather short, but exceedingly well-proportioned, a fine shape"—details his aunt had not conveyed—"a most expressive Eye, and very fair complexion: she is not a beauty but has in her Countenance, something, uncommonly interesting." He admitted that because he "had not seen enough of" her character himself yet, he would pass along what he had "collected from other Persons": "And when I become more acquainted with it, I will write you my Sentiments again." Miss Hazen, John Quincy went on, "lost her father when she was very young, which has been her great misfortune. She boarded for a time at Mrs. Sheaffe's in Boston, and was drawn into the stream of dissipation."[22]

She "has a fine natural genius; but it has been so long employ'd upon trifles, that they have almost become natural to it." The alternative was the course his aunt had attempted to impose: "Had she always been taught that prudence, and oeconomy, were qualities absolutely necessary for young People in this Country, that some knowledge in Literature, and especially in history, was a much greater ornament than a pretty face, and a fine shape; I doubt not but she would be much more universally admired than she is." "Prudence" and "oeconomy" were "absolutely necessary" because young Americans were born without fortunes and titles, the consciousness of which John Quincy believed prevented young European ladies from plunging into the stream of dissipation. The Fordycean recommendation of the further necessity of "some knowledge" was an attribute that his own mother and several of his female kin embodied. In fact, young men without his standards and implicitly the dangerous kind against which Fordyce and a raft of sentimental writers warned had been able to express their admiration for Miss Hazen during those public entertainments of which the Adamses were so ambivalent: "She has been too much celebrated, by a parcel of fops, and Vanity is her ruling passion."[23]

Included in Abigail's stream of advice to John Quincy as he was about to attend Harvard were substantial quotations from Pope's *Essay on Criticism*, directed at what the editors of the Adams correspondence call his "intellectual arrogance," and referring in Pope's phrase to "persisting Fops we know." John Adams called "fops" and "foppling" affectations. The Adamses' orientation to fops was consistent with Fordyce's. The fop was a "ubiquitous figure" in eighteenth-century imaginations, defined as "a parody of a man who has precisely followed the prescription for achieving politeness," but excessively so, and was ostentatiously vain in such self-presentation. The fop marked another contrast, along with the rough, barbaric symbols against which men of feeling or successful masking measured themselves. It was a figure that could also be combined with that of the rake, as Billy Dimple was soon to illustrate in Tyler's play *The Contrast*, a figure modeling his behavior on the advice of Lord Chesterfield. He scorns "sentiment," a value elevated and Americanized by Tyler.[24]

But then John Quincy softened his criticism, holding out hope for Nancy's reformation of manners. "Vanity is her ruling passion," he wrote, alluding to Pope. "Nature has been liberal to her in mind, and person but . . . her foibles are probably owing to Education. She has worn off many, I have been told since, she came here—and I hope the rest will disappear." In fact, despite Aunt Shaw's having written Nabby in June that Nancy "left our family last February," John wrote in this October letter that "she boards here," so Aunt Shaw must have readmitted her, although one can only guess the reasons; they may have included Nancy's declaration of an intention to reform and a strengthening of Aunt Shaw's hope that she would do so. John Quincy's final paragraph to Nabby on the subject illustrates the significance of such "dissipation" for Nancy's future and the family that sheltered her as well as those words we saw illustrate the control the man of sensibility exercised over his sincerity in the interests of delicacy: "When I write to you, I endeavor to give you the Sentiments of my heart as they arise. To any one else I should give a much more advantageous Character of this Lady, and yet speak nothing, but what I believe. But to you, I mean to speak only the truth, but the whole truth."

A month later, John Quincy admitted in his journal: "I have heretofore more than once been obliged to exert all my Resolution to keep myself from a Passion, which I could not indulge, and which would have made me miserable had I not overcome it." That passion was for Nancy Hazen, as East has elicited. She had represented the same kind of threat to his ambition as Hannah Quincy had to his father: "I have escaped till now more perhaps owing to my good fortune, than to my own firmness, and now again I am put to trial. . . . I never was in greater danger." Nancy had left the house for a while, and, during her absence, he exhorted himself: "May it be my lot, at least for years to come, never to have my heart exclusively possessed by any individual of the other sex." This was an exclusivity of which Aunt Shaw would warn Nabby.[25]

As his remarks on the fops who flattered Nancy Hazen's vanity illustrate, John Quincy criticized the manners of American men, too. When he and his brother Charles visited Francis Dana in Cambridge in April 1786, he had to listen to "a vast deal of small talk" between a "gentleman," whose name he could not recollect, and "Miss E, upon matrimony and so forth." The editors of this letter suggest that "Miss E" was Almy Ellery, Dana's sister-in-law. John Quincy described her as "unfortunately somewhat deaf, but . . . uncommonly sensible, and (what I am griev'd to say is still more uncommon in this country) her mind is much improved by reading: so that she can entertain a company with a larger variety of conversation, without having recourse to the stale, and trivial topics of common-place, or to the ungenerous, and disgraceful topic of scandal." He was in favor of the improvement of women's minds by the right kind of reading, as were Fordyce and the *Spectator*. "She is not handsome, and is I suppose 27 years old," he continued, hinting, perhaps, that she was on her way to old maidenhood, "yet if she was in company with twenty of the most beautiful young ladies in the State, and in this company I had to choose my seat, it should certainly be by her side." He concluded this part of the letter by admitting, "I have been endeavouring, my Sister, ever since I returned from Europe, to find a female character like this," like Miss Almy Ellery, but "united to great beauty of person." This, then, was one motive in his participation in the public entertainments he also criticized.[26]

In his January 1787 letter to Nabby, John Quincy included a description of "two young Ladies, . . . happy that I can give you a few traits of their characters without incurring your centure, for *severity*." This referred to Nabby's reaction to his criticism of Nancy Hazen, a reaction to which I will turn shortly. The young ladies were the cousins Catherine Jones and Peggy Wigglesworth, the niece and daughter, respectively, of the Hollis Professor of Divinity at Harvard, with whom John Quincy and another "young gentleman by the name of Bridge" were also boarding. (Frank Bridge and John Quincy had "a deep mutual affection.") Catherine Jones, "just turned eighteen," had a face whose features, "taken all together," entitled her "the appellation of beauty." "Her person is large," he noted, "though not inelegant. I would say she was *stout built*, if the expression, were not more applicable to a man of war, than to a young lady." Her mind, taken altogether, "might be to her disadvantage. She has a share of wit, and a share of good nature, which is however, sometimes soured, by a small tincture of caprice." And, here, he reveals more of the reaction to women's intellectual assertiveness that he shared with Fordyce. Miss Jones "is not wholly exempt from Vanity; but as her understanding, rather than her person is the object of this Vanity, she endeavours to appear sarcastic, because she supposes, a satirical talent, must imply, an uncommon share of wit." Ultimately, this turned John Quincy off, as Fordyce warned such behavior would. John Quincy could "esteem her as a Friend . . . love her as a Sister, but I should never think of her as the companion for my life." What Catherine Jones wished for from him we do not know, although she expressed some sarcasm to him.[27]

Peggy Wigglesworth, however, was without such mental flaws. The same letter continues: "Two years older than her Cousin," her "complexion is of the browner order; but this defect, if a defect it be, is compensated, by a rosy variety of colour." That is, she could blush. Miss Wigglesworth's "face is not beautiful, but it is remarkable for expressing, all the candor, benevolence, and sincerity of her heart," a consistency of feeling and face that John Adams had wished for in Hannah Quincy: "her shape, would be genteel in France or England, though her size, would seem to give her the title of a *pretty woman* as Fielding expresses it. As to her mind, should I attempt to give you a just description, of its virtues, I fear you would suspect me of writing a panegyric, rather than a character." She conformed to the Fordyean ideal: "She does not make such a display of wit, as her cousin, but she has an open frankness, and a generous candor, infinitely more amiable in my opinion, than an incessant endeavour to appear smart, and as she is equally acquainted with the enjoyment, and the solicitudes, which attend great sensibility, she is entirely free from that Vanity, who gratification consists in the mortification of others." This suggests that Miss Jones's exercise of her satiric talent, expressing her "Vanity," had mortified John Quincy.

Miss Wigglesworth's "greatest imperfection, which the severest critic of her conduct could discover, would be a degree of sincerity and unreservedness which is considered as a fault only because the taste of mankind is vitiated by dissimulation." Why, John Quincy had himself dissimulated his views for this reason, he admitted to Nabby. But, despite "all this," he could no more love Peggy than he could Catherine: "when I search my own mind to find the causes of it, I am reduced to condemn, either the Passion; of Love, or the sentiments by which it is produced." The source of love lay in physical passion, rather than in the kind of cool assessment he believed he had made of these cousins.

Three weeks after writing to Nabby about Catherine Jones, Peggy Wigglesworth, and Almy Ellery and telling her of his fantasy of choosing the latter out of a bevy of twenty beauties, John Quincy found himself in a circumstance very like it, at a "dancing party" in Mystic, Massachusetts, a town where there were "about thirty five young Ladies, of what is called the *ton*," but only two young gentlemen, in this a sexuosocial ratio resembling the Braintree Abigail had described in that letter to Thaxter praising Fordyce (see chapter 3 above). John Quincy, Frank Bridge, and another Harvard classmate "were introduced into a large company of Ladies. . . . Many of them were handsome, but female beauty is so universal in this country, that I pay little attention to it. We soon went to dancing and this circumstance assisted me greatly to become acquainted with the Ladies." He rationalized his subsequent unbending in scientific terms: "Where human beings are unacquainted with ridiculous solemnity of formal ceremony, the social spirit which is natural to them, will always produce its effect. Before the evening was ended, I felt free from restraint, as I could in familiar company." He was able to pursue his ideal combination: "It fell to my lot, at first, to dance with the handsomest lady in Company. I endeavoured to enter into conversation with her, but to every thing I could say the only answers were, 'yes,' 'no,' 'I think so,' 'indeed!' I was soon tired of her, and concluded she was too much occupied in thinking of herself, to give any of her attention to other people." But, if she had beauty without conversational ability, the next partner he "drew" reversed these qualities: "One of these Ladies could be seen, the other was heard with pleasure."[28]

Nabby began her reply to what her brother had written her of Nancy

Hazen by telling him that the daughter of his former tutor in Holland had got married, preparing him by saying, "Call all your fortitude to your aid," and implying that he had a bit of a crush on her. In response to what he had written of Nancy, she wrote: "I think, my brother, that you do not discover Candor enough for the foibles of others, especially the Ladies." John had twice praised Peggy Wigglesworth for her "candor." The eighteenth-century definition of *candor* included consciousness of and even sympathy for others, a meaning comparable to that of sensibility (with which Nabby linked it elsewhere). She implied that John had been too harsh in his judgement: "The best dispositions are not Convinced by Severity and austerity. Only reflect upon your own disposition, and I am sure you will be convinced of this." John Quincy was persuadable only by criticisms that took his feelings into consideration. That this was the result of his childrearing is suggested by Nabby's next sentence: "Remember, if a young lady is Capable of inconsistencys, if she is deficient in judgement prudence &c. that the fault is not half so much her own, as those who have had the Care of her education. We are like Clay in the Hands, of the Artist, and may be moulded to whatever form, they please." Just as Lockean psychology opened up potentials for any child's future, whatever the sex, so, too, it made parents and other adults vulnerable to fundamental criticism.

Nabby continued that, the "more knowledge and judgement they," that is, young ladies, "possess, the fewer faults will be found in their productions." Her point had been sharpened, it seemed, by declaring that "severity and austerity" were not effective in changing the "foibles of others, especially ladies." Now, however, Nabby reiterated her Cartesian, Lockean explanation in gender-neutral terms, which held inestimable promise for women: "I believe that the earliest impressions of the Mind are too generally neglected, and it is those which often have the greatest effect." Such a view of childhood still had to make headway against neglectful childrearing or worse. As we shall see, Nabby believed that insensitive, tyrannical fathers were the rule rather than the exception, although, in Nancy Hazen's case, her father had died when she was very young, as Nabby knew from John Quincy's letter—indeed, it had suggested that this had been a cause of her not being able to resist "dissipation." Elaborating her psychological point, and continuing to illustrate to her younger male sibling how to criticize with candor, she wrote: "You may if you attend to it, observe in many of your acquaintance, habits and [faults] which have from not being early enough attended to, Grown up, and proved so forcible as to resist all future attempts to correct them." This, she implied, had been the case with Nancy's father-absent childrearing.

Nabby explained how persons well-enough attuned to others could detect the evidence, illustrating her own sensibility: "You may observe it in the most trifling circumstances"—a view characteristic of other exponents of sensibility, among them Adam Smith, Fordyce, and Hannah More as well as both of Nabby's parents in, for example, their reading faces and gestures—"and you may generally decide, by hearing a Person converse an hour what has been their early education. You may judge from their Language, the very frases they use to express their ideas." She then applied her view of the valuable sensitivity of judgment to Nancy Hazen and John Quincy's "Severity, and austerity," toward her: "And tho they"—that is, persons with the kind of "early education" it seems Nancy had had—"may be sensible in some degree of those faults, I am inclined to believe it is not in their power to correct them." She makes explicit her point about the significance of this for heterosocial relations: "A Gentleman who is severe against the Ladies, is also, upon every principle very impolitick." He is impolitic because of the effects of such severity on himself: "His Character is soon established for a Morose severe ill Natured Fellow." This referred to her brother's consistently negative responses to young ladies that he communicated to his sister. David Musto refers to John Quincy Adams's "harsh and critical judgement of the opposite sex" in describing his general relations with women.[29]

And here Nabby showed herself to be as willing to begin to explore the psychological origins of sexism as her mother had been in suggesting why men do not want to give women equal education ("I cannot help sometimes suspecting that this neglect arises in some measure from an ungenerous jealousy of rivals near the Throne").[30] Nabby wrote her brother: "And upon my word, I think it the most Convincing proof that he can give, that He feels their Power importance, and (equallity) Superiority." She cancelled the word *equallity*, perhaps a more provocative or tougher-minded one than *superiority*. Here, she implied a still more deeply psychological, modern-sounding analysis of that feeling (such a man's sense of woman's power): "It is I assure you a want of Generosity, and I will challenge you to produce one instance of a Person of this disposition who did not at some period of his Life, acknowledge his dependence upon them." A candid conversation about a young lady's deficiencies in judgment and prudence, conducted sympathetically and generously because the gentleman is aware of the upbringing that has caused them, would avert the danger that he be thought morose and ill-natured because he is insecure, the result of the impression a woman has made on him. That, not irrelevantly, was one explanation Richardson gave for Lovelace's treatment of women, including Clarissa.[31]

The woman on whom John Quincy had been most dependent was his mother. This may well have been the woman Nabby had in mind, and, if so, her observation was consistent with what her father had written her of the influence of mothers on sons, whether they turned out "good or bad." Richard Alan Ryerson remarks that young "Johnny's diffidence towards his mother, which contrasted with her formal yet eager and solicitous address towards him, was clearly evident from his 14th year, and probably earlier." The more formally psychohistorical Musto notes the "powerful ability to control and instill guilt that Abigail exercised upon her young children during her husband's long absence." He suggests that this propensity reflected "her own special needs," but it was also a significant potential in the childrearing investment generally propounded by the culture of sensibility. East exclaims, "Wonderful indeed was the maternal influence exercised by Abigail Adams," and then details her decisive interference in John Quincy's relationship with Mary Frazier, reinforced by John's keeping his son economically dependent. This followed the same kind of impact that, as we shall see, Abigail had had on Nabby's relationship with Royall Tyler. Of course, the psychiatrist Musto links John Quincy's harsh judgments of other women to this relationship with Abigail, although it was consistent with what Fordyce's *Sermons* suggests was an explanation of men of feeling's reaction to assertive young women, wanting them to be more sentimental than themselves. In any case, Nabby's insight, and its echoes in the analyses of East, Ryerson, and Musto, further suggests that one root of modern psychology lay in the culture of sensibility.[32]

Still advising him how to treat ladies and, in effect, criticizing him for his behavior toward them so far, Nabby told John Quincy: "Persons who are conscious of their superiority in any subject, are generally diffident in proclaiming their own merit, they will prefer to prove it by their actions and Conduct, rather than discover their own knowledge of it." She had concluded this subject by adding, "I would never dispute with you, were you to assert that we were your inferiors incapable even of those improvements which you would be the superiors," but she canceled this sentence. That she first thought she should say it presumably reflected her knowledge of John Quincy's "own disposition" to be sensitive to severe and austere remarks on his "foibles." To have sent it to him would have resembled Abigail's habit of adding such deferential remarks to the complaints of his behavior she wrote to John, who had the same prickly irascibility as his son. Nabby's letter had already recorded her awareness of John Quincy's sensitivity to the question of his superiority to women by its hesitation over the word *equality*. The deleted sentence's "those improvements which you would be the superiors" (the latter noun's number showing that she was thinking of men generally, not just her brother) refers, perhaps, to her brother's current preparation for and entrance to Harvard, a level of education automatically denied women, as her father and, implicitly, her brother reminded her. That reminder may have given added force to her decision to delete this acknowledgment of men's superiority and, conversely, sustain the element of equality intimated by the word *persons* in the previous sentence.[33]

Nabby then demonstrated that she was more "sensible," not only of Nancy Hazen's faults and those of young women like her, but of the reasons for them; she showed her consciousness, too, of the reason some men treated women who had been weakened in this way by a sexist upbringing. Implicit was that women, as well as men, should become more conscious and that that, perhaps, was a first step toward the reform of both sexes.

Nabby's advice to her brother that he restrain his severe judging of women had not taken effect by the time he wrote a two-hundred-line poem modeled on Pope's "Epistle to a Lady of the Characters of Women," one of that pair of poems on each gender that had followed *An Essay on Man*. John Quincy entitled his poem "A Vision," restating his assessment of what kind of women would not and would arouse his love. By 1790, it was circulating among his young lady acquaintances, who presumably recognized its pseudonymous subjects. It resembled his fantasy of Almy Ellery and the twenty beauties as well as the experience he had had in Mystic in being able to choose partners from all those beautiful young ladies. (A few years later, he told a friend that "he had never been cut out," in East's phrase, "to be a 'rake,'" in his own self-conception, and that he "performed the part with 'as little grace as enjoyment.'" Again, we recall his father's youth, this time in his repression of a rakish route.) The context for this poem, which he wrote in Newburyport during his legal apprenticeship after Harvard, was precisely that kind of literary society described by Shields as having existed in many American towns and cities at the time. It manifested John Quincy's own "essential concern with 'the Ladies'" and was a contribution to a "veritable battle of the sexes." One of the ladies whom "A Vision" satirized would reply in kind. John Quincy had already gained a reputation in Boston as "a mag-

isterial and puckish critic of female literary 'genius,'" but, given the nature of the criticism of young women that he expressed in his letters to
Nabby, we might see it as sharing something with Fordyce's reaction to
women's assertion of intellectual equality.[34]

John Quincy had already written a "sarcastic" "Epistle to Delia," a
poem critical of Nancy Hazen, in 1785, some lines of which he would
apply to "Narcissa" in "A Vision." He also wrote an acrostic revealing
the name Catherine Jones. There were other precedents and names for
those he incorporated in "A Vision," including a poem on Mary Frazier, the "Clara" of "A Vision," which he published in the *Massachusetts
Magazine* in 1789.[35]

"A Vision"[36] opened with Cupid's leveling his dart at the male poet,
John Quincy Adams's persona, who begged to be spared on various
grounds. One of them was that the "blood of passion" was not yet "boiling in his veins." The vision had come to him while he was "fatigued
with labor, and with care opprest." Cupid refused to spare him but did
allow him to "Choose for [himself] the object of [his] pain." His wand
then conjured up a "throng" of beauties, including the stereotypes of
the "prude that pouted, the coquette that leered," and "the stale virgin,
withered, pale, and lean." The first to be named was Lucinda,

> Deficient in a single part,
> She wanted nothing but a *feeling heart!*

Pope had written of one of his pseudonymous characters: "'Say, what
can Cloe want?'—she wants a Heart."[37] His imitator here continued:

> Next Belinda advanced with stride,
> A compound strange of vanity and pride.

When to this deficiency her "tawny skin" is added, we recall that John
Quincy saw Peggy Wigglesworth's "browner" complexion as a "defect." Narcissa seemed to have a "winning softness," capable of registering the poet's heart's "rapture":

> But soon I found those ardent hopes were vain,
> Narcissa viewed my passion with disdain.

This, the poet suggested, was unnatural in a woman:

> And can the sex by nature formed for love,
> Each soft impression from the heart remove?

Vanessa might have filled the bill if only she

> could be taught
> To store her mind with larger funds of thought,
> Her volubility of tongue repress
> *Think* somewhat more, and *prattle* somewhat less.

Nature had been generous to Corinna:

> With innate warmth of constitution blest,
> Her greatest pleasure is to be caressed;
> Her lips sip rapture from an amourous kiss,
> Viewed as a pledge of more endearing bliss.

But to go along with this she had "With so much love a slender share of sense," which latter quality, in this era, had to be adequate to control such excessive sexual feeling. Nerea read the wrong kind of books:

> Why will Nerea spend her youthful days
> In wild romances and insipid plays;
> Where idle tales, in flimsy language told,
> Exhibit folly in a pleasing world?
> Fictitious evils enervate the breast,
> Deprave the morals and corrupt the taste.

These were faults that Aunt Shaw detected in Nancy Hazen.

That Almira's "face is female, masculine her mien," significantly led the poet first to ask about the gendering of qualities, for example, "why was strength dispensed to man alone," but then to warn such women as Almira:

> Attempt not then, ye fair, to rule by fear,
> The surest female weapon is a tear.

Finally, however, "the fleeting vision vanished from my mind," and the perfect Clara was left "behind," to be celebrated by John Quincy's "poetic fires,"

> Whose tender strains describe with matchless art
> The soft emotions of a feeling heart.

He bade lovers bring tribute to "the lovely Clara's shrine." The gods had given her beauty as well as worth:

> Nature formed of purest white her skin,
> A emblem of the innocence within.

Clara's complexion showed the color of roses in her cheeks,

> While Venus added to complete the fair,
> The eyes blue languish and the golden hair.

Just how *languish* works in that line is not clear, but its application to sentimental heroines was widespread because it connoted a refined, feminine nervous system:

> But far superior charms exalt her *mind*,
> Adorned by nature and by art refined;
> Hers are the lasting beauties of the *heart*,
> The charms that only nature can impart;
> The generous purpose and the soul sincere,
> Meek sorrow's sigh and gentle pity's tear.

Clara has been born beautiful, and she has been educated to refinement, including, presumably, prudence, economy, and some literature and history, to that degree that Abigail advised Lucy Cranch that a woman should make herself "a pleasing companion to a man of science and sensibility," the basis for Fordyce's argument to improve women's education. Clara would know, too, how to repress any "volubility of tongue" and had enough "sense" properly to measure out amorous kisses and more extensive sensual pledges:

> Ah, lovely Clara! can a heart like this
> Accept the tribute of a muse like mine?
> Should these poor lays attract thy beauteous eye
> Say, would they raise one sympathetic sigh?

If his blood had not yet reached boiling point, John Quincy's heart had begun to rise in temperature:

> For thee, my heart with vivid ardor glows,
> For thee, my blood with rapid impulse flows.

Deeming himself a man of sensibility, John Quincy wanted a wife exhibiting a still greater degree of it in accordance with the definition supplied by Fordyce, illustrating, it seems, the dynamic relation between these two manifestations of gendered sensibility.

# PART II

# Particular Applications

CHAPTER 6

# A Woman's Struggle
# over Sensibility

## A Kind of Freedom

Abigail's experience of feminine sensibility and what she said of it corresponded to a considerable extent to what Fordyce and other writers and preachers said. By no means, however, did she simply subordinate her feelings to her husband's wishes: she had to struggle to do so. She did wish, in accordance with her praise of Fordyce, to improve John's sensibility, a wish that coincided with his own, up to a point.

In October 1775, Abigail wrote John about her mother's death, then told him: "I know I wound your Heart. Why should I? Ought I go give relief to my own by paining yours?" She wished to trust him with her feelings and went on to tell him that the act of writing allowed her to do so: "My pen is always freer than my tongue. I have wrote many things to you that I suppose I never could have talked." She had read in Fordyce's *Sermons* about "the honest sensibilities of ingenuous nature checked by the over-cautious dictates of political prudence." *Political* here denoted the broader meaning of "self-interested calculation." "No advantage, obtained by such frigidity, can compensate the want of those warm effusions of the heart into the bosom of a friend, which are doubtless among the most exquisite pleasures." But, Fordyce admitted, by the same token—the capacity for exquisite feeling—"it must be owned they often, by the inevitable lot of humanity, make way for the bitterest pains which the breast can experience." This ambiguity of refined sensibility was something that Abigail bemoaned.[1]

She described to John a process whereby she unconsciously gave way to overwhelming emotion in the aftermath of her mother's death, setting the scene, one where John was absent and her children were in bed: "In the day time family affairs take of my attention but my Evenings are spent with my departed parent." This meant: "My Evenings are lonely and Melancholy. . . . I then ruminate upon all her care and tenderness, and am sometimes lost, and absorb'd in a flood of tenderness e'er I am aware of it, or can call to my aid, my only props and support." Her father had prayed by her mother's deathbed and then, in church, had "a tender scene to pass through—a young Granddaughter Betsy Cranch joining herself to the church, and a Beloved Wife dying to pray for—weeping children, weeping and mourning parishioners all round him, for every Eye streamed, his own heart allmost bursting as he spoke. How painful is the recollection, yet how pleasing." We have seen other illustrations of this very characteristic feature of cultures of sensibility, pain combined with pleasure.[2]

One possible explanation on this occasion, in addition to Abigail's witnessing of a communal freedom of expression, sanctioned by ritual, was its beneficial effects on her that she described later in the same letter: "My heart is made tender by repeated affliction. It never was a hard Heart." Pain enhanced the sensibility in which a person could take pleasure. Abigail's observation on affliction's tenderizing of her heart resembles John's sensibility's improvement by seeing the sufferings of the poverty-stricken Peacocks in Boston. The uneven material advances signified by the phrase *consumer revolution* provided corresponding cultural circumstances. Seeing the emotional pain that her imminent departure for Europe caused these around her, Abigail wrote John in April 1784: "I derive a pleasure from the regret of others, a pleasure which perhaps I might never have experienced if I had not been called to quit my Country, the blessing and regret of the poor and the needy, who bewail my going away." Parting juxtaposed other contrasting feelings. This particular case, however, points both to the fact that middle-class cultivators of sensibility were able to enjoy occasions when they could contrast their delicacy of feeling with the sea of poor who surrounded them and to the argument that such contrasts in feeling were linked to the social transformation of newly significant numbers of people from subsistence to the material abundance of the consumer revolution.[3]

Abigail could construe her freedom of feeling and its expression as superior to John's restraint on the basis of his declared prudence in his public life—his letters might be intercepted—although at times she deferred to it, too. In March 1778, she wrote him: "Freedom of sentiment the life and soul of friendship is in great measure cut of[f] by the Danger of Miscarriages, and the apprehension of Letters falling into the hands of our Enemies." Then in May she wrote: "I must omit many domestic matters because I will not risk their comeing to the publick Eye." But later the same year she complained that John had not mentioned receiving her letters, then declared: "I have not been so parsimonious as my Friend, perhaps. I am not so prudent but I cannot take up my pen with my Heart overflowing and not give utterance to some of the abundance which is in it." And a couple of months after she told him:

> I love to amuse myself with my pen, and pour out some of the tender sentiments of a Heart over flowing with affections, not for the Eye of a cruel Enemy who no doubt would ridicule every Humane and Social Sentiment long ago grown Callous to the finer sensibilities—but for the sympathetick Heart that Beats in unison with
>
> *Portias*

Here she conjured up a picture of herself as virtue in distress.[4]

Abigail indicated that she expected the same kind of sentimental effusion of the heart that she asked of him in other letters. Her metaphor for John's failure to write in such a way, to free himself up as it were, was in keeping with her abundant overflow; in fact, it invoked both the hardness of the stereotypical antitype and John's frequent claim that his heart could melt. In that letter telling John that she had to give utterance when her heart was overflowing, she exclaimed: "By Heaven, if you could you [would] have changed Hearts with some frozen Laplander or made a voyage to a region that has chilld every Drop of your Blood." In *Tristram Shandy*, Sterne had said that North Lapland was "where the passions of a man, with every thing which belongs to them, are as frigid as the zone itself." Fordyce contrasted "frigidity" with the "warm effusions of the heart" that should be poured "into the bosom of a friend." Here, however, Abigail recognized that her overflow had become one of anger rather than tenderness, so she was able to bring it under control: "But I will restrain a pen already I fear too rash, nor shall it tell you how much I have sufferd from this appearance of inattention." Perhaps she feared provoking his answering anger, but this, too, was *occupazio*: she was telling him how much she suffered, and, moreover, her pause before *inattention* expressed to him that this was a euphemism for what she had already said of his frozen heart.[5]

When she faced the prospect of becoming a public figure like Martha Washington were John to be elected president, Abigail wrote him: "I have been so used to a freedom of sentiment that I know not how to place so many gaurds about me, as will be indispensable to look at every word before I utter it, and to impose a silence upon my self when I talk." She had felt free in her privacy to talk as well as write.[6]

This was not apparently the case when it came to sex: "I dare not

express to you at 300 miles distance how ardently I long for your return."
Yet the unexpressed ardor triggered the feelings she did write: "The Idea
plays about my Heart, unnerves my hand whilst I write, awakens all the
tender sentiments that years have encreased and matured, and which when
with me were every day dispensing to you." What Abigail was writing
here, she reflected, was an irresistible overflow, akin to that "flood of tenderness" that had absorbed her when thinking of her recently departed
mother as well as her overflow when thinking of John's absence and inattention: "The whole collected stock of ten weeks absence knows not
how to brook any longer restraint, but will break forth and flow thro my
pen." She had presented her writing her letter of condolence to Jefferson
in similar terms. John's barriers, she thought, stemmed from his public
obligations: "May the like sensations enter thy breast, and (in spite of all
the weighty cares of State) Mingle themselves with those I wish to communicate, for in giving them utterance I have felt more sincere pleasure
than I have known since the 10 of August." That was the last date they
had been together before he left for Philadelphia.[7]

Another letter to John more directly illustrates the connection between this freedom to express feelings and the new material circumstances that increasing numbers of women could enjoy, that is, in domestic space marked by a proliferation of consumer items. During a visit
to Boston, Abigail wrote John in Philadelphia: "I have possession of my
Aunts chamber in which you know there is a very convenient pretty
closet with a window which looks into her flower Garden. In this closet
are a number of Book Shelves, which are but poorly furnished, however,
I have a pretty little desk or cabinet here where I write all my Letters and
keep my papers unmolested by any one. . . . I should like to be the owner
of such conveniences. I always had a fancy for a closet with a window
which I could more peculiarly call my own."[8] Richardson had written
that a young lady "makes her closet her paradise."[9] Abigail's here was the
setting for the outward and inward action she next recounted: "Here I
say I have amused myself in reading and thinking of my absent Friend,
sometimes with a mixture of paine, sometimes with pleasure, sometimes
anticipating a joyfull . . . meeting whilst my Heart would bound and pal-
pitate with the pleasing Idea, and with the purest affection I have held you
to my Bosom till my whole Soul has dissolved in Tenderness and my pen
fallen from my Hand." Possessing her aunt's chamber, Abigail enjoyed
that "autonomous hedonism" (Colin Campbell's phrase)[10] progressing in
her illustration by way of reverberations between thoughts and "Idea,"
on one side, and feelings, on the other, until the latter category absorbed

the former, a process symbolized by her losing her grip on her pen. Her representation to John of the outer expression (plus prop) of the climax of her inner feelings makes this a kind of self-staging, allowing him to see it more literally as a "scene." The dissolution that she describes, between her sense of self and her idea of the other, she then projected onto John's reading the scene. More precisely, she presents him with a second scene in which she imagined his responsiveness to her first: "How often do I reflect with pleasure that I hold in possession a Heart Eaqually warm with my own, and full as Susceptable of the Tenderent impressions, and Who even now whilst he is reading here, feels all I discribe." Susceptibility to the tenderest impressions that triggered entirely sympathetic feelings was synonymous with having sensibility. Abigail linked her freedom to imagine such emotional equality to the power of her "possession," circumscribed, of course, by the legal freedom and material power of her husband. Her pleasure depended on the pain of John's absence, a Platonic pleasure, a pleasure of the imagination, in the *Spectator*'s phrase, to an extent made more widely possible by literacy and by the material advances symbolized by that writing closet.[11]

Abigail's next paragraph shows her to have regarded this as self-indulgence, its pleasure enhanced, it seems, by John's using his power to allow her such freedom: "Forgive this Revere, this Delusion, and since I am debared real, suffer me, to enjoy, and indulge In Ideal pleasures—and tell me they are not inconsistant with the stern virtue of a senator and a Patriot." In other words, she wants John to reassure her that his sensibility can equal hers without surrendering the stern virtue his public life required. The latter phrase connoted the masculine value she wrote of to John Thaxter, two years later, in reflecting that "the stern virtue of Cato" could not save a people "grown wicked and Effamanate."[12] John gave one of his definitions of *stern virtue*—"resistance to passion"—in a 1795 letter he wrote Abigail, in commenting on "Men who have more Ambition than Principle": "I have gone through a Life of almost three Score Years, and how few have I found whose Principles could hold against their Passions, whose honor could contend with their Interests, or even whose Pride could Struggle with their Vanity." The fact that he could be charged with passionate ambition, with self-interest and vanity, is illustrated by his rationalization in his *Discourses on Davila*.[13]

Campbell has argued persuasively for the significance of the term *luxury* as the link between sensibility and consumerism. That 1786 poem, "On Sensibility," had called the "joys refin'd," given by "reading" to the person of sensibility, "that luxury of the exalted mind," and the capac-

ity "to feel each line" was "to taste the luxury of woe." The cultivation and culture of sensibility required more time, along with the advance in material circumstances that Abigail's aunt's closet represented.
Of course, John's being too busy with politics and diplomacy to write
of his feelings to Abigail (her married work obligations were still more
constant but at least relievable by servants) was different from a peasant's
dawn-to-dusk absorption in subsistence. Prior to his full-scale career,
John had been able to begin a letter to Cotton Tufts: "I have nothing to
do but to play with my Pen." Having time—freedom from the necessity of work—long had been another mark of gentility, identical with
leisure, a sign of "the stark separation between the leisured few and a
laboring many." Perhaps the most significant step Franklin made in his
gentrification was his decision to become "a master of [his] own time."
One can think of time as well as consumer goods prospectively increasing, first for the middle class in certain countries, heralding a far wider
distribution over the next centuries, to the point that E. P. Thompson
and Daniel Boorstin, for example, discuss from different perspectives
what postindustrial workers in England and America should or could do
with the remarkable increases in their leisure time.[14]

Frequently, Abigail took time to "recover" or "compose" herself after
indulging in or being overwhelmed with feeling, then turned to write
John about these processes. For example, in October 1775, she wrote
him that she had not been "composed enough to write you since Last
Sabbath." Sixteen years earlier, Eliza Lucas Pinckney had written to her
"dear friend" Mrs. Evance describing her grief at the death of her husband and adding: "I would describe to you . . . his last sickness and dying scene . . . but 'tis too much for me! My Eyes fail and I can write no
more." She shows that she had, indeed, put down her pen, as Abigail had
dropped hers when her "whole soul was dissolved in Tenderness," because her next sentence opens: "Tho' I take up my pen again I will not
resume the distressful subject."[15]

Abigail showed her consciousness of John's power even as she freely
expressed herself, this time after her mother died: "You will pardon
and forgive all my wanderings of mind. I cannot be correct." This was
a sentence immediately followed Abigail's writing "to be mindful of
the correcting hand, that I may not be rebuked in anger." In that case,
it was God's hand, it seems, Abigail interpreting her mother's death as
God's "Stroke," but the overlap between God's and John's corrections
was not merely fortuitous. Abigail's wish for restraint often accompanied her consciousness of giving way to emotional expression. Again in

the aftermath of her mother's death, she described the feelings caused by her distress as "selfish": "I cannot overcome my too selfish sorrow, all her tenderness to me . . . indear her memory to me, and highten my sorrow for her loss. At the same time I know a patient sorrow is my duty. I will strive to obtain it."[16]

This was precisely the lesson that, in Jane Austen's *Sense and Sensibility*, Elinor Dashwood was to teach her sister, Marianne, who (with their mother) indulged herself in excessive grief over the death of her father, one expression of her excessive sensibility. Eliza Lucas had written a friend long before: "The languishing condition of my brother Tommy is almost insupportable to so tender and indulgent a mother as my poor Mama; and indeed if there be any excuse for such an excess of grief as hers, it might be pleaded on this occasion." Tommy was dying a protracted death in "extream pain."[17] In her letter, Abigail justified her tears because they mirrored those of the kind of softened, Protestant God described by "M.B." and by Fordyce: "He who deigned to weep over a departed Friend, will surely forgive a sorrow which at all times desires to be bounded and restrained by a firm Belief that a Being of infinite wisdom and unbounded Goodness will carve out my portion in tender mercy towards me!" She expressed the same mixture of an urge to control her feelings and a justification of them—in this case, on the grounds of human nature—in her October 25 letter about the effects on her of her mother's death: "My wounded Heart . . . will sometimes when of my Guard swell and exceed the bounds I endeavor to set to it. It is natural to mourn the loss of any comforts in proportion to the pleasure and satisfaction we derived from them."[18]

## Abigail's Conflict

If Abigail continued to find freedom in the private, emotional expression of sensibility, albeit sometimes ambivalently, she also found severe limitations in it, which she linked to women's gendered nerves. In 1771, she wrote her cousin, Isaac Smith Jr.: "From my infancy I had always felt a great inclination to visit the Mother Country . . . and had nature formed me of the other Sex I should certainly have been a rover." She explained that what we can call the *naturalization* of women's delicacy of nerves was reinforced by what people thought should be their confinement to domestic space, effected by both opinion and the threat from men beyond it: "Women you know are considered as Domestick Beings, and although they inherit an Eaquel Share of curiosity with the other

Sex, but few are hardly eno' to venture chroad, and explore the amaiz-
ing variety of distant Lands. The Natural tenderness and Delicacy of our
Constitutions, added to the many Dangers we are subject to from your
Sex, makes it almost impossible for a Single Lady to travel without injury to her character." There seems to be resentment here, one widely
expressed in sentimental novels, and one that perhaps carried over to her
next sentence in the same letter: "And those who have a protector in an
Husband, have generally speaking obstacles sufficient to prevent their
Roving, and instead of visiting other Countries; are obliged to content
themselves with seeing but a small part of their own. To your Sex we
are most indebted for all the knowledge we acquire of Distant lands."
In making the point that Abigail yearned to be more than a "republican
mother," Donald Meyer quotes her response to the public lectures on
science she was able to attend when she finally got to London: "It was
like going into a beautiful Country which I never saw before, a Country
which our American females are not permitted to visit or inspect."[19]

With Abigail in London was the twenty-year-old Nabby, who wrote
John Quincy, already widely traveled: "[For] my part I should like above
all things to make one of a *Party to go* round the World. . . . I cant see
why People who have the *inclination* and *ability* . . . should not gratify
themselves by indulging it and seeing as many and various parts of the
World as it should Lead them to visit. If they are possessed of proper
Principles, it will not injure them but make them wiser and better and
happier." This was an argument against the opposite view, parallel to
the "obstacles" her mother had believed were placed around women to
prevent them roving to distant lands. By the same token, however, that
same passage expressed the wish that her brother (whom elsewhere she
asked for correction of her behavior) be one of said traveling party.[20]

As Nabby had written of "People," so her mother's letter to Isaac
Smith had been part of her discussion of differences in national manners in general and of whether they reflected nature or nurture: "As to
a Knowledg of Humane Nature, I believe it may as easily be obtained
in this Country as in England, France or Spain." Despite her having to
repress her urge to rove, Abigail thought herself just as qualified as men
to address the subject of "Humane Nature." There was significant common ground among Americans, English, French, and Spanish: "Education alone I conceive Constitutes the difference in Manners. Tis natural
I believe for every person to have a partiality for their own Country."
(*Education* in the eighteenth-century meant the whole of childrearing as

well as what we mean by the word today.) So she believed that women
and men ("persons"), were the same in respect of national manners, in
contrast to their delicacy of constitution.[21]

Abigail again addressed the subject of gendered sensibility in 1780,
again prompted by her responses to John's absence. She began by exclaiming over her customary "My Dearest Friend": "How fondly can
I call you mine, bound by every tie, which consecrates the most invio-
lable Friendship, yet separated by a cruel destiny, I feel the pangs of absence sometimes too sensibly for my own repose." The next sentence
shows this to be the result of the inner conflict in which she has again
lost: "There are times when the heart is peculiarly awake to tender impressions, when philosophy slumbers"—so, for example, reading John's
recommended Epictetus would not work—"or is overpowered by sentiments more conformable to Nature." She identifies nature with gender differences: "It is then I feel myself alone in the wide world, without any one to tenderly care for me, . . . yet my cooler reason [somehow
reawakening] dissaproofs the repineing thought, and bids me bless the
hand whence my comforts flow." Does she mean God? It is ambiguous
because the two lines of verse she then quotes address "Man," referring
to John:

> "Man active resolute and bold
>   is fashioned in a different mould."

More independent by Nature, he can scarcely realize all those ties which
bind our sex to his.[22]

Abigail continued in this letter to define such gender difference as
natural, its effect women's dependence: "Is it not natural to suppose that
as our dependence is greater, our attachment is stronger?" She turned
from the general sex difference to its particular manifestation in herself,
turning pain into pleasure: "I find in my own breast a sympathetic power
always operating upon the near approach of Letters from my dear absent
Friend." Perhaps because it was "natural," philosophers might measure
this power, but "I cannot determine the exact distance when this secret
charm begins to operate." So she finds this sympathetic power more
amenable to being described in literary or religious terms: "The time is
sometimes longer and sometimes shorter, the Busy Sylphs are ever at my
ear, no sooner does Morpheus close my Eyes, than 'my whole Soul unbounded flies to thee.' Am I superstitious enough for a good Catholic?"

Then, typically, she turns away from the language of sensibility to a direct report of her receipt of the letters: "A Mr. Ross arrived lately from Philadelphia, and punctually delivered your Letter's."

But, writing John in Amsterdam in 1782 after another two years of unrelieved separation, she was less able to be positive about a gendered sensibility: "Desire and Sorrow were denounced upon our Sex; as a punishment for the transgression of Eve. I have sometimes thought that we were formed to experience more exquisite Sensations than is the Lot of your Sex. More tender and susceptable by Nature of those impression[s] which create happiness or misiry, we Suffer and enjoy in a higher degree. I never wondered at the philosopher who thanked the Gods that he was created a Man rather than a Woman."[23] Abigail could luxuriate in her heart's susceptibility, but, when she was enduring John's more protracted absence, she said that she had "a Heart too susceptible for its own repose"; in fact, she believed her sensibility to be even more acute than that of other women. She wrote Mercy Otis Warren that she sometimes wished "the wisdom of the continent had made choise of some person whose seperation from his partner would have little or no pain, or mortification—many such might have been found I dare say." The following year she exclaimed: "My habitation, how disconsolate it looks! My table I set down to it but cannot swallow my food. O Why was I born with so much Sensibility and why possessing it have I so often been call'd to struggle with it?"[24]

Polly Rogers, Abigail's young Massachusetts contemporary, was brought to the same point, her consciousness of her susceptibility to emotional pain drawing on her sentimental reading. In 1785, she recorded sending "the amiable Woodbridge his shirt and a letter—What the Consequence is I know not." It seems she was trying to win him back. Apparently sick with her sense of loss, or even mere uncertainty, she turned to the kind of book the doctor thought would help: "Read in a *sweet novel* the D[octor] brought me. It affected me so, I could hardly read it, and was often obliged to drop the book to suppress my grief!" Among the novels she recorded reading was Sterne's *Sentimental Journey*. Behaving as a sentimental heroine, or, rather, as authors knew their readers did, she "*thot* of the Lovely Woodbridge—shed a *torrent* of tears—at the *Recollection* of past interviews with him." Did she select the underlined words from the sweet and deeply affecting novel that brought out her grief? She then re-created what she recollected: "[Woodbridge] press'd me to his *Bosom* with a *fondness* I thought expressive of approbation [she

quotes him] *never never* P[oll]y hesitate a *moment* to Let me Know if 'tis
in my power to make you happy! Would you would you no Sir! Said I,
at the same time kissing his Hand with *trembling* Lips! . . . I flew to my
Chamber, & with the *avidity* of a *Lover opened* the Seal and read! Shed-
ing tears as I read." After it was clear that Woodbridge had, in Kerber's
phrasing, "transferred his affections to someone else," Polly questioned
the extent of her emotional pain in the same terms as Abigail employed,
informed by the literature they both knew so well: "O had I less sensibility I should not *feel* so much, nor so *severely* my present situation."[25]

The African-British letter writer Ignatius Sancho, who modeled his
writing on Sterne, wrote a female friend of a mutual acquaintance: "Lydia
is exceedingly unwell—They who have least sensibility are best off in
this world." But, of course, in the same paragraph, he wished his correspondent: "May you know no pain but of sensibility!"[26] The apparent
complaints against possession of sensibility were a convention of later
sentimental novels, too. The heroine of Samuel Relf's *Infidelity* (Philadelphia, 1797) wished: "Oh, that I were cased against sensibility, that
thereby I might endure without a sigh these meditated marks of indifference." Susanna Rowson exclaimed in *Trials of the Human Heart* (Philadelphia, 1798): "Oh! How blest the heart whose sensibility has never been
awakened, who, though dead to all the joys of love and friendship, feels
not the pang of disappointment, or the piercing sting of ingratitude."[27]

Abigail also cast her struggles against her sensibility in the terms supplied by the idealization of Roman matrons, signified by her taking the
name "Portia." But the virtues of a Roman matron identifiable with stoicism had been modified, as had those of the male equivalent, Cato.[28] It
was along these lines that Carter had qualified her praise of Epictetus.
Fordyce, representing the view of Scottish moralists, said that Roman
matrons had been regarded "as the summit of human excellence and felicity," from which "the female mind" "might derive" "force or gran-
deur." But such qualities were, in this view, "far overbalanced by the
loss or the diminution of that gentleness and softness, which ever were
and ever will be the sovereign one of the female character." "Portia" was
susceptible to Fordycean sensibility. She wrote John in France in 1782:
"My dear Sir, when I can conquer the too soft sensibility of my Heart, I
feel loth you should quit your station until an Honorable peace is established." She was capable of applying what, very significantly, had been
adopted as the conventional phrase for a woman of excessive sensibility, saying in 1785 that Mrs. Amelia Bromfield Rogers, an American she

met in London, had "too much of 'the tremblingly alive all over' to be calculated for the rough Scenes of Life." She took the phrase she quoted from a line of Pope's *Essay on Man*, and, in 1788, Wollstonecraft used it the same way.[29]

Abigail may well have felt that Fordyce was addressing herself in his sermon 13: "Where an easiness of temper is particularly prevalent, and the heart uncommonly susceptible of warm emotions in the way of love and friendship; there, without question, a peculiar strain of prudence and fortitude is required, to prevent a young person's being betrayed into great inconveniences, and dangerous tendencies." He warned against another kind of emotional overload, "when the heart overflows with gaiety" and there was a "danger of its bursting its bounds." It, too, required "the check of self-command," although a young woman could "resort to the company of the sober and sedate" and there find help in "restraint." Abigail believed that women's sensibility allowed them to "enjoy in a higher degree" of pleasure, expressed, for instance, in that letter describing her dropping her pen out of feeling or the one describing it as the "secret charm" of "sympathetic power." But she also looked to John's stern, manly virtue to help her restrain herself, even as she also resented his refusal or inability to be more effusive in his expression of feeling to her.[30]

Those expressions of wishes for insensibility were disingenuous; in fact, they were expressions of the great moral value that sentimental heroines and actual women of feeling placed on the exquisiteness of their sensibility. But, despite her use of such a convention, Abigail's intrapsychic struggles over her sensibility were real. She both prized her sensibility and recognized that it made her painfully dependent. Early in 1784, agonizing over whether she should cross the ocean to rejoin John in Europe, she wrote him:

> coward as I am; without Husband or son to protect or support me; it is one thing to encounter dangers or difficulties with you; and an other without you.
>
> With such a Heart Susceptable of every tender impression, and feelingly alive, have I so often been called to stand alone and support myself through Scenes which have almost torn it asunder, not I fear, because I have more resolution or fortitude than others, for my resolution often fails me and my fortitude wavers.

A woman's standing alone was precisely what was at issue in the sentimental and antisentimental arguments, respectively, of Fordyce and Wollstonecraft.[31]

## Abigail's Wish

Abigail told John directly that she wanted his letters to express more feeling: "All the Letters I receive from you seem to be wrote in so much haste, that they scarcely leave room for a social feeling. They let me know that you exist, but some of them contain scarcely six lines. I want some sentimental Effusions of the Heart. I am sure you are not destitute of them or are they all absorbed in the great publick. You used to be more communicative a Sundays, I always loved a Sabeth days letter, for then you had a greater command of your time." John had given her such effusions of the heart in that July 7, 1775, letter that Abigail said was "the longest and therefore most Sentimental." He constantly sent her explanations, apologies, and excuses for why he did not write her as often or as effusively as she wished. For example, in 1775: "I am often afraid you will think it hard that I don't write oftener to you. But it is really impossible. Could I follow the Inclinations of my Heart I should spend half my Time in this most agreeable and pleasurable Employment: But Business presses me so close that I am necessitated to mortify myself. From 7 to ten in the Committees and from six to ten in the Evening in the same, and from 10 to four in the Congress. Many Letters to write too upon Business." He told her that she could get "News" from the "public Papers" of events that "the strongest Ties of Honour, Virtue and Love of my Country" obliged him "to keep secret." Here and elsewhere, he was able to explain to Abigail and to himself that morality was on his side in choosing work for the public good rather than following his heart's inclination, that is, to give Abigail what she asked, because his work for the public good required him to lay aside such personal, familial feeling.[32]

John did write Abigail in 1779 that he had recalled the anniversary of his departure for France, although less precisely than she, writing her on February 9: "It is now a year within a Day or two of my Departure from home." But he was not effusive: "It is in vain for me to think of writing of what is passed." He knew what Abigail wanted of him because he had evidence during his absence from her when in Philadelphia. He answered this unspoken request: "The Character and Situation in which I am here, and the Situation of public Affairs absolutely forbid my Writing, freely." He insisted: "I must be excused. So many Vessels taken, and there are so many Persons indiscreet, and so many others inquisitive, that I may not write." Then he appealed to her on the grounds of suffering, turning the tables on her: "God knows how much I suffer for Want of Writing to you. It used to be a cordial to my Spirits."[33]

Abigail wished to draw him back to the personal level in the matter of style as well as substance, looking for sensibility in him. She said of her own writing: "Style I never studied. My language is warm from the *heart*, and faithful to its fires: the faithful effusion of friendship." This was consistent with Richardson's and Fordyce's definitions of woman's familiar way of writing. John thought that he "could not have written any Thing in so manly and striking a style" as Paine's *Common Sense*, "nor his Eloquent Simplicity, nor his piercing pathos," and he acknowledged, too, that his own writing was distinct from Abigail's; he wrote her in the same letter as this comment on Paine: "Your Distresses which you have painted in such lively Colours, I feel in every Line as I read."[34] This was an effect at which Abigail aimed. First telling her that her letters gave him "the greatest Pleasure"—this from Philadelphia in 1775— he continued: "And altho every one, which has yet come to Hand is replete with melancholy Tidings, yet I can truly say I never was so earnest to receive them." He admitted: "If I could write as well as you my sorrows would be as eloquent as yours, but upon my Word I cannot."[35]

Abigail told him in 1777: "ever remember with the tenderest Sentiments her who knows no earthly happiness equal to being tenderly beloved by her dearest Friend."[36] She complained of the paucity of his "tender tokens" to alleviate his painful absence in 1778 and of having to take up the pen herself to "relieve a Heart too susceptible for its own repose." She had hoped that his writing frequently to her would be valuable to him for the same reason it was to her, "a release to you after the cares of the day, to converse with your Friend." She sent other forms of positive reinforcement, telling him (after she asked to be informed "constantly of every transaction" in 1776 Philadelphia): "Every expression of tenderness is a cordial to my Heart. Unimportant as they are to the rest of the world, to me they are *every Thing*."[37] Once, three of John's letters arrived together, and Abigail felt her "sufferings amply rewarded in the tenderness" he expressed for her, even though one of them brought her intense emotional pain: "In one of your Letters you have drawn a picture which drew a flood of tears from my Eyes, and rung my Heart with anguish inexpressible."[38]

How John wrote to Abigail remained an issue between them in 1795, one they both associated with gender differences. Abigail had complained about John's letter describing their son Charles: "The account you gave me of Charles situation, and increasing business was very agreeable to me. You did not mention Sally [Charles's wife]." She saw this neglect as a male characteristic: "Gentleman are not half [as] particular as the

Ladies are in their details." In fact, she went on, the American minister for foreign affairs had also "found fault" with John. The reason? "You was not minute enough in your description of the looks, behaviour &c of those with whom your business connected you." She noted that John had tried to supply more such details of his work in France, even relating how he had handed "Madam La Countess, to Table." This was a sharp reminder of John's insensitivity to Abigail in his praising French women long ago. Here, however, she allowed that diplomacy might have required him to be insensible: "I cannot but figure to myself how immoveable and like the Marble Medallion you ought to keep your countenance whilst differing parties address you." Her simile resembled her sarcastic accusation that the unresponsive John would "have changed Hearts with some frozen Laplander" if he could, and she had used the conventional simile of a "stone" to characterize others who lacked sensibility.[39]

John tried to say something of Sally in his reply to this: "Your new Daughter behaves prettily in her new Sphere. . . . Mrs. Adams shewed me an elegant bed which she politely said she had made up for me." He knew this was not what Abigail wanted: "As to the details in which you say the Ladies excel Us. I have not Patience." Well, not the kind of patience she wanted: "I who have the Patience of Job, have not Patience to write in the style of Grandison or Lovelace." Abigail had contrasted John to her ideal of Grandison earlier in their marriage and now to conflate this paragon of sensibility with the archetypal rake was nearly to sneer at her wishes in this regard. Rakes made themselves trusted by ladies by writing to them as if they were men of sensibility attentive to women's wishes. This apprehension shaped John's response to Abigail's report of Tyler's literary "courtship" of her in his attempt to win their daughter's heart.[40]

Abigail warned John early in their relationship to "never say a severe thing" lest he wound her feeling heart. She illustrated the kind of restraint ideally exercised by a person of sensibility, the kind he was to show her in her April 17, 1777, letter. She was pregnant, which brought her "many anxieties," and reminded him of a promise he had made to be with her under these "particular circumstances." She then referred to Mrs. Howard," a Lady for whom I knew you had great respect," whose death "yesterday" was "to the inexpressible Grief of her Friends": "She was delivd of a Son or Daughter . . . yesterday week, a mortification in her Bowels occasiond her Death. Everything of this kind naturally shocks a person in similar circumstances. How great the mind that can overcome the fear of Death!" After elaborating this picture of her own circumstances, including her apprehension of leaving her "family of young and helpless children," she declared: "But I will quit [the] Subject least it should excite painfull Sensations in a Heart that I would not willingly wound." Despite this claim of sensibility, this again was virtual *occupazio*, the denial of wounding sharpened by her reminder of his broken promise.[41]

Abigail was able to thank John later that year for a letter that gave her "a most agreeable Sensation": "It was because my Heart was softned and my mind enervated by my sufferings, and I wanted the personal and tender soothings of my dearest Friend, that [ren]derd it so valuable to me at this time. I have [no] doubt of the tenderest affections or sincerest regard of my absent friend, yet an expression of that kind will sooth my Heart to rest amidst a thousand anxieties." The editors supplied the *no*, Abigail's omission of which could well have been a telling Freudian slip. She felt particularly vulnerable because of the troubling symptoms of the very late stage of a pregnancy, soon to end in a stillbirth.[42]

We can see Abigail's wishes for more sentimental effusions from John as her particular version of the insistent representation in her contemporary sentimental literature of women's conversion of too stern, too hard men to a greater degree of sensibility, which they could then share with women.[43] That this could be merely a frustrated hope is suggested by the marriage of Grace Growden Galloway, who, during the 1750s and 1760s, wrote sentimental poems expressing her desperate unhappiness with her husband, the loyalist Joseph Galloway. Her daughter explained it by telling her children: "Your grandfather was a good man, but your G[ran]-mother . . . had great sensibility."[44] This disparity was also a theme in sentimental literature, originating, perhaps, in the complaints against Sir John Brute in Vanbrugh's *The Provoked Wife*, and demonstrated in Clarissa's rejection of Solmes as a suitor. In 1780, Abigail posed a woman with a "Bosom of Sensibility and Innocence" against "a Gambling Rake, . . . the most Profligate of the Sex," and the same apprehension would shape the Adamses' ultimate rejection of Tyler's suit. That a woman's wish for a husband of greater sensibility persisted is symbolized by Margaret Fuller's 1843 story of the marriage between Mariana and Sylvain, although she recognized, too, that the disparity could exist between a refined husband and a "coarse" wife of "low habits."[45]

Clearly, Abigail hoped an appeal to John on the basis of his having sensibility would carry weight with him. The same can be said of a December 1777 letter she wrote to James Lovell, a congressional delegate from Massachusetts, focused on the news of John's about to be separated from her. Congress had selected him to be "commissioner at the court of France." Lovell, a member of the Congressional Committee for Foreign Affairs, had written to John at the Adamses' Braintree house to "press your acceptance of the Commission which has this day been voted you." Lovell appealed to Hutchesonian values: "The great sacrifices which you have made of private happiness has encouraged them to hope you will undertake this business." Later in the letter, he returned more specifically to that private subject, well aware of Abigail's likely response: "I am ripe in hope about your acceptance, however your dear amiable Partner may be tempted to condemn my Persuasion of you to distance yourself from her farther than Baltimore or York Town." Lovell attempted to mitigate his culpability by telling Adams that "Brother Geary"—his fellow delegate Elbridge Gerry—had been still more in a hurry to notify him: "He threatens to take his Pen in hand because I am not enough urgent with you; he feels all the Callosity of a Bachelor. I am but too ready to pardon his hard-heartedness on this occasion where the eminent Interest of my Country is pleaded to excuse for him."[46]

Abigail took it on herself to reply because John was away, but Lovell had known that she would read the letter. Her first sentence described the action of Congress to Lovell as "your plot against [Mr. Adams]." It had caused Abigail what one of her biographers calls "the most difficult moment of her life." She chose the terms of sensibility to address the friend who brought her this critical news: "O Sir you who are possessed of Sensibility, and a tender Heart, how could you contrive to rob me of all my happiness?"[47]

In this, Abigail capitalized on Lovell's claim to feel more, but, in fact, she suggested that, if he truly was a man of sensibility, truly tenderhearted, he could not have joined with others in attempting to get John to take up public business at her expense. Furthermore, she was more ready than Lovell to forgive Gerry his entire lack of feeling: "I can forgive Mr. Geary because he is a stranger to domestick felicity and knows no tenderer attachment than that which he feel[s] or his country, tho I think the Stoickism which every Batchelor discovers ought to be attributed to him as a fault." Much later, when John was president in Philadelphia and Abigail remained at home in Quincy, she wrote him that they sighed separately, "without being able to afford each other any comfort, or Genial warmth." He had told her he was "fractious," and she responded that "nothing tends so much to render a Man Fractious as living without Females about him." Women knew, she continued, "how . . . to Sooth into good humour the jarring elements," the latter a phrase from Pope's

*Essay on Man* quoted by John on his *Discourses on Davila*, although, in this case, Abigail's agent is woman, not God. She shared the widespread hope that men learn more tender attachments from women as wives, augmented subsequently by their attachments to their children, in accordance with the psychology laid out by the Scottish moralists.[48]

John himself believed that having a "dearly beloved Wife and four young children, excited Sentiments of tenderness, which a father and a Lover only can conceive, and which no language can express." So, too, John Quincy explained to Nabby the fact that the unmarried John Winthrop, the librarian and a governor of Harvard, was "without one particle of softness, or anything that can make a man amiable, in him." He had heard from others that Winthrop was "severe in his remarks upon the ladies," as they were to him. Womenless men, he asserted, were "apt to despise, what they are wholly ignorant of. . . . Old bachelors too . . . are apt to talk of sour grapes; but if Mr. W. ever gets married, he will be more charitable towards the ladies." This is what Aunt Shaw predicted of the young, unmarried John Quincy himself. He completed his analysis of Winthrop by suggesting that, if he were thus softened up by a wife, he could carry the effects out into his other relationships.[49]

Abigail wanted men generally to have sensibility. She wished not only preachers, but also "Politicians, friends, Lovers and Husbands," to have and show "all Sensations which sweeten as well as embitter our probationary State!" Sentimental literature made central the conversion of men to sensibility at the hands of sentimental heroines. Such a wish would help sustain women in their subsequent efforts to reform men by an array of humanitarian societies.[50]

Abigail's varied assertions to John that she knew that he was a man of sensibility were powered by her wishfulness, or the wish that he was more so. Abigail said that she wanted to maintain John's health and to watch over him when he was sick, "to soften his repose." He had written her prior to their marriage, showing a connection in his mind between, on the one hand, such softening and tending and, on the other, the "refinement" of his sentiments, an improvement in his social affections: "You who have always softened and warmed my Heart, shall restore my Benevolence as well as my Health and Tranquility of mind. You shall polish and refine my sentiments of Life and Manners, banish all the unsocial and ill natured Particles in my Composition, and form one to that happy Temper, that can reconcile a quick Discernment with a perfect Candour." This was the womanly role that Fordyce endorsed and Wollstonecraft repudiated.[51]

Abigail may have been able to forgive Gerry for his ignorance of the tenderer attachment, but she still maintained that his "Stoickism" was a fault, in keeping with the culture of sensibility's origins and continuing standards. In that 1777 letter to Lovell, Abigail had imagined Gerry's asking whether he was not happier than a married man: "For tho destitute of the highest felicity in life, he is not exposed to the keen pangs which attend a Seperation from our dear connexions. This is reasoning like a Batchelor still." It was also to restate her experience of her own sensibility, the source of the highest felicity (expressed, e.g., in her ecstatic pen-dropping letter to John, in her response to the Hallelujah Chorus, and to Trumbull's "Death of General Warren"), but, by the same token, the source of so much pain that she could ask, "O Why was I born with so much Sensibility?"[52]

Abigail then turned to Lovell's feelings as a married man "who so lately had experienced what it was to be restored to your family after a painfull absence from it, and then in a few weeks torn from it by a call from your Country." The British had imprisoned him because of his revolutionary views, and, on his release, he was elected to Congress. (In his five years in Congress, he "never once returned to Boston to see his wife and children." Akers suggests that this was because he needed "income and position," McCullough adding that he "enjoyed the company of several women in Philadelphia.")[53] Abigail remarked with apparent praise: "You disinterestedly obeyed the Summons." She then asked him rhetorically: "But how could you so soon forget your sufferings and place your Friend in a more painfull situation considering the Risk and hazard of a foreign voyage. I pittied the conflict I saw in your mind, and tho a Stranger to your worthy partner sympathized with her and thought it cruel in your Friends to insist upon such a Sacrifice." Lovell, then, was being cruel, but Abigail characteristically backed off this implication, so contrary to the sensibility with which she had credited him, and she attributed his attempted persuasion to republican values: "I know Sir by this appointment you mean the publick good, or you would not thus call upon me to sacrifice my tranquility and happiness." This little paragraph began with a concession, but, in its second clause, she squarely replaced Lovell's own focus on the sacrifice he was asking of John with the sacrifice that only implicitly he had asked of Abigail.[54]

His sacrifice, Abigail then noted, had earned John "the esteem of his Country." Her wishes that he confine his abilities "to private life" were more "selfish" but, she suggested, were "according to his [John's] own inclinations." She could reap the rewards of public life only vicariously.

She had, she wrote Lovell, "often experienced the want of [John's] aid and assistance in the last 3 years of his absence," still more so as their children were growing. "And can I Sir consent to be separated from him whom my Heart esteems above all earthly things, and for an unlimited time? My life will be one continued scene of anxiety and apprehension, and must I cheerfully comply with the Demand of my Country?" How much choice did she have, aside from whether it was made cheerfully or not? She had detected Lovell's answer to this question: "I know you think I ought, or you [would] not have been accessory to the Call."

But, finally, she could report her abilities to think about it more philosophically: "I have improved this absence [of John's] to bring my mind to bear on the Event with fortitude and resignation." Abigail comments on her own letter in terms that she assumes she can write to a person of sensibility: "I beg your Excuse Sir, for writing thus freely, it has been a relief to my mind to drop some of my sorrows through my pen, which had your friend been present would have been poured only into his bosom." This passage illustrates that correspondents' possession of sensibility allowed them the freedom to express a greater range of sentiments, to experience such freedom as "relief," to insist on the sheer physical dimension of such self-expression, in this case again through the handheld pen, and to combine the near pleasure of relief with the pain of sorrow. Abigail also suggested to Lovell that she resented John's absence in the context of preceding passages, for example, about her "want" of his aid and assistance, and that she was willing to put Lovell in John's place of emotional intimacy.

Abigail wrote to Lovell in this way because he presented himself to her as a man of sensibility. He had adjured her: "Call me not a Savage, when I inform you that your 'Allarms and Distress' have afforded me *Delight*. I assure you, Ma'am, that my Intimates think me not devoid of the most tender Sensibilities." Here he paused to suggest that she may have been looking for something different, non- (or less) sexualized, from him: "But, if you expect that your Griefs should draw from me only sheer Pity, you must not send them to call upon me in the most elegant Dresses of Sentiment and Language; for, if you persist in your present course, be it known to you before hand, that I shall be far more prompt to admire than to compassionate Them."[55] The editors of the Adams correspondence note that, even in the context of a "streak of flirtatiousness" and women's "notable susceptibility to flattery," Abigail's enjoyment of Lovell's "queer sort of gallantry"—he was "an addict of Shandean suggestiveness"—and her "acceptance with only mock protests of a constant flow of letters from him in this view" meant that she ran "considerable risks."[56]

We can see their correspondence as the eighteenth-century type that Maynard Mack labels *epistolary gallantry*. Abigail had wished John to be more Grandisonian in his courtship of her and wanted him to write letters to her more like those of heroes of feeling in Richardson's epistolary novels. Knott describes the same type of correspondence between young Philadelphia women and men, notably alluding to Sterne, to demonstrate the existence there of sentimental culture. It was a convention that Abigail put to existential use. Shaw writes that, "in compensation" for John's absence and inadequacies as a correspondent, Abigail adopted a "literary style of her age," indulging "herself in a sentimental correspondence in a mode borrowed from Laurence Sterne." Lovell's name was "as suggestive as Richardson's Lovelace." Ferling suggests that Abigail began to write Lovell because she was particularly despondent over John's absence and sought in her words "to Give sorrow vent," although she was also "intrigued by this rakish man." It had been Clarissa's clandestine correspondence with Lovelace that initiated the series of events culminating in her rape. At the same point where Abigail had said she preferred men capable of "all Sensations" to "cold phlegmatic" men, she had swerved into doubts about men of feeling: "May I ask if the same temperament and the same Sensibility which constitutes a poet and a painter will not be apt to make a Lover and a Debauchee?"[57]

Like Sterne, Lovell combined sensibility with more explicit sexual suggestiveness. In a later letter to Abigail that first told her, "I know that *you* judge from Sensibilities to which the herd of worldlings, are intire strangers," Lovell noted that it had been "near 11 months" since John left her in Braintree and confessed: "I find myself relieved by that period from a certain anxiety, which was founded on my tenderness towards your dear Sex that Mr. A's *rigid patriotism* had overcome." This was double entendre; presumably, it would have been John's wish to breed more children for the state that would have led his erect penis to impregnate Abigail. Lovell continued: "He used, in that Spirit to contemplate with pleasure, a circumstance in you [being pregnant], the like of which in Mrs. L[ovell] aggravated my absence from home exceedingly. In spight therefore of his past reproofs to me, I will take pleasure in your *Escape*." His claim to particular sympathy for women (and defiance of masculine authority) coupled with sexual suggestiveness was a very rakish technique.[58]

Abigail responded to this with conventional sentimental language:

"In reply to a certain congratulation, can only say that the Idea of suffering for those who are dear us beyond the power of words to express, raise sensibilities in the Heart which are blendid with a delicate pleasing Melancholy, and serve to mitigate the curse upon us." This muted Lovell's sexual point, in fact, transformed it into proper, biblical terms. The language of sensibility, even when apparently espousing emotional freedom, properly showed adherence to formal limits, in fact, to delicacy, as Abigail's exchange with Jefferson over Polly's death has illustrated. Lewis says the same of the expression of sentiment among Virginian gentry in general.[59]

Sheridan's contemporary *The School for Scandal* (1777) provides a useful perspective on Abigail's correspondence with Lovell. It was a play that had absorbed Sterne's development of sensibility and was soon to demonstrate its own influence on Tyler, Abigail's near son-in-law. In the play, Lady Teazle seems to rebuff Joseph Surface: "You know I admit you as a lover no farther than fashion sanctions." To this he replies: "True—a mere Platonic cisisbeo [companion]—what every wife is entitled to." Lady Teazle replies to that: "Certainly one must not be out of the fashion." "However," she continues, "even though Sir Peter's [her husband's] ill-humour may vex me ever so, it shall never provoke me to—" commit adultery, expressed, in Joseph's completion of her sentence, as "the only revenge in your power." That reminds us of the element of resentment in Abigail's feelings about her own husband's leaving her, a feeling she expressed to Lovell.[60]

But the most salient aspect of her December 1777 letter to Lovell at this point was her appeal to him in the matter of John's posting by Congress. Lovell had protested: "Must I suppress Opinion, Sentiment and just Encomium upon the Gracefulness of a lovely suffering Wife or Mother? It seems I must or be taxed as a flatterer." In fact, Abigail had appealed to him as a suffering wife and mother, as, indeed, she appealed to John. One theme in sentimental literature, from *The Spectator* through Richardson, Sterne, and their followers, was that women's asking men for pity, presenting themselves tearful, drooping, languid—even sickening and subordinate—turned men on, particularly the rakishly inclined. This was merely an exaggeration of the gendered sensibility that Fordyce recommended.[61]

Just as his letter acknowledged that Abigail could interpret his words as hard or soft, savage or sensitive, so Lovell attributed to her a choice of self-presentation to him. Abigail, Lovell suggested by way of the sexually charged metaphor of "dress," had chosen to write him in sentimental language. That she was capable of coming very close to charging such language sexually is clear in her letters to John. That, too, she had at times the power to put on or lay aside the sentimental strain is also evident. On the other hand, it was clear to her as well as to us that often she found it impossible to control the way she poured out her feelings. The possibilities here are complicated by the fact of her continuous and powerful resentment over John's leaving her in favor of public business.

Another, larger point may be made because of some similarity of the epistolary gallantry between the married Abigail Adams and James Lovell to that between the married Maria Cosway and Thomas Jefferson. Cosway, although having great admiration for her husband's art (Richard Cosway was "one of the most successful of any artist based in London in the last two decades of the eighteenth century"), was fundamentally thwarted by him, too, and found in Jefferson an admiring correspondent to whom she could express her feelings because he presented himself to her as a man of sensibility. Jefferson compared himself explicitly to Sterne in relation to his "Maria." If cultures of sensibility came into existence in large part as manifestations of women's wishes, Abigail and Maria Cosway illustrate how they supplied the language women wanted for emotional relief, for the communication of particular feelings to men (as well as to women), and even for emotional equality, not to say superiority. Of course, women ran risks, not the least because men could turn such communication to their own purposes.[62]

## CHAPTER 7

# Sensibility and Reform

## Entertaining Reform

Abigail's continuing wish for more sensibility from John is one perspective from which to view her now well-known "Remember the Ladies" letter of March 31, 1776.[1] It was a typical wish of the gendered culture of sensibility, widely articulated in the modes I have described. Ministers like Collier, other Latitudinarians, Wesley, Whitefield, Fordyce, and Bacon preached the reformation of manners to women in response to their pursuit of public consumer pleasures but also to the rakes who they feared preyed on them and on women generally. They preached, too, the reformation of all men, of a popular male culture they deemed barbaric, hard, and violent.

One vehicle for reform had been the tea table, in both metropolitan Britain and Britain's American colonies. As we saw, the authors of the *Spectator* had associated their venture—its goal, the reformation of manners—with the "tea-equipage." Its dates, 1710–11 and 1714, remind us that its context was the libertinism addressed by Collier and the Society for the Reformation of Manners. Ladies pursuing pleasure had to reform, too, but in conjunction with degrees of consumer pleasure: "Fashionable hostesses replaced popular amusements with the more refined pursuits of literary conversation and tea drinking."[2] According to Shields, such heterosocial minglings became nodes for wider reform, one purpose being the cultivation of "sympathy" in men as well as in women: "The movement of masses of genteel ladies out-of-doors marked [a] revision in the manners of the town. . . . In British America's provincial capitals, women forced innovation in the conduct of diversion, . . . [opposing] gentility to crudity." First motivated by pleasure, the tea table became "the superintending agency in the spread of manners and taste among British American women by the 1720s." Shields suggests that middle-class women's access to public places in Boston, for example, was the fruit of tea-table networking and the transformation of one of its pleasures, gossip, to the serious purpose that would be attractive to men, instead of provoking their hostility. By midcentury, "tea drinking became a popular habit, . . . not limited to the tables of the elite," one in which women exercised the ritualistic power implied by the contemporary naming of teatime as the "unfortunate shrine of female devotion." Men who spent too much time drinking tea with women ran the risk of effeminacy; such effeminate tea drinkers were "stock comic characters" of the period.[3]

Brown describes "Tea-Table Discourses" hosted by white women in Virginia and cites a letter published in a 1737 issue of the *Virginia Gazette* describing a "Company of Young Ladies" who were "met to pay their Visits and drink their beloved Tea." One subject was the kind of sermon on "the subjects of fashion and pride" that would be reiterated throughout the century, keeping pace with women's part in the consumer revolution. A male guest at a Virginia tea party remarked that the discourses there "ended in Detraction," which provoked the ladies, acknowledging the effect of caffeine, to retort, "Men are addicted to worse things than we," that is, their drinking alcohol in taverns.[4]

The other ladies hosting the tea parties characteristic of their class and including at least some men had common ground with the refined men Bushman describes, who wished to show their "wit, vivacity, taste, and sensibility" in conversation and wanted young women to be educated to a point where they could "afford great pleasure in their Conversation with others." Those enlightened Scots argued that men could, thus, enhance their social skills, to be implemented in a marriage market where women's wishes increasingly had more weight. Such skills were invaluable in business, too. Gentlemen had other reasons to attempt to reform the boisterous, even politically assertive manners of men generally, as John Adams illustrated. According to Teute, later-eighteenth-century American salons "inculcated standards of civil society, moderating political incivilities and tempering the hierarchical tendencies of gentility with the moral conduct of republican virtue." All this made for common ground between the sexes, provoking in their opponents the bogeys of masculine women and effeminate men.[5]

Sentimental literature embodied the same purpose as the reformative tea table. Women wanted men to be more conscious of women's feelings, to become men of feeling in accordance with the heroes so constantly held up by sentimental literature, as Abigail held Sir Charles Grandison up to John. The tea table, other heterosocial gatherings, and literature, as well as the sermons preached by Crane's divines and their successors, together seem to have been powerful influences on manners and on self-conception—at least that is what participants, writers, readers, congregants, and subscribers to the societies for the reformation of manners hoped. They could rely, too, on the powerful updraft from aspirants to gentility.

## Remember the Ladies

Earlier in her 1776 letter, Abigail had discussed the war in Virginia, asking John whether that colony was so "situated as to make an able Defence." She thought it was populated by "Gentery Lords and . . . vassals" and asked: "are they not like the uncivilized Natives Brittain represents us [Massachusetts inhabitants] to be?" She hoped that Virginia's "Riffel Men who have shown themselves very savage and even Blood thirsty, were not a specimen of the Generality of the people." Those riflemen were specimens of a male culture against which "civilized" American men of feeling defined themselves.[6] Abigail also expressed a qualm about Virginia slaveholders, immediately after she praised Washington: "I have sometimes been ready to think that the passion for Liberty cannot be Eaquelly Strong in the Breasts of those who have been accustomed to deprive their fellow Creatures of theirs." Abigail was "certain that it"—slaveholders' passion for liberty—"is not founded upon that generous and Christian principal of doing to others as we would that others should do unto us." Her first sentence resembles Dr. Johnson's expression of the same sentiment in his rhetorical, "How is it we hear the loudest yelps for liberty among drivers of negroes?" in his pamphlet, "Taxation No Tyranny," a "quasi-official" British response to the grievances and resolves issued by the first Continental Congress in 1774. John wrote "the final draft" of these documents, and it seems likely that Abigail had read Johnson's response prior to writing that sentence in her 1775 letter.[7] Still, the year before, Abigail had written John to report "a conspiracy of the Negroes" in Boston and commented: "I wish most sincerely there was not a Slave in the province. It always appeared a most iniquitous Scheme to me—fight ourselfs for what we are daily robbing and plundering from those who have as good a right to freedom as we have." Evidently, she had told him this before: "You know my mind upon this Subject." In fact, both Dr. Johnson and Abigail Adams were two among hundreds of others who pointed out the "monstrous inconsistency" in white Americans' claiming liberty for themselves while keeping black people enslaved.[8] In any case, Abigail's expression of apprehension over male revolutionaries' keeping fellow creatures in bondage was the precedent for her raising the issue of men's treatment of another group of fellow creatures.[9]

Abigail then described the condition of Boston, now that the British had evacuated it. She described her sense of personal liberation. "I feel a gaieti de Coar, to which before I was a stranger." How far might she pursue such happiness?

She opened the paragraph in which she expressed her desire that John and his fellow male legislators would attend the wishes of "Ladies": "Tho we felicitate ourselves, we sympathize with those who are trembling least the Lot of Boston be theirs. But they cannot be in similar circumstances unless pusillanimity and cowardice should take possession of them." The recent history of Boston should be salutary: "They have time and warning given them to see the Evil and shun it." A dash then introduced the wish: "I long to hear that you have declared an independancy." Inspired by Boston to large-mindedness and bravery, the legislators were to rise above trembling out of pusillanimity and cowardice and succumbing to British triumph. A second dash showed her next thought to be an associated one, that is, a second effect of learning to stand up against a weakness manifested in trembling, a resistance that had led her to her personal sense of liberation: "and by the way in the new Code of Laws which I suppose it will be necessary for you to make I desire you would Remember the Ladies, and be more generous and favorable to them than your ancestors. Do not put such unlimited power into the hands of the Husbands. Remember, all Men would be tyrants if they could." There is an element of insistence, even imperiousness, in "I desire you," and, if Abigail at first merely asked John and his fellows to reorient themselves, she now introduced gender into the republican paradigm signified by "tyrants."

In his 1763 "An Essay on Man's Lust for Power," John had himself quoted the sentence, "all men would be Tyrants if they could," a line from a poem by Defoe, choosing it, he said, as "the old Maxim . . . for the Motto of this Paper." His "Meaning" was that "the selfish Passions are stronger than the social, and that the former would always prevail over the latter in any Man, left to the natural Emotions of his own Mind unrestrained and uncheck't by other Power extrinsic to himself." Shaw remarks that John's "overriding political emotion was hatred of tyranny"—John's *Discourses on Davila* reiterated the point of "Man's Lust for Power"—an attitude characteristic of the republicanism that was also the context for Wollstonecraft's full-throated expression of feminism in 1792. Of course, Abigail knew what John's "overriding political emotion" was firing his ambition for public life, and we can compare his belief that "the selfish Passions are stronger than the social" to his reading of the *Essay on Man*. My next chapter will describe Abigail's continuing struggle to reconcile herself to John's willingness to leave her in pursuit of the public good that brought him the fame he craved. Elaine Forman Crane observes of her adaptation of the Defoe line from "Man's Lust for Power": "Abigail was quite capable of such delicious irony."[10]

By 1776, the application of the term *tyranny* to men's oppression of women had a long history. Elsewhere, Abigail drew in 1778 on another metropolitan source, the Reverend John Shebbeare's *Letters on the English* (1755), to quote to John: "'Tis an inhumane Tyranny to debar [women] of the privileges of ingenious Education."[11] Poems written earlier in the century by contemporaries of Defoe referring to men's tyranny also reflected the argument made by the Cartesian feminist Poulain de la Barre's *Discourse de l'égalité des deux sexes* (translated into English in 1677) that the belief that women are inferior and should be dependent on men is "based only on interest or on custom," expressing men's prejudice. Sarah Egerton wrote:

> Say, tyrant Custom, why must we obey
> The impositions of thy haughty sway
> From the first dawn of life into the grave,
> Poor womankind's in every state a slave,
> The nurse, the mistress, parent and the swain.

And Elizabeth Thomas:

> Unhappy sex! How hard's one fate,
> By Custom's tyranny confined.[12]

Art matched life, Pope's friend Henrietta Howard writing in 1717 that, whereas her husband should have treated her with "justice as well as . . . humanity," instead he "Govern'd with Tyranny." In his "Epistle to a Lady," Pope suggested that Martha Blount, its addressee, had benefited from the fact that her parents had left her without the "pelf / That buys your sex a tyrant o'er itself." Certainly, Abigail had read this and, in all likelihood, no. 236 of the *Spectator* on "the Subject of Marriage," in which Steele gave in explanation for British youths' "treating their Wives with the most barbarous Disrespect" because they harbor "the Desire to appear to their Friends free and at Liberty, and without those Trammells they have so much ridiculed. To avoid this they . . .

grew Tyrants that they may seem Masters." Fordyce wrote that some of his female congregants called their parents "cruel and tyrannical." Widely read and influential on the revolutionary generation, Montesquieu's *The Spirit of the Laws* followed Poulain de la Barre in arguing that women were not "subject to men by the law of nature." Speaking for men, Montesquieu declared: "Our authority over women is absolutely tyrannical; they have allowed us to impose it only because they are more gentle than we are, and consequently more humane and reasonable."[13]

Art matched life in America, too. Nancy Shippen, who identified herself with "Sweet sensibility," would as a teenager in 1781 be pushed by her father into marriage with a man she did not love; unable to divorce him, like Henrietta Howard (and, one surmises, a host of trapped wives), she called herself "a wretched slave—doom'd to be the wife of a Tyrant I hate." the republican feminist Wollstonecraft would refer to "the tyranny of man" in the *Vindication of the Rights of Woman*, and, in 1800, a male republican "Citizen" in Morristown, New Jersey, asserted that the "history of women is forever obtruding on our unwilling ears, bold and ardent spirits, who no tyrant could tame, no prejudice enslave." It must be emphasized, however, that the convention of declaring men to be tyrants in their oppression of women was congruent with the still more widely known figure of virtue in distress, even as the former rhetoric implied the potential for resistance and rebellion.[14]

In her 1776 letter, Abigail drove her "desire" that John remember the ladies firmly into the heart of the innermost, personal circle of social affections, that is, into the relation of wives and husbands: "If particular care and attention is not paid to the Ladies we are determined to foment a Rebelion, and will not hold ourselves bound by any Laws in which we have no voice, or Representation." This, too, was parallel to the claims made by male American republicans, already fomenting rebellion and on the verge of declaring independence.

Abigail's next paragraph focused on explaining her letter's application to men of the term *tyrants*: "That your Sex are Naturally Tyrannical is a Truth so thoroughly established as to admit of no dispute, but such of you who wish to be happy willingly give up the harsh title of Master for the more tender and endearing one of Friend." Crane has discovered that this is, in fact, a quotation from Frances Brooke's *The History of Emily Montague* (1769), "a feminist novel" in which the heroines are outspoken and the men have sensibility. The hero, Colonel Edward Rivers, Crane writes, "is everything that John Adams is not." He has eyes "only for Montague and cannot bear to be separated from her."

It is he who speaks the lines quoted by Abigail. (Nancy Shippen copied the same passage into her journal.) Crane calls *Emily Montague* "the most tedious sentimental novel ever published," but the literary tradition it manifested had helped carry forward from the seventeenth century the feminist characterization of men as tyrants and women as figures of virtue in distress. Not coincidentally, the second of the novel's heroines is named Belinda, after the chief protagonist of Pope's *Rape of the Lock*. But Colonel Rivers also reads and quotes extensively from Madame de Maintenon's *Advice to the Duchess of Burgundy*, a contribution to the *querelle des femmes* that preceded seventeenth-century English feminism and on which Poulain de la Barre could also draw.[15]

Abigail wished men to abjure tyranny in the interest of *happiness*, another term prominent in the Declaration of Independence, its meanings derived from Locke, Hutcheson, subsequent Scottish moralists, and Sterne. Quoting Hutcheson, Garry Wills points to the Scottish moral sense school to emphasize the political value that the promotion of happiness held for Jefferson and for subsequent framers of American governments. The politicization of happiness was linked by Hutcheson to that fundamental value of cultures of sensibility, "to be pleased and happy when we reflect upon our having done virtuous actions," its converse being "to be uneasy when we are conscious of having acted otherwise." This expressed the moral sense, the motive from "self-interest" that allowed those "who duly consider it [to] pursue their own advantage wisely," such a notion derived from and perpetuated by Latitudinarian tradition and promulgated by Pope. If Abigail had not heard it from her father or read it in her husband's copy of Hutcheson, she had read something very close to it in Fordyce's *Sermons to Young Women*, where he declares that one of the higher "springs of self-love" is "the pleasure . . . of conferring felicity." This sense, Hutcheson had continued, was "the most probable means of promoting the natural good of every individual." (It was this that Tocqueville would have in mind when explaining antebellum Americans' individualism as not yet quite selfishness but the pursuit of self-interest, "rightly understood.") In Hutcheson's words: "The general happiness is the supreme end of all political union." In Abigail's condensed application to "Ladies," men who wished to promote their own "private happiness" in that innermost circle of social affection could do so by framing their new, public "Code of Laws" so that it would restrain husbands at home.[16]

The coincidence of such a legislative proposal with the goals of sentimental fiction and other expressions of the culture of sensibility is obvious. John's gender would reform its treatment of women by exchanging harsh domination for tender friendship. This hypostasized a husband/wife relationship recommended by the *Spectator* (itself responding to women's wishes) and one to which Abigail long before had asserted John should conform by calling him "Lysander." The next sentence of her letter invoked another element of the culture of sensibility, one related to her plea that men treat ladies with generosity, favor, and tenderness: "Why then, not put it out of the power of the vicious and the Lawless to use us with cruelty and indignity with impunity." *Lawless* was synonymous with the more common *licentious*, and both were close to *libertine*, in its noun form denoting the villainous proponent of values against which virtue in distress was defined. More directly, Abigail had been deeply impressed by Fordyce's *Sermons to Young Women*, which as we saw warned his audience that even men nominally reformed and who "in a sober mood were open to the tenderest feelings of humanity" gave rein to "lawless desire" when their "blood" rebelled and were "as ungovernable and fierce as any beast in the forest." Abigail seems also to have chosen *lawless* rather than *licentious* or *libertine* here in echo of her letter's addressing John's making "the new Code of Laws." Not coincidentally, Maria Edgeworth (a writer whose works were reprinted in America) would name the rake in her 1801 novel *Belinda* "Lawless," also reasserting the value of gendered sensibility to women in a revolutionary (and post-Wollstonecraftian) context.[17]

Perhaps it was in mollification, as well as in modification, that Abigail concludes her "Remember the Ladies" letter: "Men of Sense in all Ages abhor those customs which treat us only as the vassals of your Sex. Regard us then as beings placed by providence under your protection and in imitation of the Supreem Being make use of that power only for our happiness." In the same letter, Abigail has implied that Virginia slaveholders should liberate "their fellow Creatures," "vassals," that is, their slaves. This was not what she desired the Philadelphia revolutionaries to do for women. Men of sense were to retain hierarchical, literally godlike power, but, as God was now seen as the benevolent sponsor of human happiness, so men should construe themselves in their continued power over women.

In short, Abigail's "Remember the Ladies" letter called for the same reform that was so prominent throughout sentimental fiction and other manifestations of cultures of sensibility, far short of Wollstonecraft's feminism, which was centrally an assault on the gendered sensibility in which Abigail continued to believe.[18]

In answering Abigail, John first conceded the justice of her complaint about the shortness of his letters and excused himself on the grounds of "the critical State of things and the multiplicity of Avocations." He addressed her question "what Sort of Defence Virginia can make," elevating the status of those she had thought of as savage riflemen by calling them "militia and minute men" who "have been some time employed in training themselves." He gave more encouraging views of Virginia's and North Carolina's military capacity. As to the issue of Southern social structure that she had raised, he replied: "the Gentry are very rich, and the common People very poor. This Inequality of Property gives an Aristocratical Turn to all their Proceedings, and occasions a strong Aversion in their Patricians, to common Sense." Even here he reassured her: "But the Spirit of these Barons, is coming down, and it must submit." He ignored the question troubling Abigail, the obvious disparity between those barons' "passion for Liberty" and their enslavement of their "fellow Creatures."[19]

John's letter also told Abigail that hers had "given [him] some Pleasure" in her account of the burning of the solicitor general's house in Boston, going on to explain that that could act as a "warning" that "Whenever Vanity, and Gaiety, a Love of Pomp and Dress, Furniture, Equipage, Buildings, great Company, expensive Diversions, and elegant Entertainments get the better of the Principles of Men or Women there is no knowing where they will stop, nor into what Evils, natural, moral, or political, they will lead us." In this, John suggests that street violence was to be categorized with natural phenomena, a kind of providential punishment. "Men or Women" should share "Principles" in their opposition to ostentatious consumption. His introduction of gender, however, anticipated what he was about to say in response to Abigail's demand that he remember the ladies.

First, John told Abigail in answer to her description of her sense of liberation when the British withdrew from Boston: "Your Description of your own Gaiety de Coeur, charms me. Thanks be to God you have just Cause to rejoice—and may the bright Prospect be obscured by no Cloud." One can see this as the kind of sympathetic response she craved, but, notably, the significance of her feeling was the pleasure it gave her husband, in preference, say, to any connection with women's being liberated.

Then John wrote a brief paragraph on answer to another of her questions: "As to Declaration of Independence, be patient. Read our Privateering Laws and our Commercial Laws. What signifies a Word." This dismissal introduced another one: "As to your extraordinary Code of Laws, I cannot but laugh." The following August, Abigail imagined the "world perhaps would laugh at [her] and accuse [her] of vanity" for propounding a more liberal education that would produce "learned women," and, indeed, John had replied by declaring "the Femmes Scavans, are contemptible Characters," an American expression of the hostility aroused by Bluestockings and their predecessors in England, illustrated by Fordyce. Such hostility fulfilled the apprehension of women of sensibility that "the world" was made up of men hostile to their wishes. Ten years later, Nabby told John Quincy Adams: "Now do not Laugh at me, for, writing Politicks to you, and tell me I am a *dunce*, for I assure you all I mean to do is to indeavour at giving you some little information respecting *us*."[20]

John's reply to Abigail's "Remember the Ladies" continued by speaking on behalf of the white gentlemen gathered in Philadelphia: "We have been told that our Struggle has loosened the bands of Government every where. That Children and Apprentices were disobedient—that schools and Colledges were grown turbulent—that Indians slighted their Guardians and Negroes grew insolent to their Masters." The apparent connection between what Abigail had said in the same letter of Virginians' keeping their fellow creatures in slavery and her assertion of men's wish to tyrannize over women perhaps helps explain John's avoidance of that issue earlier in his reply. In effect, he repudiated the antislavery view she had expressed (and showed his willingness to join with his fellow white men from the South when he felt under attack) by disdaining the spread of the spirit of revolution to "Negroes": "But your letter was the first Intimation that another Tribe more numerous and powerful than all the rest were grown discontented.—This is rather too coarse a Compliment but you are so saucy, I wont blot it out." The coarseness lay in categorizing white ladies in the same way Indians and blacks were categorized, but Abigail's transgression of the gender line sanctioned John's contravention of the delicacy of a gentleman, which also should have restrained his laughter.

John opened his next paragraph, "Depend upon it, We know better than to repeal our Masculine systems," including those "bands of Government" that restrained women: "Altho they are in full Force, you know they are little better than Theory. We dare not exert our Power in its full Latitude. We are obliged to go fair, and softly, and in Practice you know We are the subjects. We only have the Name of Masters, and rather than give up this, which would completely subject Us to the Despotism of the Petticoat, I hope General Washington and all our brave Heroes would fight." Abigail had conceded that there were men of sense who did not treat women as vassals and who were capable of exercising generosity and fairness toward them. John here implies that he and all his fellow delegates were such men of feeling. Significantly, however, in light of Fordyce's posture and that of other men who registered the coming into existence of "feminist tendencies," John explained that the "we" who behaved thus sensibly did so owing to their fear of women ("we dare not"), and he saw the alternatives—either men have "full Force" over women, or women will be despots over men—as mutually exclusive. From the outset of his own revolutionary activities, he had wished to enjoy "perfect Peace at home," and he said that he believed that his wife's opposition would "unman" him, albeit "not wholly."[21]

In her letter to her brother about Nancy Hazen, Nabby suggested that, if a man used severity toward women, he could be suspected of having been too much influenced by them or even by his mother. To avoid such suspicion, he would have to be more responsive to his wife. For her part, Abigail had to go easy in her letters to John, apprehending and enduring not only his brevity, his silences, and his corrosiveness but also his anger. His insistence that his absences were for the public good and that, to be virtuous, a wife had to support a husband's choices rested on the "Masculine system" whose "full Force" to make those choices, even when they hurt her, he now reasserted. Ultimately, that force would be exerted by soldiers deployed to put down a rebellion by women seeking liberty: this was a joke to accompany his sarcastic laughter at her plea. John might claim that all gentlemen were men of feeling in their treatment of women, but that was to ignore the distinction her letter made between such men and "the vicious and the Lawless" who treat women "with cruelty" and who, under John's code of laws, would still be able to apply to women the full force of masculine systems.

Abigail soon replied to this, but we must bear in mind that John had written other letters to her in the meantime, including his expression of "Concern to think of the many Cares you must have upon your mind," his contrast between her achievements as "a Farmer or any Thing else you undertake" and his own "Character as a Statesman," which was "far more Problematical," his constant expressions of yearning for "domestic felicity," and that romantic desirousness in response to her own where he told her: "the Conclusion of your letter makes my Heart throb, more than a Cannonade would. You bid me burn your letters. But I must forget you first." He had also made his customary request of her for military news, and he reported to her the political and other news from Philadelphia: "Governments will be every where before Midsummer, and an end to the Royal Style." Evidently, he saw no inconsistency between the latter elements, say, and his rejection of her request that he and his fellow delegates take women into consideration when framing a government.[22]

That last sentence quoted represented in a nutshell the transition from monarchy to republicanism that Wood describes, one that had not been intended to lead to democracy. In fact, John's continuation at this point illustrated that his sharp reaction to Abigail (referring to the loosening of the bands of government) was deadly serious, in spite of its coating of jocularity: "Such Mighty Revolutions make a deep Impression on the Minds of Men and set many violent Passions at Work." He listed them, not dividing them into good and bad, as Descartes had, and including "Feeling, Sentiment, Principle and Imaginations," along with "Hope, Fear, Joy, Sorrow, Love, Hatred, Malice, Envy, Revenge, Jealousy, Ambition, Avarice, Resentment, Gratitude." Never, John wrote, "were they in more lively Exercise than they are now, from Florida to Canada, inclusively." The previous year, Abigail observed the ubiquity of "the Spirit of Liberty" among all degrees, ages, and sexes and implicitly the enslaved, too. John and his fellow gentlemen had uncorked a revolution: their acceptance of conflict, "in the market and polity too, subsequently," writes Lewis, made them "less willing to tolerate it at home. The insistence upon feminine deference revealed fears about conflict in society and nation and not just merely concern about unhappy marriages."[23]

Here, John followed his list of the violent passions that the Revolution unleashed with the prayer, "May God in his Providence overrule the whole, for the good of Mankind," feeling that he was riding in a "Whirlwind." He did not mention sex among those passions, but "Love" and "Sentiment" could have stood for it. In any case, he believed that a republican government depended on "national morality" to survive and that national morality depended on the "utmost purity and chastity in women." The newly designed republican government would depend still more on maintaining itself as a Masculine system, able to subordinate the passions of women.[24] John was provoked to this reactionary view long before his restatement of it in the still more reactionary circumstances of the 1790s, when he wrote to his son Thomas, "cautioning him against marriage"—he referred to his regret in not dictating to two others of his children when they seemed to have been following

their "wild but . . . very fickle and transient passions." That he reiterated this view may well have been influenced by his reading of Godwin's
revelations about Wollstonecraft's passions, first for Gilbert Imlay and
then for himself. John declared that the "source of revolution, democracy, Jacobinism . . . has been systematic dissolution of the true family
authority." His own failure to exercise it had been the result of his ambition for the public good, leaving the (from the Adamses' point of view)
nearly tragic entanglement of Nabby with Tyler in the oversentimental
hands of Abigail: "There can never be any regular government of a nation without a marked subordination of mothers and children to the fathers." He did not want Thomas to mention this view of his mother. If
she heard of it, she would "infallibly raise a rebellion." Her 1776 threat
had remained in his mind.[25]

Before she replied to his rebuff, Abigail wrote to Warren about her
exchange with John over improving women's legal position, introducing the subject with an account of John's unsatisfactoriness as a correspondent, a vital subject to her: "He is very sausy to me in return for a
List of Female Grievances which I transmitted to him. I think I will get
you to join me in a petition to Congress." The reference here is to the
traditional form of protest to the British government used by colonists
in the run-up to the Revolution.[26] Women had signed such documents
but none, so far, against their treatment by men, although their signing
of nonimportation agreements had included their particular interests
as women. Abigail continued: "I ventured to speak a word on behalf
of our Sex, who are rather hardly dealt with by the Laws of England
which gives such unlimited power to the Husband to use his wife Ill."
She had been consulting John's Blackstone, for instance, on coverture:
"Even the disabilities, which the wife lies under, are for the most part
intended for her protection and benefit. So great a favorite is the female
sex of the laws of England." In asking that the American legislators reform their "protection" of wives, she may well have been referring to
Blackstone's notion.[27]

Abigail told Warren that she had "requested our Legislators would
consider our case and as all Men of Delicacy and Sentiment are averse to
Exercising the power they possess"—and, in women's eyes especially,
the fundamental definition of men of feeling lay in their reformed treatment of women, including their responsiveness to women's feelings—
"yet as there is a natural propensity in Humane Nature to domination,
I thought the most generous plan was to put it out of the power of the

Arbitrary and tyranick to injure us with impunity by establishing some Laws in our favour upon just and Liberal principals." It is not clear why, in this report to Warren, she muffled the point she had made to John by ascribing the propensity to domination ("all Men would be Tyrants if they could") to "Humane nature" rather than to males, but she probably thought that Warren preferred such muffling. Abigail implied that she had not kept a copy of the letter she was here reporting: "I believe I even threatened fomenting a Rebellion in case we were not considered, and assured him we would not hold ourselves bound by any laws in which we had neither a voice, nor representation."[28]

Abigail may have not had John's reply to hand while writing to Warren, but she paraphrased it closely, from his laughing at her "Extrodonary Code of Laws" through his not blotting out his "coarse complement" because "I am so sausy," the same characterization that she applied to him in opening this part of her letter to Warren: "So I have help'd the Sex abundantly, but I will tell him I have only been making a trial of the Disintresstedness of his Virtue, and when weighed in the balance have found it wanting." In other words, she told Warren that what she asked of John in relation to women was merely a hypothetical case; her real concern was the validity of his acting above the "personal" in favor of the public good, his explanation for the brevity of his letters of which Abigail has just complained. To Warren, fellow wife and potential fellow petitioner on behalf of "the Sex," she could be more honest in the matter. She implied, it seems, that, while John will consciously believe her sole concern was his disinterestedness, he would have to act in women's favor.

To Warren, Abigail presented John's rebuttal to her wish that men formally give up some of their power, in her own words, adding a line of Pope's: "It would be bad policy to grant us greater power say they [men] since under all the disadvantages we Labour we have the ascendancy over their Hearts 'And charm by accepting, by submitting sway.'"[29] John's rejection letter had told Abigail that her "Gaiety de Coeur charm[ed] [him]" and that "we" men "are obliged to go fair, and softly, and in Practice . . . We are the subjects." Fordyce told his "fair friends" that they deceived themselves if they thought that they could take men's hearts "by storm": "When you show a sweet solicitude to please by every decent gentle, unaffected attraction; we are soothed, we are subdued, we yield ourselves your willing captives." If they betrayed "confidence" in their charms and were resolved to "force" men's admiration, they put men on their guard, and then, Fordyce warned, their "assaults are in vain."[30]

The line of poetry Abigail quoted was from Pope's "Epistle to a Lady," the same poem that referred to dowries that bought women tyrants in the form of husbands, and a poem that, as we have seen, John knew well. In the "Epistle to a Lady," Pope wrote that women's character was derived from "Nature" but that it also reflected the fact they are "by man's oppression cursed." Hence, women are ruled by two passions, the "line of pleasure and the line of sway":

> in public men sometimes are shown,
> A woman's seen in private life alone.
> Our bolder talents in full light displayed;
> Your virtues open fairest in the shade.
> Bred to disguise, in public 'tis you hide;
> There, none distinguish 'twixt your shame or pride,
> Weakness or delicacy; all so nice,
> That each may seem a virtue or a vice.

Despite his clear recognition of the profound effects of sexism on women, Pope's implicit recommendation was that women stay home and behave as Fordyce recommended and certainly not criticize their husbands directly. The line Abigail quoted was from the poem's concluding praise for a woman, actually Martha Blount, with whom the poet was in love:

> Oh! Bless'd with temper, whose unclouded ray
> Can make to-morrow cheerful as today;
> She who can love a sister's charms, or hear
> Sighs for a daughter with unwounded ear;
> She who ne'er answers till a husband cools,
> Or, if she rules him, never shows she rules;
> Charm by accepting, by submitting sways,
> Yet has her humour most when she obeys,
> Let fops or fortune fly which way they will
> . . . . . . . . . . . . . . . . . . . . . . . . . . . . . . .
> . . . Mistress of herself, though China fall.

The notion that women rule men by their soft submission, an expression of gendered sensibility, was challenged from early in the century, for example, by the feminist Mary Astell, who observed that men made themselves supplicants in courtship but, after marriage, reversed their position, making women slaves. Hogarth's paired prints *Before and After* (ca. 1731) made the same point. In writing to another woman, Abigail stated that Pope's line was merely a rationalization to keep women down. She assumed that Warren knew the "Epistle to a Lady."[31]

## "The idea of a year dissolves all my Phylosophy"

Abigail's reply to John's dismissal of her "Grievances" was dated ten days after her letter to Warren on the subject. She began by describing her loneliness and expressing the same, perhaps resentful, characterization of John's usual excuse for the brevity of his letters that she had conveyed to Warren: "How many are the solitary hours I spend, ruminating upon the past and anticipating the future, whilst you are overwhelmd with the cares of State, have but a few moments you can devote to any individual. All domestick pleasures and injoyments are absorbed in the great and important duty you owe your Country." And here Abigail quoted a long passage beginning "for our Country is as it were a secondary God . . . to be preferred to Parents, Wives, Children" and supplying the rationale for her repression of herself: "Thus do I supress every wish, and silence every Murmer, acquiescing in a painfull Seperation from the companion of my youth, and the Friend of my Heart."

She explained why she had not written for ten days: "I have not felt in a humour to entertain you. If I had taken up my pen perhaps some invective might have fallen from it." That invective would have been directed, not, nominally, against John, but against the "Lethargy" of the Boston government, but she first turned to his sexism with some directness: "I cannot say that I think you very generous to the Ladies, for whilst you are proclaiming peace and good will to Men. Emancipating all Nations, you insist upon retaining an absolute power over Wives." That she still focuses on "Wives" reflected her relation to her correspondent and, through him, to other husbands making the laws. Other categories of women may have appeared to be not so immediately subordinated to men's tyranny: it was single, propertied women who were granted the vote in New Jersey in 1776.[32] "But you must remember," she continued, "that Arbitrary power is like most other things which are very hard, very liable to be broken"—Crane points out this was Abigail's adaptation to American feminist purpose of the Marquis of Halifax's *Miscellanies*, referring to England's Glorious Revolution—"and not withstanding all your wise Laws and Maxims we have it in our power not only to free ourselves but to subdue our Masters, and without voilence throw both your natural and legal authority at our feet." Just what this power was (John has described the effects of her words on him as a "Cannon-ade") she tells him by way of the same line from Pope's "Epistle to a Lady" that she had quoted to Warren, but she added the line following it, modifying it by changing the possessive pronoun from *her* to *our*:

"Charm by accepting, by submitting sway
Yet have our Humour most when we obey."

To threaten rebellion against men's power on this basis was tantamount to acceptance of "the full Force" of "Masculine systems."[33]

To Warren in 1776, however, Abigail had presented Pope's lines as a rationalization of men's perpetuation of their unqualified tyranny over women. The context of those lines there had been Abigail's distinguish-ing between her "help[ing] the Sex abundantly"—the claim she made to her female correspondent—and telling John what, presumably, she knew he would prefer to hear, an argument to which he was more likely to respond favorably. Similarly, John had just made quite clear to her his belief in the idea that "in Practice you know We are the subjects," which she now recycled back to him.

Abigail followed the two lines of poetry with a description of the ef-fect on her of receiving several letters from John, perhaps recalling their sexual custom in former days: "They alleviate a tedious absence, and I long earnestly for a Saturday Evening, and experience a similar pleasure to that which I used to find in the return of my Friend upon that day after a weeks absence. The idea of a year dissolves all my Phylosophy." It dissolved her challenge to his power over her, or, at least, that is what she wanted him to believe, whatever she told Warren. In 1782, Abigail would write John of "the absolute power you have ever maintained over my heart." If we take her letter to him at face value, sensibility offered an argument for the reformation of men, but its very gendering also un-dercut women's power to carry it beyond wish.[34]

Wollstonecraft had faced this proclivity in herself, that is, to give in to feminine sensibility, and subsequently targeted the masculine system that undercut women in this way. One of that system's most notable proponents was Abigail's admired Fordyce, although more revolution-ary possibilities had opened up since she had read him. To illustrate what Wollstonecraft called Fordyce's "sentimental rant," she had quoted this passage from his *Sermons*, introducing it by writing that he "shall speak for himself, for thus he makes Nature address man": "Behold these smil-ing innocents, whom I have graced with my fairest gifts, and committed to your protection, . . . treat them with tenderness and honour. They are timid and want to be defended. They are frail; O do not take advantage of their weakness! Let their confidence in you never be abused." The next sentences, also quoted by Wollstonecraft, suggest rape even more explicitly and might have referred to Lovelace's rape of the drugged Clarissa, given Fordyce's special admiration for that novel: "But is it possible, that any of you can be such barbarians, so supremely wicked, as to abuse it? Can you find it in your hearts to despoil the gentle, trusting creatures of their treasure, or to do any thing to strip them of their native robe of virtue? Curst be the impious hand that would dare to violate the unblemished form of Chastity! Thou wretch! Thou ruffian! Forbear; nor venture to provoke heaven's fiercest vengeance." After "hearts," Wollstonecraft had appended the note, "Can you?—can you? Would be the most emphatical comment, were it drawled out in a whining voice," referring either to the preacher's sentimental style, or, perhaps, to his Scottish accent, or to both. She noted that she had "heard rational men use the word indecent when they mentioned" such "very sentimental passages" with "disgust."[35]

Wollstonecraft also took on Pope's view of women and the passions, although, in Valerie Rumbold's words, Pope and Wollstonecraft were "momentarily at one in identifying male oppression as the cause of women's grasping at power." But among the passages from Pope that Wollstonecraft targets in the *Vindication of the Rights of Woman* is the one Abigail quoted to both Warren and John. While there is common ground in their "portrait of modern female decadence" (common to Abigail, John, and Fordyce as well as Pope and Wollstonecraft), and while Wollstonecraft saw her book as a contribution to the reformation of manners, in referring to the *Essay on Man* and the "Epistle to Cobham," as well as the "Epistle to a Lady," she pointed out that Pope had significantly contributed to the gendering of sensibility.[36]

Three years after this exchange, John drafted a constitution for Massachusetts that has been called "the most sophisticated and influential constitution produced during the Revolutionary period." Its most clearly sentimental section, influenced by Hutcheson and his Scottish disciples, was section 2, laying out the "duty of legislators and magistrates . . . to encourage the principles of humanity and general benevolence" as well as "sincerity, good humour, and all social affections and generous sentiments among the people." There, it seems that the collective noun included both sexes, but, elsewhere, John's constitution was gender specific: "All elections ought to be free; and all the male inhabitants of this commonwealth, having sufficient qualifications, have an equal right to

elect officers, and to be elected, for public employments." Women did
not have such a right, whatever their other "sufficient qualifications."
John, then, had implemented the view that he had been provoked to articulate by Abigail's desire he remember the ladies, having written to a
delegate to the Massachusetts assembly after her "Remember the Ladies"
letter and their subsequent correspondence that to give vote to proper-
tyless men would "prove that you ought to admit women and children."
There would be "no end of it": "New claims will arise, women will demand a vote, lads from 12 to 21 will think their Rights not enough attended to." And such a cry for equality tended "to confound and destroy
all Distinction and prostrate all Ranks to one common level."[37]

The article confining the vote to "male inhabitants . . . having sufficient qualifications" was listed under "A Declaration of the Rights of
the Inhabitants of the Commonwealth of Massachusetts." Its opening
article had followed the language of the Declaration of Independence:
"All men are born equally free and independent, and have certain natural essential and unalienable rights [and so on]." Article 7 used both the
general collective term and the gender specific one, so it seems: "Government is instituted for the common good; for the protection, safety,
prosperity, and happiness of the people; and not for the profit, honor, or
private interest of any one man, family or class of men." So far, "common good" and "family" incorporated women, and the "happiness of
the people" must have done, too, its Hutchesonian meaning consistent
with the distinction and subordination of "private interest." But Adams's constitution had continued: "therefore the people alone have an
incontestable, unalienable, and indefeasible right to institute government; and to reform, after or totally change the same, when their protection, safety, prosperity and happiness require it." The powers here
signified by those transitive verbs were those John had denied to Abigail,
reserving them to "Masculine systems."[38] The possessive *their* governed
families. When taken together, the passages I have quoted, including
that one referring to humanity, social affections, and generous sentiments, as well as Adams's use of *protection*, approached what Abigail had
asked for, but they failed to address the crucial dimension in the domestic circle, a husband's power over a wife.

## CHAPTER 8

# Abigail's Perspective, Public versus Private

## Our Country Is a Secondary God

From the first, Abigail found that John's absence gave her emotional discomfort. She wrote him in August 1763: "If I was sure your absence to day was occasioned, by what it generally is, either to wait upon Company, or promote some good work, I freely confess my Mind would be much more at ease than at present it is. Yet this unease does not arise from any apprehension of Slight or neglect, but a fear least you are indisposed, for that you said should be your only hindrance." Her denial of any sense of slight or neglect indicated, perhaps, her susceptibility to such feelings and such treatment as well as her awareness that John might thus interpret her letter. It was in her next paragraph that Abigail showed her sensibility in terms of "irresistible compassion": "Humanity obliges us to be affected with the distresses and Misery of our fellow creatures." But this was to emphasize the strength of the most personal degree of feeling, the "tye" between lovers, "which makes us anxious for the happiness and welfare of those to whom it binds us." In this relation, one internalized the pain of the other: "It makes their Misfortunes, Sorrows, and afflictions our own." One can construe this in various ways when directed at a dear husband engaged in public activities. Abigail admitted that she was bound by every degree, humanity, friendship, and love, and she hoped coyly: "Nor do I [believe] that you are wholly free from it. Judge[e you then] for your Diana has she not this day [had sufficien]t cause for pain and anxiety of mind?" She engaged her Lysander to think of what she was feeling, if not to show that he, too, made her sorrow (caused by him) his own. She then made it clear that she was already taking on the wifely duty of caring for his health, before concluding that "this hasty Scrawl [came] warm from the Heart of Your Sincere Diana," the spontaneous, sincere directness—valued by cultivators of sensibility—excusing the quality of the writing. John replied: "The Disappointment you mention was not intended, but quite incidental."[1]

Abigail was not oblivious to the fact that ambition, self-interest, and worse could motivate men to take part in public life—to the contrary. She wrote Warren in February 1774, adapting some lines from *Paradise Lost* to a recent incident in Massachusetts politics, and exclaiming: "What a pitty it is that so much of that same Spirit which prompted Satan to a revolt in heaven should possess the Sons of men and eradicate every principal of Humanity and Benevolence. How unbounded is ambition and what ravages it has made among the human Species." She bemoaned "party Spirit"—as John so often did—seeing it as contrary to "good nature and humanity" and to "that precept of Christianity thou shallt love thy Neighbour as thy self." This she associated with Hutchesonian precepts because she wrote next: "I have some where met with an observation . . . that Zeal for a publick cause will breed passions in the hearts of virtuous persons to which the Regard of their own private interest would never have betrayed them."[2]

Abigail seemed to excuse John from this kind of ambition. In 1783, with the Revolution won, "a different scene of Life opening before [her]," she wrote to Thaxter that John was "still connected with publick life in his own Country." She would "became a spectator" of his "anxious cares and tormenting perplexities of which I have hitherto only heard." This alludes, with a trace of bitterness, perhaps, to John's by then protracted absences in Philadelphia and Europe and the stream of complaints he wrote to her. Those absences were in "service to his Country," but they would also express his manhood: "A State of inactivity was never meant for Man; Love and the desire of glory as they are the most natural, are capable of being refined into the most delicate and rational passions." In a draft passage that she omitted, Abigail added that "an unmanly indolence and security would unfit him for the social and relative duties of life," these words followed by her quotation of "Strength of mind is exercise not rest," another line from Pope's *Essay on Man* (epistle 2, line 104). The omitted passage added: "He is truly the noble minded man whose enlarged soul can embrace the whole Human Race, who is charmed alone by that applause which is the Fair attendant of virtue." The sentence alludes to both Hutchesonian circles and, I think, the choice of Hercules. She then distinguishes between the self-aggrandizing ambition of Alexander and refined ambition "employed for the benifit of . . . fellow mortals" and, in this unomitted part of the letter, quotes appropriate lines from *An Essay on Man*, including lines 201–2 of epistle 2:

The same ambition can destroy or save
And makes a patriot, as makes a knave.

This is identical to the notion of the ruling passion, also derived from Pope, to which John referred in *Discourses on Davila* as he wrestled to reconcile his hunger for fame with virtue. The omitted words, however, asserting that somehow refined ambition fits a man for "the social and relative duties of life" correspond to that aspect of the *Essay* that Abigail had urged against John Quincy's mere individualism. The omission (in a letter she knew Thaxter would show to John) reflected the extreme caution Abigail usually exercised in saying anything that could provoke her thin-skinned husband, who, conversely, would find satisfaction in her concurrence with his view of ambition and virtue.[3]

In June 1775, the year before Abigail's "Remember the Ladies" letter, John was one of the five Massachusetts delegates to the Continental Congress in Philadelphia. At that time, Abigail expressed her apparently wholehearted devotion to the cause. She wrote John during the battle of Bunker Hill: "The Day: perhaps the decisive Day is come on which the fate of America depends. My bursting Heart must find vent at my pen. I have just heard than our dear Friend Dr. [Joseph] Warren is no more but fell gloriously fighting for his Country—saying better to die honourably in the field than ignominiously hang upon the Gallows." Abigail had witnessed the battle from the hill next to their house, holding the seven-year-old John Quincy by the hand. She told John that she would stay in Braintree "till thought unsafe by my Friends, and then I have secured myself a retreat at your Brothers . . . house." She concluded the first part of this letter: "I cannot compose myself to write any further at present." Two days later she was "not able to give . . . any authentick account of last Saturday," the first day of the battle, but she was sure of "the Doctors Death," and she introduced her quotation of William Collins's ode "How Sleep the Brave" by telling John: "The tears of multitudes pay tribute to his memory. Those favorite lines [of] Collin[s] continually sound in my Ears."[4]

Collins's poem represented dead, buried soldiers as "Hallowed Ground," concluding:

freedom shall a while repair
To Dwell a weeping Hermit there.

Collins was a sentimental poet who wrote odes to pity, fear, simplicity, and the passions and was an advocate of the sublime. He had pub-

lished his poem in London nearly forty years earlier, to commemorate
the English soldiers killed at Culloden in fighting Bonnie Prince Char-
lie. Abigail adapted English literary sentimentalism to an event—Bunker Hill—that became a centerpiece of American nationalism. The
title of Collins's poem would be perpetuated in Francis Scott Key's national anthem.[5]

Two weeks after the battle, Abigail again demonstrated to John her
identification with the public good it represented, similarly couched in
the terms of sensibility. She began the passage with an expression of
concern for his feelings about her: "I would not have you be distressed
about me. Danger they say makes people valiant. Heitherto I have been
distress'd, but not dismayed. I have felt for my Country and her Sons, I
have bled with them, and for them. Not all the havock and devastation
they have made, has wounded me like the death of Warren." She continued with a repeated pronoun showing that her own wishes regarding public life coincided with her countrymen's as a whole: "We wanted
him in the Senate, we want him in his profession, we want him in the
field. We mourn for the citizen, the senator, the physician and the War-
riour. May we have others raised up in his room."[6]

Another letter Abigail sent to John on Warren's death, this one on
July 31, 1775, did distinguish such public life by gender. She opened: "I
do not feel easy more than two days together without writing to you.
If you abound [in letters] you must lay some of the fault upon yourself, who have made such sad complaints for Letters, but I really believe I have wrote more than all my Sister *Delegates*." The last phrase,
referring to all wives whose husbands were at the congress in Philadelphia, seems to have been without irony, but it connoted her sharing with
other women a vicarious commitment to the public good, and we can
even see it as a step toward her subsequent attempt to give input on those
delegates' Code of Laws.[7]

Abigail turned to "the diabolical crimes" of "Britain" as it planned
"to bring Misiry, Slavery, and Death upon thousands"—again sharing
in the male revolutionaries' overdetermined, republican vision of resisting enslavement. She told John of the Britons' savage treatment of the
corpse of "our ever valued Friend Warren, dear to us even in Death,"
severing his head, carrying it to General Gage (presumably in the posthumous treatment of a traitor that the regicides of Charles I had also
enjoyed), whom, Abigail imagined, "'grin'd horrible a gastly smile'" (an
unidentified literary quotation), expressing Gage's gratification with
"so horrid a Spectacle," in contrast to Caesar's response to the head of

Pompey; Caesar had felt "disgust and gave vent to his pitty in a flood of tears." This she must have derived from her reading of Plutarch's life of Pompey. Abigail quoted: "How much does pagan tenderness put Christian benevolence to shame." This referred to Caesar's tearful pity and the British officer who, Abigail explained, on the basis of sharing Masonic "Brotherhood" with Warren, had attempted to save his body from being mangled and to "find a decent interment for it." He had been too late. Inspired by Warren's burial in a common grave, Abigail quoted lines having the same sense as Collins's, referring to "Hallowed Mould."

Abigail has, then, reiterated that Americans are on the side of friendship, pity, tenderness, Christian benevolence, and humanity, arrayed against Britain's diabolical, sadistic savagery. In short, she declared that the Revolution identified the colonists with sensibility, just as they claimed to uphold the republican principles that Britain has betrayed. It was in this same letter that she thanked John for his of July 7, in which he had charged Britain with "Cruelties more abominable than those . . . practiced by the Savage Indians."[8]

Mercy Otis Warren acknowledged Abigail's sentimental identification with the Revolution: "Your last I perceive was wrote with a heart trembling with the Laudable feelings of Humanity Least your suffering Country should be driven to Extreemities, and its Inocent inhabitants be made the sacrifices to Disappointed Ambition and Avarice." The letter went on to combine republicanism with such sentimental visions of virtue in distress and then to offer an extended consideration of the nature of women's support for husbands who had chosen to put public happiness above personal interest.[9]

Abigail wrote Warren that she could not easily sacrifice her personal wishes to the public good, this in the letter in which she said she wondered sometimes about her apparent "degree of . . . insensibility" amid scenes of war: "You will be sensible no doubt from a communication of the last paquet which your Friend [husband] received, that they [our husbands] have to combat not only other provinces but their own—a doubly difficult task when those who ought to aid, become stumbling blocks—but how hard is it to devest the Humane mind of all private ambition, and to sacrifice ourselves and all we possess to the publick Emolument." Her "private ambition" was to have John home, which, in the Hutchesonian scheme of values and in the male political culture in Philadelphia, ranked lowest among those concentric circles. Abigail had read Fordyce's urging sacrifice on young women, linking it to the ideology of feminine sensibility to declare: "To virtuous love the spirit

of sacrifice is essential." Here was another pain that could be a source of
pleasure: "What hazards, hardships, losses, pains, has not this generous
attachment encountered, with pleasure and even with extasy; happy in
manifesting its zeal by the most arduous proof!"[10]

The day before John's departure from home after a brief visit in August 1775, Abigail wrote Warren: "I find I am obliged to summons all
of my patriotism to feel willing to part with him again. You will readily believe me when I say that I make no small sacrifice to the publick."
Abigail wrote about partings more frequently and more fully than John
did. Of course, both of them gave up their personal relationship, or reduced it to one of letters, but this was fundamentally John's decision,
and his sacrifice served his ambition as well as the public. Abigail felt her
alternatives were to be cheerful/willing about his leaving her or not to
be so, in her phrase, to be "a stumbling block," presumably to be critical
or angry, as, indeed, she sometimes was after he had gone, although she
always apologized and backed off, only to ask him at least to show her
more feeling in his letters.[11]

Early the following year, Abigail wrote Warren an extended account
of the tension she felt over John's leaving her. It illustrates that the language of sensibility supplied her the terms in which to articulate her di-
videdness. She had opened this letter to "My Dear Marcia" with a declaration that might seem ironic, were it not for what followed: "Our
country is as it were a Secondary God, and the first and greatest parent. It is to be preferred to parents, to wives, children, Friends and all
things the Gods only excepted. These are the considerations which prevail with me to consent to a most painfull Seperation." That she is writing of men's duty to the public good is clear ("preferred to . . . wives"),
but that this statement of values had been made by John prior to his departure this time is not apparent, especially in light of the rest of the letter, although he had made similar statements to her before. Here, Abigail
made it to Warren as if it were her own, but it set the stage for her more
elaborate account of the inner conflict it merely intimated ("prevail with
me"), itself preceded, however, by an emotionally charged hesitation: "I
have not known how to take my pen to write to you. I have been happy
and unhappy. I have many contending passions dividing my Heart, and
no sooner did I find it at my own option whether my Friend should go
or tarry and resign; than I found his honour and reputation much dearer
to me, than my own present pleasure and happiness, and I could by no
means consent to his resigning at present, as I was fully convinced he must
suffer if he quitted." Thus, she suggested to Warren that it had been in

her power to prevent John from going to Philadelphia, or at least that she had believed that to have been the case.[12]

It cannot be said whether John would have relinquished public life had Abigail refused that "consent" of which she wrote Warren, although it seems unlikely. Akers observes that the Adamses came to regard James Warren "as an insincere patriot for repeatedly refusing to abandon the comforts of home for public service; and they considered Mercy Otis Warren a poor example of republican womanhood, since she had been unwilling to give up her husband to the state for long periods." By 1780, Warren demanded her husband finally come home. "Ready," she wrote him, "to think you could serve the public better unencumbered by anxieties for me, . . . I am not Hipocrite Enough to Conceal the secret Regrets that pray upon my mind and Interrupt my peace." Now in their fifties, they had "sacrificed enough," she believed, and he returned home. Akers also suggests that the judgments the Adamses made reflected their attribution to the Warrens of "the shortcomings they feared in themselves." Shaw observes, however, that, throughout John's relationship with James Warren, the latter "held the special moral advantages . . . of having repeatedly retired from public life instead of only promising to do so." Another of Abigail's biographers remarks that, despite "twinges of guilt over his duties to his family, politics and public service became, and remained John's main commitment," another that Abigail "would always concede in the end to his ideals and ambition."[13]

The context was what Abigail knew John believed to be her wifely duty to support his decisions, and it seems likely that her disapproval of them would have made him "miserable" as well as depriving her of the feeling of "satisfaction at the Consciousness of having discharged my duty to the publick," a version of that inner feeling of pleasure in a virtuous deed aggrandized in the sensibility on which Abigail particularly prided herself.[14] To John she quoted in 1775 that "'To Bear and Suffer is our portion here'" a stance complementary to her belief that men's virtue and ambition naturally led them to public activity. Still, given that independence was to be the outcome of Congress's work this time and that John Adams was its leading and, perhaps, most persuasive proponent, the alternative that Abigail hypothesized (and the Warrens represented) is dramatic. When push came to shove, however, she found that her happiness was contingent on what she knew to be his. The reasons, however, for her giving her consent included her belief that this was to be a separation limited in time (hence the repetition of the word *present* in that passage on the contending passions dividing her heart), a belief that throws into relief her own protracted suffering as John took up one public office after another, above all, those that took him abroad in 1778.[15]

In that early 1776 letter, Abigail had gone on to spell out to Warren the source of his "sufferings" were John to "resign," elaborating the meanings of his "honour and reputation." They were the circumstances under which he had to work for "the publick": "The Eyes of every one are more perticuliarly upon that assembly, and every motion of every member is inspected, so that he can neither be droped nor resign without creating a thousand Jealousies in the minds of the people." Then she added another problem that suggests that she or John had broached an alternative to resignation or separation: "nor even obtain leave for a few weeks absence to visit his family without a thousand malicious Suggestions and Suspicions." This was entirely consistent with John's repeated views as well as his proclivity to the paranoia that was characteristic of his era's politics.[16] More to the point, however, was the apprehension of which John wrote Abigail when he was president, explaining why he could not return home to her: "I shall be charged with diserting the Presidency, forsaking the secretary of State, betraying my friend Jay, abandoning my Post and Sacrificing my Country to a weak Attachment to a Woman and a weaker fondness for my farm, if I quit at this moment." Jefferson was subject to the same criticism, and, evidently, it was a feature of gendered public life. Adams was not apologetic, his tone, perhaps, implying a degree of agreement with the charge he conjured up. "So be then thankful alone," he told her, "that thou hast a good Husband here, that thy Children are safe and in Honour in Europe, and that thy Daughter has given thee a fine Granddaughter." Finally, she should be thankful for "innumerable Blessings to thy Country."[17]

In the 1776 letter to Warren, Abigail had followed her remark about John's being liable to "a thousand jealousies" with: "All those who act in publick life have very unthankful offices and 'will often sigh to find the unwilling Gratitude of base Mankind.'" And, in case Warren judged her merely "petulant," she specified such prejudicial treatment, showing the kind of ingratitude visited on someone who, like John, "is giving up to distruction of all their own private concerns, depriving themselves of all the pleasures and comforts of domestick life, and exerting all the powers both of Body and Mind, and spending their lives in the Service of their Country." She added, bitterly, on John's behalf: "Thus does it reward them whilst it will hug a canting hypocrite who has been drawing out its vitals." This referred to Robert Treat Paine. Then she extended dis-

gust for politics: "The post of honour is a private Station." This reverses
the Hutchesonian values expressed in that criticism by men of those men
who, like Warren, put personal, private life above the public in favor of
entirely sentimental ones. But then she reversed this reversal. A private
life was "certainly the most comfortable Station. Yet in these days of
peril whilst the vessel is in a storm, it would be guilt in an able passenger
not to lend his assistance."[18]

Abigail's profoundly mixed feelings this year, her consciousness of
what John was asking of her in pursuing the revolutionary public work
in Philadelphia, was another context in which to place her adjuration
that he "Remember the Ladies" as he and his brother delegates made the
new nation's Code of Laws.

Two months after that letter, John asked Abigail: "What shall I do
with my Office—I want to resign it for a Thousand Reasons. Would
you advise me?" The office was chief justice of Massachusetts. This may
have been disingenuous; the rest of the letter gave few expressions of
concern for his "private Affairs" and much more on the Revolution and
his reiteration of his "pity" for his fifty or sixty fellow delegates. Abigail interpreted this, however, as another opportunity for her to fulfill
her private wishes: "You ask my advice with regard to your office. If I
was to consult only my own private Satisfaction and pleasure I should
request you to resign it, but as that is of small moment when compaird
to the whole, and I think you qualified and know you disposed to serve
your Country I must advice you to hold it, at least for the present year."
Again, we see republican values interwoven with marital particularities.
Abigail's next sentence was its own separate paragraph: "And in saying
this I make a Sacrifice which those only can judge of whose Hearts are
one." This was not how Hutcheson and his peers had described the sacrifice of personal interest, even if, nominally, along with the preceding
sentence, it was conformable with it. It implied severe emotional pain; it
also elevated those capable of that, just as cultivators of sensibility conventionally appealed to those "who can feel," directed at readers of sentimental fiction, aggrandizing them, and, conversely, denigrating those
who could not.[19]

Abigail next reported to John: "I was very much affected the other day
with a Letter." She then paraphrased what "the Lady of the late worthy
General Montgomery" had written on news of his death, that is, on discovering she was permanently separated from him. John might die as Dr.
Warren and General Montgomery had. "Speaking of him," Montgomery's widow's letter asked her correspondent, "suffer me to repeat his

last words to me; you shall never Blush for your Montgomery." Bravely she had declared: "Nobly has he kept his Word. As a wife I must ever mourn the Husband, Friend and Lover of a thousand virtues, of all domestick Bliss, the Idol of my warmest affections and in one word my every dream of happiness." Pinckney mourned her husband in similar terms. She described the "general and sincere" concern for his loss even among those "for whom the spirit of party . . . had estranged for some time" and asked: "What then must be my grief . . . that knew him intimately, that knew his in most thoughts, that knew the goodness of his heart, the piety of his mind, the pleasure he took in relieving and assisting the afflicted by every means in his power." The latter, as well as the politics to which the passage also refers, stands for Colonel Pinckney's public virtue, but, while further insisting on that in discribing "the amiableness of his whole deportment," his widow concluded: "All his virtues added to his partial fondness and tenderness to me surely makes my grief, pardonable if ever woman was." It was, in Abigail's account, as "a wife" that Mrs. Montgomery praised the fact that her husband, in addition to his noble, public role, was a "Lover . . . of all domestick Bliss."[20]

In this Montgomery resembled "Mr. [Joseph] Foster . . . an other passenger on Board" the *Active*, of which Foster was part owner, the ship that carried Abigail to Europe in 1784. Foster was, she wrote to Mary, "a Merchant; a Gentleman soft in his manners; very polite and kind, Loves domestick Life, and thinks justly of it. I respect him on this account." Evidently, there were men who neither loved nor thought justly of domestic life. Benjamin Vaughan had those in mind when he told Franklin that, by continuing his *Autobiography*, he would inspire his male audience by demonstrating the compatibility of being "domestic as well as great," although still maintaining the priority of the latter. This illustrates Abigail's wish that John acknowledge the importance of her and her feelings in her domestic circle was not only widespread but had some effect on husbands. Mrs. Montgomery concluded with the thought that she was now "like the poor Widow in the Gospel": "Having given my Mite, I sit down disconsolate." John's parting words to Abigail could have been his final ones, as Montgomery's had been, leaving Abigail, too, a disconsolate widow, along with thousands of others; "plausibly in the Revolution, 8,000 to 12,000 women lost their husbands . . . the equivalent of a million women [in 2004], . . . leaving tens of thousands of children fatherless."[21]

A year after Abigail had written Warren of her separation from John, she again told her that she had had it in her power to prevent him from

going to Philadelphia: "O Marcia how many hundred miles this moment separates us—my heart Bleads at the recollection." This, "the
most grievous" separation, rendered her "at times very unhappy": "I had
it in my Heart to disswade him from going and I knew I could have pre-
vaild, but our publick affairs at that time wore so gloomy an aspect that
I thought if ever his assistance was wanted, it must be at such a time."
She anticipated the cost to herself but perhaps not that it was to be so
grievous: "I therefore resignd myself to suffer much anxiety and many
Melancholy hours for this year to come." That Warren was a woman of
feeling gave Abigail sanction to reveal her pain: "I know you have a sympathetick feeling Heart or I should not dare indulge myself on relating
my Griefs." Those "only can judge" the pain of her "Sacrifice" "whose
Hearts are one."[22]

Another letter of Abigail's elaborated her feeling of her heart's one-
ness with her separated husband's in the terms of mutual sensibility: "I
this day Received . . . a large packet, which has refreshed and comforted
me. Your own sensations have ever been similar to mine. I need [not]
tell you how gratified I am at the frequent tokens of remembrance with
which you favor me, nor how they arouse every tender sensation in my
Soul, which sometimes find vent at my Eyes nor dare I discribe how earnestly I long to fold to my fluttering Heart the dear object of my warmest affections. The Idea sooths me I feast upon it with a pleasure known
only to those whose Hearts and hopes are one." While Abigail expressed
restraint ("nor dare I"), her words pointed to the sexual potentials of
the sensational psychology on which sensibility depended. The "need"
not to tell, along with "known only," signifies the wordless mutuality
characterizing a person of feeling, refined above those without it. Abigail again illustrates the value of sensibility in reconciling herself to, or
at least ameoliorating, the public-private split, and her letter demonstrates the power of John's words to her on the subject: "The approbation you give to my conduct on the Management of our private affair[s]
is very gratefull to me and sufficiently compensates, for all my anxieties[,] and endeavours to discharge the many duties devolved upon me
in consequence of the absence of my dearest Friend." In return, she sent
him sympathy: "I pity you and feel for you under all the difficulties you
have to encounter."[23]

Abigail's expression of trust in their mutual sensibility also preceded
her response to John's reaction to his appointment to the Massachusetts
Superior Court. She then showed him her sympathy with his feelings
and shored him up by her declaration of faith in the superior morality

of his motives: "I am sorry to find from your last . . . that you feel so dissatisfied with the office of which you are chosen. Tho in your acceptance of it, I know of no person here so well qualified to discharge the important Duties of it." She "would not urge" him to it because of its inadequate recompense, although this was the source of still more praise for his acting "the disintrested part." Her own ambition, however, was for a peaceful life focused on the family: "All my desires and all my ambition is to be Esteemed and Loved by my Partner, to join with him in the Education and instruction of our Little ones, to set under our own vines in Peace, Liberty and Safety." This encouragement was very similar to others she gave him, including an April 10, 1782, letter anticipating "the well earned Fame of having Sacrificed those prospects, from a principal of universal Benevolence and good will to Man, descend as an inheritance to our offspring." This was in keeping with John's— and Hutcheson's—scheme of values. But the *our* in the previous letter quoted, of parenting, is Abigail's noteworthy adaptation to her own ambition of the biblically inspired and, therefore, patriarchal idyll signified by "our own vines," modified in accordance with the marital ideal laid out by the *Spectator*.[24]

## "Bereft of my better Half"

Abigail had described wrestling with her feelings over her separation from John while he was in Philadelphia, writing him in September 1776: "Your Letter damp't my Spirits; when I had no expectations of your return till December, I endeavourd to bring my mind to acquiess in the too painfull Situation, but I have now been in a state of Hopeful expectations." Failing to acquiesce, she expected "every Letter" from John "to find the day set for your return." "Enemies" told her with "malicious pleasure" that he could never return (this was the context in which she exclaimed: "How unfeeling are the world! They tell me they Heard you was dead with as Little sensibility as a stock or a stone"), provoking her declaration, "I cannot consent to your tarrying much longer," first on the grounds of his "Health," but then because "whilst you are engaged in the Senate your own domestick affairs require your presence at Home and . . . your wife and children are in Danger of wanting Bread." She described the loss and degradation of their property but then wrote: "I know the weight of publick cares bye so heavey upon you that I have been loth to mention private ones."[25]

Then John accepted his commission to Paris. We saw Abigail's flabbergasted letter to Lovell on hearing the news ("O Sir you who are possessed of Sensibility") and her effort to think about his leaving more rationally at the same time as she admitted: "I am sometimes almost selfish enough to wish his abilities confind to private life." In fact, at that time, as John wrote Elbridge Gerry, Lovell's collaborator in getting John to accept his appointment to France, Abigail had agreed only with a very significant stipulation: "[Her] Concurrence, may be had upon one Condition, which is that her Ladyship became a Party to the Voyage, to which she had a great Inclination." He then gave Gerry his argument against it: "She would run the Risque of the Seas and the Enemies for the sake of accompanying her humble servant." The deferential terms (reported to another man) were mere gendered courtly convention—he was "Lord." He added: "But I believe it will not be expedient." This is cryptic and unsentimental, interpretable as evidence for Ferling's view that "John did not want his wife at his side," at least until the achievement of independence, which, Ferling suggests, John identified with his own "achievement of recognition," yearned for since his youth.[26]

Abigail wrote to Thaxter right after John had sailed away with the eleven-year-old John Quincy, asking him: "Imagine me seated by my fire side Bereft of my better Half, and added to that a Limb lopt of to heighten the anguish." Her account of the case John had made to her, to leave her in this state, was slightly but significantly different than John's account of it to Gerry. She said: "My desire was . . . to have run all hazards and accompanied him, but I could not prevail upon him to consent." John had, she went on, asserted: "The Dangers from Enemies was so great, and their treatment to prisoners so inhuman and Brutal, that in case of a Capture my sufferings would enhance his misery, and perhaps I might be subjected to worse treatment on account of my connection with him." Instead of referring to expediency, to her John had elaborated the "Risques of Seas and Enemies" in the terms of sensibility. He knew the value that Abigail placed on his description of such feelings as well as her constant apprehension that she caused him emotional pain. He was persuasive: "These arguments prevailed upon me to give up the favorite wish of my Heart." As she wrote Thaxter: "I . . . look for my satisfaction in the Consciousness of having discharged my duty to the publick."[27]

Abigail kept her daughter posted on their absent menfolk, John Quincy as well as John, as she conveyed to her, too, her feelings on that subject. In 1779, she began a letter to Nabby, then fourteen, with the figure of incapacity: "It is with inexpressible pleasure that I endorse to you a letter from your brother." And she notes that she had just received four "from your papa." She could not bear "to part with them," that is, the material objects her husband had handled, so she quoted them. She did so "upon politics," including the British cabinet's threat of mercenaries, the "descent upon Georgia," and European reaction to recent events in the war. The last section of this letter bore directly on John's motive for leaving his family and on what Abigail thought of it. He had enclosed a letter in French from a Mme la Grand, "a venerable old lady, in this Neighbourhood, the Wife of Monsr. Grand the Banker." The letter was the result of a question Mme la Grand had posed to John. He introduced his summary to Abigail of "the Subject" by saying of his own reply: "there was not so much Vanity and Ostentation on my Part as you will suspect from her account of it." He was frustrated, it seems, by her response to him: "But as I speak French very imperfectly and she understands not a syllable of English I suppose she did not understand me." This was what he had told her: "All that I maintained was that it was the Duty of a good Citizen to sacrifice all to his Country, in some Circumstances." He then added to Abigail: "God grant I may never be called to do this again so often as I have done already; for I have hazarded all very often and done as much as sacrifice all sometimes." It was this sacrifice in which he conceded he had a degree of "Vanity" and "Ostentation," the latter, presumably, in declaring it.[28]

Mme la Grand was unable to believe the extent of John's sacrifice. The letter she wrote to Abigail has been lost, but Abigail summarized it to Nabby: "in consequence of your papa's saying that, in some cases, it was the duty of a good citizen to sacrifice his all for the good of his country. She tells him that the sentiment is worthy of a Roman and a member of Congress, but cannot believe he would sacrifice his wife and children [by coming to France for such a long stretch of time]." Abigail continued her summary: "In reply, he tells her that I possessed the same sentiment. She questions the truth of his assertion, and says nature would operate more powerfully than the love of one's country"—she seems to have been writing of John's nature here—"and whatever other sacrifices he might make, it would be impossible for him to resign those very dear connections, especially as he had so often given her the warmest assurances of his attachment to them; and she will not be satisfied till [he] has related the conversation, and appealed to me for my sentiments on the subject." She told Nabby that she would forward the letter to her once she had "fully translated it."[29]

John had instructed Abigail how to reply to Mme la Grand: "You will have a delicate Task to answer her. Write to her in English—she has a son about five and twenty who is Master of English and will interpret." Abigail had adequate French—she could translate Mme la Grand's letter for Nabby—but John did not want to take any chances in this matter. The editors of the Adams family correspondence suggest that this was because Mme la Grand's husband, "the Banker," handled financial transactions between the French government and the new United States.[30]

While her reply has not survived, Abigail agreed entirely with John's spoken reply to Mme la Grand. Two days after her enclosure to Nabby, she wrote John, enclosing, she told him, "a Letter wrote at your request," that is, to Mme la Grand: "and if rewarded by your approbation, it will abundantly gratify your Portia."[31] The letter was circulated in French, perhaps in the translation by the la Grand son that John had expected—and with which he may have helped. One must imagine why the views of the wife of the American representative in France on the subject of American women's willingness to interfere with her husband's political work should have been deemed significant. This was a world in which the political activities of Frenchwomen—aristocrats, that is— could be decisive or were thought to be so. (Jefferson was horrified by Frenchwomen's political participation.)[32] If, say, John thought that Mme la Grand herself wished to uncover whether he was likely to continue as the American representative or had been set up to do so, or even if Adams himself engineered the message to his French audience, Abigail's reply would make plain the fact that he would stay the course.

Thaxter reported to Abigail in a February 1780 letter: "Your Letter to Madam G is rendered into French and (*I am told*) admired by every one that reads it, for its excellent Sentiments . . . its Admirers discover pure Taste and good Judgement." Thaxter wrote her later that year: "[The] Abbies Chalut and Arnoux have Copies of the Celebrated Letter of Madam A[dams] to Madam Grand. It is a Subject of Panegyrick, and very justly. It is full of good Sense, and Affection—no Husband of Sensibility can read it without Encomiums and Tears." It is quite clear that, in it, Abigail told Mme la Grand that she "possessed the same sentiment" as her husband and that it was his duty to "sacrifice his wife and children" "for the good of his country."[33]

The letter with which Abigail enclosed John's requested reply to Mme la Grand assuring her of his complete compliance was, evidently, in sharp contrast to those qualities of "pure taste and good Judgement" of which Abigail knew John would approve. She must have hoped that he would note the contrast between the self-discipline she had used in a letter intended for other eyes and the freer expression of sensibility just for his. She wrote it on February 13, 1779, beginning: "This is the Anniversary of a very melancholy Day to me [the day John departed for Europe]." "It rose upon me," she continued, "with the recollection of Scenes too tender to Name." They were inexpressible because the naming would intensify the pain unbearably. But she can, she tells her husband, trust his sensibility: "Your own Sensibility will supply your Memory and dictate to your pen a kind remembrance of those dear connections to whom you waved an adieu, whilst the full Heart and weeping Eye followed your footsteps till intervening objects obstructed the Sight." He had just refused to bring her with him. She did not have to describe the scene anyway, she said, because he possessed a physiologically operated consciousness refined to the pitch to match her tenderness and could write for himself what she could not; or she could have meant him to send her back a letter giving his version, in effect, supplying the kind of effusion of his heart for which she hungered. Then, as was so often the case with letters of sensibility claiming inexpressibility, she went on to spell out the scene or the part of it that he had not directly witnessed because his back had been turned.[34]

Abigail's next paragraph cemented the significance of the anniversary and imagined the commensurately charged reunion: "It shall ever be more particularly Devoted to my Friend till, the happy Day arrives that shall give him back to me again. Heaven grant that it may not be far distant and that the blessings which he has so unweariedly and constantly sought after may crown his Labours and bless his country." One notes, however, that this was at the end of the two opening paragraphs detailing the pain that John's departure and absence has caused Abigail and foregrounding the comparable pain she suggests those circumstances caused him, as he frequently assured her they did. The sentence praising John's search for his country's blessings as unwearied and constant also underscored the duration of the period he was absent from his suffering spouse.

She continued: "It is with double pleasure that I hold my pen this day to acquaint my Friend that I have had a rich feast indeed [i.e., the four letters from John she mentioned to Nabby]." Consistent with the metaphors, she reports what else she has feasted on to make the pleasure double: "The Hankerchiefs in which the[y] were tied felt to me like the return of an absent Friend—tis Natural to feel an affection for every thing which belongs to those we love, and most so when the object is far—far distant from us." We have seen that a garment worn by John raised a

"mixture of . . . pleasure and pain in [her] Bosom." Handkerchiefs held
to the eyes or otherwise serving as ostentatious props had, because they
were not only associated with tears but also imbued with them, become
conventional signs, popularized by sentimental novels, that the user was
a person of sensibility.

Abigail continued by responding to John's criticism of her complaints
for his not writing, indicating her pain over his absence on public business: "You chide me for my complaints, when in reality I had so little
occasion for them." He had written those four letters; she just had not
received them. Defensively, she continued: "I must intreat you to attribute it to the real cause—an over anxious Solicitude to hear of your
welfare and an ill grounded fear lest a multiplicity of publick cares might
render you less attentive to your pen than I could wish." She was blame-
worthy, but only insofar as a good quality was excessive—Elizabeth
Carter had written as much of sensibility. The second emotion, "fear,"
"ill grounded" insofar as John had found time to write to her as frequently as he had, expressed her tension over "his work for the good of
his country," with which, presumably, she had to deal, whether or not
he wrote. Necessarily it made him far less attentive to her all the time he
was away. This came close to being another complaint.

Characteristically, however, Abigail then asked John: "But bury my
dear Sir, in oblivion every expression of complaint—erase them from
the Letters which contain them, as I have from my mind every Idea so
contrary to that regard and affection you have ever manifested towards
me." After a couple of paragraphs fulminating over enfeebling luxury
and extravagance on the part of Americans, she concluded with that
sentence: "Enclosed you will find a Letter wrote at your request, and if
rewarded by your approbation, it will abundantly gratify your Portia."
While its "excellent Sentiments" assuring Mme la Grand of the patriotic, even Roman, republican sacrifice of an American wife's wishes on
the altar of her husband's duty may have brought a tear to those abbés'
eyes, the letter could not have included such painfully ambivalent expressions of sensibility.

While, in July 1782, Abigail suggested that Nabby might come to
France to keep house for her father, in August she asked John, or, rather,
rhetorically complained: "But will you, can you think of remaining
abroad?" She warned him of the damage it would do to her feelings for
him: "Should a peace take place I could not forgive you half a years longer absence." And, again, she followed her declaration of restraint with
its near contradiction: "O there are hours, days and weeks when I would

not paint to you all my feelings—for I would not make you more unhappy. I would not wander from room to room without a Heart and Soul
at Home or feel myself deserted, unprotected, unassisted, uncounseled."
John's choosing to remain abroad would cause—had caused—her to feel
that way and unforgivably so: "I begin to think there is a moral evil in
this Seperation, for when we pledged ourselves to each other did not the
holy ceremony close with, 'What God has joined Let no Man put asunder.' Can it be a voluntary seperation? I feel that it is not." Abigail's feeling, her moral sense, was that they—well, she—had not consented, and
she was close to telling John that he had forced it on her.[35]

   In October 1782, Abigail was reaching the end of her tether over John's
absence in Europe and pressed him to let her come to him: "Permit me
my Dearest friend to renew that Companionship [i.e., in person]. My
Heart sighs for it. I cannot O! I cannot be reconcild to living as I have
done for 3 years past. I am serious." She timidly threatened "I could be
importunate with you. May I?" She wanted him to unbend from the
stern virtue required by his masculine business in order to be receptive to
further effects: "Will you let me try to soften, if I cannot wholly releave
you, from your Burden of Cares and Perplexities?" In encouraging herself to face the hazards of a transatlantic crossing, she again asserted that
the degree of his affection matched hers, the latter "an affection pure
as ever burned in a vestal Heart—Warm and permanent as that which
glows in your own dear Bosom."[36]

   Importunate she may have been, but, as ever, she continued: "I re-
solve with myself to do as you wish." She knew that his wish would be
that she do her duty, so she asked rhetorically: "If I can add to your Happiness, is it not my duty? If I can soften your Cares, is it not my duty? If
I can by tender attention and assiduity prolong your most valuable Life,
is it not my duty?" His "Life" is "most valuable" insofar as he is working for the public good. She casts these wishes, then, as "Calls" to duty.
She must overcome her "Female apprehensions of storms" to answer
them and asked should she "Sacrifice them to my personal ease?" She
abandoned rhetorical argument for her direct expression of the suffering his absence brings her: "Alass I have not even that [ease], for wak-
ing or sleeping, I am ever with you." And with this, she confessed that
it was all up to him and that she was reduced to asking him "if you do
not consent so much is my Heart intent upon it, that your refusal must
be couched in very soft terms," that is, even as he remained fundamentally inflexible. Her next sentence effectively dismissed her own request
for such a pledge on the grounds that it expressed a degree of sensibility

that she was now self-critically able to repress: "Yet my dear sir when I can conquer the too soft sensibility of my Heart; I feel loth you should quit your station until an Honorable peace is established."

Abigail's next letter showed the development of her belief that John's protracted absence could mean that his love for her was fading: "I have lived to see the close of the third year of our seperation. This is a Melancholy Anniversary to me; and many tender Scenes arise in my Mind upon the recollection. I feel unable to sustain even the Idea, that it will be half that period e'er we meet again." Why Abigail began with "I have lived to see" etc. becomes clearer with her second paragraph: "Life is too short to have the dearest of its enjoyments curtailed." She was now thirty-eight, more than halfway through the Biblical biblical span of "three score Years and ten" that her letter said "circumscribes the Life of Man." At this point, she brought to mind the effects of the separation on the nervous system that underlay the sentimental metaphor and simile of this passage:

> The Social feelings grow Callous by disuse and lose that pliancy of affection which sweetens the cup of Life as we drink it. The rational pleasures of Friendship and Society, and the still more refined sensations to which delicate minds only are susceptible like the tender Blosom when the rude Northern Blasts assail them shrink within themselves together, deprived of the all chearing and Beamy influence of the Sun. The Blossom falls, and the fruit withers and decays—but here the similitude fails—for tho lost for the present—the Season returns; the Tree vegetates anew, and the Blossom again puts forth.

Was being without her developing the callosity of a bachelor in John? In any case, over the course of the paragraph, it seems that she identified herself with the blossom and John with the sun. The picture represents her sense of the power that John literally exercised over her vitality.

She then denied for herself the apparent hopefulness of the last sentence: "But alas with me; those days which are past are gone forever; and time is hastning on that period when I must fall, to rise no more; untill Mortality shall put on immortality, and we shall meet again, pure and unembodied Spirits." This presented John with a picture of widow and widower. "Perhaps I make you unhappy," she continued, and again she fantasized a responsiveness in him that corresponded perfectly to hers, indeed, that effortlessly understood her. "No you will enter with a soothing tenderness into my feelings; I see in your Eyes the Emotions of your Heart, and hear the sigh that is wafted across the Altantick to the Bosom of Portia. But the philosopher and statesman stiffels these Emotions, and regains a firmness which arrests my pen from my Hand." The differences from the very similar passage she had written John from her aunt's house in Boston in 1776—in which she had said her "Ideal pleasures" included John's, her absent husband "Who even now whilst he is reading here, feels all I discribe," and hoped that such self-indulgence was "not inconsistant with the stern virtue of a senator and a Patriot"— were charged with her criticism of his lack of effusiveness and her apprehension that his emotions for her had faded.[37]

Twelve days later, she made a lengthy addition to this as yet unsent letter: "You are neither of an age or temper to be allured with the Splendor of a Court—or the Smiles of princesses. I never sufferd an uneasy sensation on that account." This was simply not true and reveals what it denies. Abigail further reassured herself about the reason for John's absence, which the body of her letter suggests had diminished his affection: "such is my confidence in you that if you was not withheld by the strongest of all obligations those of a moral Nature, your Honour would not suffer you to abuse my confidence." She cannot tell him "any thing in the political way worth noticing," and she returned to her self-pity: "Who is there left that will sacrifice as others have done? Portia I think stands alone, alone alas! In more senses than one." Telling him that "Your daughter your Image your Superscription desires to be affectionately remembered to you," she exclaimed, "O! how many of the sweet domestick joys do you lose by this Seperation from your Family. I have the satisfaction of seeing my children this far in life behaving with credit and honour." Despite this outpouring of emotional pain of which John was the cause, Abigail managed to end on a conciliatory note, acknowledging his public good rationale and his hunger for public approval, and reiterating that hope for their enjoyment together of well-earned fame: "God . . . return to me the dear partner of my early years Rewarded for his past sacrifices by the consciousness of having been extensively usefull, not having lived to himself alone, and may the approveing voice of his Country crown his later days in peacefull retirement in the affectionate Bosom of Portia."[38]

Abigail's next letter continued to describe the state of her heart: "in the domestick way should I draw you the picture of my Heart, it would be what I hope you still would Love." The apprehension that John did not was still looming, but her love was unchanged, "tho it contained nothing New": "the early possession you obtained there; and the absolute power you have ever maintained over it; leaves not the smallest space unoccupied." In the last letter, she had said that her sense of time passing brought her pain, even the wish to die. Here, however, she wrote him: "With an indescribable pleasure I have seen near a score of years roll over our Heads with an affection heightened and improved by time"—contradicting her previous account of separation's causing a hardening of social feelings and a loss of affection, as if she later had imagined his interpreting that as an account of her feelings for him, instead of what she apprehended were his feelings for her—"nor have the dreary years of absence in the smallest degree effaced from my mind the Image of the dear untitled man to whom I gave my Heart." Her complaints to the contrary were only "sometimes": "I cannot sometimes refrain considering the Honours with which he is invested as badges of my unhappiness."[39]

In fact, Abigail now asserts, her affection had not been diminished by protracted absence: "The unbounded confidence I have in your attachment to me"—a confidence that, reading her November letter, John might well have questioned—"and the dear pledges of our affection"—their children—"has soothed the solitary hour, and rendered your absence more supportable." She now writes that she was worried she had caused him pain by giving him the impression she had doubted he loved her as much as she loved him: "for had I have loved you with the same affection, it must have been misiry to have doubted." In writing as she had, she had reflected the effect on her of "the world's" question: "Yet a cruel world to often injures my feelings, by wondering how a person possessd of domestick attachments can sacrifice them by absenting himself for *years*." The "world" here was her American one, although Mme la Grand had raised the same question.

Abigail then identified an individual representative of said cruel world, against which she posed herself as a woman of injured feelings, reporting to John that "the other day" someone had asked her: "If you had known . . . that Mr. A would have remained so long abroad; would you have consented that he should have gone?" The questioner assumed that she had the power of consent. Abigail told John: "I recollected myself for a moment"—and we must imagine what her immediate, emotional responses were to this question—"and then spoke the real dictates of my Heart." We have seen how profoundly hurt she was and the painful doubts she had felt lately, her inability sometimes to "reconcile" herself to his absence, and her efforts to persuade him to return home. But her reply did not come "warm from the heart," although she made out to her questioner, and, therefore, to her reader, John, that they were "the real dictates" of her heart: "If I had known Sir that Mr. A. could have affected what he had done; I would not only have submitted to the

absence I have endured; painful as it has been; but I would not have opposed it, even tho 3 years more should be added to the Number, which
Heaven avert!" She admitted the pain but asserted that she had learned
from John to derive the same pleasure from it that he had: "I feel a pleasure in being able to sacrifice my selfish passion to the general good,
and imitating the example which has taught me to consider myself and
family, but on the small list of the balance when compaird with the
great community." When she had written to Warren in 1776 that one's
"Country . . . is to be preferred to parents, to wives, children, Friends,"
she had done so to describe the "many contending passions dividing
[her] Heart," making her "happy and unhappy."[40]

This questioner, however, was a man, and it may have been because
of his gender (potentiating public life) or social distance that Abigail did
not tell him of the pain and ambivalence. Most obviously, however, her
audience for this letter was John, whom she wished to reassure after the
ambiguity of her previous letter. She spent much of the rest of this one
introducing Royall Tyler to John because he was a suitor to Nabby. At
the end, she returned to the question of her "coming to you," but, if he
was against it, she said, she would "not urge it further" and would not
"embarrass" him "by again requesting it."[41]

A couple of weeks following this report to John of a man who had
raised a question that Abigail wished John to know troubled her, she
gave him a report of others who found it impossible to sympathize with
John's leaving his family "for the publick service." These were their children, perhaps the youngest two especially, although she had recently intimated that Nabby had been troubled by her father's absence. First, she
described her own feelings, including some resentment that she had not
recently heard from him about the peace negotiations: "Could I look
forward to any given period, when I might hope again to embrace my
dearest Friend in his Native Land it would serve to mitigate the painfull
absence." She claimed credit for her patience, looking for "the reward
and happiness to my country," and quoting the poet/playwright James
Thomson's version of the hierarchy of values expounded by his fellow
Scot Francis Hutcheson. Abigail wrote,

With Sophonisba I can say,

"My passions too can Sometimes Soar above,
The Household task assign'd me, can extend
Beyond the Narrow Sphere of families,

And take great States into th' expanded Heart
As well as yours."

And the editors note that she substituted *my* for *our* and *me* for *us*, emphasizing her particular individual merit in this.[42]

The ensuing account of her children's inability thus to transcend their sense of their father's relinquishment of his family was incorporated into a picture of the domestic scene whose pleasures, Abigail reiterated, John had lost. She described the "little social circle" around her as she wrote to John, "Sewing, reading, Studying grammer &c . . . jointly and severally present[ing] their duty and affection." She continued: "Mamma is never so highly delighted . . . [as when telling them of] Some excellent precept, and example, whom she recollected from [their father's] writings, or his Lips. But she cannot make them enter into the Idea of his quitting his Native Land, and relinquishing all his domestick pleasures for the publick Service." She then referred to the potential effects on both parties, children and father, to pray: "May they never Suffer any diminution by absence; but may they ever rise to your view as the objects of all the others the dearest to you, and for which no foreign pleasure or amusement can compensate." There was, perhaps, a sting in this as well as in her concluding prayer that what John professed to her should come true: "Heaven Grant the day may not be far distant when you may realize all your Heart wishes; in the fond embraces of your children, and in the Reciprocal endearments of your Ever affectionate Portia."

At the end of this same month, January 1783, John told Abigail of the possibility that Congress would renew his commission to make a commercial treaty with Britain, despite "the first desire of [his] Soul to go home": "But if it should happen, I beg you would come to me with it, for nothing but your Company will make it acceptable." In fact, as the editors of this letter point out, this "commission" was John's own idea, with obvious implications for his ranking of public and private interests, of ambition and family. He "coveted the appointment as America's first minister to Great Britain." Yet he would consistently let Abigail believe that it was all in Congress's power whether he could return home and that return was the dearest wish of his heart, sacrificed on the altar of public duty.[43]

In that April 10, 1782, letter, after receiving one of his frequently passionately disillusioned and self-righteous ones, Abigail had reassured John: "Can I believe that the Man who fears neither poverty or danger, who sees not charms sufficient either in Riches, power or place to tempt him in the least to swerve from the purest Sentiments of Honour and Delicacy; will retire, unnoticed, Fameless to a Rustick cottage there by dint of Labour to earn his Bread. I need not much examination of my Heart to say I would not willing[ly] consent to it." But now, she entirely repressed her own deepest wish in favor of identifying herself with what she knew to be John's, in order to stiffen his backbone. She asked rhetorically: "Have not Cincinnatus and Regulus been handed down to posterity with immortal honour?" It was after those classical references that she had written the passage (quoted earlier) forecasting that "well earned Fame" would be their offspring's inheritance. Douglass Adair writes of the "tradition of fame" invoked by eighteenth-century writers and leaders that they self-consciously linked themselves to classical exemplars. "Fame [in their eyes]," he noted, "in contrast to honor, is more public, more inclusive, and looks to the largest possible human audience, horizontally in space and vertically in time." In the end, the benefits would rebound to the family, that is, to future offspring. The most extensive and accessible galaxy of models was supplied by Plutarch's *Lives of Noble Greeks and Romans*, a book the Adamses read, although Abigail also imbibed Plutarch by way of Shakespeare's incorporation of Sir Thomas North's English translation. According to Adair: "The American Revolutionaries found in Plutarch . . . one very specific type of fame that became most meaningful to the greatest of our Revolutionary leaders after 1776." He illustrates this by way of John Adams's "passion for fame," in fact, his "lust" for it (a "lust" John also criticized), quoting his 1777 letter to Richard Henry Lee: "You and I my dear friend, have been sent into life at a time when the greatest law givers of antiquity would have wished to live. How few of the human race have ever enjoyed an opportunity of making election of government . . . for themselves or their children."[44]

"I must submit," Abigail told John in June 1783. She knew he would stay in Europe if he stayed "for the general good," but she was "satisfied" that he would then share her pain over their continued separation: "you would not subject me to so heavy a disappointment, or yourself so severe a mortification as I flatter myself it would be." This was a hope of and a consolation in equality of feeling that she had wished for throughout their marriage. She was well able to make a nonsentimental case for his return, although it shared some terms with the culture of sensibility. Rather than accepting the "commission for forming a commercial treaty with Britain," she argued that John was needed in America: "Perhaps there has been no juncture in the publick affairs of our country; not even in the hour of our deepest distress, when able statesmen and wise Counsellors were more wanted than at the present day." Here, she used the larger meaning of *domestic*: "Peace abroad leaves us at leisure to look into our own domestick affairs." The latter phrase seems to be free of any consciousness of a double entendre, although John's return to politics at home would also return him to the smaller domestic circle, at least temporarily.[45]

In the midst of writing this, Abigail received his letter of March 28, in which, after telling her that once he had received "Acceptance of my Resignation" he would "embark in the first ship" for home, John admitted the possibility that he was to be sent on a mission to England: "I tremble when I think of such a Thing as going to London. If I were to receive orders of that sort, it would be a dull day to me. No Swiss ever longed for home more than I do." At the same time, he wrote: "I cannot bear the Thought of transporting my Family to Europe. It would be the Ruin of my Children forever. And I cannot bear the Thought of living longer Seperate from them." Foreign affairs were "a Scaene of Faction" and uncertainty: "Dont think of coming to Europe . . . unless you should receive a further desire from me, which is not at all probable. My present Expectations are to pay my Respects to you at Braintree, before Midsummer." He went over his sources of "Distress," including the dangers in Tyler's courtship of Nabby and John Quincy's journey from St. Petersburg to Hamburg. He complained of the hardship of his lot, in comparison to that of his male relatives who had remained at home. The greatest source of "the Anxiety [he had] Suffered for these Three Years," however, was the prosperity of America's commerce, for which he had been laboring diplomatically, but it would have been lost without him: "I cannot therefore repent of all my fatigues."[46]

Abigail reassured John that she was not disappointed over the uncertainty of his time of return. As far as his forbidding her to join him in Europe was concerned: "I have not a wish to join in a scene of life so different from that in which I have been educated." Her home she represented in sentimental, pastoral terms, one of "tranquil Scenes," with the "whisp'ring Zephyr, and the purling rill," as well as one of modern domesticity: "Well ordered home is my chief delight, and the affectionate domestick wife with the Relative duties which accompany my highest ambition." She had not really wanted to come, as she had written him the previous July: "It was the disinterested wish of sacrificing my personal feelings to the publick utility, which first led me to think of

unprotectedly hazarding a voyage, I say unprotectedly for so I consider
any lady who is not accompanied by her husband." Now, however, such
an exposure, and such a sacrifice, was not necessary because her husband
can return, "with honour and well earned Fame": "I cannot any longer
consider it as my duty to submit to a further Seperation, and when it
appears necessary that those abilities which have crownd you with Laurels abroad, should be exerted at home for the publick Safety." That is,
John's rationale for leaving her that previously had prevailed and made
her "submit" no longer held up. He had attained what he aimed for
abroad; he should accept her assessment of public affairs and return.[47]

Abigail opened her next paragraph with the unvarnished: "I do not
wish you to accept an Embassy to England, should you be appointed." For
the first time she attempted to exercise that option she believed she had
when facing John's departures. She followed it with a reiteration of sentimental polarities: "This little Cottage has more Heart felt satisfaction
for you than the most Brilliant Court can afford, the pure and undiminished tenderness of weded Love, the filial affection of a daughter." And,
here, Abigail tried to reassure John about Tyler's courtship of Nabby,
about which his March 28 letter had shown he was worried. She concluded with news of Charles and Tommy's being placed with the Shaws,
with her telling John that she longed to see John Quincy, and with the
request that, if he "should continue abroad until fall," he would send her
some money: "Goods will not answer. We are glutted with them." But
she did want John to send her some things for her "family use," namely,
"a few pieces of Irish linen and a piece of Russia sheeting together with
two green silk umbrellas."

Abigail continued to express her unhappiness about their separation,
ten days later explaining: "Maternal duties prevented me from accompanying you." She asserted that John's literal orientation was domestic: "Few persons who so well Love domestick Life as my Friend; have
been calld, for so long a period, to relinquish the enjoyment of it; yet
like a needle to the pole you invariably turn towards it, as the only point
where you have fixed your happiness." She implied that, if his needle
had been drawn to public life, she would have given up on him: "It is
this belief which has supported me this far through the voyage, but alass
how often have I felt the want of my pilot, 'to act my part alone.'" She
had, perforce, taken charge of their economic circumstances, but the evidence supplied by this account of her sensibility shows how powerfully
she still felt herself dependent on the absent John. She again presented
him with a "picture of domestick felicity" to lure him home: "O! May

we taste, may we drink of the cup of happiness without alloy, and be as blest as we can bear, 'all Various Nature pressing on the Heart.' Let us retire into ourselves, and rejoice in the purity of our affections, the simplicity of our manners and the Rectitude of our Hearts."[48]

Meanwhile, John still had not heard the official response to his offer that he undertake the British mission, but "publick Concerns oblige[d]" him to go to the Hague, where he was to enjoy one of his greatest diplomatic triumphs. He anticipated that he would not be able to return that summer or fall as he had said, but, learning that Charles and Tommy were to live with the Shaws, he wrote Abigail: "With . . . yourself and Miss Nabby and Mr. John with me I could bear to live in Europe another Year or two. But I cannot live much longer without my Wife and Daughter and I will not." His reason for wanting them complemented her conventionally dutiful wish to take care of him physically and psychologically, which lately she had expressed with increasing concern because of the damage that, he reported, the European climate and his work were doing him: "I want two Nurses at least: and I wont have any, at least female ones but my Wife and Daughter." Yet again, he wrote her with feeling: "I tremble, least a Voyage and a change of Climate should alter your health."[49]

Nor had John forgotten his anxiety over the "awful Problem" of whether a "lady" could resist "the Dress" and "Show of Europe." He told Abigail that, if she and Nabby were not capable of putting "off these Fooleries like real Philosophers," he would advise her "never to come to . . . Europe but order Your Husband home" and, without apparent explanation of the connection, entered into the subject of the "Precariousness" of diplomatic posts, in contrast to the "Bread that is earned on a Farm," which "is simple and sure": "That which depends upon Politicks is as uncertain as they." The connection was that, if Abigail's and Nabby's heads were "turned" by aristocratic, European consumption, he would not be able to afford it and be spent into beggary, an old worry.

In August, having told Abigail, "I always learn more of Politicks from your Letters, than any others," John said, "I expect, very soon, to be a private Man, and to have no other Resource for my family but my Farm." He would collect all their debts and "lay it out in Lands in the Neighborhood of our Chaumiere," that is, a thatched cottage, connoting the same sentimental picture that we have seen appears elsewhere in his and Abigail's letters. The house to which the Adamses referred as a *chaumiere* and a *cottage* was a "five room New England saltbox . . . built in 1681 . . . around a massive brick chimney." The symbolism of those nouns embraced the gendered values of sensibility. We have noted the meaning that her domesticity held for Abigail, but the values could be extended to John's achievement of fame and America's national political identity. That same April when Abigail encouraged John not to "retire . . . Fameless to a Rustick cottage," she also told him she imagined their reunion would take place, not in Europe, but "in our own Republican cottage, with the Simplicity that has ever distinguished it." That this was a sentimental/republican trope adapted by American revolutionaries is further illustrated by the Adamses' dear friend Joseph Warren's "Boston Massacre Oration" of 1772, when he told his audience: "If you really prefer the lonely cottage (whilst blest with liberty) to gilded palaces . . . you may have the fullest assurances that tyranny . . . will hide [her] hideous [head] in . . . despair." After she had authorized Cotton Tufts to buy "a large house and farm in Braintree" for their homecoming (to contain all their European stuff), Abigail wrote from London in 1787: "I feel I can return to my little cottage and be happier than here."[50]

In September 1783, when finally he had received the congressional commission to make a commercial treaty with Britain, that is to say, when Congress had acceded to his own wish, John asked Abigail: "Will you come to me this fall and go home with me in the Spring?" "The moment I hear [of your arrival]," he wrote, "I will fly with Post Horses to receive you." He left the decision up to her, saying that she knew the political circumstances in Philadelphia better than he did. "I am determined," he said, "to be with you in America or have you with me in Europe." And he assumed that he and Abigail would accomplish one of those purposes "consistent with private Prudence and the publick Good." Now that Congress had passed the resolution that was "highly honourable" to him and, therefore, had restored his "Feelings," John said: "I am now perfectly content to be recalled . . . or Stay in Europe, until this Business is finished, provided you will come live with me." He had dropped his concern that she and Nabby might be corrupted by exposure to European luxury: "We may spend our time together . . . as Public Business may call me and then return to our Cottage with contented Minds." The pronouns neatly represented the hierarchy of his and her wishes. He placed the decision when to come unambiguously in Abigail's power: "I must submit your Voyage to your Discretion and the Advice of your Friends." If she decided against it, he "must submit." But, if she postponed it in the fall: "I shall insist on your coming in the Spring." He sent the same message in a letter to her three days later: "I shall be Supreamly happy to see you." A month later, he repeated his "earnest Request that you and our Daughter would come to me as soon as possible."[51]

When Abigail wrote to John in October, she still did not know whether he would return or stay. She emphasized, however: "I beg you not to accept [another appointment]. Call me not to any further trials of the kind!" This expressed her awareness of the fact that, if, at some level, she had imagined that she had had the power to prevent his leaving her for public business, he had always wanted her to bear his going. "Reflect upon your long absence from your family," she continued. "Your Children have a demand upon You." He also needed to recover "that Health" that he had "unhappily impaired and lost abroad." Furthermore, if earlier she had felt "willing to cross the Seas" to be with him, now she was not: "Nothing short of an assurance from you, that your happiness depended upon it, would induce me to alter my opinion." She devoted the rest of this long paragraph to a sentimental/republican vision of the corrupt nature of public life, which, she suggested, had racked John's constitution and debilitated his faculties. (He had very often written to her in the same vein.) She also implied that his "Love of praise" had made him vulnerable and that it was, therefore, time for him to return.[52]

By November, however, John was already in London, whence he wrote Abigail: "My Life is Sweetened with the Hope of embracing You in Europe. Pray embark as soon as prudently you can, with Nabby. . . . Yours in haste, but most tenderly." He wrote her a second time the same day, excited to report all the paintings he had just seen at "Buckingham House," "by Special Permission from their Majesties": "Come to Europe with Nabby as soon as possible, and Satisfy your Curiosity, and improve your Taste, by viewing these magnificent scenes. Go to the Play—see the Paintings and Buildings—visit the Manufactures." These would provide a common fund of experience when she were to "return to America" with him "to reflect upon them." Not only could he not be happy without her, but he "really" thought "one Trip across the Sea would be of Service" to her and Nabby, "to whom my Love." Nothing here of the dangers of dress and show. "I shall expect you constantly until you arrive." He concluded: "Yours with Tenderness unutterable."[53]

When Abigail learned that John would be staying in Europe another winter, but before she had received his letter from London, she wrote him that she was not surprised but that, "so much of a coward" was she "upon the Water," she could "not possibly think of encountering" a winter voyage. She had "a still stronger objection." She knew that Congress had not yet made "any appointment to the Court of Britain." "Of this I am sure," she told him, "that I do not wish it." It was not the voyage that daunted her now but the destination: "I should have liked very well, to have gone to France, and resided there a year, but to think of going to England in a publick Character, and resideing there; engageing at my time of life in Scenes quite New, attended with dissipation parade and Nonsense; I am sure I should make an awkward figure." The public character would be as an ambassador's wife, to which she objected because she believed she would not be able to play her part as the American minister's wife. She continued: "The retired Domestick circle, 'the feast of reason and the flow of soul' are my Ideas of happiness, and my most ardent wish is, to have you return and become Master of the Feast." The quotation was from Pope's translation of Horace and one she had used in other letters. Its value to both the republican idealization of retirement and the sentimental idealization of domesticity with which Abigail here aligned it is evident. Her wish that John give up the ambassadorship in favor of being master of the domestic feast is pointed. She insists that she wants him back home, whatever her European destination. Yet, as usual, once having expressed her own wish, she acknowledged that she might well defer to him: "if I cannot prevail upon you to return to Me in the Spring—you well know I may be drawn to you." And she gave a couple of reasons that would make that easier. One was the death of her father. Another was that the Cranches might move to Boston, "almost the only [cord]" binding her "to this place": "Braintree would indeed become a lonely spot to me."[54]

In December, Abigail received John's "pressing invitation" to come to Europe: "O my dearest Friend what shall I say to you in reply?" She referred to her fears of a winter voyage and stated: "My friends are all against it." Moreover, she needed time to place her "affairs . . . in that method and order I would wish to leave them in." Then she turned to that apprehension of self-presentation in the public scenes she had expressed in her previous letter: "I think if you were abroad in a private Character, . . . I should not hesitate so much at comeing to you. But a mere American as I am, unacquainted with the Etiquette of courts, taught to say the thing I mean, and to wear my Heart in my countenance, I am sure I should make an awkward figure." John's official capacity required her to put on a "public Character." The etiquette of courts was contrary to the sincerity of word and facial expression, values of sensibility that she associated with privacy, with informality, but also with the American, republican, national character. Her assertion here of that set of values was only perhaps tinged with self-deprecatoriness. Still, such circumstances would be emotionally painful because of the damage her apparent awkwardness would do to John's public reputation: "And then it would mortify my pride if I should be thought to disgrace you."[55]

Abigail asserted sentimentalism's egalitarianism in almost Shakespearian terms: "Yet strip Royalty of its pomp and power, and what are its votaries more than their fellow worms? I have so little of the Ape about me, that I have refused every publick invitation to figure in the Gay World, and sequestered myself in this Humble cottage, content with rural life and my domestick employments, in the midst of which; I have sometimes Smiled, upon recollecting that I had the Honour of being allied to an Ambassador." It was, she acknowledged, the "Gay World" of pleasure that drew women out into the public sphere, much more generally than selected attendance at court. The "Humble cottage," of course, she expressly associated with republicanism. She concluded the paragraph with a comparison of herself to "the chaste Lucretia," about to be raped by Tarquin, the classical subject of a Shakespeare poem.

It is probable that Abigail also read Joseph Warren's comparison of the figure of Lucretia to American women, victimized by the British, incorporated into his "Boston Massacre Oration" where he described his fellow Bostonians' "children subjected to the . . . raging soldiers, our beauteous virgins subjected to all the violence of unbridled passion, our virtuous wives, endeared to us by every tender tie, falling a sacrifice to more than brutal violence, and perhaps, like the famed Lucretia, distracted with anguish and despair, end their wretched lives." These helpless, virtuous victims Warren juxtaposed with a picture of British soldiers, "the authors of our distress parading in our streets." In a 1777 letter to Isaac Smith Jr., now a loyalist in England, Abigail contrasted American bravery, fortitude, and generosity with the "savage malice" of the British, perpetrated in "crimes" against the "oppressed," including making "our women a sacrifice to brutal Lust." In short, Americans were identified with virtue in distress, although the assault provoked them to communal self-assertion—"our hearts beat to arms, we snatched up our weapons"—motivated, as Jefferson was to say in his Head vs. Heart letter, by the moral sense of the heart.[56]

This letter of Abigail's expressed pleasure at another of sensibility's contrasts, her humble station belying her connection with a great official. She expressed her pleasure in John's public accomplishments elsewhere, in accordance with the ideals of wifely duty, indeed, of the orientation of ideal feminized sensibility to pleasing men, as well as with

what she believed was the love of glory natural to them. She asserted
that she took pleasure in sacrificing her personal interest to her husband's
pursuit of the public good. Taking "vicarious" pleasure in his success
was a corollary of the same binary system, of gender and of private/
public, one consistent with Fordyce's and Hume's recommendation that
ladies safely read history rather than participate directly in it.[57]

But Abigail's earlier elaboration of sacrifice placed a different value on
the relation that vicariousness stood for. In June 1782, peace with Britain was looming, and John was directly engaged with the negotiations.
Abigail wrote John in Holland: "Ardently as I long for the return of my
dearest Friend, I cannot feel the least inclination to a peace but upon the
most liberal foundation [i.e., independence]." That is, she was willing
to endure the further separation that successful negotiation necessitated.
Here, however, she did not express vicarious pleasure in John's patriotic work but instead asserted women's distinct version of it: "Patriotism in the female sex is the most disinterested of all virtues." Men's—
John's—work on behalf of the public good embodied self-interest and
gained them rewards, too: "Excluded from honours and from offices, we
cannot attach ourselves to the State or Government from having held a
place of Eminence." She then alluded to revolutionary America: "Even
in the freest countrys our property is subject to the controul and dis-
posal of our partners, to whom the Laws have given soverign Authority." This was a fact that Abigail daily faced in John's absence: "Deprived
[as we are] of a voice in Legislation"—written six years after John had
laughed at her request to "Remember the Ladies" as he helped draw up
the Articles of Confederation—"obliged to submit to those Laws which
are imposed on us, is it not sufficient to make us indifferent to the publick Welfare?"[58]

Abigail then answers her own question this way: "Yet all History and
every age exhibit Instances of patriotick virtue in the female Sex; which
considering our situation equals the most Heroick of yours." Wood emphasizes that virtue, and "the concept of honor," "lay at the heart of all
prescriptions for political leadership." Still writing of men, he continues: "If virtue was based on liberty and independence, then it follows
that only autonomous individuals free of any ties of interest . . . were
qualified to be citizens." Women were placed automatically in the much
larger category of dependents, including children, servants, slaves, ten-
ants, and wage earners; in the case of women, *virtue* and *honor* signified
merely a negative aspect of their essentially affiliative status, their beings
devoted to reproduction, their virtue and honor really their family's.

Abigail accepted the definition of *virtue* as "disinterestedness": men's denial to women of political rewards meant that women did not have to agonize, as John Adams did, to distinguish between personal ambition for office and zeal to perform the public good. But she again registered the amount of emotional pain her acceptance of his absence had cost her: "I will take praise to myself. I feel that it is my due, for having sacrificed so large a portion of my peace and happiness to promote the welfare of my country . . . tho it is more than probable unmindfull of the hand that blessed them."[59]

John acknowledged her due the following year in a letter to his recently married acquaintance Charles William Frederic Dumas. He told him to ask his bride "whether she think she has Patriotism enough to consent that you should leave her for nine years pro bono publico? If she has she another good title to the character of an Heroine." Anticipating Abigail's soon rejoining him, John added: "I hope to be married once more myself . . . to a very amiable lady whom I have inhumanly left a widow in America for nine years, with the exception of a few weeks only."[60]

## CHAPTER 9

# John Adams and the Reformation of Male Manners

## The Choice of Hercules

At seventy-seven, John Adams wrote Rush an account of his childhood and youth in the third person. His first "15 years went off like a fairy tale," his being "at schools male and female" coexisting with truancy, and variegated play, and "running about to gentling and huskings and frolics and dances among the boys and girls!!" They were followed by a big change: "He then spent 4 years at college. He had begun to love a book. Farewell, skating, swimming, and all the rest. . . . Seeking books and bookish boys, devouring books without advice and without judgement." This made him subject to regret, if not guilt.[1] In 1760, he confided in his journal: "Ran over the past Passages of my Life;—Little Boats, watermills, wind mills, whirly Gigs, Birds Eggs, Bows and Arrows, Guns, singing, pricking tunes, Girls, &c. . . . By a constant Dissipation among Amuzements, in my Childhood, and by the Ignorance of my Instructors in the more advanced years of my Youth, my Mind has laid uncultivated so that at 25, I am obliged to study Horace and Homer.—Proh Dolor!" But he was dissatisfied with study alone and, in effect, perpetuated his earlier, even rebellious love of variety, asking himself rhetorically: "Is not such uniformity tiresome? Is not variety more agreeable and profitable, too?" He was tempted "to spend the whole day in perpetual variation, from reading to thinking, exercise, company, &c." But he also apprehended that this was "a wavering life . . . a habit of levity." He decided, at least at that point, that this was what he was like, unable to finish a book without taking up his pen to write a letter, taking another book from the shelf, "or thinking about girls." He declared that his "thoughts are roving from girls to friends, from friends to court to Worcester, Newbury, and then to Greece and Rome, then to law; from poetry, to oratory, and law. Oh! A rambling imagination." The range of John Adams's activities—in politics, of course, but also in the law; in bringing the histories of Greece and Rome and other countries to bear on his political science; in diplomacy; in oratory, but not poetry; in farming, too, although his choice of politics and public life left the management of his farm to Abigail for long periods of time—illustrates that "diversity of pursuits" nourished by "the demands of life and the impulses of passion" from which Fordyce said women were "precluded by decorum, his softness, and by fear." Abigail's moving beyond her circle was inflected by decorum, by softness, and by fearfulness.[2]

Yet, once, in 1784, when finally on board ship en route to join John in Europe—the voyages there and back were, significantly, the only times she kept a journal—Abigail wrote her sister Mary: "You can hardly judge how urksome this confinement is; when the whole ship is . . . little better than a prison; . . . O dear variety! How pleasing to the humane mind is Change; I cannot find a fund of entertainment within myself as not to require outward objects for my amusement." Her subject was the "humane mind," regardless of gender: "Nature abounds with variety, and the mind unless fixed down by habit, delights in contemplating new objects, and the variety of Scenes which present themselves to the Senses, were certainly designed to prevent our attention from being too long fixed upon any one object." Part of the stimulus to this latter reflection was her reading William Buchan's *Domestic Medicine; or, The Family Physician* (1769). Buchan (another Scot) argued, consistent with John's notion, that such variety, in Abigail's words, "greatly contributes to the Health of the animal frame. Your studious people and your deep thinkers, he observes, seldom enjoy either health or spirits." It was a book, Knott writes, "riven through with the physiology of sensibility and the nervous system," that psychophysiology elevated, I have suggested, in association with the proliferation of material goods and a greater range of experience for many more people. John's protracted wartime and postwartime absences perforce provided Abigail the opportunity to extend her domestic activities to running the family's finances and led her to amplify her interest in politics. In these respects, she illustrated the general point that Norton has made about American women, that the Revolution could break the "constant pattern of women's lives" and begin to free them from "the small circle of domestic concerns." Eliza Lucas stands for the fact, however, that some elite women were already able to experience pleasures beyond that circle.[3]

Amid his variety and ambivalences, John Adams narrowed his alternatives to those that had faced one of the greatest heroes of antiquity, confiding to his diary that, one night in 1759, "the Choice of Hercules came into my mind and left Impressions there which I hope will never be effaced, nor long unheeded." Perhaps to strengthen the impression, he went on to write out a version of the same fable, amending it to fit his own case. He began it by having a personified Virtue ask him: "Which, dear Youth, will you prefer, a life of Effeminacy, Indolence or Obscurity, or a Life of Industry, Temperance and Honour?" He had Virtue advise him to "rise and mount [his] Horse" at dawn, to clear his stomach and brain, then "return to [his] Study and bend [his] whole soul" to studying law: "Let no trifling Diversion, or amuzement, or Company decoy you from your Books; i.e. let no Girl, no Gun, no Cards, no flutes, no Violins, no Dress, no Tobacco, no Laziness, decoy you from your Books." John then interpolated in his own parenthetical voice: "(By the Way, Laziness, Languor, Inattention, are my Bane. I am too lazy to rise early . . . too languid to make me apply with spirit to my books . . . at 10 o'clock my Passion for knowledge, fame, fortune, or any good liable to be called off from Law by a Girl, a Pipe, a Poem, a Love Letter, a *Spectator*, a Play, &c., &c.)." John conflated the choice of Hercules with the Protestant ethic and, more pointedly, with the movement for the reformation of manners.[4]

Then he berated himself: "Friday, Saturday, Sunday, Monday, all spent in absolute idleness, or, which is worse, gallanting the girls." Elsewhere he wrote: "I was of an amorous disposition and very early from ten or eleven Years of Age, was very fond of the Society of females, I had my favorites among the young Women and spent many of my Evenings in their Company and this disposition although controlled for seven Years after my Entrance into College returned and engaged me too much till I was married." He had apprehended that courting the wrong woman could be his utter downfall. He confessed: "Here are 2 nights, and one day and an half in a softening, enervating, dissipating series of hustling, prattling, Poetry, Love, Courtship, Marriage." Again, he construed the alternatives he faced as equivalent to the choice of Hercules: "During all this Time I was seduced into the Course of unmanly Pleasures, that Vice describes to Hercules, forgetful of the glorious Promises of Fame, Immortality and a good Conscience, which Virtue, makes to the same Hero, as Rewards of a hardy, toilsome, watchful Life in the service of Man kind."[5]

In 1776, Adams proposed "the Choice of Hercules, as engraved by Gribeline in some Editions of Lord Shaftesbury's Works," for a "Device for a Great Seal for the confederate States." The "icons" incorporated in this myth were widely familiar in the revolutionary period, in

Virginia as well as New England.[6] For the national seal, John translated Shaftesbury's version into words: "The Hero resting on his Clubb. Virtue pointing to her rugged Mountain, on one Hand, and persuading him to ascend. Sloth, glancing at her flowery Paths of Pleasure, wantonly reclining on the Ground, displaying the Charms both of her Eloquence and Person, to seduce him into Vice." Shaftesbury's commentary on the picture, itself an intrinsic part of a book aimed at reforming men's manners by making them men of feeling, emphasized Hercules' "Agony, or inward Conflict which indeed make the principal Action here."[7]

John associated his wish to reform his manners with Shaftesburian ideals of manhood. The gender component of his thinking here is very evident, from his boyhood's dancing with girls, his own figure of Virtue urging him to give up "Effeminacy," his apprehension that a girl could be a "decoy," and his reproaching himself for gallanting the girls, along with the distractions of "Love, Courtship, Marriage," all symbolized by the seductive female figure of Sloth/Pleasure, wantonly reclining and displaying her charms. The standard that Shaftesbury's Hercules represented shaped the Adamses' ideas of raising their own sons, especially John Quincy, whom Abigail called the "Young Hercules," and who banteringly called himself "young Hercules" in a letter to her. John wanted such manhood to be an emblem of America, resting his hopes for its future on men's choice of "pure Virtue," "the only foundation of a free Constitution." The description of "the new American nation as . . . an 'infant Hercules'" was common, Shaw suggests, but Adams's apprehension of the American character, writes Wood, "sprang from his knowledge of himself."[8]

Soon after the choice of Hercules entered his mind, John almost took the wrong path, coming within a hairbreadth of marrying Hannah Quincy, prevented only by the kind of accident he said governed marriages. His friend Jonathan Sewall and Sewall's girlfriend, Esther, had broken in "upon H and me and interrupted a Conversation that would have terminated in a Courtship, which would in spight of the Dr. [i.e., Bela Lincoln, John's rival for Hannah's affections] have terminated in a Marriage, which Marriage might have depressed me to absolute Poverty and obscurity, to the end of my Life. But the Accident separated us, and gave room for Lincolns addresses, which have delivered me from very dangerous shackles, and left me at Liberty, if I will mind my studies, of making a Character and a fortune." John went on to explain Hannah's state of mind at the time. Because he had not yet broached the subject of marriage when Sewall and Esther interrupted them, Hannah "was obliged to act without certain knowledge." And, given the presence in her home of a "young and very fruitful" new stepmother, "on whom her father," Colonel Quincy, "fondly doat[ed]," "she had peculiar reasons to desire an immediate Marriage." Colonel Quincy and his father wanted her to marry Dr. Lincoln because of Lincoln's "family Business, and Character." She suspected that John "was apprised of the Drs. Designs" and— quite wrongly—that he "was determined to see her no more." John had Hannah's calculation in mind in exclaiming with ironic sentimentality: "A tender scene."

"Now let me collect my Thoughts," he continued, "which have long been scattered, among Girls, father, Mother, Grandmother, Brothers, Matrimony, Hushing, Chatt, Provisions, Cloathing, fewel, servants for a family, and apply them, with steady Resolution and an aspiring Spirit, to the Prosecution of my studies." Instead of such scattering, "Let me form the great Habits of Thinking, Writing, Speaking." Instead of "girls" like Hannah, "Let my whole Courtship be applied to win the Applause and Admiration of Gridley, Prat, Otis, Thatcher, &." According to Ferling, the latter were Boston's "four most eminent lawyers." "Let Love and Vanity be extinguished, and the great Passions of Ambition, Patriotism, break out and burn." The former were irrelevant distractions. "Let the little objects be neglected and forgot, and the great ones engross, arouse, and exalt my soul."[9]

The path that John had accidentally avoided and now was determined to resist would be illustrated by a couple—the Webbs—he met some years later. They were "the Opposites of every Thing great, spirited, and enterprising. His father was a dissenting Parson, and a Relation of [John's], a zealous Puritan and famous Preacher." But the son degenerated. He had not "the least Regard to his Education, his Connections, Relations, Reputations"; "at Colledge," a place of vulnerability for young men, he was merely "a silent Hearer of a few Rakes" and afterward "continue[d] the same Man, rather the same softly living Thing that creepeth upon the face of the Earth." He was living the kind of life that, as we shall see, John felt could be a prospect for himself, "slow, silent . . . creeping." Don Webb had "attempted Trade, but failed in that—now keeps School and takes Boarders; his Wife longs to be genteel, to go to Dances, Assemblies, Dinners, suppers &c.—but cannot make it."[10]

In that journal entry recording his escape from being diverted this way by Hannah, John resolved that "the mind must be aroused, or it will slumber," aroused, that is, by passion, but not the wrong kind, that is, the "Passion," he confessed, that had been "growing in his heart, and a consequent Habit of thinking, forming, and strengthening in [his] Mind, that would have eat out every seed of ambition," an ambition corresponding to the liability he would later feel in response to the charge that leaving public office was to "sacrifice his country" to "a weak Attachment to a Woman." Here, he added, however, that to repress love in the interests of engaging the great passion of ambition did not mean that he lacked that other passion: "A young fellow of fond amorous Passions, may appear quite cold and insensible. The Love of Knowledge may prevail over the Love of Girls." But, he continued, those "Old Men" who thought him incapable of Gallantry and Intrigue were "mistaken." In this masculine case, sensibility unambiguously connoted sexuality.[11]

## Wrestling with Dissimulation: The Requirements of Public Life

John found that he was able to incorporate that agreeable public/private variety into his Herculean ambition. Soon after his account of his rambling imagination, he contrasted the pleasures of sociability with those of "Retirement," recognizing that the "Arts of Gain are necessary" and that spending time with men—"in a Tavern, in the Meeting House, or the Training Field"—and, thus, to "grow popular" by "agreeable assistance in the Tittle-tattle of the hour" would be more valuable than study of "the deep hidden Principles of . . . Law," which would give him "a gloomy Countenance and a stiff Behavior." But to participate in social, public life was not merely to make money: "retirement [i.e., studying on his own, in private] will lose its charms if it is not interrupted by business and activity." Public activity would enhance the pleasures of retirement, and the opposite was true: "I must converse and deal with Mankind, and move and stir from one scene of Action and Debate and Business, and Pleasure, and Conversation to another, and grow weary of all, before I shall feel the strong Desire of retiring to contemplation on Men and Business and Pleasure and Books." Shaw observes that although he "continued to ransom his life to his political fortunes Adams cared above all for books and ideas." John's uniquely extensive marginalia were one expression of this transcendent appetite, the nature and extent of his writings another, but, if his devotion to politics was a "ransom," he was passionate about it, too, and Shaw, like other biographers, emphasizes his hunger for political fame.[12]

Even before John had established a home with a family in it to which

he could turn from his public activities, and vice versa, he was attracted
by a very similar kind of division between private and public life: "After
a hard Labor at Husbandry, Reading and Reflection in Retirement will
be a relief and a high refined Pleasure; after attending a Town Meeting,
watching the Intrigues, Acts, Passions, Speeches, that pass there, a Retreat to reflect, compare, distinguish will be highly delightful. So after a
Training Day, after noting the Murmurs, Complaints, Jealousies, Impru-
dence, Envy that pass in the field, I shall be pleased with my solitude."
He enjoyed the "Transitions from study to business" and "from Business to Conversation and Pleasure," not only because they made "the
Revolution of study still more agreeable," but also because they would
prevent him, he thought, if "in total Retirement" from forgetting the
sciences, and smoking, and trifling, and droning too much. We can compare John's appetite for transitions with what Wood writes of Franklin:
as a young tradesman, he had worked at home with his wife, and his later
"separating his home from his business was a graphic reminder of his
mastery of his own time," to study, to experiment, to work for the public good, in short, for the fuller flowering of his personality.[13] Perhaps,
too, we can see John's coupling of his dedication of himself to his pursuit
of fame by way of public service with his insistence that he would rather
be at home, as a version of this fundamental self-conception, along with
his making the choice of Hercules, or, rather, continually remaking it.

Entering those varied scenes challenged presentations of self. John
recorded that he was "very thankful" for those who "checked" him—
with irony, say. He was particularly responsive to other people's signals.
At twenty, he wrote in his diary after spending an evening "at Mr. Mc-
Carty's": "the Love of Fame naturally betrays a man into several weaknesses and Fopperies that tend very much to diminish his Reputation,
and so defeats itself." He had become conscious that this was his proclivity and one on which he implied he had to bring further consciousness to
bear in order to control. The passage continued: "Vanity I am sensible, is
my cardinal Vice and cardinal Folly, and I am in continual Danger, when
in Company, of being led an ignis fatuus Chase by it, without the strictest Caution and watchfulness over myself."[14]

John had addressed vanity's danger in that passage in his diary in
which he expressed his gratitude to those who had checked him. "Good
Treatment" misled him by making him think that he was "admired, beloved," and his "vanity" was "indulged." The result was that he dismissed his "Gard" and grew "weak, silly, vain, conceited, ostentatious."
On the other hand, he continued: "A check, a frown, a sneer, a Sarcasm,

rouses my Spirits, makes me more careful and considerate." Evidently, he was adept at reading such signals, and his responsiveness came close to conforming to part of the definition of *sensibility* that Hannah More gave in her 1779 poem of that name. A person of sensibility registered, she wrote,

> The hint malevolent, the look oblique,
> The obvious satire or implied dislike,
> The sneer equivocal, the harsh reply,
> And all the cruel language of the eye.

The convention that More poeticized was available to represent a particular characteristic of John's. Abigail wrote him in 1776 with the same kind of language: "I know your delicacy must be wounded by the unjust and malicious." In that same 1759 diary entry describing his letting down his "Gard," John had questioned whether the positive signals of "good Treatment," "Smiles, kind Words, respectful Action," didn't betray him "into Weaknesses and Littleness," whereas "bad" treatment, "frowns, Satirical Speeches, and contemptuous Behavior," made him avoid them. Sensibility could serve distinctively male ambition.[15]

In spite of the private pain its pursuit could bring him, John declared: "Reputation ought to be the perpetual subject of my Thoughts, and Aim of my Behavior. How shall I gain a Reputation?" He asked himself if he should frequently visit "the Neighborhood, and converse familiarly with Men, Women, and Children, in their own Style," a style that included uneducated speech, and he specified as its subjects "the common Tittle-tattle of the town and the ordinary Concerns of a family." In those "Visits," he would show such people his "Knowledge in the law." He imagined another route: "Shall I endeavor to renew my Acquaintance with those young Gentlemen in Boston, who were at Colledge with me?" This would require of him to employ a different "Style," presumably including the way he spoke usually, "and to extend [his] Acquaintance among Merchants, Shop keepers, Tradesmen, &c., and mingle with the Crowd upon Change, and trapes the Town house floor, with one and another, in order to get a Character in Town." Then he imagined himself getting the sort of reputation appropriate to his professional peers: "Shall I, by making Remarks and proposing Questions [to] the Lawyers at the Bar, endeavor to get a Great character for understanding and learning among them?"

He concluded, however, that "Neither of these projects," that is, of getting those Characters, "will avail." The first because it would "re-

quire much Thought, and time, and a very particular Knowledge of the
Province Law and common Matters, of which I know much less than I
do of the Roman law," and the second because it would be "slow and
tedious, and will be ineffectual, for Envy, Jealousy, and self-Interest,
will not suffer them [the other lawyers observing his efforts] to give a
young fellow, a free, generous Character, especially me." John was himself mulling over the best ways to advance his own self-interest, presenting a variety of selves crafted—or "self-fashioned"—to suit different
communities and groups. He had not yet exhausted the possibilities of
self-presentation, the last being more directly political, though the others would have served political ambition, too: "Shall I look out for a
Cause to Speak to, and exert all the Soul and all the Body I own, to cut
a flash, strike amazement, to catch the Vulgar." He combined the previous potentials into one in order to contrast them with the last: "In short,
shall I walk a lingering heavy Pace, or shall I take one bold determined
Leap into the midst of some, Cash, and Business? That is the question; a
bold push, a resolute attempt, a determined Enterprize, or a slow, silent,
imperceptible creeping. Shall I creep or fly." We might compare—or
contrast—this with Abigail's adaptation to herself of Thomson's lines
quoted in the previous chapter:

> My passions too can Sometimes soar above
> The household task assign'd me.[16]

Four days later, John wrote: "I feel vexed, fretted, chafed; the
Thought of no Business mortifies, stings me. . . . But let me banish these
fears; let me assume a Fortitude, a Greatness of mind." He consciously
put on a particular character, manifested in his determination to repress
certain feelings. One motive was to bring himself immediate and greater
pleasure: "In such a gradual ascent to fame and fortune, and Business,
the Pleasure that they give will be imperceptible, but by a bold, sudden
rise, I shall feel all the Joys of each at once. Have I Genius and Resolution and Health enough for such an achievement?" And he apprehended
that his ambition required an external stimulus: "I shall never shine till
some animating Occasion calls forth all my Powers."[17]

John continued to present apparently contradictory views of the
masking of feelings. In his edition of the diary, Charles Francis Adams
included an early piece that John wrote "for the newspapers" in the persona of "an old man, turned of seventy," giving a history of the change
in his views of "human nature." People were divided between a few,
"the anglers," "whose constant attention and pursuit was to allure and

take," and "the multitude," who "allowed themselves to be caught by hooks and snares." The second subject was his emotional reaction to this discovery: "My compassion and indignation [were] raised alternately. I pitied poor deluded simplicity on one hand, and I raged against cruelty and wickedness on the other." He planned "to rescue the lamb from the jaws of the wolf," which he thought "a noble adventure," one in which he would take on the role of "a reformer," a noun taking its meaning from campaigns for the reformation of manners, but it seemed "impracticable" and "odious": "The knaves would arise in combination to ruin the reformers, and the fools would be managed in no other way than that of their appetites and passions." The writer reveals that the particular relation of knaves and fools with which he was concerned was a political one: "To avoid the pungent misery of a disappointed, despised patriot, I determined to make a total alteration in the course and nature of my ideas and sentiments." That is, he would no longer attempt the reform of others. This alteration was the repression of his sensibility: "Whenever I heard or saw an instance of atrocious treachery, fraud, hypocrisy, injustice, and cruelty, the common effects of excessive ambition, avarice, ambition, and lust, instead of indulging the sentiments of nature, which I found were a resentment bordering on rage, I resolved instantly to set up a laugh and make myself merry." Sensibility could sponsor feelings of resentment and high anger, positive in relation to evil human actions and motives, or at least that is what we have seen John argued elsewhere on several occasions, as did Jefferson. Abigail taught the young John Quincy the same thing. Positive, too, was the "indulgence" of such sentiments.[18]

The next sentence could be the sketch of a sentimental plot: "Whenever I saw a simple, deluded creature brought by the craft of others to brutal debauchery, sickness, cold, prison, whipping-post, pillory, or gallows, instead of indulging sympathy and feeling, I set myself to laughing." Because the former were "the sentiments of nature," the writer had to struggle to put on a different face: "I must own I found a good deal of difficulty to command myself at first in this bold attempt to alter the whole system of morality; and in spite of my attention, a flash of vengeance, or a thrill of pity would sometimes escape me before I could bring my muscles into a risible position." Eventually he succeeded.

The rest of the article laid out the career of "a young fellow" who operated within the corrupt, unfeeling system and evinced a similar ambition to that John had himself admitted to elsewhere, including using forms of self-presentation—masks—to pursue it. The masks included false sensibility, "compassionating," as well as "wheedling himself into some connection with the people." To "those not already grappled to his interest by fear or affection," he "becomes . . . very assiduous and obliging." By these and other means, this young fellow was "presently extolled as a public blessing, as the most useful man in town, as a very understanding man." Eventually, he attained his goal of election to public office. One can see a self-serving, self-righteous note in this, but what is valuable for my purpose is that John's persona adopted an ironic orientation toward the system, "the affair of English privileges, British liberty, and all that," that was not just republican but that of a man of sensibility, to whom, ostensibly, the manipulation of feature and emotion was unnatural and immoral.

But Adams took a more complex view of self-presentation in the aftermath of his praise for one of the Reverend Robert South's sermons, which argued against a man's having "to maintain a constant Course of Dissimulation, in the whole Tenor of his Behavior." While this was, in South's 1662 judgment, "the wisdom of the world," it was "Foolishness with God." Writing the day after this entry, Adams made a distinction in dissimulation: "The first Maxim of worldly Wisdom, constant Dissimulation, may be good or evil as it is interpreted. If it means only a constant Concealment from others of such of our Sentiments, Actions, Desires, and Resolutions, as others have not a Right to know, it is not only lawful, but commendable." That is, it was in the individual's power to make that distinction. Here, Adams emphasized that the reason for concealment was to prevent being wounded by "Enemies," in accordance with what he had written earlier of his apprehensions of his treatment by his fellow lawyers. Or one could see here intimations of the emerging individualism celebrated early in the century by Mandeville's much denounced *The Fable of the Bees: Private Vice Is Public Virtue*, the book that Royall Tyler Sr. recommended to John before sending him South's *Sermons*.[19]

Adair sympathizes with the view, expressed by both John and Abigail, that "the pursuit of fame was a way of transforming egotism and self-aggrandizing impulses into service," but Wood has observed that the revolutionaries' "vision" of their "sacrifice of individual interests to the greater good of the whole" was "divorced from the realities of American society" and, at worst, Wood implies, a fantasy.[20] But John knew this, as did Abigail, even if they wished to sustain such self-sacrifice as an ideal. Here, John had gone on to say that the concealment of potentially wounding "Sentiments, Actions, Desires, and Resolutions" was not total at all: "So that some Things, which ought to be communicated to some of our Friends that they might improve them to our Profit, or Honour, or Pleasure should be concealed from our Enemies and from indiscreet friends, least they should be turned to our Loss, Disgrace or Mortification." Revelations, then, were entirely calculable in terms of self-interest, consistent with a very largely competitive, public world. John then specified what should and should not be concealed.[21]

Franklin and Washington were also preoccupied with public self-presentation, an aspect of the "performance" of refinement (including sensibility) that Bushman describes as characterizing eighteenth-century colonial elites. We can refer it to the popularization of the "self-fashioning" that Stephen Greenblatt detects first among sixteenth-century aristocratic Englishmen. In the 1771 section of his *Autobiography* where he deemed male vanity valuable to the public good, Franklin also showed himself as a young man to have been as conscious of his "public appearance" as John Adams was and as desirous of "making a good figure" and "obtain[ing] a character," there being a relation between "character and credit." Franklin recorded other young men doing the same. He distinguished between what he called his "public appearance in business" and his "state of mind with regard to [his] principles and morals," the latter category including an account of the evolution of his religious views, resulting in this: "I grew convinced that *truth*, *sincerity*, and *integrity* in feelings between man and man were of the utmost importance to the felicity in life." Like Adams, Franklin did not think of this as inconsistent with his continuing to present different masks or selves in his varied activities as politician and diplomat, as well as businessman, in which success brought him great pleasure. Perhaps the best-known fact about Franklin's writing his *Autobiography* is that he thought that the "means" by which he had "raised" himself "to a state of affluence and celebrity in the world" was "fit to be imitated." One lesson was the value and pleasure in putting on masks, "the humble enquirer," for example. In fact, "this homespun, hardworking, prototypical American was at the same time, the European, the most cosmopolitan, the most sophisticated, indeed the most aristocratic of the founding fathers." While Franklin and Adams were able to strut their stuff on European stages, their youths illustrate that the potentials for versatility of selfhood were becoming more widely available to young American men.[22]

In Wood's interpretation, the transatlantic preoccupation with duplicity, manifested in the fact that "masquerades and hidden designs formed the grammar and vocabulary for much of the thought of the eighteenth century," flowed "from the expansion and increasing complexity of the political world," in contrast to its context in, say antiquity. Unprecedented "economic developments," as well as demographic ones, meant that "more people were more distanced from the apparent centers of political decision making." The results held promise—"conceptual worlds of many individuals were being broadened and transformed." Other scholars have described how relationships spanning such widened horizons, notably in imperial and international commerce, depended on the extension of trust, formalized in legal contracts. Wood's focus is the more pained consequence in political and historical thinking, the tendency to interpret events as the result of conspiracies: "The more people became strangers to one another and the less they knew of one another's hearts, the more suspicious and untrustful they became, ready as never before in Western history to see . . . deception at work."[23]

But one must also bear in mind the pleasure that men—overwhelmingly, those engaged in this dimension were male—took in their ability to navigate these political reaches, even in their virtuosity in self-presentation and detection: "Relationship between superior and subordinates now became disturbingly problematic. . . . Growing proportions of the population were more politically conscious . . . with what seemed to be the abused [abusive] power . . . of elites." Such fresh complexities coincided with that new confidence of "the most enlightened" to understand human psychology scientifically. The belief in conspiracy, Wood suspects, was "the consequence of a political world expanding and changing faster than its available rational modes of explanation could handle."[24] One must add to this that a profoundly complicating factor was the admission into scientific psychology and into laudable human behavior of the validity of passions, all (bad and good) of which Descartes had argued had their uses. Elites in eighteenth-century transatlantic societies refined certain passions into feeling, partly prompted by the potential that such admission held for women. Even in that form, feeling posed severe problems when it came to the matter of control, above all, because of its association with sex.

Leaving aside other reasons for their identification of themselves with the "social affections"—sympathy, compassion, benevolence, humanity, and pity, say—or their arranging them in a different order of importance, one can see that women were deeply conscious of a disparity in self-presentation between themselves and men. It was men who had the widest opportunities for versatility of personality because of their kinds of engagement in public life, even though some women's opportunities were significantly increased by way of the creation of a leisured, hetero-

social infrastructure and even by the incorporation of shopped-for objects at home, including books. In contrast to men, women were, by and
large, restricted to the household and denied participation in worldly
business, yet they now had rising expectations encouraged by literacy
and the public pleasures of heterosociality, albeit associated with the
marriage market and exposure to disrepute and worse. It is evident, then,
why sentimental women would pose sincerity, private virtue, and their
moral superiority to men's worldliness. That men of sensibility adhered
to the same values is striking, explicable in part by their being reared in
ways corresponding to a new world of consumption and to the influence
of women, mothers, wives, lovers, and friends. Men had other reasons,
too, to aggrandize sincerity, not the least being their wish for credit and
trust in commerce and politics.

These considerations supply a perspective on James Flexner's juxtaposition of two of Alexander Hamilton's letters, written on "almost the
same day" in 1780, soon after he became engaged to Elizabeth Schuyler, a
match extremely advantageous to his career. To his friend John Laurens,
another of Washington's aides-de-camp, Hamilton wrote:

> Have you not heard that I am on the point of becoming a benedict? . . .
> Next fall completes my doom. I give up my liberty to Miss Schuyler.
> She is a good-hearted girl who I am sure will never play the terma-
> gant; though not a genius she has good sense enough to be agreeable,
> and though not a beauty, she has fine black eyes—is rather handsome
> and has every other requisite of the exterior to make a lover happy. And
> believe me, I am a lover in earnest, though I do not speak of the perfec-
> tions of my Mistress with the enthusiasm of Chivalry.

This, too, was convention, the man-to-man, wry hyperbole of being captured and shackled by marriage (an image that, as we have seen, John Adams used), only ironically self-pitying since it was the wife who gave up
the power ascribed to her in courtship by the suitor. Hamilton conveyed
his possession of the iron hand in a velvet glove by his assurance that "she
has good sense enough to be agreeable"—common ground between this
tone and that pleasingness to men central to the style of feminine sensibility. There is realism in his judging Elizabeth Schuyler "rather handsome"
and physically attractive enough to give him sexual satisfaction, ending
the passage with his acknowledgment of the existence of a different literary convention in which lovers exaggerated the qualities of mistresses.
"Chivalry" (part of romance) had been absorbed by sentimentalism.[25]

The second letter was to Elizabeth Schuyler herself: "I love you more and more every hour. The sweet softness and delicacy of your mind and manners, the elevation of your sentiments, the real goodness of your heart, its tenderness to me, the beauties of your face and person, your unpretending good sense and that innocent simplicity and frankness which pervade your actions; all these appear to me with increasing amiableness and place you in my estimation above all the rest of your sex." Her feminine sensibility is manifest in innocent simplicity and that good heart that is a common factor in the two letters, although "a good-hearted girl" is not quite the same as telling Betsy Schuyler of "the real goodness of [her] heart." Similarly, being "agreeable" to him resembles her showing "tenderness to [him]," but expressed differently to male chum and female lover. He told Laurens that he was "a lover in earnest," whereas to Betsy he claimed: "I love you more and more every hour." This, with his placing her "above all the rest of your sex," comes closer to the style in which he chose not to speak of her to Laurens.

Flexner notes in connection with these two illustrations that Hamilton "tailored" each letter for its recipient but that, "however contradictory, each reflected . . . aspects of Hamilton's emotions." Certainly, they attest to his versatility and cast light on the culture of sensibility's preoccupation with the unanswerable question of sincerity. Other examples of Hamilton's ability to write in conventional, sentimental style include in his first publication in St. Croix, which helped launch him; in his poem of consolation on the death of a child of one of his patrons; and, on occasion, in *The Federalist*.[26]

Women must have known that men wrote to each other less sentimentally than they wrote to women, although by no means without sentiment, but it seems highly likely that women expected to hear from lovers predominantly in the language of sensibility, as Abigail wished to hear from John and did hear from James Lovell, despite her occasional deflections. Colonel William Smith, with Hamilton and Laurens one of Washington's "family" of young officers, flavored his letters to Nabby with references to Sterne and also with his own Sterne-like passages, with the "chivalry" of his account of Diane de Poitiers, and with pastoral sentimentalism. Like Royall Tyler, he wrote the same kind of sentimental letters to Abigail when opening his courtship of Nabby. They were in sharp contrast to those he wrote at the same time to his close male friend Baron Friedrich von Steuben, in which "he appeared another man, this one ambitious, striving, impecunious, flirtatious." This is not to say that women were not capable of other styles and degrees of versatility themselves, but those styles and degrees of versatility corresponded to the restricted range of experience among many literate women, regretted by Abigail and marked by the line of which both sexes were so keenly aware.[27]

## Sensibility in the Courtroom

John imagined that success in public life might require him to give up the values of sensibility, but he put them to use in his work as a lawyer, which brought him into contact with the distressed. In 1761, he represented an apprentice, whom he described as "a poor, fatherless Child . . . his Mother Unable to provide for him," in an action against his master, who had broken his covenant to teach him to read and write as well as to weave. Adams recorded his address to the jury, which opened: "The Law, Gentlemen, is extreamly tender and indulgent to such Actions as these. For such is the Benignity and Humanity of the English Constitution that all the weak, and helpless, and friendless part of our Species are taken under its Peculiar Care and Protection. Women, Children, and Especially Widows and fatherless Children, have always from the Compassion of the Law peculiar Privileges and Indulgences allowed them." The extension of such a view to slaves by some whites was illustrated in the works of Granville Sharp, so notable a part of Adams's library.[28]

In a 1774 case stemming from a mob attack on Richard King, a supporter of the Stamp Act, Adams wrote out in full what his modern editors call an "emotional harangue to the jury," concentrating to a significant extent "on the physical damage to King's property, the intangible damage to his 'Credit in Trade' . . . and the anguish suffered by the whole family from the malice and cruelty of the mob." He said he wanted the jury to imagine the dimensions of what King's family suffered: "The Cruelty, the Terror, the Horror of the whole dismal scene. It would be affectation to attempt to exaggerate, it is almost impossible to exaggerate, the distresses of this innocent Family." He incorporated a very similar passage to Abigail in a letter describing the same scene, notably elaborating it literally in terms of sensibility: "The Terror, and Distress, the Distraction and Horror of this Family cannot be described by Words or painted upon canvass. It is enough to move a Heart of Stone, to read the Story. A Mind susceptible of Feelings of Humanity, an Heart which can be touch'd with Sensibi[li]ty for human Misery and Wretchedness, must reluct, must burn with Resentment and Indignation, at such outrageous Injuries." He hoped to move the jury with such language because he believed that they shared the values it expressed. Whether his use of it in both private and public was because of his own irresistible feelings on the issue cannot be said. Indubitably genuine was the feeling that he added in words to Abigail but did not tell the men of the jury: "These private Mobs, I do and will detest."[29] Again, his strong feelings ranged to anger, a proclivity of which he was well aware. Angered by the attribution of ambition to him, he wrote Abigail: "There are very few People in this World, with whom I can bear to converse. I can treat all with Decency and Civility, and converse with them when it is necessary, on Points of Business. But I am never happy in their Company." This speaks to the freedom to show such feelings that he reserved for her.[30]

In the Richard King case, John distinguished "private" mob action from crowd action aimed at the public good. He had continued in his letter about it to Abigail: "If Popular Commotions can be justified, in Opposition to Attacks upon the Constitution it can be only when Fundamentals are invaded, nor then unless for absolute Necessity and with great sanction." John's revolutionaryism went only so far, or, rather, like other republicans, he rationalized it as conservative, defensive, against novel, licentious imperialism, but we can see, too, that his distinction was consistent with the lengthy criticism of popular and overwhelmingly male culture that he made elsewhere: "But these Tarrings and Featherings, these breaking open Houses by rude and insolent Rabbles, in Resentment for private Wrongs or in pursuit of private Prejudices and Passions, must be discountenanced, cannot be even excused upon any Principle which can be entertained by a good Citizen—a worthy Member of Society." Again, we see John's adherence to the Hutchesonian, republican distinction between private passion and, implicitly, public good, attributing mob action to the former, an attribution he did not feel free to express to the jury. It was one he would carry into his apprehensions of postrevolutionary democracy, which he forecast in an 1814 letter to Jefferson would be "revengefull bloody and cruel."[31]

Sensibility, however, the elevation of certain kinds of feeling, could provide common ground under certain circumstances. This is how John's courtroom appeal continued: "The Excellency of a Tryal by Jury is that they are the Partys Peers, his equalls, men of like passions, feelings, Imaginations and Understandings with him. If your Passions are not affected by this Occasion, you will not be the Plaintiffs Peers. It is right and fit, it is reasonable and just that you should feel as he did, that you should put yourselves in his Place, and be moved by his Passions." This latter was the basis for those 1754 Boston gentlemen's appeal I quoted in the introduction, and both appeals could be said to illustrate Smith's *Theory of Moral Sentiments*.[32] In the post-1960s and continuing debate over "the radicalism of the American Revolution" between those who uphold the decisive and shaping actions of white, male, elite "founders" and those wishing to interpret it as a revolution "from the bottom up," one element of agreement among some is the existence of "a shared belief in equality."[33] More apparent, perhaps, is the ostensibly shared and growing belief in the value of feeling, assisted by the inroads of evangelism, but qualified by the existence of a popular male culture to which I have alluded, and coexisting with the continuous history of the domination of American democracy by those of wealth and power. The founding fathers apprehended the ability of elites to manipulate the feelings of those they wished to rule, but Waldstreicher writes of postrevolutionary politics that opposition "ritual and rhetoric . . . maintained the vital link between street theater and sentimental culture, a link that allowed cross-class mobilization."[34]

John attempted further to "affect" the 1774 jurymen's passions on the basis of his Smithian definition of sympathy: "Be pleased then to imagine yourselves each one for himself—in Bed with his pregnant Wife, . . . [the household] all asleep, suspecting nothing—harbouring no Malice, Envy, or revenge in your own Bosoms." In other words, imagine a family entirely innocent and safe. We must imagine John then suddenly raising his voice and speaking more rapidly, to say: "All of a sudden, in an Instant, in a twinkling of an Eye, an Armed Banditti of Felons, thieves, Robbers, and Burglars, rush upon the House." His next simile Americanized the assault with a vision driven deep "into the white American psyche" by experience, by memory, and by captivity narratives: "Like Savages from the Wilderness, or like Legions from the Blackness of Darkness, they yell and Houl, they dash in all the Windows and enter—entered the[y] Roar, they stamp, they yell, they houl, they cutt, break and burn all before them." John wanted his words to activate the jury's mind's eye. "Do you see," he continued, "a tender and affectionate husband, an amiable deserving Wife near her time . . . The Husband attempting to run down stairs, his Wife laying hold of his Arm, to stay him and sinking fainting, dying away in his Arms. The Children crying and clinging round their Parents—*father will they kill me*—father save me!" He then argued that the family had been traumatized. The "Impressions" could never be "erased," becoming "a continual Sourse of Grief."[35]

Quite soon thereafter, John was confronted by tears of pain in his Boston office. They were being shed by James Forrest, a customhouse agent who had "been over half the city looking for a lawyer" to take the case of Captain Thomas Preston, the commander of the British troops who had just committed "the Boston Massacre": "With tears streaming from his Eyes, he said, 'I am come with a very solemn Message from a very unfortunate man, Captain Preston, in Prison.'" Adams recognized the significance of the case but warned Forrest that Preston "could expect no Art or Address" in his presentation of it. Yet his introductory address to the court quoted this passage from Beccaria's *Essay on Crimes and Punishments* (another illustration of the international dimension to sensibility): "If, by supporting the rights of mankind, I shall contribute to save from the agonies of death one unfortunate victim of tyranny . . . the blessing and tears of transport will be a sufficient consolation to me for the contempt of all mankind."[36] John Quincy Adams recorded that he had "often heard from individuals, who had been present among the crowd of spectators at the trial, the electrical effect produced upon the jury and upon the immense and excited auditory by the first sentence with which he [his father] had opened his defence, which was the following citation from the then recently published work of Beccaria."[37]

John Adams showed in his diary that he found that that same passage from Beccaria's book represented the feelings that his own practice of law generally brought him. He declared: "I have received such Blessings and enjoyed such Tears of Transport—and there is no greater Pleasure, or Consolation!" He went on to specify his response to a man he saved from a rape conviction. This client exclaimed: "God-bless Mr. Adams; God bless his soul. I am not to be hanged" "His Blessing and his Transport . . . gave me," Adams wrote, "more Pleasure, when I first heard the Relation and when I have recollected it since, than any fee would have done." He added: "This was a worthless fellow; but *Nihil humanum, alienum*. His joy, which I had in some Sense been instrumental in procuring, and his Blessings and good Wishes, occasioned very agreeable emotions in the Heart." Such self-satisfaction was central to the culture of sensibility.[38]

That sentimental lawyering coexisted with an older form is suggested by Edmund Randolph's contrasting the practices of Jefferson and Patrick Henry in the late 1760s: "Mr. Jefferson drew copiously from the depths of the law, Mr. Henry from the recesses of the human heart." (This was not to say that, in other settings, Jefferson did not speak like a man of feeling.) A lawyer from Connecticut shared Henry's approach, stating proudly in 1786: "The feelings of my Heart . . . inspire my head, give expression to my pen, and a voice [to his letters]." John Adams's potential son-in-law, Royall Tyler Jr., "bred to the law," as he was described in 1797, was said to have "a most benevolent heart": "Does misery need an advocate? Mr. *Tyler* eagerly steps forth, its unpurchased champion." That is, he combined advocacy with knight-errantry. "Does guilt (when not atrocious) sink down heart-broken and desponding? in Mr. *Tyler* it finds a man, who . . . feels for the errors of others, pities their vices, and compassionates their wants." He showed this in his courtroom oratory, as John Adams had done, and his was one of "resistless power," in its invocation of compassion: "He rouses every sympathizing passion of their souls, attacks them in every vulnerable part; awes, soothes, softens, and finally prevails." Like Adams and Henry, Tyler assumed that his audience, including juries, would be men of feeling, responsive to his power and his art, which he also put to use in writing sentimental comedies and other literary forms. In 1810, a judge wrote Tyler, by then a judge, too: "[When] we come to be judged for our judgements, my friend, the question will not be whether we pursued legal forms or technical niceties, but have you heard the cry of the poor and relieved them from their oppressors."[39]

In short, the practice of law was already significantly marked by the culture of sensibility before the period in which Perry Miller discerned that, when faced with accusations of self-serving chicanery, lawyers defended themselves by arguing on behalf of "legal benevolence." Professionalism required the "amiable affections of the heart," which imparted "lustre to the utility of learning." The New York lawyer James Kent said in an 1827 lecture that no "man can preserve in his own breast a constant and lively sense of justice, without being insensibly led to cherish the benevolent affections." He and his fellows "allied themselves with the sentimental version of benevolence" that Miller detected in the 1820s. Similarly, Daniel Walker Howe writes that, "from the 1830s on, judge made, legal innovation often reflected increased compassion for the underdogs . . . judicial opinions often cited 'the common feelings of mankind' . . . in justification for their compassion." Knott demonstrates that members of another professional group, physicians, presented themselves as men of feeling in the later eighteenth century, and, of course, ministers had led the way.[40]

## John's Campaign for the Reformation of Men's Manners

John did not limit his efforts to reform men's manners to himself. In 1811, he wrote Rush that he had been "a churchgoing animal of seventy-six years" and "could not recollect a single insinuation against [him] of any amorous intrigue or irregular or immoral conduct with a woman." In his twenties, he wrote, he "had been fired with a zeal amounting to enthusiasm against ardent spirits, the multiplication of taverns, retailers, dram shops, and tippling houses." Teaching schoolboys, he recorded that he would rather "sit in school and consider which of [his] pupils will turn out in his future Life, a Hero and which a rake." He was not only projecting his own Herculean potentials but also reflecting what he saw of other adult men around him: "Let others waste the bloom of Life at the Card or biliard Table among rakes and fools, and when their minds are sufficiently fretted with losses, and inflamed by Wine, ramble through the Streets assaulting innocent People, breaking Windows, or debauching young Girls."[41]

The men's manners targeted by such reformers as John Adams should be seen as the marks of a distinct culture. In metropolitan Britain, that culture was popularly based on taverns, the sites for the drinking that accompanied "every commercial bargain, every commercial ritual," a center for the "craftsman culture" of men's societies. On occasion, and encouraged by drink, men would issue from these bases to assault representatives of status, law, and order—and also vulnerable women venturing out in public. Leisure activities proliferated from the sixteenth century, and, by the early seventeenth century, the alehouse became a new kind of economic center, outside the regulated medieval market, more modern in its range and improvisatoriness. Alehouses and taverns took on greater importance as employment exchanges, meeting places, too, for travelers, and centers for "popular religion" and for resistance to official and semiofficial sabbatarianism.[42]

Such combinations of tradition and innovation were brought across the Atlantic. By 1660, Richard Gildrie writes, "a fairly coherent variant of English popular culture"—including tavern culture—"emerged in New England," embraced by "respectable solid citizens." Their gambling, drinking, violence, and fornication provoked the jeremiads bewailing "declension," from the Puritan establishment's point of view, and the institutionalized efforts of its would-be "Reformation of Manners."[43]

Rhys Isaac has described popular male culture in eighteenth-century Virginia as focused on the "ordinary" and the courthouse, comparable to the popular male culture in New England described by Gildrie. Travel narratives by Dr. Alexander Hamilton and the Reverend Charles Woodmason, their perspectives identical to that of would-be reformers of manners, testify to its existence among men living on the Atlantic seaboard and in the backcountry of the Carolinas. Later in the century, the

Quaker Henry Drinker articulated the same cultural clash, bringing a middle-class, Quaker reformer's vision to bear on those riverboatmen in whom Rourke detects one powerful source of the American "national character" and whose culture Mark Twain later recorded. Drinker wrote his land agent in 1792: "[Every] piece of information relative to a reformation of manners amongst the people your way I shall be pleased to hear—a more contemptible set of Beings are hardly to be found than many of those who make their appearance in Spring and Fall with Boats and Rafts from your parts." Those parts were on the upper Delaware River in western New York. "If they can be brought off from their habits of Drunkenness and Profanity it will be good work, to which I wish much success. Some books shall be thought of." The manly culture of the riverboatmen and rafters, shared with backcountry inhabitants, was an oral one, although some participants left literary evidence.[44]

Cities, too, were centers for the expression of popular male culture. That fact can be detected in Carl Bridenbaugh's history *Cities in Revolt*, chronologically overlapping with the onset of Revolution and shaping itself to Revolutionary goals and ideology. In Boston, New York, Newport, Philadelphia, and Charleston, "mobs" included "Gentlemen Rakes" and "middle-class citizens," a finding about the mixing of men of different classes consistent with Gildrie's and Isaac's accounts of popular culture in New England and Virginia, as well as sailors and "unemployed dock and shipyard workers." Their actions expressed "boorish boisterousness," Bridenbaugh's phrasing perpetuating the views of reformers of manners.[45]

The persistence of this public street culture, largely of young men, is indicated by Michael Meranze's account of it in postrevolutionary Philadelphia. They congregated in taverns, said by a contemporary to be "the bane of youth, the nocturnal haunts of shoppers, robbers, and ruffians of every description." They set off firecrackers, fired their fowling pieces in the streets, and rattled carriages, frightening women and children in particular. One "frolick" resulted in the death of an "ancient woman," who "from the supposition she was a witch [they repeatedly] cut in the forehead, according to ancient and immemorial custom."[46]

While, as Sharon V. Salinger notes, Adams "began each day with a tankard of hard cider," he devoted page after page in his diary to taverns' proliferation, degeneration, and destructive effects. He believed that "Licensed Houses" originally had been designed to accommodate "Strangers" and, "perhaps, Town Inhabitants on public occasions." The only "excusable Designs" of a liquor retailer were "to supply the Neighborhood with

necessary Liquors in small Quantities to be consumed at home." Those
in charge, John averred, "should be selected from the most virtuous and
wealthy People," who accepted such positions as a "Trust." But, in 1760,
they were run by "Multitudes" and were "the haunt of loose, disorderly
People," a "trifling and nasty vicious Crew," rendering taverns "offen-
sive and unfit for the Entertainment of a Traveller of the least delicacy";
he put his own well-traveled self in the latter category, the term *delicacy* connoting sensibility and politeness, in contrast to the looseness
and disorderliness of people who were unwilling to restrain their appetites. John listed several of the damaging effects of taverns, first tempting
young people to waste their time and money, then following down the
slope to beggary, vice, prison, and the gallows, ruining "the Reputation
of our Country among strangers"; but "the worst Effect of all" was that
taverns had become "in many Places the Nurseries of our Legislators. An
Artful Man, who has neither sense nor sentiment, may by gaining a little
sway among the Rabble of a Town, multiply Taverns and Dram shops,
and thereby secure the Votes of Taverner and Retailer, and of all." Voting took place in taverns, when "Riotous drinking was typical." John's
proposal to get legislators to limit the number "and retrieve the Character of Licensed Houses" was intended to inhibit "that Impiety and Pro-
phaneness, that abandoned Intemperance and Prodigality, that Impudence and brawling Temper" they daily propagated.[47]

John identified the positive side of the implicit sociopsychological
polarity in manners with the Christianity that the goal of "reforming"
them implied. In that 1761 piece where he wrote in the guise of an old
man, Adams implied that men who controlled themselves had greater
sensibility as well as "sense and sentiment." If such men had passions,
they were not violent ones, or confused, but controlled by reason and
therefore channelable into positive political action. Among them was an
indignation prompted by that betrayal of the fantasied English political heritage, belief in which was central to the republican tradition that
American revolutionaries saw themselves rescuing. Local elections were
being won by men securing "the favor of taverners," in turn securing
"the suffrages of the rabble . . . perhaps the largest number of voters."
They provoked his republicanism as well as his sensibility. "Good God!"
he exclaimed, "where are the Rights of English men! Where is the spirit
that once exalted the souls of Britons, and emboldened their [faces] to
look even Princes and Monarchs in the face!"[48]

Like his predecessors among Puritan campaigners for the reformation of manners, John was appalled by the public behavior of men whose

lives were based on taverns: "Quarrels, Boxing, Duels, oaths, Curses, affrays, and Riots are daily hatching from Eggs and Spawns deposited in the same Nests . . . these Houses." He had engaged in similar physical activities in his youth, but he had done so apart from the tavern and with self-improvement in mind: "Instead of an unmanly Retreat to the Chimney-Corner of a Tavern, the young fellows of my Age were out in the Air improving their strength and Activity by Wrestling, running, leaping, lifting, and the like vigorous Diversions, and when satisfyed with these, resorted every one to his Mistress or his Wife." Expounding on that latter return to womenfolk led John to explain how such men's heterosexual relations differed from those of the unmanly, public house–based sort: "Love, that divine Passion which Nature has implanted for the Renovation of the species, and the greatest solace of our Lives: virtuous Love I mean, from whence the greatest Part of human Happiness originates, and which these modern seminaries have almost extinguished, or at least changed into filthiness and brutal Debauch, and then considered as God intended it, both a Duty of our Nature and the greatest source of our Bliss."[49]

John was capable of repressing the passion of love as a petty distraction from the great, ennobling passion for fame. But, with his reformer's hat on, he suggested that love held the courtly, romantic qualities widely elevated by sentimental literature, including colonial magazines,[50] and combined them with scientific and religious sanction. To call taverns "modern" was to endorse the characterization of irreligious materialism that the classically trained "ancients" had applied to their opponents and the interpretation of popular, male culture suggested elsewhere. John's phrase "filthiness and brutal Debauch" pointed to sex with the prostitutes who found customers in taverns, whence respectable women went rarely and only under highly restricted conditions.

Dueling, too, was a longtime target of reformers of manners.[51] John attacked it in papers on "Private Revenge" published in 1768, wishing "to eradicate the Gothic and pernicious principles of private revenge," principles he identified with "rusticity and barbarity," which, he said, had "been lately spread among [his] countrymen." He conceded that it was the case that "a competition and a mutual affectation of contempt is apt to arise among the lower, more ignorant, and despicable of every rank and order in society." Men who believed that revenging themselves on an offender by drawing a sword and killing, or "by wringing noses, and boxing it out," was an expression of spirit and "gallantry" were no better than cocks on a dunghill, or enraged bulls, or rivalrous stallions.[52]

Those who thought the justification for extreme and private violence was derived from the army were wrong: "For every gentleman, every man of sense and breeding in the army had a more delicate and manly way of thinking, and from his heart despises all such little, narrow, sordid notions." John was talking of officers. Other ranks might well show the effects of a machismo that they shared with civil society in a vision consistent with his comparison of men of spirit to cocks on a dunghill. In fact, however, "the culture of honor," to which notions of spirit and gallantry appealed, was not entirely class bound. John said that competition had been socially ubiquitous lately, that is, in the protorevolutionary circumstances under which he was writing, as a man who himself was deeply animated by personal ambition. He clarified his class point by conceding that a few of the competitive sorts of men affecting contempt, that is, the "coxcombs and brutes," were to be found "in every profession, among divines, lawyers, physicians, as well as husbandmen, manufacturers, and laborers."[53]

In fact, John's most telling description of the manners of an unreformed man was of those of Bela Lincoln, the doctor who had been a classmate at Harvard and had married Hannah Quincy the year after the moment when John himself had been about to propose to her. This was the context for John's description of Lincoln's behavior at a small social gathering at Hannah's parents' house soon after her marriage, both description and behavior apparently still influenced by the previous rivalry. John began with a summary: "The Dr. gave us an ample confirmation of his Brutality and his Rusticity. He treated his Wife, as no drunken Cobler, or Clothier would have done, before Company. Her father never gave such Looks and answers to any of his slaves in my Hearing." Rural bullies, their characteristics sometimes combined with those of the rake, were frequent emblems of the manhood targeted by novelists. One of them was Fielding, whose Squire Western in *Tom Jones* exemplified the type. The squire's tyrannical treatment of his wife was exacerbated by drink. Like Squire Western, Bela Lincoln used a strain of language at this polite, heterosocial domestic gathering that Adams believed men should reserve for each other elsewhere, in taverns, for instance: "He contradicted, he Squibed, shrugged, scouled, laughd at the Coll [Colonel], in such a Manner as the Coll, would have called Boorish, ungentlemanly, impolite, ridiculous, in any other Man. More of a Clown is not in the World." *Boorish* and *clown* held the same econnotations as *rusticity*, that of the country bumpkin, in contrast to the politeness of urbanity: "A hoggish, ill bred, uncivil, haughty, Coxcomb, as ever I saw." Dr. Hamilton gave the pseudonym "Mr. Hog" to a man he witnessed verbally denigrating his wife before company, including the declaration that she needed a good "mowing," or what his industrialized descendants would call a good screw.[54]

It might be thought that these two Harvard-educated professionals had more common ground than their relations with a woman, but John represented Bela's wit and theological knowledge (mingled with his unsuccessful polish) as pretentious, degraded, and false, in implicit contrast to his own: "His Wit is forced and affected, his Manners, to his father, Wife, and to company brutally rustic, he is ostentatious of his Talent at Disputation, forever giving an History like my Uncle Hottentot, of some Wrangle he has had with this and that divine." Adams used the word *Hottentot* to represent the barbarian on other occasions. Jordan cites the characterization of "the Hottentot" ("of all People they are the most Bestial and sordid") as one source for white American "attitudes toward the Negro." During the eighteenth century, the word was "transferred," according to the *OED* (1928), from the group of people indigenous to the Cape of Good Hope and conquered by the Dutch to any "person of inferior intellect or culture; one degraded on the scale of civilization, or ignorant of the usages of civil society." One illustration of this meaning the authors of the *OED* took from Chesterfield's letters to his son, aimed at teaching him such usage for elite, white, Anglophone circles. Adams's comparison of his old rival to "Uncle Hottentot" illustrates the racist border described in my introduction.[55]

"[Dr. Lincoln's] treatment of his Wife amazed me. Miss Q [Hannah's stepmother] asked the Dr. a Question[.] Miss [Mrs.] Lincoln[,] seeing the Dr. engaged with me," Adams continued, "gave her Mother an Answer, which however, was not satisfactory. Miss Q repeats it. 'Dr. you did not hear my Question.'—'Yes I did, replies the Dr., and the Answer to it, my Wife is so pert, she must put in her Oar, or she must blabb, before I could speak.' And then shrugged. And affected a laugh, to cow her as he used to, the freshman and sophymores at Colledge." John read Hannah's feelings from her nonverbal response: "She sunk into silence and shame and Grief, as I thought.—After supper, she says 'Oh my dear, do let my father see that Letter we read on the road.' Bela answers, like the great Mogul, like Nero or Caligula, 'he shant.'" In John's view, this man was a tyrant. Hannah begged: "Why, Dr. do let me have it! do!—He turns his face about as stern as the Devil, sour as Vinegar. 'I wont.'—Why sir says she, what makes you answer me so sternly, shant and wont?—Because I wont, says he." This was not the stern virtue that

Abigail expected from John, and it did not accompany any signs of sensibility toward his wife, as the rest of the passage makes clear.[56]

"Then the poor Girl, between shame and Grief and Resentment and Contempt, at last strives to turn it off with a Laugh.—'I wish I had it. Ide shew it, I know.'—Bela really acts the Part of the Tamer of the Shrew in Shakespear. Thus a kind Look, an obliging Air, a civil Answer, is a boon that she cant obtain from her Husband." John imagines that Hannah wants from her husband what the other men and women present, as well as even drunken craftsmen, expect husbands to give wives. It was not the "shrew" who should be tamed but her husband. In fact, John writes, returning to his point about cobblers' and clothiers' treatment of their wives: "Farmers Tradesmen, Soldiers, Sailors, People of no fortune, Figure, Education, are really more civil obliging, kind to their Wives than he is." It seems that Dr. Lincoln's taming Hannah and treating her as a slave has led to her internalization of subordination: "She is always under Restraint before me. She never dares shew her endearing Airs, nor any fondness for him." Once John had been impressed by her raising questions about Pope's *Homer* in mixed company.

If Harvard reinforced John's self-improvement in the direction of showing greater sensibility, it had not had the same effect on Bela Lincoln, who, John records, had bullied the college underclassmen, although such bullying was common at the time. In fact, college life posed the same temptations as taverns to young men. Eighteenth-century colleges and their surroundings could be the riotous center of male culture against which sentimental literature warned.[57] Two vulnerable youths were the Adamses' sons, Charles and Tom, the latter perhaps first led "astray" at Harvard "by the spice of fun in his composition." His older brother, John Quincy, had been exposed to "high jinks" in his first evening there when some sophomores "got drunk, and sallied out and broke the windows of three of the tutors before staggering back to their chambers." But John Quincy and his father had been able to restrain themselves, making the same choice as Hercules. Eventually, Charles would leave his wife, Sarah Smith, the sister of Nabby's husband, Colonel William Stephens Smith, "with two small daughters," having become "bankrupt, faithless, and an alcoholic." Charles's abandoned wife invoked John's sympathy. "I pitied her, I grieved, I mourned," he wrote Abigail, "but I could do no more." Charles was, his father said, "a mere rake, buck, blood, and beast." He declared: "I renounce him." These terms placed father and son on opposing sides of the conflict over manhoods represented by the reformation of manners.[58]

## CHAPTER 10

# The Pleasures and
# Pains of Public Life

## Men of Feeling

John, then, construed himself as a man of feeling, quite apart from his relation with Abigail, although, typically, he believed that marriage would improve his sensibility. In 1771, a thirty-six-year-old married lawyer riding on the Eastern Circuit in Massachusetts, he came to share a lodging and a bed with an old neighbor, Joseph Barrell, whose young wife had recently died: "His Grief is intense indeed. He spent the whole Evening and a long Time after we got into Bed in lamenting the Loss of his Wife." John paraphrased Barrell's words, including that he "Heartily wishes himself with her." It had been a love match: "He married from pure Regard, utterly against the Will of his Mother and all his Friends, because she was poor"—this was not the woman John would have married—"but she made him happy." Barrell told John of her final moments: "She beckoned to me but a few Minutes before she died, when her Hands were as cold as clods. She whispered to me,—I love you now—if I could but carry you and the Children with me, I should go rejoicing." Barrell's eloquence occasioned John "Millions of Thoughts." The next day they rode together, every "Object" recalling "the Subject of Grief." John concluded: "this Man's Mournings have melted and softened me beyond Measure." The effect was comparable to that the poverty of Peacock's family had had on him a couple of years previously.[1]

John represented himself to his friends as a man who could give way to feeling, writing to Christopher Gadsden, whom he had known since that first 1774 meeting of Congress: "[I] Perceive that your friendly sentiments for me are as kind and indulgent as they were six-and-twenty years ago . . . and with a tenderness which was almost too much for my sensibility." Because the subject of his May 14, 1810, letter to Rush was the death of Benjamin Lincoln, "my ancient, my invariable and inestimable friend," Adams wrote that it "will be full of sentiment, sympathy, and feeling." John expressed his sensibility elsewhere in his correspondence with his old friend Rush, for example, in response to news of the 1812 war,: "My heart bleeds for the frontiers and much more for the unfeeling insensibility which to much prevail in this quarter." The latter phrase referred to the Kentucky and Ohio frontier, the seat of that far harder, male counterculture to which John opposed himself.[2]

John found noteworthy those men who showed the characteristics of sensibility: "Mr. Reed is a very sensible and accomplished Lawyer, of an amiable Disposition—soft, tender, friendly, &c." "Mr. Dickinson . . . has an excellent Heart." Reed and Dickinson were members of the Continental Congress whom John met in 1774. "This [September 17]," he wrote, "was one of the happiest days of my life. In Congress we had generous noble sentiments, and manly eloquence." The next day, in a letter to Abigail, he expanded that brief characterization in the terms of sensibility: "The Esteem, the Affection, the Admiration, for the People of Boston and the Massachusetts, which were expressed Yesterday, And the fixed Determination that they should be supported, were enough to melt an Heart of Stone. I saw the Tears gush into the Eyes of the old, grave pacific Quakers of Pennsylvania." Two weeks later, he wrote her that the Congress professed "to consider our Province as suffering in the common Cause, and indeed they seem to feel for Us, as if for themselves."[3] This was a quality that Abigail longed to know about. She thanked John for a letter he sent her the following June but asserted: "I want you to be more particular. Does every Member feel for us? Can they realize what we suffer?" Gentlemen's weeping together in public illustrates the reputability of such a display of sensibility. At John's first appearance as president in "the Chamber of the House of Representation," he wrote Abigail on March 5, 1797, there was "a Multitude as great as the Space could contain"—there were women there, too—"and . . . Scarcely a dry Eye but Washingtons." John thought Washington was happy to be leaving office.[4]

## John's Expression to Abigail of His Conflict over Public versus Private Life

John distinguished between correspondence between family members and correspondence with those outside, a distinction we have seen made by Abigail, John Quincy, Franklin, and Jefferson, for example. The difference lay in the quality of feeling. In 1782, John wrote his "dear Son" John Quincy, then fifteen: "It is with Pleasure that I enclose this amiable Letter from your Sister, which breaths a very commendable affection for You and solicitude for your Welfare." Nabby was sixteen. He continued: "There is nothing more tender than these Correspondences between Families"—he meant among family members—"it is a moral and religious duty to cultivate these amiable Connections by constant Correspondence, when we cannot by Conversation." Another "Motive" was "Pleasure," so, in urging his son to correspond with his daughter, John noted that he "need not recur to any Thing so austere as the idea of Duty."[5]

From early in his letters to Abigail, John had contrasted his life in the public world with being home with her. In February 1763, he wrote her of that

> noisy, dirty town of Boston, where Parade, Pomp, Nonsense, Frippery, Folly, Foppery, Luxury, Polliticks and the soul-Confounding Wrangles of the Law will . . . give me the Higher Relish for Spirit, Taste and Sense, at Weymouth, next Sunday.
>
> My Duty, w[h]ere owing!

He had gotten such pleasure from comparable transitions before he met her. Now he described one in terms more markedly of sensibility, the town negatively juxtaposed with the country, that is, with Weymouth, where Abigail lived. Those last four words, however, represented the reason he consistently gave her to justify the absences—or, at least, their duration—that she had not anticipated.[6]

I have quoted the letter to Abigail in which John told her that his increasing affections for her, moving out across Hutchesonian circles, quickened his affections for everyone else, until he wondered whether "the fires of Patriotism" would not soon "begin to burn!" This was a love letter, in which he looked forward to marrying her. He liked Weymouth better than Braintree at the time because Abigail was there, but he told her: "Something prompts me to believe I shall like Braintree next Winter better than Weymouth." That something was the fact that, next winter, married, they would be living there together. One context for his subsequent adjuration was the prospect of sex: "Patience, my Dear! Learn to conquer your Appetites and Passions!" In his next paragraph, after advising Abigail read Epictetus, he attributed to such "Ancient Principles of Morals and Civility" "a Feeling for our Fellow men," himself, therefore, merging Epictetus to a significant extent with the eighteenth-century emphasis on the social affections propounded by the culture of sensibility. The 1774 writer of "Thoughts on Matrimony" in the *Royal American Magazine*, published in Boston, sketched the same process, reflecting the same scheme of values. By "giving pleasure," the married man "receives it back again with increase. By this endearing intercourse of friendship and communications of pleasure, the tender feelings and soft passions of the soul are awakened with all the ardour of love and benevolence. . . . In this happy state, man feels a growing attachment to human nature and love to his country."[7]

John eventually directed his "amorous Passions" into marriage with the highly suitable Abigail, and he quickly begot children. He could have construed the subsequent rearousal of his patriotic ambition as the development articulated in the *Royal American Magazine*, but his feelings were now complicated by his awareness of the effects on his family: "I have a Zeal at my Heart, for my Country and her Friends, which I cannot smother or conceal: it will burn out at Times and in Companies where it ought to be latent at my Breast. This Zeal will prove fatal to the Fortune and Felicity of my Family, if it is not regulated by a cooler Judgement than mine has hitherto been."[8] An active opponent of the Stamp Act, and then elected selectman in Braintree, John was by the late 1760s "Boston's busiest attorney." In 1770, as we have seen, he successfully defended Captain Preston, which, he said, was "one of the most gallant, generous, manly and disinterested Actions of my whole Life." That year he was elected by "a large majority" as one of Boston's representatives to the Massachusetts General Court, then in the throes of protorevolutionary activity: I will return to his memory of his bringing the news to Abigail.[9]

During the first period of extended separation that ensued, John wrote frequently of his affection for the little family he evidently missed. The year after his first election, his health was "exhausted" by several things, "especially the constant Obligation to speak in public," and he was "compelled . . . to throw off a great part of the Load of Business, both public and private, and return to [his] farm in the Country." Staying in his Braintree home, away from "the Air of the Town of Boston, which was not favourable" to him, he wrote: "the daily rides on horseback and the Amusements of Agriculture always delightfull to me soon restored my Health." But again he made the transition to the "vagabond life" of the lawyer's circuit, and again he wrote Abigail that he yearned for home: "This wandering, itinerating Life grows more and more disagreeable to me. I want to see my Wife and Children every Day, I want to see my Grass and Blossoms and Corn, &c every Day." If the latter wish assumed the ancient meaning of the home economy, of personal domain and interest, he added, "I want to see my Workmen, nay I almost want to go and see the Bosse Calf," irony at the cost of sentimentality. The prior wish, to see his wife and children, was for the private life identified as domesticity and reflected that his earlier ambivalence had been augmented, if not transformed, by his marriage.[10]

John had bought a house in Boston in 1772 because of the extent of his business, and he wrote that he was "pretty well determined" to bring his family there that fall: "If I do, I shall come with a fixed Resolution to meddle not with public Affairs of Town or Province. I am determined my own Life and the Welfare of my Family, which is much dearer to me, are too great Sacrifices for me to make." *Sacrifice* represented the Hutchesonian value of giving up personal, private self-interest to devote oneself to the public good: "I have served my Country and her professed Friends, at an immense Expense, to me of Time, Peace, Health, Money, and Preferment, both of which last have courted my Acceptance, and been inexorably refused, least I should be laid under a Temptation to forsake the Sentiment of the Friends of this Country." His rejection of the job of advocate general in the Court of Admiralty presumably had been motivated by what John called the "great passions of ambition, patriotism," but, if he saw himself as a "Friend of [his] Country," he contrasted such genuineness of sentiment with that of his country's "professed Friends," that phrase referring to the deceptiveness against which the culture of sensibility, as well as republicanism, posed genuineness and sincerity. The degree of self-interest rather than sacrifice with which he had entered politics, despite his demurrals, becomes apparent, as was the frustration driving him to imagine leaving it for private life: "These last [i.e., the 'professed Friends'] are such Politicians as to bestow all their Favours upon their professed and declared Enemies. I will devote myself wholly to my private Business, my Office and my Farm, and I hope to lay a Foundation for better Fortune to my Children, and an happier Life than has fallen to my Share." John reiterated this resolution a few pages later: "Above all Things I must avoid Politicks, Political Clubbs, Town Meetings, General Court, &c. &c."[11]

He was drawn back into politics later in 1772, this time by his wish to answer Governor Hutchinson's claim that "Parliament was our sovereign legislature," but not by way of the "democratical" principles already drafted by some of his acquaintances. John was invited by Sam Adams, John Hancock, and others to read another draft, which, he remarked, while full of "elementary principles of liberty, equality and fraternity . . . founded in nature, and eternal, unchangeable truth," did not answer "the Governor's legal and constitutional arguments." It was much later, in an 1817 letter after Abigail's and Nabby's deaths, that John described the conflict this caused him, not just in criticizing his friends' draft, but, more fundamentally, between his private and public commitments.[12]

We can note that news of death elicited the language of sensibility from John, as the news of Polly Jefferson's death elicited it from Abigail. John wrote Abigail: "I am wounded to the Heart, with the News this Moment of J[osiah] Quincy's death." Similarly, he wrote her on the death of her mother: "I bewail more than I can express." His heart was "too full of Grief for you and our Friends . . . to say any Thing of News or Politicks," although he went on to do just that. Here, he echoed Abigail's expression of the sentimental value that private pain could sometimes trump news of public life. She had written him: "Such has been my distress that I know nothing of the political world." But she, too, had then gone on to discuss the same irresistible subject that John had dropped his grief to discuss.[13]

Time and again John would write to Abigail when away on revolutionary business, first, that he wished he were with her and the children at home but, second, that his obligation to the public good required him to sacrifice such personal interest. In a letter of 1775, he began by telling her: "In every part . . . [of the] almost three Months since I left you . . . my Anxiety about you and the Children, as well as our Country, has been extreme." His anxiety for them already placed in the larger context of his anxiety for the country, in the rest of the letter, he detailed his supervening cares, beginning: "The Business I have had upon my Mind has been as great and important to me as can be entrusted to [One] Man, and the Difficulty and Intricacy of it prodigious." Because of the task undertaken by "the 50 or 60 men" of the Congress in Philadelphia, of creating a constitution to govern such a huge "empire," with "Millions to arm and train," the beginning of a navy, the regulation of commerce, negotiations with "numerous Tribes of Indians," and raising and running an army of "Twenty thousand Men," John told Abigail that he "really [would] pity those 50 or 60 men," a hint, perhaps, that she should pity him. He added: "I must see you e're long." He might feel very alone amid the torrent of business in Philadelphia and even declare, "I never will come here again without you," but he reiterated that "Calls of . . . private Affection must give Place to those of Duty and Honour."[14]

On occasion, John came close to admitting his ambition more directly to Abigail. In February 1776, he wrote that "the martial spirit" was evident at "the beginning of a War" and among a "People unaccustomed to Arms." He continued: "I feel upon some of these Occasions, a flow of Spirits, and an Effort of Imagination, very like Ambition to be engaged

in the more active, gay, and dangerous Scenes." These included revolutionary politics in Philadelphia, for which he and his fellows knew they
could be executed as traitors: "(Dangerous I say but recall that Word, for
there is no Course more dangerous than that which I am in.)" The fulfillment of his early-felt ambition transcended even "such Passions . . .
to be a Soldier." He recalled that, in 1757, during the French and Indian
War, he had "longed more ardently to be a Soldier than a Lawyer."[15]

John's letter of April 28, 1776, to Abigail was tinged with self-pity,
even as he rationalized ambition, or the pursuit of "fame" as self-sacrifice,
along with a sense of his moral obligation to the "sublime, universal
good": "Instead of domestic Felicity, I am destined to public Conten-
tions. Instead of rural Felicity, I must reconcile myself to the Smoke and
Noise of a city. In the Place of private Peace, I must be distracted with
the Vexation of developing the deep Intrigues of Politicians. . . . And
think myself, well rewarded, if my private Pleasure and Interest are sacrificed as they ever have been and will be, to the Happiness of others."[16] A
month later, John wrote her: "I am a lonely, forlorn, Creature here. . . .
It is a cruel Reflection, which very often comes across to me, that I
should be separated so far, from those Babes, whose Education And Welfare lies so near my Heart. But greater Misfortunes than these must not
divert us from Superiour Duties." He then ascribed to Abigail the same
public-over-personal hierarchy of values, corresponding to those concentric degrees, from loved ones outward to humanity (he saw the outer
public circles "descend" to the inner ones: this could be said to correspond to a "vortex"): "Your Sentiments of the Duties We owe to our
Country"—specifying the Superior Duties of the previous sentence—
"are such as become the best of Women, and the best of Men." John
made clear to Abigail his belief that she shared this hierarchy as the result
of both her intelligence, her "Capacity [that] enabled her to compre-
hend," and her "pure Virtue [which] obliged her to approve the Views
of her Husband." That he could believe this (implicitly in contrast to the
incapacity and immoral views of a wife who would have disagreed with
his values and/or refused to go along with the absence they entailed)
was, he told her, "the cheering Consolation of [his] Heart, in [his] most
solitary, gloomy and disconsolate Hours." Conversely, her disapproval
of his views would have made him "the most miserable Man alive."[17]

This was the period when Abigail called on John and his fellow delegates to remember the ladies and when he vigorously rejected her call.
Her separation from the world coupled with her ability to "compre-
hend" him provided him with place where and a person with whom he

could freely express himself, in fact, precisely the resource Fordyce said a husband looked for in a wife, rather than a challenge. In August 1776, John wrote Abigail, reflecting on the "odd Mixture" of things his letters expressed: "You will see a Proportion of Affection, for my Friends, my family and Country, that gives a Complexion to the whole. I have a very tender feeling Heart." The categorizations were significant. The specific feeling he had in mind, in addition to "Affection," was emotional pain, rendered as metaphoric torture according to sentimental convention: "The Country knows not, and never can know the Torments, I have endured for its sake." His keeping them private, confining their expression to Abigail within that inner circle, was a measure of his sensibility to those outside it, his constancy attunement from his premarital years: "I am glad they never can know, for it would give more Pain to the benevolent and humane, than I could wish, even the wicked and malicious to feel." He posed such a sensibility against "the World" that did not value the man of feeling, who prized the social affections, but, instead, respected the selfish man, "who grasped for himself, under specious Pretenses, for the public Good." John was expressing his ne "Mortification" to Abigail that he was suspected of being "actuated by private Views, and have been aiming at high Places." To the contrary, he declared to her: "Let me have my Farm, Family, and Goose Quill, and all the Honours and Offices this World has to bestow, may go to those who deserve them better, and desire them more. I covet them not." He realized that the high ground he here claimed also reflected his own, special thin-skinnedness. It was here that he wrote: "There are very few People in this World, with whom I can bear to converse. I can treat all with Decency and Civility, and converse with them, when it is necessary, on Points of Business. But I am never happy in their Company. This has made me a Recluse, and will one day make me an Hermit."[18]

The latter fancy was another sentimental convention, the ultimate and self-righteous retreat from a corrupt world, akin to John's and Abigail's deeming their house a chaumiere and a cottage. Sentimental literature was sprinkled with hermits; to mark the eleventh anniversary of their mother's death, Elizabeth sent Abigail two 1746 lines by William Collins:

> "*she* shall a while repair
> To dwell a weeping Hermit there."

One of the earliest and, perhaps, most influential of sentimental works was "The Hermit," two hundred and fifty lines of heroic couplets by the Reverend Thomas Parnell, the "graveyard" poet, whose work was published posthumously in 1721 by his friend Pope. Eliza Lucas wrote her future husband, Charles Pinckney, about the challenge that learning "Docr. Parnels Hermit" posed (later in life and widowed, she described their small, noncommercial plantation called Belmont, a place where she venerated an oak that the now dead Pinckney had planted, as "a little hovel"). The Hermitage was the first name Jefferson gave to the incipient mansion he would later call Monticello.[19]

John's self-conception as a recluse and hermit came close, too, to the kind of deceptive presentation that Wood and Bushman see as a characteristic of his culture, his apparent civility masking different and truer inner feelings. In this case, the passage was an expression of resentment occasioned by his treatment by other men in public life, particularly Hancock and Robert Treat Paine, also from Massachusetts, men who desired honors and office more than he did, his phrasing freighted with self-righteousness. He elaborated his resentment in a passage he "decided not to entrust to the post": "I have been wounded, more deeply than I have been willing to acknowledge, more deeply than the World suspects, by the Conduct of those Persons, who have been joined with me here."[20]

"The love of fame," Adair writes, summarizing the eighteenth-century view, encouraged "a man to make history; to leave the mark of his deeds and his ideals on the world," to "refuse to become the victim of events," but we should note that John often did thus present himself, especially to Abigail, or, rather, as a victim of other men—competitors or detractors—a temptation fostered by the interweaving of the masculine ideals of republicanism with men's acculturation to sensibility. Here, John added to the same convention by representing one of his victimizers as a grand deceiver: "The sordid meanness of their Souls is beneath my Contempt. One of them covers as much of it, as ever disgraced a mortal, under the most splendid Affections of Generosity, Liberality, and Patriotism." This scratched-out passage also elaborated the connection with his preference to live as a hermit: "I had rather shut myself up in the Cell of an Hermit, and bid adieu to the human face, than to live in Society with such People."[21]

Saliently, John made Abigail the audience for this empty and unsent threat, assuming that she would recognize it for what it was (or oblivious to what she might think of his preferring such a life alone to one at home with her). The distinction between audiences his letter assumes—Abigail, on the one hand, and the repressed audience of politicians, on the other—can be seen as parallel to those (Abigail and Gerry) to whom he had directed his different arguments against Abigail's accompanying him to France in 1778.

That John consistently presented himself in this way to Abigail was evidently in expectation of her sympathy. In 1777, he described his alienation to her with a Rousseauistic scene that included her, at least as a sometime participant. He had opened the letter with a little pastoral sentimentalism, of which she, too (like Pinckney), was capable: "The Spring advances, very rapidly, and all Nature will soon be cloathed in her gayest Robes. The green Grass, which begins to show itself, here, and there, revives in my longing Imagination my little Farm and its dear Inhabitants." His loss was not his choice: "What Pleasures has not this vile War deprived me of! I want to wander, in my Meadows, to ramble over my Mountains, and to sit in Solitude, or with her who has all my Heart, by the side of Brooks." In this case, however, he placed a positive value on the revolutionaries' work in Philadelphia: "These beautiful Scaenes would contribute more to my Happiness than the sublime ones which surround me." The distinction between the beautiful and the sublime was the one Burke had made in his development of the aesthetics of sensibility. John wrote here that he longed "for rural and domestick scaenes, and the prattle of [his] children," in self-consciously literary style, one he singled out with a pair of dashes: "—Dont you think I am somewhat poetical this morning, for one of my Years, and considering the Gravity, and Insipidity of my Employment.—" His action, that is, his leadership in the claim for independence, was his implementation of the insistent wish of his youthful diary for fame, to be exalted by "great" objects, and his expression of his "great passions of ambition, patriotism." Yet, here, to Abigail, he wrote: "As much as I converse with Sages and Heroes, they have very little of my Love or Admiration. I should prefer the Delights of a Garden to the Dominion of a World. I have nothing of Caesars Greatness in my Soul. Power has not my Wishes in her Train."

Instead, John continued: "The Gods, by granting me Health, and Peace and Competence, the Society of my Family and Friends, the Perusal of my Books, and the Enjoyment of my Farm and Garden, would make me as Happy as my Nature and State will bear." This is a vision of retirement also derived from alternative classical, Roman ideals, epitomized by Cincinnatus, who, after a military victory, "returned to his farm beyond the Tiber," a figure from whom the order of ex-revolutionary officers took its name and with whom Washington was identified. In this letter, John illustrates how it could be associated with sentimental retirement, as the older definition of the household evolved into domesticity.

John added: "Of that Ambition which has Power for its Object, I dont believe I have a Spark in my Heart. . . ." The ellipses here were signs to Abigail. "There [are] other kinds of Ambition of which I have a great deal." To her, of course, this was an undeniable fact.[22]

During his self-initiated mission to the United Provinces in May 1781, John replied quite briefly to a letter from Abigail he had received the day before, explaining how little time he had, but reporting that Charles was "yet weak from his Fever, but is getting better daily." He outlined the difficult international political situation facing him, then asked: "My dear Nabby and Tommy, how do they do? Our Parents, our Brothers, sisters and all Friends how are they?" Then he made a terse, qualified promise: "If I could get back gain I would never more leave that Country, let who would beg, scold, or threaten." Abigail replied to this with a cold eye, if not a degree of anger: "You flatter me with a pleasing Illusion that if ever you see your Native land again you will not quit it. If you once see it at peace, I should hope you would not, but until then, I can have little faith in the promise." Her characteristic tempering of this at first included her reference to John's susceptibility to those who had flattered him with the argument Lovell had made in 1778, getting him to go to Europe in the first place: "For tho you should return with that desireable object unaccomplished, the same principle which first led you to quit your family and Friends would opperate again, when ever you could be brought to believe that you could render your Country more Service abroad than at Home." But she quickly added that it had been "providence" that had "been pleased to separate" them, John deputed to implement "the Benevolent wishes of the United States."[23]

A year later, John had triumphed in Holland and could say: "I must come to you or you must come to me, I cannot live, in this horrid Solitude, which it is to me, amidst Courts, Camps and Crowds." But he then dismissed the possibility because of practical considerations. Telling Abigail, "I envy you, your Nabby, Charly and Tommy," he declared: "The Embassy here however has done great Things." He had gained crucial financial aid and recognition from the United Provinces. His embassy "has not merely tempted a natural Rival, and an imbittered, inveterate, hereditary Ennemy, to assist a little against G[reat] B[ritain] but it has torn from her Bosom, a constant faithfull Friend and Ally of an hundred Years duration." His triumphant list suggests that this was the kind of fulfillment of great ambition to which he had aspired. Despite the belittling of his achievement that he anticipated, he declared: "Very well! Thank God it is done, and that is what I wanted." It could be said of his aim what Meyer writes in connection with a later and literary revolutionary: "Home is not the locus of heat and daring."[24]

A month later, John expressed his pleasure to Abigail in "the Air of the Hague, and the Return of warm Weather," allowing him to mount "on Horse back every Morning," and even wrote, "You can scarcely imagine a more beautiful Place than the Hague," before adding: "Yet no Place has any Charms for me but the Blue Hills [of Braintree]. My Heart will have in it forever, an acking Void, in any Place. If, you and your Daughter were here! But I must turn my Thoughts from such Objects, which always too tenderly affect me, for my repose or Peace of mind, I am so wedged in with the Publick Affairs that it is impossible to get away at present." The phrase "acking Void" alluded to the same lines from Pope's "Eloisa to Abelard" that Abigail quoted to him. The thought of bringing his wife to Europe, however, was a source of emotional pain, reiterating the terms with which he had refused her in 1778, "opening a scaene of Risque and Trouble for you that I shudder at." Still, he continued to revel in his unique success, in spite of the personal pain that he assured her the separation caused him. "The American Cause has obtained a Tryumph in this Country more signal, than it ever obtained before in Europe," he wrote, despite "the Dangers, the Mortifications, the Distresses ['Your Friend'] has undergone in Accomplishing this great Work."[25]

Two months later, and still in Holland, John confided to Abigail: "People say I was born for such Times." This was true, he admitted, "but [I] was not made for them. They affect too tenderly my Heart." As in the case of that August 1776 letter, in which he confided to Abigail, "I have a very tender feeling Heart," Abigail could infer that John's public roles frustrated the kind of freedom her private experience of sensibility gave her.[26] By December 1782, John could foresee "a Peace this Winter," that is, with Britain, and, in any case, said: "I shall come home in the Summer." He again promised what he knew Abigail yearned for: "You may depend upon a good domestic husband, for the remainder of my Life, if it is the Will of Heaven that I should once more meet you. My Promises are not lightly made with any body. I have never broken one made to you, and I will not begin at this time of Life." Along with being "a good domestic husband" came taking up fatherhood in person: "My Children I hope will once at length discover, that they have a Father, who is not unmindfull of their Welfare. They have had too much Reason to think themselves forgotten, although I know that an Anxiety for their happiness has corroded me, every day of my Life." He conveyed his promise and this statement of feeling with "a Tenderness which Words cannot express" and closed: "I am theirs and yours forever."[27]

After they were reunited in 1784, Abigail and John were never separated for so long again, although Abigail remained at home in Quincy from April 1792 until April 1797, John returning to visit her. After months of separation in 1794 (while he was vice president), the "old dilemma," "public duty version private happiness," as Withey terms it, was renewed, and Withey quotes Abigail's May 10 letter to John: "I check every rising wish & suppress every anxious desire for your return, when I see how necessary you are to a Country which I love."[28]

## John Explains His Absence to His Daughter

John used superlatives and the figure of incapacity to demonstrate his sensibility in his letters to his children, ending one letter to the twelve-year-old Nabby: "Remember me with the tenderest Affection to your Mamma and your Brothers. I am with inexpressible Affection, Your father, John Adams."[29]

John wrote directly to Nabby to explain why he was absent so often. One such letter he sent to her from the Hague when she was seventeen, after that proposal that she come to Europe. He replied: "Your proposal of coming to Europe to keep your papa's house and take care of his health, is a high strain of filial duty and affection, and the idea pleases me much in speculation, but not at all in practice." Her rationale had been an expression of her consciousness of women's prescribed focus. John had taken two of her brothers to Europe to further their education and widen their horizons, in effect, to prepare them for public life. He turned Nabby down with the same sentimental argument he had used to deny Abigail's coming with him to France: "I have too much tenderness for you, my dear child, to permit you to cross the Atlantic. You know not what it is." The perils of such a voyage, in sailing ships and in wartime, were real, but John's work on behalf of the public good required him to face such risks, as his gendered ambition for his sons did: "If God shall spare me and your brothers to return home, which I hope will be next Spring, I never desire to know of any of my family crossing the seas again."[30]

Nabby had asked her father to send her presents. John criticized her choice but said that he would consider it, taking the opportunity to tell her to learn patience. This occasioned his explanation to her of the value to be placed on the work for which he had sacrificed his family happiness: "If you have not yet so exalted sentiments of the public good as have others more advanced in life, you must endeavor to obtain them. They are the primary and most essential branch of general benevolence, and therefore the highest honour and happiness both of men and Christians, and the indispensable duty of both." It is not entirely clear if he is using *men* here in its gender- or species-specific sense, although, evidently, he wanted his daughter to absorb this "primary" value.

John linked this value both to sensibility and to that Hutchesonian vision of which he wrote to Abigail. John wrote his daughter: "Indifference to the happiness of others must arise from insensibility of heart, or from a selfishness still more contemptible, or rather destestable." He elaborates the meaning of *selfishness*: "But for the same reason that our own individual happiness should not be our only object, that of our relatives, however near or remote, should not; but we should extend our views to as large a circle as our circumstances of birth, fortune, education, rank, and influence extend, in order to do as much good to our fellow men as we can." The outward reach of benevolence, the expression of unselfishness and sensibility of heart, extended to a wider circle, concentric with the personal, private, domestic sphere. John had refused Nabby the extension of its dimensions (keeping house and nursing) to him in Europe, and he wrapped this decision—or even grounded it—in his sensibility. That she should still learn that "the sentiments of the public good . . . are the primary and most essential branch of general benevolence" was, presumably, in order that she might respect her father's kind of work, accept his absence, and prepare herself for the same orientation when she was a wife. Her interest in luxurious consumer items would not help such a purpose: "You will see, my dear child, that jewels and lace can go but very little way in this career."

John continued with that conventional, characterological distinction to which he referred elsewhere, telling Nabby that "knowledge in the head and virtue in the heart . . . instead of show and pleasure" is how one can be happy. This was Jefferson's view of the function of head and heart. Nabby could reinforce her sense that there was an alternative here, one that deeply bothered her father; indeed, it was a major political theme of the era. He insisted: "Your happiness is very dear to me. But depend upon it, it is simplicity, nor refinement nor elegance can obtain it. By conquering your taste, (for taste is to be conquered, like unruly appetites or passion, or the mind is undone), you will save yourself many perplexities or mortifications." Her request for jewels and lace touched directly on that charged subject of taste, a symptom of the increasing profusion of consumer goods, no longer confined to those, in John's phrase, of "birth, fortune, education, rank, and influence." Still, such an elite could mark its superiority with the ability to repress appetites and, instead, extend sensibility to "general benevolence." There was a familial note as well as a conventionally gendered one in his message that his daughter's passion was for jewels and lace, rather than, God forbid, other "unruly appetites." Fordyce had illustrated the conventional apprehension over the progression of consumer passions in young women. John had had to conquer unruly passions in himself, in favor of higher goals. Might Nabby show the same fault he occasionally admitted to himself? "There were more thorns sown in the path of human life by vanity, than by any other thing." *Human* underlined that this was a potential that John and Nabby shared. He added that he knew his daughter's "disposition to be thoughtful and serene" but that, still, "nobody can be guarded too much against it [vanity], or too early."

Such observations bespoke a knowledge of his young daughter and a concern with her previous years on which his extraordinarily protracted absences might cast doubt. This seems to have been the thought that led John to the final paragraph of this same letter, for which all the foregoing, above all, his insistence on the primacy of his work, can be seen as prelude: "Overwhelmed as I have been ever since you was born, with cares such as seldom fall to the lot of any man, I have not been able to attend to the fortunes of my family." He had chosen to pursue an ambition on behalf of the public good at the expense of making money, another reason Nabby had to conquer her taste: "They [his family] have no resource but in absolute frugality and incessant industry, which are not only my advice, but my injunction upon every one of them."

John concluded this letter with a sentimental expression, perhaps to ameliorate the effects of the toughness of that underscored paternal injunction: "With inexpressible tenderness of heart, I am Your affectionate father, John Adams." And he opened his next letter to Nabby, written three weeks later, to say that he had received hers of September 3 (a letter now lost) and read it "with all the tenderness of a father deprived of the dearest, and almost the only enjoyment of his life, his family." In a moment, he was to expand that *almost*, but, right off, this seems to have been intended to make a very strong impression on the family member to whom it was addressed. He next described an emotional pain, in addition to deprivation of happiness, caused by reminders of what he had not had: "I never receive a packet from your mamma without a fit of melancholy that I cannot get over for many days." Nabby might well have imagined that "tenderness" with which he received and read her letter was felt with similar emotional pain. He then put it in longer perspective, opening with an account of his suffering: "Mine has been a hard lot in life, so hard that nothing would have rendered it supportable, especially for the last eight years, but the uninterrupted series of good fortune which has attended my feeble exertions for the public." He wanted Nabby to think of him as deprived, subject to extended periods of melancholy, enduring a nearly insupportably hard lot. The end of the next sentence finally got around to his "almost . . . only enjoyment": "If I have been unfortunate and unhappy in private life, I thank God I have been uniformly happy and successful as a public man." It could be said that he had succeeded in the Herculean task he had chosen, fulfilling "the glorious promises of fame, immortality and a good conscience . . . the rewards of a hardy, watchful life in the service of mankind." This was a choice he had made premaritally, and he could continue to justify it in the terms supplied by republican values. It seems, too, that he felt some urgency in justifying this to his family, prompted, not only by his own feelings, but also by their expression of emotional pain. Here, sensibility supplied at least the appearance of common ground.

This letter to Nabby concluded with John's describing his equanimity at that date: "This happiness [i.e., 'as a public man'] may not always last, and I am now very little solicitious whether it does or not." John had succeeded diplomatically in France and in Holland, and the independence for which he had been a leading proponent had been won: "The great cause of our country is established and out of danger, both in America and Europe, and therefore it does not matter, in my judgement, how soon I return to my family."[31]

## Abigail and John's Retrospective View

Abigail had endured the conflict that last sentence represents all along, but, as we have seen, it was often agonizing. After she and John were reunited, however, and with memory's inevitable operation, they adjusted their narratives.

John wrote his *Autobiography* in three parts between 1802 and 1807. The whole had a "chaotic" structure, its editors write, and the first part, addressing the period up to October 1776, was written mostly "from unaided memory," so it was particularly susceptible to modifying the past. Included is his account of his 1770 election to the Massachusetts legislature. "I went down," John remembered, "to Phanuel Hall and in a few Words expressive of my sense of the difficulty and danger of the Times; of the importance of the Trust, and of my own Insuffi[ci]ency to fulfill the Expectations of the People, I accepted the Choice." He recorded that only afterward did he present himself to Abigail, to whom he "broached all of [his] Apprehensions," including the potential effects on her and the children: "I considered the Step as a devotion of my family to ruin and myself to death." He was giving up "more Business at the Bar, than any Man in the Province." He was "throwing away as bright prospects [as] any Man ever had before him," replacing them with "endless labour and Anxiety if not to infamy and death, and that for nothing, except, what indeed was and ought to be in all, a sense of duty." It was a Herculean choice. He had been married to Abigail for six years, although they had been a couple for nearly ten, they had three children at the time of his election, the youngest just a month old, and they had suffered the death of a fourth. On telling Abigail of his election, he wrote: "That excellent Lady, who has always encouraged me, burst into a flood of Tears, but said she was very sensible of all the Danger to her and to our Children as well as to me, but she thought I had done as I ought, she was very willing to share in all that was to come and place her trust in Providence." Tears were, in this analysis, offset by her expression of consciousness and, it appears, self-control in her willing assent to what John had already decided. She had helped him with the emotionally charged accompaniment of his decision. His "sense of duty"—"to the People," perhaps, but certainly to the public good—had dictated his decision, and Abigail's sense of her duty as a wife dictated her willing support of a decision based on that sense. Very important here, precisely because it is a generalization, is his assertion about Abigail, "who has always encouraged me," a clause that edits out the severe conflict that he had known his partings and absences caused her because she wrote him about them. The unqualified acceptance he had wished for he could enjoy retrospectively.[32]

John elaborated his account of their 1770 exchange in dialogue form in a still later (1809) letter to Rush: "I said to my wife, 'I have accepted a seat in the House of Representatives, and thereby have consented to my own ruin, to your ruin, and to the ruin of our children. I give you this warning that you may prepare yourself for this fate.' She burst into tears, but instantly cried out in a transport of magnanimity; 'Well, I am willing in this cause to run all risks with you and be with you and to be ruined with you.'" Abigail's instantaneity of compliance is dramatic. John added: "These were the times my friend, in Boston which tried women's souls as well as men's." He could now afford some generosity toward women in connection with the Revolution and even grant them a kind of equality when he had not been so unambiguous at the time.[33]

The long view also stimulated John to elaborate the picture of what had been at stake in his wife's willingness to go along with his 1770 decision. To his account of that moment he added a description of the opposition that John Dickinson got from his "Mother and his Wife" on his election to the Continental Congress: "[They] were continually distressing him with their remonstrances. His Mother said to him 'Johnny you will be hanged, your Estate will be forfeited and confiscated, you will, leave your Excellent Wife a Widow and your charming children Orphans, Beggars and infamous.'" John recalls his putting himself in Dickinson's shoes: "From my Soul I pitied Mr. Dickinson. I made his case my own. If my Mother and my Wife had expressed such Sentiments to me, I was certain, that if they did not wholly unman me and make me an Apostate, they would make me the most miserable man alive."[34] Dickinson "agonizingly hesitated" before refusing to break what John Randolph called that "ligament" tying America to Britain. John, however, was supported in his drive for independence. "I was very happy," he remembered, "that my Mother and my Wife and my Brothers, my Wife's Father and Mother"—and all the other members of his and Abigail's families—"had uniformly been of my Mind, so that I always enjoyed perfect Peace at home." This had not quite been the case "always," but it helps explain why Abigail repeatedly failed to use the power that she told Warren she could have exercised in opposing John's departures in his pursuit of fame, identifiable with elevating the public over the personal: John had staked the best part of his manhood on such a pursuit, a quality vulnerable to the sentiments of his wife and mother.[35]

Then there was that choice John had made in 1772, in drafting a response to Governor Hutchinson's assertion of Parliament's sovereignty over Massachusetts. In 1817, the year before Abigail's death, and when they had long been retired together, he wrote William Tudor of the severe conflict the call for his political reengagement had caused him: "I had a wife—and what a wife! I had children—and what children!" On the one side, he "was determined never to accept any . . . employment from the government of Great Britain." On the other, that is, the revolutionary side: "There was nothing for me to depend on but the popular breath, which I knew to be as variable and uncertain as any of the thirty two points of the compass." He invoked the sentimental alternative he had so frequently offered to Abigail: "In this situation I should

have thought myself the happiest man in the world, if I could have retired to my little hut and forty acres, which my father left me in Braintree, and lived on potatoes and sea-weed for the rest of my life." She
had to recognize his preference for fame, rather than a rustic cottage, although she was susceptible to imagining that he really wanted the same
thing she did.[36]

Two years after his wife's death, John wrote to his granddaughter,
Nabby's daughter, Caroline de Windt, again praising Abigail for her un-
stinting encouragement. A mutual friend had recently sent him "a life
of Lady Russell," widowed when her husband was executed for trea-
son. He told Caroline: "I bought the life and letters of Lady Russell, in
the year 1775, and sent it to your grandmother, with an express intent
and desire, that she should consider it a mirror in which to contemplate
herself; for at the time I thought it extremely probable, from the daring and dangerous career I was determined to run, that she would one
day find herself in the situation of Lady Russell, her husband without
a head." Abigail had been deeply apprehensive over that prospect, and,
as she and John both said, she was virtually widowed by his protracted
absences. He continued, his "Lady" (i.e., Abigail) "was more beautiful
than Lady Russell, had a brighter genius, more information, a more refined taste, and at least her equal in virtues of the heart; equal fortitude
and firmness of character, equal resignation to the will of Heaven, equal
in all the virtues and graces of the Christian life." Notable, so far, is that
the first context for his sending Abigail this exemplary life was that he
was "determined to run" this "daring . . . career," and, therefore, what
he required of her was resignation to his will, perfectly consistent with
his wishes at the time, not, however, with hers: "Like Lady Russell, she
never by word or look discouraged me from running hazards for the salvation of my country's liberties; she was willing to share with me, and
that her children should share with us both, in all the dangerous consequences we had to hazard."[37]

As we see, John's later regrets also embraced the lives of his children.
To his *Autobiography*'s recording his marriage to "Miss Smith" in 1764,
John added: "[It was] a Connection which has been the Source of all my
felicity. Although a Sense of Duty which forced me away from her and
my Children for so many Years has produced all the Griefs of my heart
and all that I esteem real Afflictions in Life." In old age, he wrote Jefferson, mortified by the strength of his regrets: "Education! Oh Education!
The greatest Grief of my heart and the greatest Affliction of my Life! To
my mortification I must confess, that I have never closely thought, or

very deliberately reflected upon the subject, which never occurs to me now, without producing a deep Sigh, or heavy groan, and sometimes Tears. My cruel Destiny separated me from my Children, almost continually from their Birth to their Manhood." We can note that, implicitly, his being separated from Nabby was not a source of mortification—or such a big one—because her gender made her the responsibility of her mother. Here John continued, regarding his sons, one of whom by then had come to a very bad end: "I was compelled to leave them to the ordinary routine of reading, writing, and Latin school, Accademy and Colledge. John alone was much with me, and he, but occasionally." In his *Autobiography*, he wrote, recalling his feelings on sending young Charles back to Abigail: "I thus deprived myself of the greatest pleasure I had in life, the society of my children." In fact, at the time, he kicked himself for having brought Charles to Europe with him in the first place. He was probably not so mortified in telling Abigail in 1794 of what he had written to Jefferson, and she reassured him: "With respect to what is past, all was intended for the best, and you have faithfully served your generation . . . at the expence of all private Considerations. . . . You do not know whether you would have been a happier Man in private, than you have been in publick life." To her, then, he had continued to present his choice as the result of a painful conflict.[38]

In truth, Abigail, as well as John, could look back and see that she had frequently encouraged him and, in the end, always sacrificed her own wishes so that he could fulfill his ambition to attain fame for the country's good. But sometimes she had outright balked, declaring herself opposed to his wishes; usually she suffered conflict; and always she felt great emotional pain. After peace and independence, she had an interest in emphasizing her compliance, but she was reluctant to repress the memory of her sufferings. For example, there was her letter describing her response to the Reverend Clark's December 14, 1783, Boston sermon, celebrating the Treaty of Paris, when she exclaimed: "How did my heart dilate with pleasure, when as each event was particularized I could trace my Friend as a Principal in them, could say, it was he, who was one of the first in joining the Band of Patriots." Then she gave her version of his leaving her after his 1770 election to the Massachusetts legislature. John, "tho happy in his domestick attachments, left his wife his Children: then but Infants"—no mention of the magnanimous compliance that, in retrospect, John attributed to her. Just as his account attributed entire consistency to her throughout, so she here asserts: "Trace his conduct through every period, you will find him the same undaunted Character." It was truly heroic, comparable to that shown by mythic and literary heroes: "Encountering the dangers of the ocean; risking Captivity, and a dungeon; contending with wickedness in high places; jeopardizing his Life, endangerd by the intrigues, revenge, and malice, of a potent; tho defeated Nation." Their correspondence demonstrates that John's conduct and character were more complicated and flawed, vulnerable to disheartenment, apt to be vitiated by the intrigues and malice of his American rivals, and liable to interpretation as merely ambitious.

Abigail recognized that this retrospective account might appear biased and seem to edit out any negative aspect: "These are not the mere eulogiums of conjugal affection; but certain facts and solid truths." After that reference to his being "happy in his domestick attachments" but leaving his wife and children, "then but Infants," she added that John had done so when they "were surrounded by the Horrours of war; terrified and distress't." He "left them," she repeated, "to the protection of Providence" while he remained "undismayed." She also added, after acknowledging that she could be seen to have glossed reality because of her own, praiseworthy "conjugal affection": "My anxieties, my distresses, at every period; bear witness to them." It had been her conjugal affection, facing the unchallengeable truth of John's wishing to behave like a hero like Hercules, that had caused Abigail so much distress. Here, she concluded this section of the letter: "tho now by a series of prosperous events; the recollection is more sweet than painfull." She could not bring herself to omit the central feature of her life during John's heroic feats.[39]

Nonetheless, the Adamses left enough evidence to help establish the picture of a joint commitment to the cause of independence, on which subsequent writers were to capitalize in perpetuating a myth of unalloyed, archetypal marital harmony.

# PART III

# Private Perpetuation

CHAPTER 11

# Raising Children
# with Sensibility

## Some Childrearing Parameters

Jürgen Habermas argued that eighteenth-century bourgeois childrearing linked the public to the private. The "closeness, the ideas of freedom, love, and cultivation of the person . . . grew out of the experience of the conjugal family's private sphere." There originated "the individual," an autonomous self-governing person, prepared for the public sphere. "Demarcation of the private," in Gurpreet Mahajan's words, "constitutes a moment in the idea of individualism," the word *individualism* having perhaps first been used by Tocqueville in his 1840 characterization of democratic, American men.[1] Another psychological element generated in that private sphere was *subjectivity*, in Habermas's phrase, "the innermost core of the private." Habermas associated this eighteenth-century form of subjectivity with sentimentality, which entered that much-enlarged public sphere by way of fiction and, I would add, sermons, poetry, and music as well as the discourse of republicanism.[2]

Sensibility was created in the private circle that such writings aggrandized, wherein genteel mothers and aspirants to gentility, enjoying eventually abundant "supplies of domesticity," to apply Meyer's characterization of comparable conditions in the antebellum United States, and drawing on religious and literary resources to implement their wishes (with degrees of husbandly/fatherly collaboration), taught their children the value of feeling, their own and its extension to others, one might say self-love and social love.[3]

Among the eighteenth-century writers on the public and private on whom Habermas could have drawn was Fordyce. His *Sermons to Young Women* aimed to convince young, unmarried women "how much the calm and rational pleasures of the home are preferable to the noisy and giddy diversions usually found abroad," although, like other Scots, he saw the value of such heterosociality for improving—softening—the manners of men. No woman, however, he asserted, aiming to orient young women to an effective domestic life, "ought to think it beneath her to be an economist . . . a character truly respectable, in whatever station." Women should spend their time "in examining the accounts, regulating the operations," that is, of servants, "and watching over the interests of perhaps a numerous family." A man should choose a wife to be "what is called a Good Manager." Her management included the aesthetic and financial skills to make the best of consumption, that is, to be "so exquisitely versed" in the "art . . . of housewifery" that, while "her dress, her table, and every other particular, appeared rather splendid than otherwise . . . her bills . . . were a fourth less than most of her neighbours, who had hardly cleanliness to boast in return for their awkward prodigality." "Domestic Accomplishments" included, above all, the obtaining of "every possible light with relations to the nursing, management, and education of children," and Fordyce urged women to value such accomplishments, rather than to "despise any one of them as trivial or dull." Implicitly, some women did so regard such domestic accomplishments. Lord Kames, another enlightened Scot, urging the reform of women's education, went further than Fordyce in his criticism of wives and mothers: "Married women . . . destined by nature to take the lead in educating their children, would no longer be the greatest obstruction to good education, by their ignorance, frivolity, and disorderly manner of living. Even upon the breast, infants are susceptible of impressions; and the mother hath opportunities without end of instilling into them good principles, before they are fit for a male tutor." Fordyce, Kames, and the other Scots had absorbed Lockean psychology, including Locke's application of it to "education," with the childrearing meaning I have mentioned. Locke, too, had registered the coming into existence of consumerism as a context for his recommendations.[4]

Abigail subscribed to the ideals outlined by Fordyce and Kames: "I consider it as an indispensable requisite that every American wife should herself know how to order and regulate her family; how to regulate her domestics, and train up her children. For this the all-wise Creator made woman a helpmate for man, and she who fails in these duties does not answer the end of her creation." Like many other women, however, for significant periods she had to go it alone.[5]

John Dwyer points out that Edinburgh had become "the focal point for luxurious consumption, as well as intellectual and fashionable refinement," whereas "the Scottish highlands were . . . an economic backwater." The same kind of contrast was fundamental to the emergence and definition of the culture of sensibility in America.[6] In America, the back-country offered the same self-aggrandizing possibilities to literate inhabitants of the urban seaboard, also undergoing the consumer revolution, some of them attempting to implement a reformation of manners. This topography could be seen to correspond to the stages-of-history model of progress created by Scottish historians and philosophers, even as the backcountry began to be reevaluated as "frontier" later in the century. Benjamin Rush was one of its American articulators. The relation between such a vision and the rise of sensibility can be indicated by William Robertson's 1777 *History of America* (a book that John Adams read in 1779). In the first stage, wrote Robertson, that "state of domestic union towards which nature leads the human species, in order to soften the heart of gentleness and humanity, [was] rendered so unequal, as to establish a cruel distinction between the sexes, which forms the one to be harsh and unfeeling, and humbles the other to servility and subjection."[7] Jefferson subscribed to this vision, as far as whites were concerned.[8]

Scottish writers advanced the importance of sentimental childrearing in its relation to public life, but they were opposed to unfettered individualism. According to Dwyer, Scottish moralists "illuminated private life and the domestic circle, both as a protection against a commercial 'society of strangers' and as an ideal environment for the stimulation of interactive sensibility." And, in effect, their vision of childrearing and family dynamics attempted to harmonize the individualism that it also encouraged.[9]

Looking to environmental psychology, Hutcheson in 1725 had "depicted the family as a transmitter of customs, habits, morals and manners as the basic building blocks of a larger society." Hume declared the family "the first and original principle of society," emphasizing "custom and habit" over "blood or instinct." He went on to say that "sexual attraction between men and women provided the primary bond," an idea to which Abigail referred ("a tye more binding"). She had read in Fordyce that marriage was the "tenderest of all connexions." Those "truest pleasures and fairest prospects are the pleasures which are enjoyed at home, and the prospects which include a family." Children, writes Rosemarie Zagarri in her summary of this Scottish vision, "provide a further 'principle of the union' between couples," which children themselves when grown were to carry out into other relationships from which society exfoliated. She points out that Adam Smith extended Hutcheson's notion of social affections to sympathy, which was also "learned in the family." Affection was "nothing but habitual sympathy," and it meant that "the origins of political sentiment and society lay in the family." Because of her role in generating affection, therefore, a mother was very important to "a citizen's political socialization," the view that postrevolutionary Americans adapted.[10]

Smith exclaimed over the pleasure brought him by viewing the feelings generated in middle-class family life, able to afford such psychological luxuries as careful childrearing as well as material ones, in contrast to poor people's families: "With what pleasure do we look upon a family, through the whole of which reign mutual love and esteem, where the parents and children are companions for one another, without any other difference than what is made by respectful affection on one side, and kind indulgence on the other; where freedom and fondness, mutual raillery and mutual kindness, show that no opposition of interest divides the brothers, nor any rivalship of favour sets the sisters at variance, and where everything presents us with the idea of peace, cheerfulness, harmony, and contentment." Poverty, Smith wrote, could not supply such circumstances: "[It] is extremely unfavourable to the rearing of children . . . the common people cannot afford to tend them with the same care as those of the better station." Another Scot, James Glen, the governor of South Carolina, while visiting the backcountry in 1753, remarked on the sheer numbers of children there, noting that parents did not "Bestow the least Education on them, they take so much Care in raising a Litter of Piggs, their Children are equally naked and full as Nasty. The Parents in the back Woods come together without any previous Ceremony, and it is not much to be wondered at that the offspring of such loose Embraces should be little looked after." Glen compared these frontier manners to Indians, and his implicit standards recall Crèvecoer's in his sympathy for African American slaves' being deprived of the resources to rear children as Scottish theorists recommended.[11]

Smith further demonstrated his own capacity for sympathy in his remarkable description of the relations between mother and baby, one both scientific and sentimental, with which he illustrated his theory of sympathy: "What are the pangs of a mother, when she hears the moanings of her infant that during the agony of disease cannot express what it feels?" She is in a position analogous to what he said "we"—men in particular—feel in conceiving of "our brother . . . upon the rack." The baby stimulates a kind of reflex introjection: "In her idea of what it suffers, she joins, to its real helplessness, her own terrors for the unknown consequences of its disorder; and out of all these, forms for her own sorrow, the most complete image of misery and distress." Smith then turns to the baby, who, while not blank, is undeveloped, unsocialized: "the infant, however, feels only the uneasiness of the present instant, which can never be great. With regard to the future, it is perfectly secure, and in its thoughtlessness and want of foresight, possesses an antidote against fear and anxiety, the great tormentors of the human breast, from which reason and philosophy will, in vain, attempt to defend it, when it grows up to be a man."[12]

Smith's vision assumes, in fact, sketches, the specific kinds of interactions between adults and babies that generated sensibility. We can juxtapose it with Hildred Geertz's 1957 account of emotional acculturation: "The range and quality of emotional experience is potentially the same for all human beings. . . . In the course of the growth of a given person, this potential range of emotional experience becomes narrowed, and out of it certain qualitative aspects are socially selected, elaborated, and emphasized." The "growth" is mediated by "interaction with . . . bearers of a particular culture," most saliently parents. The terms are a variety of signs, necessarily all nonverbal on one side, but emotions are intimately associated with words from the beginning. Words are most evidently the culturally distinct clues that change over time. Geertz's article is entitled "The Vocabulary of Emotion," and we can construe sensibility's "family of words" according to social-psychological model that she describes. She continues: "[The adults around the child] provide not only the situation for his learning about himself and his world, but also definitions and interpretations of this situation, and conceptualizations of their feelings and his feelings within it. This aspect of the child's learning, this progressive narrowing of situation, self, and feeling-states, can be a key to understanding of personality differences found between members of different cultures."[13]

Evidently, Geertz's model pertains to the European American, African American, and Native American cultures coexisting within the borders of the British American colonies and, then, the United States.[14] The model also assimilated features of class and gender. Girls and boys were reared differently, even within cultures of sensibility, as Smith assumed by referring to brothers and sisters in his description of family interrelations.

## Looking to Advice

Pinckney, Warren, and Adams each acknowledged their sense of the great importance of mothers to childrearing, in part because of their agreement with Locke's analysis of the operation of the mind as it developed after its birth as a blank slate. Locke explained this process in *An Essay concerning Human Understanding* and in *Some Thoughts on Education*, which were to be popularized by the *Spectator*, Richardson, and many other vehicles. Pinckney intended to teach her first son, she recorded when he was three months old, "according to Mr. Locks method," which she had "carefully studied." Later, when she had had more children, she resolved "to watch over their tender minds, to carefully root out the appearing and buddings of vice, and to instill piety, Virtue and true religion into them." Because young minds were tender, they were deemed particularly susceptible to impression, this belief intimately connected with the tenderness aggrandized by devotees of sensibility, a culture that arose in conjunction with new emphases in childrearing. Pinckney wrote to her two young sons in London, where she and Colonel Pinckney had left them for what they construed as a better education (bringing their daughter home with them to South Carolina), to tell them of their father's unexpected death: "How shall I write to you! What shall I say to you! My dear, my ever dear Children! But if possible more so now than Ever, for I have a tale to tell you that will pierce your tender infant hearts!"[15]

In a letter to Abigail, Warren called "cultivating the minds and planting the seeds of Virtue in the infant Bosom" a "mighty task," her terms ignoring the hypothetical existence of an innate moral sense. It was a "duty that is of the utmost importance to society." For Warren this was suffused with her sense of religion. The task was that "important Charge (by providence devolved on Every Mother)," and she would "Esteem it a happiness indeed" if she could acquit herself of it, "to the approbations of the judicious Observer of Life," but then she wrote: "A much more noble pleasure is the Conscious satisfaction of having Exerted our utmost Efforts to rear the tender plant and Early impress the youthful mind, with such sentiments that if properly Cultivated when they go out of our hands they may become useful in their several departments on the present theatre of action, and happy forever when the immortal mind shall be introduced into more Enlarged and Glorious scenes." The self-conscious pleasure she describes at the beginning of this sentence manifested her Cartesian, liberal Protestant inheritance, so fundamental to the culture of sensibility.[16]

Before she was married, Abigail wrote to her cousin: "In youth the mind is bent like a tender twig, which you may bend as you please, but in age like a sturdy oak and hard to move." Like Warren, she expressed some dismay over the disparity between the responsibility that childrearing entailed and her lack of preparation for it. Abigail wrote to her older friend in 1776: "I find myself dear Marcia, not only doubled in Wedlock but multiplied in cares to which I know myself uneaqual, in the Education of my little flock I stand in need of the constant assistance of my Better half," a need of which we saw she also complained to Lovell. It was four months later that she wrote to John with a degree of indignation over the "neglect of Education in . . . daughters," illustrating its effects on herself: "With regard to the Education of my own children, I find myself soon out of my debth, and destitute and deficient in every part of Education." This became a chief reason for her advocacy of improving women's education.[17]

When first she became a mother, Abigail turned to Fordyce's *Sermons to Young Women* for advice about childrearing, but just how to practice it was not the focus of his book. With four live children, she turned specifically to a British popularizer of Locke, John Hill, masking his gender under the pseudonym Julianna-Susannah Seymour. In her first letter to Warren, written soon after visiting her in July 1773, Abigail sent her a copy of "Mrs. Seymore upon Education," that is, *On the Management and Education of Children* (1754). It was because Warren had expressed a desire to see Hill's book when Abigail "mentiond" it during her recent visit that she had complied with Warren's request: "Not from an opinion that you stand in need of such an assistant, but that you may give me your Sentiments upon this Book, and tell me whether it corresponds with the plan you have prescribed to yourself and in which you have so happily succeeded."[18]

Abigail was more complimentary over Warren's own mothering: "I was really so well pleased with your little offspring, that I must beg the favour of you to communicate to me the happy Art of 'rearing the tender thought, teaching the young Idea how to shoot, and pouring fresh instruction o'er the Mind.'" Warren's "little offspring" were aged sixteen, thirteen, eleven, nine, and seven. Warren herself was forty-five. Her admiring visitor, then twenty-nine years old, had children of eight, six, three, and one. "May the Natural Benevolence of your Heart," Abigail continued, "prompt you to assist a young and almost inexperienced Mother in this Arduous Business, that the tender twigs allotted to my care, may be so cultivated as to do honour to their parents."[19]

But, given Abigail's interest and the correspondence between the book's recommendations and the Anglophone cultures of sensibility, it is worth considering some of what Hill wrote in 1754, five years before Smith's *Theory of Moral Sentiments*, and long before the postrevolution-

ary republican mothering recommendations described by Norton and
Kerber, but in the wake of Locke and the high point that sentimental
literature had reached in the novels of Richardson, published between
1740 and 1754.[20]

## How to Raise Children with Sensibility

John Hill wrote in a female persona because he addressed a female readership, ostensibly giving advice in letters to "her" supposed niece, "newly
Married" and "newly widowed," wishing to make her "a good Mother."
More "than the welfare of our own Sex depends on [that] Character."
The fundamental influence of the first adult figure to whom an infant is
exposed is the reason for the author's opposition to putting babies out to
nurse: "Children imbibe their Principles with their Milk; 'tis certain that
from those who are about them when they first began to exercise their
little Faculties, they do receive Impressions, which are never afterwards
to be eradicated." Abigail did nurse her babies herself ("for about a year"),
although she probably did not need Hill's book to tell her to do so. So did
Warren, according to one of her biographers, intending in that way to inhibit fertility, illustrating the claim made generally for late eighteenth-
century American women. But, given the importance elite American
women gave to their superiority to working-class women, including servants (I have quoted Abigail's condescending "even by one's Servants"
[see the introduction]), there is no reason not to think that such a reason
played a part, too.[21]

The emphasis on a mother's power was the corollary of the environmental, Lockean psychology on which Hill insisted throughout. He
presented such a view as an innovation, stating that it was "common
Opinion, that People's Dispositions and Temper are born with them;
but . . . it is a very false one." His authority here was scientific psychology.[22] "Nature has formed the Mind as she has formed the Body, tender,
and susceptible in its infancy, of all Impressions." These were grounds
for a parent's paying great attention, becoming more conscious, or more
sensitive. "In the Mind the slightest and least Tendency to Ill may be increased into the worst imaginable Disposition by false Management." It
was up to mothers to "implant" principles "in tender" minds, precisely
as Warren thought. Elsewhere, Hill modified this vision, noting that "almost all Children are born with the Seeds of a good Temper . . . and all
the Care that is necessary is preserving them," although that orientation
can be "lost by many in the Course of their life." The qualifications are

important since they allowed for the existence of bad people and the existence of an immoral "world."[23]

This Lockean psychological perspective had democratic potential: "It is certain, that the Minds of all People, are in their Infancy a kind of Blank, the greatest as well as the least. They are ready to receive whatever Character shall be written on them, and what they do receive at this time is fixed upon them forever . . . the original Characters appear the deepest coloured and are the last to be entirely eradicated." Such a view dictated a new kind of childrearing as well as which parent was to implement it. The "Rod is unnecessary on all Occasions" because the emotion it aroused was not effective enough: "They are but half cured of their Faults who omit to practice them through Fear of Punishment; but when Children are brought into a better Course by Rewards; it is as it is with Men." That is to say, those adults who now were being rewarded materially on a much wider scale, and not unrelatedly, were able to construe God as more benevolent. "The habit becomes Nature. The Rod only cows and sours the Temper; Encouragement exalts and enlarges the Mind." Hill believed that his advice here was as unusual as the view that disposition was not innate: "I know Severity is the common Method of governing, but I would do all with Mildness." Wood writes of this period: "[Nearly] all of the traditional child-rearing manuals advocated the physical punishment of children. Heads of households . . . beat their children with a readiness and fierceness that today leaves us wincing." The more enlightened vision expressed by Hill in 1754 had its political as well as its theological corollary: the result of impressing children's minds with mildness would be that they would "grow up into a State of natural Freedom, which will not bear absolute Slavery."[24] Teaching school in 1759, after graduating from Harvard, John Adams wrote in his diary: "I find by repeated experiment and observation, in my School, that human nature is more easily wrought upon and governed, by promises and incouragement and praise than by punishment, and threatening and Blame." Shaw, who notes the influence on John of conflict with his father, remarked that his next sentence anticipated the "central thesis" of the *Discourses on Davila*: "Corporal as well as disgraceful punishments, depress the spirits, but commendation enlivens and stimulates them to a noble ardor and emulation." We can repeat Fliegelman's characterization of the American Revolution as one "against patriarchal authority." It was this note in prerevolutionary Whiggish, British childrearing advice that would be adapted by the "Republican motherhood" of post-revolutionary America.[25]

The tenderness and susceptibility to all impressions evinced by a baby meant that the parent, paying close attention, could be subtle in response. Hill wrote: "I will have the Parent look grave and seem uneasy. This will not be difficult to a rational Person for it need not be affected. This is all the Punishment I would inflict on the little Offender." Such looks will capitalize on a child's natural affection, and the child will learn to read them: "If the Child be fond of the Parent (as naturally, we all are) it will, in Time, have enough Reason and Gratitude to grow ashamed of what it sees produce this Effect." While the child "is thus taught to avoid the Occasions of Uneasiness to its Parent by the Perverseness and Sourness of its Temper, it may be lured to the Practice of every thing opposed to its fault by Rewards." These rewards, like punishments, re-inforced a child's need to read expressions and gestures: "A kind Look, or a Kiss from a Parent, on every such Occasion, will do well; but, beside this, every the least Tendency to Affability and Good-humour is to be rewarded by some little Matter of which it is fond. All that is required, therefore is Attention on the Part of the Parent." The attention was to accompany the parent's careful exercise of self-control, calibrated to the child's capacities: "only some one Sentiment can be impressed upon the Infant Mind at once, and this only by slow Degrees; it is of great Importance to determine which, of many that are right, shall be selected." This, the author makes clear, is the exercise of "Power."[26]

Hill denied that the management he recommended was merely the application to children of the method used in the training of dogs and horses, one we would call *Pavlovian*: "Brute Beasts . . . may be taught Obedience on the Principle of Rewards and Punishments; but rational Creatures should be treated otherwise. . . . Believe me . . . Education does as much in setting Men above the Brutes, as their Inherent Superiority." Children were to be treated as "rational" creatures, not just with rewards and punishments. The distinction lay in the subtlety of emotional clues: "I would have your particular Favor and Indulgence be the great Reward for the Children's acting as they ought; and your Coolness and Disregard to them the Punishment for their doing otherwise. . . . Nothing can be so mean as to place some little Indulgence to the Appetite, as a Reward, or the Stroke of a Rod as a Punishment; the one will lead Children to set their Hearts upon those Things they ought to despise, and the other will place, singly, Fear and Meanness of Spirit in the stead of a Sense of Right and Wrong." The clergy, Hill asserted, had dropped the ball in the latter regard, in favor of abstruse theology, and next "to the Authority of Heaven—its immediate Minister, the word of a Parent . . . is the greatest Sanction." In spite of his suggestion that babies had a "natural Tendency" toward the "Good," Hill did not assume the existence of an innate moral sense; that would have run counter to the pure Lockeanism on which his system of management depended. Still, it was a "sense" that mothers were to "place" in their children.

Hill criticized parents who are "indulgent to [children] at all Times, while they are thus young; whether they are doing Right or Wrong; and it is therefore impossible the Infant can form any Notion of what is Right or what is Wrong." The author specified the motives of such parental failures: if their children "do Right, they are by these Parents fondled for it, because it pleases: if they do wrong, they are fondled to put them in better Humour; . . . and this being the Management, it is impossible they should know what deserves Encouragement, what Blame." In effect, "indulgence" of children was self-indulgence creating self-indulgence.[27]

Moral sense transcended rank, but, despite his assertion that virtue and vice nominally united lord and peasant, Hill conflated a sense of right and wrong with what was "proper and becoming." These latter two terms carried particular meaning for girls; the author illustrated how the teaching of morality included the double standard. Boys could, in fact, learn from the psychological as well as the physical freedom of peasants: "There is a rough Freedom, and open Honesty in the Hearts of these Villagers, which though it must be new modeled for the Service of those whose Scene of Action will be in the polite World, yet is itself right." On the other hand, for girls to take such a sense of "Freedom" into the polite world for which they were being shaped would be extremely dangerous: "There is nothing they can learn of the mean Persons, whose Conversations they first hear, whose Principles they will imbibe." Young women of fashion obtain "low Ideas and Indelicate Sentiments" among servants, whereas "delicacy" and "generosity" are "the very Sentiments" for which children "will afterward be respected and applauded."[28]

Mothers were to teach their children how to act their gender: "As you would your Sons always act like Men, you would doubtless wish to have your Daughters always behave like Women. These things, do not happen my Dear, by Miracles; they are the natural Effects of natural Means; and if you omit to employ the one, you must not expect to find the other." Again, to square environmental psychology with nature, parents' management is deemed natural, but implicit in this statement was the possibility that gender was malleable and that girls raised in other ways would not be conventionally feminized or boys masculinized. As we have seen, these were persistent and widespread apprehensions in the contexts of self-assertion by women, the change in manhood and its ideals, and the consequences of Locke's notion of a blank state. If Hill said, "Custom . . . when it is begun from Infancy, becomes Nature," Poulain de la Barre had ascribed gendering to "Custom" long before, and eighteenth-century feminists reiterated the point.[29]

Hill lays great emphasis on the fact that the women he is addressing are—or should be—more delicate than men. He refers to "the natural Delicacy of the Sex" and "their naturally delicate Constitution" as well as "the natural softness of my [putative] Sex," both *delicacy* and *softness* connoting behavior as well as denoting nerve quality. Softness was more or less synonymous with the tenderness with which Hill also associated delicacy. He declared: "[I] would not have the Mind neglected in Women more than in Men; only in the latter it is the sole Consideration; whereas, in the soft Sex the body is expected to be so much taken Care of." Both genders should get fresh air and exercise, but girls in significantly greater moderation than boys. Too much sun and air "would turn your Daughters brown, and give them the Appearance of Milkmaids." Care of the "Complexion" in boys is "effeminate and out of Character"; in girls, "it is essential."[30]

Hill directed his addressee, his "niece," to her mother as her model: she had "exceeded all in Delicacy." In so doing, he explained more precisely what delicacy was and how a lady, not servants, should teach it: "She could sooner pardon the Person who let slip a Double-meaning Expression, tending to Obscenity, than one who spoke coarsely or indecently." His objective was to show mothers how to impart such sensibility to infants, rather than leave it to the later, less impressionable stages of life: "Whenever you find [your . . . little Daughter] tending but the least toward a Word or Expression of that kind, check her, and convince her thoroughly how wrong it is. It will become natural to her, thus to fear the least Syllable that tender to this Character; and being accustomed to condemn it in herself, she will, from Early Example from others, hear it with Abhorrence." The strength of feeling in relation to the slightest provocation marked the existence of a level of sensibility from which even the exemplary niece's mother had exempted gentlemen, who, nonetheless, prized it in women.[31]

Hill writes that the conclusion of child management is to bring "sons to a Time of mixing among the World, and . . . Daughters to the Period of their being solicited to enter a State of marriage." In getting married, the supposedly female author declares, boys have the advantage over "the . . . unhappy Infants of our Sex." Chillingly, Hill tells mothers that it is their "Business to represent Marriage" to their daughters "as the most Hazardous of all Engagements." If the latter's military connotations are doubtful here, Fordyce made such a perspective clear: "The greater part of either sex study to prey on one another. The world in too many instances, is a theatre of war between men and women." This had been Lovelace's conception in laying siege to Clarissa. But women were far more likely to lose. Aunt Shaw told Nabby after the latter's marriage to Colonel Smith (and in a letter replete with Fordycean advice) that to "place ourselves under quite a new kind of Protection, cannot but strike a reflecting Mind with awe, and the most fearful Apprehensions—as it is *the* important Crisis, upon which our Fate depends." Colonel Smith turned out to be a disaster of a husband.[32]

Young ladies entered the world in order to find husbands, but, according to Hill, men were being primed from their boyhood to treat women very badly indeed. Hill regarded "the Stories of the Heathen Gods" not just "frivolous and trifling" but "infamous and dangerous." There were "Sentiments of Honour and Virtue" in Horace, but other ancients wrote of "Lewdness and Debauchery." (He probably had Ovid in mind.) So he imagined selecting "such Parts" of the classics as "tend to inculcate Virtue; at least such only as are innocent," and printing versions for "Youth" that should have all the "bad Passages omitted." As it was, boys read that "Jupiter, the greatest of all the Gods of the Time, was a most debauched Person, always in Intrigue, and continually . . . debauching Peoples Wives and innocent Daughters." Thomas Bowdler, who gave his name to such censorship because of a life's work excising all sexual references in Shakespeare, was born the same year Hill made this recommendation.[33]

Hill went on to argue that boys should be educated at home because of the "debauched Principles" propagated "so strongly at university and Schools." Sons should be taught Greek and Latin at home, where mothers could influence their emotional "Manners": "I should certainly think their Hearts a first Consideration, and should rather they were left a little less finished in the Heads than that these should be spoiled." But their "Genius and Imagination" had to be instructed, too, for which task mothers were unqualified. Hill advised his audience: "Take the Advice of some learned and ingenious Person in that Head: But you are qualified to do a Job of his Manners." If the tutor did not have manners, the mother should fire him. The results of such an educational program, at home, with a vetted tutor, and under the eye of the mother, would be, "instead of Profligates and Rakes, good Men and sufficient Scholars."[34]

Meanwhile, the young daughter entering the world found men there who had not been so reared: "There are among the Men a Number of idle People, who though never think of Matrimony talk of nothing but Love. These are everywhere in public Places. They mix themselves in all Parties, and employ their mean Flattery, and their prostituted Tenderness, on every Woman equally." These were the artful male predators, able to put on whatever face necessary to insinuate themselves into young women's favor. Hill advised a young woman to ask a "Friend to enquire after men who make address to her," in an era when increasingly young women wished to marry for love. While earlier he had stressed the importance of leading young children to tell the truth, in this section of the book he pointed out that "sincerity" made women vulnerable to rakes.[35]

## Abigail Attempts to Instill Sensibility into Her Sons

Married in 1764, Abigail had five children between 1765 and 1772, one of whom, Susanna, died before her second birthday. She had a stillborn daughter in 1777. Soon after Nabby's birth in 1765, Abigail wrote Hannah Storer Green that she had "become a Mamma—can you credit it?" She said that she had been "Bless'd with a charming Girl whose pretty Smiles already delight my Heart, who is the Dear Image of her still Dearer Pappa." "You my Friend," she continued, "are well acquainted with all the tender feelings of a parent, therefore I need not apologize for the present overflow." Reading a baby's face elicited feelings that could be expressed in the uncontrolled words of sensibility, at least to a fellow parent. Babies, Abigail thought, "endeard" themselves to her by their "smiles and graces." In October 1765, Abigail wrote to her sister Mary, thanking her for a letter that brought her "both pleasure and pain." Abigail pleased herself, she wrote, "with the thoughts of seeing you in November." She then specified that vision of "My Dear Betsy," Mary's little daughter, as a second source of pleasure: "what would I give to hear her prattle to her Cousin Nabby, to see them put their little arms round one an others necks, and hug each other, it would really be a very pleasing Sight, to me. But to leave these little charmers. . . ."[36]

The experience of being a parent led Abigail to realize why parents in general overflowed with words corresponding to the powerful feelings elicited by having children and watching them carefully: "How every word and action of these little creatures, twines around one's heart[.] All their little pranks which would seem ridiculous to relate, are pleasing to a parent. How vex'd have I felt before now upon hearing parents relate the chitt chat of little Miss, and Master said or did such and such a queer thing—and this I have heard done by persons whose good Sense in other instances has not been doubted." She realizes that she can now behave as ridiculously by chitchatting the same way to others who were not parents or were distant enough to be considered "company": "This tho really a weakness I can now more easily forgive, but hope in company I shall not fall into the same error." This would be to check the overflow of feeling with "good Sense."[37]

Abigail used the term *parent* in these illustration, applying it, however, to herself and two other mothers. John found strong feelings elicited in himself as a father, but women illustrated the belief, in keeping with such feelings' theorization, that mothers were especially susceptible to feeling, making of *maternal tenderness* a conventional phrase.[38] Elizabeth Smith Shaw used it in a passage that also suggested that sisterhood gave her a special sympathy for Abigail's maternal feelings. In the spring of 1786, while Abigail was in England, her three sons, then aged nineteen, sixteen, and fourteen, were staying with their Aunt Shaw, who wrote this to their mother: "I went up after they were abed to see if they were warm, and comfortable . . . but *really* to enjoy the satisfaction of seeing the three Brothers embracing each other in Love, Innocence, Health, and Peace." She had chosen to indulge an emotional pleasure in an actual "Sight," one she could then present as a scene to Abigail: "All my Sister rose within me—Joy-Love-Gratitude, and maternal Tenderness sparkled in my Eye." She writes that she had imagined herself her sister too successfully, that she was able to feel her sister's feelings, an act of sensibility repeatedly idealized in such correspondence and the kind on which Smith built his theory: "What said I, 'would your Mother give to look upon you all, and see you all happy as I do.' Would she were here. I know that you can have no greater pleasure, than to hear that your 'Children walk in the Truth.'" She conveyed sympathy for Abigail's pain, along with the pleasure she reported.[39]

Because John was absent on public business for so many years, Abigail was left to rear their children, enhancing still more the power that, as we have seen, her favored theorists emphasized mothers should exercise. She told him in September 1767, "I know from the tender affection you bear me, and our little one's that you will rejoice to hear that we are well, our Son is much better than when you left home"—John Quincy had been born that July—"and our Daughter"—then aged two—"rock's him to Sleep, with the Song of 'Come pappa come home to Brother Johnny.'"

She followed that with: "Sunday seems a more Lonesome Day to me than any other when you are absent." So, from their earliest years, Abigail oriented her children to yearning for their father's return and again told him that her writing to him of their emotional pain would affect his feelings. She wrote him in April 1777, for example: "It would have grieved you if you had seen your youngest Son [Tommy] stand by his Mamma and when she deliverd out to the others their Letters, he inquired for one, but none appearing he stood in silent grief with the Tears running down his face, nor could he be pacified till I gave him one of mine.—Pappa does not Love him he says so well as he does Brothers, and many comparisons are made to see whose Letters were the longest." The letters John had written to Charles, aged seven, and John Quincy, ten, described the casting of cannon and other warlike preparations that John had observed. Nabby does not seem to have gotten a letter either.[40]

Abigail's place in John Quincy's young imagination is illustrated by that occasion when the seven-year-old held his mother's hand as they watched the Battle of Bunker Hill. In old age, John Quincy recalled his mother's transmission of her views of Warren's death in that battle, in so doing revealing his internalization and perpetuation of the culture of sensibility. He wrote to an English Quaker of the war's effect on his family when it was under Abigail's direction: "My father was separated from his family on his way to attend the . . . continental Congress in Philadelphia." For twelve months afterward, he recalled, "my mother with her infant children dwelt liable every hour of the day and of the night to be butchered in cold blood." "I saw with my own eyes," he continued, "those fires burning [in Charlestown], and heard Britannia's thunders at the Battle of Bunker's hill and witnessed the tears of my mother and mingled with them my own, at the fall of Warren, a dear friend of my father, and a beloved Physician to me." (He loved Warren in part because the doctor had saved his forefinger from amputation.) The spring and summer following Bunker Hill, John Quincy recalled:

> [My mother] taught me to repeat daily after the Lord's prayer before rising from the bed the Ode of Collins, on the patriot *warrior* who fell in the War to subdue the Jacobite rebellion of 1745.
>
> How sleep the *brave*, who sink to rest. . . .

And he went on to quote Collins's whole poem accurately. He then described what his remembering these lines signified in terms of the psycho-perceptual model of sensibility: "Of the impression made upon my heart by the sentiments inculcated in these beautiful effusions of patriotism and poetry, you may form an estimate by the fact that now, seventy-one years after they were thus taught me, I repeat them from memory without reference to the book."[41]

Collins's poem was itself a sentimental one: Abigail had wished to implant delicacy of responsiveness in her sons as well as in her daughter. In 1774, she had kept little Johnny out of the Braintree school because of the appointment of a master of whom she disapproved, sending him instead to John Thaxter, her cousin and a man of sensibility, to be tutored. She explained to her husband: "I am certain that if he does not get so much good, he gets less harm, and I have always thought it of very great importance that children should in the early part of life be unaccustomed to such examples as would tend to corrupt the purity of their words and actions that they may chill with horrour at the sound of an oath, and blush with indignation at an obscene expression. These first principal[s] which grow with their growth and strengthen with their strength neither time nor custom can totally eradicate." This shares assumptions with Hill, namely, that children are born pure and that the moral sense should be implanted to be registered by the feelings signified by blushes and horrified chills.[42]

We saw that Abigail trained her other son, Charles—perhaps named for her male ideal, Sir Charles Grandison—to console her for the absence of her husband by teaching him to sing that simple "Scotch song" to her. Reading her account in 1778, John could infer that Charles's singing to her both stimulated her sensibility and allayed its distressing effects. We can imagine one of the duo putting arms around the other or both of them doing so. More important for my purpose than invoking Oedipus (although wanting John to behave like Sir Charles and the song's fantasizing the return of her lover would be pertinent), Abigail drew her eight-year-old into her emotional mix of pleasurable pain, imbuing him with the value of emotional responsiveness of sensibility.

Rearing sons in this way could make them vulnerable—Hill had insisted on mothers' calibrating their interaction with children in accordance with their gender. In 1778, John took Charles as well as John Quincy with him across the Atlantic, in accordance with the parents' wishes that boys be raised to noble manhood. John Quincy was happy to go, but, Abigail admitted, "young as he is a Mothers Heart will feel a thousand Fears and anxieties." Tommy was too young to go and Nabby excluded by gender. During the voyage, John reported to Abigail: "Charles [now nine years old] . . . lies in my Bosom a nights." Abigail had "horrours both day and night," thinking of them at sea: "My dear sons, Little do they know how many veins of their Mothers Heart bled when she parted from them." She was particularly worried about Charles: "My delicate Charles, how has he endured the fatigues of his voyage? John [Quincy] is a hardy Sailor, seasoned before, I do not feel so much for him." Abigail wrote Charles, asking him, "How many times did you wish yourself by mammas fireside?" and telling him: "[You are] a favorite in the Neighbourhood at home, all of whom wonder how Mamma could part with you. Mamma found it hard enough tis true, but she consulted your good more than her own feelings." Evidently, however, he was to keep her feelings in mind because she hoped he would "not disapoint her hopes and expectations by contracting vices and follies, instead of improveing in virtue and knowledge."[43]

Charles and John Quincy (then twelve) traveled with their father across Spain and then studied in Leyden and outside Paris. John put Charles to school to "keep him steady" but soon came to feel, not that Charles was too young to be away from his mother, but that he had "too exquisite sensibility for Europe." Perhaps this was linked to Charles's health being "much affected by this tainted Atmosphere" of Amsterdam. Charles himself, John wrote Abigail, "had set his heart so much upon going home." It would "have broken it [his heart], to have refusedJanuary 30, 2010 him." His next sentence was self-critical: "I desire I may never again have the Weakness to bring a Child to Europe." He did not regard the older John Quincy as a child, and he remained. John's weakness was, presumably, either self-indulgence because he missed his children or perhaps that he acceded to Abigail's wish that he take more fatherly responsibility in raising his sons. Or perhaps we can categorize John's weakness here with his liability to being charged with a "weak Attachment to a Woman," supervening over his manly activity in public office.[44]

Given Charles's exquisite sensibility, it is not surprising that among the "many anxieties" relieved by his safe return, Abigail wrote her sister Elizabeth, was that he had been "restored . . . to his Native Land, undepraved in his mind and morals, by the fascinating allurements of vice." Instead, the "fond Mother would tell you that you may find in him the same solid sober discreet Qualities that he carried abroad with a modesty bordering upon diffidence"—the self-conscious phrase, the "fond Mother would," suggesting, perhaps, that Abigail realized that this was an exaggeration, even a wish, superimposed on John's judgment of Charles's exquisite sensibility.[45]

Abigail was similarly concerned in writing to the thirteen-year-old John Quincy in May 1780: "You my dear son are formed with a constitution feelingly alive, your passions are strong and impetuous and tho I have sometimes seen them hurry you into excesses, yet with pleasure I have observed a frankness and Generosity accompany your Efforts to govern and subdue them." In the previous paragraph, she had quoted Pope: "'Passions are the Elements of life' but Elements which are subject to the controul of Reason." She quoted the *Essay on Man* as advice to John on other occasions, too. John Quincy's subsequent modeling his "Vision" on Pope may have been charged with Abigail's transmission to him of the value she placed on the great and popular poet.[46]

Abigail's identifying John Quincy here as "formed with a constitution feelingly alive," the same terms in which we have seen she characterized herself, led her to refer next to the ambiguous potential in such special sensibility, sometimes leading to passionate excess (note that, inevitably, feeling and passions ran into each other, despite efforts to distinguish them), but capable, too, of contributing to frankness and generosity, even as John Quincy reined in his passions. This was the struggle Abigail believed her own heightened sensibility forced her to endure, one she helped transmit to her sons by such direct characterization as well as by example. John Quincy's father, Abigail believed, could temper his sensibility with the "stern virtue" of Cato or Hercules, the latter a figure with whom she explicitly encouraged John Quincy to identify. She reiterated that it was of the greatest importance that her son govern his passions, being "particular upon the passion of Anger, as it is generally the most predominant passion of your age," and, one can add, the one to which her husband was most susceptible. Yet again, she qualified this by explaining: "I do not mean to have you insensible to real injuries"—as in the case of others, including John and Jefferson, Abigail had suggested that it had been sensitivity to abuse that had provoked Americans to revolution—"yet if you can preserve good Breeding and decency of Manner you will have an advantage over the aggressor and will maintain a dignity of character which will always insure you respect even from the offender."

Abigail had written John Quincy with the same coupling of advice two months earlier, warning him of his particular "failing": "You must curb that impetuosity of temper, for which I have frequently chid you, but which properly directed may be productive of great good." She told him: "When a mind is raised, and animated by scenes that engage the Heart, then those qualities which would otherwise lay dormant, wake into Life, and form the Character of the Hero and Statesman." Thus was a post-Cartesian, psychophysiological belief widely held and illustrated by the words of Elizabeth Smith Shaw and Thomas Jefferson as well as by Pope. It was this model that, presumably, Abigail had in mind in reading Collins nightly to her little son following the scene of Bunker Hill, thereby elevating his mind toward heroism and statesmanship.[47]

Abigail had laid aside the March 1780 letter for seven or eight weeks, then added more advice, including that John Quincy should remember that his "example will have great weight" with his brother Charles. She then attempted to stimulate another feeling in him by making him conscious of her feeling: "If you could once feel how gratefull to the Heart of a parent the good conduct of a child is, you would never be the occasion of exciteng any other Sensations in the Bosom of your ever affectionate Mother, AA."[48]

Abigail had continued to apprehend that her sons were susceptible to the dangers of an immoral world. In 1783, she reported to John that her two younger sons had begun "to think of a Colledge Life, as not more than a year and a half distance. Charles is very desirous that he may be ready at 15, and Master Tommy is determined that he shall not out strip him, in his learning." Abigail imagined John's response to these college prospects: "You will tell me, that the season for temptation is not yet arrived, that altho they are carefully Guarded against evil communications, and warned of the danger of bad examples"—in accordance with the kind of childrearing advice Abigail admired in Hill's book— "no humane foresight can effectively preserve them from the contagion of vice." On the basis of the now conventional model of psychophysiology, she thought that the early inculcation of Christian morals had armed them: "I have a great opinion of early impressions of virtue. . . . They recall the wanderer to a sense of his Duty, tho he has strayed many many times. . . . If the Heart is good, all will go well." Nonetheless, she continued: "I have a thousand fears for my dear Boys, as they rise into Life, the most critical period of which is I conceive, at the university; there infidelity abounds, both in example and precepts, there they imbibe the specious arguments of a Voltaire a Hume and Mandeville."[49]

Abigail had read Hill's recommendation that boys be educated at home because of the "debauched Principles" propagated "so strongly at university and Schools." Here, she continued: "Thus is a youth puzzled in Mazes and perplexed with error untill he is led to doubt, and from doubting to disbelief." In contrast to the views of Voltaire, Hume, and Mandeville: "Christianity gives not such a pleasing latitude to the passions. It is too pure [and thus an invaluable check]. It teaches moderation humility and patience, which are incompatable, with the high Glow of Health, and the warm blood which riots in their veins." But, with those three un-Christian writers, "to enjoy, is to obey." She hoped that John would "return and assist by [his] example and advise, to direct and counsel them; that with undeviating feet they may keep the path of virtue." Sons needed an input from fathers that daughters did not, and John's example included that "stern virtue" that moderated sensibility as well as passions.

In 1788, when Tom was at Harvard, John wrote Nabby that he was "as fine a youth, as either of the three" of his sons, qualifying this ominously, "if a spice of fun in his composition should not lead him astray." Abigail anticipated the same Hogarthian progress that John would see in Charles. In 1789, she wrote John Quincy as she had nine years before regarding Charles, but now asking him in her absence: "attend to your Brother Tom, to watch over his conduct & prevent by your advice & kind admonitions, his falling prey to vicious Company." For the moment, she could report, "[Tom] seemes desirious of persueing his studies preserving a character and avoiding dissipation, but no youth is secure whilst temptations surround him." The following year, John Adams wrote Tom, still at Harvard, urging him: "Go on my son pursue your mathematics and your morals."[50]

Later Tom took to drink, but, even after a period in Europe, returned home in 1799 "an honest Sober and virtuous citizen." Abigail wrote John: "I hope he will continue an honour and a comfort to his Parent's tho it is allotted them to experience different Sensations with respect to one of whose reformation I can flatter myself, with but faint hopes." The psychological model represented by the word *sensations* accompanied the narrative intimated by *reformation*, both, of course, expressions of sensibility, as was Abigail's accompanying account of her suffering: "It is so painfull and distressing a subject to me, that what I suffer in silence." She could find some relief were she able to write to someone else. "I cannot write upon it, but to him," continued, noting that doing so was a "painfull" "duty." "I wish however some means could be devised to save him, from that ruin and destruction with which he must soon be overwhelmed if he is not already." As a mature adult, Tom was characterized by his nephew, Charles Francis Adams (the son of Tom's dauntingly successful brother John Quincy), as "a brute in manners and a bully in his family," terms very similar to those with which John Adams had dismissed his other son, Charles.[51]

John had approached Charles with the same mind frame that Abigail brought to the problem Thomas posed. He told Abigail in 1794: "[I write] oftener to Charles than to his Brothers to see if I can fix his Attention in which design I flatter myself I shall have success." But, in 1800, Charles was overwhelmed. Two months before his death, Abigail wrote her sister Mary: "[In] New York I found my poor unhappy son, for so I must still call him [an allusion to John's having disowned him as a buck and a beast] laid upon a Bed of sickness, destitute of a home. . . . You will easily suppose that this scene was too powerfull and distressing to me. Sarah was with him. . . ." John passed through the city without stopping, on route to Washington.[52]

From Washington, Abigail wrote Mary on hearing of Charles's death: "I know my loved Sister, that you will mingle in my sorrow and weep with me over the Grave of a poor unhappy Child who cannot now add an other pang to those which have pierced my Heart for several years past." She hoped that he had been redeemed, that her "supplications to Heaven for him, that he might find mercy from his maker might not have been in vain." She saw signs that he was on the way to a softened heart: "His disease was through the last period of his Life dreadfully painfull and distressing; He bore with patience & submission his sufferings and heard the prayers for him with composure." Abigail suggested that Charles's emotional behavior was linked to a degree of reconciliation with his wife: "[Sarah] took him into her care. She has a satisfaction in knowing that she has spared no pain to render his last moments less distressing to his Parents and relatives than they could have been else where." She referred to Charles's alcoholism: "Food has not been his sustenance, yet he did not look like an intemperate Man—he was bloted but not red." Finally, she insisted that Charles "was beloved in spight of his Errors, and all spoke with grief and sorrow for his habits."[53]

If, then, John had dismissed Charles as a "rake," Abigail went some way to represent her son as converted on his deathbed as Rochester also had been, including being converted to faithful husbandhood. Notably, however, Charles had approached that point by way of his mother's pious agency, not by the formal intercession of a minister, as Bishop Burnet had acted for Rochester, although one can say that her sentimental orientation had been shaped in part by the religious tradition represented by the Latitudinarian Burnet. More immediately, Abigail's account resembled the sentimental heroine's wish, constantly reiterated in novels since *Clarissa*, that she be able to convert hard, rakish men into men of sensitivity to women, a wish on which Hannah Quincy Lincoln appears to have given up.[54]

## Fathering from a Distance

John's orientation to his children and to Abigail's relation with them was sentimental. Long before he had any of his own, and in a diary entry in which he mulled over divorce and its effects, he had said that if either divorced parent "retained all the Children the other would be deprived of the Pleasure of educating and seeing [them]." But this was a fate he would make for himself by his choice of fame. As we have seen, he had to live merely with the "hope" that his "Children . . . will once at length discover, that they have a Father, who is not unmindfull of their Welfare," despite their "Reason to think themselves forgotten," which Abigail conveyed to them. She told John that they could not understand why he chose to be away so long. Even her attempts to make John vivid to them would remind them of his absence.[55]

John's letters contained sentimental messages to his children, including the last one quoted, which concluded, "With a Tenderness which Words cannot express I am theirs and yours forever," to be relayed to his children by their mother. John asked Abigail in 1769: "Give my Love to my little Babes . . . kiss my little Suky, for me." He wrote Abigail from the 1774 revolutionary convention in Philadelphia, where he was playing a leading role in promoting independence: "Pray remember me to my dear little Babes, whom I long to see running to meet me and climb up upon me, under the Smiles of their Mother." Soon after, he wrote her: "My Babes are never out of my Mind, nor absent from my Heart." And then he asked her: "Remember me in the tenderest Language, to all our little Folks."[56]

When, in 1776, Abigail wrote John of the six-year-old Charles's potentially fatal illness following his inoculation for smallpox, he replied: "Yours of the Eighteenth has fixed an Arrow in my Heart, which will not be drawn out, untill the next Post arrives, and then, perhaps, instead of being withdrawn, it will be driven deeper. My sweet Babe, Charles, is never out of my Thoughts.—Gracious Heaven preserve him!—The Symptoms you describe, are so formidable, that I am afraid almost to flatter myself with Hope." But then he checked himself in his account of his emotional pain and resistance to the idea that his little son might die by turning to religion, the convention in contemporary sentimental poems on the death of children. He asked: "Why should I repine? Why should I grieve? He is not mine, but conditionally, and subject to the Will of a Superiour, whose Will be done." And, if Abigail had told him that his son was in crisis, this same reply told her: "Every Moment grows more and more critical at New York. We expect every Hour, News of serious Joy, or Sorrow. The two Armies are very near each other, at Long Island."[57] John wrote Abigail of his "Joy" on hearing from her of Charles's recovery: "I feel quite light. I did not know what fast Hold that little Pratler Charles had upon me before." His daughter had been inoculated at the same time: "Give my Love to my little Speckeled Beauty, Nabby. Tell her I am glad she is like to have a few Pitts." This expressed his consciousness of gender. "She will not look the worse for them. If she does, she will learn to prize looks less and Ingenuity more. The best Way to prevent the Pitts from being lasting and conspicuous is to keep her out of the sun . . . to prevent her from tanning." John shared this concern shared with Hill.[58]

In 1775, John wrote Abigail: "I never observe in the World, an Example of any Person brought to Poverty from Affluence, from Health to Distemper, from Fame to Disgrace by the Vices and Follies of the age, but it throws me into a deep Rumination upon Education [i.e., childrearing]." He had been brought to this 1775 rumination by an excursion he had taken with Dr. Thomas Bond Jr. out to "his [Bond's] Father's Seat in the Country" outside Philadelphia, a welcome relief from the "suffocating Heats of the City, and the wasting, exhausting Debates of the Congress." Bond had "lost his wife" and had two "pretty little Girls," one of them "about Ten Years old who sings most sweetly and dances, delightfully." This was Nabby's age. After losing "five or six thousand Pounds sterling," of his father's money "in Trade," Bond had returned to "the Study and practice of Physic." He was "fat and jolly, a Lover of Pleasure," wrote John, who in the interest of the public good had himself laid aside such a life as well as forgone the prosperity that afforded the Bond family seat. John continued: "the Farm is large the Gardens very spacious, the orchards noble, and the Fruit Trees, very numerous and of great Variety." Bond's pleasures included sex. "Wine and Women he uses freely," John observed, and he was "supposed to have Connections" with "a pretty Girl in a Chamber opposite his Lodging in the City." This illustrated the general contrast between Philadelphia and Boston: "Epicurism and Debauchery are more common in this Place than in Boston."[59]

"My poor Children," John had continued in this monitory letter about a son's blowing his paternal inheritance, "I fear will loose some Advantages in Point of Education, from my continual Absence from them." He wanted then armed against the mistakes and vices of which Dr. Bond was an emblem: "Truth, Sobriety, Industry should be pe[r]petually inculcated upon them." John believed that his children should be taught "A System of Morality." They should be taught "Geography and . . . drawing Plans of . . . Countries—especially of America. . . . But Their Honour, Truth, in one Word their Morals, are of most importance. I hope these will be kept pure."

John brought the same psychology to bear on his sons as he had in teaching schoolboys in 1759, writing Abigail on October 29, 1775: "Human nature with all its infirmities and depravation is still capable of great things. It is capable of attaining to degrees of wisdom and goodness [i.e., by its own training and effort] . . . [heights that] appear respectable in estimation of superior intelligences[, not only to God]. Education makes a greater difference between man and man, than nature has made between man and brute. The virtues and powers to which men may be trained, by early education and constant discipline, are truly sublime and astonishing." His two examples of such sublimity were Newton and Locke, but it was illustrated in its lesser degrees by "your common mechanics and artisans," by "a watchmaker, . . . a pin or needlemaker," this in the year before Smith's illustration of the enormous economic advantage of the mechanization of production by way of the manufacture of pins in *The Wealth of Nations*. While his first observation of these potentials had been made of "human nature" and his use of *man* had been species generic, his illustrations were all gender specific.[60]

"It should be your care, therefore, and mine," John continued, "to elevate the minds of our children and exalt their courage; to accelerate and animate their industry and activity; to excite in them an habitual contempt of meanness, abhorrence of injustice and inhumanity, and an ambition to excel in every capacity, faculty, and virtue." "Abhorrence of inhumanity" was a mark of sensibility, comparable to Abigail's wishing little John Quincy would be chilled with horror. For John, such ends and means had the same characterological goal of self-assertion, of independence: "If we suffer their minds to grovel and creep in infancy, they will grovel all their lives." He had chosen to fly rather than "creep." It was on the same day that, in a second letter, John wrote Abigail his version of Hutchesonian degrees of social affection, strongest "as We descend" to "Family, which We call our own," at which point it was "so powerful" as "to darken our Understandings and pervert our Wills." It was an "Infirmity, in [his] own Heart," to be struggled against, to free himself for the national efforts that he had embraced in Philadelphia. This had provided him and Abigail a rationale for his turning over his part of parental "care" to her, despite its fundamental importance.[61]

That same relation between his public responsibility and his parental one shaped John's further remarks on his children's education in April the following year, as the American revolutionaries awaited the last efforts at negotiation with British commissioners: "What will come of this Labour Time will discover. . . . I am sure the Public or Posterity ought to get Something." The latter included his own children: "I believe my Children will think I might as well have thought and laboured, a little, night and Day for their Benefit. . . ." The letters' editors note that those four latter "suspension points" in the manuscript were actually "curled dashes, a device J[ohn] A[dams] began to use at this time, evidently to indicate elisions of thought more pronounced than dashes would . . . indicate." That is to say, they were intended to convey to his reader that he had feelings so strong he could not express them in words. Dashes had come into increasing use for the same purpose or to indicate informally the process and quality of association and the degree of feeling, reaching one apogee in the novels of Sterne.[62]

In this case, the "curled dashes" led to: "But I will not bear the Reproaches of my Children." John's imagining how their responses would feel to him further illustrated that his relations with them were fraught with sensibility. So, should they reproach him in this way in the future, he would defend himself—in effect, he was defending himself against his pain over his absence from them at the time of this letter—by telling them: "I studied and laboured to procure a free Constitution of Government for them to solace themselves under, and if they do not prefer this to ample Fortune, to Ease and Elegance, they are not my Children, and I care not what becomes of them. They shall live upon thin Diet, wear mean Cloaths, and work hard with Chearfull Hearts and free Spirits or they may be the Children of Earth or of no one, for me." This was to link the Revolution's goal to values John had expressed in 1765 when, writing as "Humphrey Ploughjogger" for the *Boston Gazette*, he had registered consumerism's appeal to the young of both genders: "All the young men b[u]y them[selves] blue surtouts with fine yellow buttons, and boughten broad cloth jackets and breeches—and our young women wear calicoes, chinces and laces, and other knickknacks to make them fine."[63]

As we have seen, the Adams children expressed themselves to each other in the terms of sensibility. John Quincy illustrates how his parents influenced him in this regard. Attempting to motivate his eight-year-old brother Charles to study French, the twelve-year-old John Quincy transmitted the following from France so that Charles would prefer such serious study to the "frivolous amusements" of childhood: "Pappa laments very much his having neglected this study in his youth, in terms so pathetical, as to have made a deep impression upon my mind, & I wish to make the same upon yours." Similarly, John had painted a verbal picture for Nabby of himself suffering "a fit of melancholy" on receiving a packet of letters from her mother. He was able to help shape John Quincy into a man of feeling more directly, even as he precociously embarked on "publick affaires" with his father.[64]

Forty years later, on Abigail's death in 1818, John Quincy asked his father: "How shall I offer you consolation for your loss when I feel my own is irreparable?" His letter of condolence illustrated several features of his sensibility, including awareness of the intended recipient's pain and the belief that words could "sooth" "the anguish" he knew was "preying" on his father's heart. It illustrated apprehensiveness, too, over what the other might think of the absence of a letter: "Do not impute, my dear and only parent the silence that I have kept to the neglect of that sacred duty which I owe to you." Just as Abigail had had to compose herself before writing, so her son explained to his father: "If I have refrained from good words it was because, in the agitation of my own heart, I knew not how to order my speech, nor whether on receiving my letter, it would come to you seasonably to sympathize with your tears of gratitude or of resignation." Gratitude was for the fact that Abigail had passed "the pangs of dissolution" and, he hoped, "is a spirit." John Quincy had heard that his father "endured the agony of [Abigail's] illness with the fortitude that belongs to [his] character" and that, after "the fatal event," his father's "fortitude" had been renewed. Now John Quincy hoped that John would be able to let his son's words soothe him: "Will the deep affliction of your son now meet in congenial feeling with your own, without probing the wound which it is the dearest of his wishes to alleviate?"[65]

Abigail may have tried to model John Quincy on Sir Charles Grandison, and he was also "young Hercules." Sons could benefit from the openendedness of Lockean childrearing, even model themselves as Newton and Locke, but, in John's view, daughters could not. In 1775, he wrote the ten-year-old Nabby: "[I] condole with you, most sincerely, for the loss of your most worthy grandmamma. I know you must be afflicted at this severe stroke." Such knowledgeable sympathy both conveyed the fact of her father's sensibility and was a parental instruction, but it was female examples a daughter required. Of this grandmother (Elizabeth Quincy Smith), he wrote: "Her piety and benevolence; her charity; her prudence, patience, and wisdom, would have been . . . an admirable model for you to copy." The ancient virtue of charity was capitalized on in the culture of sensibility, and supplied a root for women's involvement in humanitarian benevolence and reform. Other qualities of piety and patience also were traditional, urged on women in keeping with their identification with suffering. John continued: "I hope you will remember a great deal of her advice and be careful to pursue it." Nabby could compensate for the loss of this female example with those supplied by Abigail and her sisters: "I hope you will be more attentive than ever to the instruction and examples of your mamma and your aunts. They I know will give you every assistance in forming your heart to goodness and your mind to useful knowledge, as well as to those other accomplishments which are peculiarly necessary and ornamental to your sex."[66] Abigail's success in instilling sensibility in Nabby is a subject of the next chapter.

When John defended himself in that 1776 letter against the imagined reproaches of his children, he first turned to his oldest sons, ages nine and six: "John has Genius and so has Charles. Take Care that they dont go astray. Cultivate their Minds, inspire their little Hearts, raise their Wishes." This, presumably, was by way of the kind of emotional management that his earlier teaching had attempted and that Hill exemplified. He continued: "Fix their Attention upon great and glorious Objects, root out every little Thing, weed out every Meanness, make them great and manly." They should "scorn Injustice" and "revere nothing but Religion, Morality, and Liberty." In a subsequent letter to "Portia," John described a book just published in Amsterdam that included "representation of the Gods and Heroes of Antiquity, with most of the fables of their Mithology." He first said that "such a Book would be very usefull to the Children in studiing the Classicks" but then reminded himself and "Portia" that, if there was "every Thing here that can inform the Understanding, or refine the Taste, and indeed one would think that could purify the Heart[s]"—here his apprehensions were identical to Hill's—"it must be remembered there is every thing here too, which can seduce, betray, deceive, deprave, corrupt and debauch it." One representation was of Hercules, and in recommending his example to his children John explicitly identified himself with them at his age: "Hercules marches here in full View of the Steeps of Virtue on one hand, and the flowery Paths of Pleasure on the other—and there are few who make the Choice of Hercules. That my Children may follow his Example, is my earnest Prayer: but I sometimes tremble, when I hear the syren songs of sloth, least they should be captivated with her bewitching Charms and her soft, insinuating Musick." Shaw notes that John's letters in the 1820s to his grandchildren—grandsons—"were filled with warnings to make the choice of Hercules and control their passions."[67]

In his 1776 letter urging Abigail to make his older son "great and manly," John turned to his daughter, eleven, and youngest son, only three: "Nabby and Tommy are not forgotten by me altho I did not mention them before. The first by Reason of her sex, requires a Different Education from the two I have mentioned. Of this you are the only judge." Raising sons was a shared venture, although that did not mean that John's gendered input should not predominate. Raising daughters was, however, the mother's job, augmentable by the models of adult female relatives. Precisely how gendered John construed girls and boys lives to be is suggested by the analogies he gave to Rush during the election of 1808: "I look at the presidential election as I do at the squabbles of little girls about their dolls and at the more serious wrangles of little boys, which sometimes come to blows, about their rattles and whistles."[68]

John's letter to Nabby, written three days after he had told her mother that her education was to be different because she was female, again conveyed the fact of his fatherly sensibility to her and illustrated that, in his view, she had learned the lesson of a good heart from her mother and aunts, identifiable with that sensibility that her mother and the experts she read prized in women particularly: "I cannot recollect the tenderness and dutiful affection you expressed for me, just before my departure, without the most sensible emotion, approbation, and gratitude. It was the proof of an amiable disposition, and a tender feeling heart." This was the other side of the daughter-father dyad that Fordyce encouraged.[69]

A year later, John wrote Nabby: "You have discovered, in your Childhood, a remarkable Modesty, Discretion, and Reserve." These were qualities he had praised in Abigail when courting her and the qualities that Hill had wished to be emphasized in the rearing of daughters, although he said that sons should be modest, too. He continued "I hope these great and amiable Virtues will rather improve, in your riper Years. You are now I think, far advanced in your twelfth Year—a Time when the Understanding generally opens, and the Youth begin to look abroad into that World among whom they are to live." That world held very limited prospects. "To be good, and to do good, is all We have to do." He reported "a remarkable Institution for the Education of young Ladies" that he had seen recently in Bethlehem, Pennsylvania, but, while he said that he wished Nabby could see "the curious Needle Work, and other manufactures" done there, he said he would not like her to live there because the "young Misses keep themselves too warm with dutch Stoves, and they take too little Exercise and fresh Air to be healthy." This, too, was consistent with Hill as well as with Wollstonecraft's subsequent recommendations for the education of girls. He concluded: "Remember me, with the tenderest Affection to your Mamma and your Brothers. I am with inexpressible Affection, your Father."[70]

John wrote the fourteen-year-old Nabby in December 1779 from Europe, just after he had arrived there with John Quincy and Charles, promising to inform her "of any Thing" he encountered in his "Journeys . . . which may contribute to your Improvement or Entertainment," a value her subsequent letters to her brother showed her to have internalized. Her father could not benefit in the same way: "But you must remember that my Voyages and Journeys are not for my private Information, Instruction, Improvement, Entertainment, or Pleasure; but laborious and hazardous Enterprises of Business." He could not yet say that of his sons, abroad, therefore, for other reasons: "I shall never be much polished, by Travel, whatever your Brothers may be. I hope they will be improved. I hope they will increase in Knowledge as they go: but I am not anxious about their being very much polished." This led him to a general rumination about polish, in turn leading him to think of Nabby's education, to which a significantly different kind of polish was required: "I dont mean by this however to suggest, that Arts and Accomplishments which are merely ornamental, should be wholly avoided or neglected especially by your Sex." His final admonition makes it quite clear why nowhere has he directly addressed why Nabby should not have been "improved" by foreign travel: "I hope your Attention will be fixed chiefly upon those Virtues and Accomplishments, which contribute the most to qualify Women to act their Parts well in the various Relations of Life, those of Daughter, Sister, Wife, Mother, Friend." The theatrical metaphor offered a narrower repertoire of roles to women, to be played overwhelmingly in domestic scenes. Long before he had a daughter, John had written a letter of advice to young ladies (as Hill's book was, addressed to hypothetical "Nieces"), in which he stated that "the Principal Design of a young Lady from her Birth to her Marriage, [is] to procure and prepare herself for a worthy Companion in Life."[71]

## CHAPTER 12

# A Reformed Rake?

## Melting the Ice

Royall Tyler Jr. first entered Nabby's correspondence in 1781 as the kind of predator against whom Richardson, Hill, Fordyce, and a host of sentimental writers warned. He was lodging with her cousin Betsy's family, the Cranches, and may have been making a play for Betsy. Perhaps Betsy and her mother, Abigail's sister Mary, saw him as an eligible bachelor. Nabby wrote Betsy from Boston, where she was attending a boarding school for young ladies. She wrote only, she explained, "as they [her letters] are dictated by a heart that rearly loves you. My affection for you is an inducement for my writing you at this time more particularly, I have my friend been in company with many persons since I have been in town who *were formerly* acquainted with the gentleman that lately has resided in your family." Her underlining indicated that those Boston persons had dropped Tyler because he was disreputable. They may well have heard that Tyler had sired a son on a "cleaning woman" while at Harvard, three years before. She continued: "Every one expresses great surprise at the event [his lodging with the Cranches], these persons say [that] he is practicing upon Chesterfield's plan, that he is the essence and quintessence of artfulness and fear he will in some way or another ingratiate himself into the good opinion of your self." Those Bostonians had dropped Tyler socially just as in Foster's novel *The Coquette* Eliza's friends had urged her to drop Major Sanford owing to his reputation as a seducer. Nabby reported that they had said of Betsy: "You are not acquainted with his character." Otherwise, they implied, Tyler would not have been admitted into her family.[1]

Nabby knew that Betsy would understand her Chesterfieldian reference, and she told her she had reassured her Boston acquaintances. She continued: "I have no fear about the matter, that I think you are too well gaurded against art in any shape and that you would despise the attempt,

and detest the action." Nabby, however, thought her cousin's guard
might need reinforcement: "But my friend I don't know but a word by
way of caution is nesesary. Perhaps you will laugh at me as I have at others who have made the supposition but I know that your heart is at present uncommonly softened by affliction [i.e., her father's illness]." The
model of psychological vulnerability (a heart softened by suffering), always potential in a person of sensibility, was one Nabby's mother used
to explain her feelings to John in asking for the balm of his words. It
was a condition, too, on which moralists like Fordyce warned that men,
merely pretending sympathy, would capitalize, as Lovelace had capitalized on Clarissa's emotional pain. Nabby said of Tyler: "Should he learn
your disposition and find a way to sooth your sorrows I will not answer
for you, that will not at least esteem him." Esteem would be a first step,
signifying Tyler's engagement of Betsy's feelings. Nabby insisted: "His
character and his conduct are not deserving the least degree of your
friendship and I dare say you will discover it soon if you have not at present." She had herself been forbidden his acquaintance and articulated
the sense of solidarity among women provoked by such a man: "I was
told the other day that I could not see him and not become acquainted
with him. I am determined to avoid the least degree of acquaintance if
anything short of affrontery will answer his whole study, his dissimulation; our sex cannot be too carefull of the characters of the acquaintance
we form." Her social posture was precisely that her mother's authorities
had recommended. It was for a "world" requiring the delicate performance of gesture and word to which Foster was to expose her monitory
"coquette" and one that destroyed her real-life counterpart.

The seventeen-year-old Nabby's marital prospects were soon on her
mother's mind, and Abigail apprehended that they were being reduced
by John's absence as well as by that dearth of marriageable gentlemen in
Braintree on which Abigail had remarked in her praise of Fordyce. In
August 1782, she reported to John that Nabby proposed coming to Europe "to keep House" for him, although she was as daunted by the voyage as her mother was: "Could you make a Bridge she would certainly
present herself to you"—the verb intimates a degree of psychological
distance—"nor would she make an ungracefull appearance at the Head
of your table." Abigail explained this unenthusiastic observation in the
next sentence: "She is rather too silent." And she took the opportunity
tartly to remark: "She would please you the better." This referred to
John's objections to women's speaking out in mixed company.[2]

The implicit criticism was a prelude to her account of the social and psychological suffering that John's paternal absence was causing his daughter: "She frequently mourns the long absence of her Father, but she knows not all she suffers in consequence of it." Because Abigail followed the class convention that a lady should not go out into "society" without her husband, she was unable to introduce her marriageable daughter into mixed company. Her father, Abigail went on, "would prudently introduce her to the world, which her Mamma thinks proper in great measure to seclude herself from, and the daughter is too attentive to the happiness of her Mamma to leave her much alone, nor could repeated invitations nor the solicitation of Friends joined to the consent of her Mamma, prevail with her to appear at [Harvard's] commencement this year." Typically for her, though still more significantly in the context of contemplating Nabby's entering the sexuomarital phase, Abigail refers to "the daughter" throughout, emphasizing conventional familial roles rather than the particularity represented by a name.

But immediately Abigail expressed a preference: "But much rather would the Mamma and daughter embrace the Husband and Father in his Native Land." She did not want to be separated from her daughter. She asked John: "Will the cottage be sweet? Will Retirement be desirable? Does your Heart pant for domestick tranquility, and for the reciprocation of happiness you was once no stranger to." Abigail began by representing this as both mother's and daughter's longing for the translation of the sentimental idyll into reality, but she concluded by making the "we" an "I" as she extended the familiar republican/sentimental trope until she was carried away by her sensibility: "Is there ought in Courts, in Theaters or Assemblies that can fill the void? Will Ambition, will Fame, will honour do it? Will you not reply—all, all are inadequate, but whither am I led? I cannot assume an other Subject—the Heart is softned. Good night." The feeling that she showed him as carrying her into inexpressibility could have included resentment. Nabby recorded witnessing her mother's emotional reaction to John's absence, if not here, then on other occasions, as Abigail records her brother Charles had, too. All her children saw it.

Abigail was also worried about Nabby's characterological deficiencies in the marriage market. Later that year, she told John that he "would be proud" of his daughter: "Not [that] she is like her *Mamma*. She has a Stat[el]iness in her manner which some misconstrue into pride and haughtiness, but which rather results from a too great reserve; she wants

more affability, but she has prudence and discretion beyond her years."
Nabby was, Abigail continued, "in her person tall large and Majestick"—
Abigail herself was "tiny"—this contrast between them corresponding,
it seems, to the differences in sensibility: "Her sensibility is not yet sufficiently a wakend to give her Manners that pleasing softness, which at-
tracts whilst it is attracted. Her Manners rather forbid all kinds of Intimacy; and awe whilst they command." Abigail repeated: "Indeed she is
not like her Mamma. Had not her Mamma at her age too much sensibility, to be *very prudent*. It however won a Heart of as much sensibility—
but how my pen runs." Her use of *prudence* and *prudent* in this context
recalls Fordyce's remark that sometimes prudish behavior "may . . . arise
from an original frigidity, or a strange insensibility of make." But Abigail believed that Nabby's sensibility could be awakened.[3]

Tyler had turned his attention to Nabby. In December 1782, Betsy
wrote her cousin that suggesting she was falling in love with him. Nabby
denied it, replying: "[The] most reasonable construction I can put on
this curious *rant* of yours, is that your own feelings are so greatly influenced by this said soft awakening *passion*, that in your eyes, all your acquaintances are in the same net with yourself." Betsy's "said passion,"
it transpired from later in the letter, was now for Henry Warren: "Your
usual susceptibility and softness of disposition, has led me to believe that
you only esteemed, where I am now fully convinced you love." Nabby
thought Betsy's too intense feelings were attributable to Boston's dangerous influence, although her terms are playful hyperbole. If Betsy was
revealing that she thought herself in love, Nabby continued, "I should
suppose your late excursion to, that *detestable* town has affected your
sentiments, I would not by aney means have you give place, to those romantick sentiments of *Love* that you talk about, they are very daingerous,
I am told. I would advise you to consult, prudence, discretion, reason
caution and all the discretionary powers, that ever influenced wisdom, or
indifferance—ere you harbour aney other ideas than those of mere cold
indifferent esteeme."[4]

That was much closer to Nabby's own character, she explained, contrary to Betsy's projection: "You was never more extravagantly mistaken, my friend. Your Amelia"—Nabby's middle name—"is the same
cold indifferent Girl she ever was, she knows not the person on earth she
could talk or write (about) [deleted] so romantickly upon [i.e., as Betsy
had written of her]. I'll certainly become your pupil, do indeavour to
diffuse into me a little of your susceptibility. I long to be in Love, it must
be a strange feeling, it seems to me." Here, then, Nabby grants Betsy

superiority. Or if, as Nabby reiterated, Betsy was too susceptible—had too great a degree of sensibility—Nabby represented her own putative coldness as a deficiency. Her declaration to Betsy that she was "the same cold indifferent Girl" may have served to divert Betsy's suspicions that Nabby herself was falling in love with Tyler, Betsy's own erstwhile interest, and the rake against whom Nabby had warned her. This would have been an irony tinged with a double guilt. Perhaps Nabby was trying not to fall in love with a suitor she had recently believed to be a Chesterfieldian deceiver.

The next paragraph, playful as it may seem, presented the cause of Nabby's coldness even more dramatically: "I have sometimes been at a loss to know whether I have a heart or not, but at last have made this conclusion, that in the days of my very youth I was deprived of it. I believe I then used to have what are stiled the symtoms of this passion, you may remember I was remarkable for my blushing diffidence. I guess those were the days of my weakness." In fact, Tyler had just given Nabby an ice carving of a heart, as Abigail reported in a letter to John (first reporting Nabby's "growing attachment" to Tyler) in all likelihood written the same day Nabby questioned whether she had a heart. One could see Tyler's gift as a reference to the result of the *Spectator*'s dissection of "a Coquette's Heart," initially finding it hard to grasp, however, because "it glided through the fingers like a smooth piece of Ice." The writer, Addison, made use of Descartes and Malebranche in describing this heart's "fibres." He found that "those little Nerves in the Heart . . . affected by the Sentiments of Love, Hatred, and other Passions, did not descend to [it] . . . from the Brain, but from the Muscles which lie about the Eyes." Perhaps in her witty conversations with Tyler that Abigail described in this selfsame letter they referred playfully to Sterne's notion of the frozen heart of a Laplander, to which Abigail had once compared John's unresponsiveness, as well as to the popular *Spectator*.[5]

It was the day following her daughter's letter describing her heartlessness to Betsy that Abigail broached the subject of Tyler's courtship of her to John. Before doing so, she told him: "[Nabby] has had a strong desire to encounter the dangers of the sea to visit you." She had prefaced that with: "Your daughter most sincerely regrets your absence, she sees me support it, yet thinks she could not imitate either parent in the disinterested motives which actuate them." Nabby had seen the emotional costs to her mother of subordinating her own wishes to her husband's. Inevitably, Abigail's account of the courtship, and the courtship itself, was bound up with John's absence: "I however am not without a sus-

picion that she may loose her realish for a voyage by spring." Nabby's
change of heart would be due to her feelings for Tyler, whom Abigail
now introduced as one of a social circle composed principally of her and
the Cranches: "We have in the little circle an other young gentleman
who has opend an office in Town [Braintree], for about nine months
past, and boarded in Mr. Cranch['s] family." Tyler also had a connection
with John: "His father you knew," Abigail told him, although she may
not have known anything more of that relationship. "His name is Tyler." He had yet another connection with John: "he studied Law upon
his coming out of colledge with Mr. Dana." (He also studied with Oakes
Angier.) Francis Dana, like John, was a Harvard graduate and Massachusetts revolutionary. He had gone to France with John as secretary to the
American legation; John would soon entrust the sixteen-year-old John
Quincy to him as his secretary when Dana was the American minister
to the Russian court.[6]

Then Abigail turned to an admission of Tyler's youthful faults, sand-
wiched between an explanation of them and an account of his remorse:
"Loosing his father young and having a very pretty patrimony left him,
possessing a sprightly fancy, a warm imagination and an agreeable person, he was rather negligent in persueing his buisness by way of his profession; and dissipated two or 3 years of his Life and too much of his
Fortune to reflect upon with pleasure; all of which he now laments but
cannot recall." Tyler had reformed on "comeing to B[osto]n, taking the
resolution" of "withdrawing from a numerous acquaintance." According to Nabby's earlier account, those acquaintances had withdrawn from
Tyler because of his reputation for a Chesterfieldian past. Abigail continued this introduction of the potential son-in-law to John, telling him
that Tyler "resolved to pursue his studies; and his Buisness; and save his
remaining fortune," the loss of which had not been so much his fault, she
implies, as that of "the paper currency." He had only half of the original
seventeen thousand pounds left, "as he told me a few days past," a piece
of information that prospective parents-in-law might regard as a potential gain. To this, Tyler had added that his "Mamma is in possession of
a large Estate and he is a very favorite child." Then Abigail returned to
the young man's current, more mature resoluteness, a quality that he
combined with other signs of his reformation of manners. "When he
proposed comeing to settle here he met with but little encouragement,
but he was determined upon the trial. He has succeeded beyond expectation, he has popular talants, and his behaviour has been unexceptionable
since his residence in Town; in consequence of which his Buisness daily

increases—he cannot fail making a distinguished figure in his profession if he steadily persues it."

Abigail also suggested to John that the reformed and successful young lawyer was a man of sensibility: "I am not acquainted with any young Gentleman whose attainments in literature are equal to his, who judges with greater accuracy or discovers a more delicate and refined taste." This might be a powerful attraction for the literary John: "I have frequently looked upon him with the Idea that You would have taken much pleasure in such a pupil." All this was a prelude to her main point: "I wish I was as well assured that you would be equally pleased with him in any other character, for such I apprehended are his distant hopes." That is, she anticipated that John would not favor Tyler as a suitor as he might as a law student. For her own part, however, Abigail wished that he would. She prided herself on so soon recognizing Tyler's potential as a husband for Nabby, although she assured John of her proper caution: "I early saw that he was possessd of powerful attractions and as he obtained and deserved, I believe the character of a gay; though not a criminal youth"— this may be evidence that Nabby had passed on what her Boston acquaintances said of Tyler—"I thought it prudent to keep as great a reserve as possible." She said she then waited to see whether he had reformed, although her letter asserted that he had.

Here Abigail introduced Nabby into her story. "In this," she continued, that is, keeping her own reserve, "I was seconded by the discreet conduct of a daughter, who is happy in not possessing all her Mother's sensibility." Abigail implied that, had it been she herself who was thus being courted by the powerfully attractive Tyler, she would not have been able to hide her feelings. But Nabby's being cool had only encouraged Tyler: "Yet I see a growing attachment in him stimulated by that very reserve." The latter was a quality in a woman on which Hill, Fordyce, and John Adams placed high value, even though a woman's show of it, entirely proper as it was, could turn men on, whether they were rakes or men of genuine feeling.

Abigail's own sensibility so far, then, had both positive and negative value, insofar as she had the special discernment to register emotional process and potential but also the susceptibility to showing her feelings prematurely, without at first having been sure that Tyler was adequately reformed. That sensibility, in its very ambivalence, expressed itself in her wish for her husband's authority, including, perhaps, his gendered ability to temper his and her feelings: "I feel the want of your presence and advise." Yet again, John's absence had forced Abigail to put herself in his shoes: "I think I know your sentiments so well that the merit of a gentleman will be your first consideration, and I have made every inquiry which I could with decency; and without disclosing my motives."

It had been at Harvard and then staying on in Cambridge to study law with Dana that Tyler had led the kind of exuberant, youthful male life against which sentimental moralists warned and, presumably, of which Nabby's Boston acquaintances had known. Tyler, as well as his brother John and other young men, had congregated in the painter John Trumbull's rooms for a variety of purposes, regaling themselves in that revolutionary time "with a cup of tea instead of wine, and disscuss[ing] literature, politics, and war," but also, on one occasion at least, they burst out into "horrid Profanity, riotous & Tumultuous Noises, & breaking of Windows at College," grist, of course, for campaigns for the reformation of manners. It was in this period, in 1779, that Tyler in all likelihood sired a son with Katherine Morse, a year older than he and from a different and, perhaps, from Tyler's point of view, an unmarriageable class. Their son was named Royal Morse (he grew up to be a prominent and respected figure in Cambridge).[7] In short, it could have been said that Tyler seduced and abandoned one woman and might well do the same again. Of whom and in what terms did Abigail make the inquiries to which she referred in this long letter introducing their potential son-in-law to John? In any case, the result of her discreet detective work had been reassuring enough to her; evidently, she hoped that it would be to the more cautious John: "Even in his most dissipated state he always applied his mornings to study; by which means he had stored his mind with a fund of usefull knowledge."[8]

Tyler's manners evinced Christian purity and a good heart: "I know not a young fellow upon the stage"—the metaphoric stage of being in public—"whose language is so pure—or whose natural disposition is so agreeable." Abigail knew how he spent all his time: strikingly, he had made his afterbusiness hours visible to her: "His days are devoted to his office, his Evenings of late to my fire side." He had already put his feelings for Nabby into words, including his wish to marry her, and he expressed them in other ways discerned by Abigail at her fireside or in other venues enjoyed by what Abigail called their little "Beau Mond": "His attachment is too obvious to escape notice." Giving her an ice heart would be a bit of a clue. Nabby, she implied, had noticed, but that discretion that had bolstered her mother's restraint of her own sensibility while she made prudent inquiries meant that Tyler had been unable to read the daughter's feelings. "I do not think the Lady wholly indifferent,"

Abigail told John, not revealing whether she had talked to Nabby about her feelings, "yet her reserve and apparent coldness is such that I know he is in misirable doubt." As I suggested, Nabby's apparent resistance to Tyler's "powerfull attractions" must have owed something to what she knew of his reputation in the eyes of Boston acquaintances as well, perhaps, as awkwardness in recalling her warning Betsy away from him, and it was consistent with the incessant warnings given young women by sentimental culture, although Nabby's caution may have been undercut by self-doubt in the matter of her sensibility.

It was to express more of her sympathy for him that, following some "conversation one Evening of late" between herself and Tyler at her fireside, Abigail reported to John that she was led "to write him [Tyler] a Billet" in which she told him: "I might quit this country in the Spring; . . . I never would go abroad without my daughter, and . . . I wished to carry her with a mind unattached, besides I could have but one voice; and for that I held myself accountable to you [i.e., John]." Also, she continued, he was "not yet Established in Buisness sufficient to think of a connection with any one." So Tyler was to infer that he was going to have to wait for some time, even if one parent made it clear she favored his suit.

Abigail then quoted Tyler's answer. It displayed his "delicate and refined taste" to a woman who prided herself on her sensibility. "Madam," Tyler began, "I have made an exertion to answer your Billet." He has had to raise himself out of that "miserable" state he had also shown her, stemming from the same source, that is, his susceptibility to feeling. "I can only say," he continued, "that the second impulse in my Breast is my Love and respect for you"—the first, he wanted her to infer, was his love for her daughter—"and it is the foible of my nature to be the machine of those I Love and venerate," that is, to be entirely responsive to such persons. (Jefferson as well as John Adams illustrated the conventionality of mechanical, Cartesian psychology.) Tyler explained he was willing to trust Abigail because she was a woman of sensibility who had shown her sympathy for his plans. It is hard not to bring to mind Hamilton's diction when writing to Elizabeth Schuyler (see chapter 9 above) or to think of Tyler as an embryonic playwright and novelist, capable of creating a suitor of false sensibility (as he would in *The Contrast*), which does not mean that he was not sincere in his feelings for Nabby: "Do with me as seemeth good unto thee." This was to reiterate the utter passivity of being a "machine," to make himself vulnerable, but, he continued, "I can safely trust my dearest fondest wishes in the hands of a Friend that can feel"—the last phrase, as we have seen, a distinguishing marker of

sensibility—"that knows my situation and her designs." Tyler was on
the side of reason, however, and he recommended that Abigail "hesitate" if "reason pleads against [him]," personifying that part of himself
that Jefferson would in his "Head vs. Heart" letter to Maria Cosway. He
continued: "[But if] friendship and reason unite"—and he has just let
Abigail know as forcefully as possible the extent to which he believed
her to be his "Friend"—"I shall be happy—only say I shall be happy
when I *deserve*." If she would concede just this: "it shall be my every exertion to augment my merit, and this you may be assured of, whether I
am blessed in my wishes [to marry Nabby] or not, I will endeavour to
be a character that you shall not Blush once to have entertaind an Esteem
for." The subject here was his past. He was willing to wait, implicitly
until he had further demonstrated his reformation.

Having given Tyler's story, described Nabby's feelings and her own
course of action, and quoted this letter, all composed as a narrative conforming with sentimental convention, Abigail asked John: "What ought
I to say?" In conjuring up her feelings for John, parallel to those Tyler
felt for Nabby, Abigail evidently wished to invoke John's for her and so
get him to "be equally pleased with him" as a suitor for Nabby. "I feel
too powerful a pleader within my own heart," she continued, a personification matching Tyler's and another illustration of the convention Jefferson elaborated, "and too well recollect the Love I bore to the
object of my early affections to forbid him to hope. I feel a regard for
him upon an account you will smile at, I fancy I see in him Sentiments
opinions and actions, which endeared me to the best of friends." Not
only would John "take pleasure" in Tyler's literary tastefulness; Tyler
resembled John in his powerful attractions.

Abigail told John that she "daily saw that he will win the affections
of a fine Majestick Girl who has as much dignity as a princess." But she
next repeated that contrast between her own sensibility and Nabby's that
she had described in her October letter: "She is handsome, but not Beautifull. No air of levity ever accompanies either her words or actions.
Should she be caught by a tender passion, sufficient to remove a little of
her tender reserve and soften her form and manners, she will be a still
more pleasing character." Tyler's eliciting her affection would be good
for her—Fordyce's fundamental goal in advocating feminized sensibility was to make a woman more pleasing to a man, above all, to an eligible
bachelor. Abigail reported to John that Nabby was "daily improving,"
evidently in concert with Abigail's "daily" seeing that Tyler would win
her affection: "She gathers new taste for literature perhaps for its appear-

ing in a more pleasing form to her." Here, Abigail was punning about the physical attractions of Tyler, a gentleman also with unsurpassed literary attainments. "If I can procure a little ode which accompanied an ice Heart I will inclose it to you." It is hard to imagine that, persuaded that Tyler was qualified as a husband and that, if he had been a rake, he was now a reformed one, Abigail had not told Nabby that she should attempt to be more pleasing to Tyler by removing a little of her tender reserve and by melting her "apparent coldness."

Another letter to John a week later repeated Abigail's account of Tyler in briefer form and made more pointed her view that it would take his unusual masculine charms, even the natural warmth that in his youth helped lead him a little bit astray, to break through Nabby's reserve: "His disposition appears exceedingly amiable—his attractions too powerfull even to a young Lady possesst with as much apparent coldness and indifference as ever you saw in one character, and with such a reserve as has awed to the greatest distance the least approach to her." Nabby's behavior seems to have evinced that degree of female moral scrupulosity that was exemplified by Hill's putative niece but that could be counterproductive in the marriage stakes. "I cannot however help noticeing," Abigail continued, "the very particular attention and regard of this Gentleman towards her, and that it daily becomes more pleasing to her." No longer did she describe her daughter as "happy in not possessing all her Mothers sensibility." She also declared that Tyler's daily behavior was, in fact, moving Nabby, rather than hoping to do so, as she had said in her previous letter. In this briefer version, she told John: "I [had previously] mentiond that he had opend his mind to me; declared his attachment, but asked for my countanence no further than he should in future merit it." She added to the admission that he had "foolishly squanderd" a now unspecified amount that he was "trying to purchase a farm in Town," one that belonged to "Mr. Borland," a dispossessed loyalist, a valuable property she knew John would recognize.[9]

Despite Abigail's claim that Tyler's demonstration of his regard for Nabby was "daily . . . more pleasing to her," that pleasure did not yet match Tyler's "regard": "If he should obtain the regard of the Lady he wishes for, I suppose he would think himself authorized to address you." At the moment, Tyler shared Abigail's "state of suspence." Both of them wanted Nabby to melt. Abigail again referred to the ode that had accompanied Tyler's gift to Nabby of a "Hea[r]t of Ice." He had given a copy of the poem to Abigail, which she said she would enclose: "Possibly it may draw you a moment from the depths of politicks to family." So an expression of Tyler's courtship overlapped with Abigail's deep wish, and Tyler's hopes for Nabby paralleled Abigail's for John. Anticipating one of John's concerns, that his choice of public life had prevented him from amassing a dowry, she added: "Merit I know will ever be the first consideration with you. This Gentleman well knows that he has no fortune to expect here, should he be admitted to a connection."

The letters between Tyler and Nabby have not survived, so there is a "remarkably indirect" quality of evidence about their relationship.[10] Other letters of Nabby's do survive, however, written during the period of Tyler's "powerful" presence in the Braintree "Beau Mond," and especially at her mother's fireside, and we must make the best of them. They suggest that she was conflicted and unhappy, a state of mind she explained to Betsy a few days after that second letter of her mother's describing Tyler's courtship of her by writing: "A heart of Adamant when separated from a parent and Brother who claims its tenderest affections, could not know happiness." This was a self-deprecating or, perhaps, resentful self-justification in the face of the characterization of hard-heartedness she was hearing from her mother and Tyler: "My friends and acquaintances tell me I ought to be happy." This makes more sense if one interprets this to mean that those "friends and acquaintances" were telling her that she should be happy because she was being courted by an attractive and wealthy young man, not that they were advising her to be happy despite the continuing absence of her male kin.[11]

She should, Nabby wrote, show a happy face out of consideration for her mother's feelings, presumably including her feelings about her daughter's feelings for Tyler as well as her pain over the absence of her husband and son. Nabby told Betsy: "I indeavour to appear so, it would be wrong to wear a sorrowfull countenance, it would give them pain and embitter the Life of a Mamma who feels too much to be happy at all times." The first reason she should, therefore, mask her true feelings illustrates a general conflict within persons of sensibility—sometimes sympathy for others required them to be insincere. The second reason demonstrated that Abigail had implanted in her daughter her own self-conception as a person whose particular sensibility could be a source of pain. It was against this that Nabby must have measured herself as deficient, although she may have had at least mixed feelings about her mother's susceptibility.

Nabby's next sentence was: "I do not talk upon the subject, (but) [deleted] there is not a day passes over my Life but this subject occupies my thoughts, and disbelieve it if you please, I can seldom reflect upon it without tears." This could also refer to Nabby's being "seperated from a parent and Brother," but she had been separated from them without tears, in fact, apparently had been happy enough for a considerable time despite their absence. The editors note of the sentence, "Your solicitation to know the cause of why I am not really happy": "The specific cause of this solicitation is not known. . . . For [Nabby's] recent expression of unhappiness see her letters of [9 *Nov.*] and [ca. 22 Dec. 1782] above."[12] Given the coincidence of these letters with Abigail's to John supplying him with an account of Tyler's application to her for Nabby's hand, it is highly probable that "the subject" that occupied her thoughts and brought her to tears was that suit as well as Abigail's support of it, including her knowledge of Nabby's wish to make her mother happy.

But then Nabby allowed: "Perhaps I am now happier than I deserve." Did she refer to the fact that she was being courted, even loved, despite her deficiency of feeling? She continued: "I feel that I . . . enjoy many blessings and many pleasures that others are deprived of, and I hope I am not ungratefull. I believe that were a few of my, *perhaps imaginary* wishes granted, I should enjoy too much pleasure." The range of such wishes in this context was circumscribed. Perhaps one was that her father and brother were back and another that she was in love with Tyler or that, in love with him, she wished that he had not had a rakish past. "We need not fear too great a share of happiness, in this varied scene of Life. Those to whom fortune and fate are most favourable"—she means "even those"—"have some wishes ungratified." She ends this line of thought simply: "It is best—It is right." This could mean that she accepted the public good rationale for John's absence and even John Quincy's being with him, but, as we have seen, she said elsewhere that "she could not imitate either parent" in such "disinterested motives." So did this simple statement mark her acceptance of Tyler's suit and deference to her mother—to please them both? Or did it mean that it was "right" because she now loved Tyler and that negated the problem of his Chesterfieldian past?

## John's Reaction

Abigail's December 23, 1782, letter about Tyler, her first one, had made quick passage across the wintry Atlantic, reaching John in Paris on January 22, 1783, just as he had begun to write her about the signing of the preliminary peace articles between Britain and the United States. This was, he wrote, the denouement of this most decisive phase of his life on the public stage: "Thus drops the Curtain upon this mighty Trajedy. It has unraveled itself happily for Us." He would be free "to come home in the Spring Ships," once the American government accepted his resignation. But that orientation was galvanized by the news of Nabby's being courted by Tyler: "I had written thus far when yours of 23 decr. was brought in. Its Contents have awakened all my sensibility"—this perhaps with irony in response to Abigail's criticism of their daughter's insufficiency in that regard—"and shew in stronger light than ever the Necessity of my coming home." One must allow for the possibility that Abigail had wanted her tale of Tyler and Nabby to stimulate John to come home. By far Abigail's most powerful wish throughout this phase of her life was to be together with John, trumping all other feelings.[13]

First John said: "I confess I don't like the Subject at all." This was a direct expression of an emotion not characteristic of the feeling to be expressed by sensibility. He continued: "My Child is too young for such Thoughts." Then he seized further on the sentimental terms with which Abigail had framed Tyler's qualifications to marry Nabby: "and I don't like your Word 'Dissipation' at all. I don't know what it means, it may mean every Thing." That is, it could mean that Tyler has been dissipated to the Richardsonian, Hogarthian uttermost, most saliently in sex. "There is not Modesty and Diffidence in the Traits you Send me." Here, he was getting at the imbalance in Abigail's picture of the courtship, her suggestions throughout that Tyler assumed that he was worthy of Nabby, his approach to her justifiable, and Nabby's response deficient. "My Child is a Model, as you represent her and as I know her, and is not to be the Prize, I hope of any, even reformed Rake." This was to make explicit the culturally charged issue that had animated Abigail's "inquiry" and, in all likelihood explained, Nabby's reserve, given her earlier characterization of Tyler.

John agreed that a "Lawyer would be [his] Choice," but not the kind of lawyer Abigail's letter had shown Tyler to be: "it must be a lawyer who spends his Midnights as well as his Evenings at his Age over his Books not at any Ladys Fire side." He criticized Abigail still more directly, touching a point, her self-control, on which she had repeatedly told him she doubted herself, including in the letter to which he was now replying: "I Should have thought you had been enough to be more upon your Guard than to write Billets upon such a subject to such a youth." He knew that she liked men to show sensibility and taste, and here she had been drawn into being a kind of substitute correspondent with a suitor. If he did not know of the nature of her letters to Lovell, the convention of epistolary gallantry was on his radar. John was not impressed by Tyler's literary attainments, even if he was not a rake: "A youth who has been giddy enough to Spend his Fortune or half his Fortune in Gaieties, is not the Youth for me, Let his Person, Family, Connection and Taste for Poetry be what they will. I am not looking out for a Poet, nor a Professor of belle Letters."

John then invoked a standard to suggest that Abigail contradicted her claim of a mother's sensibility and to vindicate Nabby's: "In the Name of all that is tender dont criticize Your Daughter for those qualities which I am amazed to hear you call want of Sensibility. The more Silent she is in Company, the better for me in exact Proportion and I would have this observed as a Rule by the Mother as well as the Daughter." This was to reassert a preference for which Abigail recently had dared criticize him. The sensibility he thus defended was the feminized, self-subordinating kind, much closer to Fordyce's definition. It dramatized the extent to which Abigail had left that behind in pushing the interests of a young man of at least questionable credentials. John reversed the value that Abigail placed on her own sensibility in contrast to Nabby's deficiency in it.

John next accused Abigail of being insufficiently sympathetic to himself, contrary to her letter's claim to know his sentiments. This was in regard to his public obligations' having deprived him of the private, legal career that would have brought him the kind of thousands that Tyler still had, despite his relative inapplication to legal work: "You know moreover or ought to know my utter Inability to do any Thing for my Children, and you know the long dependence of young Gentlemen of the most promising Talents and Obstinate Industry at the Bar." If Abigail was to juxtapose the young man's writing "Billets" with what she knew of her husband at that age, it should be to contrast them. Tyler, moreover, had been left a fortune by his father: "My Children will have nothing but their Liberty and the Right to catch fish, on the Banks of Newfoundland." This is bitter irony, a sum of Adams's achievements to date in the Revolution and the looming, postrevolutionary commercial settlement, the fruit of selfless public service, rather than self-interested extravagance. "This is all the Fortune that I have been able to make for myself or them."

John then seemed to back off: "I know not however, enough of this subject to decide any Thing." That is, he was not ready to decide whether Tyler was, after all, disqualified from being a suitor to Nabby. He asked, "Is he a Speaker at the Bar [as Adams himself had been]? If not he will never be any Thing." He seems to allow for the possibility that Abigail's account of Tyler's reformation was accurate: "But above all I positively forbid, any Connection between my Daughter and any Youth upon Earth, who does not totally eradicate every Taste for Gaiety and Expense." He grumbled out his skepticism: "I never knew one who had it and indulged it, but what was made a Rascall by it, sooner or later." He could have referred to the younger Dr. Bond, of Philadelphia, enjoying illicit sex. Nor was he impressed by his own knowledge of Tyler's family. His brother was "a detestible Specimen," and their "father had not those nice sentiments" that he would wish, "although an Honorable Man." Royall Tyler Sr. had taken "the popular side" in the early years of the Revolution and "cultivated the good will and support of the Boston 'mechanicks.'"[14]

But John continued to back away from his initially angry and negative tone: "I think he and you have both advanced too fast, and I should advise you to retreat." To retreat would allow more time to see if Tyler had, in fact, reformed, somehow purged of "the Qualities which by your own Account have been in him." "And if they were ever in him," he continued, "they are not yet out." As parents, they should not take chances: "This is too Serious a Subject, to equivocate about." John again voiced direct dislike: "I don't like this method of Courting Mothers." It was the other side of John's representation of Abigail's being so unguardedly responsive as to have written "Billets upon such a subject to such a youth." Tyler's literary ability could be seen in a different light: "There is something too fantastical and affected in all this Business for me." He implied that Tyler's sensibility was false: "It is not nature, modest, virtuous, noble nature. The Simplicity of Nature is the best Rule with me to Judge of every thing, in Love as well as State and War." He knew Abigail shared this sentimental value with him, expressing it, for example, in her letter describing the effects on her sensibility of the simplicity of that Scotch song. John closed this subject with, "This is all between you and me," a deliberately cutting terseness, although his letter's final paragraph was mollification: "I would give the world to be with you Tomorrow. But there is a vast Ocean. No Enemies [because of the peace treaty]." But his sentence, "if I were to stay in Europe another Year I would insist upon your coming with your daughter but this is not to be and I will come home to you. Adieu ah ah adieu," can be seen to have referred to Abigail's report of her conversation with Tyler, telling him that it was possible she would join John in Europe.[15]

The editors note unequivocally: "This is the harshest among JA's letters to AA that survive." Consequently, it took decisive effect.[16]

John wrote Abigail again on January 29, first describing the effect on his feelings of receiving two letters she had written him prior to the December 23 one: "A packet from you is always more than I can bear." His second subject was his resignation; should Congress accept it, he would "embark for home as soon as it arrives." The Tyler-Nabby issue was subordinate to that. He next directly addressed Nabby: "My 'Image,' my 'superscription,' my 'Princess,' take care how you dispose of your Heart.— I hoped to be at home and to have chosen a Partner for you. Or at least to have given you some good Advice before you should choose." The salient fact was his long absence, but he called on Nabby to think of their mutuality to stress the emotion behind his advice. The second two sentences stand for the patchy transition from patriarchal to paternal authority and, conversely, that daughterly power of marital choice that was a running theme of sentimental writing.[17]

John's next words to Nabby were intended to get her to go beyond the "form" of Tyler, however much Abigail celebrated it: "If I mistake not your Character it is not Gaiety and Superficial Accomplishments alone that will make you happy. It must be a thinking Being, and one who thinks for others good and feels anothers Woe." The last phrase is from Pope's very popular poem "The Universal Prayer," its sentiment central to the culture of sensibility, directly counter to the essentially unfeeling rake.[18] While Tyler had presented himself to Abigail as a man so responsive to others as to be their machine, John judged his behavior "affected, . . . not nature." The man to make Nabby happy must be, in other words, a man of genuine feeling but also one who had the kind of stamina the younger John himself had demonstrated in the early years of his lawyering: "It must be one who can ride 500 miles upon a trotting Horse"—as well as his subsequent efforts on behalf of the Revolution— "and cross the Gulph streams with a steady Heart." His "superscription" would do well to choose a husband like himself: "One may dance or sing, play or ride, without being good for much." Finally, he assured her with the inexpressibility of sentimentalism that "no Words can express the Feelings of my Heart, when I subscribe myself Yours forever."

In the next of his letters to Abigail, John told her that the two of hers regarding Tyler he had received were "never out of [his] mind." Because of Tyler's family and connections, as well as the qualities of his mentors Dana and Angier, "Health, Talents, and Application" would lead him to "full Business." "But I dont like his Character," he continued, "his Gaiety. He is but a Prodigal Son, and though a Penitent, has no right to your Daughter, who deserves a Character without a Spot." The prodigal son

had asked his father for his inheritance early, then "wasted" it "with riotous living" before being driven home by need and, penitent, was there
forgiven by his father, who, seeing him coming, "had compassion, and
ran, and fell on his neck, and kissed him" (Luke 15:20). Fliegelman has
found that the story took on newly resonant meanings in the eighteenth
century, not only in an America contemplating a break with its British
parent, but also in sentimental culture in general, articulated, for example, in the Reverend Sterne's *Sermons of Mr. Yorick*, where that "arch-
sentimentalist . . . shifts allegiance to the prodigal, gently disagreeing
with the father," thus marking a transition to "the new family relations"
also marked by John's letters to Nabby. Here, however, John conflated
the parable with the question of the reformability of a rake "That frivolity of mind, which breaks out into Such Errors in Youth, never gets out
of the Man but Shews itself in some mean Shape or other through life."
John was again critical of Abigail, "You seem to me to have favoured this
affair much too far, and I wish it off."[19]

But, in light of his dependence on Abigail for information and of his
nominal acceptance of Nabby's decisive power in the matter, John again
had second thoughts: "I must Submit, my Daughters Destiny, to Her
own Judgement and her own Heart"—but along with crucial family input—"with your Advice and the Advice of our Parents and Brothers and
sisters and Uncles and Aunts &c." He acknowledged his previous hope
for "a few Years of the society of this Daughter, at her Fathers House":
"But if it must be otherwise I must submit." Here was the potential for
a different outcome, wherein Abigail could have gone along with her
daughter's eventually melted heart, seeing her married in America prior
to being reunited to John. Despite his uneasiness "about this Subject,"
his public obligations kept him in Europe. Indeed, he gave equal space
to his account of his own, passionate feelings about his public reputation in connection with Congress's renewal of his ministerial commission and could not have made it clearer that, whatever was going on in
that personal circle of "[his] Family," his public work transcended it in
importance.

Waiting to hear whether Congress would officially send John to Great
Britain and the consequences of that decision for his being reunited with
Abigail were subjects that continued to dominate their correspondence
at this time. While their letters always discussed these prospects, they often did not mention the courtship, and John did not receive any more of
Abigail's letters until August 1783. Still, John wrote her in his March 28,
1783, letter, chiefly focused on the subjects just mentioned: "My dear

Daughter's happiness employs my Thoughts night and Day. Dont let her form any Connection with any one, who is not devoted entirely to study and to Business. To honour and Virtue. If there is a Taint of Frivolity and Dissipation left, I pray that She may renounce it, forever."[20]

## Abigail's Responsiveness to John's Reaction

By April 7, Abigail had received several of John's letters, one of them including the words he addressed to Nabby. She had to paraphrase Nabby's rejection of John's implication that Tyler's attractions were merely superficial because Nabby could not tell him so directly herself, presumably out of the strong sense of deference she always displayed to her father, enhanced by the distance in time since she had last seen him (she had been fourteen), but most obviously because she had to disagree with him. Abigail wrote: "'Your' Image your 'Superscription,' Your Emelia would tell you, if she would venture to write to you upon the subject; that it was not the superficial accomplishments of danceing, singing, and playing; that led her to a favorable opinion of Selim [i.e., Tyler]; since she knew him not when those were his favorite amusements." That she spelled Nabby's second name with an *E* here connected her with "one of the most popular" numbers of the *Spectator* (no. 302): "Who ever beheld the charming *Emilia*, without feeling, in his Breast the Glow of Love and the Tenderness of virtuous friendship? The unstudied Graces of her Behaviour, and the pleasing Accents of her Tongue, insensibly draw you on to wish for a nearer Enjoyment of them; but even her Smiles carry in them a silent Reproof to the impulses of licentious Love. Thus, tho the Attractions of her Beauty play almost irresistibly upon you and create Desire, you immediately stand corrected not by the Severity but the Decency of her Virtue."[21] Of course, this was to agree with John's characterization of Nabby and, perhaps, was intended to reassure him of her invulnerability to the "licentious Love" at which John had hinted in referring to Tyler as a (possibly) "reformed rake." It would be the name Abigail would use for Nabby in relation to her suitor from here on out. "Selim" was the hero of Charles Johnstone's sentimental novel *The History of Arsaces, Prince of Betis* (1774), interestingly a figure exemplifying the positive effects of the benevolent treatment of slaves.[22]

The *Spectator*'s Emilia was a figure of female sensibility and impregnable virtue: the "Sweetness and Good-humour which is so visible in her face, naturally diffuses it self into every Word and Action," thereby exerting a power that Hill advised mothers to cultivate in daughters. "A

Man must be a Savage," the *Spectator* noted, "who at the Sight of *Emilia*,
is not more inclined to do her good than to gratify himself." Her naturally beautiful "Person" "is a fit lodging for a mind so fair and lovely;
there dwell rational Piety, modest Hope, and cheerful Resignation."[23]
The last was a quality on which Abigail was soon to call.

The word *playing* in that list of "superficial Accomplishments" to which
Abigail referred in her April 7 letter was a response to John's assuming
that it had been in card "play" that Tyler had lost thousands of pounds.
Abigail continued: "Nor has he ever been in the practise of either, since
his residence in this Town; even the former Beau, has been converted to
the plain dressing Man." He was, then, now like those whom Fordyce
called "truly men," signified by their wearing "a plain coat," the kind Sir
Charles Grandison wore, and showing "manly deportment," rather than
those men displaying themselves to women with "embroidery, finery,
and foppish manners." And Abigail suggested that this was not merely
appearance but behavior, too: "the Gay volatile Youth, appears to become the studious Lawyer."[24]

Nonetheless, Abigail next told John, presumably referring to something suspicious remaining in Tyler (at least, that is what her sequence
intimated): "Yet certain reasons which I do not chuse to enumerate here,
have led me to put a present period, as far as advise and desire would
go, to the Idea of a connection." Having exerted her parental power to
foster the relationship so far and seen it to have been effective in the aftermath of John's vehement disapproval, Abigail now has exerted it by
way of advising "Emelia and Selim" to postpone thinking of marriage,
although she admitted: "to extirpate it from the Hearts and minds of either is not I apprehend in my power, voilent opposition never yet served
a cause of this nature." This resembles the same psychological observation she had made in her January 10 letter to John. "It means that I see
what I scarcely believe in my power to prevent without doing voilence
to Hearts which I hope are honest and good." But, at that time, she had
not expressed, either to Tyler or to Nabby, a wish to limit their relationship. Indeed, her letters could be read to indicate her pleasure that
Nabby finally had expressed reciprocity.

Abigail reported the couple's response to her putting a "present period" to the idea of getting married: "Whilst they believe me their best
Friend and see that their Interest is near my Heart, and that my opposition is founded upon rational principals, they submit to my prohibition,
earnestly wishing for your return, and more prosperous days; as without
your approbation, they can never conceive themselves happy. I will be

more particular by the first direct conveyance." In Abigail's eyes, Nabby and Tyler have become a couple, thinking as one about marriage, and deferring, as one, to her. They believed, as one, that she wanted the best for them, even that she would approve their marriage eventually. They respected Abigail's "rational principals." Among the subjects the three of them may have had in mind was the necessity for Tyler to continue to demonstrate the permanence of his reformation, of his erasing all "Taint of Frivolity and Dissipation," by way of his successful conduct of himself in his profession. John's approval remained a decisive factor, and, although he had reluctantly said in his February 4 letter, "I must submit [to Nabby's judgment]" (coupled with Abigail's and the family's "Advice"), evidently Abigail could not bring herself to sanction the marriage and thereby go against his first, harsh opposition.

John had not received this letter when he wrote Abigail from Paris in April, listing "many Things" that for the past few months "put my Patience and Resignation to the Tryal." The first was that he had not heard from John Quincy, then en route from Northern Europe to the Hague. He continued: "2. Your Letters concerning Miss N. have given me as much Concern as they ought—not knowing the Character"—that is, of Tyler (so Abigail's defensive account had been inadequate, at least)— "nor what to advise, but feeling all a Fathers Tenderness, longing to be at home that I might enquire and consider and take the Care I ought." Fathers, John assumed, naturally felt tenderly toward daughters, along with considering practical concerns (the material as well as the characterological prospects of suitors), subsumed by taking "the Care [he] ought." The other three of the "tryals" John here compared to Job's included the contrast in his isolated circumstances with John Jay's, "a friend to his Country, without Alloy": "I shall never forget him, nor cease to love him, while I live. He has been happier than I, having his Family with him, no Anxiety for his Children, and his Lady with him to keep up his Spirits. His Happiness in this particular, has made me more unhappy for what I know under Seperation from mine."[25]

In June, John wrote Abigail again on the same subject: "I am astonished . . . that we have heard nothing from Congress nor from you. If you and your Daughter were with me, I could keep up my Spirits." They would serve his purpose the same way Jay's family did. John did not expect those emotional rewards for his diplomacy ("the 'Tears of Gratitude,' or 'the Smiles of Admiration,' or the 'Sighs of Pity'") that the revolutionary army enjoyed, but he asserted its worth. So he adjured his sons in the letter: "Boys! if you ever Say one Word, or utter one Complaint,

I will disinherit you. Work you Rogues and be free. You will never have so hard Work to do as Papa has had." His work had opened their futures to freedom, despite his absence and his lack of money.[26]

Then he directed a longer paragraph at Nabby. Her prospect was marriage, not freedom: "Daughter! Get you an honest Man for a Husband, and keep him honest. No matter whether he is rich, provided he be independent." The latter prospect was more likely now, as it was for her brothers, because of the success of his Revolution: "Regard the Honour and moral Character of the Man more than all other Circumstances. Think of no other Greatness but that of the soul, no other Riches but those of the Heart." The Revolution had advanced romance, too. John next might have had his own, ideal self in mind: "An honest, Sensible humane Man, above all the Littlenesses of Vanity, and Extravagances of Imagination, labouring to do good rather than be rich, to be usefull rather than to make a show, living in modest Simplicity clearly within his Means and free from Debts or Obligations, is really the most respectable Man in Society, makes himself and all about him the most happy." Nabby could infer that, in her father's opinion, Tyler fell short.

Before she received this, but after Abigail had written to John to tell him that she had advised Nabby and Tyler that they had to submit to her prohibition of their thinking of marriage, Nabby wrote to Thaxter. She knew he knew of Tyler and her relation with him and in all probability thought he would pass her letter on to her father. She referred to the "misfortune and unhappiness" of the Palmer household—to whom both she and Tyler were connected—which included General Palmer's finances and "the nervous disorder" of the elder Mary Palmer as well as the 1780 death of Betsy Palmer's fiancé. Nabby reflected that "events so . . . fraught with happiness do not claim so great a degree of an amaizement and surprise, as the contrary." She believed there was "a happiness to have arrived at that state of mind in which we can look calmly and composedly on all events of fortune and meet its decrees without repining." The decree that she had herself met most directly was Abigail's, that she put her relationship with Tyler on hold. Nabby continued: "[Such] a calm and composed state of mind was seldom attained by youth, for where it does exist in young minds there is generally a want of that sensibility and feeling, which, constitutes it a virtue." For stoicism to be a virtue it had to be the result of a struggle with one's own feelings. Her mother struggled in this way and claimed to succeed, but she criticized Nabby for a lack of feeling, and Nabby believed it of herself. (That summer she referred to "my natureal insensibility" in a letter to Betsy.) She may have been telling Thaxter, and therefore her father (whom she knew would also be hearing from Abigail), of the stalled state of the relationship with Tyler, in accordance with her father's apparent wishes and that she felt calm and composed about it, although nominally she felt that way in regard to the "misfortunes" of the Palmer household.[27]

The day after this, Abigail wrote John a letter principally concerned with the peace treaty and the question of whether he would return to America or she would "come to [him]": "I shall not run the risk unless you are appointed minister at the court of Britain." Her second, much shorter paragraph began: "With Regard to some domestick affairs which I wrote you about last winter, certain reasons have [pre]vented their proceeding any further—and perhaps it will never again be renewed. I wished to have told you so sooner, but it has not been in my power." This sentence was not in Abigail's draft of the finished letter. Instead, that draft had continued from the preceding sentence: "I wish exceedingly to come to you if you continue abroad, and should congress as is expected give you a commission to the British court, unqualified as I feel myself for public Station in life, I believe I shall venture"—then a clause omitted—"as I have a reason for wishing to come with our daughter to you." It was this that, perhaps, the editors had in mind when they wrote: "Tyler's courtship of [Nabby] had a definite part in the Adams ladies' subsequent voyage to Europe." In that billet to Tyler, of which she sent a copy to John, Abigail had hypothesized that she might take Nabby to Europe with her, but this had not been for the purpose of separating lovers whose relationship she now wished to downgrade.[28]

That same day Abigail did make explicit the "certain reasons" that "[pre]vented" Nabby and Tyler's "proceeding any further," which explained the other, censored "reason" for her wish that she and Nabby come to Europe. One can only speculate why this indirectness and why it had not yet been in her power to tell John herself. It may well have been related to her own ambivalence, her ambiguous words and actions at home, and her apprehension over John's reactions. In any case, she told him via an intervening party. This second letter of April 28, 1783, was directed to Charles Storer, four years older than Nabby, "a distant family connection" of Abigail's, and "an intimate of the Adams and Smith family circles in Braintree and Boston." He had temporarily replaced Abigail's cousin Thaxter as John's secretary in Paris. In this letter Abigail agreed to be Storer's correspondent, insisting: "you must be able to write to me with that freedom and unreserve which I so much admire in your Letters." One of his qualifications, she told him, was "the confidence of my best

Friend towards you." Her letter was a reply to Storer's of February 10, in which he had written that John had told him he "shall return with pleasure to his plow. A civil Cincinnatus!" He also told Abigail that John had "again flattered [him], with Confidence about a certain affair, mentioned in your last letters." John may well have quizzed young Storer on his fresh, firsthand knowledge of Tyler and Nabby. Storer reported that John "will return you his Sentiments, thereupon," and that it did not become him "to speak, further than to assure *Amelia* of my best wishes for every happiness and pleasure the married state will afford." So John, too, was under the impression that his daughter was to marry Tyler, not having received Abigail's latest news of her "prohibition."[29]

Storer had signed his letter to her "Eugenio," an apparent reference to "Eugenius," a character appearing throughout *Tristram Shandy*, an "idealized depiction of John Hall-Stevenson," whom Sterne met as a fellow undergraduate at Cambridge, and who was his lifelong friend. It was Eugenius to whom Yorick had addressed his apostrophe to "Sensibility!" in Sterne's *Sentimental Journey*. After Sterne's death, a sequel to the novel was published by one "Eugenius." Participants in sentimental correspondence in Philadelphia, contemporaries of Storer and Abigail and fans of Sterne, also used the name Eugenius, and it seems very likely that there were others. Storer had added: "NB I trust *Portia* will excuse the signature of *Eugenio*, since both are in mask." Abigail had opened her letter to Storer, "May I address you by the Epithet of my dear Charles? For I really feel towards you a Maternal Regard" (as she told Tyler she also felt for him, reciprocating his courtship), and she signed her letter to Storer "Portia." Such affection and such literary names mark their correspondence as one of sensibility.[30]

Writing that John's discussion of the Nabby-Tyler courtship was "proof" of his confidence in Storer, indicating that what she wrote now was a subject Storer could/should convey to John, Abigail had continued: "the words, 'It becomes not me to speak,' express more than a page." This might be seen as reserve, but, in fact, Abigail wished Storer to know that she could read his invaluable inexpressibility. "Believe me I know your thoughts"—this, too, signifying that they shared sensibility—"the person whom they concerned [i.e., Tyler] is a different Character from what in very early Life you knew him at least I presume so." Storer had entered Harvard in 1779, when Tyler was still enjoying his dissipated life in Cambridge. His illegitimate son was born that year. Abigail's last five words are ambiguous and might be seen to communicate some doubt as to Tyler's reformation. She continued: "I wish him well, I wish him prosperous and happy, and that every juvenile deviation from the Path of Rectitude, may teach him wisdom and prudence in future, but he will never be in any other character in Life to Emelia, than an acquaintance." Storer's belief that they were set for marriage was contradicted. Abigail added: "I speak not this from any recent misconduct, but from a full conviction that it is right."[31]

Abigail then turned at considerable length to how a young man's prospects could be spoiled forever by a false step and a contravention of principles. Her perspective here on the doubtfulness of a gay youth's ability to reform was now far closer to John's. Indeed, she added another difficulty. She had turned to this by way of her expression of the effect of an unstable education on her younger sons, explaining why she had sent them to the Shaws: "Youth are peculiarly liable to this frailty [i.e., instability], and if it is not early curbed and restrained both by example and precept, it takes root and saps the foundation, it shoots out into unprofitable branches, if the Tree blossoms, they wither and are blown by every change of the wind so that no fruit arrives to maturity." Contributing to the danger to her sons was her inability to find "a Suitable preceptor," and from what follows it could be inferred that she apprehended that Tyler's presence around them offered bad "precepts": "The Character which a youth acquires in the early part of his Life is of great importance towards his future prosperity—one false step may prove irretrievable to his future usefulness." A "false step" such as the juvenile Tyler had made in Cambridge could be a sign of instability, even if he seemed to have been resolute and steady since. The perception of a false step made a young man vulnerable to the "World": "The World fix their attention upon the behaviour of a person just setting out, more particularly so if they stand in a conspicuous light with Regard to family or estate, and according to their discretion, prudence or want of judgement, pronounce too precipitately on the whole of their future conduct."

But imprudent and injudicious though the world's pronouncement may have been, Abigail concluded, "of how great importance is it, that good principals be early, inculcated and steadily persued in the Education of youth?" So, however careless or precipitous adverse pronouncements on Tyler's prospects had been, he had damaged himself, and the false steps he had taken could be irretrievable. Abigail's sentence reiterated her apprehensions for her sons in terms identical to those we have seen her express in another letter, where she faced their going off to the college Tyler had attended.

Portia added a little paragraph to this unreserved letter to Eugenio:

"But whither does my imagination lead me, and why all this to me[?] Madam! methinks I hear you inquire. My thoughts are not difficult to trace, I dare say you will find the thread." The most obvious "thread" was that which connected "why all this to me" to "the confidence of my best Friend towards you." In short, she asked him to give "all this" to John, so her questions, "whither . . . my imagination?" and "why all this," apparently asked with the spontaneity of sensibility, were disingenuous.

Ten days later, Abigail was able to write directly to John on the subject, telling him that she was sorry he had "sufferd so much anxiety with regard to a domestick occurrence" and that, in fact, the relationship between Nabby and Tyler had been "done with . . . soon after my last Letter to you . . . in December." This was despite what she had written him in April of the impossibility of extirpating the thought of marriage from "the Hearts and Minds of either." "In Jan'ry" Nabby "went to Boston and spent the rest of the winter there." Here, then, Abigail implied that this stay had been the beginning of the breach that had now occurred. She gave John the impression that, sensitive to what she intuited his wishes would be, Nabby had already distanced herself from Tyler. The April letter, then, which emphasized Abigail's decisive role in putting a perhaps permanent end to the marital prospect, merely consummated what had begun before, and John could infer that that, too, had been under Abigail's guidance.[32]

Yet she also conveyed that Tyler had borne out her own, early feelings about him. She told John: "[None] of those Qualities you justly Dread have appeared in this Gentleman Since his residence in this Town." His reformation of manners had taken hold: "His conduct has been Regular and his Manners pure—nor has he discovered any Love of Gaiety inconsistent even with your Ideas." Abigail had been right on this point: "I say this as it appears to me to be the truth, and in justification of my having had a partiality in his favor." Her wish to justify her action to the husband she had angered explains this tergiversation. Then she wrote about "the world's" opinion, just as she had to Storer some days earlier: "The world look back to the days in which I knew him not: and remember him as a Beau and a Gay volatile young fellow, and tho I never heard any vices asscribed to him"—either she was splitting hairs, or she had not heard of Tyler's likely sexual relationship with Katherine Morse, but she is motivated by defensiveness—"yet I think with Some of my Friends a longer period necessary to Establish a contrary Character. It has therefore been my advise and wish to put an end to the connection." This was a more emphatic version of what she had said of her words to the lovers in her letter to John of exactly a month before, expressing her "advice and desires," but then merely to postpone the idea of marriage until John returned. Now Abigail represented herself as having been conclusive, not for those two earlier reasons, but because of other people's apprehensions of Tyler's reputation and potential for gaiety. Notably, one of those had been Abigail's "dearest Friend."

## Tyler and Nabby's Resistance and Abigail's Ambiguities

The same letter then recorded the response of Nabby and Tyler to a more permanent period to their marital wishes: "I cannot affirm that it is wholly eradicated from their minds, but time will do it." She suggested that Nabby's own response to the distancing of her marital prospects endorsed John's view of her: "your daughter has a firmness of mind and a prudence beyond her years." This acknowledged the value that John placed on Nabby's distinction from Abigail's less controllable sensibility. Nabby's self-control, however, also reflected the weight she gave the opinion of others, who included not only her father and Thaxter but, still more apparently, her mother, first in accepting Tyler, and now, apparently, in rejecting him, at least as a husband: "She will not act contrary to the advise of her Friends, and in a particular manner her parents."

Abigail then returned to Nabby and Tyler's joint response. "It <is> [significantly deleted] has not been a matter of indifference to either of them. Yet it is now so far laid aside as gives me reason to think it will never again be renewed; he visits here but seldom." This did leave slightly ajar the possibility that they could reopen their prospects: "When I received yours of Febry 4th and found your anxiety"—this was the letter in which John had said he was "so uneasy about the subject"—"it gave me a pleasure to think I could tell you it was wholy done with." Her description of her response to it supports the notion that her intimation to John that the breach had begun in "Jan'ry" was a self-justifying, retrospective interpretation, a sign to him that she was in tune with his feelings, even at three thousand miles. Establishing that, and pleasing him (both marks of her feminine sensibility), became paramount once she knew what he thought of a family connection between the rakish Tyler and his daughter, his "Image."

Three days later, Nabby herself wrote to John, as she had not done for months: "No opportunity has presented since I was so happy to receive two excellent letters from my Dear Pappa [the previous fall]." This was because not "a vessel" had sailed for Europe since. She did not mention the dramatic turn in her life, at least directly, but she described the intensity of her moral dependence on him: "All the return that it is in my power to make, is to indeavour to assure you Sir that I feel a greater degree of gratitude for all your favours, than it is possible for me to express. It is the foundation of virtue, and I hope is fully impressed on my heart." Having acknowledged her father's power in the matters of her heart, Nabby turned to his public life: "Permit me my Dear Pappa to join the general voice in addressing my congratulations on your late happy success in your publick station." She echoed his complaint about those who would withhold such praise out of "self interest," but this led gracefully to her own personal interest (entirely in keeping with Abigail's) because she could now "look forward with pleasure" to his return. Her alternative wish indicates that she had been talking with her mother: "Yet I still have an ardent desire to cross the atlantick, it is quite as powerfull as ever. Was you to continue abroad I should not feel contented with the distant prospect I have had for these few years past." It is important to note that this was clearly a qualified view, certainly an expression of strong feeling, but, here, leaving Braintree was merely hypothetical.[33]

Abigail wrote to Tyler a month later and placed on John the responsibility for preventing (or postponing) his hoped-for family connection. Her introductory sentence is ambiguous: "I had thought of writing to you before I received my last Letters from abroad [i.e., from John], because you have flattered me with an assurance that my advice is not unacceptable to you." This could refer both to her previous advice in handling his end of the relationship with Nabby and to the advice this letter contained. She continued: "I thought I had some hints to drop to you which might Serve your interest. I feel an additional motive to take my pen, and communicate to you a passage from my last Letter [i.e., from John]." She then quoted the passage from John's March 28 letter (only slightly altered in the matter of capitalization) that included the direct command: "Do not let [my dear Daughter] form any Connection with any one, who is not devoted intirely to Study and to Buisness—To honour and to virtue." John had prayed that Nabby would "renounce" the connection if there was "a Trait of frivolity and Dissapation left." Abigail's quotation of this paragraph to Tyler included more of what John had said he wanted in his daughter's husband: "I ask not Fortune nor favour for mine, But prudence Talents and Labour—She may go with my consent wherever she can find enough of these."[34]

So John's words were the basis for the advice that Abigail then gave to the at least distanced suitor, and they included phrasing ("not intirely" and "if there was a Trait . . . left") that could offer Tyler hope: "You have before you sentiments and principals which your reason must assent to, and your judgement approve, as the only Solid foundation upon which a youth can Build." It was with this that Tyler would have "a prospect of happiness for his connections." Abigail added, with apparent sympathy and condescension: "Talants are not wanting, shall they lack Labour for improvements, or industry for cultivation?" One can see this as disingenuous: if she had expressed concerns earlier, she had resolved them, not only to her own satisfaction, but also to the extent of attempting to persuade John that Tyler had overcome his earlier faults and was fully acceptable husband material. She now went back on this, in light of John's objections, restating and elaborating the paragraph she had just quoted: "Honour and virtue, are they not in[ti]mates and companions? Is there a Trait of Frivolity and dissapation left?" Previously, she had been convinced by her inquiries and Tyler's assertion. Now she told him: "Examine your own Heart with candour, let it not deceive you." She conveyed her certainty that it had and then advised him to cure his "dissapation" by "method and order," which she spelled out in detail. By implementing "a determined Resolution"—a quality that previously she had declared he had—he would, in accordance with eighteenth-century psychological theory, fix habits "which would not be easily shaken." John attempted to fix his son Charles's habits, to check his descent into rakery. Abigail speculated: "Perhaps more industery and application, are necessary, in the . . . Law to become Eminent." This, too, was to echo John's criticism of Tyler. She added, suggesting a process whereby she had been persuaded by her husband: "if it is, as I realy believe, in the power of my young Friend, to become so; it is also a duty incumbent upon him." She then paraphrased the parable of the talents (Matt. 25: 14–30: Luke 19:12–27).

There was more of the same and further reference to John's authoritative standards in advising Tyler how "to become an honour to his profession." But then, Abigail wrote: "If you can find in your own breast any additional motives, let them serve to enforce my Recommendations." The letter's only previous reference to Tyler's wishes for Nabby had been by way of Abigail's quotation of John's letter ("My dear daughters happiness employs my Thoughts Night and day" etc.). Here, however, Abigail suggested that, should Tyler form the right habits, resist dissipation, and become eminent, he might overcome John's reservation and win his lady. She continued after "Recommendations": "I have so far interested myself in your advancement in Life, as to feel a peculiar satisfaction in your increasing Business. I shall rejoice in your success, and in the consistency of your Character."

Abigail made clear that this quality was a masculine ideal, one that she had in mind in sending her sons to John Shaw for a stable education: "There is a strength of mind, a firmness and intrepidity which we look for in a masculine character—an April countance, now Sunshine and then cloudy, can only be excused in a Baby faced girl—in your sex it has not the appearance of Nature, who is our best guide." This was to perpetuate the same gender stereotypes on which she had quoted Pope. Both she and John took pride in John's manly "stern virtue." At some level, she might also have been excusing her own apparent change of attitude toward Tyler's suit, although she was no baby-faced girl.

Abigail followed her hint that Tyler could still attain Nabby with: "Be assured you have my best wishes that you may merit and obtain whatever may conduce to your happiness, for I am most sincerely a Friend to your Fame and a Love of your Virtues.—Adieu—" So Tyler could read this to say that, in Abigail's view, the relationship with Nabby was not yet done with, although its prospects were more remote.

On the evidence of Abigail's next letter to him a week later, Tyler had sharply disagreed, in person or in a letter, and he had asked her, in her summary of what he had said, "to devote half an hour to [him] in [him] absence," to write to him again, not only in further explanation, but also, it seems, to provide him greater hope, contrary to what Abigail had represented as her husband's opposition. She replied:

> You requested and I comply, to shew you I have a disposition to oblige, but I am very unequal to the task you have assigned me for I have no Herculean properties [again signifying her difference in sensibility from her authoritative husband], but can say with [John] Gays Shephard,
>
> > "the little knowledge I have gaind
> > is all from simple nature draind."

She explained that her "late advise" to Tyler had been guided by "nature," "for our actions must not only be right, but expedient, they must not only be agreeable to virtue but to prudence." This was her own natural, feminine prudence, protecting Nabby from, at the worst, marrying a rake who had not really reformed.[35]

Tyler's reply, Abigail indicated, had "differd so widely from [hers] in sentiment" that she determined "never again to tender an opinion unaskd," although she assured him she had meant it only to help him succeed: "yet I did not wish you any further influenced by it than . . . to conduce to your own happiness." Then, in another extended application of conventional, Lockean, gardening psychology, Abigail reiterated her previous letter's condescending, maternalistic advice: "Let it be our study to cultivate the flowers, and root out the weeds, to nourish with a softening care and attention those tender Blossoms"—and here her extended analogy is ambiguous—"that they be neither blasted in their prime nor witherd in their bloom but as the blossom falls may the fruit . . . ripen into maturity until the Beauty of its appearance shall tempt some fair hand to pluck it from its native soil and transplant it to one still more . . . conducive to its perfection." This could be read as a forecast for Tyler's successful marital prospects, even with Nabby, but certainly it referred to the assumption that Abigail shared with her daughter, with Fordyce, and with the culture of sensibility generally, that ladies had the power to reform gentlemen's manners. It was an "observation" that she attributed to Sterne. She followed it with Poor Richard's aphorism that God "helps those who help themselves," but she coupled that with her warning against "a mutability of temper and inconsistency with ourselves" that "render us little and contemptible in the Eyes of the World." She urged Tyler to be "unchangeable in [his] justice, temperance [and] fortitude."

Abigail had concluded by telling Tyler that she missed him, in so doing further describing those evenings when he was courting her at her fireside and figuring out how he could win Nabby's heart:

> My Weymouth Friends dined with me [today] together with my sister and cousins. You was kindly enquired after, and the vacant Chair lookt solitary. The provision too was not carved with that dexterity and alertness which your hand is accustomed to. This evening I know you think of your solitary friend. . . . You wish yourself at hand to read me some amuseing or entertaining subject, or to beguile the hour with the incidents of the past day, or to converse upon some literary subject. . . . My Candle and my pen are all my companions. I send my thoughts across the broad Atlantick in search of my associate and rejoice that thought and immagination are not confined like my person to the small spot on which I exist.

She signaled her own continuing "partiality" for him, whatever the state of his relationship with Nabby and John's feelings on that score. The paragraph's shift in subject suggests that, in her imagination, Tyler filled the shoes of the absent John to some extent, doing so, perhaps, with more satisfyingly effusive and immediate expressions of attentive sensibility. It was John's absence that required her, by her standards of propriety, to be "confined," hungrier for the kind of heterosocial conversation Tyler was eager to supply.

Tyler's biographer sees this as an "encouraging but restrained letter." Had Tyler read Abigail's next one to John (written a few days after this), he might have been still more encouraged, and it seems that, in writing what she did, Abigail was complying with Tyler's request. It was the same letter in which Abigail told John that she did "not wish" him "to accept an Embassy to England" (see chapter 8). Then she had turned to that picture of sentimental feelings toward home characterizing its inmates by their feelings for him—hers "the pure and undiminished tenderness of weded love" and Nabby's "the filial affection of a daughter who will never act contrary to the advise of a father." Abigail first reiterated to John: "Be assured that she will never make a choice without your approbation which I know she considers as Essential to her happiness." Nabby had just demonstrated this in her letter to her father, using virtually the same language. Abigail continued: "That she has a partiality I know, and believe, but that she has submitted her opinion to her Friends, and relinquished the idea of a connection upon principals of prudence and duty, I can with equal truth assure you." That this was still more laudable she implied by beginning her next sentence's account of Tyler's behavior with the word *yet* since the only grounds Nabby had for giving Tyler up were those of deference to her father's opinion as it was transmitted and subscribed to by her mother: "Yet nothing unbecoming the Character which I first entertained has ever appeard in this young Gentleman since his residence in this Town"—her own first impression had been borne out, and she was still able to observe him by way of those visits that he had resumed after that absence when Abigail had written to tell him she missed him—"and he now visits in this family with the freedom of an acquaintance, tho not with the intimacy of a nearer acquaintance." To John, at least, Abigail represented Tyler as capable of reining himself in, in accordance with his erstwhile prospective father-in-law's wishes. In fact, Tyler had obliged Abigail not only to defend John's opposition to his suit but also to renew his challenge to it.[36]

Abigail's reply to his request had expressed her own strong feelings for Tyler and her wish to enjoy his company at her fireside. To John, however, Abigail explained that the continuance of Tyler's visits were the result of Nabby's wish: "It was the request of Emelia who has conducted [herself] with the greatest prudence, that she might be permitted to see and treat this Gentleman as an acquaintance whom she valued."

Abigail quoted her justification for her request: "'Why said she should I treat a Gentleman who has done nothing to forfeit my Esteem, with neglect or contempt, merely because the world have said, that he entertained a preferable regard for me? If his foibles are to be treated with more severity than the vices of others, and I submit my judgement and opinion to the disapprobation of others in a point which so nearly concerns me, I wish to act in other respects with becoming decency.'" Nabby's initial view that Tyler was "practicing upon Chesterfield's plan" had been replaced by one wherein his "foibles" had been exaggerated. It was the world's opinion of Tyler's youthful behavior that, as Abigail had explained (not only to Storer but evidently to Nabby, too), had led to the prohibition of the marriage. In this account, however, Abigail suggests that it had been a downgrading rather than an ending of the relationship. One can read this reported speech of Nabby's as a veiled criticism of John's judgment, too.[37]

Abigail followed her report of Nabby's limited self-assertion with: "And she does and has conducted [herself] so as to meet with the approbation of all her Friends. She has conquerd herself." She still has "a partiality" for Tyler, Abigail has said, and still wants Tyler to spend time with her in the family circle, but Nabby was able to conform to the change in prospects transmitted to her by her mother. She was able, in Abigail's account to John, to repress her feelings in the way Abigail so often tried to do.

Here, Abigail referred to a poem of Tyler's: "An extract from a poetick piece which Some months ago fell into my Hands may give you some Idea of the Situation of this Matter. You will tell me you do not want a poet, but if there is a mind otherwise well furnished, you would have no objection to its being a mere amusement." That Tyler's was a mind qualified in the way John has written he wanted Abigail now asserted yet again: "You ask me if this Gentleman is a speaker at the Bar. He attends Plimouth Court and has spoke there." She can add to what she has said of Tyler's qualification previously that he "is proposed to be sworn in" to the Superior Court "with his contemporaries": "I cannot say what he will make, but those who most intimately know him, say he has talants to make what he pleases, and fluency to become a good Speaker." (Tyler was sworn in as an attorney to the Supreme Judicial Court of Massachusetts the following month; he had been officially recommended for that step the previous February.)[38] Abigail continued by telling John that Tyler's business in Braintree was increasing and that "I know nothing but he is well esteemed."

From Tyler's public, professional reputation, Abigail turned to the evidence of his private behavior. The Cranches, with whom Tyler still boarded, "find no fault in his conduct: He is Regular in his living, keeps no company with Gay companies, seeks no amusement but in the society of two or 3 families in Town, never goes to Boston but when Business calls him there." So far, then, all the evidence demonstrated Tyler was reformed: "If he has been the Gay thoughtless young fellow which he is said to have been and which I believe he was"—this was both to credit John's apprehension and to exonerate Tyler from the charge of having been a rake—"he has at least practiced one year of reformation." His reformation was the fundamental issue. Then, squaring this reiterated defense with what she had written to Tyler, even as the whole implicit burden of it was to hold out the potential of his complete reformation and, therefore, being qualified to marry Nabby, Abigail concluded: "Many more [years of reformation] will be necessary to Establish him in the world, whether he will make the man of worth and stediness time must determine." Tyler would go on to become, not only a distinguished playwright, novelist, and orator, but chief justice of Vermont. He also became a well-loved husband.[39]

John, meanwhile, still had not gotten Abigail's news of her apparent prohibition. In mid-July 1783, he asked her to let him "know the History of the Affair" and, along with his earlier willingness to "submit" if he had to, here stating unequivocally: "I hope there is an end to it. I hope never to be connected with frivolity. Youths must study to make any Thing at the Bar. . . . An Idler I despise." He told her: "You will keep this to yourself but I don't like the Affair at all." This secrecy would spare Nabby's feelings, especially if in the end she was to marry Tyler, but it gave Abigail latitude in representing John's reaction to the couple. John reiterated his January criticism of Abigail: "My Daughter is very dear to me and need not be in haste to form Friendships. Let her keep her Reserve I say. I wish her Mother had been more so than she has been upon this Occasion." They were now in that phase of their correspondence wherein, having decided that he was not yet returning to America, instead taking up the post in England (which Abigail had directly opposed), John insisted repeatedly that he wanted his "Wife and Daughter" with him.[40]

In August, John wrote that he had received Abigail's May 7 and June 20 letters with the news that the couple had accepted the postponement of any talk of marriage and Abigail's prediction that they "never" would raise it again. All John said to this was: "I learn with great Satisfaction the Wisdom of my Daughter, whom I long to see." His overwhelming concerns were his own immediate prospects and the effects on himself of his own Herculean effort in diplomacy: "I feel my self very happy to have got through it, in no worse a Condition. Adieu."[41]

But John had registered the fact that the relationship was not definitely over. In October, he repeated his request that Abigail and Nabby come to him "as soon as possible." At the end of this letter, he saw the advantage of such a sojourn as a test of Nabby and Tyler's feelings: "The Family affair . . . may be managed very well. . . . If the Parties preserve their Regard untill they meet again and continue to behave as they ought, they will still be young enough. Lawyers should never marry early." He declared himself "unqualified to decide upon the matter." He had depended almost entirely on Abigail and had fallen back on what he knew of Tyler's brother and his father, but chiefly on literary stereotype: "To your Judgement, with the Advice of our Friends, I must leave it." He could contribute only something of his own experience: "One thing I know, that Knowledge of the Law comes not by Inspiration, and without painfull and obstinate Study no man will ever have it."[42]

That same month, Abigail wrote John: "You call upon me to write you upon a subject that greatly embarrasses me." The editors note that this referred to John's asking her about "the Affair" in his July 13 letter and his terse: "I hope there is an end to it." Abigail continued: "Yet I ought to tell you what I conceive to be the Truth." Then came her own explanation for her embarrassment: "I wrote you the Truth when I informed you that the connection was broken of[f]." But the affair was not over: "Yet it is evident to me, as well as to the family [the Cranches] where he lives, that his [Tyler's] attachment is not lessned." "He conducts prudently," she continued, showing the behavior and manners that, unbeknownst to John, she had advised him, in order to win Nabby. With clearer deceptiveness, Abigail wrote: "tho nothing is said upon the subject, I do not immagine that he has given up the Hope, that in some future Day he may be able to win your approbation."[43]

Abigail then paraphrased Nabby's words, saying that "she could never be happy" without her father's approbation. Abigail herself was "satisfied" that Nabby "will not act contrary to the opinion of her Friends." So far this was nearly word for word what Abigail had written John in June, but, here, she continued: "her sentiments with regard to this Gentleman she says are not to be changed but upon a conviction of his demerit." In the end, this was to prove very significant: "I wish most sincerely you was at Home to judge for yourself. I shall never feel safe and happy until you are." Did she fear they might marry, Tyler turn out to be a rake,

and she, Abigail, be blamed for it? That Tyler might seduce and abandon
Nabby? We can see that Abigail was caught among her daughter's determination and the authoritative men Tyler and John, the latter of whom
had largely discredited her judgment in the affair, doing so with the anger from which, perhaps, she also wished to be safe: "I had rather you
should inquire into [Tyler's] conduct and behaviour, his success in Buisness, and his attention to it, from the family where he lives"—she had
already tried to bolster her opinion by associating it with theirs—"than
say any thing upon the subject myself." She again defended her previous truthfulness: "I can say with real Truth that no Courtship subsists
between them." She then returned to the wish John had expressed in
the letter to which she was replying: "I believe it is in your power to
put a final period to every Idea of the kind, if upon your return you
think best."

Meanwhile, Nabby left Braintree for her customary winter in Boston,
and Abigail had Tyler try to collect some of the debts due to the Adamses. On December 27, 1783, she wrote to John that he had been able
to complete "the purchase" of the Borland Farm for "a thousand pounds
Lawfull Money." But she had to reiterate the embarrassing modification
of her account of the end of the affair she had written him in October
because she had received his of August 14, in which he had declared his
"great Satisfaction" in hearing of Nabby's wisdom in deferring to her
mother's translation of John's wishes: "I should deceive you if I did not
tell you that I believe this Gentleman has but one object in view, and that
he bends his whole attention to an advancement in his profession and to
own economy in his affairs . . . he looks forward to some future day with
a hope that he may not be considered unworthy a connection to this
family." Her October letter illustrates her vulnerability to the charge
of deceit. Nabby shared Tyler's goal of marriage: "The forms of courtship as the world stiles it, do not subsist between the young folks, but I
am satisfied that both are fixed, provided your consent may one day be
obtained." But this time, realizing that John was not coming back as she
said she wished in her October letter, Abigail added: "She intends however to take a voyage with me, provided I cross the water." She could in
Europe attain the safety of turning the matter over to her husband.[44]

In her letter to John a week later, Abigail quoted Nabby's encouraging
her mother to join him: "O Mamma what have we not to fear from his
continuance abroad in climates so enemical to his Health? I shudder at the
thought." Nabby also told Abigail: "I know perfectly well how I should
act with regard to Pappas requests, were I exactly in your situation tho I

own, I now dread the result." She said nothing about accompanying her mother. She went on: "Yet my duty and my fears for the critical state of his Health, operate so powerfully upon my mind being never absent from my thoughts, that I would rather influence than dissuade you from going." This was not yet "we" or "us," even though Abigail had told Tyler early on that she "would never go abroad without [her] daughter."[45]

Abigail followed this quotation from Nabby's letter with: "In consequence of your last Letter I shall immediately set about putting our affairs in such a train as that I may be able to leave them in the spring." When she wrote the week before, "[Nabby] intends . . . to take a voyage with me, provided I cross the water," she had not yet ascertained whether that was, in fact, her daughter's intention.

Three days after Nabby had written her mother, "I would rather influence than dissuade you from going," she replied to her mother's query to her on that score. Fortunately, Nabby quoted the letter because the original has been lost. She first said that she would have liked to know more of her mother's sentiments but continued: "I presume you do not propose the question, 'whether I would consent to your leaving this country without me,' without an intention of being influenced by my reply, if you did." Nabby confessed, "I should not know what to determine," but she said that, if she were free to choose, she would not go. On her first reporting Tyler's courtship of Nabby in that 1782 letter to John, Abigail had said that she suspected that Nabby would lose her relish for a voyage to see John in favor of being with Tyler. Now Nabby wrote: "I would rather go from necessity than choice—the latter would never carry me, the former must. My inclination and wishes must be subservient to my duty. Willingly would I sacrifice my happiness, my peace, my pleasure, and every agreeable idea, for a time, did I only involve myself in the event." If, previously, she had always subordinated her own wishes to those of others, now her sacrifice required her to hurt Tyler. While her mother appeared to leave her a real choice in the matter, Nabby had made it clear that, if she said no, it was likely her mother would not go. Moreover, she continued: "It is my opinion that by your going my father will return much sooner than otherwise he would." So, even if she had to part from Tyler temporarily, Nabby believed, we can infer, that, once her father was home, he would put an end to Abigail's equivocations. The state of his health was critical. "The life you must live," she continued to her mother, "will not be agreeable to you, and I flatter myself that twelve months or eighteen at farthest, will not elapse ere he is influenced to return." She knew the emotional power that Abigail could exert over the issue of bringing John home: "I have known your sacrifices. I have shared them with you, in some degree of the anxiety and unhappiness you have suffered, and to dread their continuance or repetition. ✱✱✱✱✱✱[.]" She followed these marks with this: "What I have said is all I shall ever say on this subject." Later, her Aunt Shaw praised Nabby for her "strength of Mind and coolness of Judgement": "Possessed of these Sentiments, with which she left America, her *Conflict* must have been great."[46]

A month later, with arrangements for her and Nabby's departure well in hand, Abigail wrote John of the grief her going away was causing his aged mother, leading her to reflect: "However kind sons may be disposed to be, they cannot be daughters to a Mother." This lay behind Abigail's getting Nabby to go with her, but her next words suggest that Nabby could not help showing her unhappiness over Abigail's treatment of her, her unkind inconsiderateness of her daughter's feelings, in favor of relieving her own suffering: "I would endeavour in the discharge of my duty towards her, to merit from her the same testimony which my own parent gave me, that I was a good kind considerate child as ever a parent had."[47]

CHAPTER 13

# The Question Answered

## Parting

Abigail's decision to sail for Europe with the reluctant Nabby provoked Tyler to write directly to John the same month, January 1784. He began: "When a man's views are direct and Intentions consistant with Honour and Virtue he seldom affects Concealment." This was to assert his own moral value with precisely the phrase that John had used in his letter to her that Abigail had quoted to Tyler the previous June. ("Do not let her form any Connection with any one, who is not devoted entirely to Study and Buisness—To honour and to virtue. If there is a Trait of fFrivolity and Dissapation left I Pray that She may renounce it forever.") Tyler continued: "I not will presume . . . that my Attentions to your Daughter are Unknown to you." Relying so much on Abigail hitherto left him needing to apologize: "If you demand why an affair of so much importance to your Domestick Concerns was not communicated by me sooner, I hope that my Youth, the early progress of my professional career, and the continual expectations of your daily return to your Family will be accepted as sufficient apology." This was to touch very lightly indeed on the fact that the design had been to have enough time elapse for Tyler to demonstrate that he had grown past his youthful dissipation, not only fully to have reformed, but also to have risen to more eminence in the law.[1]

According to his letter, however, the delay had an unforeseen consequence that Tyler now reported as fresh news to his hoped-for father-in-law, whose sentence on Nabby ("My dear daughters happiness employs my Thoughts Night and day") Abigail had quoted to Tyler in her June 1783 letter to him: "The encrease of the strongest attachments is often imperceptible; while I every day Anticipated your return I heeded not that every day encreased my esteem for her [Nabby's] Virtues." He implied that he would have preferred to speak to John face-to-face before his feelings had reached that pitch, but "that Event [John's return] must now be viewed as distant as she is about to leave the country," a change in perspective that, if not simply disingenuous, suggests that the "many years" demonstration of his reformation that Abigail had asked Tyler (and Nabby) to endure before they revived the issue of marriage had been drastically telescoped and coupled with the expectation that John's return would be followed by his quick approval of Tyler's suit. Now, however, Nabby's departure, together with the increase in his esteem, forced him to act: "my own sense of propriety forbids me any longer to Defer the soliciting the Sanction of your Approbation to my Addresses, and 'tho I do not think myself entitled to your Consent to an immediate Union Yet I cannot suffer this separation without requesting your permission to expect it when ever she shall return to Her Native country." Among many possible comments on this passage, one can note the double meaning of *suffer*, by which Tyler endorsed Nabby's point that her deferring to her parents' wishes involved the feelings of the man they both anticipated would eventually be allowed to propose to her.

The letter's other paragraph reflected Tyler's knowledge of the letters Abigail had sent: "It will I presume be needless to trace the rise and progression of that attachment which now Authorizes me to apply, solely to her parents for the Completion of my Wishes." This was to repeat that the degree of his "esteem" for Nabby was reciprocated, but he added: "suffice it to say: that our mutual Esteem was formed under the Inspection of your Lady and with the knowledge of the worthy Family [the Cranches] with whom I reside." This reminded John that one of Nabby's parents had already approved of his suit. And John could infer that, prior to this letter, both Nabby and Tyler had let themselves be guided by Abigail's sense of propriety and that it had been she who argued on that basis that Tyler should not contact John. There had been no attempt by either Tyler or Nabby to conceal their relationship from him. This, too, referred back to the first paragraph, which had opened with a denial of "Concealment," a significant subject manifest in cultures where clandestinity in courtship, reflecting self-assertion by courting couples against the traditional control (of daughters especially) by "hard-hearted" parents, could result in pregnancy, followed either by marriage or abandonment. Clarissa's first step on the road to ruin had been the clandestine letters she had secretly exchanged with Lovelace, the epitome of a man lacking in honor and virtue.[2]

Tyler, then, tells John that he has been honorable and virtuous in his suit for Nabby. That he insisted that he recognized "her Virtues" and esteemed her for them suggests that he knew John had written Abigail that he had not. And to confine his history to "the rise and progression" of their relationship was entirely to ignore his putatively dishonorable earlier history. The brief letter concluded: "Permit me, then, to apply to you Sir, for your Approbation and Consent to my looking forward to a Connection with your Daughter as the reward of my Deserving her, and if I know my own Heart, on no other Terms would I solicit it." This did allude to the question of his own character, to assert that he was now a man of "Honour and Virtue"—what he might have been in the past was irrelevant. One can add that, in this self-conscious self-assertion, the letter was literally manly as well as man-to-man. If Tyler recognized that he had to get the demanding father's consent, his tone in doing so was the opposite of Nabby's submissive approach.

His letter was enclosed in one from Richard Cranch, John's very old friend as well as brother-in-law. That enclosure literalized the fact that Tyler and Nabby had formed their relationship "with the knowledge of the worthy Family with whom I reside." Cranch expressed his sorrow that John's return to America had been postponed, wrote that the "unhappiness that you and your dear Partner must feel from your mutual Absence, must be great: and the Loss that we on our part must sustain in parting with [Abigail and Nabby] by their taking a voyage to Europe . . . will be truly great on our part," and prayed that their "Voyage, whenever it is undertaken, may be prosperous and happy." He then turned to Tyler: "Inclosed is a Letter from my esteemed Friend Mr. Tyler, the subject of which is not unknown to me." Tyler must have asked Cranch to write John in support of it. Cranch continued: "As you are not personally acquainted with that young Gentleman, I would take the liberty of informing you that he has boarded at our House for near two Years past, and from my acquaintance with him, he appears to me to be possess'd of Politeness, Genious, Learning and Virtue." The editors note that crossed "out in the draft at this point is: 'His Gaiety and sprightfulness when at Colledge (which he entered very young) led him perhaps into some youthfull.'" Cranch may simply have debated this within himself before deciding that he would purge it from the fair copy, either because he knew John's views or because it might undercut what he wanted to be an unqualified endorsement of Tyler's present character. Perhaps, however, he consulted with Tyler on the point, following as he did Tyler's repression of the issue in his own letter. Cranch continued with the same prediction his sister-in-law made: "I think he will make a very respectable Figure in his Profession of the Law. His Business in that Department increases daily." He finally explained: "I tho't it my duty thus freely to give you my Sentiments of a Gentleman, who, I have reason to think, is making honourable Addresses to your Daughter, grounded on mutual Affection." This, too, seems to have been coordinated with Tyler's letter.[3]

A few days after Tyler and Cranch wrote their letters to him but long before he received them, John referred to Nabby in a letter to Abigail. He entreated Abigail to come to him: "my Happiness depends so much upon it, that I am determined, if you decline coming to me, to come to you." So powerful was that wish to be rejoined with Abigail that he now restated less reluctantly what he had written in his February 4, 1783 ("I must submit"), letter: "If Miss Nabby is attached, to Braintre, and you think, upon Advizing from your Friends, her Object worthy, marry her if you will and leave her with her Companion in your own House, Office, Furniture, Farm and all. H[is] Profession is, the very one, I wish. His Connection[s] are respectable, and if he has sown his will [wild] Oats and will Study, and Mind his Business, he is all I want." To have sown wild oats was a metaphor that implied the subject had, like the prodigal, reformed.[4]

The editors suggest here that Abigail "may not have received this letter before sailing to England in June," especially in light of a letter she would write her sister Mary after a conversation with John on the subject, to which we will turn in chronological order. When she and Nabby sailed, if the editors are right, Abigail still believed that she was complying with John's wishes, having "come to see a separation between AA2 and Tyler as a suitable test of the strength of their love." John had suggested that in his October letter, but, more evidently, Abigail postponed the match on the grounds that Tyler's reformation needed further testing and that, as she told the couple, they still needed John's consent. In fact, as we have seen, John had grudgingly consented the previous February, but he made that submission to his daughter's wishes contingent on Abigail's "Advice," and Abigail chose to postpone the marriage. I suggest that this was because paramount to her was compliance with John's initial, unambiguous opposition and, even more so, deference to his very harsh, emotionally laden criticism of her; she also took the opportunity to rejoin him as soon as she could.[5]

On April 3, the day after he received their letters, John wrote replies to both Richard Cranch and Royall Tyler, telling Cranch at the outset: "I hope to See Mrs. and Miss Adams before this reaches you. . . . They may be on their way." John had opened by telling Cranch: "Mr. Tyler's Letter inclosed is here answered. Your Opinion has great Weight with me." He began his letter to Tyler by explaining why the "Subject" of Tyler's letter "has for some time been to [him] an Occasion of Solicitude," but in the most general of terms, which minimized, if they did not conceal, his particular reasons. It was "chiefly on Account of the Uncertainty" in which he had been "too long left respecting every thing which concerns" him and his family. Tyler's family and his education were, John wrote Tyler, "too respectable for me to entertain any objections to them": "Your Profession is that for which I have the greatest Respect and Veneration." The objections to which he had alluded by saying that his "chief" cause of worry in effect had been the subordination of his family to his obligations to the public had now been answered: "The Testimonials I have received of your personal Character and Conduct are such as ought to remove all scruples upon that head."[6]

In the end, however, John now wrote, he would have agreed to Tyler's marrying Nabby, even if his scruples had not been removed. "It is a Serious affair which most of all concerns the Happiness of the Parties: So that I should scarcely in any case have opposed the Final Judgement and Inclination of my Daughter." This was to reiterate what he had told Abigail in his February 4, 1783, letter, and it was in keeping with the kind of fathering Clarissa's father should have exhibited, instead of attempting to force her to marry the uncouth Solmes. At the same time, however, John had had decisive influence in putting off the day of that "Final Judgement," and he knew it would be postponed further by Nabby's coming to Europe with her mother, a postponement he had told Abigail would test the relationship. So he followed his accession to "my Daughter" with "But the Lady is coming to Europe with her Mother" and coupled that with his virtual order that Tyler not follow her. "It would be inconvenient to you to make a voyage to Europe, perhaps, and when the time will come for her to return to America, is Uncertain." In his simultaneous reply to Cranch he twice said he hoped to return in a year.

Yet again, John further extended his positive orientation toward Tyler: "I approve very much of your Purchase in Braintree"—Abigail's account of the Borland Farm had been effective—"and if any of my Library may be of use to you, in the prosecution of your Studies or your Practice, the loan of *it* is at your Service." This would help sustain Tyler's reform: "Finally, Sir, you and the young Lady have my Consent to arrange your Plans according to your own Judgements, and I pray God to bless and prosper you both together or asunder." The last two words were a reminder that Tyler still could not bank on the marriage.

Nine days after John sent these letters, Abigail wrote John: "I have adjusted all my affairs and determined upon comeing out, I summon all my resolution that I may behave with fortitude upon the occasion. The Hope . . . of meeting my dearest best Friend . . . and rejoicing with him, buoys me up . . . in parting with my Dear connexions." Bringing one of them with her—Nabby—had been part of her decision. Here, she mentioned Nabby only to say: "I press our Daughter to write and hope she will." A few days later, Elbridge Gerry wrote Abigail to tell her that Congress was likely to appoint Adams to the commission to negotiate commercial treaties with "sixteen nations," including France, and that it might be "best to have every Thing in Readiness to embark on the shortest Notice." Gerry confirmed this plan a month later.[7]

Thus, on May 25, Abigail was able to write John: "Let me request you to go to London some time in july if it please God to conduct me there [to Auteuil] in safety." She was acutely aware that she was "embarking . . . without any Male Friend connection or acquaintance," but she anticipated finding resources in herself. Nabby was not such a resource, although worry about leaving her at home lessened the drain on her own spirits: "I have to combat my own feelings in leaving my Friends and I have to combat encourage and Sooth the mind of my young companion whose passions militate with acknowledged duty and judgement." This was the conflict that Nabby had outlined to Abigail when agreeing to accompany her: her feelings for her lover versus what her parents had taught her and what she knew they wanted. Her mother's wish supervened. Abigail immediately preceded this account of Nabby's being parted from Tyler by writing to John: "I dare not trust my self with anticipating the happiness of meeting you; least I should unhappily meet with a bitter alloy." She followed that with her brief statement of her own conflict, then Nabby's, and then this: "I pray Heaven conduct me in safety and give me a joyful and happy meeting with my long seperated best Friend and ever dear companion and long absent son."[8]

Abigail and Nabby sailed from Boston a month later, on June 20, 1784. Abigail recorded in her diary, written on the boat after they left: "I have great satisfaction in the behaviour of my daughter. The Struggle of her mind was great, her passions strong, never before calld into opposition." She had quite recently praised Nabby for her self-conquest in the enforced downgrading of her relationship with Tyler, but this further diminution was to be unalleviated by the tangible hope represented by Tyler's continued welcome at the fireside. By contrast, Abigail could now expect the renewal of her own relationship with John. Nabby's struggle to command her passions was the same that Abigail had attempted throughout her years of separation from her lover and on which she prided herself when successful. Here, she added the two perspectives offered by the conventions of sensibility: "the parting of two persons strongly attached to each other is only to be felt; discription fails." Abigail's next paragraph began: "Yet once the struggle was over, she has obtain'd a Calmness and a degree of cheerfulness which I feard she would not be able to acquire." To Nabby's apparent "Calmness" and "degree of cheerfulness" on thus having parted from Tyler "the kindness and attention of Dr. Clark [another passenger] has contributed, tho he knew not that there was more than ordinary occasion for them."[9]

Abigail wrote Tyler from "On Board ship Active," beginning:

As well in compliance with your request, as to gratify my own inclination I take my pen after 3 weeks absence to inquire after you: you have been frequently in my thoughts during this interval and I have traced you in my imagination. . . . I fanc'd you rising wih the morning sun,

"And Sprin[g]ing from the bed of Sloth enjoying,
The cool, the fragrant, and the Silent hour
To meditation due, and sacred song."

Thus, she represents Tyler to himself as a man of feeling, before imagining herself accompanying him on his stern, virtuous, daily round of legal study in pursuit of laudable ambitions, her letter geared, nominally at least, to urge him on in his demonstration of reformation, to make him "what [he] ought to be," to attain eminence as a thinker, a speaker, and a reasoner, "but above all [as] a Man of the strickest honour and integrity." She then again segues into a highly self-conscious literary mode before quoting Montaigne: "Nothing makes a Man truly valuable but his Heart. . . . If [our inclinations] are such as lead to trifling passions, we shall be the Sport of their vain attachments. They offer us flowers, but says Montaigne, always mistrust the treachery of your pleasures." This resembles the advice young John took from the choice of Hercules, but, of course, Abigail alluded to Tyler's past of gaming, dissipation, and, perhaps, rakery.[10]

The letter continued at some length, referring to Nabby by making the shipboard experience one "we" shared: "From Dr. Clark we have received every attention of a Gentleman and Physician, both of which we stood in need of." She concluded with a paragraph that sympathized with Tyler, a passage that is sentimental, personal, and intimate, but one in which the change in pronouns is salient: "Pray how does Braintree look, is the Season favourable? On ship Board we are almost frozen; the old camblet cloak is of Emminant Service upon deck to wrap around us, and our Baize gowns are rather thin without the addition of a cloak. Has not habit led you to visit the cottage altho deserted? Recalling to your rembrance what it once was; I have vanity enough to commisirate all your Situations, and Benevolence enough to wish my place happily supplied by pleasures from some other Scource." She "assured" him: "you have a share and that not a small one in the affectionate Regards of A Adams." According to the reminiscences of Tyler's widow, following the departure of mother and daughter, time "healed his feelings, and some time afterwards, when a tremendous packet containing several sheets sealed with U.S. seal was delivered to him his spirits revived."[11]

Mother and daughter landed in England in order to rejoin John in London before going on together to Paris. Living with her father in August 1785, Nabby wrote that her earlier views of him were the result of misinformation, this observation in response to a thoughtful action of his: "Read Shakespeare after dinner. Papa purchased his works this morning, upon my saying I had never read them. I discover a thousand traits of softness, delicacy, and sensibility in this excellent man's character. I was once taught to fear his virtues." Taught by whom? one might ask, and one recalls the apprehensiveness John caused Abigail during their courtship as well as her observation of his "stern virtue," the quality that rationalized his separation from his wife and children all those years. But, now with him, Nabby was relieved: "I had been taught to think him severe, and as he would demand my obedience, I found him far otherwise, he never demanded of me even acquiescence to his wishes, but left me to follow my own, in the most important concerns of life."[12]

This referred to what she believed to be her forthcoming marriage to Tyler. Nabby attributed this freedom to John's behavior as a modern father, behavior to which his sensibility was central: "How amiable—how respectable—how worthy of every token of my attention, has this conduct rendered a parent—a father—to whom we feel due even a resignation of our opinions!" That is to say, John's worthiness depended in part on his restraint of his familial power. Nabby's feeling that she should resign "even" her own opinions also referred to her relations with Tyler. Here, she exclaimed that she knew of fathers who perpetuated an unenlightened, archaic form of power, the kind for which her mother, in her "Remember the Ladies" letter of 1775, had said all men yearned, albeit with husbands' power in mind: "How many are there who usurp the power Nature has given them a right to use, and who act rather as tyrants over their families than as parents of their children; how much is the want of this gentleness, delicacy and sensibility observed in that sex, whose worth and amiability of character depends upon the possession of it." Abigail illustrated the wish that a man have more of those latter qualities and the fact that some men were merely "Stoickal." Conventionally, she believed that family life could soften a man and develop his feelings, but here Nabby suggests that this was not necessarily the case at all, that the feelings fathers had could be authoritarian, rather than those of the near-synonymous "gentleness, delicacy, and sensibility."

In this, Nabby was at one with what Jan Lewis describes as "the anti-patriarchalism of Revolutionary ideology," although Fordyce had written in 1766 that some of his lady readers complained that their parents were "cruel and tyrannical" in regard to marriage choice: it had been a literary theme since the Restoration, most notably in *Clarissa*, but the American Revolution gave it fresh momentum and a new context. Revolutionaries, including John Adams, had compared themselves to young people revolting against arbitrary parents in Great Britain. Stephen Mintz writes that it was "not accidental that early participants in the Revolutionary cause called themselves 'sons' and 'daughters' of liberty." A little later than Nabby's observation, a writer in the *American Museum* (1791) declared that parents had "no right to act the part of tyrants to their children" because children had "natural rights," too, and, after 1789, another woman could publicly accuse a father of establishing "a *domestic bastille*" over his daughters, provoking them to revolt against him by marrying men of whom he did not approve. The author of "The Inexorable Father" in a 1791 issue of the *Massachusetts Magazine* (Boston) characterized her subject as "unfeeling as adamant, hard of heart as the nether mill stone." Nabby, however, concluded her thought here by adding women to the category of the unfeeling: "How many ladies, within my knowledge, . . . do not possess one iota of [gentleness, delicacy, or sensibility]." Her mother had suggested Nabby herself could use more.[13]

The following September, Trumbull's portrait of John Adams led Nabby back to the subject. She said that John felt that no artist "had yet caught his character"—clearly she was paraphrasing his observations. "The ruling principles in his moral character, were candour, probity, and decision." She agreed, but wrote: "I add another which is sensibility." The quality she most admired in him was the first one he listed, "candour": "I hope if I inherit any of his virtues it may be this. . . . In whatever intercourse we have with society, we find it necessary in a greater

or less degree; and in the mind of a woman, I esteem it particularly amiable." P. N. Furbank points out that, in the eighteenth century, *candid*
and *candour* referred, "not to telling the truth even if painful, but to doing one's very best to think well of others."[14] At the beginning of her sojourn in Europe, then, and still anticipating a marriage to Tyler that her
mother maintained depended on her father's decision, Nabby saw him
(with sentimental eyes) as a man of feeling, praising him for his willingness to leave her free to marry whomever she wanted and for an orientation that would lead him to think well of the calumniated Tyler.

## "*Cruel* Suspence": Reading Signs That
## Tyler Had Not Reformed

Abigail had relied on letters from John to convey the feelings on which
she was dependent. The most frequent subject of them had been the letters themselves—how many, how long, their emotional adequacy, their
arrival, and their loss, all reflecting the unpredictable vagaries of distance,
means of delivery, warfare, and censorship, factors that Abigail could feel
reflected John's feelings about her, knowing as she did that he had chosen
to place the public above the private. She had been able to mitigate her
dependence by taking up the responsibilities of farm and business as well
as household and childrearing, and she had been called on to supply him
with a continuous stream of political news, feeding his successful public
career, in which she could take some pride. Even so, she had been obsessed with his letters. She had now put Nabby in a similar position, but
Nabby lacked comparable responsibilities—she was a leisured daughter in France living an even more aristocratic life than she and her peers
did in New England. Tyler's worse than inadequacy as a letter writer,
coupled with broad hints from Mary Cranch that he was an unfeeling,
unreformed rake after all, led to the breakup.

   Abigail, believing herself to be carrying out John's wishes regarding
the relationship as well as the presence of his wife and daughter with him
in Europe, had engineered the separation of Nabby and Tyler. But "in
conversation" with John Quincy about August 1, 1784, she made a "discovery," as she told Mary in a letter she immediately wrote, that John
had, in fact, already "acquiesced to his daughter's marriage" in that January 25, 1784, letter, one that was mailed prior to mother and daughter's
sailing for Europe but that, apparently, Abigail had not received. On August 2, she wrote Mary that, until the day before or so, she had had "no
opportunity to ask Master John"—John Quincy—"a question but in

company." It seems that this question was about John's having agreed to Nabby's marriage and/or about Nabby's knowledge of such an agreement (consistent with what can be seen as the relieved and grateful feelings toward him that she expressed in her journal). Nabby must have said something along the same lines to John Quincy. Abigail continued: "I find by his accounts that Some Letters are gone to America." These were, not only that January 25, 1784, letter ("marry her" to Tyler "if you will . . . if he has sown his [wild] Oats . . . he is all I want"), but also a second one, written on July 3, 1784, wherein John had said to Abigail "if you conclude to come to me, you may marry your Daughter before hand if you will and bring her Husband with her. If you do not come, you may still marry your Daughter if you think proper."[15] But there had been that February 4, 1783, letter wherein John had said, "I must submit, my Daughters Destiny, to Her own Judgement and her own Heart, with your Advice," a sentiment of which it seems Nabby had learned. Abigail had certainly received this letter. Somehow the real potential it embodied had not registered with Abigail, and one can hypothesize various reasons, including her sensibility to the harshness of John's first, unambiguous hostility to the match. She had been reading his feelings, especially toward her. It was also the case, moreover, that, had Nabby married Tyler and stayed in America, Abigail may not have had the psychological wherewithal to voyage alone to rejoin John. And, of course, John had changed his mind again in the interim—or could have been read to have done so.

Whatever the case, Abigail told Mary in August 1784: "Some letters are gone to America the contents of which should they come into your hands; I hope you will keep wholly to yourself. I own I am rather surprized at them, and I think I may rely upon your prudence, and all connected with you to keep them intirely to yourselves. I have thought it a very fortunate circumstance that they did not reach me before I saild, as they would have greatly embarrassed me." She would have been embarrassed because she had already had to reverse her original work on behalf of the relationship in deference to John's first angry opposition and criticism of her. That is, having assisted Tyler to melt Nabby's heart, Abigail then had to attempt to refreeze it; having wholeheartedly endorsed Tyler's suit on the grounds that he was reformed (let alone his own Grandisonian courtship of her), she then had attempted to put distance between him and his goal by requiring him to show evidence that he had, in fact, reformed. Had she known of (or believed in) John's acceptance of the match, she would have had to reverse her approach again. Her rationale for bringing Nabby with her across the fearsome ocean to fulfill her own heart's desire would not have existed. We should note, too, that Abigail already had been embarrassed by having to admit to John that, contrary to her previous assertion of their permanent disconnection, Nabby and Tyler were still determined on marriage.[16]

If by August 2, 1784, what was done was done, we can still observe the paramountcy of Abigail's own feelings on discovering that John had said yes to the marriage—relief at having avoided further embarrassment, along with her assumption that her sister would sympathize with such feelings. Even more to the point was the cause of that hypothetical embarrassment, her unquestioned deference to John's will. It was at this point in her letter to Mary that Abigail fell back on something he had said, supplying the editors with explicit evidence for her coming "to see a separation between AA2 and Tyler as a suitable test of the strength of their love": "The present trial must be a test, if the Gold is genuine failing neither in weight or value, time will not diminish it— But should such a mixture of alloy be found in it, as to prove the coin either counterfeit, or base, it will not pass for current where it is now valued as intrinsick." She reinforces our knowledge of the particular bond between the sisters in this matter by adding that she was "anxious" that Mary "should receive this" and that, if Mary wanted to "communicate with [her], any thing that no other person ought to see, let it always be inclosed in an other Letter with such a mark upon the outside as this ⊖." One could say that Abigail had given Mary a motive to help tank the relationship. Tyler always suspected that Mary had played a decisive part in that result.

Subsequently, Mary kept her sister and niece posted on Tyler, who was involved in her own family's to-ings and fro-ings. We can assume that she marked the envelopes containing negative reports of Tyler with a ⊖. She wrote in August: "I suppose Mr. Tyler will write, he is well. Tell Cousin Nabby that she has left a sorrowful looking Picture behind her. I dont like it." She was already intimating what a later letter on Tyler's response to Nabby's departure spelled out, that he was putting on an act. This was enclosed with her husband's acknowledgment of John's replies to his and Tyler's April letters, replies that had arrived right after Mary reported Tyler's sorrowful self-representation. Cranch sent Tyler's on to him at Borland Farm in Braintree, where the previous owner, still in possession, was allowing Tyler to make repairs: this Tyler reported to John in some detail in his reply to John's to him, written two days after he got it.[17]

Tyler suggested that it was "from the very great Interest in the subject, or some more latent cause," that he "never Felt more at a loss to Express myself with Propriety," that is, the extent of his "Gratitude, which, a Man of Ingenuity may be supposed to render to the person to whom he shall have been indebted in High Degree, for the Principal Enjoyment of his Life." This could be read to mean that he was writing this out of convention, rather than wholeheartedly, although it could be read as an irony. At the same time, Tyler challenged John's condescension in telling him that marriage was serious: "Marriage is indeed a '*Serious Affair.*'" This, like the other doubly emphasized words, were Tyler's quotations from John's letter to him: "But the '*Parties*' have not proceeded thus far in their endeavours to attain it, without suitable Reflections upon its importance, as involving their own Happiness and that of their Friends and Relatives." Tyler might have made this up in self-assertion, but it is the best evidence of one of the subjects, perhaps the most salient one, that he and Nabby had discussed during their courtship, forced as they were to make it contingent on her parents' feelings. In any case, there is no doubt that Nabby's contribution was shaped by her parents' definition of the process whereby a daughter accepted a husband.[18]

Tyler noted the irony of getting John's apparent permission after Nabby's departure had made it impossible to act on it: "The Young Lady probably Arrived in England, before I received Your Letter, but if it had been received previous to her Departure, and even countenanced her remaining in the Country and the State of my Affairs had renderd an immediate Union Feasible and Prudent." Here, Tyler did not complete the thought signified by *if*. Anyway, he seems to have known that John had countenanced an immediate marriage. He suggests, too, that the responsibility and power for delaying the marriage lay in his own hands. Certainly, he knew of the terms of the struggle that Nabby had described in her letter to her mother, wherein she said that her choosing to stay and marry Tyler would have prevented Abigail's rejoining John in Europe: "Nevertheless, the many Filial Incitements she had to cross the Atlantic, would have silenced every selfish suggestion, and have induced her to Accompany her Mother." Nabby must have shown Tyler that letter to her mother (or discussed its terms) describing her conflict between inclination and filial duty. Its mentioning the pain that deference to the latter would cause him may well have reflected his response. Now this one was tinged with the bitterness consistent with the manly pride of his letters to John, a quality present, too, in his expression of gratitude for John's offer of his library: "Accept Sir my thanks for the kind Proffer of the Loan of your Library. I shall endeavour to make that Use of it,

which is becoming a Man, who wishes to be serviceable to his Friends
and his Country." All the previous correspondence had articulated Abigail and John's requirement that Tyler's agenda in pursuing his legal career should be to demonstrate his reformation. Here, however, Tyler
repudiates that humiliating goal in favor of an entirely noble ambition,
one that was the same as John's.

His final paragraph opened with similar self-assertion against John's
terms even as it could be read to comply with them: "Our present 'Arrangements' not withstanding your Liberality, We—I venture to speak
for your Daughter—shall chearfully submit to your Inspection and Advice, and I hope that our Union will afford you and your Lady, that En-
viable Satisfaction, which Parents experience when they Perceive their
Children, Usefull, Worthy, Respectable and Happy." He implicitly rejected the possibility that he and Nabby would each "prosper . . . asunder" with which John had concluded his letter to Tyler.

Although only one of Nabby's and Tyler's letters to each other has
survived, other letters indicate that they wrote and even how often. They
also show indirectly what Nabby, at least, felt. She wrote Betsy Cranch
from Auteuil in September 1784 that to return to America was "the first
wish of my heart, and (*only*) [deleted] three months absent." Her remark
about letters, "No arrivals from America since I received yours by Mr.
Tracy's Ship," referred to her not hearing from Tyler and is a reminder of
the way in which she felt in the same position vis-à-vis him as her mother
had toward her "Friend" when he had been across the Atlantic. Her next
sentence was a message to be relayed to Tyler: "I am impatient to hear,
from my friends. If they knew what a pleasure and satisfaction they
would confer upon me sure I am that they would never permit a Ship to
sail without letters." She asked Betsy to tell her "all about" their "circle,"
and, in discussing the possible marriages of mutual friends, right after the
phrase "after I left Boston," she remarked: "Interested friends should be
very cautious that their influence does not lead them to advise too great
a sacrifice." Nabby had, we have seen, told her mother that manipulating
her to leave Tyler and go with her to Europe had been to "sacrifice [her]
happiness, [her] peace, [her] pleasure, and every agreeable idea." She
told Betsy: "Remember me affectionately to your family—*all* of them."
Tyler was their lodger and, thus, one of the "*all*." She concluded this letter to Betsy with: "Remember me to every one who takes the pains to
inquire or feels interested enough to think of your friend." The implicit
criticism of the insensibility of those who did not could be applied to
Tyler, illustrating Nabby's susceptibility to such suspicions.[19]

Abigail wrote Betsy the day after Nabby did: "I will write to Mr. Tyler I hope to be able to send at least a few lines." But she had to leave off writing because she heard the carriage wheels of "your uncle" arrive: "I go to hasten tea of which he is still fond." She also wrote to both Betsy's mother and her sister and accompanied these with a letter she wrote the same day to Tyler, in which she first explained to him the difficulties and delays he could expect in receiving letters—"we can convey them" "only by private hands." She assumed that he was thinking about her and Nabby as she always assumed John had been. She said that he would have had news, she hoped, "long before this will reach you what may set your Heart and mind at ease," and she combined this with a reminder of the long-range plan for reformation and marriage: "And I hope you are going on in Such a way as to give those who are disposed to (befriend) [deleted] assist you no cause to repent their friendly disposition towards you."[20]

In her view, Abigail told Tyler in this letter, "manners more than conversation" distinguished a fine woman, so ignorance of French was immaterial: "A woman whose manners are modest and decent cannot fail of having some merit. Emelia on this account strikes where ever she appears." Some old "Abbes who are Mr. Adamses particular Friends called her une Ange," while Madam Helvetius "threw herself into a chair with this exclamation, *une Belle figure.*" While Abigail went on to describe Madame Helvetius's dress to Tyler, an urbane gentlemen who she thought would be interested in it, she did not develop the highly negative view of this lady that she wrote to her other correspondents at the same time. Her point was to remind Tyler what an attractive prospect he had in Nabby, even to suggest that the qualities that might have betokened an ice heart were highly prized in fashionable Europe. Evidently, her letters to Tyler were now shaped by the realization that John had agreed to the marriage, and she was doing her part to keep Selim in contact with Emilia.[21]

In October 1784, Mary Cranch reported a more tangible reminder that Tyler kept Nabby in mind: "Mr. Tyler has received another Letter from Mr. Adams and from Cousin with her Picture"—this was one of the miniatures that were so popular and fashionable among those who could afford them—"which we think is very well done and a pretty good likeness but I would rather see the original Dear Girl." (Nabby had such a miniature of Tyler.) But Mary had opened this letter with a remark about Tyler that soon would grow into full-blown criticism: "When I return'd from Haverhill I hurry'd over a very incorrect Scrowl, being as I thought very much in danger of not getting it on board Capt. Scott before he saild, but here Mr. Tyler just return'd from Boston and tells me he will not Sail till Teysday. I don't Love to have Letters lay by so. They will seem such old things when you get them that their value will be lost."[22]

Early in November, Mary reported that Tyler had written several letters to Nabby. She described his doing so: "Shut [i]n his chamber three Days writing to France." He tried to keep their contents confidential in spite of Mary's efforts: "We have insisted upon his giving us the Heads of his discourses least we should give you nothing but a repetition of anecdotes. He has not yet done it." But by December, Abigail wrote, Nabby had heard nothing from Tyler since she sailed for Europe. Acquaintances had received letters recently, but "we have none, how can this be? . . . Emelia lookd sad but said nothing. Six months and not one line was hard accounting for." The last package from Mary had nothing from Tyler in it, "no Letters for her. I kept the knowledge of it wholy from her." The family had waited on tenterhooks for two days after hearing that American acquaintances had received letters from America—John Quincy went from Auteuil to Paris to find out. Eventually, some letters were brought to them. Abigail described their anxious expectation and the scene of waiting, including "Emelia setting . . . in a low chair in a pensive posture," the eagerness with which the packet arrived, and John's distribution of its contents. It may have been one of these wherein Tyler informed Abigail that a farm in which he knew she was interested was coming onto the market.[23]

Abigail received another one from Tyler early in January. Her long reply to it opened: "Half the Pleasure of a Letter consist in its being written to the moment and it always gave me pleasure to know when and Where Friends received my Letter." She assumed that he would get the same pleasure. Her description demonstrates the emotional importance of the event and can be categorized with other expressions of the self-consciousness of the material circumstances of letter writing (dropping the pen, sitting at a particular desk, trembling, or dropping tears) that we have seen characterized the correspondence of persons of sensibility: "I was sitting by my fire side at one end of a table and at the other my best friend was studying his favorite Author Plato. I was reading a French comedy called the procurer which I saw acted a few evenings ago." She then quoted that part of Philippe Poisson's *Le procureur arbitre* that she was reading when a servant brought in two large packets. On seeing the packets, she said: "I cried out from America and seized my sizer [scissor] to cut them open." "Emelia" had gone into Paris with her brother, so, she wrote: "I have tuckd away [her letter from him] with an intention of teasing her a little." She recorded that it was included in the second packet "received from you since [their] arrival."[24]

Abigail told Tyler: "the receipt of this second Letter has determined me to Seaize my pen this very moment and thank you." This was to re-iterate her reminder of the value of a letter being "written to the moment," in contrast to Tyler's reported dilatoriness in writing. "To discribe to you the pleasure that a packet from America gives me," she continued, "must take a theatrical stile and Say it is painted upon my face it sparkles in my Eyes and plays around my Heart. . . . I Love to hear every domestick occurrence then I live with you tho absent from you." Abigail told him she was having "pleasures and amusements" but "not what the Beau Mond would esteem such." She described her usual daily activities, an account in which she incorporated "Emelia's." After her own fire was laid in the morning and her room cleaned, she repaired "to Emelia's Chamber and rouse[d] her." Later, Emelia went back "to her room to translating Telemack," and at noon the "Ladies"—herself and Emelia—"repair to the toilite." In the afternoon, Emelia "reads or plays with her Brother which they can do with a game of Romps very well."

She turned this into a running record of the time she was writing to show Tyler how she "teased" Nabby by not telling her that a longed-for letter from Tyler had at last arrived: "Ceasar barks and the gate bell rings, which announces the return of the Carriage." Abigail reported the dialogue to Tyler, and her stage directions made it still more a play, consistent with the "theatrical stile" she said she adopted earlier, or, more specifically, given her game and Nabby's yearning, allowed Tyler to read it as a sentimental comedy:

Enter Miss A, "What are you cold?"
Enter Mr. JQA with a set of Mathamatical instruments,
"Pray what Spectacle have you been at to Night?"

Nabby replies, "A Variety, into the palais Royal. I have seen (*the*) [deleted] du palais de bon goüt l'Intendant comedian malgre lui; le Memsouge excusable, et le nouveau parvenu." These were four plays—or extracts from them. Abigail then supplied Tyler, her confidante, with her unspoken thought: "Now what had I best do, give her these letters to night which will keep her up till 12 or give them for her Breakfast to morrow morning?" She switches back to her comedy: "Hem, come take of[f] your Cloak in an instant, and I will give you an entrennes"—explaining in an aside to Tyler—"which in plain English is a new Year's Gift." She continued: "Off went the Cloak in an instant, then I delt out the letters one by one, at every one Miss calling out for more, more until I had exhausted the bugget; but so secret and so affraid that one can hardly get a peep at a single line." Abigail recognized all this as "trifling," but it resembled the scene where, at her American fireside, an enamored mother had conspired with the suitor to affect her daughter's feelings toward him.

Abigail continued by reassuring Tyler that French manners led her to "believe you need be under no apprehensions respecting a young Lady of your acquaintance, who has never yet found her self so happy in Europe as America, and who . . . will ever find in herself a preference to the manners of her Native Country." She went on to describe the immodesty of French ladies and French manners, declaring that "the Pythagorian doctrine of Reverencing thyself is little practiced among the Females of this Nation" and that the "Affections of the Heart are never traced." She implied that both of these qualities were American characteristics, and the context implied that Emelia's and Selim's relation was one of "Affections of the Heart."

Abigail's concluding paragraph was her clearest statement of her expectation that Tyler would marry Nabby, although she introduced it by her reiteration that he keep up his reformation: "you are pleased to say you feel disposed at all times to attend to" her "advice," which Abigail said had "ever been of that kind to promote both your honour and Reputation." She assured him: "I am no less solicitous when I view you with more confidence as the person to whose care and protection I shall one day resign a beloved and only daughter." She now assumed that such a statement was in keeping with John's view, but she still had to gain "more confidence" in Tyler and would do so if he continued to follow her advice and, thus, completely persuade her and the world of his reformation: "Industry integrity frugality and honour are the Characterisstick Virtues which will recommend and ensure to you parental Regard and Fraternal affections and which will continue to you the Friendship the Esteem and the Maternal Regard of A. Adams." In this listing she left Nabby aside, having made it clear that she was still in love with Tyler and hungered for his letters.

Mary reported to Abigail in January that Tyler had planned on taking her three grown children (Betsy, Lucy, and their brother William) to visit the Shaws in Haverhill in his sleigh but had been prevented by an unexpected continuation of the Boston court's sitting: "His business I think increases, and as far as I can judge he attends it with steadiness." She was keeping an eye on the course of Tyler's reformation, and Abigail could not miss the qualification in her report.[25] In April, Mary was explicit in her criticism. She opened her letter by describing Tyler's response to the receipt of two packets of December and January letters from Auteuil, after a six-month interval: "Mr. T. receiv'd only one from Emelia, Dated September in the first Pacquit. He look'd very cross. It was nothing but a scolding letter he said." Nabby must have told Tyler what she thought and felt about not having heard from him. Mary continued: "I told him I was very glad of it. Such an one was all he deserv'd, and that had my Cousin possessed my Spirit he would not have had one." She reported to him that Abigail had gotten his letters: "But I refused to read him that part of your Letter in which you so Pictures[q]uely describe the reception of them." In her view, he did not deserve that pleasure. Indeed, it was Mary's way of adding to the punishment she thought he deserved instead: "Ask'd him whether after setting such an example of neglect and exerciseing the Power he knew he had to give Pain, He thought he tlineought to expect any more." Giving such emotional pain was precisely what a man was not to do to a susceptible woman: "He was nettled and I design'd he should be I had no doubt but that he had more [letters] on Board ship, but it was hard that one should suffer so long Such *Cruel* Suspence and the other none." Nabby was suffering at the hands of this cruel, unfeeling man, who made her yet another figure of virtue in distress.[26]

After he "pouted away all Sunday," Tyler sent off for the other letters, and his messenger came back "with a volume of Letters for him and several for others." Mary told Abigail: "I gave him yours to him Which was included in Mr. Cranchs. I have heard parts of Emelias, and you may if you please assure her that he never fails of reading that part in one of them, wherein She tells him that Mrs. Hall told her Papa that Mr. T was a very handsome Man." She devoted another paragraph to Tyler, giving a detailed story that further discredited his character, showing him to be insensitive, ignorant, willful, vain, foolish, cruel in his treatment of horses, and similar in his treatment of ladies. Later in the same letter, she returned to the subject of Abigail's description of her and her family's feelings on receiving the letters from America. She waxed sentimental over young John Quincy's: "Sweet Youth! I could have shed Tears at your description of his walking away a little mortified upon not finding any Letters for him among those he had taken so much pain to procure." And she promised that he would get letters from her, her husband, and their daughters. This led her to Nabby and Abigail's account of her hunger to hear from Tyler: "If I have time I shall write to Cousin Nabby. Dear Girl she does not know how anxious I am for her Happiness."

Tyler—or Nabby's feelings about his writing to her—was still on her mind when Mary came to the end of this very long letter. She had heard that Captain Lyde (who had commanded the boat that had taken Abigail and Nabby to Europe the year before) was to sail very soon. Again, Tyler was willful: "Mr. T would not write till the Court . . . was over, so that unless he writes in Boston which I think he may, he will not write by this vessel." She wished he would take every opportunity he had to send a letter, rather than save them up for a larger "volume." She also criticized him for the way in which he composed his letters: "I wish you could see him when he is writing. Shut up in his chamber for a week together with about forty books round him: I told him one day, that one Letter warm from the Heart and sent *in Season* was worth all of them." Not only was this to invoke the polarity in styles connoted by sensibility: immediacy of reply showed the spontaneous, heartfelt, yet considerate versus the labored, authoritative, and artful that represented the self-definition of persons of sensibility, a contrast manifested in the familiar, normal style of the sentimental novel versus the formal, classically informed style of traditional publications, the former associated above all with subordinated women, the latter with hierarchically educated men. The former was also the kind Abigail wanted more of from John, telling him as she did during their courtship that her words came "warm from the *heart*" (see chapter 6). It could be inferred from this that Tyler was a polished wit and not a man of genuine feeling.

That Tyler sat down to write surrounded by published books may well have signified his self-consciousness as a literary artist—here we have the advantage of knowing that Tyler was soon to burst on the public scene as a professional dramatist. One irony is that the heartfelt writing that Mary limited to correspondence was in Abigail's case loaded with allusions to her reading and, further, that her conception of Emelia's and Selim's relationship had a very literary and dramatic shape, largely stage-managed as well as represented by herself, although her artfulness in this regard was a perspective of which she was, perhaps, not fully conscious. Finally in this letter to her sister, Mary spelled out her accusation that Tyler was careless of Nabby's feelings, in effect, that he lacked sensibility: "I ask'd him also what excuse he could make for his neglect. He said he should make none. I confess I felt too much to answer him." Thus, for Mary to present herself experiencing the highest pitch of feeling was to give emphasis to her definition of Tyler, in keeping with the contrast in the speed with which they replied to letters. We cannot say what Tyler's refusal to respond to Mary's charge meant. Perhaps a proud and learned

man simply resisted his nosey landlady. She, however, combining some
knowledge of his youth with sentimental stereotype and with what she
picked out from his recent behavior, above all in his manner of correspondence with her niece and his supposed beloved, felt herself qualified
to say that he did not feel what he should have.

Meanwhile, and before she heard from Mary, Abigail engaged another
member of her family, her trusted uncle Cotton Tufts, to prod Tyler
to keep up his reformation. She wrote Tufts in May 1785 telling him:
"[Nabby] is well and a Good child. I hope she will ever be a happy one
and to this purpose sir, I wish you to give advise to a Young Friend of
hers, when ever you see it necessary." She linked this request to anxiety,
which she appeared to imply Nabby shared: "I was not without anxiety,
as every thoughtfull young person must be, when they are going to connect themselves for Life, when I changed a Single for a Married State.
I need not say to you Sir that my own union has been of the happiest
kind"—this was to leave aside all the pain of separation and near widowhood to which Abigail's letters testify, exactly the pain Abigail now
witnessed her daughter suffering, the more painful to Abigail, perhaps,
because it was suffering that Abigail herself had doubly engineered—
"but I am not the less desirous that my daughter should prove so too,
tho I have had more fears and more anxieties for her than ever I felt for
myself. This Sir is between ourselves."[27]

The month after Abigail had written to Uncle Tufts, Mary again
wrote her of Tyler's worse-than-unsatisfactory handling of correspondence, detailing his failure to pass along the letters to others that Nabby
had enclosed in the "Paquit" she sent him: "It is one of his whims not to
deliver Letters for a long time after he has recev'd them. He would not
like to be Serv'd so himself." Here, however, Mary raised the issue of
what Abigail was to say of this to Nabby: "You may read this to her or
not, as you may think best." She hinted that she could have said more.
She wanted to write "with more freedom": "If there is any thing which
you may wish to be inform'd of which I have not told you ask me, and I
will endeavour to satisfy you." This was certainly a letter marked with
a ☉. She was worried that her letters might be opened. The editors
suggest that her July 19 letter to Abigail may have been showing caution with regard to the same mysterious subject. She told Abigail that
she had written her two letters recently that, when done, she "thought
proper to commit to the Flames": "There are many things which would
do to be said, that it would not be prudent to commit to writing." She
did refer explicitly to Tyler later in the letter, to say that as for news of

"Mr. Palmer's family Mr. Tyler must give you an account of them. He knows much more about them than any one else." This points to the subject that Mary was endeavoring to repress and that she would explain in subsequent letters.[28]

## Dismissal

On or about August 11, 1785, Nabby sent Tyler this note, or one very like it:

> Sir
> Here with you receive your letters and miniature with my desire that you return mine to my Uncle Cranch, and my hopes that you are well satisfied with the affair as is.
>
>                                                                    AA

This survived only in Tyler's wife's memoir, written long after the event—and it was an inaccurate copy insofar as the uncle thus commissioned was Cotton Tufts.[29] The day before its most likely date, Colonel William Smith, two years older than Tyler, Adams's secretary in London, and residing with the Adamses there, left them for a trip to continental Europe. This was because Abigail, discerning his interest in Nabby, had told him, as she later wrote John Quincy, that Nabby was still "under engagements" with Tyler.[30] Abigail, however, was encouraging Smith's suit. Smith wrote a note to her from Harwich, en route, having previously, Abigail said in her reply to him (two days after Nabby dismissed Tyler), "tendered [her his] services and asked [her] commands." She told him that she wanted him to think of her on his trip while he wrote a "journal" that they would enjoy together on his return. She intimated that Nabby thought positively of him: "I presume that the family would join me in their regards to you, if they knew that I was writing; you will, from the knowledge you have of them, believe them your well wishers and friends, as well as your humble servant, A. Adams."[31]

Two days after that letter, Abigail wrote Mary an account and explanation of Nabby's dismissal of Tyler. Because she had wanted to seize the chance to send her reply to Mary's of April 25 on June 24, she told Mary that had not "noticed certain parts of your Letter, some of which gave me anxiety, particularly that which related to a certain Gentleman, of whose present affairs, or future intentions we know nothing of." Mary's April 25 letter had addressed the subject of Tyler's behavior extensively, but Abigail's reply had been an extremely detailed account of her and Nabby's reception by the British queen, and she had responded hardly at all to the contents of Mary's letter. "Captain Dashwood came [while] I have not half done," she had said.[32]

In this letter of August 15, Abigail continued: "I had written you upon this Subject but not having time to transcribe more than half my Letter, that part was omitted." This unsent section of the letter, it can be inferred, addressed the subject of Tyler as if Nabby was, in Abigail's retrospective phrase, still "under engagements" with him: "I am not sorry that it was [omitted], as neither he or his affairs in future will be of any material importance to us, for when this reaches you it will accompany a *final* dismission of him."

Prior to this dramatic turn of events, Abigail implied, she had to glean indirectly what was going on in her daughter's mind: "I have for sometime observed a more than common anxiety in the appearance of your niece, which I sometimes attributed to the absence of her Brother." It is true that Nabby and John Quincy had grown very close in France, and their subsequent long letters to each other show how much they missed one another after he returned to Massachusetts. But, Abigail went on, "several times she had dropt hints as if returning to America soon was not the object nearest her Heart and I knew that nothing had taken place here to attach her." The editors note that this "ignores William Stephens Smith's recent interest in [Nabby], which may not have been reciprocated by her,"[33] although Abigail was already encouraging Smith's hopes.

Abigail's letter to Mary continued: "[A] few days since, something arose which led [Nabby] to ask me if I did not think a Gentleman of her Acquaintance a Man of Honour." Given the date of Smith's departure (August 9), that the reason for his doing so included his unreciprocated feelings for Nabby, and that Abigail had told him she was still engaged to Tyler, this was Colonel Smith. Abigail seized the opportunity to contrast this "Gentleman" with Tyler: "I replied yes, a Man of strict honour, and I wisht I could say that of all her acquaintances." She must have given the word *all*, and probably *acquaintances*, particular emphasis and, perhaps, accompanied the sentence with facial expressions to make sure that Nabby could read her: "[As] she could not mistake my meaning, instead of being affected as I apprehended she said, a breach of honour in one party would not justify it in the other." Nabby felt free to raise the issue that, according to this exchange, had been causing her anxiety: whether she was now free to repudiate Tyler, even if she was now convinced of his "demerrits."

"I thought this the very time to speak," Abigail continued. "I said if she was conscious of any want of honour on the part of the Gentleman, I and every Friend she had in the world, would rejoice if she could liberate herself." What did Nabby think Tyler had said or done that showed a "want of honour?" Existing letters point to the fact that, in the eyes specifically of Mary and now Abigail, Tyler had not reformed his manners. His inability to send Nabby letters "warm from the *heart*" and his willingness to cause her emotional pain contravened any notion that his feelings for her were still genuine, and that idea may have revived her first impressions of him, that he was a Chesterfieldian deceiver. She was imbued with the same sentimental values her parents were. So long as her mother had argued against stereotype or Tyler had seemed to have reformed, or at least was on the way to becoming so, Nabby had allowed her heart to melt. But, if Mary could interpret Tyler's failures in his writing to his fiancée as the intentional giving of pain to a lady of sensibility and his failure to distribute Nabby's letters as a breach of trust, how much more was that the case with Nabby herself?

Abigail's next paragraph supplies evidence of Nabby's thinking prior to sending Tyler her "dismission": "Here ended the conversation she retired to her Chamber and I to mine. About two hours after she sent me a Billet, with the copy of two Letters which she desired one to communicate if I thought proper." Nabby did not want to speak to her mother face-to-face, although she did want to continue to question her: "In the Billet she asks if her Father was included in the Friends I mentioned." They were those who would "rejoice if [Nabby] could liberate herself" from her engagement to Tyler. Nabby "adds"—the verb's present tense suggesting that Abigail was now paraphrasing the billet directly—"that she dreads [her father's] displeasure, and will not in future take a step unapproved by him."

Realizing that Nabby was ready to ditch Tyler, Abigail paused in her account to exclaim to Mary: "Thanks Heaven that her mind is in not so weak a state as to feel a partiality which is not returnd." This is what Nabby's billet had also said, and it confirms that Nabby had come to believe that Tyler no longer loved her, if he ever had, although he had not told her so. (Her mother, also suffering from an absence of letters from John, had been brought to a similar fear.) Abigail went on: "There is no state of mind so painfull as that which admits, of fear, suspicion doubt, dread and apprehension." This was a paraphrase of what Nabby's billet conveyed to her mother, of what she had come to feel about Tyler in light of his "neglect" of her. Abigail moved into a direct quotation of it: "'I have too long' says she 'known them all—and I am determined to know them no longer.'" Nabby here may have extended that "too long" a period back to her original deep suspicion of Tyler that she had expressed in her letters to Betsy Cranch.

Nabby's billet asked what her father thought about Tyler and about her ending her engagement to him, so Abigail next told Mary: "You may be sure I did not fail of communicating the whole to her Father, the result of which was a conversation with her." She reported: "He told her that it was a serious matter, and that he hoped it was upon mature deliberation that she acted"—one is reminded of his favorable remarks on Nabby's earlier reserve, in contrast to her mother's precipitousness— "that he was a perfect stranger to the Gentleman, that his Character had been such as to induce him to give his consent not so freely as he would wish: but because he conceived her affection engaged." This was consistent with that letter in which he did give his reserved consent, deferring to his daughter's feelings. The next sentence of his reported words to Nabby was in response to the question she now directly asked him, having tried it out first on her mother (and we do not know whether Abigail was present during the interview, but it does seem likely). John pinpointed the evidence for Nabby's doubts: "But if she had reason to question the strictest honour of the Gentleman, or supposed him capable of telling her that he had written Letters when he had not, he had rather follow her to her Grave, than see her united with him." This was the familiar, passionately extreme John, at last able to vent directly to Nabby what previously he had confined to his letters to her mother.

Abigail then explained to Mary in detail what John had summarized: "[Nabby] has not received but one Letter since last December, and that a short one, and by what I can learn only four since she left America." That was between June 20, 1784, and August 15, 1785. "He says that he had written to her and to her parents by way of Amsterdam." Abigail declared now: "I doubted it when [Nabby] told me, tho I kept silence, but I find now she is of the same opinion." Now Nabby requested more restraint of her mother and everyone else "that neither the Name or subject may ever be mentioned to her," and Abigail then expressed the hope that none of Nabby's "Friends will be so unwise to solicit for him. The Palmers will be most likely, but the die is cast." A striking detail in this account of the denouement of the relationship, as in the case of its beginning, is that nowhere does Abigail refer to her daughter by name, instead introducing her in the letter as "your Neice" and referring to her subsequently as "she."

Abigail wrote Mary another account of this decisive episode ten months later, the day after Nabby married Colonel Smith, having dreamed of Tyler the night of the marriage: "I have felt for him I own," she said in explanation, "[but] sure I own that his conduct in neglecting to write to her as he did for months and Months together, was no evidence of regard or attachment. Yet I have repeatedly heard [Nabby] tell him"—presumably when they had been in Braintree and while she was overcoming her apprehensions that Tyler was operating in a Chesterfieldian manner— "that she would erase from her Heart and mind every sentiment of affection how Strong so ever, if she was conscious that it was not returnd and that She was incapable of loveing the Man, who did not Love her."[34]

In this account, Abigail summarizes Nabby's "fear, suspicion doubt, dread, and apprehension" as: "Much and many Months did she suffer before She brought herself to renounce him for ever." Still, Nabby had not "given any incouragement to Col. S." Abigail was vehement in placing the responsibility for the breakup on Tyler's behavior, rather than a new prospect entering a scene where John, finally, could play the decisive role Abigail wanted. According to this version of events, during Colonel Smith's "absence," Nabby "received a Letter from him," Tyler, that is, which "she laid . . . before her Father and begged him to advise her, if upon perusing it he considered it a satisfactory justification," that is, for her dismissal of Tyler. Here Abigail added: "May he [Tyler] never know or feel, half the Misiry, She sufferd for many days. Upon perusing the Letter mr A. was much affected. I read it—I knew his *cant* and *grimace*, I had been too often the dupe of it myself." In retrospect, Tyler had behaved as the artful, predatory deceiver against whom Fordyce, typically, had warned, and Abigail, a woman of sometimes excessive sensibility, had been his first victim in the immediate Adams family, her admission here touching on her own responsiveness to this apparent man of feeling who only seemed to put himself in her power. In John's hardeyed view, she had let herself be courted. At this point in the second version of the process whereby Tyler was dismissed, with John now "much affected," Abigail told Mary: "I then thought it my duty to lay before mr A some letters from you, which he had never seen." She continued: "He returned the letter of mr T's to your Niece and told her the Man was unworthy of her, and advised her not to write him a line." He also "thought it proper" that Abigail write to him. She did, but the letter has not been found. Again Abigail does not name her daughter until the conclusion of the letter, where she emphasizes: "*Mr and Mrs Smith* present their regards to all their Friends and mine." It is hard to resist repeating John's fundamental view that "the Principal Design of a young Lady from her Birth to her Marriage [is] to procure and prepare herself for a worthy Companion in Life."[35]

In her earlier account of the dismissal, Abigail reported that Nabby "appears much more cheerful since she has unburthend her mind" but that the wrong words could still touch a nerve. Abigail had reiterated the request Nabby had made, in terms expressing the operation and values of sensibility: "There is however a degree of delicacy necessary to be preserved, between persons who have thought favorably of each other, even in their seperation. I do not wish that a syllable more may be said upon the subject, than just to vindicate her, and I believe very little will do that, in the Eye of the world." That Nabby had broken the engagement when Tyler's friends might "continue to solicit for him" in the belief that he still wanted to marry her needed vindication, although, here, the Adamses could capitalize on what Abigail had said "the World" already believed of Tyler's character.[36]

Meanwhile, Colonel Smith wrote Abigail early in September from Berlin, addressing her as "My dear Madam," and opening by excusing himself for writing to her rather, say, than to John: "Your benevolence I know will excuse the particularity of this address, when you confide in the assurance of its proceeding from a sincere heart nourishing the most exalted sentiments of the virtue and sensibility of yours." This, too, could be construed as courting a mother. Smith continued with further indirection: "I feel myself complimented by your confidence and believe I am not capable of abusing it. I hope for an advocate in you, should Mr. Adams think my absence long." Smith's prolongation of his journey was of considerable annoyance to John, "who found himself coping with an extensive correspondence in the fall without a secretary." Smith represented his journey as a sentimental one, asking Abigail in reference to John: "Tell him—what will you tell him? Can you say with Stern that it is a quiet Journey of the heart in pursuit of those affections which make us love each other, and the world better than we do(?)"—this was a quotation of *A Sentimental Journey* and presumably he hoped Nabby would move from well-wishing and friendship to love—"or will you say he is flying from?" He hints that he was escaping the pain of unrequited love, or worse, his beloved's being engaged to another: "Hush, madam not a lisp?"—that is, to Nabby or even John—"but I will not dictate, say what you please. Whatever you say and do (confiding in the spring of your actions) I will subscribe to it." The letter then described his journey, Smith at times self-consciously imitating Sterne's *Sentimental Journey*.[37]

Abigail replied to this letter on September 18, the day after the evening on which she received it. As far as Smith's hopes for Nabby's hand were concerned, Abigail wrote: "Prudence dictates silence to me. . . . There are entanglingment as Lady G. terms them"—this reference to Richardson's third novel (whence Abigail took her masculine ideal) sustained the sentimental-literary tone that she adopted with her new prospective son-in-law—"from which Time the great solaces of Humane woe only can relieve in." She became more positively reassuring: "And Time I dare say will extricate those I Love from any unapproved Step, into which inexperience and youth may involve them." The correspondence tells a different story of the approval of Nabby's responsiveness to Tyler, but who was to enlighten Smith? Abigail concluded the subject: "But until that period may arrive Honour, Honour, is at stake—a word to the wise is sufficient." Extrication was at hand; in this same letter, Abigail told Smith that Charles Storer was about to sail to New York, as he did shortly thereafter, bearing Nabby's letter that ended the "entanglement" with Tyler.[38]

In sum, the sequence eligible suitor is attracted to daughter and is recognized, encouraged, and mediated by mother until daughter reciprocates repeated the sequence of the Tyler-Abigail-Nabby triangle. Colonel Smith proposed to Nabby in a December 1785 letter to Abigail, and the letter's terms show that he was in close touch with Abigail. The breach was still fresh: Abigail was preoccupied with placing the blame for it on Tyler, rather than on her daughter, let alone explaining how soon a new suitor had replaced Nabby's fiancé. After telling Abigail of his "increasing interest in her sentiments," Smith wrote disingenuously: "I have some reason to believe that the late Connection which appeared an Obstacle to the accomplishment of the Wish nearest my heart exists no longer. And from the opinion I have of the Lady, am persuaded, that nothing dishonourable on her part could have occasioned it." He next proposed to connect himself for life to Abigail's "Amiable Daughter" and then hypothesized that "perhaps" this "Communication," Abigail "might think, ought to be made to Mr. Adams," but he explained: "I feel more easy in the communication with you." "[This] mode"—a letter to Abigail, rather than the "long and formal Letter" to John—"may answer every end, as I suppose you will be in a great measure governed by his sentiments on the Subject, it is probable, you will submit this to his perusal."[39]

Ensuing transatlantic correspondence addressed Tyler's reaction and the extraordinary precipitousness of Nabby's acceptance of Colonel Smith.

The wedding took place on June 12, 1786. In that letter to Mary describing the wedding, Abigail told her to tell "Betsy and Lucy that they would Love [Colonel Smith] for that manly tenderness, that *real* and *unaffected* delicacy of Mind and Manners which his every sentiment and action discovers." Smith's sensibility was Grandisonian, in implicit contrast to Tyler's, now characterized as a mask, as John had apprehended at the beginning. Abigail ruminated: "Who that had told your Neice two years ago, that an English Bishop should marry her, and that to a Gentleman who she had then never seen. . . ? Had Such an Idea been Started, she would never have consented to have come abroad."[40]

Mary had one more and most damning revelation of Tyler's rakery to convey, spelling out why she had said that Abigail need not fear any repercussions from General Palmer's family. Tyler fathered a child, Sophia, on Betsy Palmer during the absence of her husband, Joseph. Betsy was only two years older than Tyler; she and her four sisters were "celebrated for their beauty." Tyler had "made frequent visits" to the Palmer's house in Germantown while still boarding with the Cranches, and "Joseph Pearse Palmer became one of his closest friends." Mary Palmer "recalled that the two were 'twin souls,' and that Tyler was repeatedly [the Palmer's] 'friend in a time of need.'" One reason for his shifting his lodging from the Cranches to the Palmers (adding to Mary Cranch's hostility, perhaps) had been to contribute rent to the desperate Palmers. The date of the baby's birth, September 2, 1786, was the clue that set Mary on the track of its mother's adultery. "We live in an age of discovery," she had written in punning hyperbole to Abigail. "One of our acquaintances has discovered that a full grown, fine child may be produc'd in less than five months as well as nine, provided the mother should meet with a small fright before its Birth. You may laugh: but it is true. The Ladys Husband is so well satisfied of it that he does not have the least suspicion of its being otherways, but how can it be? for he left this part of the country the beginning of september last, and did not return till the Sixth of April, and his wife brought him this fine Girl the first day of this present month."[41]

So Mary had now revealed the "reason" that Abigail need not fear the "disapprobation" of the Palmers, of which she had written mysteriously the same October, coupling it with "[Tyler] boards at Mrs. Palmers." Mrs. Palmer—Betsy—conceived Sophia with Tyler two months or so after he received Nabby's letter of dismissal. It seems likely that the two letters that, as Mary wrote Abigail, she "committed to the Flames" in July had contained observations or rumors of an improper degree of intimacy between Tyler and Betsy; before the evidence of the baby's birth, Mary had somehow "picked up a Letter" written by Betsy in Joseph's absence, "directed to a gentleman" who, she made clear, was Tyler, "with such sentences as this in it. 'I am distress'd, distress'd by many causes, what can we do. I know you would help me if you could. Come to me immediately.'—'O, think of me, and think of your Self.'" This presentation of a female self to a male self was a convention of sensibility: Abigail presented herself to John in this way. It was the fictional Maria's tearful distress that turned on Sterne's Yorick, and Maria Reynolds presented herself to Alexander Hamilton as a lady in distress when wishing to seduce him, at least in Hamilton's account. Mary reported her response to this letter: "It alarm'd me. It was so mysterious but it is no longer so."[42]

The size of what she said was the "full grown" baby was further evidence that it had been brought to term, rather than being premature: "It was the largest she ever had her Mother says. I thought So myself, but I could not say it." Others in the neighborhood gossiped, but it was Mary who acted: "It was a matter of so much speculation that I was determin'd to see it. I went with trembling Steps, and could not tell whether I should have courage enough to see it till I had Knock'd at the Door. I was ask'd to walk up, by, and was follow'd by her Husband. The Lady was seting by the side of the Bed suckling her Infant and not far from her ———"—here she represents Tyler with a dash, but the context makes it clear that it was him—"with one slipper off, and one foot just step'd into the other." They had not been face-to-face since May, and Mary knew Tyler blamed her for Nabby's rejection of him, writing to vindicate himself "at [her] expense," she would reiterate, blaming her for "enjuring him so." When, self-righteously determined, she came into the room, Mary reported: "[Tyler] look'd, I cannot tell you how. He did not rise from his seat, perhaps he could not. I spoke to him and he answer'd me, but hobble'd off as quick as he could without saying any thing more to me. There appear'd the most perfect harmony between all three." Mary concluded her account of this visit: "I make no remarks Your own mind will furnish you with sufficient ematter for sorrow and joy, and many other sensations, or I am mistaken." The "joy," of course, would be relief that Nabby had escaped Tyler.[43]

Mary went back to the Palmers a few days later, reporting the visit to Abigail. After describing what in her view was Tyler's elaborate but fruitless act to gain "consolations" from her and her daughters on Nabby's departure and his blaming her and others for fatally injuring his reputation with Nabby, she described the following conversation with Betsy Palmer. Nabby, Betsy said, "never would have treated him [Tyler] in such a manner only for not writing him." Mary commented: "That was not all, and he knows it." Betsy replied: "Well he has Suffer'd for it I am sure, poor creature. He had nobody but me to open his mind too." This followed Mary's account of her family's "unfeeling" refusal to be taken in. Mary told Abigail her unspoken response to the new mother: "and happy had it been for *you* and *yours*, if he had not open'd so much of it to you unhappy woman I could have said." Betsy had gone on to give her opinion of Nabby's marriage to Colonel Smith: "She has not better'd herself by what I can hear. My Brother and Sister know him, and say he is a man of no abilities and is of no profession and in any thing will not bear a comparison with [Tyler]."[44]

Mary compared her recent three letters' account of this affair to a sentimental novel, one she knew Abigail had read: laid "together," they would lead Abigail to "think of the Pupil of Pleasure, of Philip Sedley, and be thankful." The editors note that Sedley, "the title character of Samuel Jackson Pratt's *The Pupil of Pleasure*, 1778, employs dissimulation, hypocrisy, and a pleasing façade to increase his personal profit and pleasure, the consequences of which introduce greater sorrow and vice into the community." The putative "editress" of this epistolary novel presented it as "a biographical commentary on the text of Chesterfield." Mary said that she could send Abigail still more "anecdotes" of Tyler's recent "gallantry in this Town" and asked: "Is it not astonishing that he should be continu'd in the family and no notice taken?" A theory by "Some" was that, while Joseph Palmer "felt" it "severly," he needed Tyler's rent so much that "they have made a bargain." Whether this was simply that he would accept Tyler's insemination of Betsy or that Tyler and Betsy could go on making love is not clear.[45]

Mary returned yet again to view this remarkable ménage à trois, writing of the Palmers: "They seem all of them to be very Sensible of the Injury that has been done the family." She described Tyler as "this disturber of the peace of Familys," like Philip Sedley: "It is a serious affair to break up such a large one, besides the disgrace which will forever attend even the Innocent ones of it." The latter included baby Sophia and, perhaps, her older sister, Mary Palmer. But it was Joseph Palmer whom Mary Cranch had particularly in mind: "A man looks very Silly with a pair of horns stuck in his Front—and yet to suffer the enemy of ones peace to be under the same roof and to See—dividing her leering (I will not say tender) looks between himself and her Paramour is too much for

Human nature to bear." "O my sister," she exclaimed to Abigail in this letter, "you do not half know him yet, he will not long have any thing to do at Braintree, I believe I should not wonder if he should pack up and go to new york. I hope he will pay us first."[46]

To New York Tyler went, and to a dramatic triumph, but only after military and diplomatic adventures in New England, to which he subsequently returned, establishing himself as a successful lawyer in Guilford, Vermont. Thence he "made periodic trips south to visit the Palmers" and eventually found Joseph a job in Vermont. He proposed to Mary when she was seventeen and he was thirty-seven, but their engagement was kept secret for two years because of the opposition of her mother, Betsy Palmer, who was herself only thirty-nine. In 1798, the twelve-year-old Sophia went to live with the Tylers in Vermont. The editors of the Adams correspondence, earlier in the same note writing that she was "allegedly fathered by Royall Tyler," conclude that, while "her "paternity was never openly acknowledged, . . . it was known to later generations of the Cranch and Tyler families."[47]

Ryerson refers to the marriage of Nabby and Colonel Smith as the "tragic result" of "her mother's courting," although he baulks at crediting "Nabby's disastrous choice of a husband to Abigail": "Smith turned out to be an unprincipled and improvident disaster and Nabby spent over 25 years trapped in an increasingly insecure and finally hopeless marriage." Ten years after her glowing letters to her relatives about the colonel's sterling moral qualities, a judgment she reiterated the day after his marriage to Nabby (he was a "Man of strict honour, unblemished reputation and Morals"), Abigail wrote John that the "col. Is a Man wholly devoid of judgement . . . and has led his Family into a state of living which I fear his means would not bear him out in." A few months later, she wrote: "[He has] gone a journey, I knew not where, I could not converse with [Nabby]. I saw her Heart too full." After months, he returned to face his creditors. Abigail wrote: "I am glad he has returnd. It really seemd to me at times as if Mrs. Smith would lose herself. She has sometimes written me that life is a burden to her and she was little short of distraction." John wrote of Colonel Smith in 1799: "All the Actions of my Life and all the Conduct of my Children have not yet disgraced me so much as this Man." The previous month he had exclaimed over the suffering Smith had brought his daughter, a woman and wife "without fault:" "Unfortunate Daughter! Unhappy Child!"[48]

# PART IV

# Conclusion

## CHAPTER 14

# The Americanization
# of Sensibility

## Republicanism and Sensibility

Following Robbins's book on the metropolitan "commonwealthman"
and "True Whig," or "republican," political thought, Bernard Bailyn,
Gordon S. Wood, and J. G. A. Pocock demonstrated that it supplied the
ideological origins of the American Revolution. As Addison's *Cato* illustrates, republicanism had long overlapped with the ideology of sensibility. According to Robbins, the essays of Addison and Steele, including
the *Spectator*, "spread mild Whiggery everywhere." They presented it
with the language of sensibility: Addison's more directly Whig *Guardian*
of September 15, 1713, consistent with that change in manly ideals epitomized by Dryden, described certain men as having a "fine and delicate"
"sense of honour" and contrasted them with those who treated that sense
of honor with "ridicule" because "their imaginations have grown callous,
and have lost all those delicate sensations which are natural to minds that
are innocent and undepraved." John Adams prided himself on precisely
this kind of honor; so did Richardson's heroes, and his novels show his
general sympathy for the political views of his Whig contemporaries.
That Francis Hutcheson and Adam Smith, primary exponents of the
intellectual and moral rationale for sensibility, are subjects of Robbins's
*Eighteenth-Century Commonwealthman* also illustrates the fact that republicanism and the culture of sensibility long had common ground.[1]

Wood's 1992 *The Radicalism of the American Revolution* makes explicit
a relation between republicanism and sensibility: "enlightened and re-
publicanized gentry," finding common ground with "their inferiors,"
"gave birth to . . . humanitarian sensibility—a powerful force that we of
the twentieth century have inherited and further expanded." His metaphor of causation, however, can serve to remind us that the influence
of women played a significant part, along with the values propagated
by religion and sentimental literature. Wood quotes Josiah Quincy's

1770 exclamation against the British government's minion Governor Hutchinson: "Good Good! What must be the distress, the sentiments, and feelings of a people, legislated, condemned and governed, by a creature so mercenary, so dependent, and so—but I forbear: my anguish is too exquisite—my heart too full!" David Waldstreicher writes of "republican sentimentalism" in America during the period 1776–1820, and Sarah Knott notes that sensibility served "as a congenial complement to the antique austerity of republicanism." For both sensibility and republicanism, the "world" was one of duplicity and power-hungry, self-interested politicians, and, in both, the innocent and virtuous yearned for reform.[2]

John Adams immersed himself in republican writings as he adapted them to American opposition to Britain's imperial power. He also owned and autographed the works of John Milton, another commonwealthman, whose "vast compass" astonished him. Abigail quoted a passage from *Paradise Lost*, "adapted for her purpose," in a letter to Mercy Otis Warren. Because of Milton's profoundly influential views of gender and marriage (despite the absence of sentimental language in his great poem), Jean Hagstrum argues in *Sex and Sensibility* that they stood at the headwaters of the art that celebrated sensibility: they were sharply gendered and, for that reason, targeted by Wollstonecraft.[3]

Another republican book that Adams owned, and one to which Abigail referred, was John Trenchard and Thomas Gordon's *Cato's Letters*, its title identifying its authors' political ideals with the figure deemed emblematic of republican Roman virtue and popularized in the revised form presented by Addison's sentimental tragedy. Gibbon's *The Decline and Fall of the Roman Empire* was not published until 1776, but its history, to which Gibbon, like Hume, applied sensational psychology, reinforced the lesson that his republican predecessors had held up to Augustan Britain, that "the subordination of republican manhood to tyranny, imperial ambition, the corruption of courtly manners, and the degenerative effects of luxury . . . led to effeminacy" and the triumph of Caesarism. This, too, was a book John had in his library. Abigail read Hume's history.[4]

An ideology that attacked government as corrupt and tending toward Roman imperialism had been of great value to Tories in opposition (to Whigs), as well. One of the best known of them was Henry St. John, Viscount Bolingbroke, to whom Pope dedicated the *Essay on Man*. Bolingbroke compared the British government to that of the emperor Augustus, writing: "We must not wonder that the people who bore the *tyrants*, bore the *libertines*." Eventually, John's library held several volumes of the writings of Bolingbroke, who became "one of his favorite authors." Early during her sojourn in France, Abigail referred to Bolingbroke's "Reflections on Exile" in a letter she wrote to her sister, whom she assumed knew of Bolingbroke's views.[5]

One eighteenth-century commonwealthwoman whose five-volume history of England John owned, and with whom Abigail as well as John corresponded, was Catherine Macaulay. Warren, too, corresponded with Macaulay—for ten years—and the British republican writer helped inspire the American republican's *History of the American Revolution*. It was Macaulay's *Letters on Education* on which Wollstonecraft drew in *A Vindication of the Rights of Woman*, a book known by both Adamses.[6] Like Macaulay, Wollstonecraft was an eighteenth-century commonwealthwoman. The self-consciously gendered analysis in this republican tradition, which characterized the damage done to manhood by corrupt government as "effeminizing," held potential for women. Wollstonecraft had begun to develop this point in her reply to Burke's *Reflections on the Revolution in France*, which had referred to the same gendered view of women as creatures of disabling sensibility, as had his earlier book on the sublime and the beautiful, debated by John Adams and his friends, and quoted and scorned by Wollstonecraft in her *Vindication of the Rights of Men* (1790). John owned Wollstonecraft's *Historical and Moral View of the French Revolution* (1794), which he annotated heavily.[7]

## Sensibility Adopted by American Revolutionaries

In the 1760s, and prior to the Revolution, alienated and violent frontiersmen—the Regulators of backcountry South Carolina and the "Paxton Boys" of backcountry Pennsylvania—put the language of sensibility to use, ironically presenting themselves as figures of virtue in distress, persecuted by their hard-hearted governments, hoisting the gentry with its own, moralistic petard.[8]

In January 1766, John wrote a series of pieces opposing a defender of Parliament's power to pass the Stamp Act. He began by voicing the suspicions that this defender's "humanity was counterfeited" and that his "ardor for liberty cankered with simulation." The counterfeiting of humanity was equivalent to "licentiousness," from which the counterfeiter had made a "sudden transition . . . to despotism." The origin of this revolution lay in the heart, and, here, Adams's republican language coincided

even more apparently with that of sentimental fiction. In the same series, John characterized American people's virtue in a way that implied
the kind of historical development of sensibility assumed by Shaftesbury,
the Latitudinarians, and Carter, "with the high sentiments of the Romans, in the most prosperous and virtuous times of that commonwealth,"
not, that is, of degenerate and imperial times, but "with the tender
feelings of humanity, and the noble benevolence of Christians."[9]

And, having asserted in this 1766 series, "All men are born equal,"
Adams warned that, because British judges—part of "the executive
branch"—were uncommonly rich and great, "they might learn to despise the common people, and forget the feelings of humanity." As we
have seen, *humanity* reflected the scientific view of human nature and,
therefore, was something everyone had in common, but, like the *Spectator*, Adams also preserved the cultural, class distinctions reflected in his
qualifying *people* as *common*. He was to defend the Constitution in 1788
by writing that "the people of all nations are naturally divided into two
sorts, the gentlemen and the simplemen, a word here chosen to signify
the common people."[10]

Long having shared a "transatlantic culture of sensibility" with the
metropolitan British, many colonists had hoped that their suffering
would move those in power to compassion and to change their policy.
In 1768, Phillis Wheatley represented the repeal of the Townshend Act
in such terms, and, in his 1772 Boston Massacre Oration, Joseph Warren
declared that, "so sensible" was Britain of her interest "in the prosperity of the colonies, she must eventually feel every wound given to their
freedom," and he told his Boston audience: "She must from a sympathy of soul . . . pray for your success." That her correspondent was English helps explain why, in 1773, Abigail composed for Edward Dilly
a particularly sentimental representation of virtuous Bostonians' being
distressed by the British and those colonists who joined them in "trai-
torously betraying their Country." She cried out to Dilly as a representative of people of sensibility in Britain: "What is next to take place God
only knows but we think if you love us if you feel for us you cannot any
longer suffer a Spirit of blindness and infatuation to delude you."[11]

Americans were disillusioned, their attempt to elicit British compassion futile. A letter in 1775 from the "Continental Congress to the Inhabitants of Great Britain" reported: "If justice and humanity have lost
their influence on your hearts, still motives are not wanting to excite
your indignation at the measures now pursued." The British immigrant

Thomas Paine ended his introduction to *Common Sense* (1775) with this version of virtue in distress:

> [Britain's] laying a Country desolate with Fire and Sword, declaring War against the natural rights of all Mankind, and extirpating the Defenders thereof from the Face of the Earth, is the concern of every Man to whom Nature hath given the Power of feeling: of which Class, regardless of Party Censure, is the
>
> *Author.*

Americans could be aroused and united on the basis of their loyalty to the values of sensibility, while metropolitan Britons had betrayed those values. The Declaration of Independence expressed the theme of disillusionment; like the tyrant king, "our British brethren . . . have been deaf to the voice of justice and consanguinity." This was an appeal based on family feeling.[12]

In the "Taxation No Tyranny" pamphlet of 1775 to which I referred in chapter 7, Dr. Johnson identified the Americans' appeal as sentimental but dismissed it as insincere. He observed of those documents issued by the First Continental Congress that their authors used "many artifices" to "perplex the opinion of the publick," adding that these artifices "lose their force when counteracting one another," which "usually happens when falsehood is to be maintained by fraud." The first artifice was sentimentality: "The nation is sometimes to be mollified by a tender tale of men who fled from tyranny to rocks and desarts." This was the vision of the original settlement by English colonists widely propounded during the Revolution (one such proponent was Joseph Warren). Johnson observed that Britain is "persuaded to lose all claims of justice, and all sense of dignity in compassion for a harmless people . . . who are now invaded by unprecedented oppression, and plundered . . . by the harpies of taxation." He then specified the intrusion of a counteracting artifice by the resolutions' authors (the most prominent was John Adams): "But while we are melting in silent sorrow, and in the transports of delicious pity, dropping both the sword and balance from our hands," other language was aimed "to awaken another passion and tries to alarm our interest, or excite our veneration, by accounts of [the Americans'] greatness and their opulence."[13]

Johnson also described "the delirious dream of republican fanaticism," his irony addressed to "ye sons and daughters of liberty." Among the republican writers to whom he referred was "a female patriot bewailing the miseries of her 'friends and fellow citizens,'" quoting Macaulay's *An Address to the People of England, Scotland and Ireland, on the Present Important Crisis of Affairs* (1775). "Slavery," he wrote, "glides too cold into our hearts, by the soft conveyance of female prose." Abigail wrote Macaulay at this time to answer a question Macaulay had asked John about "our American ladies," doing so in the sentimental language that Johnson deemed insincere: "Should I attempt to describe to you the complicated miseries and distresses brought upon us by the late inhumane acts of the British parliament my pen would fail me."[14]

Johnson's reference to daughters as well as sons "of liberty" picked up on a phrase frequently used in American newspapers from 1769 in reference to women's boycotts of tea and other British imports. The Continental Congress had adapted the goals of the reformation of manners (an ideal that republicans shared with cultivators of sensibility) to patriot purpose. For example, "card playing, cockfighting and horseracing were discouraged as frivolous," and ostentatious mourning, including "the customary giving of scarves and gloves," was "curtailed." Those "superfluities of life" marking the consumer revolution were to be sacrificed, their curtailment enforced where necessary by committees of safety. Critics of women's excessive consumption of British goods said that it undercut "the efforts of American men to develop a national culture." Fordyce's argument that British women—of course, American women had been at least nominally British when they bought his book in Philadelphia or Boston—contributed to national prosperity, national identity, by purchasing British goods rather than the more fashionable French ones was Americanized.[15]

Most famously, Americans boycotted tea. Hannah Griffitts called on ladies:

> Come, sacrifice to Patriot fame,
> And give up your Tea.

Men's chucking of the tea into Boston Harbor and calling it a *tea party*, however, illustrates that not all Americans identified themselves with the polite culture of sensibility and virtue in distress; there were other sources of national identity, represented, too, by those Virginia riflemen to whom Abigail referred in asking John to remember the ladies. Shields suggests that men "throughout the British Empire recognized the tea table as the critical institution in the assertion of women's presence in the emerging public sphere" and that women's writings about the tea table were "rejoinders to male censors," as demonstrated by the exchange in the *Virginia Gazette* quoted in chapter 7 above. The unlawful, public demonstration by the Boston men Americanized the comment: that they were dressed as "Mohocks" was another and multilayered irony, given their frolic, because the Mohocks were also a London street gang (having taken its name from American Mohawk visitors) the knowledge of which had been popularized by the would-be reformer of manners the *Spectator*. To call the demonstration a *tea party*, an irony also comparable to the sentimentality of the Regulators and the Paxton Boys, was to assert the emergence of the "American humor" described by Rourke, essentially masculine, and essentially critical of genteel, Anglophile manners.[16] This was the context for Warren's writing Abigail in regard to the Boston Tea Party that she hoped that "we have less to Dread than you then apprehended, for an Cathartick and sometimes pretty Violent Exercise is recommended by the physicians as Beneficial"—she referred to the dressed-up, male Bostonians as "Tuscureros," rather than Mohocks—and also that the demonstrators' "Violent Exercise" would be thus "salutary," a view of populist, patriotic acts that John Adams expressed. Warren hoped, too, that "the Beautiful Fabrick" might be "repaird and reestablished on so Firm a Basis that it will not be in the power of the Venal and narrow hearted on Either side the Atlantick to break down its Barriers and threaten its total Dessolution." Salutary that male violence may have been, but it also threatened with dissolution a beautiful fabric that was manifested in civilized tea parties.[17]

Of course, because of its gendering, there were masculine elements in the Americanization of sensibility, as we saw illustrated in Paine's introduction to *Common Sense* and in the Declaration of Independence's breaking the bonds with "our British brethren." In 1776, Henry Laurens recorded the breach "with generosity," Burstein suggests: "God grant that our success may work the happiness of both parties, that out of seeming Evil, solid good may grow. I triumph not, in Britain's blushes; when an Englishman bleeds, I feel the blow; when my Mother Country, my old friend suffers disgrace, I droop." Burstein quotes the account of the 1770 Boston massacre in the *Boston Gazette*, which called it "the most cruel and inhuman Massacre, perpetuated by the Hands of Men, who may be justly stiled more savage than savage Beasts." The same paper assumed, as Paine and Jefferson would, that American men were united in nonblood kinship by way of their common feeling (replacing the fellow feeling of "consanguinity"); it reported that, when the city's bells called in to mourn the slain, "many thousands of our brave Brethren in the Country [were] deeply affected with our Distress." John developed the notion in his *Novanglus*, no. III (1774): "when a number of persons were slaughtered . . . such was the brotherly sympathy of all the colonies, such their resentment against a hostile administration, that the innocent blood then spilt has never been forgotten, nor the murderous minister and governors, who brought the troops here, forgiven by any part of the continent, and never will be." This was evidence of "union," and, he continued, were his readers to "look over the resolves of the several colonies," they would "see that one understanding governs, one heart animates the whole." Head and heart were combined, the former directing the feelings of the latter. "The congress of Philadelphia have expressed the same sentiments with the people of New England," and so it went with all the other colonies, of which Adams then gave "proofs."[18] But, when Abigail asked John "if every Member feels for Us," his answer distinguished between those who did and those who only "professed" to do so: "Every Member says he does—and most of them really do. But most of them feel more for themselves. In every Society of Men . . . you find some who are timid . . . some who are selfish and avaricious, on whose callous Hearts nothing but Interest and Money can make Impression." He picked out merchants in New York and Philadelphia to illustrate the latter type.[19]

Abigail and Mercy Otis Warren represented themselves responding to revolutionary events as women of sensibility. "O my dear Friend," Abigail wrote Warren, August 14, 1777, "when I bring Home to my own Dwelling these tragical Scenes which are every week presented in the publick papers to us, and only in Idea realize them, my whole Soul is distress'd. Were I a man I must be in the Field. I could not live to endure the Thought of my Habitation desolated my children Butcherd, and I am inactive Spectator."[20] The same year, Warren wrote Hannah Storer Lincoln: "as every domestic enjoyment depends on the decision of the mighty contest, who can be an unconcerned and silent spectator? Not surely the fond mother, or the affectionate wife who trembles lest her dearest connection should fall victim to lawless power, or at least pour out the warm blood as a libation to liberty." This justified speaking of politics but was also to construe oneself as a woman of gendered sensibility, a victim, "bound" by gender in a contest over liberty, another figuration of virtue in distress. Nearly a quarter of a century later, Warren wrote of the "Quasi-War" with France: "I dread it as a Woman, I fear it as a friend to my country; yet think (as a politician) I see it pending over this land." So she assigned feeling to the part of herself identified by gender and assigned thought to a part conventionally beyond such a line, that of the politician. Her public rationale for undertaking the *History of the Rise, Progress and Termination of the American Revolution*, eventually published in 1805, was the same she had given Lincoln in 1774 for wives and mothers not standing by unconcerned and silent: "The horrors of civil war, rushing . . . events to the quiet cottage, where only concord and affection reigned; stimulated to observation a mind that had not yielded to the assertion that all political attentions lay out of the road of female life." She agreed that style followed sex, that "manly eloquence" should "describe the blood-stained field." "Sensible of this," her "trembling heart . . . recoiled at the magnitude of the undertaking," but, recalling that "every domestic enjoyment depends on . . . civil and religious liberty," she noted that "a concern for the welfare of society ought equally to glow in every human breast." This was to declare the common ground that each sex had in sensibility: Warren had asserted in 1774 that "every mind of the least sensibility must be greatly affected with the present distress." But she also said that she "never laid aside the tenderness of the sex in writing [the] *History*."[21]

Chapter 8 demonstrated Abigail's growing identification of American patriots with the figure of virtue in distress, she and other revolutionaries applying the binary values of the culture of sensibility to their opposition to the "barbarean Britains." The latter were uncivilized, savage, and committed "inhuman acts."[22] This was to reverse the post–Seven Years' War's application of the same vision by Englishmen, then reveling in imperial nationality. For them, "the term 'American' often conjured up images of unrefined, if not barbarous persons, degenerate and racially debased," living among the criminals that metropolitan Britain dumped there, all associated with "African slaves and Indian savages thousands of miles from civilization." Americans were seen as "coarse, rowdy, and prone to breaking the law."[23]

Three years after her appeal to Dilly, Abigail wrote her sister Elizabeth that she called for "the just vengance of Heaven" on Britain because it had betrayed its responsibility to protect virtue in distress—in fact, it had persecuted it. Britons "had not only deprived individuals of happiness, but by their cruelty, Rage and rapine laid waste oppulent cities, populus Towns, fruitfull villages and pleasent Feilds, but reached misiry and famine the widow, the Fatherless and the orphan." John came to insist that civility, humanity, and generosity were American qualities that contrasted with British savagery. Furthermore, Abigail's vision of British generals' willingness to employ Indian allies against Euro-Americans illustrates the projection of the early colonial trope into nationalism:

"The History of the Events of the present day must fill every Humane Breast with Horrour. Every week produces some Horrid Scene perpetuated by our Barbarous foes, not content with a uniform Series of cruelties practiced by their own Hands, but they must let loose the infernal Savages. . . . Cruelty, impiety and an utter oblivion of the natural Sentiments of probity and Honour with the violation of all Laws Humane and Divine . . . characterize a George, a How and a Burgoine." In this, Abigail elaborated the grievance expressed in the Declaration of Independence the year before that the British king "had endeavoured to bring on the inhabitants of our frontiers, the merciless Indian Savages, whose known rule of warfare is our undistinguished destruction of all ages, sexes, and conditions." A New Jersey woman wrote of American female "martyrs," asserting that the British "waged war against our sex": "Who that has heard . . . of the tragical death of Miss M'Crea, torn from her house, murdered and scalped by a band of savages hired and set on by British emissaries . . . but would wish to avert [such a fate from themselves]." One of Americans' particular versions of virtue in distress—the Indian captivity narrative—was assimilated to another, their victimization and potential enslavement by British tyranny. Triumph in war meant that at least part of the trope could be reversed, a 1782 print representing "America Triumphant and Britannia in Distress."[24]

## The Racial Politics of Sensibility

"White" emerged in partial answer to Crèvecoeur's famous 1782 question, "What is the American, . . . this new man?" just as slavery "emerged from the Revolution more firmly entrenched than ever in American life." This was after serious challenge, perpetuated thereafter by a burgeoning free black community, abolitionism, and the ending of slavery in the North.[25]

Eric Foner writes that the United States was "founded on the premise that liberty is the entitlement of all humanity," going on to refer to the link between such an entitlement and the appeal of the Declaration of Independence to "the Laws of Nature and Nature's God." The translation of humanity into a qualification for liberty, that is, for a degree of political power, made human nature the subject of renewed debate, one drawing on a scientific and literary preoccupation dating back to Descartes and the reassessment of the passions. Humanity connoted sensibility. Chris Jones writes: "Sensibility, itself a new movement in the progress of nations towards perfection, looked to the development of men's affective nature as a source of improvement beyond the limits of a fallen nature, and in the political sphere was given immense impetus by the American Revolution and American rhetoric." How far did "men's affective nature" extend? White women had sensibility, but it had been invidiously gendered for a century. What of Africans and their descendants? The momentum of sensibility was identifiable with what American contemporaries called "the contagion of liberty," spreading to the potential rebellion and emancipation of black slaves. If white men were truly men of feeling, surely they would find that the sufferings of the enslaved stimulated irresistible compassion.[26]

The first white, English objections to race slavery originated during that fifty-year period, 1675–1725, identified by Fiering and Crane with the rise of the view that the source of the moral judgment lay in the feelings. One could mention various types of writing by, for instance, the Quaker William Edmundson (1676); Thomas Tryon (1684), whose book Davis says foreshadowed "the cult of sensibility"; Aphra Behn, whose 1688 novel *Oroonoko* (and the 1689 stage adaptation by Thomas Southerne) presented an African man of feeling, albeit a king; and the Harvard-educated Samuel Sewall, whose *The Selling of Joseph* (1700) "contributed to a transatlantic transmission of ideas which faintly anticipated the exchanges of Benezet, Sharp, and Wesley." The Society for the Propagation of the Gospel (SPG) was established in London in 1699, by the now Latitudinarian establishment, contemporaneously with the Society for the Reformation of Manners. Both preached the ideology of the man of feeling described by Crane. Bishop William Fleetwood's 1711 sermon before the SPG argued for the baptism of slaves, declaring with hortatory intent that, while slaveowners in "all our Plantations abroad" used slaves "cruelly," they "see them"—he means they *should* see them—"equally the Workmanship of God, with the same faculties and intellectual Powers; Bodies of the same Flesh and Blood, and Souls as certainly immortal." He asserted that "These People," the lineenslaved, were "made to be as Happy" as their owners. Fleetwood called the refusal to baptize slaves "inhumane," although, as Davis points out, this attribution of humanity did not yet entitle them to British "liberties."[27]

That same year, the issue of enslaved Africans' equal humanity was still more widely posed to the Anglophone reading public by the *Spectator*. Two months after its exposition of "humanity," the *Spectator* had expressed indignation that "we" did not put "Negroes" on "the common foot of Humanity." "Negroes"—slaves, the writer assumed—demonstrated their humanity by the feeling they had for their masters, hanging themselves on a master's death or "upon changing their service." What excuse was there for "the Contempt with which we treat this Part of our Species" and, by contrast, setting only "an insignificant fine upon the Man who murders them"? the *Spectator* asked rhetorically. There followed Hutcheson's argument, further elevating "the ethics of feeling," and publications by individual Quakers, some pointing out that the luxuries afforded by the famous Quaker economic proficiency "were made possible by Negro slavery." Davis also acknowledges that sentimentalism generally "conditioned people to . . . support antislavery."[28]

It was in the 1760s, coinciding with the publication of the later volumes of Sterne's *Tristram Shandy*, that Anthony Benezet played a key role in initiating "the great age of Quaker philanthropy." His language was that of sensibility. Writing his own "scenes," and frequently quoting the words of others—including participants in the slave trade describing family separation, extreme labor and physical deprivation, punishment, and atrocity—Benezet insisted in *A Caution and Warning to Great Britain and Her Colonies* (1766) that the capacity to sympathize was a mark of "humanity": "Can any human heart, that retains a fellow-feeling for the sufferings of mankind be unconcerned at relations of such grievous affliction?" It was a demonstration of the "laws of humanity" that Africans being "men"—evidently he meant human beings—have "the same sensibility" as "we" do. Conversely, those who inflicted the horrors Benezet described had lost "the common feelings of human nature." That loss was the result of God's "displeasure," and it showed God's own responsiveness to "the groans of the afflicted": "What greater calamity can befall any people who have become prey to that hardness of heart . . . and insensibility to every religious impress." Benezet warned Britons on both sides of the Atlantic "whose hearts had not yet hardened and who prided themselves on their humanity." He hoped that his words and quotations would have the same effect on his readers as those George Whitefield had "feelingly set forth" in 1739 in his letter from Georgia to other southern colonies which Benezet quoted: "As I lately passed through your provinces . . . I was sensibly touched with a fellow-feeling of the miseries of the poor Negroes!" The Quaker Benezet was touched by the Anglican Whitefield just as the white preacher had been touched by black slaves, and both hoped that their accounts of their feelings and the feelings of slaves would touch their readers, all linked by humanity. Enslavement broke the "tender attachment" of family members, according to Benezet, and he asked his readers to imagine such a breach in their own lives, making the same assumption of the significance of families in the creation of the social affections as did his Scottish predecessors and contemporaries.[29]

But that Sternean traveler Josiah Quincy wrote indignantly of the views of whites in the Carolinas: "The Africans are said to be inferior, in point of sense and understanding, sentiment and feeling, to the European and other white nations. Hence one can infer a right to enslave the other." Eliza Lucas Pinckney, who encountered the teachings of Whitefield, was a woman of sentimental but racist culture; she would feel "robbed" of her property when some of her slaves took the opportunity offered by the Revolution to liberate themselves. Slaveholders in Virginia as well as South Carolina, facing British commanders who offered freedom to slaves who joined their armies, became revolutionaries in order to maintain the institution of slavery.[30]

Still, in 1773, Patrick Henry responded to the Virginia Quaker Robert Pleasants's sending him a copy of "A. Benezets Book against the Slave Trade" by asking whether it was not "a little surprising that Christianity whose chief Excellence consists in softening the human Heart, in cherishing & improving its finer feelings should encourage a Practice so totally repugnant to the first Impressions of right & wrong," a sentence containing assumptions fundamental to the culture of sensibility. His next sentence expressed more of that culture's contrasts between "high Improvements in the Arts, Sciences & refined Morality," on the one hand, and, on the other, slavery and the slave trade, "a species of violence & Tyranny which our more rude & barbarous, but more honest Ancestors detested." He agreed that the slaves were part of humanity: "Is it not amazing, that at a Time, When, the Rights of Humanity Are defined and understood with Precision, in a Country above all others Fond of Liberty . . . we find Men Professing a Religion the most humane, Mild, meek, gentle & generous, Adopting a Principle as repugnant To humanity as it is inconsistent With the Bible & destructive to Liberty." Henry praised the Quakers for their "noble Effort to abolish Slavery" before asking Pleasants: "Would you believe that I am Master of Slaves of my own Purchase!" He explained that he was "drawn along by the general Inconvenience of living without them." He believed that, in the future, "an oppor[tunity] will be offered to abolish this lamentable Evil." Meanwhile, perhaps slavery could be improved: "If not, let us transmit to our Descendents together with our Slaves a Pity for their unhappy Lot & an abhorrence for Slavery." Thus could sensibility motivate the wish to abolish slavery and assuage the guilt of perpetuating it.[31]

The same year, Benezet's friend the Philadelphian Benjamin Rush argued that "Negroes" shared "Human Nature" with whites in spite of the toll that slavery took on their personalities, and he quoted Smith's *Theory of Moral Sentiments*, referring to "slaves' cries . . . their looks of tenderness at each other, on being separated." As further proof of their humanity, he cited black slaves' assertions of "Liberty" in South America. The following year, at their annual general meeting in Philadelphia, abolitionist Quakers first succeeded in prohibiting their fellows from owning and trading in slaves after several years of trying, using the sentimental arguments Benezet publicized. According to Nicole Eustace, however, many white Pennsylvanians "excluded Africans" from the "humanity" with which they had increasingly identified themselves from midcentury, and we have seen that the Reverends Allen and Jones, black Philadelphians, had to challenge such exclusion in the 1790s.[32]

So sensibility was racialized as well as gendered. At one point in his *Notes on Virginia*, written during and just after the Revolution to explain and vindicate his country to European questioners, Jefferson had imagined that in the future blacks might, with justice, rebel against their enslavement, just as his fellow whites had resisted being enslaved by British monarchical "oppressors."[33] (This was the passage that African American Benjamin Banneker would reprint in his *Almanac*.)[34] But, as noted earlier, Jefferson threw doubt on blacks' having sensibility at all, and he judged Ignatius Sancho incapable of refining his passions into what he and his fellow elite Virginians thought of as sensibility. Blacks' bravery, Jefferson asserted, probably proceeded "from a lack of forethought." As Foner points out, Jefferson here gave the rationale later adopted by Congress to exclude all non–"free whites" from naturalization: creatures of masked passions, they lacked "the capacity for self-control, rational forethought, and devotion to the larger community," characteristics that, as we have seen, men applied to women. (Abigail apprehended them in herself.)[35] Jefferson had added that Sancho's imagination was a powerful, unpredictable force. In "the course of its vagaries, [it] leaves a tract of thought as incoherent and eccentric as a . . . meteor through the sky."[36]

Prior to the posthumous publication of his complete letters in the period Jefferson was writing his *Notes on Virginia*, Sancho had become well-known for his correspondence with Sterne, the most famous and influential exponent in English of refined sensibility during the second half of the century. Sypher writes that the "reading public identified Sancho with Lawrence Sterne." Their correspondence had been included in two best-selling collections of Sterne's own letters, also published posthumously (in 1775 and 1780). Doubtless Jefferson read them, and, anyway,

Sancho's initial letter to Sterne was included in *Letters of the Late Ignatius Sancho, An African*. He sent it the same year, 1766, that Benezet published the little book I quoted earlier. Jefferson, then, read this:

> Reverend Sir,
> It would be an insult on your humanity (or perhaps look like it) to apologize for the liberty I am taking.—I am one of those people whom the vulgar and illiberal call "*Negurs*."

Sancho continued: "My chief pleasure has been books.—Philanthropy I adore.—" He then exclaimed: "How very much, good Sir, am I (amongst millions) indebted to you for your amiable Uncle Toby." Here he is sharing readership with all Sterne's chiefly white readers. He continued: "Your Sermons have touch'd me to the heart, and I hope I have amended it." This was a process that we have seen to be characteristic of those of sensibility, the Adamses, for example. The point of Sancho's contacting Sterne was to enlist his unrivaled power on behalf of slaves, having been brought to it, Sancho continued, by quoting the following passage from Yorick's (the Reverend Sterne's) sermon on Job: "Consider how great a part of our species—in all ages down to this"—a passage whereby Sancho, although self-identified as black, again asserts that *humanity* means all human beings—"have been trod under the feet of cruel and capricious tyrants, who would neither hear their cries nor pity their distresses.—Consider slavery—what it is—how a bitter a draught— and how many millions are made to drink it!" He and Sterne were linked to all these because they are "our species," but then Sancho referred to the color that made for his special kinship with contemporary slaves: "Of all my favorite authors, not one has drawn a tear in favor of my miserable black brethren—excepting yourself, and the author of Sir George Ellison." Sancho urged Sterne to publish something more on slavery that would, he hoped, "ease the yoke (perhaps) of many" and told him: "You cannot refuse—Humanity must comply." And in *A Sentimental Journey* (1768), Sterne incorporated the passage on slavery from his own sermon that Sancho had quoted to him, endorsing its sentiment in his rumination on a captive blackbird, with which he identified himself. Poor blacks in a part of London were called "St. Giles blackbirds." [37]

The author of *The History of Sir George Ellison*, a sentimental novel published the year Sancho wrote to Sterne, was Sarah Scott; not only was she Sterne's wife's cousin, she had a family connection with the Duke of Montagu—who had taught Sancho to read and whose widow had hired him as her butler in 1749—insofar as her sister Elizabeth had married a Montagu. Knowing of Sancho's continuing relation with the ducal branch of the Montagu family, in 1767 Sterne got him to persuade it to subscribe to the publication of *A Sentimental Journey*, reminding him: "good Sancho dun the Duke of M, the Duchess of M and Lord M for their subscriptions, and lay the sin, and the money with it too, at my door."[38]

The hero of Scott's novel, an English gentleman-merchant, became a slaveholder by his marriage to a Jamaican heiress: "The thing which had chiefly hurt him during his abode in Jamaica, was the cruelty exercised on one part of mankind by another; as if the difference of complexion excluded them from the human race, or indeed as if their not being human could be an excuse for making them wretched." Sir George was an exemplar of active, humanitarian sympathy, and his affectionate, Latitudinarian-Christian treatment of his slaves elicited their own, human affections for him. Scott intended that, in this, as in many other episodes in his life, most of them set in England, her hero was to be "a useful lesson to others."[39]

Popular in England, *The History of Sir George Ellison* was subsequently reoriented for a specifically American audience. In 1774, the Philadelphia publisher James Humphreys drastically condensed the novel so that it focused almost entirely on slavery and renamed it *Man of Real Sensibility; or, The History of Sir George Ellison*. He added an epigraph, an edited passage from Sterne's *Sentimental Journey* beginning: "Dear SENSIBILITY!—Source inexhausted of all that's precious in our joys, or costly in our Sorrows.—'Tis here I feel thee—'tis thy Divinity that stirs within me." And here Humphreys added: "For that I feel some generous care beyond my self.—All comes from Thee." The retitling and the epigraph reflected the impact of Sterne's published responses to Sancho's plea, although sentimentalism was already evident in antislavery writing. The context of Humphrey's version of Scott's novel was the "pamphlet debate over slavery in Philadelphia," beginning in 1773. Its purpose was the same as Rush's *Addresses* of 1773, to galvanize support for the finally successful antislavery push set in motion at the Philadelphia yearly meeting of 1774. That meeting was "in the forefront of the Quaker abolitionist movement," its members finally prohibiting slave ownership among themselves at the yearly meeting of 1776. It may well have been a Quaker who commissioned the publication of *Man of Real Sensibility*. Jefferson was in close touch with the Virginia delegates to the Continental Congress in Philadelphia in 1774 before coming in person in 1775, the year of the first anti-slavery convention.[40]

When he came to write about his *Letters* in the early 1780s, Jefferson, then, could see Sancho as the embodiment of the serious danger posed to slavery by his now famous exemplifications of the equal humanity of blacks, above all, in the sensibility so widely valued by the powerful and in the context of the momentum given sensibility by the Revolution. Jefferson, moreover, shared Sancho's extravagant admiration for the writings of Sterne, so generally influential among the literate in the colonies, holding him to be an invaluable force for good but one whose view of sensibility was, Jefferson believed, entirely consistent with elite Virginians' "sentimental code." He had told a nephew in 1771: "The writings of Sterne particularly form the best course of morality that ever was written." More recently, when his wife, Martha Wayles Jefferson, lay dying, he brought *Tristram Shandy* to her, she copied out a passage, he copied some more of it, and then he wrapped the paper around a lock of her hair, which he kept to the end of his life. The hair linked their respective parts of this passage because they omitted the words between them—"whilst thou are twisting that lock,—see! It grows grey." Linda Layne points out that hair "has been associated with mourning since antiquity . . . [and] used in [America] as a memento of loved ones . . . since the 18th century." Richardson's dying Clarissa bequeathed "a ring with [her] hair" to Anna Howe, "that sister of [her] heart," and more elaborate rings containing her hair to others. Adapting this ritual form of commemoration during Martha's protracted dying, the Jeffersons expressed to each other the unique value that Sterne held for them. It was soon afterward that Jefferson wrote his assessment of the self-described "*Negur*" who had known Sterne personally; in this he referred to the novel from which he and Martha had taken their quotation, first praising Sancho insofar as "his style" was "easy and familiar," but then adding "except when he affects a Shandean fabrication of words."[41]

Sancho's letters, Jefferson said, "do more honour to the heart than the head," the symbolic psychological relationship on which he was to dilate in that letter to Mrs. Maria Cosway, one in which a third figure, the writer himself was, in control, the year after his *Notes on Virginia* was published in Paris. It opened a correspondence with a woman named, like Sterne's heroine, Maria, one in which Jefferson himself attempted to be Shandean.[42]

Both Martha and Maria were fair, delicate and refined in taste, and objects of his sensibility: blacks, Jefferson had written in the passage preceding his denigration of Sancho, "are more ardent after their female; but love with them seems to be more an eager desire, than a tender delicate mixture of sentiment and sensation. Their griefs are transient."

Jefferson was in the traumatic throes of grief when he wrote this. In fact, Sancho's representation of his relation with his wife, Anne (their marriage "one of the only two known all-Black marriages recorded" in Britain "during the century"), was as Sternean as that emblematized by the Thomas-Martha memento. Sancho declared in a 1779 letter: "To my inexpressible happiness, she is my wife." To the same close friend Sancho wrote: "Dame Sancho would be better if she cared less.—I am her barometer—if a sigh escapes me, it is answered by a tear in her eye;—I oft assume a gaiety to illume her dear sensibility with a smile—which twenty years ago almost bewitched me;—and mark! after twenty years enjoyment—constitutes my highest pleasure!" They had the kind of relationship that Jefferson had prematurely lost.[43]

Blacks' "love," wrote Jefferson, as he homed in on Sancho's deficiencies in sensibility, "is ardent but it kindles the senses only, not the imagination." (Jefferson allowed blacks had a moral sense, albeit damaged by slavery.)[44] Of course, he then wrote that Sancho's imagination was out of control. He concluded, however: "though we admit him to the first place among those of his own colour who have presented themselves to the public judgement, yet when we compare him with the writers of the race among whom he has lived"—that is, with whites—"and particularly with the epistolary class, in which he has taken his own stand"—Sancho placed what he called "the simple effusion's of a poor Negro's heart" in the context of other books written "in the epistolary way," including Richardson's and Sterne's—"we are compelled to enroll him at the bottom of the column." Finally, perhaps unwilling to concede Sancho even a neo-Shandean success, Jefferson suggests very strongly that his *Letters* were entirely fabricated: "This criticism supposes the letters published under his name to be genuine, and to have received amendment from no other hand [i.e., a white one]; points which should not be of easy investigation." Subsequent slave narratives would have to assert on the title page that they were, like Frederick Douglass's, "Written by Himself." Sancho's *Letters*, already downgraded by Jefferson as the expression of "Real Sensibility," could be entirely dismissed as evidence of black humanity.[45]

The human feelings of black people were the subject for debate at the constitutional convention later in the 1780s, a debate that would result in the three-fifths clause, apportioning congressional representation and electoral college votes by counting each black inhabitant as three-fifths of a white person. The proposal was intended to gain support for the Constitution from delegates from states with large enslaved populations. During debate, Gouverneur Morris (himself actually a rake) declared, as

Madison recorded, "that the inhabitant of Georgia and S.C. who goes to the Coast of Africa, and in defiance of the most sacred laws of humanity, tears away his fellow creatures from their dearest connexions & damns them to the most cruel bondages, shall have more votes in a Govt. instituted for the protection of the rights of mankind than the Citizen of Pa. or N. Jersey who views with a laudable horror, so nefarious a practice." Conversely, Samuel Chase of Maryland argued that slaves were mere property, viewed in the South as Northerners viewed "cattle, horses, etc." To such men, their own "liberty" meant "the protection of property from the state," and, of course, property was not part of humanity.[46]

As we saw, Abigail Adams had expressed her suspicion about the strength of "the passion for Liberty" among Virginia slaveholders, and we can infer that her writing Edward Dilly in 1775 that "the Spirit that prevails among Men of all degrees, all ages and sex'es is the Spirit of Liberty" could well have included blacks. She was also conscious of her racism, showing that in her shocked response to a representation of interracial sex on the London stage in 1785: "Othello was represented blacker than any affrican. Whether it arises from the prejudices of Education or from a real natural antipathy I cannot determine, but my whole soul shuddered when ever I saw the sooty (heretik?) More touch the fair Desdemona." Sancho had once played the role of Othello and was identified with this perhaps best-known African figure in England, Shakespeare's "Moor of Venice," by a reviewer of Sterne's letters, for example, and by a man on the street who yelled "Smoke Othello" at Sancho on the street. Sancho proudly accepted the identification, turning the tables on the would-be insult by calling the man Iago. Abigail recognized that Othello's character was "Manly open generous and noble," but she had to acknowledge: "*So powerfull was prejudice that I could not separate the coulour from the Man.*" That she called Desdemona "gentle" suggests that her racist feelings were sharpened by her feeling of the contravention of the values of sensibility. She illustrates that "the concept of prejudice . . . —the very term itself!—came suddenly into wide currency in the years after 1760" and suggests, too, that such a concept had evident kinship with sensibility.[47]

But Abigail's apparent political inclusiveness was more liberal than that of her friend Mercy Warren, whose sentimental *History* of the Revolution said of the ex-Virginia governor and British antirevolutionary commander Lord Dunmore that he "had the inhumanity . . . to declare freedom to the blacks, and on any appearance of hostile resistance to the Kings authority to arm them against their masters." By the time that Warren published these words, "the contagion of liberty" had spread across the Atlantic and back again, to St. Domingue (Haiti), where, in 1804, ex-slaves finally won independence. American sympathizers explained the black rebels' inspiration the same way we have seen the Adamses and Jefferson explain their own revolution, whereby oppression galvanized feeling into justifiably angry and forceful action, "the only means [black Haitians] had to throw off the yoke of hated slavery." In 1804, the Pennsylvanian David Beard argued in Congress that slaves in the United States, if ignorant, were capable of proficiency in war: "we have only to look to St. Domingo. There the negroes felt their wrongs and have avenged them."[48]

The fierce debates over human equality persisted, inspired by the promise of the Revolution. John Quincy Adams's "The Character of Desdemona," from his "Personifications of the Characters of Shakespeare," would be unembarrassed in its racism. It was written in 1836, that is, as Lawrence Levine remarks, "even as he was waging his heroic fight against the power of the slave South in the House of Representatives." He attributed to Shakespeare his own horror of interracial sex, exclaiming over Desdemona's desire for Othello: "No! Unnatural passion! It cannot be named with delicacy." He repeated: "Her passion for him is *unnatural*; and why is it unnatural but because of his color?" Desdemona's perversity drove her to elope "in the dead of night to marry a thick-lipped, wool-headed Moor," John Quincy here adopting the language of Shakespeare's characters as his own. And even the clandestine nature of her marriage raises "a prepossession rather unfavorable to the character of a young woman of refined sensibility and elevated education." This was the standard against which he measured Desdemona. She betrayed it, too, in defending the violence of the drunken Cassio, engineered, of course, by Iago: "Is this the character for a woman of delicate sentiment to give of such a complicated and heinous offense as that of which Cassio had been guilty?" Adams answered: "No! it is not for female delicacy to extenuate the crimes of drunkenness and bloodshed, even when performing the appropriate office of raising the soul-subduing voice for mercy." His efforts on behalf of antislavery were an element of that humanitarian crusade in which women's sentimental values played a very significant part, including the reiterated juxtaposition of domestic sensibility with male drunkenness and violence.[49]

In the same place, John Quincy represented the "moral lesson" of *Othello* as one to be Americanized: that it was "of no practical utility in England, where there are no valiant Moors to steal the affections of fair and high-born dames, may be true," but that, in America of the 1830s, that lesson could be extended to a "salutory admonition against ill-assorted, clandestine, and unnatural marriage." Influenced by the Scottish vision of the rise of sensibility marking the stages of historical progress, and writing more or less at the same time that John Quincy Adams was commenting on *Othello*'s pertinence to Americans, Tocqueville remarked in *Democracy in America* that "the American," that is to say, the free white man, was "full of humanity towards his fellow creatures" but was "insensible" to the "frightful misery" and "very cruel punishments" endured by the slaves because he deemed them to be outside humanity.[50]

## John and Abigail on Sensibility and the American Character

John Adams's 1779 draft of the Massachusetts Constitution bearing on Harvard, that is, chapter 6, section 2 ("The Encouragement of Literature, &c."), declared that it was "the duty of legislators and magistrates in all future periods of this commonwealth . . . to inculcate the principles of humanity and general benevolence" into the people, the priority of these virtues striking in a list that went on to include "public and private charity, industry and frugality, honesty and punctuality in their dealings," then further, the Shaftesburian, Hutchesonian qualities "sincerity, good humor, and all social affections and generous sentiments among the people." Just previously, John had said that the legislators' and magistrates' duties had included "the promotion of agriculture, arts, sciences, commerce, trades, manufacturers, and a natural history of the country" by rewards and immunities and the "dealings" with which the moral qualities of humanity, benevolence, and generous sentiments—implicitly, sensibility—were to be conducted. Commerce and sensibility went hand in hand, the former helping spread the latter as one fruit of the civilizing process. This paragraph, John later said, was itself a manifestation of his sensibility: "The words flowed from the heart in reality, rather than the head."[51]

Consistent with Chris Jones's observation of the "impetus" that the American Revolution gave to sensibility as "a new movement in the progress of nations," Abigail wrote her niece Lucy Cranch from London in 1786 to explain how it was that Americans had taken "humane nature" to fresh heights, a vision that John had expressed in his *Novanglus* papers of 1774. She opened with a description of her response to Lucy's letter: "These tokens of Love and regard which I know flow from the Heart, always find their way to mine, and give me a satisfaction and pleasure, beyond any thing, which the ceremony of Courts and kingdom can afford." This was a particular version of the republican, sentimental model to which she then linked it: "The social affections are, and may be made the truest channels for our pleasures and comforts to flow through." She assumed that they were inborn but, at the same time, could be improved, and here she quoted that line from the end of Pope's *Essay on Man* "'and bade self Love and social be the Same.'"[52]

Abigail then turned to postrevolutionary America's superiority in this regard: "Perhaps there is no Country where there is a fuller exercise of those virtues than ours at present exhibits," attributable to those republican features with which Hector St. John Crèvecoeur, for one, also explained the American national character at the same time, that is, as Abigail continued, "to the equal distribution of Property, the Small Number of inhabitants, in proportion to its territory, the equal distribution of justice to the Poor as well as to the rich, to a Government founded in justice and exercised with impartiality, and to a Religion which teaches peace and good will to man, to knowledge and learning being so easily acquired and so universally distributed, and to that sense of Moral obligation which generally inclines our countrymen; to do to others as they would that others should do to them." This version of the moral sense was a reminder that all these were the social and political factors making up the environment that opened "the truest channels" to the "social affections" so that they could be most fully exercised, a model of the relation between government and people articulated by the male authors both of the *Federalist Papers* and of the antifederalist papers and also assumed by John when writing the Massachusetts Constitution. Abigail then, continuing the letter to Lucy, reflected: "Humane nature is much the same in all Countries, but it is the Government the Laws and Religion, which forms the Character of a Nation." The American national character, having created the circumstances that best capitalized on social affections, according to that same model led the world in humanity and sensibility.[53]

In 1783, Abigail asked Thaxter in Paris: "Shall I talk of my self and contrast my simple manners and republican stile of Life, with the pageantry, Splendour, and courtly Life you are necessitated to endure[?]" She reiterated this morally loaded contrast as one between "painted greatness," "daubing," and the "more Luxurious and refined Manners of European Courts," on the one hand, and "the Native Beauties, and comparatively Simple, Rustick, and plain manners of America," on the other. A few months later, she wrote Thaxter that, while she had been "particularly interested in the various countries," she had now "quitted all thoughts of ever visiting them." This was the context for the contrast: "Depreciated and depraved as our manners are, from the purity of former days," she still thought her own country a place where "domestick virtues are more Esteemed and cultivated, Gallantry is less practised, those passions which enoble and soften Man are not prostituted at the Shrine of Mammon." But, in the end, she came to Europe.[54]

In England, the Adamses visited "the fashionable Resort" of Bath, where, Abigail wrote Mary, "like the rest of the World I spent a fortnight in Amusement and dissipation, but I returnd I assure you, with double pleasure to my own fire side, where only thank heaven, my substantial happiness subsists." This conceded at least a measure of happiness in fashionable pleasures. "Here," that is, by her fire side, she continued, "I find these satisfaction which neither Satiate by enjoyment nor pall by reflection, for tho I like Some times to mix in the Gay World, and view the manners as they rise, I have much reason to be gratefull to my Parents, that my Education gave me not an habitual taste for what is termd fashionable Life." The pleasures she had enjoyed included "3 balls 2 concerts, one Play and two private parties, besides dinning and Breakfasting abroad." Bath was, she added in a detailed description, "one constant scene of dissipation and Gambling . . . and the Ladies set down to cards in the publick rooms as they would at a private party."[55]

As if to amplify the significance of her parents' opposition to such ladies' behavior, Abigail had opened this letter by characterizing Mary's account of Mrs. Betsy Palmer's baby being fathered during her adulterous affair with Royall Tyler as particularly shocking because, "in a Country like ours, . . . conjugal infidelity is held in the utmost abhorrence, and brands with eternal infamy the wretch who destroys it." It was otherwise in Europe, where "the Husband might have looked upon the Gallant as Men do upon their deputies, who take the troublesome buisness off their Hands." In America, "the seducer should be considered as the worst of assassins." In this therefore anomalous case, Abigail thought "the female," that is, Betsy Palmer, "more Guilty in proportion to her obligations to her Husband, her children, her family and the Religion . . . and she has sacrificed her Honour, her tranquility and her virtue." She "quit a subject so painfull" to describe her own participation in Bath's "dissipation," adding that, not only did "the Gay the indolent, the curious, the Gambler [and] the fortune hunter resort to it," but even "those who go as the thoughtless Girl from the Country told Beau Nash . . . that She cam *out of wanteness*."

Yet Abigail could be as dazzled by London's delights as were the heroines of sentimental novels, including the eponymous heroine of Fanny

Burney's *Evelina*, who reported the excitement she felt in London, "now in full splendour." Her first "entrance" to Ranelagh Gardens, Evelina wrote, " made me almost think I was in some enchanted castle, or fairy palace, for all look like magic to me." Even as Richardson had disapproved of urban delights, like Fordyce he showed women's deep attraction to them. From the outset, Abigail found, as she wrote to Mary Cranch: "I am better pleased with this city than I expected. It is a large magnificent, and Beautifull city." She wrote long, journal-like descriptions, one of which concluded: "You are ready to fancy yourself in fairy land."[56]

In Paris the following month, Nabby thought that in point of beauty and elegance it could not "bear a comparison with London." She wrote Betsy Cranch that she had enjoyed Beaumarchais's *Le Marriage de Figaro* at the Comedie Française, but she could not let go her conventional contrast: "I shall learn to prize my own Country above all others. If there is not so much elegance and beauty and so many sources of amusement and entertainment, there is what to every honest and virtuous mind will be far preferable, a sincerity and a benevolence which must be prized above every other consideration."[57] At the Paris Opéra, Abigail found, as she wrote Mary: "The first dance initially, shoked me, the Dress'es and Beauty of the performers was enchanting, but no sooner did the Dance commence then I felt my delicacy wounded, and I was ashamed to bee seen to look at them." Her detailed description shows that, despite her awareness of what others thought of her looking, she had continued to look, riveted by the dancers' virtuosity: "their motions are as light as air and as quick as lightning. They balance themselves to astonishment." She returned to her being "shoked" by asking rhetorically: "Shall I speak a Truth and say that repeatedly seeing these Dances has worn off that disgust which I first felt, and that I see them now with pleasure." The change was in her feelings, her responsiveness to the beauty, which she identified with her sensibility: "Yet when I consider the tendency of these things, the passions they must excite, and the known Character . . . which is attached to a opera Girl, my abhorrence is not lessned, and neither my Reason or judgement have accompanied my Sensibility in acquiring any degree of callousness." The softest degree of sensibility, she implied, was one that operated in accordance with reason—or morality—a faculty from which the feeling of "abhorrence" (the same as her initial "disgust") somehow flowed. This was pretty much what Fordyce and the other theorists of feminine sensibility, calibrated by an innate delicacy, wished to see. It pertained to sensibility's inevitable connection with sexuality.[58]

Nonetheless, having paused to assure her sister that she was still sensitive to immorality, in other words, to the proper relation of sense to sensibility, Abigail immediately continued to express her pleasure in the Opéra and her unbuttoned sensibility: "The Scenary is more various, and more highly decorated, the dresses more costly and rich. And O! the Musick vocal and instrumental, it has a soft persuasive power and a dying, dying Sound." It broke through all inhibitions, it seems, even to making Abigail express its cadence verbally in her memorializing of it, and we recall her responsiveness to Handel's *Messiah* in London as well as to those lectures on science. Abigail agreed with the French Catholic treatment of the dancers as harlots, but evidently her description of the seductive scene shows her to have been excited by other sentiments, as she confessed in introducing it. One could say, then, that she was moved by the sexual freedom of old France as she feared her husband had been, as Jefferson was, perhaps, by Maria Cosway, and as Franklin certainly was. More relevant, however, was her capacity for the pleasures against which Fordyce warned, implicit always in feminized sensibility. Abigail identified sensibility with emotionally expressive freedom all along, accompanying it with ambivalent attempts to guard against it.

## Gender and the Politics of Sensibility

Meanwhile, in the United States, from which mother and daughter had sailed and to which they would soon return, literate and many nonliterate Americans were bathed in sensibility. The 1780s "appear to have been the high-water mark of the cult of sensibility in America," writes Waldstreicher. According to Knott, after the conclusion of the Revolution, "sensibility was promoted in newspapers, magazines, public orations, and formal debates," including the debate over black people's sensibility.[59] Members of the upper classes, facing postrevolutionary demands and conflict, staged "impressive displays of patriotic sensibility in an attempt to domesticate Revolution." Reflecting long-standing belief, they urged that "virtue . . . could be cultivated." The "right sensations awakened the 'moral sense,'" a vision identical with that of those Philadelphians Knott describes attempting reforms extending from prisons to families, the former already targeted in England by leaders of what Langford calls "the sentimental revolution" there, the latter long a focus of sentimentalists.[60]

At first, postrevolutionary leaders promoted "polite standards of celebration," as they channeled, or surfed, the popular politics unleashed by the Revolution, attempting to make them "genteel." That perspective marks the coexistence of contrasting, even competing, cultures, although there were class interpenetrations coinciding with racial ones. The attempts at sentimentalization were yet further expressions of the continuing campaign for the reformation of manners, now linked to nationalism. Promoters had the same hopes of opening up those true channels for the social affections that Abigail believed were characteristic of America.[61]

The verbal content of fetes and other public occasions—speeches, declarations, handbills, and toasts—drew from the literary materials described earlier, from "sentimental republicanism," the documents described by Wills, Wood, Burstein, and François Furstenberg as well as Waldstreicher and Knott. Americans of both sexes wept tears of joy at scenes of patriotic celebration, insisting on their sincerity in contrast to "two-faced patriots" who shared newspapers space "with rakes who feigned love to the doom of credulous women" and "counterfeiters of all sorts." This was the context for the novels of Hill Brown, Relf, Rowson, and Foster. Symbolically, federalists "rebroadened the field of respectable, or virtuous citizenry, to include, first women of the upper classes," but also "artisans and others of 'the middling sorts'"—but we can see these women as heiresses of the Boston ladies Shields describes and of Brown's Virginia equivalents, hoping to reform the manners of men as well as women. A group of Massachusetts ladies, asserting themselves in a 1783 peace celebration, included among their own thirteen toasts number 8, "Reformation to our husbands," and number 11, "Reformation to the men in general." Sentimental reformers still had to persuade young women to redirect the feelings aroused by sentimental culture from self-indulgence to socially responsible, sympathetic action: in 1787, Rush observed "young ladies, who weep away a whole forenoon over the criminal sorrows of a fictitious Charlotte or Werter," but who disdain "a beggar soliciting 'the crumbs which fall from their father's tables.'"[62]

Women had begun emerging into public spaces long before the Revolution, expressing their appetite for pleasure, and better-off women had been able to assert themselves domestically, too, finding resources in religion, literature, and consumption, although within the interstices of sexist and patriarchal culture. Traditional hierarchical patriarchalism had long been under challenge: the crucial turn (by ministers and other social leaders) toward the sentimental ethics detailed by Fiering had been made in the period 1675–1725, and revolutionaries and postrevolutionaries identified themselves with them. It was not coincidental that the "high-tide of sensibility" accompanied a postrevolutionary outburst of "agitation about women's rights." Zagarri's account of American wom-

en's political participation—first in the streets, then in ensuing partisanship—can be added to Waldstreicher's to show that they were entering
politics, defined broadly, "in ways and on a scale that had not before been
possible." Some women's voting in New Jersey, 1776–1807, along with
free blacks, was one end of a spectrum of activity.[63]

By definition, however, the sensibility thus popularly propagated
and absorbed was gendered in the way I have described, which is why
women could be construed as civilizing influences. Waldstreicher finds
that, "since the American Revolution at least, women had served a key
symbolic role for men seeking to construct consensus." If, during the
1780s, fete leaders had sought to make popular expressions of sensibility more genteel by encouraging women's participation, federalists and
antifederalists in the 1790s looked to female supporters "to confer a kind
of respectability" on party gatherings, even to compensate for viciously
competitive partisanship. So, too, Zagarri's account of the influence that
male leaders sought from women—the instilling of moral values, the
transformation of rudeness into civility, in short the tempering of individualistic competitiveness into sociability—can also be identified with
Knott's definition of *the sentimental project*. Its leader, Dr. Rush, asserted
that "the nerves of women are more sensible, than the nerves of men,
and more susceptible to impressions of mind and body," and, therefore, that women could be more "humane."[64] The ambiguous value of
this for women is apparent, consistent with what Norton and Kerber
concluded about republican motherhood. Knott's meticulous analysis
of sentimental correspondence among "coteries" of young women and
men in Philadelphia in the 1780s shows the persistence of "issues of male
governance and female submissiveness." In addition, women's assertiveness was accompanied everywhere by outright hostility, an outpouring
of sexist satire. Women's political self-assertion had been opposed earlier, as John Adams illustrates, but Fordyce, and, before him, the *Spectator*, illustrated and helped perpetuate the reactionary motive in sensibility's gendering from the first, rationalized physiologically, "essentially,"
by Malebranche's psychoscientific definition of the nerves.[65]

The French Revolution galvanized partisanship in postrevolutionary America: antifederalists identified with Jacobins and federalists with
anti-Jacobins. At first, the former held that the French Revolution was
unleashing humanity in the same way Americans had, the republican
Hugh Brackenridge declaring on July 4, 1793, that a treaty with revolutionary France was "not necessary": "We are bound by a higher principle . . . the great law of humanity. . . . The heart of America feels the

cause of France." And, in 1794, the federalist John Quincy Adams had written to his sister describing the French government under Robespierre as "a constant violation of every principle of justice and sentiment of humanity."[66]

Despite this politicization of sensibility in the struggle between Jacobins and anti-Jacobins, or, in fact, because of sensibility's identification with social harmony, Americans continued to look to it as a source of "nationalist détente," in Waldstreicher's phrase, or what Knott calls "the imperative for national social union."[67] Letters, speeches, newspaper articles, and, those works' writers hoped, parents made the figure of Washington, "the very personification of sensibility," serve the purpose of identifying the new nation with sensibility and humanity. Washington's secretary of war wrote him that Philadelphians responded to his Farewell Address (1796), bound as a pamphlet and widely distributed, "with the strongest expression of sensibility." Many "tears were shed on the occasion" of its publication. On Washington's death, Joseph Tuckerman's *Funeral Oration* (1800) exhorted: "Let every *American* transcribe the following few words [from the Farewell Address] in letters of grateful sensibility. Ingrave them on the living tablet of the feeling heart." The 1790s speeches and the ceremonies including them were intended, declared a participant, "to contribute to the formation of a *national character*."[68]

To call Washington the *father* of his country, writes Furstenberg, was to epitomize "a model of family life grounded in bonds of sentiment, affection, and consent," assuming the kind of childrearing advocated by Hill nearly half a century earlier, but contributing, presumably, to that "revolution against patriarchal authority" described by Fliegelman to have taken place in America between 1750 and 1800, and, in theory, extending even to the paternalistic treatment of American slaves.[69] The Reverend Bancroft urged parents: "Teach your children to lisp [Washington's] praise: Instill into their minds his spirit." Another eulogist urged the preverbal infant be impressed with his words, referring to the Farewell Address's capacity to "awaken every tender emotion" as honey: "Let the infant cherub suck its honey with its earliest sustenance." It is not clear, however, who was to read the address to the baby while it sucked on the nipple. Another newspaper explained: "We preserve all the details of Americans' responses to Washington, alive and dead, so that posterity . . . may discern the . . . strong proofs of the sensibility, affection, and gratitude of his Countrymen."[70]

As president, John Adams perpetuated the identification of executive power and nationality with sensibility. Waldstreicher quotes several of the sentimental replies Adams wrote, "for more than two months," to groups of young men formed to pledge their feelings to him in the same terms. For example, Adams wrote: "An address from the youth of Augusta [Georgia], so remote from the seat of Government, and where I am personally unknown is a very high gratification to my feelings." Such official replies were published in local newspapers, the exchange testifying to and promoting the cultivation of sensibility in the backcountry as well as in the towns of the East. In 1798, in the capital city of Philadelphia, fifteen hundred young male federalists "marched to the executive mansion to perform" a "rhetorical invocation of an identity between the people (that counted) and the government." President Adams "met them in full military dress and proclaimed 'No prospect or spectacle could excite a stronger sensibility in my bosom than this which . . . presents itself before me." It is certainly possible to see this as an expression of the political "compassionating" that Adams had publicly scorned early in his career as well as of the political lesson he drew from the great British judges in 1766 not "to despise the common people and forget the feelings of humanity." Afterward, the young men attacked the print shop of the antifederalist Benjamin Franklin Bache, one among the public acts of violence characteristic of the young male Philadelphians Michael Meranze describes. Their two actions, addressing the president in terms of sensibility and performing mayhem, can be seen as an illustration of cultural interpenetration or can bear comparison with the words and actions of the Paxton Boys.[71]

## Reactions to Wollstonecraft in America

Mary Wollstonecraft was a Jacobin figure of decisive significance to women's aspirations and to the related history of sensibility. At first, her *Vindication of the Rights of Woman* (1792) was favorably received in some quarters as a contribution to the debate over the reform of women's education. Immediately excerpted in American journals, the *Vindication* saw three American editions by 1795, adding momentum to the notion of "the rights of woman," coinciding with the increase in women's political activities in the postrevolutionary period.[72]

Moreover, some American women adopted the central target of the *Vindication*, the crippling effects of gendered sensibility. One American writer it inspired was the anonymous "Lady" who published her take on Pope's widely known "Epistle to a Lady" in the *American Museum* in 1792, three years after John Quincy Adams bent it to his purpose, and the same year Wollstonecraft published her book. The lady entitled her poem "On Pope's Characters of Women" and quoted the same sexist line of Pope's that Wollstonecraft did, "fine by defect and delicately weak," and, while brief, her poem makes the same argument about the effects of gendered education on female psychology that Wollstonecraft made.[73]

She first addressed Pope's prose "Argument," preceding his poem, which read: "Of the Characters of Women (consider'd only as contra-distinguished from the other Sex.) That these are yet more inconsistent and incomprehensible than those of Men, of which Instances are given." (It was from this that was derived the kind of listing that John Quincy followed.) She then opened, "By custom doom'd to folly, sloth and ease," her first two words attributing women's characteristics to mutable sources, precisely as Poulain de la Barre and his feminist successors had done, rather than to innate, physiological ones. She continued:

> No wonder Pope such female triflers sees;
> But would the satirist confess the truth,
> Nothing is so like as male and female youth;
> Nothing is like as man and woman old,
> Tho' diff'rent acts seem diff'rent sexes growth,
> Tis the same principle impels them both.

Pope's prose "Argument" had continued: "But tho the *Particular Characters* of this Sex"—that is, "Women"—"are more various than those of Men, the *General Characteristick*, as to the *Ruling Passion*, is more uniform and confin'd. In what That lies, and whence it *proceeds*, 207, &c. . . ." And we read from line 207:

> In Men, we various Ruling Passions find,
> In Women, two almost divide the kind;
> Those only fix'd, they first or last obey,
> The Love of Pleasure and the Love of Sway.

Pope's explanation of such psychology is that it is nature coupled with the effects of sexism:

> That, Nature gives; and when the lesson taught
> To but to please, can pleasure seem a fault?
> Experience this; by Man's Oppression, curst,
> They seek the second not to lose the first.[74]

The "second" is, of course, sway, the first pleasure. In answering this, the American lady changes her subject to "we," men and women:

Whether a crown or bauble we desire,
Whether to learning or to dress aspire:
Whether we wait with joy the trumpet's call,
Or wish to shine the fairest at a ball;
In either sex the appetite's the same,
For love of pow'r is still the love of fame.

The Duke of Wharton's love of fame had illustrated man's "ruling passion" in Pope's "Epistle to Cobham," on the character of men. The lady's next line, "Women must in a narrow orbit move," seems to be in agreement with Pope's preceding:

But grant, in Public Men sometimes are shown,
A Woman's seen in Private life alone;
Our bolder Talents in full light display'd;
Your Virtue open fairest in the shade.

The lady, however, followed her observation on women's orbital confinement with:

But power, alike, both males and females love.
What makes the diff'rence, then, you may enquire.

The "diff'rence" is, not only that between men and women, but also that between men of different ranks and women of different ranks. She continues: "Ambitious thoughts the humblest cottage fill." The dwelling here is not merely the symbolically simplified one of the literary sentimentalist, but one charged with particular significance in the post-revolutionary American republic. The lady answers her question:

In education all the diff'rence lies;
Women if taught, wou'd be as learn'd and wise.

Just as many fools, their heads "toy-shops" (this an allusion to Pope's *Rape of the Lock* as well as "Epistle to a Lady"), can be found among men as among women:

Culture improves all fruits, all sorts we find
Wit, judgement, sense, fruits of the human mind.

There are men of all sorts, merchants, courtiers, soldiers, sailors, who are ignorant of "How Nature op'rates," ignorant of "Aristotle down to Newton's rules": "Reason's not reason, if not exercis'd." Young women are misled by custom, taught that their power lies in their charms and their beauty, and taught also: "By ambush Dress, to catch unwary Hearts." All this Pope has seen, too, but he explained it, in part at least, by nature; the American lady's argument is entirely Wollstonecraftian. Young women are raised

> Strangers to reason and reflexion made,
> Left to their passions, and by them betray'd;
> . . . . . . . . . . . . . . . . . . . . . . . . . . . . .
> Bred to deceive even from their earliest youth!
> Unus'd to books, no virtue taught to prize,
> Whose mind, a savage waste, unpeopl'd lies,
> Which to supply, trifles fill the void.

The writer nevertheless then gives a list of Roman matrons each of whom was not so deprived of education, above all,

> Taught by philosophy all moral good,
> How to repel in youth the impetuous blood!
> How her most fav'rite passions to subdue
> And Fame through Virtue's avenues pursue.

Thus she made the choice of Hercules.

There were other writers who published their agreement with Wollstonecraft's critique of gendered sensibility and her argument that women be educated to reason as well as to feel, for example, the author of "Reflections on What Is Called Amiable Weakness in Woman," published in the *Lady and Gentleman's Pocket Magazine* in 1796. The opening paragraph of the "Reflections" quoted Wollstonecraft's summary of the "prevailing opinion, that [women] were created rather to feel than reason," then criticized their being "educated," in the eighteenth-century sense, to be made "fine ladies brimful of sensibility, and teeming with fine fancies."[75] An unknown number of people wrote privately to each other on the subject. In a letter written the year after Wollstonecraft's book was published, Annis Boudinot Stockton wrote Julia Stockton Rush that she was "much pleased" with Wollstonecraft's "strength of reasoning and her sentiment in general" but declared that the "Slavish obedience" that European women showed "to the caprice of an arbitrary tyrant, which character she seems to apply to men as a sex," was not the case in America, where, she said, "the Empire of reason, is not monopolized by men." Stockton was more willing than Wollstonecraft to "accommodate [herself] to our [i.e., women's] situation," more orthodox in her Christianity, and critical of "the presumptuous manner, in which she [Wollstone-craft] speaks of the Deity." Some of Wollstonecraft's "expressions," she noted, were "by far, too strong for [her] Ideas," but she admitted that that reflected her limitations since Wollstonecraft "writes as a philoso-pher, and I think as a novice": "To sum up my poor Judgement upon this wonderful book, I do really think a great deal of instruction may be gathered from it—and I am sure that no one, can read it, but they may find something or other, that will Correct their Conduct and enlarge their Ideas." There was, as yet, nothing here of Wollstonecraft's sex-ual morality, although her book "raised the stakes and transformed the debate" over the education and rights of women. Stockton's husband, Elias, read Wollstonecraft's book, too. He was a federalist (and Hamilton-ian) congressman from New Jersey at a time when some women could vote, and he supported women's rights.[76]

Of course, Abigail had declared in 1776 that all men would be ty-rants if they could. From John's reference to *A Vindication of the Rights of Woman* in January 1794, we can infer that she had expressed her agree-ment with Wollstonecraft's criticism of the education of women: he ob-jected to their son Thomas's spending so much time visiting "Families with young Ladies. Time is spent and nothing learn'd. Pardon me! Dis-ciple of Wollstonecraft!" Abigail had written John of her own criticism of the education of women many years before. She had also told him that he liked women to stay silent. Here he added that he never "relished Conversation with Ladies, excepting with one at a time. . . . I liked not to loose my time."[77]

Then, in January 1798, Wollstonecraft's widower, William Godwin, published a *Memoir* of her life in which he revealed that Wollstonecraft had been thwarted in her attempt to have an affair with Henry Fuseli, a married man; had then consummated an affair with the American ad-venturer in France, Gilbert Imlay, by whom she had had a child out of wedlock; had became pregnant by Godwin before marrying him; and had ignored religion on her deathbed. Godwin had published these rev-elations (some of them bound to come out because of dates and other details in Wollstonecraft's obituaries) in order to defend her sexual un-orthodoxy on the basis of her finer sensibility, a defense that, at that re-actionary time, discredited not only Wollstonecraft's feminism but also the tendency of sensibility to excess even more than it had been discred-ited already, associated as it became with the excesses of the French Rev-olution, interpreted by counterrevolutionaries—anti-Jacobins—as the result of the unleashing of Rousseauistic feeling.[78] On both sides of the

Atlantic, the rights of women were thereafter associated with women's sexual freedom, that is, with immorality. Wollstonecraft was depicted as "lecherous Mary, of passion the slave," an irresistible association that persisted well into the next century:

> Dame Nature tells us Mary's rights are wrong,
> Her female freedom is a syren song.[79]

The link was central to the "backlash" described by Friedman and Zagarri, although, in fact, it accentuated the sexual invidiousness that had always been there. Now, however, because of the dangers in female sensibility epitomized by Godwin's Wollstonecraft and the overlap between the sexes long potentiated in making men of feeling, gender categories were hardened, sensibility still more sharply gendered.[80] In 1802, the author of an article entitled "Remarks on Female Politicians," a categorization whose rise and fall Zagarri describes, declared: "When I see a female deeply interested in politics, I tremble for her tranquility." The putatively female writer thus shows her own, appropriate sensibility: "As the sensibility of women is livelier, and their enthusiasm more ardent than that of men, they are less qualified to decide the affairs of government."[81]

While Judith Apter Klinghoffer and Lois Elkis have provided a detailed account of the specific political circumstances under which some propertied, single women in New Jersey voted from 1776 until losing the vote in 1807, the poem with which they conclude their history illustrates that sharply gendered ideology that was used to undermine them:

> Man is great in enterprise,
> Woman great in suffering lies
> Man is best abroad displayed
> Woman loveliest in the shade.

That line echoes Pope. Later lines declare:

> Man judges with facility,
> Woman with sensibility.
> Man severely just you meet,
> Woman beams in mercy sweet.

This was published in the *Genius of Liberty*, the same paper that seven years before had published that July 4 oration celebrating Wollstonecraft for her "invulnerable reason."[82]

Jefferson was elected in 1800, on the heels of Godwin's memoir, that second American "revolution" marking the broadening of the franchise for white men, in contrast to the narrowing of its prospects for white women and free black people. Another very significant factor was the impact of news and refugees from the successful black slave revolution in Haiti. Without the extra votes apportioned to Jefferson under the three-fifths clause of the Constitution, Adams would not have lost to him. After 1800, "every state that entered the Union," except Maine, "restricted the right to vote to free white males," whereas, before, only Virginia, South Carolina, and Georgia had expressly excluded blacks. We saw that John wrote "male" into voters' qualifications in Massachusetts.[83] The increasing number of white male voters since the Revolution had by definition enhanced the significance of the male aspect of gendered sensibility. Republicans as a group, moreover, had always been less sympathetic than federalists to women's involvement in politics. Jefferson was himself adamant about women's exclusion, conducting his presidency in ways that implemented his exclusiveness.[84] After his election, "both Republicans and Federalists increasingly directed their primary attention toward actual or potential voters" inhabiting the more and more states that defined them by sex and race. The extension of the franchise necessarily included many more unreformed men, adherents of the popular culture that I have described.[85]

Whatever the ambivalent potentials briefly held by the elevation of women's rights and sensibility's elevation of common feeling, they were, thus, "tamed." In a July 4, 1807, oration, the Vermonter Gardner Child told his female audience: "You are blessed with existence in a land of liberty, where the rights of women are understood and regarded. While the man protects, labors, and accumulates wealth, you have to preside over domestic affairs, to cultivate civilization, soften manners, and correct morals."[86] The only difference from Fordyce's adjuration is in the reference to "the rights of women." According to the widespread ideology that this oration represents, one in evidence since before the Revolution, both sexes were to exercise sensibility in marriage, and mothers were to do so in rearing children, in contrast to the self-indulgence of excessive sensibility now expressly associated with women's sexual freedom. The former was "true," the latter "false," a distinction in sensibility that Fordyce had made. In 1806, "Sister Adelaide" asked her fellow members of the "Boston Gleaning Circle," a female literary society, "What is Sensibility?" and answered: "There are two kinds of what is called sensibility; that which is real, and is accompanied with fortitude is one of the greatest elements of human nature; while that which is false, or affected is often troublesome, sometimes quite disgusting." Dispensers of advice insisted that true and clearly gendered sensibility could reinforce women's power within marriage: their terms drew on those popularized by the *Spectator*, which themselves had been a compromise in the face of women's demands for literacy and the feminism that had followed revolution in seventeenth-century England. American republican wives were told that marriage was to be "the basis and the cement of those numberless tender sympathies, mutual endearments, and interchanges of love between the mutual parties themselves."[87]

The postrevolutionary reform of women's education had this vision of marriage in mind. It was to be improved but not to the extent that it "unsexed" women or made them "masculine," as Fordyce had warned. Indeed, because of his ongoing influence (which Wollstonecraft noted in 1792), Norton quotes Fordyce on the point in her history of postrevolutionary efforts to reform American women's education. Reformers then were as worried about young women's appetite for freedom, which could derail them from that respectable goal. Foster, who wrote *The Boarding School; or, Lessons of a Preceptress to Her Pupils* in 1798, the year after *The Coquette* was published, followed Fordyce in observing: "Novels are the favorite, and most dangerous kind of reading adapted to the generality of young ladies. I say dangerous . . . [because they] fill the imagination with ideas that lead to impure desires . . . and a fondness for show and dissipation. . . . They often pervert the judgement, mislead the affections, and blunt the understanding." Kerber remarks that such "attacks on fiction"—and on the heterosocial pleasures it represented—"were in large part attacks on emotion, on passion, and on sexuality." They were not, however, attacks on gendered sensibility: moralists wished women to distinguish feeling from passion or, minimally, to direct the latter into maintaining reputable, bourgeois marriages.[88]

## Abigail and John in This Context

In the 1790s, Abigail, never democratic and turned antirevolutionary by Shays' rebellion, drew on the term supplied by the French Revolution to see "Jacobins behind every tree." Late in 1797, she wrote her sister that Jacobins in Philadelphia were sponsoring libels intended "to excite a spirit of opposition to the Government." The paper that published these libels was Benjamin Franklin Bache's republican *Aurora*. (Bache's grandfather, Ben Franklin, had introduced him to the printing and newspaper trades.) "Scarcly a day passes but some such scurrility appears in Baches paper, and of no concequences in the minds of many people, but it has, like vice of every kind, a tendency to corrupt the morals of the common people." In fact, she added: "Mr. Bache and his correspondents appear to be in great distress least the respect shown to the President . . . by the people of every City and Town . . . be continued as satisfaction with the Government, and an approbation of its administration." Abigail here suggests that Bache, who identified his paper with the values of feeling, was, in fact, false.[89]

At issue were the morals and manners of each side. Abigail referred to Bache's recent and ironically "polite allusion to Darby and Joan," symbols of a married pair grown old together ("the subject of a ballad called 'The Happy Old Couple'"): "I consider that as highly honorary to the domestic and conjugal character of the President, who has never given His Children or Grandchildren cause to Blush for any illegitimate offspring." This referred to the behavior in Paris of Bache's famous grandfather; Franklin had had his grandson with him then, and Abigail traced the differences between Bache and her husband back to the friction between Franklin and Adams there. President Adams, Abigail wrote her sister, exemplified "Republican," that is, republican American, "manners and habits," whereas Bache "aims to introduce True French manners in Religion and politicks." The manners for which Bache stood, tainted somehow as he was by his connection with his roué of a grandfather, were contrary to the all-American, republican values of domesticity and conjugality. When in Paris herself, Abigail had detected a contrast between sexually loose French ladies and their uxorious American counterparts, oriented toward domesticity, and we noted her ultimately horrified repudiation of those dancers at the Opéra. Now such manners threatened to cross the Atlantic.[90]

A little later, Abigail engaged Bache directly in the terms of sensibility. Bache had publicly attacked John Adams for nepotism in appointing his son John Quincy minister to Berlin. Abigail wrote to Bache, quoting a letter that John Quincy had written in response: "My son has written to me. As for Mr. Bache, he was once my schoolmate, one of those companions of those Infant years when the heart should be open to strong and deep impression of attachment, and never should admit any durable sentiment of hatred or malice." John Quincy's own heart thus had been permanently shaped: "'There is a degree of Regard and Tenderness that mixes itself in my recollection of every individual with whom I ever stood in that relation. . . . Mr. Bache must have lost those feelings, or he would never have been the vehicle of abuse upon me, at least during my absence from the country.'" Abigail sent this letter to Bache with the intention of affecting him in accordance with the same set of sentimental beliefs to which John Quincy's words were indebted: "Mr. Bache is left to his own reflections. This communication is only to his own Heart, being confident that the writer never expected it to meet his Eye."[91]

Four months later, Bache published his take on Abigail's appeal to his sensibility, one to which she responded with indignation. She introduced the subject by sending Mary "a National Song" that had been composed as part of a political exchange. "French tunes," she wrote from the then capital, Philadelphia, "have for a long time usurped an uncontrould sway." She referred to the impact of the XYZ Affair, an effort to extort bribes from the American ministers to France:[92] "Since the Change in the publick opinion respecting France, the people began to lose the relish for them, and what had been harmony now becomes discord." The result was a partisan demonstration at a public, heterosocial entertainment: "According their had been for several Evenings at the Theatre something like disorder, one party crying out for the Presidents March and Yankee Doodle, whilst Ciera was vociferated from the other." The editor of this letter notes of "Ciera": "'Ca ira,' the first popular song of the French Revolution, was sung in 1789 by the insurgents as they marched to Versailles." "Ca ira" had been suggested to its composer "by Lafayette, who remembered hearing Franklin say, when asked for news at various stages of the American Revolution: 'Ca ira, Ca ira.'" Abigail wrote that, at the song's performance by sections of the theater audience in Philadelphia, "it was hisst off repeatedly." But Bache's newspaper praised the players for their compliance with audience demands, demonstrating that "they did not forget that their audience was American." The song stimulated partisanship among Boston theatergoers, too.[93]

Theater managers tried to please both sides. In Philadelphia, they had no words to the "President's March," so Joseph Hopkinson wrote "Hail Columbia." Abigail reported: "Last Eve'ning they were sung for the first time. I had a Great curiosity to see for myself the Effect." At the end of the evening's formal program: "[The audience] calld again for the song and made [Gilbert Fox] repeat it for the fourth-time. And the last time the whole Audience broke forth in the Chorus whilst the thunder from their Hands was incessant, and at the close they gave 3 Huzzas, that you might have heard a mile." This was, Abigail asserted, "expressive of Approbations of the measures of the Executive," President John Adams, that is, as well as repudiative of Jeffersonian Francophilia. The episode only further provoked the opposition. "Yet dairingly do the vile incen-

diaries keep up in Baches paper the most wicked and base, violent & ca-
lumniating abuse," leveled not only "against the Government" but now
"contrary to their sentiments daily manifested" in "Hail Columbia," "so
that it insults the Majesty of the Sovereign People." She looked for relief
to Congress's passage of "a Sedition Bill," to be aimed at the libels that
issued from the Bache press "upon the President."[94]

Abigail described another libel in a postscript to this letter, the whole
of which supplied a context for its relation to sensibility: "Since writing
the above the song ['Hail Columbia'] is printed. Bache says this morning
that the excellent Lady of the Excellent President, was present, and shed
Tears of sensibility upon the occasion." This was heavily charged irony:
excessive sensibility had become associated with the excesses of the
French Revolution. A few months after Godwin's revelation of Wollstonecraft's unorthodox sexual behavior, defended on the basis of her
finer sensibility, the British anti-Jacobin cartoonist James Gillray, published "The New Morality" (illustrating the poem by George Canning),
in which one of the three goddesses presiding over part of the vast, satiric scene was labeled "Sensibility." In her left hand she held a dead bird,
feet upturned, representing disproportionate, if not false, sympathy—
these were false gods. Presumably, this was an allusion to the disreputable Sterne, whose protagonist in *A Sentimental Journey* responded to
the sight of a caged bird, "I never had my affections more tenderly awakened," leading to an exfoliation of his sympathetic imagination, which
throughout gained him access to sexual scenes with women and, in this
case, extended in effect to enslaved Africans. Abigail had invoked this
passage privately in that letter to Jefferson in which she mourned the loss
of her bird. One of the many Jacobin texts strewn at the feet of Gillray's
figure of sensibility was Wollstonecraft's recently published sentimental
and feminist novel *The Wrongs of Woman*. Gillray's cartoon was reprinted
and widely known, but it was only one expression of the discrediting of
excessive sensibility by its supposed association with revolution and the
unleashing of female sexuality, a reaction always latent but emerging in
the postrevolutionary 1780s. It bore an evident similarity to Rush's 1787
remark about young ladies weeping over *The Sorrows of Young Werther*
but disdaining the real needs of a beggar. (Abigail herself had agreed
with the negative typing of an excessively sentimental woman as "tremblingly alive all o'er.") Bache, then, has held Abigail up as the same kind
of figure, ironically, given his approval of the French Revolution and
his knowledge of her disapproval of it, as he had associated Abigail and
John with Darby and Joan, in order, Abigail wrote, to bring them "into

ridicule." He knew that she prided herself on her sensibility because she had told him so in the same letter that asserted that he lacked it.[95]

Abigail first coupled her account of Bache's report that she had shed tears of sensibility with a denial: "That was a lie. However I should not have been asshamed if it had been so." She was willing still to demonstrate her feeling that way on behalf of President Adams and his identification with American manners and morals, in repudiation of those associated with Jacobinism, with Bache, and with his grandfather. She then admitted that she well might have shed tears during the performance: "I laughed at one scene which was playd, [to] be sure, until the tears ran down, I believe." This may have been more scrupulous reporting, but more likely it indicated that she had become reluctant to admit that she could show the signs that opponents of the French Revolution were in the process of discrediting.[96]

John showed that he joined the reaction to Wollstonecraft provoked by Godwin's *Memoir* in twelve thousand words of commentary on her *Historical and Moral View of the Origin and Progress of French Revolution* (1794), although some of them were written prior to the publication of the *Memoir* (1798). According to Haraszti, to whom we are indebted for the publication of his marginalia, John read it on at least two occasions, 1796 and 1812. John declared Wollstonecraft to be "a lady of a masculine masterly understanding" but her *History* to be seriously flawed because she had "little experience in public affairs and her reading and reflection which would result from it." His general criticism was that her excessive feeling led her to fantasy, one currently conventional worry about the dangers of women's reading and writing, although it coincided with the federalist, anti-Jacobin view of the French Revolution: "The improvement, the exaltation of the human character, the perfectibility of man, and the perfection of the human faculties are the divine objects which her enthusiasm holds in beatific vision. Alass, how airy and baseless a fabric!" He reiterated this judgment by referring to Wollstoncraft's hopes as "ardent prophecies," which, he said, could be only partially accomplished by his favorite recipe, a form of "government, so mixed, combined and balance, as to restrain the passion of all orders of men." One recalls that 1801 attack on "female Politicians" whose inevitably female sensibility gave rise to an "ardent enthusiasm," in contrast to men's, and who were, therefore, disqualified from politics. Jefferson had disparaged black people because they were "ardent" in desire, rather than "tender and delicate" in love.[97]

Whether or not his phrase about restraining the passions characterizing all men also referred ironically to Wollstonecraft's *Vindication of the Rights of Woman*, John showed his consciousness of her sex throughout his commentary. He wrote that he had pointed out her history's defects "with too much severity, perhaps, and too little gallantry"; that last term he associated with Wollstonecraft's being a "lady," but with irony because she had excoriated it in the *Vindication*, signifying as it did profound male condescension and the double standard. Although on occasion he granted Wollstonecraft's "wisdom" and "sound sense," John called her "Indelicate" in her comparison of a government "to a dying wretch prompted by the lust of enjoyment," and, as Haraszti notes, when Wollstonecraft "spoke of the fair bosom of public opinion," John had to remind himself that 'A lady is the writer.'" Similarly, John judged "Miss Wollstonecraft . . . too fond of such words as "insinuating *voluptuous* softness." On reading "the moments of languor that glide into the interstices of *enjoyment*," John remarked: "These luscious words might have been avoided by a lady." In reaction to Wollstonecraft's comparing France to a diseased body suffering from "excrementituous humours," John declared: "This nasty rhetoric could be learned only in France. By an English lady it could be only written in the temple of Cloacina, at her devotion to the goddess." During his first years with Abigail, he had written her that the "History of Close Stools and Chamber Potts" would not be acceptable to a lady, illustrating that limits of propriety shaped by gender as well as by class. At different points, he exclaimed of Wollstonecraft "this weak woman," "this mad woman," "this foolish woman," and "this silly woman."[98]

John's reading Godwin's *Memoir* prior to rereading Wollstonecraft's book on the French Revolution enabled him, as it did his reactionary contemporaries, to link her feminism to her sexual freedom. In her *Historical . . . View of the French Revolution*, Wollstonecraft asked rhetorically: "And who will coolly maintain that it is as just to deprive a woman of all the rights of a citizen, because her revolting heart turns from the man whom she can neither love or respect, to find comfort in a more congenial or humane bosom?" Adams reacted with indignation: "Would you divorce her when she pleaded? Would you have no women because some are incorrigible prostitutes? Would you have no husbands because some are brutal? Would you have no beauty because it often seduces? Would you have no writers because some like yourself are licentious?" After commenting on her consideration of an executive's veto and her apparent "vacillations" toward it, he "angrily concluded": "This ignorant woman knows nothing of the matter. She seems to have half a mind to be an English woman; yet more inclined to be an American. Perhaps her lover gave her lessons." This was Imlay.[99]

It is hardly conceivable that John did not discuss Godwin's *Memoir* with Abigail. In any case, the same year of that book's publication and of Bache's report that she publically shed tears of sensibility, Abigail wrote John the letter in which she told him that nothing made a man more "fractious" than "living without females about him" and that women knew how to "Sooth" the jarring elements "into good humour." She then added: "You see I am willing to keep up my self consequence, as well as the honour and dignity of the Sex." In reiterating her view of a woman's proper role, Abigail has added a clear slap at the Wollstone-craftian attack on that convention (propounded by Fordyce) that women should subordinate themselves to men's needs and wishes. She continued: "I have an Authority on point, our minister at Berlin"—that is, John Quincy—"in his last Letter Speaking of his wife says, 'her Lovely disposition and affectionate heart, afford me constant consolation amidst all the distresses, cares and vexations which the publick concerns so thickly strew in my way.'" This had been what the young, unmarried John Quincy had fantasized in "A Vision," which he said came to him when he was "fatigued with labor and with care opprest."[100] Abigail's quotation of John Quincy's 1798 expression of this comfort led her back to John's comfortlessness in Philadelphia: "I hope you sleep a nights." Strikingly, however, she was now apart from him by choice, even as she subscribed to the ideal of ministering wifehood.[101]

Mary Kelley has recently demonstrated that the Americanized culture of sensibility only expanded throughout the antebellum period, continuing to move West and down the social scale. Heyrman suggests the same of the white rural South.[102] Letters written to Jefferson during his two terms indicate that white Americans, noticeably women, also continued to identify the presidency with sensibility. One poor woman claiming acquaintance with him wrote Jefferson from Williamsburg in 1801: "I think I am to well Acquainted with the goodness of your Heart, your tender Sensibility, to doubt your sending me a little Assistance." She believed that her words would stimulate his charity. He would "Pitty and feel" when she told him the story of her brother whose derangement had been brought about because of his service in the Revolution. The editor of a selection of these letters asks of one of the most "self-consciously pathetic" of them, sent Jefferson by a seventeen-year-old Baltimore girl: "Was she manipulative and melodramatic, wallowing in self-pity, or is her letter the impulsive outpouring of an innocent teenager, written in the fevered prose of the sentimental fiction she read?" To Washington's, Adams's, and Jefferson's identification with sensibility it can be added that Lincoln's speeches as president, including the first inaugural address (quoted in the introduction) as well as his speeches as candidate from Illinois to Washington, incorporated some of the language of sensibility, but Lincoln also spoke the language of male popular culture he first learned in Kentucky.[103]

Updated in terminology to an extent, its sexual potentials shriveled even more by political reaction and evangelism, the Americanized culture of sensibility, already resting on the domesticity nourished by commerce from the 1790s, could begin to capitalize on the industrial revolution. Kelley remarks that the "supposed break between 'republican womanhood' and 'Victorian domesticity' was not as decisive as has been suggested by many historians." If Bushman holds that "sensibility was at the heart of genteel culture" in the eighteenth-century, Anglo-American colonies, Shirley Samuels declares that "sentimentality is at the heart of nineteenth-century American culture." We could put *genteel* in that statement, too, provided we allow for social aspiration and penetration.[104]

The ensuing "female world of love and ritual" coexisted with that masculine culture of "American humor" that was described by Rourke, one that she demonstrates drew on African American culture or cultures, too.[105] Mark Twain has left us a detailed record of that coexistence on the Missouri frontier of the 1830s and 1840s. One item in the Grangerford household where Huck found shelter was a picture—a "crayon"— that, Huck writes, "one of the daughters which was dead made her own self when she was only fifteen years old." Its subject was descended from Sterne by way of that Gillray cartoon. "Sister Adelaide" illustrated the perpetuation of the figure in the intervening period, her definition of *sensibility* referring to the false version depicted by a woman who would "weep over the sorrows of an unfortunate heroine, turn pale at the sight of a beggar, and faint at the death of a canary bird." The crayon Huck described was of "a young lady with her hair all combed up straight to the top of her head, and knotted there in front of a comb like a chair-back, and she was crying into a handkerchief and had a dead bird laying on its back in her other hand with its heels up, and underneath the picture it said 'I Shall Never Hear Thy Sweet Chirrup More Alas.'" Huck's orientation here, and his diction, expressed the popular male culture evident throughout *The Adventures of Huckleberry Finn*.[106] The picture manifested the popularized, female sentimentality expressed literarily in *Prose and*

*Poetry by a Western Lady*, quoted by Twain in the public exercises of Tom Sawyer's female schoolfellows in "St. Petersburg," Missouri, set in the same antebellum era as *Huckleberry Finn*. Tom himself, however, one of the boys, "soared into the unquenchable and undestructible 'Give me liberty or give me death'" speech that Patrick Henry appropriated from Addison's *Cato*. True sensibility in *Huckleberry Finn* is shown by the relationship between Huck and Jim throughout, on one occasion Huck concluding: "I didn't do him no more mean tricks, and I wouldn't done that one if I'd a knowed it would make him feel that way."[107]

# NOTES

## INTRODUCTION

1. Winthrop Jordan, *White over Black: American Attitudes toward the Negro, 1550–1812* (New York: Penguin, 1969), 338 (and see 335–39).

2. G. J. Barker-Benfield, *The Culture of Sensibility: Sex and Society in Eighteenth Century Britain* (Chicago: University of Chicago Press, 1992).

3. Boston journal quoted in Rosemarie Zagarri, *Revolutionary Backlash: Women and Politics in the Early American Republic* (Philadelphia: University of Pennsylvania Press, 2007), 67; Charles Francis Adams, ed., *Familiar Letters of John Adams and His Wife, Abigail Adams, during the Revolution* (Boston: Little, Brown, 1876); *The Book of Abigail and John: Selected Letters of the Adams Family, 1762–1784*, ed. L. H. Butterfield, Marc Friedlaender, and Mary Jo Cline (Cambridge, MA: Harvard University Press, 1975), 11, 9.

4. *Book of Abigail and John*, 9; Abraham Lincoln, "First Inaugural Address," March 4, 1861, in *Collected Works of Abraham Lincoln*, ed. R. P. Basler, 9 vols. (New Brunswick, NJ: Rutgers University Press, 1953), 4:262–71, 271.

5. *Book of Abigail and John*, 8.

6. Page Smith, *John Adams*, 2 vols. (Garden City, NY: Doubleday, 1962), 1:71; David McCullough, *John Adams* (New York: Simon & Schuster, 2001), 57.

7. *Adams Family Correspondence* (hereafter *AFC*), ed. L. H. Butterfield et al., 9 vols. to date (Cambridge, MA: Belknap Press of Harvard University Press, 1963–); John Adams, *Diary and Autobiography of John Adams*, ed. Lyman H. Butterfield et al., 4 vols. (Cambridge, MA: Belknap Press of Harvard University Press, 1961); Peter Shaw, *The Character of John Adams* (Chapel Hill: University of North Carolina Press, 1976); Peter Shaw, "Diplomacy and Domesticity: An Intimate Record," review of vols. 3 and 4 of *Adams Family Correspondence*, *American Scholar* 42 (1973): 686–92, 688, 690.

8. Charles W. Akers, *Abigail Adams: An American Woman* (Boston: Little, Brown, 1980), 29, 59; McCullough, *John Adams*, 57; Lynne Withey, *Dearest Friend: A Life of Abigail Adams* (New York: Free Press, 1981), 115–16, 117; Phyllis Lee Levin, *Abigail Adams: A Biography* (New York: St. Martin's, 1987), chap. 8; Edith B. Gelles, *Portia: The World of Abigail Adams* (Bloomington: Indiana University Press, 1992), 25.

9. John Ferling, *John Adams: A Life* (Knoxville: University of Tennessee Press, 1992), 4, 132–34.

10. Margaret A. Hogan and C. James Taylor, introduction to *My Dearest Friend: Letters of Abigail and John Adams*, ed. Margaret A. Hogan and C. James Taylor (Cambridge, MA: Belknap Press of Harvard University Press, 2007), xiii–xvii, xvi. Hogan and Taylor are also

the first listed of the team that edited vol. 8 of the *Adams Family Correspondence*, the others being Hobson Woodward, Jessie Mary Rodrique, Gregg L. Lint, and Mary T. Claffey.

11. David Waldstreicher, "Founders Chic as Culture War," *Radical History Review* 84 (2002): 185–94; H. W. Brands, "Founders Chic: Our Reverence for the Founders Has Gotten Out of Hand," *Atlantic Monthly*, September 2003, 101–10; James J. Ellis, foreword to *My Dearest Friend*, vii–xii.

12. Edith B. Gelles, *Abigail and John: Portrait of a Marriage* (New York: William Morrow, 2009), ix, x, 68–69, 150, 285.

13. R. F. Brissenden, *Virtue in Distress: Studies in the Novel of Sentiment from Richardson to Sade* (New York: Barnes & Noble, 1974).

14. Constance Rourke, *American Humor: A Study of National Character* (1931; Tallahassee: Florida State University Press, 1986).

15. Herbert Ross Brown, *The Sentimental Novel in America, 1789–1860* (Durham, NC: Duke University Press, 1940); Leslie Fiedler, *Love and Death in the American Novel* (New York: Stein & Day, 1966); Cathy N. Davidson, *Revolution and the Word: The Rise of the Novel in America* (New York: Oxford University Press, 1987); Julia A. Stern, *The Plight of Feeling: Sympathy and Dissent in the Early American Novel* (Chicago: University of Chicago Press, 1997); Elizabeth Barnes, *States of Sympathy: Seduction and Democracy in the American Novel* (New York: Columbia University Press, 1997); Julie Ellison, *Cato's Tears and the Making of Anglo-American Emotion* (Chicago: University of Chicago Press, 1999).

16. Garry Wills, *Inventing America: Jefferson's Declaration of Independence* (New York: Vintage, 1979), chap. 19; Gordon S. Wood, *The Radicalism of the American Revolution* (New York: Vintage, 1992), 235; Andrew Burstein, *Sentimental Democracy: The Evolution of America's Romantic Self-Image* (New York: Hill & Wang, 1999), xi; Sarah Knott, *Sensibility and the American Revolution* (Chapel Hill: University of North Carolina Press, 2009), 105; David Waldstreicher, *In the Midst of Perpetual Fetes: The Making of American Nationalism, 1776–1820* (Chapel Hill: University of North Carolina Press, 1997), 51. Americanization is implicit in Nicole Eustace's *Passion Is the Gale: Emotion, Power, and the Coming of the American Revolution* (Chapel Hill: University of North Carolina Press, 2008), which, like Knott's book, focuses on Pennsylvania.

17. E. P. Thompson, *The Making of the English Working Class* (New York: Vintage, 1963), 9–10. For a brilliant correction of this fundamental flaw, see Anna Clark, *The Struggle for the Breeches: Gender and the Making of the British Working Class* (Berkeley and Los Angeles: University of California Press, 1991).

18. Simone de Beauvoir, *The Second Sex* (1949), trans. H. M. Parshley (New York: Vintage, 1989).

19. William Haller, *An Elect Nation: The Meaning and Relevance of Foxe's Book of Martyrs* (New York: Harper & Row, 1963); William Bradford, *Of Plymouth Plantation*, ed. Samuel Eliot Morison (New York: Knopf, 1952), 5.

20. Mary Rowlandson, *The Sovereignty and Goodness of God, Together with the Faithfulness of His Promises Displayed* (1686), ed. Neal Salisbury (Boston: Bedford, 1997). In his superb introduction to this edition, Neal Salisbury writes that it invented the genre (ibid., 51). Margaret Fuller, *Summer on the Lakes, in 1843* (1844; Urbana: University of Illinois Press, 1991), 111, 39.

21. James Everett Seaver, *A Narrative of the Life of Mary Jemison: The White Woman of the Genesee* (1824), rev. Charles Delamater Vail (New York: American Scenic and Historic Preservation Society, 1918), vii; Bernard Bailyn, *The Peopling of British North America* (New York: Vintage, 1986), 116; Christine Leigh Heyrman, *Southern Cross: The Beginning of the Bible Belt* (New York: Knopf, 1997), 150. See, too, Jan Lewis, *The Pursuit of Happiness: Family and Values*

*in Jefferson's Virginia* (Cambridge: Cambridge University Press, 1983), 219; and Rourke, *American Humor*, 10–11, 37, 38–39.

22. Kenneth Cmiel, *Democratic Eloquence: The Fight over Popular Speech in Nineteenth-Century America* (Berkeley and Los Angeles: University of California Press, 1990), 28, 29; Adams, *Diary and Autobiography*, 1:198, 97. For a thorough definition of the meaning of being a gentleman in eighteenth-century British North America, see Wood, *Radicalism of the American Revolution*, chap. 2. I realize that my application of the term *class* to the eighteenth century is a bit anachronistic; cf. Eric Foner, *The Story of American Freedom* (New York: Norton, 1998), 9–11.

23. *Spectator*, no. 294 (February 6, 1712), in *The Spectator*, ed. Donald F. Bond, 5 vols. (Oxford: Clarendon, 1965), 3:47–48; Richard L. Bushman, *The Refinement of America: Persons, Houses, Cities* (New York: Knopf, 1992), 365–70; Wood, *Radicalism of the American Revolution*, 27, 31. Compare the perspective offered recently in Keith Thomas, *The Ends of Life: Roads to Fulfillment in Early Modern England* (Oxford: Oxford University Press, 2009), 12–29.

24. Barker-Benfield, *Culture of Sensibility*, 63; *Spectator*, no. 10 (March 12, 1711), in Bond, ed., *Spectator*, 1:45.

25. Bushman, *Refinement of America*, 281; Cmiel, *Democratic Eloquence*, 56, 57 (and see 176).

26. Jackson Turner Main, *The Social Structure of Revolutionary America* (Princeton, NJ: Princeton University Press, 1983), 277–78; *The Carolina Backcountry on the Eve of Revolution: The Journal and Other Writings of Charles Woodmason, Anglican Itinerant*, ed. Richard J. Hooker (Chapel Hill; University of North Carolina Press, 1953), 223, 222; Wood, *Radicalism of the American Revolution*, 133. Richard Hooker compares Woodmason's writing to that of his contemporary, Laurence Sterne. Richard J. Hooker, introduction to *Journal of Charles Woodmason*, xxxiv.

27. Heyrman, *Southern Cross*, 44–46.

28. Rhys Isaac, *The Transformation of Virginia, 1740–1790* (Chapel Hill: University of North Carolina Press, 1982), 309; Bushman, *Refinement of America*, 80–83; Heyrman, *Southern Cross*, 33–34.

29. Barker-Benfield, *Culture of Sensibility*, 178–79; Bushman, *Refinement of America*, 403–6; Carol Berkin, *First Generations: Women in Colonial America* (New York: Hill & Wang, 1996), 136–50; Wood, *Radicalism of the American Revolution*, 184–85; Gordon S. Wood, *The Americanization of Benjamin Franklin* (New York: Penguin, 2004), chap. 1.

30. Abigail Adams to Mary Smith Cranch, January 31, 1767, in *AFC*, 1:60–61.

31. Wood, *Radicalism of the American Revolution*, 172. See, too, Gary J. Kornbluth and John M. Murrin, "The Dilemmas of Ruling Elites in Revolutionary America," in *Ruling America: A History of Wealth and Power in a Democracy*, ed. Steve Fraser and Gary Gerstle (Cambridge, MA: Harvard University Press, 2005), 27–63.

32. Adams, *Diary and Autobiography*, 1:332–33; Ian Watt, *The Rise of the Novel: Studies in Defoe, Richardson and Fielding* (1957; reprint, Berkeley: University of California Press, 1967), 188–89; Isaac, *Transformation of Virginia*, 302–5; James Deetz, *In Small Things Forgotten: The Archeology of Early American Life* (Garden City, NY: Anchor, 1977); Barker-Benfield, *Culture of Sensibility*, 161–62, xxvi, chap. 6 passim.

33. Bushman, *Refinement of America*, 123, 127; Abigail Adams to John Adams, August 29, 1776, in *AFC*, 2:112; Withey, *Dearest Friend*, 204–5, 202.

34. It was with such images that Blake illustrated Wollstonecraft's *Original Stories from Real Life* (1788). For an example by another artist, see Barker-Benfield, *Culture of Sensibility*, 230.

35. Adams, *Diary and Autobiography*, 1:333.

36. Ibid.; Abigail Adams to Mary Smith Cranch, [July 26, 1786], in *AFC*, 5:377–78; *Journal*

*and Correspondence of Miss Adams, Daughter of John Adams*, ed. Caroline Amelia Van Windt, 2 vols. (New York: Wiley & Putnam, 1841, 1842), 1:41–44. For Descartes etc., see chapter 1 below.

37. Thomas Jefferson to Robert Skipwith, August 3, 1771, in *The Papers of Thomas Jefferson*, ed. Julian P. Boyd et al., 25 vols. to date (Princeton, NJ: Princeton University Press, 1950–), 1:76–81; Elizabeth Smith Shaw to Abigail Adams, June 12, 1785, in *AFC*, 6:174–75.

38. *Society for Encouraging Industry and Employing the Poor . . .* (Boston, 1754). This document is held by the Library Company of Philadelphia. For its context, see Gary B. Nash, *Urban Crucible: Social Change, Political Consciousness, and the Origins of the American Revolution* (Cambridge, MA: Harvard University Press, 1979), 192.

39. M. J. Heale, "From City Fathers to Social Critics: Humanitarianism and Government in New York, 1790–1860," *Journal of American History* 63 (1976): 21–41; M. J. Heale, "Humanitarianism in the Early Republic: The Moral Reformers of New York, 1776–1825," *Journal of American Studies* 2 (1968): 161–75; Barker-Benfield, *Culture of Sensibility*, 77–98; David Hume, "Of Money" (1777), in *Essays Moral, Political, and Literary*, ed. Eugene F. Miller (Indianapolis: Liberty Fund, 1985), 283.

40. Abigail Adams to John Adams, March 12, [1776], in *AFC*, 1:352; Abigail Adams to Mary Smith Cranch, July 6, 1784, in ibid., 5:358–59, 373. For John's view of social hierarchy, see Shaw, *Character of John Adams*, 209–14.

41. Abigail Adams to Cotton Tufts, September 8, 1784, in *AFC*, 5:456 (writing about her efforts to achieve such harmony); Barker-Benfield, *Culture of Sensibility*, 229, 231; Abigail Adams to Thomas Jefferson, June 6, 1785, in *The Adams-Jefferson Letters: The Complete Correspondence between Thomas Jefferson and Abigail and John Adams*, ed. Lester J. Cappon (Chapel Hill: University of North Carolina Press, 1959), 28.

42. Sarah N. Randolph, *The Domestic Life of Thomas Jefferson, Compiled from Family Letters and Reminiscences* (New York: Frederick Ungar, 1958), 152. For a discussion of this passage, see Annette Gordon-Reed, *The Hemingses of Monticello: An American Family* (New York: Norton, 2008), 397–401.

43. Thomas Jefferson, *Notes on the State of Virginia* (1785; New York: Harper Torchbooks, 1964), 135–36; Lewis, *Pursuit of Happiness*, 218–19. Jefferson's views of race and slavery were changeable and contradictory over his lifetime. See John Chester Miller, *The Wolf by the Ears: Thomas Jefferson and Slavery* (New York: Free Press, 1977); and, in the richest social context, Gordon-Reed, *The Hemingses of Monticello*, passim.

44. Vincent Carreta, introduction to *Letters of the Late Ignatius Sancho, an African* (1782), ed. Vincent Carreta (New York: Penguin 1998), ix–xxxiv; Gordon-Reed, *The Hemingses of Monticello*, 494; Knott, *Sensibility and the American Revolution*, 294–95. For the paragraph's last point, see Jordan, *White over Black*, 343; and David Brion Davis, *The Problem of Slavery in Western Culture* (Ithaca, NY: Cornell University Press, 1966), 352–53.

45. Wylie Sypher, "Hutcheson and the 'Classical' Theory of Slavery," *Journal of Negro History* 24, no. 3 (July 1939): 263–80, 203, 277; Davis, *Problem of Slavery*, 333, 333 n. 1, 348 n. 41. For Sypher's skeptical view of sentimentality and antislavery, see his *Guinea's Captive Kings: British Anti-Slavery Literature of the Eighteenth Century* (1942; New York: Octagon, 1969), 260–72 and passim. Jordan distinguishes between humanitarianism and sentimentality, suggesting that the former motivated reform and that the latter was self-indulgent. *White over Black*, 365–72. In this, Jordan follows Sypher, *Guinea's Captive Kings*, 105, 266–86.

46. Julie Roy Jeffrey, *The Great Silent Army of Abolitionism: Ordinary Women in the Antislavery Movement* (Chapel Hill: University of North Carolina Press, 1998), 36, 37, and passim; Claire Midgeley, *Women against Slavery: The British Campaigns, 1780–1870* (London: Routledge, 1992), passim.

47. For the Adamses' views of race, see chapters 7 and 14 below. Davis notes that "there was an immense gulf between literary pathos and dedicated reform." *Problem of Slavery*, 357. The nineteenth-century black abolitionist David Ruggles was to declare that the "pleas of crying soft and sparing never answered the purpose of reform, and never will." Quoted in Benjamin Quarles, *Black Abolitionists* (New York: Oxford University Press, 1969), 15.

48. Bushman, *Refinement of America*, 434. See, too, Peter Kolchin, *American Slavery, 1619–1877* (New York: Hill & Wang, 1993), 82–84.

49. Brenda E. Stevenson, *Life in Black and White: Family and Community in the Slave South* (New York: Oxford University Press, 1996), 315.

50. Philip D. Morgan, *Slave Counterpoint: Black Culture in the Eighteenth-Century Chesapeake and Lowcountry* (Chapel Hill: University of North Carolina Press, 1998), 102, chap. 2 passim. There is evidence that some African Americans, slave and free, participated in the eighteenth century's consumer revolution. When they could obtain fashionable items of clothing (hand-me-downs or garb that was stolen, traded, or bought), they put them to their own cultural and subversive purposes, although, evidently, there was some common ground here with white women and lower-class white men in terms of opportunities for self-expression. Shane White and Graham White, "Slave Clothing and African-American Culture in the Eighteenth and Nineteenth Centuries," *Past and Present* 148 (1995): 149–86; Morgan, *Slave Counterpoint*, 598–99, 602; Christine Stansell, *City of Women: Sex and Class in New York, 1789–1860* (Urbana: University of Illinois Press, 1986), 93.

51. James Walvin, "Ignatius Sancho: The Man and His Times," in *Ignatius Sancho: An African Man of Letters* (London: National Portrait Gallery, 1997), 93–113, 97–98. See, too, Jordan, *White over Black*, 333.

52. Kolchin, *American Slavery*, 50; J. Hector St. John de Crèvecoeur, *Letters from an American Farmer* (1782; New York: Dutton, 1957), 157; Stevenson, *Life in Black and White*, 324–25, 325, 261.

53. Kolchin, *American Slavery*, 126, 155.

54. Donald Meyer, *The Positive Thinkers: Religion as Pop Psychology from Mary Baker Eddy to Oral Roberts* (1965; New York: Pantheon, 1980), 52.

55. Morgan, *Slave Counterpoint*, 437, 645, 638, 656, 610, 658; Heyrman, *Southern Cross*, 50. For a summary of contrasting views, see Kolchin, *American Slavery*, 145–46.

56. Morgan, *Slave Counterpoint*, xvii, 664 (and see 560–80).

57. Marie Jenkins Schwartz, *Born in Bondage: Growing Up Enslaved in the Antebellum South* (Cambridge, MA: Harvard University Press, 2000); Wilma King, *Stolen Childhood: Slave Youth in Nineteenth Century America* (Bloomington: Indiana University Press, 1997); Steven Mintz, *Huck's Raft: A History of American Childhood* (Cambridge, MA: Belknap Press of Harvard University Press, 2004), chap. 5. See, too, Kolchin, *American Slavery*, 117.

58. Morgan, *Slave Counterpoint*, 664; "Journal of Josiah Quincy, Junior, 1773," *Proceedings of the Massachusetts Historical Society* 49 (June 1916): 424–81, 456–57. Quincy referred to Sterne's novel *A Sentimental Journey* (1768). For a contrasting view to the idea that most African Americans' speech was quite different from that of whites, see Michael Patrick Ely, *Israel on the Appomattox: A Southern Experiment in Black Freedom from the 1790s to the Civil War* (New York: Knopf, 2004), 290–95. Gordon-Reed agrees. See *The Hemingses of Monticello*, 285.

59. Harriet Jacobs, *Incidents in the Life of a Slave Girl, Written by Herself* (1861), ed., with an introduction by, Jean Fagan Yellin (Cambridge, MA: Harvard University Press, 1987), 118; Jean Fagan Yellin, introduction to Jacobs, *Life of a Slave Girl*, xiii–xxxiv, xxi; B. A. Botkin, *Lay My Burden Down: A Folk History of Slavery* (Chicago: University of Chicago Press, 1945), ix; Harriet Beecher Stowe, *Uncle Tom's Cabin; or, Life among the Lowly* (New York: New American

Library, 1966), preface. In his preface to Frederick Douglass's *Narrative*, first given in spoken form, Garrison declared that "multitudes had been melted to tears by his [Douglass's] pathos." William Lloyd Garrison, preface to *Narrative of the Life of Frederick Douglass, an American Slave, Written by Himself* (1845; New York: Penguin, 1982), 33–42, 33–34.

CHAPTER I

1. Norman S. Fiering, "Irresistible Compassion: An Aspect of Eighteenth-Century Sympathy and Humanitarianism," in *Race, Gender, and Rank: Early Modern Ideas of Humanity* ed. Maryanne Cline Horowitz (Rochester, NY: University of Rochester, 1992), 378–401; Norman S. Fiering, *Moral Philosophy at Seventeenth-Century Harvard: A Discipline in Transition* (Chapel Hill: University of North Carolina Press, 1981); Norman S. Fiering, *Jonathan Edwards's Moral Thought and Its British Context* (Eugene, OR: Wipf & Stock, 1981).

2. Fiering, *Moral Philosophy at Seventeenth-Century Harvard*, 5. Suggestive, too, is Amélie Oksenberg Rorty, "From Passion to Emotions and Sentiments," *Philosophy* 57 (1982): 159–27.

3. Fiering, "Irresistible Compassion," 379 n. 3. The history of cultures of sensibility in other nations is a subject beyond the scope of this book.

4. Fiering, *Moral Philosophy at Seventeenth-Century Harvard*, 6.

5. Jon Butler, *Awash in a Sea of Faith: Christianizing the American People* (Cambridge, MA: Harvard University Press, 1990), chap. 4; David Humphreys, *An Historical Account of the Incorporated Society for the Propagation of the Gospel in Foreign Parts* (London: Joseph Downing, 1730); Rev. H. P. Thompson, *Into All Lands: The History of the Society for the Propagation of the Gospel in Foreign Parts, 1701–1950* (London: SPCK, 1951); *Journal of Charles Woodmason*, 202, 208, 210, 214, 217; Harry S. Stout, *The Divine Dramatist: George Whitefield and the Rise of Modern Evangelicalism* (Grand Rapids, MI: William B. Eerdmans, 1991), chaps. 4, 6; Barker-Benfield, *Culture of Sensibility*, 72, 76–7.

6. James Walvin, *The Quakers, Money, and Morals* (London: John Murray, 1997); Davis, *Problem of Slavery*, chap. 10; Heyrman, *Southern Cross*, 44–46, 33–35, and passim.

7. Fiering, *Moral Philosophy at Seventeenth-Century Harvard*, 178.

8. René Descartes, *The Passions of the Soul*, trans. Stephen H. Voss (Indianapolis: Hackett, 1989), 51–52, 133 n. 46. See, too, Desmond M. Clarke, *Descartes's Theory of Mind* (Oxford: Clarendon, 2003), 119–20, 128–34.

9. Susan James, *Passion and Action: The Emotions in Seventeenth-Century Philosophy* (Oxford: Clarendon, 1997), 97–108; Clarke, *Descartes's Theory of Mind*, chap. 4.

10. Descartes, *Passions of the Soul*, 29–30, 58; John Dunn, *Locke: A Very Short Introduction* (Oxford: Oxford University Press, 2003), 50; John W. Yolton, introduction to John Locke, *An Essay concerning Human Understanding*, ed. John W. Yolton (London: Dent, 1993), xix–xlii, xxxiv; Clarke, *Descartes's Theory of Mind*, chap. 1.

11. For More's and Descartes's letters to each other, see *The Philosophical Writings of Descartes*, trans. John Cottingham, Robert Stoothoff, Dugald Murdoch, and Anthony Kenny, 3 vols. (Cambridge: Cambridge University Press, 1991), vol. 3, *The Correspondence*.

12. Marjorie Nicholson, "The Early Stages of Cartesianism in England," *Studies in Philosophy* 26 (July 1929): 356–74; Danton B. Sailor, "Cudworth and Descartes," *Journal of the History of Ideas* 23, no. 1 (1962): 133–40; Fiering, *Moral Philosophy at Seventeenth-Century Harvard*, 268, 64.

13. Henry More, *Enchiridion ethicum: The English Translation of 1690* (New York: Facsimile Text Society, 1930); Fiering, *Moral Philosophy at Seventeenth-Century Harvard*, 47 n. 77; Bond, ed., *Spectator*, 1:68–69, 480, 2:423, 4:349.

14. Margaret Jacob, *The Newtonians and the English Revolution, 1689–1720* (Ithaca, NY: Cornell University Press, 1976), 28 and passim; Simon Patrick, *A Brief Account of the New Sect of Latitude Men, Together with Some Brief Reflections of the New Philosophy* (1662; Los Angeles: William Andrews Clark Memorial Library, 1963).

15. Frank Manuel, *The Religion of Isaac Newton* (Oxford: Clarendon, 1974), 63; Barker-Benfield, *Culture of Sensibility*, 4–5; Daniel Garber, *Descartes' Metaphysical Physics* (Chicago: University of Chicago Press, 1992), 299.

16. R. S. Crane, "Suggestions toward a Genealogy of the 'Man of Feeling,'" *English Literary History* 1, no. 3 (December 1934): 205–30, 207. Unfortunately, Crane ignored the impact of Descartes. For objections to Crane's argument, see Barker-Benfield, *Culture of Sensibility*, 421 n. 133. For More and Crane's subjects, see Fiering, *Moral Philosophy at Seventeenth-Century Harvard*, 262 n. 57.

17. Jan Papy, "Justus Lipsius," in *Stanford Encyclopedia of Philosophy* (Fall 2004), available at http://plato.stanford.edu/archives/fall2004/entries/justus-lipsius/; Crane, "Genealogy of the 'Man of Feeling,'" 214; Frederick C. Beiser, *The Sovereignty of Reason: The Defense of Rationality in the Early English Enlightenment* (Princeton, NJ: Princeton University Press, 1990), 142.

18. T. C. Curtis and W. A. Speck, "The Societies for the Reformation of Manners: A Case Study in the Theory and Practice of Moral Reform," *Literature and History*, no. 3 (1976): 45–64; Dudley W. R. Bahlman, *The Moral Revolution of 1688* (New Haven, CT: Yale University Press, 1957).

19. Jacob, *Newtonians*, 52–53, 45. For a contrary view, see Beiser, *Sovereignty of Reason*, 140ff.

20. Jacob, *Newtonians*, 53, 51, 52, 57; Colin Campbell, *The Romantic Ethic and the Spirit of Modern Consumerism* (Oxford: Blackwell, 1987), introduction and passim; Alexander Pope, *An Essay on Man*, ed. Maynard Mack (London: Methuen, 1950), 166 (lines 394–96).

21. There is, in addition to Curtis and Speck's "Societies for the Reformation of Manners" and Bahlman's *Moral Revolution of 1688*, a growing number of histories of this subject. For the large context, see Norbert Elias, *The Civilizing Process: The History of Manners and State Formation and Civilization* (1939), trans. Edmund Jephcott (Oxford: Blackwell, 1978). I have found Bushman's *Refinement of America*, Richard P. Gildrie's *The Profane, the Civil, and the Godly: The Reformation of Manners in Orthodox New England, 1679–1749* (University Park: Pennsylvania State University Press, 1994), and Ann Fairfax Withington's *Toward a More Perfect Union: Virtue and the Formation of American Republics* (New York: Oxford University Press, 1991) most relevant to my eighteenth-century subject. See, too, C. Dallett Hemphill, *Bowing to Necessities: A History of Manners in America, 1620–1860* (New York: Oxford University Press, 1999).

22. See Curtis and Speck, "Societies for the Reformation of Manners"; Bahlman, *Moral Revolution of 1688*; and Peter Wagner, *Eros Revived: Erotica of the Enlightenment in England and America* (London: Seeker & Warburg, 1988), 134, 256.

23. Elizabeth Howe, *The First English Actresses: Women and Drama, 1600–1700* (Cambridge: Cambridge University Press, 1992); John Harold Wilson, *All the King's Ladies: Actresses of the Restoration* (Chicago: University of Chicago Press, 1958); *The Works of Aphra Behn*, ed. Montague Summers, 6 vols. (New York: Benjamin Bloom, 1967); Maureen Duffy, *The Passionate Shepherdess: Aphra Behn, 1640–1689* (New York: Avon, 1977); Anne Conway, *The Principles of the Most Ancient and Modern Philosophy* (1690), ed. Allison P. Coudet and Taylor Corse (Cambridge: Cambridge University Press, 1966); Anne Finch, Countess of Winchilsea, *Selected Poems*, ed. Katherine M. Rogers (New York: Frederick Ungar, 1979); *First Feminists: British Woman Writers, 1578–1799*, ed. Moira Ferguson (Bloomington: Indiana University Press, 1985); Hilda L. Smith, *Reason's Disciples: Seventeenth-Century English Feminists* (Urbana: Uni-

versity of Illinois Press, 1982); Katie Whitaker, *Mad Madge: The Extraordinary Life of Margaret Cavendish, Duchess of Newcastle, the First Woman to Live by Her Pen* (New York: Basic, 2002). This is the tip of an iceberg.

24. This reflects my reading in Restoration plays, notably *The Works of John Dryden* (ed. E. N. Hooker and H. T. Swedenborg Jr., 20 vols. [Berkeley and Los Angeles: University of California Press, 1950–2002]), the *Works of Aphra Behn*, and *The Broadview Anthology of Restoration and Early Eighteenth-Century Drama* (ed. J. Douglas Canfield [Peterborough, ON: Broadview, 2001]), as well as other plays, all part of my research for a chapter in a project tentatively entitled "From Passions to Sensibility: Descartes, Dryden, and Behn to Pope."

25. Ruth Perry, *The Celebrated Mary Astell: An Early English Feminist* (Chicago: University of Chicago Press, 1980); Barker-Benfield, *Culture of Sensibility*, 193–98.

26. Jeremy Collier, *A Short View of the Immorality and Profaneness of the English Stage*, facsimile of the 3rd, 1698 ed. (Munich: Wilhelm Fink, 1967), 68.

27. John Dryden, "An Essay of Dramatick Poesie" (1668), in *Works of John Dryden*, 17:3–81; Aphra Behn, preface to *The Lucky Chance* (1687), in *Works of Aphra Behn*, 3:185–87. Other women playwrights included Frances Boothby, Susannah Centlivre, Delariviere Manley, Mary Pix, Elizabeth Polwhele, and Catherine Trotter, all described in Janet Todd, ed., *A Dictionary of British and American Women Writers, 1600–1800* (London: Methunen, 1987).

28. Collier, *Short View*, 1–2, 166, 68–69, 7, 11.

29. Nicholas Malebranche, *The Search after Truth*, trans. Thomas M. Lennon and Paul J. Olscamp, and *Elucidations of the Search after Truth*, trans. Thomas M. Lennon (Columbus: Ohio State University Press, 1980); Fiering, *Moral Philosophy at Seventeenth-Century Harvard*, 269 n. 66. See, too, Stuart Brown, "The Critical Reception of Malebranche, from His Own Time to the End of the Eighteenth-Century," in *The Cambridge Companion to Nicholas Malebranche*, ed. Steven Nadler (Cambridge: Cambridge University Press, 2000), 202–87.

30. *Catalogue of the John Adams Library in the Public Library of the City of Boston* (Boston: Trustees of the Public Library of Boston, 1917), 157. John Adams's library was "probably the greatest private collection of its day in America." Zoltán Haraszti, *John Adams and the Prophets of Progress* (Cambridge, MA: Harvard University Press, 1952), vi. For a general characterization of the library, see ibid., chap. 2.

31. François Poulain de la Barre, *The Equality of the Sexes* (1673), trans. Desmond M. Clarke (Manchester: Manchester University Press, 1990). The English translation of 1677, by "A.L.," has been reprinted as *The Woman as Good as the Man*, ed. Gerald M. MacLean (Detroit, MI: Wayne State University Press, 1988). Smith, *Reason's Disciples*, 202–3; Perry, *Mary Astell*, 70–71. Astell's view of Descartes was influenced by her close ties to the Cambridge Platonists. See Perry, *Mary Astell*, 49ff., 77ff.

32. Malebranche, *Search after Truth*, 130.

33. Ibid., 176–83; John Dryden, *All for Love*, in *Works of John Dryden*, 13:2–111; James Anderson Winn, *Dryden and His World* (New Haven, CT: Yale University Press, 1987), 192, 220; John Dryden, prologue to *An Evening's Love*, in *Works of John Dryden*, 10:214–15.

34. Collier, *Short View*, 11, 144–45 (and see 202–5).

35. Ibid., 149.

36. John Harrington Smith, "Shadwell, the Ladies, and the Change in Comedy," *Modern Philology* 46, no. 1 (August 1948): 22–33; Laura Brown, "The Defenseless Woman and the Development of English Tragedy," *Studies in English Literature* 22 (1982): 429–43.

37. Shirley Strum Kenny, "Richard Steele and the 'Pattern of Genteel Comedy,'" *Modern Philology* 70, no. 1 (August 1972): 22–37; *Spectator*, no. 231 (November 24, 1717), in Bond, ed.,

*Spectator*, 2:399; David S. Berkeley, "An Early Use of 'Sensibility,'" *Notes and Queries* (April 3, 1948): 150; More, *Enchiridion ethicum*, 101.

38. For John's criticism of Calvin's double decree and original sin, see John Adams to Samuel Quincy, April 22, 1761, in *The Works of John Adams, Second President of the United States*, ed. Charles Francis Adams, 10 vols. (Boston: Little, Brown, 1856), 1:645–46; Ralph Ketcham, "The Puritan Ethic in the Revolutionary Era: Abigail Adams and Thomas Jefferson," in *"Remember the Ladies": New Perspectives on Women in American History*, ed. Carol V. R. George (Syracuse, NY: Syracuse University Press, 1975), 49–65, 50; Akers, *Abigail Adams*, 67; Withey, *Dearest Friend*, 4, 307; and Edith B. Gelles, *First Thoughts: Life and Letters of Abigail Adams* (New York: Twayne, 1998), 20. For students, including John, at Harvard, see Ferling, *John Adams*, 15.

39. Abigail Adams to John Adams, June 25, 1775, and August 5, 1776, in *AFC*, 1:231, 2:79.

40. Adams, *Diary and Autobiography*, 2:135; John Adams to Abigail Adams, June 11, 1775, in *AFC*, 1:215.

41. Adams, *Diary and Autobiography*, 2:156, 1:43–44, 219; Joseph J. Ellis, *Passionate Sage: The Character and Legacy of John Adams* (New York: Norton, 1993), 47–48, 50–51, 52; Shaw, *Character of John Adams*, 8–9, 17–19; Ferling, *John Adams*, 16–19.

42. Adams, *Diary and Autobiography*, 1:9, 10; John Adams, *A Dissertation on Canon and Feudal Law* (1765), in *The Revolutionary Writings of John Adams*, selected by C. Bradley Thompson (Indianapolis: Liberty Fund, 2000), 21–41; *Catalogue of the John Adams Library*, 248; Abigail Adams to John Adams, October 10, 1777, in *AFC*, 2:354–55; Fiering, *Moral Philosophy at Seventeenth-Century Harvard*, 244 n. 11. See, too, John Adams to Abigail Adams, October 27, 1799, in *My Dearest Friend*, 467.

43. Adams, *Diary and Autobiography*, 2:38; James Fordyce, *Sermons to Young Women*, 2 vols. (1766; London: William Pickering, 1996), 2:112–13; John Dwyer, *Virtuous Discourse: Sensibility and Society in Late Eighteenth-Century Scotland* (Edinburgh: John Donald, 1987), 128.

44. Mary Beth Norton, *Liberty's Daughters: The Revolutionary Experience of American Women, 1750–1780* (Boston: Little, Brown, 1980), 128–32; Sarah Juster, *Disorderly Women: Sexual Politics and Evangelicalism in Revolutionary New England* (Ithaca, NY: Cornell University Press, 1994).

45. Barker-Benfield, *Culture of Sensibility*, 109, 119; Wood, *Radicalism of the American Revolution*, pt. 3.

46. *Catalogue of the John Adams Library*, 67; John Adams to John Quincy Adams, May 19, 1783, in *AFC*, 5:163.

47. *Catalogue of the John Adams Library*, 21; Fiering, "Irresistible Compassion," 384; Fiering, *Jonathan Edwards's Moral Thought*, 132.

48. Fiering, *Jonathan Edwards's Moral Thought*, 249; Fiering, *Moral Philosophy at Seventeenth-Century Harvard*, 199; *Catalogue of the John Adams Library*, 125, 122. See, too, Eustace, *Passion Is the Gale*, 173. For Hutcheson's and Shaftesbury's continuing influence on early-nineteenth-century female academies, see Mary Kelley, *Learning to Stand and Speak: Women, Education, and Public Life in America's Republic* (Chapel Hill: University of North Carolina Press, 2006), 17–18.

49. Abigail Adams to Abigail Adams Smith, August 15, 1788, in *AFC*, 7:320; Dwyer, *Virtuous Discourse*, 11, 19–20. For Shippen, see Knott, *Sensibility and the American Revolution*, 139. For the influence of the Scottish Enlightenment, in addition to works cited in n. 41 above, see Rosemarie Zagarri, "Morals, Manners, and the Republican Mother," *American Quarterly* 44, no. 2 (June 1992): 192–215; Douglass Adair, *Fame and the Founding Fathers* (1975), ed. Trevor Colbourn (Indianapolis: Liberty Fund, 1998), 134–37, 181–84; and Stanley Elkins and Eric

McKittrick, *The Age of Federalism: The Early American Republic, 1788–1800* (New York: Oxford University Press, 1993), 84–92, 107–8.

50. Adams, *Dissertation on Canon and Feudal Law*, 27; Adams, *Diary and Autobiography*, 1:9.

51. Adams, "On Private Revenge, 1 August, 1763," in *Revolutionary Writings of John Adams*, 3–7, 4, 5.

52. Adams, *Diary and Autobiography*, 1:43; John Adams, *Novanglus; or, A History of the Dispute with America, from Its Origin, in 1754, to the Present Time* (1774), in *Revolutionary Writings of John Adams*, 149–284, 152; John Adams to Abigail Adams, August 19, 1777, in *AFC*, 2:319.

53. A. R. Humphreys, "'The Friend of Mankind' (1700–1760)—an Aspect of Eighteenth-Century Sensibility," *Review of English Studies* 24 (1948): 203–18, 203; Abigail Adams to Mercy Otis Warren, February 3(?), 1775, in *AFC*, 1:183.

54. John Adams to Abigail Adams, August 19, 1777, in *AFC*, 2:319.

55. James Madison to Edmund Randolph, June 11, 1782, quoted in Noble E. Cunningham Jr., *In Pursuit of Reason: The Life of Thomas Jefferson* (New York: Ballantine, 1987), 75. For other expressions of this idea, very much a Cartesian inheritance, see Adams, *Diary and Autobiography*, 2:236; and John Adams to Thomas Jefferson, May 6, 1816, in *Adams-Jefferson Letters*, 473.

56. Adams, *Diary and Autobiography*, 1:234–35; John Tillotson, "Of Doing Good," appended to *Several Discourses upon the Attributes of God*, 6 vols. (London: Chiswell, 1700), 1:401–42, 432. See, too, A. O. Aldridge, "The Pleasures of Pity," *English Literary History* 16, no. 1 (March 1949): 76–87, 83–86.

57. Compare Knott, *Sensibility and the American Revolution*, 291–92; Karen Halttunen, "Humanitarianism and the Pornography of Pain in Anglo-American Culture," *American Historical Review* 100, no. 2 (1995): 303–36, 308 and passim. Illustrations of the schadenfreude point include Jordan, *White over Black*, 372; and Deirdre Coleman, "'Conspicuous Consumption,' White Abolitionism and English Women's Protest Writing in the 1790s," *English Literary History* 61, no. 2 (1994): 341–62.

58. Gordon S. Wood, *The Creation of the American Republic, 1776–1787* (Chapel Hill: University of North Carolina Press, 1969), 571ff. See, too, Shaw, *Character of John Adams*, 244, 221.

59. John quoted in Haraszti, *Adams and the Prophets of Progress*, 79 (and see chap. 4).

60. Abigail Adams to Mary Smith Cranch, October 6, 1766, in *AFC*, 1:55. Adams owned Hobbes's *Moral and Political Works*. *Catalogue of the John Adams Library*, 121. John had published the same view as Abigail the year before. John Adams, "An Essay on Man's Lust for Power, with the Author's Comment in 1807," in *Papers of John Adams*, ed. Robert J. Taylor et al., 13 vols. (Cambridge, MA: Belknap Press of Harvard University Press, 1977), 1:81–83.

61. Abigail Adams to John Adams, November 27, 1775, in *AFC*, 1:329. See, too, Bernard Bailyn, *The Ideological Origins of the American Revolution* (Cambridge, MA: Belknap Press of Harvard University Press, 1967), 56–57.

62. Adams, *Diary and Autobiography*, 1:28, 31 (see, too, 2:51–52); Barker-Benfield, *Culture of Sensibility*, 6; John Adams to Benjamin Rush, February 2, 1806, in *The Spur of Fame: Dialogues of John Adams and Benjamin Rush, 1805–1813*, ed. John A. Schutz and Douglass Adair (Indianapolis: Liberty Fund, 1960), 82; Ketcham, "Puritan Ethic," 50.

63. Adams, *Diary and Autobiography*, 3:272, 1:186; John Adams to Abigail Adams, October 29, 1775, in *AFC*, 1:317; John Adams to Abigail Adams, February 25, 1799, in *My Dearest Friend*, 463.

64. Haraszti, *Adams and the Prophets of Progress*, 110; Eustace, *Passion Is the Gale*, 4; John Adams to Abigail Smith, April 20, 1763, in *AFC*, 1:5; *Catalogue of the John Adams Library*, 84; Elizabeth Eger and Lucy Peltz, *Brilliant Women: Eighteenth-Century Bluestockings* (London: National Portrait Gallery, 2008), 74; *Spectator*, no. 397 (June 5, 1712), in Bond, ed., *Spectator*, 3:86.

65. Elizabeth Carter, trans., *All the Work of Epictetus* (Dublin, 1759).

66. Ibid., xiv.

67. Ibid., xii, xiv–xv; Abigail Adams to John Shaw, January 18, 1785, in *AFC*, 6:62. That the eighteenth-century Enlightenment in fact popularized seventeenth-century discourses is demonstrated in Jonathan I. Israel, *Radical Enlightenment: Philosophy and the Making of Modernity, 1650–1750* (Oxford: Oxford University Press, 2001).

68. Carter, trans., *Epictetus*, xv.

69. Ibid., xix, xxi.

70. Linda Kerber, *Women of the Republic: Intellect and Ideology in Revolutionary America* (Chapel Hill: University of North Carolina Press, 1980), 192; Carter, trans., *Epictetus*, i–ii, iii. See, too, Valerie Rumbold, *Women's Place in Pope's World* (Cambridge: Cambridge University Press, 1989), 6–7.

71. Barbara Brandon Schnorrenberg, "Elizabeth Carter," in Todd, ed., *Dictionary of Women Writers*, 75–76; Eger and Peltz, *Brilliant Women*, 69; Nicholson, "Early Stages of Cartesianism," 372.

72. Aphra Behn, "To Mr. Creech (under the Name of *Daphnis*) on His Excellent Translation of *Lucretius*," in *Works of Aphra Behn*, 6:160–70; Haraszti, *Adams and the Prophets of Progress*, 24.

73. Winn, *Dryden*, 474; Claudia N. Thomas, *Alexander Pope and His Eighteenth-Century Women Readers* (Carbondale: Southern Illinois University Press, 1994), 22, 118, 268 n. 2. John Adams and John Quincy Adams both read Dryden's translation of the *Aeneid*. John Quincy Adams to John Adams, May 24, 1783, and John Adams to John Quincy Adams, May 29, 1783, in *AFC*, 5:165, 166.

74. Steven Shankman, *Pope's Illiad: Homer in the Age of Passion* (Princeton, NJ: Princeton University Press, 1983); Thomas, *Pope and Women Readers*, 25–35 and passim; Rumbold, *Women's Place in Pope's World*, xv, 44, 269, and passim.

75. Abigail Adams to John Adams, April 10, 1782, in *AFC*, 4:306–7; Thomas, *Pope and Women Readers*, 240–44; Adams, *Diary and Autobiography*, 1:68. And see Charles Scruggs, "Phillis Wheatley," in *Portraits of American Women*, ed. G. J. Barker-Benfield and Catherine Clinton (New York: Oxford University Press, 1998), 105–19, 111, 113–15

76. Fiering, *Moral Philosophy at Seventeenth-Century Harvard*, 151 n. 7 (for Smith and manhood, see Barker-Benfield, *Culture of Sensibility*, 137–41); Eger and Peltz, *Brilliant Women*, 70; *Milcah Martha Moore's Book: A Commonplace Book from Revolutionary America*, ed. Catherine La Courreye Blecki and Karin A. Wulf (University Park: Pennsylvania State University Press, 1997), 227, 102 n. 76, 103. See, too, Sylvia Harestark Myers, *The Bluestocking Circle: Women, Friendship, and the Life of the Mind in Eighteenth-Century England* (Oxford: Clarendon, 1999).

77. Gelles, *First Thoughts*, 19; Abigail Adams to John Thaxter, July 1, 1783, in *AFC*, 5:191; Charles Francis Adams, "Memoir," in *Letters of Mrs. Adams, the Wife of John Adams*, ed. Charles Francis Adams (1840; Boston: Wilkins, Carter, 1848), xvii–lxi, xxvi.

78. Adams, *Diary and Autobiography*, 1:26, 72; John Adams to Benjamin Rush, September 1, 1807, in *Spur of Fame*, 100; Rosemary Keller, *Patriotism and the Female Sex: Abigail Adams and the American Revolution* (Brooklyn, NY: Carlson, 1994), 24; Donald F. Bond, preface to Bond, ed., *Spectator*, 1:v. For Franklin's well-known modeling of his prose on the *Spectator*, see Benjamin Franklin, *Autobiography and Other Writings*, ed. Russell B. Nye (Boston: Houghton Mifflin, 1958), 12–13. Eliza Lucas wrote a lady friend in 1742 about music, citing and quoting the *Spectator*, no. 580, on the subject. *The Letterbook of Eliza Lucas Pinckney, 1739–1762*, ed. Elise Pinckney (Columbia: University of South Carolina Press, 1997), 49. Maria Carter copied passages from the *Spectator* in the 1760s. Kathleen M. Brown, *Good Wives, Nasty Wenches,*

*and Anxious Patriarchs: Gender, Race, and Power in Colonial Virginia* (Chapel Hill: University of North Carolina Press, 1996), 257.

79. Abigail Smith to John Adams, April 12, 1764, in *AFC*, 1:25; *Spectator*, no. 522 (October 29, 1712), in Bond, ed., *Spectator*, 4:357–60. For an exploration of the significance of this marital ideal for Abigail, see Keller, *Patriotism and the Female Sex*, chap. 2.

80. For Steele's uxoriousness and that of his successor playwrights, see nn. 36 and 37 above. See, too, Jean H. Hagstrum, *Sex and Sensibility: Ideal and Erotic Love from Milton to Mozart* (Chicago: University of Chicago Press, 1980).

81. Barker-Benfield, *Culture of Sensibility*, 115–16; Joseph Addison, *Cato: A Tragedy and Selected Essays*, ed. Christine Dunn Henderson and Mark E. Yellin (Indianapolis: Liberty Fund, 2004), 5–6.

82. Agnes Marie Sibley, *Alexander Pope's Prestige in America, 1725–1835* (New York: King's Crown Press/Columbia University Press, 1949), 18, 68, 71. See, too, Eustace, *Passion Is the Gale*, 17–18, 21–22, 25–30, 44, 237; and Abigail Adams to Elizabeth Cranch, January 3, 1785, in *AFC*, 6:39.

83. For a discussion of the significance of these pen names, see Phillip Hicks, "Portia and Marcia: Female Political Identity and the Historical Imagination, 1770–1800," *William and Mary Quarterly*, 3rd ser., 62, no. 2 (April 2005): 265–94; *Julius Caesar*, 2.1.293–96.

84. Abigail Adams to John Adams, April 12, 1764, in *AFC*, 1:27; Abigail Adams to Mercy Otis Warren, December 5, 1773, in ibid., 88. Addison wrote: "What pity is it / That we can die but once to serve our country!" (Joseph Addison, *Cato: A Tragedy*, in *Cato and Selected Essays*, 84 [4.4.81–82]). Abigail also quoted *Cato* elsewhere. Abigail Adams to Elbridge Gerry, July 20, 1781, in *AFC*, 4:182–83.

85. John Adams to Abigail Adams, February 18, 1776, in *AFC*, 1:349.

86. Sibley, *Pope's Prestige in America*, 2–3, 22–25, 51; Bernard A. Goldgar, "Pope's Theory of the Passions: The Background of Epistle II of the *Essay on Man*," *Philological Quarterly* 41 (1962): 730–37. One who was upset by Pope's lines on the passions was the Philadelphia Quaker James Logan. See Eustace, *Passion Is the Gale*, 22–26.

87. Hagstrum, *Sex and Sensibility*, 121. This is the gist of the chapter on Pope in my in-progress "From Passions to Sensibility."

88. Alexander Pope to the Earl of Oxford, November 7, 1725, in *The Correspondence of Alexander Pope*, ed. George Sherburn, 4 vols. (Oxford: Clarendon, 1956), 2:337; Abigail Adams to John Adams, April 18, 1793, in *My Dearest Friend*, 362; Adams, *Diary and Autobiography*, 1:84.

89. Pope, "Epistle II to a Lady, of the Characters of Women," in *Epistles to Several Persons*, ed. F. W. Bateson (London: Methuen, 1951), 44–71 (line 288). For John Quincy Adams's imitation, see the conclusion of chapter 5 below.

90. *Catalogue of the John Adams Library*, 199, 122–23; Adams, *Diary and Autobiography*, 1:152; Akers, *Abigail Adams*, 198.

91. Autobiographical piece printed in Adams, *Diary and Autobiography*, 3:149–54, 151; Abigail Adams to Lucy Cranch, July 20, 1784, in *AFC*, 7:267–68; Abigail Adams to Mary Smith Cranch, August 2, 1784, in ibid., 5:417.

92. Abigail Adams to John Quincy Adams, March 20, 1780, in *AFC*, 3:311; Pope, *Essay on Man*, epistle 4, lines 35–40, 395–96.

93. John Adams, *Discourses on Davila: A Series of Papers on Political History*, in *Works of John Adams*, 6:226–403; Pope, *Essay on Man*, epistle 3, lines 283–84, 289–300.

94. Haraszti, *Adams and the Prophets of Progress*, 168, 169.

95. Adams, *Davila*, 246 (preface); Pope, *Essay on Man*, epistle 2, lines 117–18.

96. Pope, *Essay on Man*, epistle 2, lines 138ff.; Pope, "Epistle I, to Richard Temple, Earl of Cobham," in *Epistles to Several Persons*, pp. 13–36, lines 174, 178, 180, 181; John Adams to Thomas Jefferson, July [3], 1813, in *Adams-Jefferson Letters*, 349.

97. Pope, *Essay on Man*, epistle 2, lines 97–100, 107–8. The word *gale* is used by More, *hurricane* by Locke. More, *Enchiridion ethicum*, 2, 41; Locke, *Human Understanding*, chap. 21, sec. 12. Descartes, *A Discourse on the Method*, trans. Ian Maclean (Oxford: World's Classics, 2006), 48. Maclean notes that Descartes's analogy "like a pilot in his ship" is from Aristotle's *De anima*.

98. Pope, *Essay on Man*, epistle 2, lines 183–84.

99. Goldgar, "Pope's Theory of the Passions"; Adams, *Davila*, 245.

100. Adams, *Davila*, 245.

101. There is considerable scholarship on this point, beginning with Brown's *Sentimental Novel in America* and continuing through to, most recently, Knott, *Sensibility and the American Revolution*, 27.

102. Bushman, *Refinement of America*, 281; *Journal and Correspondence of Miss Adams*, 1:33. For valuable context for John's famous metaphor, see Jay Fliegelman, *Prodigals and Pilgrims: The American Revolution against Patriarchal Authority, 1750–1800* (New York: Cambridge University Press, 1982), 237.

103. Akers, *Abigail Adams*, 10–11; Abigail Smith to John Adams, April 30, 1764, in *AFC*, 1:41–42. For other illustrations of literary, sentimental flirtatiousness, see Knott, *Sensibility and American Revolution*, chap. 3. See, too, the discussion of letters between Abigail and James Lovell, Abigail and Royall Tyler, and Abigail and Colonel William Smith below.

104. Abigail Smith to John Adams, April 30, 1764, in *AFC*, 1:41–42. She had expressed similar sentiments to him two weeks earlier. Abigail Smith to John Adams, April 16, 1764, in ibid., 32. See Shaw, *Character of John Adams*, 47–48.

105. Abigail Adams to Elizabeth Cranch, May 12, 1785, in *AFC*, 6:141–42; Abigail Adams 2nd to Elizabeth Cranch, January 14, 1779, in ibid., 3:156. Betsy referred to *Sir Charles Grandison*, too, e.g., in Elizabeth Cranch to Abigail Adams 2nd, April 25, 1785, and September 5, 1785, in ibid., 6:91, 337. Her mother knew the novel well, referring to it, e.g., in Mary Smith Cranch to Abigail Smith Adams, October 10, 1784, in ibid., 5:469.

106. John Quincy Adams to Abigail Adams 2nd, October 19, 1785, in ibid., 6:402–3.

107. Abigail Adams to Lucy Cranch, August 22, 1785, in ibid., 312–13.

108. Eliza Lucas to Miss Bartlett, [1742], in *Letterbook of Eliza Lucas Pinckney*, 47–48.

109. Abigail Adams to Lucy Cranch, August 22, 1785, in *AFC*, 6:313.

110. Barker-Benfield, *Culture of Sensibility*, 64–65 and chap. 5 passim. The attack on *Pamela* was renewed in the 1790s. Kerber, *Women of the Republic*, 240.

111. Abigail Adams to Lucy Cranch, August 22, 1785, in *AFC*, 6:313. For Pinckney, see n. 108 above.

112. Lucy Cranch to Abigail Adams, December 8, 1785, in ibid., 484.

113. *Sterne: The Critical Heritage*, ed. Alan B. Howes (London: Routledge & Kegan Paul, 1974), passim. This is a collection of primary documents. Knott illustrates that Sterne continued to be influential in America after the Revolution. Knott, *Sensibility and the American Revolution*, 82, 219–20, 271–72.

114. Adams, *Diary and Autobiography*, 1:200; John Adams to Abigail Adams, July 25, 1782, in *AFC*, 4:353; Adams, *Diary and Autobiography*, 1:354. See, too, John Adams to Benjamin Rush, August 1, 1812, and December 8, 1812, in *Spur of Fame*, 256, 283, 284.

115. Abigail Adams to James Lovell, February 13, 1780, in *AFC*, 3:273; Abigal Adams to Mary Smith Cranch, February 10, 1788, in ibid., 8:225; James Aikin Workman, introduction

to Laurence Sterne, *The Life and Opinions of Tristram Shandy, Gentleman*, ed. James Aikin Workman (New York: Odyssey, 1940), xliii; John Adams to Abigail Adams, March 16, 1777, in
*AFC*, 2:176; John Adams to Thomas Jefferson, November 14, 1813, in *The Adams-Jefferson Letters*, 364. For Jefferson's reverence for Sterne, see Andrew Burstein, *The Inner Jefferson: Portrait
of a Grieving Optimist* (Charlottesville: University Press of Virginia, 1995), chap. 2.

116. Abigail Adams to Thomas Jefferson, June 6, 1785, and February 11, 1786, in *Adams-
Jefferson Letters*, 28, 119; John Adams to Benjamin Rush, August 1, 1816, in *Spur of Fame*, 256;
Abigail Adams to Elizabeth Smith Shaw, March 4, 1786, in *AFC*, 7:81–82; Abigail Adams to
Mary Smith Cranch, November 10, 1800, in *New Letters of Abigail Adams, 1788–1801*, ed. Stew-
art Mitchell (Boston: Houghton Mifflin, 1947), 255.

117. Abigail Adams 2nd to Elizabeth Cranch, [April 1782], in *AFC*, 4:318; *Journal and Correspondence of Miss Adams*, 1:10; Abigail Adams to John Quincy Adams, July 22, 1785, in *AFC*,
6:211; "Twenty-four Letters from Col. to Mrs. Smith," in *Journal and Correspondence of Miss
Adams*, 1:125–202.

118. Abigail Adams to John Adams, March 16, 1776, in *AFC*, 1:359; John Adams to Abigail
Adams, April 12, 1776, in ibid., 376.

119. Johnson quoted in Robert Kilburn Root, introduction to *Lord Chesterfield, Letters to
His Son and Others* (1774; London: Dent, 1929), vii–xiv, xiii.

120. Abigail Adams to John Adams, April 21, 1776, in *AFC*, 1:389; John Adams to Abigail
Adams, February 20, 1783, and June 10, 1783, in ibid., 5:98, 170 n. 1.

121. Abigail Adams to Mercy Otis Warren, February 28, 1780, in ibid., 3:289. Mercy Otis
Warren's son, Winslow, was "enamored" of Chesterfield's letters, provoking his mother to
send him "a long letter critical of Chesterfield's ethics and reasoning" and declaring that he
sacrificed "all the finer feelings of the soul to a momentary gratification." Rosemarie Zagarri,
*A Woman's Dilemma: Mercy Otis Warren and the American Revolution* (Wheeling, IL: Harlan Davidson, 1995), 110.

122. See chapters 12 and 13 below.

123. Abigail Adams to John Thaxter, July 21, [1780], in *AFC*, 3:378–79. Abigail expressed
her jealousy in several of the letters she wrote John after he wrote her in praise of French ladies at the beginning of his long separation from her, compounding her feeling in subsequent
references, including one to Franklin's dalliances. Her reply of June 30, 1778, was the first of
a series in which her anger was hardly veiled. See John Adams to Abigail Adams, April 25,
1778, in ibid., 17; and Abigail Adams to John Adams, June 30, 1778, in ibid., 51–52. Alexander
Pope, "Eloisa to Abelard," in *The Rape of the Lock and Other Poems* (Twickenham Edition), ed.
Geoffrey Tillotson (London: Methuen, 1962), 317–45 (lines 95–96).

124. Barker-Benfield, *Culture of Sensibility*, 321–22; Mary Astell, *Some Reflections upon Marriage* (4th ed., 1730; reprint, New York: Source Book, 1970), 6–7. Compare J. M. S. Tompkins, *The Popular Novel in England, 1770–1800* (1932; Lincoln: University of Nebraska Press,
1961), 84–85, 88, 90.

125. *AFC*, 3:380 n. 2. See, too, Robert East, *John Quincy Adams: The Critical Years, 1785–
1794* (New York: Bookman, 1962), 108.

126. John Thaxter to Abigail Adams, June 10, 1783, in *AFC*, 5:172.

127. John Adams to Abigail Adams, December 2, 1778, in ibid., 3:125; *Catalogue of the
John Adams Library*, 216; for John's marginalia, see Haraszti, *Adams and the Prophets of Progress*,
96–98; Kerber, *Women of the Republic*, 243. And see Knott, *Sensibility and the American Revolution*, 129.

128. Abigail Adams to John Adams, November 13, 1780, in *AFC*, 4:12.

129. Quoted in Ellis, *Passionate Sage*, 89.

130. Barker-Benfield, *Culture of Sensibility*, 260; Ellis, *Passionate Sage*, 90; Haraszti, *Adams and the Prophets of Progress*, 81, chap. 5, and passim.

131. Adams, *Diary and Autobiography*, 4:131. (He was introduced to Burke when in London. See ibid., 3:150.) He owned both an 1798 English edition of Mathias's book and an 1800 American one. *Catalogue of the John Adams Library*, 164. Adams linked the same thought to Rousseau. See John Adams to Thomas Jefferson, July 13, 1812, in *Adams-Jefferson Letters*, 355. See, too, John Adams to Thomas Jefferson, July 16, 1814, in ibid., 435; Barker-Benfield, *Culture of Sensibility*, chap. 7; and chapter 14 below.

132. Abigail Adams to John Quincy Adams, October 27, 1799, in *My Dearest Friend*, 468.

## CHAPTER 2

1. "Ode to Sensibility" quoted in Waldstreicher, *In the Midst of Fetes*, 78–79; John Adams to Abigail Adams, July 28, 1775, and October 7, 1775, in *AFC*, 1:267, 294–95. For a valuable discussion of how sentimentalists read, see Knott, *Sensibility and the American Revolution*, 53–62.

2. For Fiering, see chapter 1, n. 1, above; Abigail Adams to John Adams, December 15, 1783, in *AFC*, 5:279. For the meanings of grief to some eighteenth-century Pennsylvanians, see Eustace, *Passion Is the Gale*, chap. 7.

3. Mary Smith Cranch to Abigail Adams, October 3, 1784, in *AFC*, 5:467; John Quincy Adams to Abigail Adams 2nd, May 17, 1785, in *Journal and Correspondence of Miss Adams*, 1, pt. 2:37; Paine quoted in Jay Fliegelman, *Declaring Independence: Jefferson, Natural Language, and the Culture of Performance* (Stanford, CA: Stanford University Press, 1993), 78–79.

4. Abigail Adams to Elizabeth Smith Shaw, [July 29, 1784], in *AFC*, 5:407. See, too, Mercy Otis Warren to Abigail Adams, September 21, 1777, in ibid., 1:282.

5. Elizabeth Cranch to Abigail Adams, September 18, 1785, in ibid., 6:339.

6. Abigail Adams 2nd to Elizabeth Cranch, [ca. December 19, 1782], in ibid., 5:50; Descartes, *Passions of the Soul*, 44.

7. Thomas Jefferson to Maria Cosway, October 12, 1786, in *Papers of Thomas Jefferson*, 10:443–53, 450.

8. *Letterbook of Eliza Lucas Pinckney*, 84; Abigail Adams to John Adams, July 14, 1776, in *AFC*, 2:46; Abigail Adams to Elizabeth Smith Shaw, July [11?], 1784, in ibid., 5:395–96; Descartes, *Passions of the Soul*, 44, 100–101.

9. Abigail Adams to John Adams, October 16, 1774, in *AFC*, 1:172; Abigail Adams to Cotton Tufts, April 9, 1764, in ibid., 21.

10. Barker-Benfield, *Culture of Sensibility*, 7–8; Shaw, *Character of John Adams*, 39; John refers to Cheyne's psychophysiological views in John Adams to Samuel Quincy Adams, April 22, 1761, in *Works of John Adams*, 1:645–46; Abigail Adams to John Adams, September 29, 1781, in *AFC*, 4:221; John Adams to Abigail Adams, January 29, 1783, in ibid., 5:82.

11. Abigail Adams to John Adams, December 27, 1778, in *AFC*, 3:140.

12. Fliegelman, *Declaring Independence*, 63, 90, 96; Adams, *Diary and Autobiography*, 1:152.

13. Barker-Benfield, *Culture of Sensibility*, 73–74, 115; Billings quoted in Fliegelman, *Declaring Independence*, 69.

14. John Adams to Abigail Adams, February 13, 1779, in *AFC*, 3:170.

15. Eliza Lucas Pinckney to [Mrs. Lucas], September 25, 1758, in *Letterbook of Eliza Lucas Pinckney*, 101; Abigail Adams to John Adams, November 13, 1780, in *AFC*, 4:13; Abigail Adams to John Adams, June 23, 1777, in ibid., 2:269.

16. John Adams to Abigail Smith, [April 12], 1764, in *AFC*, 1:24; Abigail Adams to John Adams, August 19, 1774, in ibid., 143; Elizabeth Smith Shaw to Abigail Adams, June 12, 1785,

in ibid., 6:174–75; Ann Jessie Van Sant, *Eighteenth-Century Sensibility and the Novel: The Senses in Social Context* (Cambridge: Cambridge University Press, 1993), xi; Abigail Adams to Elizabeth Smith Shaw, July 28, 1784, and January 11, 1785, in *AFC*, 5:402, 6:56–58; *Journal of Charles Woodmason*, 25; and Shaw, *Character of John Adams*, 303. The first two letters cited in this note illustrate the use of theatrical metaphors.

17. Van Sant, *Sensibility and the Novel*, xii.

18. John Adams to Abigail Adams, September 29, 1774, in *AFC*, 1:163.

19. Eliza Lucas to [Mrs. Boddicolt], December 14, 1743, in *Letterbook of Eliza Lucas Pinckney*, 69; John Adams to Abigail Smith, April 7, 1764, and John Adams to Abigail Adams, October 23, 1775, in *AFC*, 1:18, 311; Abigail Adams to John Adams, May 27, 1776, in ibid., 416.

20. John Adams to Abigail Adams, February 1, 1774, in *AFC*, 1:119; Adam Smith, *The Theory of Moral Sentiments*, ed. D. D. Raphael and A. L. MacFie (1759; Indianapolis: Liberty Classics, 1982), 9; Mary Smith Cranch to Abigail Adams, August 20, 1774, in *AFC*, 1:143.

21. Abigail Adams to John Adams, [November 12–23, 1778], and November 14, 1779, in *AFC*, 3:119, 234; Abigail Adams to John Thaxter, February 15, 1778, in ibid., 2:390.

22. Abigail Adams to Mary Smith Cranch, December 8, 1800, in *New Letters of Abigail Adams*, 261–62.

23. Abigail Adams to John Adams, August 5, 1776, in *AFC*, 2:79–80; Abigail Smith to John Adams, October 4, 1764, in ibid., 1:50–55.

24. Abigail Adams to John Adams, [November 12–23, 1778], in ibid., 3:119; Abigail Adams to John Adams, May 27, 1776, in ibid., 1:415.

25. Abigail Adams to John Adams, [November 12–23, 1778], in ibid., 3:118–19; the *Liberal American* quoted in Tompkins, *Popular Novel*, 92.

26. John Adams to Abigail Adams, May 22, 1776, in *AFC*, 1:412–13.

27. Abigail Adams to John Adams, August 12, 1777, in ibid., 2:308.

28. John Adams to Richard Cranch, September 18, 1774, in ibid., 1:159; Eunice Paine to Abigail Adams, June 4, 1775, in ibid., 1:210; Mercy Otis Warren to Abigail Adams, September 21, [1775], in ibid., 281–82; Abigail Adams to John Adams, September 25, 1775, October 25, 1775, and March 11, 1782, in ibid., 284–85, 312–13.

29. John Adams to Richard Cranch, September 18, 1774, in ibid., 159; Abigail Adams to John Adams, July 31, 1775, in ibid., 219; Abigail Adams to John Adams, [November 12–23, 1778], in ibid., 3:118, and Abigail Adams to John Adams, June 18, 1775, in ibid., 1:222. The editors of *My Dearest Friend* quoted Abigail's September 23, 1776, letter to John (in *AFC*, 2:133) in support of their view that "writing about her personal afflictions also became Abigail's means of coping." Hogan and Taylor, introduction, xvii. For a contrary view, see Carol Tavris, *Anger: The Misunderstood Emotion* (New York: Simon & Schuster, 1989); and Mark D. Seery, Roxane Cohen Silver, E. Alison Holman, Whitney A. Ence, and Thai Q. Chu, "Expressing Thoughts and Feelings Following a Collective Trauma: Immediate Responses to 9/11 Predict Negative Outcomes in a National Sample," *Journal of Consulting and Clinical Psychology* 76, no. 4 (August 2008): 657–67. Confession "in the West has a long history as a culturally authorized 'idiom of distress' . . . associated with some benefits to body and soul," but, "in other cultures, confession is absent—and even actively discouraged, on the premise that the disclosure of intimate thoughts and feelings could compromise health and well-being." Eugenia George, "A Cultural and Historical Perspective on Confession," in *Emotion, Disclosure, and Health*, ed. James W. Pennebaker (Washington, DC: American Psychological Association, 1990), 11–25, 11. I am indebted to Linda Layne for this reference. See, too, Lauren M. Bylsma, A. J. J. M. Vingerhoets, and Jonathan Rottenberg, "When Is Crying Cathartic? An International Study," *Journal of Social and Clinical Psychology* 27, no. 10 (December 2008): 1165–87.

30. Abigail Adams to John Adams, October 9, 1775, in *AFC*, 1:298. See, too, Eliza Lucas Pinckney to the Honble Mrs. King, May [1759], *Letterbook of Eliza Lucas Pinckney*, 119. For an account of Jefferson and such sensational, medical language, see Andrew Burstein, *Jefferson's Secrets: Death and Desire at Monticello* (New York: Basic, 2005), chap. 2.

31. Nancy Cott, *The Bonds of Womanhood: "Women's Sphere" in New England, 1780–1835* (New Haven, CT: Yale University Press, 1977), 140; Donald Meyer, *Sex and Power: The Rise of Women in America, Russia, Sweden, and Italy* (Middletown, CT: Wesleyan University Press, 1987), 273 (and see 311–30 passim).

32. Brissenden, *Virtue in Distress*, chap. 2. William Empson uses the phrase in *The Structure of Complex Words* (1951; London: Hogarth, 1985), chap. 12, "Sense and Sensibility." Others who address these and related terms include Tompkins, *Popular Novel*, 92–95; Erik Erametsä, *A Study of the Word "Sentimental," and of Other Linguistic Characteristics of Eighteenth-Century Sentimentalism in England* (Helsinki: Helsingin Liikekirjapaino OY, 1951); and Hagstrum, *Sex and Sensibility*, introduction.

33. John Adams to Abigail Smith, May 7, 1764, in *AFC*, 1:44–45; Adams, *Diary and Autobiography*, 1:234.

34. Abigail Smith to John Adams, May 9, 1764, in *AFC*, 47; Gelles, *First Thoughts*, 6.

35. Adams, *Diary and Autobiography*, 2:55; Abigail Adams to John Adams, September 20, 1776, in *AFC*, 2:128; Fordyce, *Sermons to Young Women*, 1:478, 169–70.

36. Adams, *Diary and Autobiography*, 2:55.

37. Ibid., 1:271, 2:43.

38. Barker-Benfield, *Culture of Sensibility*, 208, 281, 303, 362–63; G. J. Barker-Benfield, "Mary Wollstonecraft's Depression and Diagnosis: The Relation between Sensibility and Women's Susceptibility to Nervous Disorders," *Psychohistory Review* 13 (1985): 15–31.

39. Abigail Smith to John Adams, September 12, 1763, in *AFC*, 1:8; Bond, ed., *Spectator*, 2:399 (and see 1:30, 193–94, 3:482); Benjamin Franklin, "Old Mistress Apology," in *Writings of Benjamin Franklin*, ed. J. A. Leo Lemay (New York: Library of America, 1987), 302–3. Franklin's absorption of Cartesian psychology is illustrated in his 1725 "A Dissertation on Liberty and Necessity, Pleasure and Pain," in ibid., 57–71, 65–69 and passim. Franklin's views of gender were close to those propagated by the *Spectator*. See Keller, *Patriotism and the Female Sex*, 24–27.

40. "On Happiness—to N.S.—U," in *Milcah Martha Moore's Book*, 189; Linn quoted in Brown, *Sentimental Novel in America*, 124.

41. Abigail Adams to John Adams, July 25, 1775, in *AFC*, 1:260–61. For difficulties in defining *sentimental* and related terms, see Knott, *Sensibility and the American Revolution*, 5off.

42. John Adams to Abigail Adams, July 7, 1775, in *AFC*, 1:241–43. Unless indicated otherwise, quotations in subsequent paragraphs are from this letter.

43. Abigail Smith to John Adams, April 12, 1764, in ibid., 27.

44. Abigail Adams to Elizabeth Cranch, August 1, 1784, in ibid., 5:414–15.

45. John Quincy Adams to Abigail Adams 2nd, August 20, 1785, in ibid., 6:289–90.

46. Barbara Hardy, *Forms of Feeling in Victorian Fiction* (Athens: Ohio University Press, 1985), 72 (Hardy cites Ernst Robert Curtius, *European Literature and the Later Middle Ages*, trans. Willard R. Trask [New York: Bollingen Foundation/Pantheon, 1953], 159–62); Eliza Lucas Pinckney to My Lady Carew of Beddington, May 1759, in *Letterbook of Eliza Lucas Pinckney*, 115; Abigail Adams 2nd to Elizabeth Cranch, [1784], in *AFC*, 5:294; Elizabeth Cranch to Abigail Adams, September 26, 1784, in ibid., 460–61.

47. Adams, *Diary and Autobiography*, 3:330; John Adams to Benjamin Rush, September 28, 1811, in *Spur of Fame*, 208; Thomas Paine, *Common Sense*, in *The Thomas Paine Reader*, ed. Michael Foot and Isaac Kramnick (New York: Penguin, 1987), 65–115, 65.

48. Adams, *Diary and Autobiography*, 2:155. See, too, Waldstreicher, *In the Midst of Fetes*, 92; Eliza Lucas to [Colonel Lucas], [1740], in *Letterbook of Eliza Lucas Pinckney*, 6.

49. Abigail Adams to Thomas Jefferson, May 20, 1804, in *Adams-Jefferson Letters*, 268−69.

50. Thomas Jefferson to Abigail Adams, June 13, 1804, in ibid., 269−71.

51. Abigail Adams to Thomas Jefferson, July 1, 1804, in ibid., 271−74.

52. Adams, *Dissertation on Canon and Feudal Law*, 33; Adams, *Novanglus*, 167. See, too, John Mullan, *Sentiment and Sociability: The Language of Feeling in the Eighteenth Century* (Oxford: Clarendon, 1988), 7−8.

53. John Quincy Adams to Abigail Adams 2nd, March 15, 1786, in *AFC*, 7:90. See, too, John Quincy Adams to Abigail Adams 2nd, April 11, 1786, in ibid., 121.

54. Abigail Adams to John Adams, December 27, 1778, in ibid., 3:140.

55. Adams, *Diary and Autobiography*, 1:32−33; Adams, *Novanglus*, 152; John Adams, "Two Replies of the Massachusetts House of Representatives to Governor Hutchinson" (1772), in *Revolutionary Writings of John Adams*, 119−45, 142, 141.

56. Adams, *Diary and Autobiography*, 3:288; Adams, *Novanglus*, 154; John Adams to Samuel Quincy, April 22, 1761, in *Works of John Adams*, 1:646; Eliza Lucas Pinckney to Mrs. Pocklington, [ca. May 1759], in *Letterbook of Eliza Lucas Pinckney*, 114; Franklin, *Autobiography and Other Writings*, 82−83.

57. Abigail Adams to Mary Cranch, December 26, 1797, in *New Letters of Abigail Adams*, 120; Abigail Adams to John Adams, November 27, 1775, in *AFC*, 1:330.

58. Francis Hutcheson, *An Essay on the Nature and Conduct of the Passions and Affections, with Illustrations on the Moral Sense* (1728; Indianapolis: Liberty Fund, 2002), 35.

59. John Adams to Abigail Adams, February 17, 1794, in *My Dearest Friend*, 360; Abigail Adams to John Adams, September 20, 1783, and July 17, 1782, in *AFC*, 5:254, 4:343.

60. Abigail Adams to Mercy Otis Warren, July 24, 1775, in *AFC*, 1:254−55; John Adams to Benjamin Rush, September 30, 1805, in *Spur of Fame*, 43.

61. Abigail Adams to Mercy Otis Warren, July 24, 1775, in *AFC*, 1:254−55.

62. Abigail Adams 2nd to John Quincy Adams, October 5, 1785, in ibid., 6:434; Abigail Adams to Isaac Smith Jr., April 20, 1771, in ibid., 1:778; *Journal and Correspondence of Miss Adams*, 1:25−26; Abigail Adams to John Adams, September 20, 177[6], in *AFC*, 2:128. For Garrick and Cumberland, see Janet Todd, *Sensibility: An Introduction* (London: Methuen, 1986), 34, 46−47.

63. Abigail Adams to Catherine Sawbridge Macaulay, [1774], in *AFC*, 1:177−78; John Adams to Abigail Adams, September 18, 1774, in ibid., 158.

64. *Journal and Correspondence of Miss Adams*, 2, pt. 1:200−201; Abigail Adams to Mary Smith Cranch, July [22], 1784, in *AFC*, 5:370−71.

65. Paul Langford, *A Polite and Commercial People: England, 1727−83* (Oxford: Clarendon, 1989), 462ff.; G. J. Barker-Benfield, "The Origins of Anglo-American Sensibility," in *Charity, Philanthropy, and Civility in American History*, ed. Lawrence J. Friedman and Mark D. McGarvie (Cambridge: Cambridge University Press, 2003), 71−89, 71−72; Cunningham, *In Pursuit of Reason*, 60−61.

66. Adams, *Diary and Autobiography*, 1:98.

67. Ibid., 43−44.

68. Ibid., 2:94; Benjamin Rush to John Adams, May 12, 1807, in *Spur of Fame*, 91; Thomas Jefferson to Maria Cosway, October 12, 1786, in *Papers of Thomas Jefferson*, 10:443−53.

69. Nancy Shippen, *Her Journal Book: The International Romance of a Young Lady of Fashion of Colonial Philadelphia with Letters to Her and about Her*, ed. Ethel Ames (Philadelphia: Lippin-

cott, 1935), 135; Sherman and the New England man quoted in Ellen K. Rothman, *Hands and Hearts: A History of Courtship in America* (New York: Basic, 1984), 37, 38.

70. Abigail Adams to Thomas Jefferson, May 20, 1804, in *Adams-Jefferson Letters*, 268–69; Brissenden, *Virtue in Distress*, 17.

71. John Quincy Adams to Abigail Adams, May 19, 1786, in *AFC*, 7:164; John Quincy Adams to Abigail Adams 2nd, August 28, 1785, in ibid., 6:291.

72. John Quincy Adams to Abigail Adams, October 6, 1785, in ibid., 409.

73. John Quincy Adams to Abigail Adams 2nd, October 16, 1785, in ibid., 443.

74. See, e.g., Elizabeth Smith Shaw to Abigail Adams, June 12, 1785, in ibid., 175–76.

75. Adams, *Diary and Autobiography*, 1:40. Compare J. G. A. Pocock, *Virtue, Commerce, and History: Essays on Political Thought and History Chiefly in the Eighteenth Century* (Cambridge: Cambridge University Press, 1985), 49; and Barker-Benfield, *Culture of Sensibility*, 84–86. Tompkins has described "gestures in which sensibility expresses itself." *Popular Novel*, 106–11.

76. Abigail Adams to John Adams, August 29, 1776, in *AFC*, 2:112.

77. Adams, *Diary and Autobiography*, 3:313, 329.

78. Stephen H. Voss, translator's introduction to Descartes, *Passions of the Soul*, vii–xiv, xii; Fliegelman, *Declaring Independence*, 31; Israel, *Radical Enlightenment*, 33; W. A. Coupe, "Lavater, Johann Caspar," in *Penguin Companion to European Literature*, ed. Anthony Thorlby (New York: McGraw-Hill, 1969), 463.

79. Abigail Adams to John Adams, November 5, 1775, in *AFC*, 1:320–21; Abigail Adams to John Adams, January 28, 1797, in *My Dearest Friend*, 432. See, too, Waldstreicher, *In the Midst of Fetes*, 84.

80. Adams, *Diary and Autobiography*, 1:65, 3:321, 315.

81. John Adams to Benjamin Rush, June 20, 1808, in *Spur of Fame*, 119; Jefferson to Abigail Adams, June 13, 1804, in *Adams-Jefferson Letters*, 271; Fordyce, *Sermons to Young Women*, 2:5–6, 237.

82. Abigail Adams to John Adams, July 16, 1775, in *AFC*, 1:246.

83. Abigail Adams to Mary Smith Cranch, September 30, 1785, in ibid., 6:392.

84. Adams, *Diary and Autobiography*, 1:68.

85. Abigail Adams to John Adams, December 7, 1783, in *AFC*, 5:277.

86. Markman Ellis, *The Politics of Sensibility: Race, Gender, and Commerce in the Sentimental Novel* (Cambridge: Cambridge University Press, 1996), 19–20; Descartes, *Passions of the Soul*, 80–81.

87. Hannah Griffitts, "On Reading the Adventurer World & et[c].," in *Milcah Martha Moore's Book*, 271.

88. *Journal and Correspondence of Miss Adams*, 1:72–73.

89. Jefferson, *Notes on the State of Virginia*, 133. Jefferson here was virtually quoting (in translation) Buffon's *Natural History* (1749–75). See Jordan, *White over Black*, 236. The narrator of Elizabeth Bonhote's Sternean novel *Rambles of Mr. Frankly* (1773) asked on meeting a black man in Jamaica: "Why did I start? That jetty countenance perhaps never blushed for guilt—and if so, his heart is as fair as his countenance is gloomy." He exclaimed: "A Slave!—The heart shuddered at a fellow creature's being a slave." (Quoted in Sypher, *Guinea's Captive Kings*, 269.) The shudder was another nonverbal expression of sensibility, as we will see. *Letters of the Late Ignatius Sancho*, 148 (and see 112).

90. John Adams to Benjamin Rush, April 18, 1813, in *Spur of Fame*, 307; Adams, *Diary and Autobiography*, 1:226 (quoting Pope, *Essay on Man*, epistle 4, lines 387–88); Eliza Lucas to [Miss Livingston], [1743], in *Letterbook of Eliza Lucas Pinckney*, 62.

91. Abigail Adams to Catherine Sawbridge Macaulay, [1774], in *AFC*, 1:177; Abigail Adams to John Adams, July 31, 1777, in ibid., 269.

92. Adams, "Instructions of the Town of Braintree to Their Representative, 1765," in *Revolutionary Writings of John Adams*, 39–41.

93. Abigail Adams to Mercy Otis Warren, December 5, 1773, in *AFC*, 1:89; Mercy Otis Warren to Abigail Adams, January 28, 1775, in ibid., 181. See, too, Knott, *Sensibility and the American Revolution*, 66. I return to this subject in chapter 14 below.

94. Mercy Otis Warren to Abigail Adams, December 11, 1775, in *AFC*, 1:339; Abigail Adams to John Adams, March 10, 1776, in ibid., 355.

95. "Sleepless nights and an aching heart occationed by poor Mr. Pinckneys severe illness makes me very unfit for this imployment as I have such a tremor upon my nerves I can but just hold my pen." Eliza Lucas Pinckney to the Right Honble Lady Mary Drayton, [ca. June–July 1758], in *Letterbook of Eliza Lucas Pinckney*, 93.

96. John Adams to Secretary [John Jay], June 3, 1785, in *Works of John Adams*, 8:255–59.

97. Abigail Adams to Elizabeth Smith Cranch, September 2, 1785, in *AFC*, 6:329–30. For another illustration of *shudder*, see Abigail Adams to Mercy Otis Warren, May 2, 1775, in ibid., 1:190. On Trumbull's painting, see Abigail Adams to Elizabeth Smith Shaw, March 4, 1786, in ibid., 7:82. Nabby wrote John Quincy about the picture's effects: "I was frozen, it is enough to make one's hair stand on end . . . . the scene is so dreadfully beautiful, or rather dreadfully expressive." Abigail Adams 2nd to John Quincy Adams, January 14, 1786, in ibid., 16–17.

98. Eliza Lucas to [Miss Bartlett], [1742], in *Letterbook of Eliza Lucas Pinckney*, 35–36.

99. Eliza Lucas to Miss Bartlett in St. Pauls Church Yard, London, [ca. May 1742], in *Letterbook of Eliza Lucas Pinckney*, 61–62; "Jan 7th, 1742," in ibid., 57–58.

100. Abigail Adams to John Adams, August 29, 1776, and July 12, 1775, in *AFC*, 2:112–13, 1:245. For an account of Abigail's running the farm while John was away, see Keller, *Patriotism and the Female Sex*, chap. 7. For Abigail's increasing self-assertion in financial matters while John was away, see Woody Holton, "Abigail Adams, Bond Speculator," *William and Mary Quarterly*, 3rd ser., 64, no. 4 (October 2007): 821–38.

101. Abigail Adams to John Adams, May 14, 1776, in *AFC*, 1:407–8; Norton, *Liberty's Daughters*, chap. 7.

102. John Adams to Abigail Smith, April 11, 1764, and [April 12], 1764, in *AFC*, 1:22, 24–25; Wagner, *Eros Revived*, 182–83.

103. Abigail Smith to John Adams, April 15, 1764, in *AFC*, 1:31, 32–33; John Adams to Abigail Smith, [April 14, 1764], in ibid., 30; Abigail Adams to Royall Tyler, [January 4, 1785], in ibid., 6:47.

104. Mira, "Reflections on the Fair Sex," *Royal American Magazine*, May 1774, 188.

105. Gelles, *Abigail and John*, 199; John Adams to Abigail Adams, December 25, 1786, in *AFC*, 7:412; Wagner, *Eros Revived*, pll. 60, 61, p. 264; Ferling, *John Adams*, 34. For a view contrary to Wagner's on the extent of pornography in America, albeit focused on the nineteenth century, see Carl Bode, "Columbia's Carnal Bed," in *The Half-World of American Literature: A Miscellany* (Carbondale: Southern Illinois University Press, 1965), 27. For John's amorousness, see chapter 9 below.

106. John Adams to Abigail Smith, September 30, 1764, in *AFC*, 1:48–49; David S. Shields, *Civil Tongues and Polite Letters in British North America* (Chapel Hill: University of North Carolina Press, 1997), passim.

107. John Adams to Abigail Smith, May 7, 1764, in *AFC*, 1:45; Abigail Smith to John Adams, May 9, 1764, in ibid., 47.

108. John Adams to Abigail Adams, May 19, 1794, and Abigail Adams to John Adams, May 27, 1794, in *My Dearest Friend*, 371, 373.

109. Abigail Adams to John Adams, December 10, 1779, in *AFC*, 3:242–43. Mary Wollstonecraft wrote: "A little sensibility, and great weakness, will produce a strong sexual attachment." *A Vindication of the Rights of Woman* (1792), ed. Carol H. Poston (New York: Norton, 1975), 189. Abigail Adams to Mary Smith Cranch, July 6, 1784, in *AFC*, 5:361; Barker-Benfield, *Culture of Sensibility*, 296, 482 n. 27; Jean-Jacques Rousseau, *Confessions*, trans. Angela Scholar (Oxford: Oxford University Press, 2000), 192; Abigail Adams to Caroline A. Smith, November 19, 1812, in *Letters of Mrs. Adams*, 411; Withey, *Dearest Friend*, ix–x.

CHAPTER 3

1. Abigail Adams to Mary Smith Cranch, January 31, 1767, in *AFC*, 1:61; Abigail Adams to John Thaxter, June 17, 1782, in ibid., 4:330–31. The quotations in the next paragraph are from this source as well.

2. Dwyer, *Virtuous Discourse*, 128, 91 n. 13; Fordyce, *Sermons to Young Women*, 1:38–39; Janet Todd, introduction to Fordyce, *Sermons to Young Women*; Wollstonecraft, *Vindication of the Rights of Woman*, 92; Barker-Benfield, *Culture of Sensibility*, 373–94, 133–41.

3. Keller, *Patriotism and the Female Sex*, 24, 27; Akers, *Abigail Adams*, 20–22; Levin, *Abigail Adams*, 28–29; Wollstonecraft, *Vindication of the Rights of Woman*, 92–93, 72–92. Jane Austen parodied Fordyce via the "ridiculous" figure of the Reverend William Collins in *Pride and Prejudice*.

4. Fordyce, *Sermons to Young Women*, 1:20, 2:40, 303.

5. Ibid., 1:51–52, 2:233–35.

6. See chapter 12 below.

7. Fordyce, *Sermons to Young Women*, 1:93, 167; Norton, *Liberty's Daughters*, 3.

8. Fordyce, *Sermons to Young Women*, 1:166–67, 138, 271–72. For Hume on Queen Elizabeth, see Barker-Benfield, *Culture of Sensibility*, 136.

9. For brief summaries of the *querelle des femmes*, see Margaret L. King and Albert Rabil Jr., series editors' introduction to *The Correspondence between Princess Elisabeth of Bohemia and René Descartes*, ed. and trans. Lisa Shapiro (Chicago: University of Chicago Press, 2007), ix–xxvii; Desmond M. Clarke, introduction to Poulain de la Barre, *Equality of the Sexes*, 1–39, 11–21.

10. Fordyce, *Sermons to Young Women*, 2:220–21, 1:229, 281–82; Barker-Benfield, *Culture of Sensibility*, 168–71.

11. Fordyce, *Sermons to Young Women*, 1:282, 2:290.

12. Samuel Richardson, *Clarissa; or, The History of a Young Lady* (1748–49), ed. John Butt, 4 vols. (London: Dent, 1932), 4:495.

13. Fordyce, *Sermons to Young Women*, 1:290–91. Compare Cmiel, *Democratic Eloquence*, 29–30.

14. Fordyce, *Sermons to Young Women*, 1:290, 291.

15. Ibid., 1:9, 2:24–25; Barker-Benfield, *Culture of Sensibility*, 385–86.

16. Fordyce, *Sermons to Young Women*, 2:78, 111 (and see 61–62).

17. Wollstonecraft, *Vindication of the Rights of Woman*, 93; Fordyce, *Sermons to Young Women*, 1:185–86.

18. Fordyce, *Sermons to Young Women*, 1:185–86; Barker-Benfield, *Culture of Sensibility*, 250–79; David Chaplin's "A Discourse Delivered before the Charitable Female Society in

Groton" (1814) quoted in Cott, *Bonds of Womanhood*, 128–29; Heyrman, *Southern Cross*, 163–67 (and see 194–95).

19. Fordyce, *Sermons to Young Women*, 1:184–85, 2:60–61, 231, 232.

20. Ibid., 1:103, 165, 126–27, 2:124.

21. Ibid., 1:208, 2:265.

22. Ibid., 1:192–93.

23. Ibid., 2:17–18, 1:283, 175; David Hume, "Of Refinement in the Arts" (1754), in *Essays Moral, Political, and Literary*, 268–80, 271.

24. *Scots Magazine* quoted in Dwyer, *Virtuous Discourse*, 126; Barker-Benfield, *Culture of Sensibility*, chap. 3; Fordyce, *Sermons to Young Women*, 1:175.

25. Fordyce, *Sermons to Young Women*, 1:248; Barker-Benfield, *Culture of Sensibility*, 139.

26. Fordyce, *Sermons to Young Women*, 2:268, 1:267, 2:30–31.

27. Barker-Benfield, *Culture of Sensibility*, 250–54, 263; Fordyce, *Sermons to Young Women*, 1:17–18, 33–34, 2:84, 85.

28. Fordyce, *Sermons to Young Women*, 1:22–23. Fordyce wrote: "Habits, we all know, are formed by many reiterated acts." Ibid., 2:138. This was a theme in Descartes, *Passions of the Soul*, 42–43, 47–81, 108–9, 132–34.

29. Wollstonecraft, *Vindication of the Rights of Woman*, 67. She had (mis)quoted Pope's line about women, "Fine by defect, and amiably weak!" (*Moral Essays*, epistle 2, line 43: "Fine by defect, and delicately weak") five pages before.

30. Fordyce, *Sermons to Young Women*, 1:23–24; Barker-Benfield, *Culture of Sensibility*, 250–58.

31. Barker-Benfield, *Culture of Sensibility*, chap. 3, "The Question of Effeminacy"; Abigail Adams to John Thaxter, May 21, 1778, in *AFC*, 3:25. Abigail wrote John Quincy pretty much the same. See Abigail Adams to John Quincy Adamns, March 20, 1786, in ibid., 7:97. Barker-Benfield, "Mary Wollstonecraft: Eighteenth-Century Commonwealthwoman," in Horowitz, ed., *Race, Gender, and Rank*, 184–204; John Adams to Abigail Adams, June 3, 1778, in *AFC*, 3:32; Crèvecoeur, *Letters from an American Farmer*, 36.

## CHAPTER 4

1. Mary P. Ryan, "The Public and the Private Good: Across the Great Divide in Women's History," *Journal of Women's History* 15, no. 2 (2003): 10–27, 19.

2. H. D. F. Kitto, *The Greeks* (Chicago: Aldine, 1964), 40 and chap. 12 passim; Gurpreet Mahajan, "The Public and the Private: Two Modes of Enhancing Democratization," in *The Public and the Private: Issues of Democratic Citizenship*, ed. Gurpreet Mahajan (New Delhi: Sage, 2003), 9–33, 9–10; Elias, *Civilizing Process*, 349.

3. Mahajan, "The Public and the Private," 11–12; Jürgen Habermas, *The Structural Transformation of the Public Sphere: An Enquiry into a Category of Bourgeois Society*, trans. Thomas Burger (Cambridge, MA: MIT Press, 1989), 55.

4. Wood, *Radicalism of the American Revolution*, 54; Carole Shammas, "The Domestic Environment in Early Modern England and America," *Journal of Social History* 14, no. 1 (1990): 3–24. And see Carole Shammas, *The Pre-Industrial Consumer in England and America* (New York: Oxford University Press, 1990), 183, 185.

5. Habermas, *Structural Transformation of the Public Sphere*, 55; Shammas, *Pre-Industrial Consumer*, 157, 186; Shammas, "Domestic Environment," 17–18. Compare Meyer, *Sex and Power*, 430. Keith Wrightson modifies Lawrence Stone's case for the coming into existence of "companionate marriage," suggesting that marriages in seventeenth-century England be placed on

a continuum between patriarchal and companionate forms. Keith Wrightson, *English Society, 1580—1680* (London: Hutchinson, 1982), 90—105; Lawrence Stone, *The Family, Sex and Marriage in England, 1500—1800* (New York: Harper & Row, 1977).

6. Habermas, *Structural Transformation of the Public Sphere*, 55.

7. Crane, "Genealogy of the 'Man of Feeling,'" 219—20; More, *Enchiridion ethicum*, 138—39.

8. Fiering, "Irresistible Compassion," 385; Crane, "Genealogy of the 'Man of Feeling,'" 208—12.

9. *Spectator*, no. 169 (September 13, 1711), in Bond, ed., *Spectator*, 2:164—67. Unless indicated otherwise, quotations in subsequent paragraphs are from this source.

10. Adams, *Diary and Autobiography*, 1:60.

11. Hutcheson, *Nature and Conduct of the Passion and Affections*, 95, 121; Fordyce, *Sermons to Young Women*, 2:111.

12. Eliza Lucas to Miss B[artlett] at the Honble. Pinckney, Esq., in Crs. Town, [1742], and Eliza Lucas Pinckney to [Lady Nicholas Carew], [1755], in *Letterbook of Eliza Lucas Pinckney*, 46, 85; Brown, *Good Wives*, 171, 336, 354, 360; Eustace, *Passion Is the Gale*, chap. 8.

13. Abigail Adams to John Adams, August 11, 1763, in *AFC*, 1:6; Adams, *Diary and Autobiography*, 3:314, 315.

14. Obituary printed in *AFC*, 1:293—94; Adams, *Diary and Autobiography*, 2:43—44.

15. Abigail Smith to John Adams, August 11, 1763, in *AFC*, 1:6; Eliza Lucas Pinckney to [Lady Carew], February 7, 1757, in *Letterbook of Eliza Lucas Pinckney*, 88.

16. Anthony, Third Earl of Shaftesbury, *Characteristics of Men, Manners, Times* (1711), 6th ed., 3 vols. (1737—38; Indianapolis: Liberty Fund, 2001), 2:45—47; Hutcheson, *Nature and Conduct of the Passions and Affections*, 19, 33. For the representation of the graphic "Circle of the Social and Benevolent Affections," printed in the February 1789 *Columbian Magazine*, see Knott, *Sensibility and the American Revolution*, 196. For Abigail's views of public vs. private affections, see chapter 8 below.

17. John Adams to Abigail Adams, July 7, 1775, in *AFC*, 1:241; *Journal and Correspondence of Miss Adams*, 2, pt. 1:193.

18. Quoted in Tony Horwitz, *Blue Latitudes: Boldly Going Where Captain Cook Has Gone Before* (New York: Henry Holt, 2002), 348. For context, see Langford, *Polite and Commercial People*, 515.

19. Mercy Otis Warren to Abigail Adams, December 1, 1776, in *AFC*, 2:142—43.

20. Elizabeth Smith Shaw to Abigail Adams 2nd, June 4, 1786, in ibid., 7:213; René Descartes, *Principles of Philosophy*, (1644), pt. 3, art. 65; Smith, *Theory of Moral Sentiments*, 313; Mary Smith Cranch to Abigail Adams, May [21], 1786, in *AFC*, 7:185; Hannah Webster Foster, *The Coquette; or, The History of Eliza Wharton: A Novel, Founded on Fact* (1797; New York: Oxford University Press, 1986), 24.

21. Elizabeth Smith Shaw to Abigail Adams 2nd, June 4, 1786, in *AFC*, 7:214, 215.

22. John Adams to Abigail Smith, April 20, 1763, in ibid., 1:5; Hutcheson, *Nature and Conduct of the Passions and Affections*, 19.

23. Fordyce, *Sermons to Young Women*, 2:201—3, 205—6.

24. Ibid., 1:38 (and see 2:296). For the adaptation to America, see chapter 14 below.

25. Elizabeth Smith Shaw to Abigail Adams 2nd, June 4, 1786, in *AFC*, 7:213; Hutcheson, *Nature and Conduct of the Passions and Affections*, 18.

26. Elizabeth Smith Shaw to Abigail Adams 2nd, in *AFC*, 7:214, 215.

27. John Adams to Abigail Adams, October 29, 1775, in ibid., 1:318 (for context, see Wood, *Radicalism of the American Revolution*, 219—20); Bernard Mandeville, *The Fable of the Bees; or, Private Vices, Public Benefits* (1714), ed. F. B. Kaye, 2 vols. (Oxford: Clarendon, 1924), 2:43—53.

28. Adams, *Diary and Autobiography*, 2:61–62; Meyer, *Sex and Power*, 253–54.

29. Adams, *Dissertation on Canon and Feudal Law*, 29, 30; Smith, *Theory of Moral Sentiments*, 190–91.

30. John Quincy Adams to Thomas Boylston Adams, 1818, in *Journal and Correspondence of Miss Adams*, 2, pt. 1:6–8. Nonetheless, Abigail herself was capable of agreeing with Hamlet's "Frailty thy Name is woman!" She thus judged Mrs. Hancock's intention to marry Captain Scot, "an able bodied rough Sea Captain." Abigail Adams to John Adams, December 6, 1794, in *My Dearest Friend*, 377.

31. Barker-Benfield, *Culture of Sensibility*, 225–26 and chap. 3 passim.

32. John Adams to Benjamin Rush, December 27, 1810, in *Spur of Fame*, 187. For Rush's context, see Michael Meranze, *Laboratories of Virtue: Punishments, Revolution, and Authority in Philadelphia, 1760–1835* (Chapel Hill: University of North Carolina Press, 1996); and Knott, *Sensibility and the American Revolution*, chap. 5.

33. Thomas Jefferson, *Notes on Virginia* (New York: Harper Torchbooks, 1964), 131–43; Benjamin Rush to John Adams, December 26, 1811, in *Spur of Fame*, 220.

34. Fordyce, *Sermons to Young Women*, 1:250.

35. Ibid., 2:9–10, 1:vi–vii, 2:22. For a listing of these historians, see Kelley, *Learning to Stand and Speak*, 2 n. 2. See, too, Jan Lewis, "'Of every age sex & condition': The Representation of Women in the Constitution," in *What Did the Constitution Mean to Early Americans?* ed. Edward Countryman (Boston: Bedford/St. Martin's, 1999), 115–40, 126.

36. Fordyce, *Sermons to Young Women*, 2:25.

37. Barker-Benfield, *Culture of Sensibility*, 325–26; Bushman, *Refinement of America*, 300–302; Elizabeth Smith Shaw to Abigail Adams 2nd, June 4, 1786, in *AFC*, 7:214.

38. Fordyce, *Sermons to Young Women*, 1:268, 81, 88; Barker-Benfield, *Culture of Sensibility*, 198–205, 185–86.

39. Fordyce, *Sermons to Young Women*, 1:88, 139; Barker-Benfield, *Culture of Sensibility*, 188.

40. Fordyce, *Sermons to Young Women*, 1:21, 35; Rodris Roth, "Tea-Drinking in Eighteenth-Century America: Its Etiquette and Equipage," in *Material Lives in America*, ed. Robert Blair St. George (Boston: Northeastern University Press, 1988), 439–62; Shammas, *Pre-Industrial Consumer*, 299; Anna Smart Martin, "Buying into the World of Goods: Eighteenth-Century Consumerism and the Retail Trade from London to the Virginia Frontier" (Ph.D. diss., College of William and Mary, 1993).

41. Fordyce, *Sermons to Young Women*, 1:286, 62–63; Wagner, *Eros Revived*, 158–59.

42. Fordyce, *Sermons to Young Women*, 1:238–43.

43. Ibid., 243, 244, 245.

44. Peter Borsay, *The English Urban Renaissance: Culture and Society in the Provincial Town, 1660–1770* (Oxford: Clarendon, 1989), 250; *Spectator* quoted in ibid., 250.

45. Fordyce, *Sermons to Young Women*, 2:16–17, 75.

46. Ibid., 1:77, 94; Roy Porter, *English Society in the Eighteenth Century* (Harmondsworth: Penguin, 1982), 97; Harold Perkin, *The Origins of Modern English Society, 1780–1880* (London: Routledge & Kegan Paul, 1972), 91; Shammas, *The Pre-Industrial Consumer*, 185; Neil McKendrick, "Home-Demand and Economic Growth: A New View of the Role of Women and Children in the Industrial Revolution," in *Historical Perspectives: Studies in English Thought and Society*, ed. Neil McKendrick (London: Europe, 1974), 152–210.

47. Fordyce, *Sermons to Young Women*, 1:95.

48. Ibid., 141, 58–59.

49. Ibid., 237, 256, 259–60, 261, 2:69; Barker-Benfield, *Culture of Sensibility*, 132–37.

50. Fordyce, *Sermons to Young Women*, 2:69. For an elaborate description of a fop, see Eliza-

beth Thomas's 1722 poem "The True Effigies of a Certain Squire: Inscribed by Clemena," in *Eighteenth-Century Women Poets: An Oxford Anthology*, ed. Roger Lonsdale (New York: Oxford University Press, 1989), 37–38. For the history of homosexuality in eighteenth-century England, see *English Masculinities, 1660–1800*, ed. Tim Hitchcock and Michele Cohen (London: Longman, 1999), 3 n. 5.

51. Fordyce, *Sermons to Young Women*, 1:60, 21.

52. Fliegelman, *Prodigals and Pilgrims*; Fordyce, *Sermons to Young Women*, 2:187–88.

53. Fordyce, *Sermons to Young Women*, 2:189–90, 191, 194.

54. Ibid., 194–95.

55. Ibid., 195; Todd, introduction, 1:xxiv; Barker-Benfield, *Culture of Sensibility*, 112.

56. Fordyce, *Sermons to Young Women*, 2:195–96.

57. Ibid., 196. Chapter 3 of Dwyer's *Virtuous Discourse* is entitled "The Construction of Adolescence in Late Eighteenth-Century Scotland."

58. Berkin, *First Generations*, 147; Kerber, *Women of the Republic*, 263–64; Davidson, *Revolution and the Word*, chap. 6.

59. Fordyce, *Sermons to Young Women*, 2:112–13, 1:44, 127.

60. Ibid., 1:128, 129–30.

61. Ibid., 1:101–2, 2:123–24; Barker-Benfield, *Culture of Sensibility*, 1–2.

62. Gordon S. Wood, "Conspiracy and the Paranoid Style: Causality and Deceit in the Eighteenth Century," *William and Mary Quarterly* 39, no. 3 (July 1982): 401–41; Fordyce, *Sermons to Young Women*, 1:130.

63. Fordyce, *Sermons to Young Women*, 1:130, 131.

64. Ibid., 34; Barker-Benfield, *Culture of Sensibility*, 238; for Burnet's Rochester, see ibid., 41–44.

65. Barker-Benfield, *Culture of Sensibility*, 128–29; Zagarri, *Revolutionary Backlash*, 20; Langford, *Polite and Commercial People*, 601–3, 606, 607; Fordyce, *Sermons to Young Women*, 1:287. Kelley has recently endorsed Nancy Cott's suggestion of the influence of Hannah More's views in America, particularly her antifeminist *Strictures on Female Education* (1799), but her earlier works, too. See the numerous citations to More in the index of Kelley, *Learning to Stand and Speak*; and Cott, *Bonds of Womanhood*, 74 n. 20.

66. Fordyce, *Sermons to Young Women*, 1:289.

67. Ibid., 288; Myers, *The Bluestocking Circle*; Eger and Peltz, *Brilliant Women*, 16–17 and passim.

68. Fordyce, *Sermons to Young Women*, 1:288, 2:128–29.

## CHAPTER 5

1. Bailyn, *Peopling of British North America*, 61–62. See, too, Berkin, *First Generations*, chap. 6.

2. Jack P. Greene, *Pursuits of Happiness: The Social Development of Early Modern British Colonies and the Formation of American Culture* (Chapel Hill: University of North Carolina Press, 1988), 188. See, too, Alan Taylor, *American Colonies: The Settling of North America* (New York: Penguin, 2002), 440–41.

3. Adams, *Diary and Autobiography*, 1:35, 8; Bushman, *Refinement of America*, 81; Norton, *Liberty's Daughters*, 23; Kerber, *Women of the Republic*, 251–58.

4. Mary Summer Benson, *Women in Eighteenth-Century America: A Study of Opinion and Social Usage* (1935; Port Washington, NY: Kennikat, 1966), 29–95, chap. 7; Fredrika J. Teute, "Friendly Conversation between Women and Men in Late Eighteenth-Century New York" (paper presented at the Early American Seminar, Huntington Library, October 25, 1997);

Stansell, *City of Women*, 23, 89–101; Bushman, *Refinement of America*, 289; Bertha Monica Stearns, "Early Factory Magazines in New England: *The Lowell Offering* and Its Contemporaries," *Journal of Economic and Business History* 2 (1929–30): 685–705.

5. Benson, *Women in Eighteenth-Century America*, 292–93; Bushman, *Refinement of America*, 81–82, 287–89; *Diary of Anna Green Winslow: A Boston Schoolgirl of 1771* (1894; Bedford, MA: Applewood, 1996).

6. Eliza Lucas to Mrs. Pinckney, [1741], in *Letterbook of Eliza Lucas Pinckney*, 46; John Kukla, *Mr. Jefferson's Women* (New York: Knopf, 2007), 32; Isaac, *Transformation of Virginia*, 77–79, 81–87; Brown, *Good Wives*, 281, 285, 299; Shields, *Civil Tongues*, 146 and chaps. 2 and 4 passim; Catherine Clinton, *The Plantation Mistress: Woman's World in the Old South* (New York: Pantheon, 1982), 177–79; Stevenson, *Life in Black and White*, 69, 135; Greene, *Pursuits of Happiness*, 5.

7. Rowlandson, *Sovereignty and Goodness of God*, 97.

8. *Letterbook of Eliza Luca Pinckney*, 9 n. 11, 78–79; Eliza Lucas to Mrs. H., [1742], in ibid., 48.

9. Eliza Lucas to Mrs. H., [1742], in ibid., 48–49.

10. Ibid., 49; *Spectator*, no. 580 (August 13, 1714), in Bond, ed., *Spectator*, 4:582–86, 585; Campbell, *Romantic Ethic*, 78–88.

11. *Diary of Anna Green Winslow*, 42, 60, 115–16.

12. Ibid., 74–75, 75 n. 1; Alice Morse Earle, foreword to ibid., iii–xx, x–xi.

13. *Diary of Anna Green Winslow*, 58, 1, 20, 40, 47, 63, 18, 57, 65, 23; *Memoir of Eliza Susan Morton Quincy* quoted in ibid., 96–98.

14. *Diary of Anna Green Winslow*, 12, 20, 28, 33, 47, 60, 64, 6–7, 20, 72, 18, 29, 15, 59, 46.

15. Ibid., 4–5, 7, 13–14, 16–17, 20, 31–32. Illustrations of the same kind of description is Abigail Adams to Lucy Cranch, April 2, 1786, in *AFC*, 7:126–27; and Entry, "Oct. 29th, 1741," in *Letterbook of Eliza Lucas Pinckney*, 23. And see the plate in the *Letterbook* of a "gold brocade dress woven from silk that Eliza Lucas Pinckney produced [i.e., produced by slaves] at the Belmont plantation."

16. *Diary of Anna Green Winslow*, 71 (and see 19). The editors of the *Adams Family Correspondence* include an illustration of the "fashion for enormous, inverted pyramids of hair, richly ornamental" (in *AFC*, 3:116, annotated xiii–xiv). See, too, Bushman, *Refinement of America*, 69–74.

17. *Diary of Anna Green Winslow*, 1–2, 2–3; Heyrman, *Southern Cross*, 171; Stansell, *City of Women*, 92–93, 53, 83.

18. John Adams to Abigail Smith, May 7, 1764, in *AFC*, 1:44–45; Elizabeth Smith to Abigail Adams, March 7, 1774, in ibid., 104. For Abigail's attempted interference with her sister's marriage, see Gelles, *Abigail and John*, 102–3.

19. Elizabeth Smith Shaw to Abigail Adams 2nd, June 4, 1786, in *AFC*, 7:214–15. Unless indicated otherwise, quotations in subsequent paragraphs are from this source.

20. John Quincy Adams's identification of the Boston boarding school Nancy Hazen attended is in John Quincy Adams to Abigail Adams 2nd, October 5, 1786, in ibid., 6:399.

21. East, *John Quincy Adams*, 22, 30, 178, 37, 24, 178; John Quincy Adams to Abigail Adams 2nd, September 22, 23, 1785, in *AFC*, 6:370–72.

22. John Quincy Adams to Abigail Adams 2nd, October 1785, in *AFC*, 6:399.

23. John Quincy Adams to Abigail Adams 2nd, October 5, 1785, in ibid., 399–400.

24. John Quincy Adams to Abigail Adams 2nd, October 15, 1786, in ibid., 400; Abigail Adams to John Quincy Adams, July 21, 1786, in ibid., 7:274–75; Adams, *Diary and Autobiography*, 1:13; Michele Cohen, "Manliness, Effeminacy, and the French: Gender and the Construction

of National Character in Eighteenth-Century England," in Hitchcock and Cohen, eds., *English Masculinities*, 44–61, 51. On his first entrance, the opening of act 3, Billy Dimple is "at a toilet, reading," and his first speech consists of a quotation from Lord Chesterfield's *Letters*, with his approving: "Very true, my lord; positively very true." Royall Tyler, *The Contrast: A Comedy in Five Acts* (1787; New York: AMS, 1970).

25. Extracts from John Quincy Adams's journal and an account of the relationship with Nancy Hazen are in East, *John Quincy Adams*, 41–45.

26. John Quincy Adams to Abigail Adams 2nd, April 15, 1786, in *AFC*, 7:157; John Quincy Adams to Abigail Adams 2nd, January 14, 1787, in ibid., 436–37.

27. John Quincy Adams to Abigail Adams 2nd, January 14, 1787, in ibid., 435–36. For John Quincy's relationship with Frank Bridge, see David F. Musto, "The Youth of John Quincy Adams," *Proceedings of the American Philosophical Society* 113 (1969): 269–82.

28. John Quincy Adams to Abigail Adams 2nd, February 5, 1787, in *AFC*, 7:437–38.

29. Abigail Adams 2nd to John Quincy Adams, April 25, 1786, in ibid., 150–51; Musto, "Youth of John Quincy Adams," 272.

30. Abigail Adams to John Thaxter, February 15, 1778, in *AFC*, 2:391–92.

31. Abigail Adams 2nd to John Quincy Adams, April 25, 1786, in ibid., 7:151.

32. Richard Alan Ryerson, "The Limits of a Vicarious Life: Abigail Adams and Her Daughter," *Proceedings of the Massachusetts Historical Society* 100 (1988): 1–14, 14; Musto, "Youth of John Quincy Adams," 280; East, *John Quincy Adams*, 16, 122–25. For another illustration of Abigail's interfering in John Quincy's life, getting President Madison to recall him from Moscow, see Gelles, *Abigail and John*, 270–71. Here, she was able to bring about what she had not in the case of her husband.

33. Abigail Adams 2nd to John Quincy Adams, April 25, 1786, in *AFC*, 7:152.

34. East, *John Quincy Adams*, 175, 107, 112, 108; Shields, *Civil Tongues*, chap. 2.

35. East, *John Quincy Adams*, 111, 227 n. 21, 111–13.

36. The complete poem is printed in *Journal and Correspondence of Miss Adams*, 2, pt. 1: 157–61.

37. "Epistle to a Lady," 60 (line 160).

## CHAPTER 6

1. Abigail Adams to John Adams, October 27, 1775, in *AFC*, 1:310; Fordyce, *Sermons to Young Women*, 1:170.

2. Abigail Adams to John Adams, November 12, and October 22, 1775, in *AFC*, 1:325, 310. See, too, Aldridge, "The Pleasures of Pity."

3. Abigail Adams to John Adams, April 12, 1784, in *AFC*, 5:318. This is a major theme in my *Culture of Sensibility*. See, too, Thomas, *The Ends of Life*, 12–29.

4. Abigail Adams to John Adams, March 8, 1778, May 18, 1778, October 25, 1778, and December 27, 1778, in *AFC*, 2:402, 3:23, 110, 140.

5. Abigail Adams to John Adams, [October 25, 1778], in ibid., 3:111; Sterne, *Tristram Shandy*, 196.

6. Abigail Adams to John Adams, February 20, 1796, quoted in Withey, *Dearest Friend*, 237.

7. Abigail Adams to John Adams, October 16, 1774, in *AFC*, 1:172.

8. Abigail Adams to John Adams, August 29, 1776, in ibid., 2:112. For context, see Withey, *Dearest Friend*, 84; and Barker-Benfield, *Culture of Sensibility*, chap. 4.

9. Barker-Benfield, *Culture of Sensibility*, 161.

10. Campbell, *Romantic Ethic*, 31, 26–27, 88–89.

11. Abigail Adams to John Adams, August 29, 1776, in *AFC*, 2:112; Bond, ed., *Spectator*, 3:536.

12. Abigail Adams to John Adams, August 29, 1776, in *AFC*, 2:112; Abigail Adams to John Thaxter, May 21, 1778, in ibid., 3:25.

13. John Adams to Abigail Adams, January 16, 1795, in *My Dearest Friend*, 381.

14. Campbell, *Romantic Ethic*, 59–60, 141–42; "On Sensibility" quoted in Waldstreicher, *In the Midst of Fetes*, 78–79; John Adams to Cotton Tufts, April 9, 1764, in *AFC*, 1:19; Wood, *Americanization of Benjamin Franklin*, 38, 62. And see Wood, *Radicalism of the American Revolution*, 33–34; E. P. Thompson, "Time, Work-Discipline, and Industrial Capitalism," in *Essays in Social History*, ed. M. C. Flinn and T. C. Smout (Oxford: Clarendon, 1974), 39–77, 68; and Daniel Boorstin, *The Democratic Experience*, vol. 3 of *The Americans* (New York: Vintage, 1972), 305–8 and bk. 2 passim (the point is implicit).

15. Abigail Adams to John Adams, October 9, 1775, in *AFC*, 1:296; Eliza Lucas Pinckney to [Mrs. Evance], [1759], in *Letterbook of Eliza Lucas Pinckney*, 104.

16. Abigail Adams to John Adams, October 1, 1775, in *AFC*, 1:289.

17. Eliza Lucas to Mrs. Chardon, [1743], in *Letterbook of Eliza Lucas Pinckney*, 68. Lucas believed that women were by "nature" too susceptible to the feelings of tender engagement, as her mother's grief was excessive, yet "feeling" was also the characteristic they prized. Eliza Lucas to the Honble. C[harles] P[inckney], Esqr., [1743], and Eliza Lucas Pinckney to the Honble. Mrs. King, May [1759], in ibid., 67–68, 118.

18. Abigail Adams to John Adams, October 25, 1775, in *AFC*, 1:312–13.

19. Abigail Adams to Isaac Smith Jr., April 20, 1771, in ibid., 76; Meyer, *Sex and Power*, 192–93.

20. Abigail Adams 2nd to John Quincy Adams, August 11, 1785, in *AFC*, 6:220.

21. Abigail Adams to Isaac Smith Jr., April 20, 1771, in ibid., 1:76.

22. Abigail Adams to John Adams, December 25, 1780, in ibid., 4:50–51.

23. Abigail Adams to John Adams, April 10, 1782, in ibid., 306. A correspondent to the *Lady's Magazine* in London declared: "Sensibility is the cause either of the greatest happiness or misery to the female sex." Quoted in Ellis, *Politics of Sensibility*, 23.

24. Abigail Adams to John Adams, [November 12–23, 1778], in *AFC*, 3:118; Abigail Adams to Mercy Otis Warren, December 10, [1778], in ibid., 132; Abigail Adams to John Adams, November 14, 1779, in ibid., 233–34. Abigail revealed consciousness of the same wish she expressed to Mercy by denying it in her letter to John, October 25, 1782, in ibid., 5:22.

25. Quoted in Kerber, *Women of the Republic*, 235–36. Cathy N. Davidson describes Rogers's diary showing her "love of novels" (including Sterne's *Sentimental Journey*); Rogers also called Woodbridge "Portius" after the young hero of Addison's *Cato*. Davidson, *Revolution and the Word*, 191. Compare Knott, *Sensibility and the American Revolution*, chap. 3.

26. Ignatius Sancho to Miss L[each], August 27, 1775, in *Letters of the Late Ignatius Sancho*, 63.

27. Both quotations are from Brown, *Sentimental Novel in America*, 97. Relf's novel may have been sparked in part by Rowson's; both are placed in context in Knott, *Sensibility and the American Revolution*, 299–300 (and see 222).

28. For the modification of Roman matrons, see Hicks, "Portia and Marcia." Malebranche described Cato (in Seneca's account of him) as having been motivated by the passions of pride and contempt. *Search after Truth*, 176–79.

29. Fordyce, *Sermons to Young Women*, 2:235; Abigail Adams to John Adams, October 8, 1782, in *AFC*, 5:5; Abigail Adams to Elizabeth Smith Shaw, ca. August 15, 1785, in ibid.,

6:281; Pope, *Essay on Man*, epistle 1, line 197; Mary Wollstonecraft, review of *Edward and Harriet; or, The Happy Recovery: A Sentimental Novel* by a Lady, *Analytical Review* 1 (1788): 207–8.

30. Fordyce, *Sermons to Young Women*, 2:237, 1:123–24.

31. Abigail Adams to John Adams, January 3, 1784, in *AFC*, 5:290–91.

32. Abigail Adams to John Adams, July 16, 1775, in ibid., 1:247; John Adams to Abigail Adams, November 12, 1775, in ibid., 326. Other illustrations of the stream of excuses he gave her for not writing are in John Adams to Abigail Adams, September 14, 1774, October 10, 1775, and April 14, 1776, in ibid., 155, 295, 381.

33. John Adams to Abigail Adams, February 9, 1779, in ibid., 3:160.

34. Abigail Adams to Judge Vanderbilt, January 2, 1818, in Adams, "Memoir," lix–lx; John Adams to Abigail Adams, March 19, 1776, in *AFC*, 1:363.

35. John Adams to Abigail Adams, October 23, 1778, in *AFC*, 1:311–12.

36. Abigail Adams to John Adams, April 17, 1777, in ibid., 2:213.

37. Abigail Adams to John Adams, [November 12–23, 1778], August 22, 1777, and July 14, 1776, in *AFC*, 3:118, 2:323, 46.

38. Abigail Adams to John Adams, August 5, [1777], in ibid., 2:301.

39. Abigail Adams to John Adams, December 20, 1795, in *My Dearest Friend*, 391. Once Benjamin Rush was accused of converting "a feeling Heart"—his own—"into a marble Monument of Stoicism!" Quoted in Knott, *Sensibility and the American Revolution*, 202.

40. John Adams to Abigail Adams, December 28, 1795, in *My Dearest Friend*, 392.

41. Abigail Smith to John Adams, October 4, 1764, in *AFC*, 1:50; Abigail Adams to John Adams, April 17, 1777, in ibid., 2:211–12. For Abigail's difficult pregnancies, see Ferling, *John Adams*, 167–68.

42. Abigail Adams to John Adams, July 10, [1777], in *AFC*, 2:278–79. In their exchange of letters about this dramatic event, Abigail's concern for John's feelings was paramount. G. J. Barker-Benfield, "Sensibility and Stillbirth" (typescript, Department of History, State University of New York at Albany, 2008).

43. Barker-Benfield, *Culture of Sensibility*, 250–58, 321–22.

44. Norton, *Liberty's Daughters*, 44.

45. Barker-Benfield, *Culture of Sensibility*, 322; Abigail Adams to John Thaxter, July 21, [1780], in *AFC*, 3:379; Fuller, *Summer on the Lakes*, 58–61, 13–15.

46. Abigail Adams to James Lovell, [ca. December 15, 1777], in *AFC*, 2:370–71; Lovell's letter quoted in ibid., n. 1.

47. Abigail Adams to James Lovell, [ca. December 15, 1777], in ibid., 370; Withey, *Dearest Friend*, 95.

48. Abigail Adams to John Adams, December 15, 1798, in *My Dearest Friend*, 452, 453. Knott addresses sensibility and bachelorhood. See *Sensibility and the American Revolution*, 227–28.

49. Adams, *Diary and Autobiography*, 4:4; John Quincy Adams to Abigail Adams 2nd, May 27, 1786, in *AFC*, 7:168.

50. Abigail Adams to John Adams, August 5, 1776, in *AFC*, 2:79; Barker-Benfield, *Culture of Sensibility*, 250–58. For the paragraph's last point, see Barbara J. Berg, *The Remembered Gate: The Origins of American Feminism: The Woman and the City, 1800–1860* (New York: Oxford University Press, 1978). A host of books on the subject have since been published.

51. Abigail Adams to John Adams, October 8, 1782, in *AFC*, 5:6. This had been her wish since before their marriage. See Abigail Smith to John Adams, April 8, 1764, in ibid., 1:19; and John Adams to Abigail Smith, September 30, 1764 in ibid., 49.

52. Abigail Adams to James Lovell, [ca. December 15, 1777], in ibid., 2:370.

53. Ibid., 371; Akers, *Abigail Adams*, 65, 64; McCullough, *John Adams*, 217.

54. Abigail Adams to James Lovell, [ca. December 15, 1777], in *AFC*, 2:371. The next two paragraphs quote this letter.

55. James Lovell to Abigail Adams, April 1, 1778, in ibid., 3:1.

56. Ibid., xxxiv.

57. Maynard Mack, *Alexander Pope: A Life* (New York: Norton, 1985), 302—3; Knott, *Sensibility and the American Revolution*, chap. 3; Ferling, *John Adams*, 209—10, 217, 234; Shaw, "Diplomacy and Domesticity," 690; Abigail Adams to John Adams, August 5, 1776, in *AFC*, 2:79.

58. James Lovell to Abigail Adams, January 19, 1776, in *AFC*, 3:150.

59. Abigail Adams to James Lovell, [February—March 1779], in ibid., 184; Lewis, *Pursuit of Happiness*, 218—19.

60. Richard Brinsley Sheridan, *The School for Scandal and Other Plays* (New York: Penguin, 1988), 216—17 (act 2, scene 2).

61. James Lovell to Abigail Adams, June 13, 1778, in *AFC*, 3:43. See, e.g., *Spectator*, no. 144 (August 15, 1711), in Bond, ed., *Spectator*, 2:69; Richardson, *Clarissa*, 3:116; Richardson, *The History of Sir Charles Grandison*, ed. Jocelyn Harris, 3 vols. (London: Oxford University Press, 1972), 1:152; Sterne, *Tristram Shandy*, 629—31; Laurence Sterne, *A Sentimental Journey through France and Italy, by Mr. Yorick* (1768), ed. Ian Jack (London: Oxford University Press, 1968), 112—17. It was the encounter between "Yorick" and Maria in *Sentimental Journey* that prompted Yorick's famous apostrophe, beginning "Dear SENSIBILITY!" Ibid., 117.

62. Stephen Lloyd, "The Accomplished Maria Cosway: Anglo-Italian Artist, Musician, Salon Hostess and Educationalist, 1759—1838," *Journal of Anglo-Italian Studies*, 2 (1992): 108—39, 113; Barker-Benfield, "Jefferson and Sensibility" (typescript, Department of History, State University of New York at Albany, 2003). This essay reflects my reading of the letters between Cosway and Jefferson.

## CHAPTER 7

1. Abigail Adams to John Adams, March 31, 1776, in *AFC*, 1:369—71.

2. Eger and Peltz, *Brilliant Women*, 21.

3. Shields, *Civil Tongues*, 110, 114, 116, 112, and chaps. 4 and 9 passim; Barker-Benfield, *Culture of Sensibility*, 159. See, too, Teute, "Friendly Conversation," 2—3; and Knott, *Sensibility and the American Revolution*, 43—44, 96—97.

4. Brown, *Good Wives*, 283, 285, 286.

5. Bushman, *Refinement of America*, 88; Barker-Benfield, *Culture of Sensibility*, 77—98, 154; Fredrika J. Teute, "Roman Matron on the Banks of Tiber Creek: Margaret Bayard Smith and the Politicization of Spheres in the Nation's Capital," in *A Republic for the Ages: The United States Capitol and the Political Culture of the Early Republic*, ed. Donald R. Kennon (Charlotte: University Press of Virginia, 1999), 89—121, 91.

6. For Abigail's letter, see n. 1 above. Isaac includes an illustration of a Virginia "Rifleman" in the unnumbered selection of pictures at the opening of *Transformation of Virginia*.

7. Samuel Johnson, "Taxation No Tyranny," in *Political Writings*, ed. Donald J. Greene, vol. 10 of *The Yale Edition of the Works of Samuel Johnson* (New Haven, CT: Yale University Press, 1958), 411—55, 454. Greene calls it "quasi-official." Donald J. Greene, introduction to Johnson, "Taxation No Tyranny," in Greene, ed., *Political Writings*, 401—11. For John's role in the First Continental Congress, see Ferling, *John Adams*, 110, 112, 147.

8. Abigail Adams to John Adams, September 22, 1774, in *AFC*, 1:162. Abigail suggested later that if "Negroes" in the South rose up against their owners—"haughty Aristocrats"—

they would be fighting "our Battles." Abigail Adams to John Adams, May 10, 1794, in *My Dearest Friend*, 369; Jordan, *White over Black*, 289–90.

9. For all quotations from Abigail's "Remember the Ladies" letter, see n. 1 above.

10. Adams, "An Essay on Man's Lust for Power," 81–83; Shaw, *Character of John Adams*, 303; Elaine Forman Crane, "Political Dialogue and the Spring of Abigail's Discontent," *William and Mary Quarterly*, 3rd ser., 56, no. 4 (October 1999): 745–74, 763.

11. Abigail Adams to John Adams, June 30, 1778, in *AFC*, 3:53. John owned a copy of Shebbeare's book and recommended it to his "Nieces" in 1761, adding: "And let me warn you against any Prejudice to him, or his sentiments on Account of that open Defyance and Contempt in which he held your sex." Adams, *Diary and Autobiography*, 1:52, 194.

12. Poulain de la Barre, *Equality of the Sexes*, pt. 1; Sarah Egerton, "The Emulation," and Elizabeth Thomas, "On Sir J—— S—— Saying in a Sarcastic Manner, My Books Would Make Me Mad, an Ode," both in Lonsdale, ed., *Eighteenth-Century Women Poets*, 31, 40. "Tyrant custom" here was a feminist adoption of an old phrase. See *Othello*, 1:3, line 228.

13. Henrietta Howard quoted in Rumbold, *Women's Place in Pope's World*, 213; Pope, "Epistle to a Lady," 71 (line 288); *Spectator*, no. 236 (November 30, 1711), in Bond, ed., *Spectator*, 2:417–18; Montesquieu quoted in Kerber, *Women of the Republic*, 20. Abigail quoted Montesquieu in a letter she wrote aboard ship and, thus, probably by heart. See Abigail Adams to Royall Tyler, July 10, 1784, in *AFC*, 5:391.

14. Shippen quoted in Knott, *Sensibility and the American Revolution*, 130–40; Wollstonecraft, *Vindication of the Rights of Woman*, 19; republican "Citizen" quoted in Judith Apter Klinghoffer and Lois Elkis, "'The Petticoat Electors': Women's Suffrage in New Jersey, 1776–1807," *Journal of the Early Republic* 12 (Summer 1992): 159–93, 179–80.

15. Elaine Forman Crane, "Abigail Adams, Gender Politics, and *The History of Emily Montague*: A Postscript," *William and Mary Quarterly*, 3rd ser., 64, no. 4 (October 2007): 839–44, 839, 841, 842; Crane, "Political Dialogue," 758; Clarke, introduction, 20–21.

16. Wills, *Inventing America*, chap. 18; Fordyce, *Sermons to Young Women*, 1:33; Alexis de Tocqueville, *Democracy in America*, trans. Henry Reeve, 2 vols. (New York: Vintage, 1990), 2:121–24; Wills, *Inventing America*, 252.

17. For Edgeworth in America, see Kerber, *Women of the Republic*, 241, 252. For an analysis of *Belinda*, see Barker-Benfield, *Culture of Sensibility*, 386–92.

18. Crane provides a useful sketch of scholars' varying views of Abigail's feminism, asserting herself that, in 1776, it was "egalitarian and revolutionary." See "Political Dialogue," 751–52. Compare Knott, *Sensibility and the American Revolution*, 150.

19. John Adams to Abigail Adams, April 14, 1776, in *AFC*, 1:381–82. All subsequent quotations of this letter are drawn from this. For John's "subordination of the issue of slavery to the question of independence," see Ferling, *John Adams*, 172–73.

20. Abigail Adams to John Adams, August 14, 1776, in *AFC*, 2:94; John Adams to Abigail Adams, August 25, 1776, in ibid., 109. Fifteen years earlier, John had advised his supposed "Nieces" (see n. 11 above): "I would not have you Pedants in Greek and Latin nor the Depths of science, nor yet over fond to talk of any Thing." Adams, *Diary and Autobiography*, 1:194. Abigail Adams 2nd to John Quincy Adams, July 31, 1785, in *AFC*, 6:216.

21. Adams, *Diary and Autobiography*, 3:316.

22. John Adams to Abigail Adams, April 28, 1776, in *AFC*, 1:400, 398–99, 401.

23. Wood, *Radicalism of the American Revolution*, pt. 2; Abigail Adams to Edward Dilly, May 22, 17[75], in *AFC*, 1:200–201; Jan Lewis, "The Republican Wife: Virtue and Seduction in the Early Republic," *William and Mary Quarterly*, 3rd ser., 44, no. 4 (October 1987): 689–721, 713.

24. John Adams to Abigail Adams, April 28, 1776, in *AFC*, 1:401. See Lawrence J. Friedman, *Inventors of the Promised Land* (New York: Knopf, 1976), chap. 4; and Waldstreicher, *In the Midst of Fetes*, 82.

25. John Adams to Thomas Boylston Adams, October 17, 1799, quoted in Smith, *John Adams*, 2:1016–17. See, too, Crane's comment on this letter. "Political Dialogue," 768–69. In 1794, John wrote Abigail that "the Author of Nature" had established "a Physical Inequality, an Intellectual Inequality" among men and declared: "Society has a Right to establish any other Inequalities it may judge necessary for its good." John Adams to Abigail Adams, February 4, 1794, in *My Dearest Friend*, 1794. For Godwin's revelations about Wollstonecraft, see chapter 14 below.

26. Abigail Adams to Mercy Otis Warren, April 28, 1776, in *AFC*, 1:396–97.

27. Keller, *Patriotism and the Female Sex*, 94; William Blackstone, *Commentaries on the Common Law* (1771), quoted in Kerber, *Women of the Republic*, 140.

28. Abigail Adams to Mercy Otis Warren, April 28, 1776, in *AFC*, 1:397.

29. Ibid., 397–98.

30. Fordyce, *Sermons to Young Women*, 1:54.

31. Pope, "Epistle to a Lady," lines 213, 199–206, 257–65, 248; Astell, *Some Reflections upon Marriage*, 7–8; Hogarth's *Before and After* reproduced in Wagner, *Eros Revived*, 278–79.

32. Abigail Adams to John Adams, May 7, 1776, in *AFC*, 1:401–402. For women's voting in New Jersey, see Klinghoffer and Elkis, "'Petticoat Electors.'"

33. Crane, "Political Dialogue," 764; Abigail Adams to John Adams, May 7, 1776, in *AFC*, 1:402–403.

34. Abigail Adams to John Adams, May 7, 1776, in *AFC*, 1:403; Abigail Adams to John Adams, December 23, 1782, in ibid., 5:54. That this was a romantic metaphor, signifying the strength of love, is endorsed by Abigail's later description of how women in the past had exercised "political Government," e.g., as absolute monarchs. "But," she continued, "my ambition will extend no further than Reigning in the Heart of my Husband. That is my Throne and there I aspire to be absolute." Abigail Adams to John Adams, February 26, 1794, in *My Dearest Friend*, 302.

35. Wollstonecraft, *Vindication of the Rights of Woman*, 93–94.

36. Rumbold, *Women's Place in Pope's World*, 266; Wollstonecraft, *Vindication of the Rights of Woman*, 62, 72–73, 188; Barker-Benfield, *Culture of Sensibility*, 285, 292.

37. Wood, *Creation of the American Republic*, 568; [John Adams], "The Report of a Constitution, or Form of Government, for the Commonwealth of Massachusetts, Agreed upon by the Committee," in *Revolutionary Writings of John Adams*, 296–322, 296; John Adams to John Sullivan, May 26, 1776, in *Papers of John Adams*, 4:211–12.

38. Adams, "Report of a Constitution," 296.

## CHAPTER 8

1. Abigail Smith to John Adams, August 11, 1763, in *AFC*, 1:6–7; John Adams to Abigail Smith, August 15, 1763, in ibid., 7.

2. Abigail Adams to Mercy Otis Warren, [before February 27, 1774], in ibid., 97–98. Here, Abigail may be recalling her own reading of Hume's influential essays on political parties "Of Parties in General" (1741) and "Of the Parties of Great Britain" (1741).

3. Abigail Adams to John Thaxter, July 1, 1783, in *AFC*, 5:192–93.

4. Abigail Adams to John Adams, June 18, 1775, in ibid., 1:222–23.

5. For the poem's context and the other poems mentioned, see *The Poems of Thomas Gray,*

*William Collins, and Oliver Goldsmith*, ed. Roger Lonsdale (New York: Longmans, 1980), 436–47, 414–27, 477–85.

6. Abigail Adams to John Adams, July 5, 1775, in *AFC*, 1:239–40.

7. Abigail Adams to John Adams, July 31, 1775, in ibid., 269–70 n. 3. Unless indicated otherwise, quotations in subsequent paragraphs are from this source.

8. John Adams to Abigail Adams, July 7, 1775, in ibid., 241.

9. Mercy Otis Warren to Abigail Adams, January 28, 1775, in ibid., 181–82.

10. Abigail Adams to Mercy Otis Warren, [July 24], 1775, in ibid., 255; Fordyce, *Sermons to Young Women*, 102.

11. Abigail Adams to Mercy Otis Warren, August 28, 1775, in *AFC*, 1:276.

12. Abigail Adams to Mercy Otis Warren, [January ?, 1776], in ibid., 422–23.

13. Akers, *Abigail Adams*, 114; Abigail Adams to John Thaxter, February 15, 1778, in *AFC*, 2:390; Zagarri, *A Woman's Dilemma*, 107; Shaw, *Character of John Adams*, 288–89; Withey, *Dearest Friend*, 32; Gelles, *First Thoughts*, 131.

14. Abigail Adams to John Thaxter, February 15, 1778, in *AFC*, 2:390.

15. Abigail Adams to John Adams, September 16, 1775, in ibid., 1:279; Ferling, *John Adams*, 149.

16. Abigail Adams to Mercy Otis Warren, [January ?, 1776], in *AFC*, 1:423.

17. John Adams to Abigail Adams, February 2, 1795, in *My Dearest Friend*, 384; Gordon-Reed, *The Hemingses of Monticello*, 137–38.

18. Abigail Adams to Mercy Otis Warren, [January ?, 1776], in *AFC*, 1:423.

19. John Adams to Abigail Adams, May 12, 1776, in ibid., 406–7 (see, too, ibid., 419 n. 6); Abigail Adams to John Adams, May 27, 1776, in ibid., 417–18.

20. Ibid., 418; Eliza Lucas Pinckney to [Mrs. Evance], 1759, in *Letterbook of Eliza Lucas Pinckney*, 104.

21. Abigail Adams to Mary Smith Cranch, July 6, 1784, in *AFC*, 5:360; Benjamin Vaughan to Benjamin Franklin, January 31, 1783, in Franklin, *Autobiography and Other Writings*, 66–71, 68; Abigail Adams to John Adams, May 27, 1776, in *AFC*, 1:418; Mintz, *Huck's Raft*, 66.

22. Abigail Adams to Mercy Otis Warren, [January ?, 1777], in *AFC*, 2:150.

23. Abigail Adams to John Adams, June 17 [1776], in ibid., 13–14.

24. Abigail Adams to John Adams, August 29, 1776, in ibid., 113; Abigail Adams to John Adams, April 10, 1782, in ibid., 4:307; Greene, *Pursuits of Happiness*, 96.

25. Abigail Adams to John Adams, September 20, 1777 [i.e., 1776], in *AFC*, 2:128–29.

26. Abigail Adams to John Adams, [ca. December 15, 1777], in ibid., 370–71; John Adams to Elbridge Gerry, December 23, 1777, in *Papers of John Adams*, 5:366; Ferling, *John Adams*, 175 (and see 261).

27. Abigail Adams to John Thaxter, February 15, 1778, in *AFC*, 2:390.

28. Abigail Adams to Abigail Adams 2nd, February [11?], 1779, in ibid., 3:161–63; John Adams to Abigail Adams, September 23, 1778, in ibid., 91.

29. Abigail Adams to Abigail Adams 2nd, February [11?], 1779, in ibid., 162.

30. John Adams to Abigail Adams, September 23, 1778, in ibid., 91 and n. 1.

31. Abigail Adams to John Adams, February 13, 1779, in ibid., 168.

32. For example, Thomas Jefferson to George Washington, November 4, 1788, in *Papers of Thomas Jefferson*, 14:330.

33. John Thaxter to Abigail Adams, February 16, 1780, and June 18, 1780, in *AFC*, 3:278, 369.

34. Abigail Adams to John Adams, February 13, 1779, in ibid., 167–68. Unless indicated otherwise, quotations in subsequent paragraphs are from this source.

35. Abigail Adams to Abigail Adams 2nd, July 17, 1782, in ibid., 4:344; Abigail Adams to John Adams, August 5, 1[7]82, in ibid., 358.

36. Abigail Adams to John Adams, October 8, 1782, in ibid., 5:4-6. The quotations in the next paragraph are from this source as well.

37. Abigail Adams to John Adams, November 13, 1782, in ibid., 35-36.

38. Abigail Adams to John Adams, November 25, 1782, in ibid., 36-37.

39. Abigail Adams to John Adams, December 23, 1782, in ibid., 54-58. Unless indicated otherwise, quotations in subsequent paragraphs are from this source.

40. Abigail Adams to Mercy Otis Warren, [January ?, 1776], in ibid., 1:422.

41. Abigail Adams to John Adams, December 23, 1782, in ibid., 5:55.

42. Abigail Adams to John Adams, January 10, 1783, in ibid., 67, 68 and n. 2. The quotations in the next paragraph are from this source as well.

43. John Adams to Abigail Adams, January 29, 1783, in ibid., 82-83; Ferling, *John Adams*, 255.

44. Abigail Adams to John Adams, April 10, 1782, in *AFC*, 4:307; Adair, *Fame and the Founding Fathers*, 18, 14, 28-29.

45. Abigail Adams to John Adams, June 20, 1783, in *AFC*, 5:179.

46. John Adams to Abigail Adams, March 28, 1783, in ibid., 107, 110-11. See, too, Shaw, *Character of John Adams*, 182-83, 198-99.

47. Abigail Adams to John Adams, June 20, 1783, in *AFC*, 5:180. The quotations in the next paragraph are from this source as well.

48. Abigail Adams to John Adams, June 30, 1783, in ibid., 189.

49. John Adams to Abigail Adams, July 17, 1783, in ibid., 202-3. The quotations in the next paragraph are from this source as well.

50. John Adams to Abigail Adams, August 14, 1783, in ibid., 221-22; Withey, *Dearest Friend*, 197-98; Abigail Adams to John Adams, April 28, 1783, in *AFC*, 5:144; Joseph Warren, "An Oration on the Second Anniversary of the Boston Massacre, March 5, 1772," in *Readings in the American Past: Selected Historical Documents*, ed. Michael J. Johnson (Boston: Bedford/St. Martin's, 2009), 106; Abigail Adams to Mary Smith Cranch, February 25, 1787, in *AFC*, 7:471.

51. John Adams to Abigail Adams, September 7, 10, and October 14, 1783, in *AFC*, 5:236, 238, 255.

52. Abigail Adams to John Adams, October 19, 1783, in ibid., 258-59.

53. John Adams to Abigail Adams, November 8, 1783, in ibid., 264, 265.

54. Abigail Adams to John Adams, November 20, 1783, in ibid., 271-72.

55. Abigail Adams to John Adams, December 15, 1783, in ibid., 279-80. The quotations in the next paragraph are from this source as well.

56. Warren, "Oration," 104-5; Abigail Adams to Isaac Smith Jr., [October 30, 1777], in *AFC*, 2:363. For rape in the ideology of the Revolution, see Kerber, *Women of the Republic*, 46-47.

57. See, Withey, *Dearest Friend*, 75; Ryerson, "Limits of a Vicarious Life"; Akers, *Abigail Adams*, 196 (and see 74); Adair, *Fame and the Founding Fathers*, 10. For another expression of Abigail's "identification" with her husband's achievements, see Abigail Adams to John Adams, July 14, 1776, in *AFC*, 2:46.

58. Abigail Adams to John Adams, June 17, 1782, in *AFC*, 4:328.

59. Wood, *Radicalism of the American Revolution*, 105, 106; Abigail Adams to John Adams, June 17, 1782, in *AFC*, 4:328.

60. John Adams to Charles William Frederic Dumas, May 16, 1783, quoted in Levin, *Abigail Adams*, 148.

## CHAPTER 9

1. John Adams to Benjamin Rush, January 4, 1813, in *Spur of Fame*, 287. See, too, Adams, *Diary and Autobiography*, 3:257.

2. John Adams to Benjamin Rush, January 4, 1813, in *Spur of Fame*, 287–88; Adams, *Diary and Autobiography*, 1:131, 86.

3. Abigail Adams to Mary Smith Cranch, July 7, 1784, in *AFC*, 5:363; Knott, *Sensibility and the American Revolution*, 88–89; Holton, "Abigail Adams, Bond Speculator"; Norton, *Liberty's Daughters*, chaps. 7–8. The quotations are Norton's titles for pt. 1 and chap. 1, respectively.

4. Adams, *Diary and Autobiography*, 1:72.

5. Ibid., 73, 3:260–61.

6. John Adams to Abigail Adams, August 14, 1776, in *AFC* 2:96–97 (see, too, Adams, *Diary and Autobiography*, 2:75); Isaac, *Transformation of Virginia*, 289.

7. John Adams to Abigail Adams, August 14, 1776, in *AFC*, 2:97; Shaftesbury, *Characteristics*, 3:211–39, 215–16. Shaftesbury, who regarded the dozen engravings published with his book "to be as much a part of the *Characteristics* as the words themselves," described the picture in a section of the book, "Treatise VII," entitled "A Notion of the Historical Draught of Tablature of the Judgement of Hercules." See Douglas Den Uyl, foreword to Shaftesbury, *Characteristics*, 1:vii–xii, xi. For Shaftesbury's reform of manners and the rise of sensibility, see Barker-Benfield, *Culture of Sensibility*, 105–19.

8. Akers, *Abigail Adams*, 89; John Quincy Adams to Abigail Adams, December 28, 1785, in *AFC*, 6:505; Shaw, *Character of John Adams*, 176; Wood, *Creation of the American Republic*, 571. Abigail also told John Quincy that she wanted him to be "a Hero and a Statesman." Abigail Adams to John Quincy Adams, January 19, 1780, in *AFC*, 3:268.

9. Adams, *Diary and Autobiography*, 1:87; Ferling, *John Adams*, 23.

10. Adams, *Diary and Autobiography*, 1:358.

11. Ibid., 87–88.

12. Ibid., 96; Shaw, *Character of John Adams*, 242.

13. Adams, *Diary and Autobiography*, 1:96; Wood, *Americanization of Benjamin Franklin*, 57.

14. Adams, *Diary and Autobiography*, 1:69, 24–25.

15. Ibid., 69; Hannah More, "Sensibility, a Poem," in *Sacred Pieces, Chiefly Intended for Young Persons* (1784; Philadelphia: Thomas Dobson, 1787), 177–94. Abigail Adams to John Adams, February 21, 1776, in *AFC*, 1:350.

16. Adams, *Diary and Autobiography*, 1:78. Ferling entitles chapter 2 of *John Adams* "Shall I Creep or Fly?" The phrase *self-fashioned* refers to Stephen Greenblatt, *Renaissance Self-Fashioning from More to Shakespeare* (Chicago: University of Chicago Press, 1980). See, too, Barker-Benfield, *Culture of Sensibility*, 82ff.

17. Adams, *Diary and Autobiography*, 1:80, 84, 133.

18. *Works of John Adams*, 2:120–23. Unless indicated otherwise, quotations in subsequent paragraphs are from this source.

19. Adams, *Diary and Autobiography*, 1:362–63. South's text is 1 Cor. 3:19. Wood writes that John Adams "filled his diary and other writings with lengthy analyses of Dissimulation." "Conspiracy and the Paranoid Style," 423. For Tyler Sr.'s conversation about Mandeville and South, see Adams, *Diary and Autobiography*, 1:362.

20. Adair, *Fame and the Founding Fathers*, 16; Wood, *Creation of the American Republic*, 53–54.

21. Adams, *Diary and Autobiography*, 1:363.

22. Bushman, *Refinement of America*, 32–33, 39; Greenblatt, *Renaissance Self-Fashioning*; Franklin, *Autobiography and Other Writings*, 29, 27, 53, 51–52, 1, 14–15; Gordon S. Wood, "Not So Poor Richard," *New York Review of Books*, June 6, 1996, 47–51, 47. See, too, Fliegelman, *Declaring Independence*, 67, 81–82. For masking and the American national character, see Meyer, *Sex and Power*, 256–57.

23. Wood, "Conspiracy and the Paranoid Style," 407, 410; Barker-Benfield, *Culture of Sensibility*, 84–89.

24. Wood, "Conspiracy and the Paranoid Style," 410, 411.

25. James Flexner, *The Young Hamilton: A Biography* (1976; New York: Fordham University Press, 1997), 279. Subsequent quotations related to Hamilton are from this source.

26. The St. Croix piece includes as one effect of the hurricane it describes an account of a starving baby, to whom its mother was unable to give "relief": "Her breast heaves with pangs of maternal pity, her heart is bursting, the tears gush down her cheeks. O sight of woe! O distress unspeakable! My heart bleeds." Quoted in ibid., 48–49. Lafayette said that Hamilton's letter on the death of Major André was "a masterpiece of literary talent and amiable sensibility." Quoted in Sarah Knott, "Sensibility and the American War of Independence," *American Historical Review* 109, no. 1 (2005): 19–40, 21. Antifederalists drew on the same language, too. See G. J. Barker-Benfield, "Sensibility in *The Federalist* and in Antifederalist Papers" (typescript, Department of History, State University of New York at Albany, 2007).

27. Col. W. S. Smith to Mrs. Abigail Adams Smith, April 27, and May 19, 14, 1786, in *Journal and Correspondence of Miss Adams*, 1:127, 146–48, 141–42. An example of Smith's literary, sentimental correspondence with Abigail is Col. W. S. Smith to Mrs. Abigail Adams Smith, September 5, 1785, in *AFC*, 6:340–42. For Smith to Steuben, see Levin, *Abigail Adams*, 217–18.

28. Adams, *Diary and Autobiography*, 1:219; *Catalogue of the John Adams Library*, 227–28. For Sharp's correspondence with Adams, see Simon Schama, *Rough Crossings: Britain, the Slaves, and the American Revolution* (New York: Harper Collins, 2006), 166–67.

29. *AFC*, 1:132–33 n. 3; John Adams to Abigail Adams, July 7, 1774, in ibid., 131.

30. John Adams to Abigail Adams, August 18, 1776, in *AFC*, 2:100. He said of himself that he was, "like my friend [Samuel] Chase, of a temper naturally quick and warm." Adams, *Diary and Autobiography*, 3:311.

31. John Adams to Abigail Adams, July 7, 1774, in *AFC*, 1:131; John Adams to Thomas Jefferson, July 16, 1814, in *Adams-Jefferson Letters*, 435.

32. *AFC*, 1:133 n. 3.

33. The debate is summarized in Edmund S. Morgan, "The Other Founders," review of *The Unknown American Revolution: The Unruly Birth of Democracy and the Struggle to Create America*, by Gary B. Nash, *New York Review of Books*, September 22, 2005, 41–43. Nash is the leading proponent of the populist view.

34. Fraser and Gerstle, eds., *Ruling America*; Waldstreicher, *In the Midst of Fetes*, 144.

35. *AFC*, 1:133 n. 3. On captivity narratives, see n. 19 of the introduction.

36. Adams, *Diary and Autobiography*, 3:292–93. See, too, Smith, *John Adams*, 1:121–26.

37. John Quincy Adams quoted in *Works of John Adams*, 2:238 n. 1.

38. Adams, *Diary and Autobiography*, 1:352–53.

39. Randolph quoted in Cunningham, *In Pursuit of Reason*, 12; Connecticut lawyer quoted in Rothman, *Hands and Hearts*, 9; John A. Graham's *A Descriptive Sketch of the Present State of*

*Vermont* (London, 1797) quoted in G. Thomas Tanselle, *Royall Tyler* (Cambridge, MA: Harvard University Press, 1967), 38; Jonathan Robinson to Royall Tyler, February 4, 1810, quoted in Tanselle, *Royall Tyler*, 37–8.

40. Perry Miller, *The Life of the Mind in America: From the Revolution to the Civil War* (New York: Harcourt, Brace & World, 1965), 189; Daniel Walker Howe, *What Hath God Wrought: The Transformation of America, 1815–1848* (New York: Oxford University Press, 2007), 559–60; Knott, *Sensibility and the American Revolution*, 98–104.

41. John Adams to Benjamin Rush, August 28, 1811, in *Spur of Fame*, 209; Adams, *Diary and Autobiography*, 1:14.

42. Barker-Benfield, *Culture of Sensibility*, 45–55; Keith Thomas, *Religion and the Decline of Magic* (New York: Scribner's, 1971), 17, 19; J. M. Golby and A. W. Purdue, *The Civilization of the Crowd: Popular Culture in England, 1750–1900* (New York: Schocken, 1985), 87, 22–23.

43. Gildrie, *The Profane, the Civil, and the Godly*, 12, xiii; Greene, *Pursuits of Happiness*, 59–60. For a history of taverns, including attempts at regulation, see Sharon V. Salinger, *Taverns and Drinking in Early America* (Baltimore: Johns Hopkins University Press, 2002).

44. Isaac, *Transformation of Virginia*, 94–98; *Gentleman's Progress: The Itinerarium of Dr. Alexander Hamilton, 1744*, ed. Carl Bridenbaugh (Chapel Hill: University of North Carolina Press, 1984); *Journal of Charles Woodmason*, 31–32, 47, and passim; Rourke, *American Humor*; Drinker quoted in Alan Taylor, *William Cooper's Town: Power and Persuasion on the Frontier of the Early American Republic* (New York: Vintage, 1995), 116. For literary evidence, see Rourke, *American Humor*, passim.

45. Carl Bridenbaugh, *Cities in Revolt: Urban Life in America, 1743–1776* (New York: Capricorn, 1964), 113–14 and chap. 3 passim. See, too, Paul A. Gilje, *The Road to Mobocracy: Popular Disorder in New York City, 1763–1834* (Chapel Hill: University of North Carolina Press, 1987), chap. 1.

46. Michael Meranze, "Class, Seduction, and the Dream of Society in the Post-Revolutionary City" (paper presented at the annual meeting of the Organization of American Historians, Atlanta, 1994). For the connotations of *frolick* in this context, see Barker-Benfield, *Culture of Sensibility*, 40, 45, 47–49. Other illustrations are *Peter Kalm's Travels in North America: The English Version of 1770*, rev. and ed. Adolph B. Benson (1931; New York: Dover, 1964), 24; and Edward Jarvis, *Tradition and Reminiscences of Concord, Massachusetts, 1779–1878*, ed. Sarah Chapman (Amherst, MA: University of Amherst Press, 1993), 101–3.

47. Salinger, *Tavern and Drinking in Early America*, 2; Adams, *Diary and Autobiography*, 1:128–29; Zagarri, *Revolutionary Backlash*, 36. See, too, Isaac, *Transformation of Virginia*, 111–12.

48. See n. 18 above.

49. Adams, *Diary and Autobiography*, 1:190–92.

50. Herman R. Lante, Margaret Britton, Raymond Schmidt, and Eloise C. Snyder, "Pre-Industrial Patterns in the Colonial Family in America: A Content Analysis of Colonial Magazines," *American Sociological Review* 33 (1968): 413–20; Mildred Davis Doyle, "Sentimentalism in America Periodicals, 1741–1800" (Ph.D. diss., New York University, 1941).

51. Joanne B. Freeman, *Affairs of Honor: National Politics in the New Republic* (New Haven, CT: Yale University Press, 2001), 159–98. For metropolitan Britain, see Barker-Benfield, *Culture of Sensibility*, 80–81. An illustration of opposition to dueling on the grounds of sensibility is Reverend Frederic Beasley, *A Sermon on Duelling, Delivered in Christ-Church, Baltimore, April 28, 1811* (Baltimore: Joseph Robinson, 1811).

52. Adams, "On Private Revenge, 1 August, 1763," 6. And see John Adams, "On Private Revenge, 5 September, 1768," in *Revolutionary Writings of John Adams*, 12–17.

53. Adams, "On Private Revenge, 1 August, 1763," 6. On the relation between class and

sensibility among officers and men, see Knott, "Sensibility and the American War of Independence." Knott quotes Hamilton: "Let the officers be men of sense and sentiment, and the nearer the soldiers approach to machines perhaps the better." Ibid., 21.

54. Adams, *Diary and Autobiography*, 1:176; Barker-Benfield, *Culture of Sensibility*, 240–42; *Gentleman's Progress*, 177.

55. Adams, *Diary and Autobiography*, 1:176; John Adams to Samuel Quincy, April 22, 1761, in *Works of John Adams*, 1:646; Haraszti, *Adams and the Prophets of Progress*, 215; Jordan, *White over Black*, 226–27.

56. Adams, *Diary and Autobiography*, 1:176–77. The quotations in the next paragraph are from this source as well.

57. Ferling, *John Adams*, 15; Shields, *Civil Tongues*, 211; Joseph F. Kett, *Rites of Passage: Adolescence in America, 1790 to the Present* (New York: Basic, 1977), 53; Barker-Benfield, *Culture of Sensibility*, 46–47.

58. John Adams to Abigail Adams, July 11, 1781, in *AFC*, 4:170; John Adams to Abigail Adams Smith, July 16, 1788, in ibid., 8:279; East, *John Quincy Adams*, 29; John Adams to Abigail Adams, October 12, 1799, quoted in McCullough, *John Adams*, 529.

### CHAPTER 10

1. Adams, *Diary and Autobiography*, 2:36–37.

2. John Adams to Christopher Gadsden, April 16, 1801, quoted in E. Stanly Godbold Jr. and Robert H. Woody, *Christopher Gadsden and the American Revolution* (Knoxville: University of Tennessee Press, 1982), 250; John Adams to Benjamin Rush, May 14, 1810, and February 23, 1813, in *Spur of Fame*, 178.

3. Adams, *Diary and Autobiography*, 2:131, 133, 134; John Adams to Abigail Adams, September 18, 27, 1774, in *AFC*, 1:157, 163.

4. Abigail Adams to John Adams, June 22, 1775, in *AFC*, 1:225; John Adams to Abigail Adams, March 15, 1797, in *My Dearest Friend*, 441.

5. John Adams to John Quincy Adams, August 18, 1782, in *AFC*, 4:366.

6. John Adams to Abigail Smith, February 14, 1763, in ibid., 1:3.

7. John Adams to Abigail Smith, April 20, 1763, in ibid., 5; "Thoughts on Matrimony" quoted in Lewis, "The Republican Wife," 689.

8. John Adams to Abigail Adams, July 9, 1774, in *AFC*, 1:135.

9. McCullough, *John Adams*, 63; Adams, *Diary and Autobiography*, 2:79. For the politics of the decision to defend Preston, see Ferling, *John Adams*, 67–69.

10. Adams, *Diary and Autobiography*, 3:296; John Adams to Abigail Adams, May 1772, in *AFC*, 1:83.

11. Adams, *Diary and Autobiography*, 2:63, 67.

12. Ibid., 3:304–5; John Adams to William Tudor, March 8, 1817, in *Works of John Adams*, 2:312–13 and nn. 310–11.

13. John Adams to Abigail Adams, April 30, 1775, and October 13, 1775, in *AFC*, 1:190, 300, 301; Abigail Adams to John Adams, October 9, 1775, in ibid., 298.

14. John Adams to Abigail Adams, July 24, 1775, in ibid., 255–56.

15. John Adams to Abigail Adams, February [13], 1776, in ibid., 347.

16. John Adams to Abigail Adams, April 28, 1776, in ibid., 399.

17. John Adams to Abigail Adams, May 22, 1776, in ibid., 412–13.

18. John Adams to Abigail Adams, August 18, 1776, in ibid., 2:99–100. John recorded that he was frequently subject to "mortification." Shaw, *Character of John Adams*, 292–94.

19. Elizabeth Smith Shaw to Abigail Adams, October 1, 1786, in ibid., 7:351; "Parnell, Thomas," in *Oxford Companion to English Literature*, ed. Margaret Drabble (Oxford: Oxford University Press, 1985), 740; *Letterbook of Eliza Lucas Pinckney*, 66, 185; Gordon-Reed, *The Hemingses of Monticello*, 111.

20. John Adams to Abigail Adams, August 18, 1776, in *AFC*, 2:100 n. 4.

21. Adair, *Fame and the Founding Fathers*, 14; John Adams to Abigail Adams, August 18, 1776, in *AFC*, 2:100 n. 4.

22. John Adams to Abigail Adams, March 16, 1777, in *AFC*, 2:175–76; Piero Treves, "Cincinnatus, Lucius Quinatius," in *Oxford Classical Dictionary*, ed. N. G. L. Hammon and H. H. Scullard (Oxford: Clarendon, 1970), 241; Garry Wills, *Cincinnatus: George Washington and the Enlightenment* (Garden City, NY: Doubleday, 1984).

23. John Adams to Abigail Adams, May 22, 1781, in *AFC*, 4:121–22; Abigail Adams to John Adams, in ibid., 229–30.

24. John Adams to Abigail Adams, May 14, 1782, in ibid., 323; Meyer, *Sex and Power*, xxvi.

25. John Adams to Abigail Adams, June 16, 1782, in *AFC*, 4:324–25.

26. John Adams to Abigail Adams, [ca. August 15, 1782], in ibid., 361; John Adams to Abigail Adams, August 18, 1776, in ibid., 2:99.

27. John Adams to Abigail Adams, December 28, 1782, in ibid., 5:60.

28. Withey, *Dearest Friend*, 230; Abigail Adams to John Adams, May 10, 1794, in *My Dearest Friend*, 370. For a detailed account of Abigail and John's relationship in the years subsequent to their return from Europe, see Gelles, *Abigail and John*, chaps. 11–14.

29. John Adams to Abigail Adams 2nd, March 17, 1777, in *AFC*, 2:179.

30. John Adams to Abigail Adams 2nd, September 26, 1782, in ibid., 4:383–84. Unless indicated otherwise, quotations in subsequent paragraphs are from this source.

31. John Adams to Abigail Adams 2nd, October 16, 1782, in ibid., 5:17–18.

32. Adams, *Diary and Autobiography*, 1:xlv, 3:294–95.

33. John Adams to Benjamin Rush, April 12, 1809, in *Spur of Fame*, 156.

34. Adams, *Diary and Autobiography*, 3:316.

35. Wood, *Creation of the American Republic*, 45; Adams, *Diary and Autobiography*, 1:316. Ferling suggests that Adams's sense of manhood was at stake throughout his career, until the successful diplomatic conclusion of the war for independence, and that John became most sure of his manhood once he was vice president. Ferling, *John Adams*, 21–22, 131–33, 280–81, 319–21.

36. John Adams to William Tudor, March 8, 1817, in *Works of John Adams*, 2:312–13.

37. John Adams to Mrs. [Caroline] de Windt, May 12, 1820, in *Journal and Correspondence of Miss Adams*, 2:246–47. This is the letter with which de Windt, the editor of her mother's journal and correspondence, chose to conclude her two volumes.

38. Adams, *Diary and Autobiography*, 3:280–81; John Adams to Thomas Jefferson, July 16, 1814, in *Adams-Jefferson Letters*, 438; Abigail Adams to John Adams, May 10, 1794, in *My Dearest Friend*, 370.

39. Abigial Adams to John Adams, December 15, 1783, in *AFC*, 5:278–79.

## CHAPTER 11

1. Habermas, *Structural Transformation of the Public Sphere*, 48; Mahajan, "The Public and the Private," 13 (and see 11); Tocqueville, *Democracy in America*, 2:98. Tocqueville is the *OED*'s first illustration of the use of *individualism*. There were, of course, other sources of individualism.

2. Habermas, *Structural Transformation of the Public Sphere*, 49. For republicanism and sensibility, see chapter 14 below. Lynn Hunt argues something very similar in her account of the relation between the novel and family psychology in eighteenth-century France. See *The Family Romance of the French Revolution* (Berkeley and Los Angeles: University of California Press, 1992), xiii, 21, 188–90.

3. Meyer, *Sex and Power*, 271.

4. Fordyce, *Sermons to Young Women*, 1:227, 231, 232, 233; Kames quoted in Zagarri, "The Republican Mother," 199–200; *The Educational Writings of John Locke*, ed. James L. Axtell (Cambridge: Cambridge University Press, 1968), 141–42, 208–9, 317–18.

5. Abigail Adams quoted in Gelles, *First Thoughts*, 70.

6. Dwyer, *Virtuous Discourse*, 57, 15. See, too, Barker-Benfield, *Culture of Sensibility*, 132–33.

7. Robertson quoted in Dwyer, *Virtuous Discourse*, 5; Adams, *Diary and Autobiography*, 2:398. For a valuable assessment of the significance to women of Robertson's and others' histories, see Zagarri, *Revolutionary Backlash*, 16–19. See, too, Karen O'Brien, *Women and Enlightenment in Eighteenth-Century Britain* (Cambridge: Cambridge University Press, 2009). On the backcountry/frontier, see John Clive and Bernard Bailyn, "England's Cultural Provinces: Scotland and America," *William and Mary Quarterly*, 3rd ser., 11, no. 2 (April 1954): 200–213; *Journal of Charles Woodmason*, xi–xxxix; J. A. Leo Lemay, "The Frontiersman from Lout to Hero: Notes on the Significance of the Comparative Method and the Stage Theory in Early American Literature and Culture," *Proceedings of the American Antiquarian Society* 82, no. 2 (1978): 187–223; "To Thomas Perceval: An Account of the Progress of Population, Agriculture, Manners, and Government in Pennsylvania" (October 26, 1786), in *Letters of Benjamin Rush*, ed. Lyman H. Butterfield, 2 vols. (Princeton, NJ: Princeton University Press, 1951), 1:400–406; Frederick Jackson Turner, "The Significance of the Frontier in American History," in *Does the Frontier Experience Make America Exceptional?* ed. Richard W. Etulain (Boston: Bedford/St. Martin's, 1999), 18–43.

8. Jefferson, *Notes on the State of Virginia*, 57–58.

9. Dwyer, *Virtuous Discourse*, 5, 96, 6. For another exploration of anxiety over social disintegration and its expression in the language of sentimentalism, see Mullan, *Sentiment and Sociability*.

10. Dwyer, *Virtuous Discourse*, 209, 195, 196; Mintz, *Huck's Raft*, 59 (quoting Hutcheson's view of children); Fordyce, *Sermons to Young Women*, 1:111; Zagarri, "The Republican Mother," 196–97.

11. Smith, *Theory of Moral Sentiments*, 39; Glen quoted in *Journal of Charles Woodmason*, xxv.

12. Smith, *Theory of Moral Sentiments*, 12.

13. Hildred Geertz, "The Vocabulary of Emotion: A Study of Javanese Socialization Processes," *Psychiatry* 22 (1959): 225–37, 205–6. I am indebted to Linda Layne for this reference.

14. Nicole Eustace addresses Native American and African emotions in the eighteenth century. See *Passion Is the Gale*, 71ff. And see Anthony F. C. Wallace, *The Death and Rebirth of the Seneca* (New York: Vintage, 1969), chaps. 3–4. On African American childrearing, see Mintz, *Huck's Raft*, passim; and the introduction, n. 57, above.

15. Pinckney quoted in Constance B. Schulz, "Eliza Lucas Pinckney," in Barker-Benfield and Clinton, eds., *Portraits of American Women*, 64–81, 75, 76; Eliza Lucas Pinckney to "My dear Children Charles and Thomas Pinckney," August 1758, in *Letterbook of Eliza Lucas Pinckney*, 94.

16. Mercy Otis Warren to Abigail Adams, July 25, 1773, in *AFC*, 1:86–87. For a description of Warren's childrearing practices, see Zagarri, *A Woman's Dilemma*, 20, 23–30.

17. Abigail Smith to Isaac Smith Jr., February 2, 1762, quoted in Withey, *Dearest Friend*, 11;

Abigail Adams to Mercy Otis Warren, April 13, 1776, in *AFC*, 1:377; Abigail Adams to John Adams, August 14, 1776, in ibid., 2:94.

18. Akers, *Abigail Adams*, 22–23; Abigail Adams to Mercy Otis Warren, July 16, 1773, in *AFC*, 1:84–85; Juliana-Susannah Seymour [John Hill], *On the Management and Education of Children* (1754; New York: Garland, 1985).

19. Abigail Adams to Mercy Otis Warren, July 16, 1773, in *AFC*, 1:85.

20. The original definitions of republican motherhood are Kerber, *Women of the Republic*, chap. 9; and Norton, *Liberty's Daughters*, conclusion.

21. Seymour, *Management of Children*, 6, 149; Withey, *Dearest Friend*, 29; Mintz, *Huck's Raft*, 16; Zagarri, *A Woman's Dilemma*, 25; Norton, *Liberty's Daughters*, 233–34; Robert V. Wells, "Family Size and Fertility Control in Eighteenth-Century America: A Study of Quaker Families," *Population Studies* 25 (1971): 73–83; Abigail Adams to Mary Smith Cranch, January 31, 1767, in *AFC*, 1:60.

22. Seymour, *Management of Children*, 22 (and see 105). In fact: "Custom . . . when it is begun from Infancy, becomes Nature." Ibid., 108.

23. Ibid., 105–6, 107, 10, 22–23.

24. Seymour, *Management of Children*, 145, 119; Wood, *Radicalism of the American Revolution*, 49.

25. Seymour, *Management of Children*, 119, 130 (and see 133–34). Adams, *Diary and Autobiography*, 1:9. "John Adams's defiance of his father was representative of a gradual erosion of parental control in eighteenth-century New England." Shaw, *Character of John Adams*, 11, 21. Fliegelman, *Prodigals and Pilgrims*.

26. Seymour, *Management of Children*, 120. Much earlier in the century, and despite his promulgation of an innate moral sense (but consistent with his general absorption of sensational, environmental psychology), Shaftesbury, "the father of sentimental ethics," reared under Locke's direction, had observed the beneficial operation of "Reward and Punishment . . . in the Publick, so, . . . as to *private family* . . . the Master of the family using proper Rewards and gentle Punishments towards his Children, teaches them Goodness." Shaftesbury, *Characteristics*, 2:37.

27. Seymour, *Management of Children*, 140, 141–42, 259–60, 261–62, 124, 131–32.

28. Ibid., 165–66, 167, 156.

29. Ibid., 164, 108.

30. Ibid., 44, 83, 84, 78, 77–79.

31. Ibid., 126, 170–71, 172.

32. Ibid., 286, 190; Fordyce, *Sermons to Young Women*, 2:87; Elizabeth Smith Shaw to Abigail Adams 2nd, November 27, 1786, in *AFC*, 7:404. On Colonel Smith as a husband, see the conclusion to chapter 13.

33. Seymour, *Management of Children*, 223, 225, 227, 229.

34. Ibid., 197, 198, 205–6, 187.

35. Ibid., 243, 247, 262.

36. Abigail Adams to Hannah Storer Green, [after July 14, 1765], in *AFC*, 1:51; Abigail Adams to John Adams, August 12, 1777, in ibid., 2:308; Abigail Adams to Mary Smith Cranch, October 6, 1766, in ibid., 1:55.

37. Abigail Adams to Mary Smith Cranch, January 12, 1767, in ibid., 1:57–58.

38. See, e.g., John Quincy Adams to Thomas Boylston Adams, 1818, *Journal and Correspondence of Miss Adams*, 2, pt. 1:6–8 (writing of Abigail on her death).

39. Elizabeth Smith Shaw to Abigail Adams, March 18, 1786, in *AFC*, 7:95.

40. Abigail Adams to John Adams, September 14, 1767, in ibid., 1:62; Abigail Adams to

John Adams, [April 1777], in ibid., 2:229; John Adams to Charles Adams, March 30, 1777, and John Adams to John Quincy Adams, March 30, 1777, in ibid., 190–91.

41. John Quincy Adams to Joseph Sturge, March 2, 1846, in ibid., 1:223–24 n. 3.

42. Abigail Adams to John Adams, September 16, 1774, in ibid., 153.

43. Abigail Adams to John Thaxter, February 14, 1778, in ibid., 2:390–91; John Adams to Abigail Adams, November 29, 1779, in ibid., 3:237; Abigail to John Adams, December 10, 1779, in ibid., 242; Abigail Adams to Charles Adams, January 19, 1780, in ibid., 270.

44. John Adams to Abigail Adams, July 11, 1781, and December 2, 1781, in ibid., 4:170, 249. For John's supervision of his sons in Europe, see Ferling, *John Adams*, 222–23.

45. Abigail Adams to Elizabeth Smith Shaw, [February–March 1782], in *AFC*, 4:284–85.

46. Abigail Adams to John Quincy Adams, March 20, 1780, in ibid., 3:312. The quotations in the next paragraph are from this source as well.

47. Abigail Adams to John Quincy Adams, January 19, 1780, in ibid., 269.

48. Abigail Adams to John Quincy Adams, May 8, 1780, in ibid., 313.

49. Abigail Adams to John Adams, November 11, 1783, in ibid., 5:267, 268. The quotations in the next paragraph are from this source as well.

50. John Adams to Abigail Adams Smith, July 16, 1788, in ibid., 8:279; Abigail Adams to John Quincy Adams, May 30, 1789, in ibid., 363; John Adams to Thomas Boylston Adams, September 2, 1789, in ibid., 407.

51. Abigail Adams to John Adams, February 14, 1799, in *My Dearest Friend*, 461; Charles Francis Adams quoted in McCullough, *John Adams*, 634.

52. John Adams to Abigail Adams, January 21, 1794, in *My Dearest Friend*, 350; Abigail Adams to Mary Smith Cranch, August 19, 1789, in *AFC*, 8:400. And see John Adams to Thomas Boylston Adams, September 2, 1789, in ibid., 407; and Abigail Adams to Mary Smith Cranch, November 11, 1800, in *New Letters of Abigail Adams*, 255.

53. Abigail Adams to Mary Smith Cranch, December 8, 1800, in *New Letters of Abigail Adams*, 261–62. Compare the terms of Eliza Lucas to [Thomas Lucas], [1744?], in *Letterbook of Eliza Lucas Pinckney*, 70.

54. Barker-Benfield, *Culture of Sensibility*, 43, 247–58.

55. Adams, *Diary and Autobiography*, 1:111; John Adams to Abigail Adams, December 28, 1782, in *AFC*, 5:60. For a summary of John's views on childrearing and education, see Levin, *Abigail Adams*, 41–44.

56. John Adams to Abigail Adams, June 29, 1769, July 2, 1774, September 14, 1774, and September 17, 1775, in *AFC*, 1:66, 121, 155, 281.

57. John Adams to Abigail Adams, August 28, 1776, in ibid., 2:111. For the sentimental convention, see, e.g., poems in *Milcah Martha Moore's Book*, 132, 135, 139; *The Poems of Phillis Wheatley*, ed. Julian D. Mason Jr. (Chapel Hill: University of North Carolina Press, 1989), 57. And see Wendy Simonds and Barbara Katz Rothman, *Centuries of Solace: Expressions of Maternal Grief and Popular Literature* (Philadelphia: Temple University Press, 1992). I am grateful to Linda Layne for this reference.

58. John Adams to Abigail Adams, August 30, 1776, in *AFC*, 2:115.

59. John Adams to Abigail Adams, July 17, 1775, in ibid., 1:251–52. The quotations in the next paragraph are from this source as well.

60. John Adams to Abigail Adams October 29, 1775, in ibid., 317.

61. John Adams to Abigail Adams, October 29, 1775, in ibid., 318; John Adams to Abigail Adams, October 29, 1775, in ibid., 318–19.

62. John Adams to Abigail Adams, April 15, 1776, in ibid., 383, 385 n. 4.

63. Ibid., 383; "Humphrey Ploughjogger" quoted in Ferling, *John Adams*, 39.

64. John Quincy Adams to Charles Adams and Thomas Boylston Adams, October 3, 1778, in *AFC*, 3:102; Shaw, *Character of John Adams*, 316–17; Keller, *Patriotism and the Female Sex*, 139–40.

65. John Quincy Adams to John Adams, November 2, 1818, in *Journal and Correspondence of Miss Adams*, 2, pt. 2:155–56.

66. John Adams to Abigail Adams 2nd, October 20, 1775, in *AFC*, 1:304.

67. John Adams to Abigail Adams, April 15, 1776, in ibid., 383–84; John Adams to Abigail Adams, [April–May 1780], in ibid., 3:333; Shaw, *Character of John Adams*, 317.

68. John Adams to Abigail Adams, April 15, 1776, in *AFC*, 1:384; John Adams to Benjamin Rush, July 25, 1808, in *Spur of Fame*, 122.

69. John Adams to Abigail Adams 2nd, April 18, 1776, in *AFC*, 1:387–88.

70. John Adams to Abigail Adams 2nd, March 17, 1777, in ibid., 2:179; Wollstonecraft, *Vindication of the Rights of Woman*, 168.

71. John Adams to Abigail Adams 2nd, December 12, 1779, in *AFC*, 3:247–48; Adams, *Diary and Autobiography*, 1:194.

CHAPTER 12

1. Abigail Adams 2nd to Elizabeth Cranch, June [1782], in *AFC*, 4:335–36 (the quotations in the next paragraph are from this source as well); Foster, *Coquette*, 31. Lyman Butterfield comes close to the eighteenth-century characterization of the rake, calling Tyler "ingratiating," a man who "so artfully and disturbingly entered the close-knit Adams family circle." *The Earliest Diary of John Adams*, ed. L. H. Butterfield et al. (Cambridge, MA: Belknap Press of Harvard University Press, 1966), 24, 22. Here, Butterfield outlines the story of the relationship between Nabby and Tyler. Ibid., 18–28. His successor as editor in chief of the *Adams Family Correspondence*, Richard Alan Ryerson, does so in *AFC*, 5:59; and in "Limits of a Vicarious Life," 8–11. See, too, Tanselle, *Royall Tyler*, 9–19; Paul C. Nagel, *The Adams Women: Abigail and Louisa Adams, Their Sisters and Daughters* (New York: Oxford University Press, 1987), chap. 6; Akers, *Abigail Adams*, 75–79, 101–3; Keller, *Patriotism and the Female Sex*, 170–76, 180–81; Ferling, *John Adams*, 263; Gelles, *Portia*, chap. 5; and Gelles, *Abigail and John*, 184–87. I have concentrated on the evidence that the relationship—extending to the part played by Nabby's family members—gives of the power of the culture of sensibility.

2. Abigail Adams to John Adams, July 17, 1782, in *AFC*, 4:344–45. The quotations in the next two paragraphs are from this source as well. John's objection to women's speaking "in mixed Companies" was deep-seated. See, e.g., Adams, *Diary and Autobiography*, 1:194.

3. October 8, 1782, in *AFC*, 5:7; Withey, *Dearest Friend*, 22; Fordyce, *Sermons to Young Women*, 2:240.

4. Abigail Adams 2nd to Elizabeth Cranch, [ca. December 22, 1782], in *AFC*, 5:52. Unless indicated otherwise, quotations in subsequent paragraphs are from this source.

5. *Spectator*, no. 281 (January 22, 1712), in Bond, ed., *Spectator*, 2:594–97 (and see no. 247 [December 13, 1711], in ibid., 459–60). Compare Sterne, *Sentimental Journey*, 65.

6. Abigail Adams to John Adams, December 23, 1782, in *AFC*, 5:54–58. Unless indicated otherwise, quotations in subsequent paragraphs are from this source.

7. Tanselle, *Royall Tyler*, 7, 8, 225–26 n. 15.

8. For a helpful introduction to Tyler's writing, see Davidson, *Revolution and the Word*, 192–200.

9. Abigail Adams to John Adams, December 30, 1782, in *AFC*, 5:61–62. The quotations in the next paragraph are from this source as well.

10. *AFC*, 5:59 n. 4.

11. Abigail Adams 2nd to Elizabeth Cranch, [ca. January 4, 1783], in ibid., 63–64. Unless otherwise indicated, the quotations in the next three paragraphs are from this source as well.

12. *AFC*, 64 n. 2.

13. John Adams to Abigail Adams, January 22, 1783, in ibid., 74–75. Unless otherwise indicated, the quotations in the next several paragraphs are from this source as well.

14. "This youth has had a brother in Europe, and a detestible Specimen he exhibited"— i.e., a specimen of the Tyler family. Ibid., 75. John Steele Tyler, who served with his brother in the revolutionary army, was commissioned as a lieutenant colonel; able in 1780 to reach London via Paris, with John Trumbull he "called on John Adams late in June." In 1781, he "offered to serve in the British forces," provided he was compensated for the American property he would thereby lose, but his offer was not accepted. If Colonel Tyler "later returned to Boston without damage to his reputation," John Adams in London seems to have heard of his Arnoldian turnabout. *AFC*, 3:321 n. 1.

15. See, too, Ferling, *John Adams*, 263.

16. *AFC*, 5:76 n. 7.

17. John Adams to Abigail Adams, January 29, 1783, in ibid., 82–83. The quotations in the next paragraph are from this source as well.

18. Pope's "Universal Prayer" was among the most frequently reprinted of his poems in colonial America. Sibley, *Pope's Prestige in America*, 3, 25, 39, 53, 71, 93. The phrase is from line 37.

19. John Adams to Abigail Adams, February 4, 1783, in *AFC*, 5:88–89 (the quotations in the next paragraph are from this source as well); Fliegelman, *Prodigals and Pilgrims*, 65, 66, and chaps. 2–3 passim.

20. John Adams to Abigail Adams, March 28, 1783, in *AFC*, 5:110.

21. Abigail Adams to John Adams, April 7, 1783, in ibid., 116, 118; *Spectator*, no. 302 (February 15, 1712), in Bond, ed., *Spectator*, 3:78–80, 78–79. Bond notes that it was "one of the most popular." Ibid., 79 n. 2.

22. Sypher, *Guinea's Captive Kings*, 268–69. But see, too, *AFC*, 5:119 n. 4. The *Spectator*'s popularized female ideal may well have influenced the Adamses' giving their daughter her middle name, manifesting Henry Fielding's absorption of it into the eponymous heroine of his *Amelia* (1752). Emelia was also a major protagonist in Richardson's third novel, in love with Sir Charles Grandison.

23. *Spectator*, no. 302 (February 15, 1712), in Bond, ed., *Spectator*, 3:80.

24. Abigail Adams to John Adams, April 7, 1783, in *AFC*, 5:118. The quotations in the next two paragraphs are from this source as well.

25. John Adams to Abigail Adams, April 16, 1783, in ibid., 124.

26. John Adams to Abigail Adams, June 9, 1782, in ibid., 168–69. The quotations in the next paragraph are from this source as well.

27. Abigail Adams 2nd to John Thaxter, April 22, 1783, in ibid., 138–39, 140 n. 5; Abigail Adams 2nd to Elizabeth Cranch, August 20, [1783], in ibid., 225.

28. Abigail Adams to John Adams, April 28, 1783, in ibid., 141, 143–44. Compare Ferling, *John Adams*, 263.

29. Abigail Adams to Charles Storer, April 28, 1783, in *AFC*, 5:146 (for Storer's relation to the Adamses, see *AFC*, 4:124 n. 1); Charles Storer to Abigail Adams, February 10, 1783, in ibid., 5:90.

30. Sterne, *Tristram Shandy*, 28 n. 1; Sterne, *Sentimental Journey*, 117; Knott, *Sensibility and the American Revolution*, 109ff.; Abigail Adams to Charles Storer, April 28, 1783, in *AFC*, 5:145. For Abigail's expression of maternal feelings for Tyler, see below.

31. Abigail Adams to Charles Storer, April 28, 1783, in *AFC*, 5:147. The quotations in the next three paragraphs are from this source as well.

32. Abigail Adams to John Adams, May 7, 1783, in ibid., 151. The quotations in the next three paragraphs are from this source as well.

33. Abigail Adams 2nd to John Adams, May 10, 1783, in ibid., 156.

34. Abigail Adams to Royall Tyler, June 14, 1783, in ibid., 173–75. The quotations in the next four paragraphs are from this source as well.

35. Abigail Adams to Royall Tyler, [after June 14, 1783], in ibid., 175–76. The quotations in the next two paragraphs are from this source as well.

36. Tanselle, *Royall Tyler*, 228 n. 28; *AFC*, 5:191 n. 1; Abigail Adams to John Adams, June 20, 1783, in ibid., 181.

37. Abigail Adams to John Adams, June 20, 1783, in *AFC*, 5:181–82. Unless otherwise indicated, the quotations in the next three paragraphs are from this source as well.

38. Tanselle, *Royall Tyler*, 13, 228 n. 29.

39. Tanselle, *Royall Tyler*, 34; *Grandmother Tyler's Book: The Recollection of Mary Palmer Tyler (Mrs. Royall Tyler), 1775–1866*, ed. Frederick Tupper and Helen Tyler Brown (New York: Putnam's, 1925), passim.

40. John Adams to Abigail Adams, July 13, 1783, in *AFC*, 5:199.

41. John Adams to Abigail Adams, August 14, 1783, in ibid., 221–23.

42. John Adams to Abigail Adams, October 14, 1783, in ibid., 255–56.

43. Abigail Adams to John Adams, October 19, 1783, in ibid., 259–60, 261 n. 4. The quotations in the next paragraph are from this source as well.

44. Abigail Adams to John Adams, December 15, 1783, and December 27, 1783, in ibid., 279, 286.

45. Abigail Adams to John Adams, January 3, 1784, in ibid., 291. The quotations in the next paragraph are from this source as well.

46. Abigail Adams 2nd to Abigail Adams, January 6, 1784, in ibid., 296–97; Elizabeth Smith Shaw to Abigail Adams, March 18, 1786, in ibid., 7:94.

47. Abigail Adams to John Adams, February 11, 1784, in ibid., 5:304.

## CHAPTER 13

1. Royall Tyler to John Adams, January 13, 1784, in *AFC*, 5:297–98. The quotations in the next three paragraphs are from this source as well.

2. *Clarissa* is archetypal in respect to clandestinisty. See Barker-Benfield, *Culture of Sensibility*, 326. For a real episode of self-assertion in sexual clandestinity, see the story of Lucy Barnes and Joseph Hosmer in Concord, Massachusetts, in the 1750s, in Robert A. Gross, *The Minutemen and Their World* (New York: Hill & Wang, 1976), 99–101.

3. Richard Cranch to John Adams, January 20, 1784, in *AFC*, 5:300.

4. John Adams to Abigail Adams, January 25, 1784, in ibid., 301.

5. *AFC*, 5:302 n. 5, 417 n. 2.

6. John Adams to Richard Cranch, April 3, 1784, and John Adams to Royall Tyler, April 3, 1784, in ibid., 315–16, 316–17. The quotations in the next two paragraphs are from this second letter as well.

7. Abigail Adams to John Adams, April 12, 1784, in ibid., 318; Elbridge Gerry to Abigail Adams, April 16, 1784, and May 18, 1784, in ibid., 320, 328.

8. Abigail Adams to John Adams, May 25, 1784, in ibid., 331.

9. "Abigail Adams' Diary of Her Voyage from Boston to Deal, 20 June–20 July 1784," in Adams, *Diary and Autobiography*, 3:154–66, 160–61.

10. Abigail Adams to Royall Tyler, July 10, 1784, in *AFC*, 5:390–91.

11. Ibid., 392–93; *Grandmother Tyler's Book*, 80.

12. *Journal and Correspondence of Miss Adams*, 1:ix–x ("Introductory Remarks"). The "Introductory Remarks" quote extensively from Nabby's unpublished journal entries, in this case, one attributed to August 27, 1785. Unless otherwise indicated, the quotations in the next two paragraphs are from this entry as well.

13. Lewis, "The Republican Wife," 693–94; Mintz, *Huck's Raft*, 55, 61; *American Museum* and "another woman" quoted in Norton, *Liberty's Daughters*, 236; "The Inexorable Father" quoted in Lewis, "Republican Wife," 693–94.

14. *Journal and Correspondence of Miss Adams*, 1:80–81; P. N. Furbank, "Cultivating Voltaire's Garden," *New York Review of Books*, December 15, 2005, 68–70, 70.

15. John Adams to Abigail Adams, July 3, 1784, in *AFC*, 5:354.

16. Abigail Adams to Mary Smith Cranch, August 2, 1784, in ibid., 417. Unless otherwise indicated, the quotations in the next paragraph are from this source as well.

17. Mary Smith Cranch to Abigail Adams, August 8, 1784, in ibid., 421; Richard Cranch to John Adams, August 8, 1784, in ibid., 422–23.

18. Royall Tyler to John Adams, August 22, 1784, in ibid., 425–26. The quotations in the next two paragraphs are from this source as well.

19. Abigail Adams 2nd to Elizabeth Cranch, September 4, 1784, in ibid., 429.

20. Abigail Adams to Elizabeth Cranch, September 5, 1784, in ibid., 435; Abigail Adams to Royall Tyler, [September 5, 1784], in ibid., 4:445–46 (the quotations in the next paragraph are from this second source).

21. One letter presenting Madame Helvétius very negatively was to Lucy Cranch, written apparently on the same day she wrote this to Tyler. See Abigail Adams to Lucy Cranch, September 5, 1784, in ibid., 5:436–37.

22. Mary Smith Cranch to Abigail Adams, October 10, 1784, in ibid., 470.

23. Mary Smith Cranch to Abigail Adams, November 6, 1784, in ibid., 479 (and see 480 n. 2); Abigail Adams to Mary Smith Cranch, December 12, 1784, in ibid., 6:17–18; Abigail Adams to Cotton Tufts, January 3, 1785, in ibid., 41–42.

24. Abigail Adams to Royall Tyler, [January 4, 1785], in ibid., 45–50. The quotations in the next four paragraphs are from this source.

25. Mary Smith Cranch to Abigail Adams, January 16, 1785, in ibid., 59, 61.

26. Mary Smith Cranch to Abigail Adams, April 25, 1785, in ibid., 93, 94, 96. The quotations in the next three paragraphs are from this source.

27. Abigail Adams to Cotton Tufts, [April 22, 1785], in ibid., 107.

28. Mary Smith Cranch to Abigail Adams, June 4, 1785, in ibid., 164; Mary Smith Cranch to Abigail Adams, July 19, 1785, in ibid., 231.

29. Abigail Adams 2nd to Royall Tyler, [ca. August 11, 1785], in ibid., 262, reprinted from *Grandmother Tyler's Book*, 76. While Tyler procrastinated, Tufts was finally able to retrieve her letters and the miniature. Cotton Tufts to Abigail Adams, April 13, 1786, and August 15, 1786, in *AFC*, 7:143, 326. See, too, Abigail Adams to Cotton Tufts, August 18, 1785, in ibid., 6:285.

30. *AFC*, 6:280 n. 4; Abigail Adams to John Quincy Adams, March 16, 1786, in ibid., 7:64.

31. Abigail Adams to William Stephen Smith, August 13, 1785, in ibid., 6:266–67.

32. Abigail Adams to Mary Smith Cranch, August 15, 1785, in ibid., 276–77. Unless otherwise indicated, quotations in subsequent paragraphs are from this source.

33. *AFC*, 6:280 n. 4.

34. Abigail Adams to Mary Smith Cranch, June 13, 1786, in ibid., 7:220. Unless otherwise indicated, quotations in the next paragraph are from this source.

35. Adams, *Diary and Autobiography*, 1:194.

36. Abigail Adams to Mary Smith Cranch, August 15, 1785, in *AFC*, 6:277.

37. William Stephen Smith to Abigail Adams, September 5, 1785, in ibid., 340–42; *AFC*, 6:267 n. 1. *Sentimental Journey*, 84–85.

38. Abigail Adams to William Stephen Smith, September 18, 1785, in ibid., 365–69; *AFC*, 6:369 n. 4.

39. William Stephen Smith to Abigail Adams, December 29, 1785, in ibid., 508–9.

40. Abigail Adams to Mary Cranch Smith, June 13, 1786, in ibid., 7:218.

41. Tanselle, *Royall Tyler*, 25; Mary Smith Cranch to Abigail Adams, September 24, 1786, in *AFC*, 7:342–43.

42. Mary Smith Cranch to Abigail Adams, October 9, 1785, in *AFC*, 7:358; "Printed Version of the 'Reynolds Pamphlet,'" in *The Papers of Alexander Hamilton*, ed. Harold C. Syrett et al., 27 vols. (New York: Columbia University Press, 1974), 21:238–69, 250, 252, 253.

43. Mary Smith Cranch to Abigail Adams, September 24, 1786, in *AFC*, 7:343.

44. Mary Smith Cranch to Abigail Adams, October 8, 1786, in ibid., 354–55.

45. Mary Smith Cranch to Abigail Adams, October 8, 1786, in ibid., 355, 356 n. 3; Tompkins, *Popular Novel*, 81–83.

46. Mary Smith Cranch to Abigail Adams, October 9, 1786, in *AFC*, 7:358.

47. Tanselle, *Royall Tyler*, 27–29; *AFC*, 7:344 n. 4.

48. Ryerson, "Limits of a Vicarious Life," 12; Abigail Adams to John Adams, January 28, 1797, in *My Dearest Friend*, 431; "I am glad . . . distraction" quoted in Gelles, *Abigail and John*, 160; John Adams to Abigail Adams, January 5, 1799, and December 17, 1798, in *My Dearest Friend*, 458, 455. Stewart Mitchell, who edited a number of letters in which Abigail expressed her feelings over the pain Smith caused Nabby, remarked that his "extravagance and long, silent absences from home were a source of great displeasure to Mrs. John Adams." *New Letters of Abigail Adams*, 111 n. 7. Jefferson's daughter Martha also married in haste, with horrible results. Gordon-Reed, *The Hemingses of Monticello*, 420–21, 603.

## CHAPTER 14

1. Caroline Robbins, *The Eighteenth-Century Commonwealthman: Studies in the Transmission, Development, and Circumstances of English Liberal Thought from the Restoration of Charles II until the War with the Colonies* (1959; Indianapolis: Liberty Fund, 2004), 82 (and see 84 and 99); Bailyn, *Ideological Origins of the American Revolution*; Wood, *Creation of the American Republic*; J. G. A. Pocock, *The Machiavellian Moment: Florentine Political Thought and the Atlantic Republican Tradition* (Princeton, NJ: Princeton University Press, 1975); Joseph Addison, *The Guardian*, no. 161 (Tuesday, September 15, 1713), in *Cato and Selected Essays*, 194–96; John Adams to Abigail Adams, December 2, 1781, in *AFC*, 4:250. For Richardson's political views, see Jocelyn Harris, *Samuel Richardson* (Cambridge: Cambridge University Press, 1987), 1–3 and chap. 4 passim; and Robbins, *Eighteenth-Century Commonwealthman*, chap. 6.

2. Wood, *Radicalism of the American Revolution*, 7, 235, 175; Waldstreicher, *In the Midst of Fetes*, 77; Knott, *Sensibility and the American Revolution*, 190. See, too, Gordon S. Wood, *Creation*

*of the American Republic, 1776–1787* (1969), with a new preface by the author (Chapel Hill: University of North Carolina Press, 1998), vii, x, ix, x; and Wood, *Radicalism of the American Revolution*, 216.

3. *Catalogue of the John Adams Library*; Adams, *Diary and Autobiography*, 1:23; Abigail Adams to Mercy Otis Warren [before February 27, 1774], in *AFC*, 1:97; Hagstrum, *Sex and Sensibility*, chap. 2; Wollstonecraft, *Vindication of the Rights of Woman*, 100, 102. See, too, Shaw, *Character of John Adams*, 219–21; and Haraszti, *Adams and the Prophets of Progress*, 162–64.

4. Barker-Benfield, *Culture of Sensibility*, 3, 148; Withey, *Dearest Friend*, 47.

5. Robbins, *Eighteenth-Century Commonwealthman*, xiv, 267–68, 289; Bolingbroke quoted in James Sambrook, *The Eighteenth Century: The Intellectual and Cultural Context of English Literature, 1700–1789* (London: Longman, 1986), 169; Adams, *Diary and Autobiography*, 1:35, 40; Ellis, *Passionate Sage*, 89; Abigail Adams to Mary Smith Cranch, December 9, 1784, in *AFC*, 6:14 and n. 3.

6. Zagarri, *A Woman's Dilemma*, 55, 141; Wollstonecraft, *Vindication of the Rights of Woman*, 137.

7. Barker-Benfield, "Mary Wollstonecraft"; John Adams to Abigail Adams, January 22, 1794, in *My Dearest Friend*, 351; Haraszti, *Adams and the Prophets of Progress*, chap. 11.

8. *Journal of Charles Woodmason*, 213–46; Eustace, *Passion Is the Gale*, chap. 8; Waldstreicher, *In the Midst of Fetes*, 79.

9. John Adams, "The Earl of Clarendon to William Pym, 13 January, 1766," in *Revolutionary Writings of John Adams*, 45–56, 45, 50.

10. John Adams, "Clarendon to Pym," 54–55; John Adams, *Defence of the Constitution of the United States*, in *Works of John Adams*, 6:185.

11. Eustace, *Passion Is the Gale*, 387; *Poems of Phillis Wheatley*, 125–26; Warren, "Oration," 103–6; Abigail Adams to Edward Dilly, May 22, 17[75], in *AFC*, 1:200–201.

12. The 1775 letter quoted in Eustace, *Passion Is the Gale*, 387, 433; Paine, *Common Sense*, 66.

13. Johnson, "Taxation No Tyranny," 412–13.

14. Ibid., 428, 429; Abigail Adams to Catherine Sawbridge Macaulay, [1774], in *AFC*, 1:177–78.

15. Norton, *Liberty's Daughters*, 166; Zagarri, *A Woman's Dilemma*, 66. For a history of this moral campaign, see Withington, *Toward a More Perfect Union*; Kerber, *Women of the Republic*, 362.

16. Griffitts quoted in Kerber, *Women of the Republic*, 39; Shields, *Civil Tongues*, 104; Barker-Benfield, *Culture of Sensibility*, 46, 48–49, 415 n. 55; Rourke, *American Humor*.

17. Mercy Otis Warren to Abigail Adams, January 19, 1774, in *AFC*, 1:91–92.

18. Burstein, *Sentimental Democracy*, 106, 63; Adams, *Novanglus*, 168–69.

19. John Adams to Abigail Adams, September 29, 1774, and July 7, 1775, in *AFC*, 1:163, 242.

20. Abigail Adams to Mercy Otis Warren, August 14, 1777, in ibid., 2:314.

21. Mercy Otis Warren to Hannah Storer Lincoln, September 3, 1774, quoted in Kerber, *Women of the Republic*, 84; Mercy Otis Warren, *History of the Rise, Process and Termination of the American Revolution*, 2 vols. (1805; Indianapolis: Liberty Classics, 1988), 1:xli–xlii. According to Nina Baym, Warren's application of the gendered language of sensibility contributed to its Americanization. Nina Baym, "Mercy Otis Warren's Gendered Melodrama of Revolution," *South Atlantic Quarterly* 90, no. 3 (Summer 1991): 531–54, 533.

22. John Adams to Abigail Adams, August 19, 1777, in *AFC*, 2:319; Abigail Adams to Catherine Sawbridge Macaulay, [1774], in ibid., 1:177.

23. Wood, *Americanization of Benjamin Franklin*, 113–14.

24. Abigail Adams to Elizabeth Smith Shaw, [March 1778], in *AFC*, 2:407; Abigail Adams to Mercy Otis Warren, August 14, 1777, in ibid., 313–14; New Jersey woman quoted in Kerber, *Women of the Republic*, 105; print from *Weatherman's Town and Country Almanack* reproduced in ibid., 72–73. See, too, Waldstreicher, *In the Midst of Fetes*, 31.

25. Foner, *American Freedom*, 38–39, 28; Ira Berlin, *Slaves without Masters: The Free Negro in the Antebellum South* (New York: Oxford University Press, 1974), chap. 1. For the apparent broadening of possibilities in the revolutionary era and the ensuing narrowing, see Kolchin, *American Slavery*, chap. 3; Jordan, *White over Black*, pt. 4.

26. Foner, *American Freedom*, xix, 15; Chris Jones, *Radical Sensibility: Literature and Ideas in the 1790s* (London: Routledge, 1993), 60; Jordan, *White over Black*, 386–91. See, too, François Furstenberg, *In the Name of the Father: Washington's Legacy, Slavery, and the Making of a Nation* (New York: Penguin, 2006), 70.

27. For Fiering and Crane, see chapter 1 above. For Edmundson, Tryon, and Sewall, see Davis, *Problem of Slavery*, 307, 371–74, 342–48, 210. (Davis's history of the intellectual origins of the rise of sentimentalism is in general agreement with what I say in chapter 1, but there are significant differences. See David, *Problem of Slavery*, 348–64.) Bishop Fleetwood's sermon is printed in Frank Klingberg, *Anglican Humanitarianism in Colonial New York* (Philadelphia: Church Historical Society, 1940), 195–212, 203, 206. Still more explicitly sentimental was Bishop Porteous's *Sermon to the SPG*, given in 1784, at one height of antislavery (London: J. F. and C. Rivington, 1784). The scope of the SPG in Britain's American mainland colonies in the earlier period is described in Humphreys, *Historical Account*. See, too, Jordan, *White over Black*, 180–83, 197–98.

28. *Spectator*, no. 215 (November 6, 1711), in Bond, ed., *Spectator*, 2:338–41; Davis, *Problem of Slavery*, 319, 357.

29. Davis, *Problem of Slavery*, 303; Anthony Benezet, *A Caution and Warning to Great Britain and Her Colonies in a Short Representation on the Calamitious State of the Enslaved Negroes in the British Dominions, Collected from Various Authors, and Submitted to Serious Consideration of All, More Especially of Those in Power* (Philadelphia: Henry Mill, 1766), 32, 22, 10.

30. "Journal of Josiah Quincy," 463.

31. *Letterbook of Eliza Lucas Pinckney*, 42 n. 9; Schulz, "Eliza Lucas Pinckney," 79; Schama, *Rough Crossings*, 57, 67, and chap. 3 passim; Woody Holton, *Forced Founders: Indians, Debtors, Slaves, and the Making of the American Revolution in Virginia* (Chapel Hill: University of North Carolina Press, 1999); "A Letter from P. H. to R. P. Hanover January 18th 1773," in *Milcah Martha Moore's Book*, 191–92. Jordan describes some of Pleasants's antislavery efforts in Virginia. His account also illustrates that slaveholding sentimentalism was expressed in unenforceable laws prohibiting the "gross maltreatment of slaves." *White over Black*, 357, 359 n. 43, 367–68.

32. Benjamin Rush, *An Address on the Slavery of Negroes in America* (1783; New York: Arno, 1969), which includes both Rush's "Address to the Inhabitants of the British Settlements on the Slavery of the Negroes in America" and his "A Vindication" (my quotations taken from p. 22 of the former and pp. 22–23 of the latter); Jean R. Soderlund, *Quakers and Slavery: A Divided Spirit* (Princeton, NJ: Princeton University Press, 1985), 172; Eustace, *Passion Is the Gale*, 252 (and see 255, 299). For a concise account of slavery and the black community in Philadelphia, see Gordon-Reed, *The Hemingses of Monticello*, 459–63.

33. Jefferson, *Notes on the State of Virginia*, 156, 177. Some of what follows first appeared in Barker-Benfield, "Ignatius Sancho vs. Thomas Jefferson: An Afro-British Ex-Slave's View of Sensibility Contrasted with a Slavemaster's View of Sensibility" (paper presented at the In-

ternational Conference of Eighteenth-Century Studies, University of California, Los Angeles, August 2003).

34. *Banneker's Almanack and Ephemera from the Year of Our Lord 1793* (reprint; Philadelphia: Rhetoric Publication, n.d.), n.p.

35. Jefferson, *Notes on Virginia*, 133–34; Foner, *American Freedom*, 40. And see Lewis, "'Of every age sex & condition,'" 129–30.

36. Jefferson, *Notes on Virginia*, 135.

37. Sypher, *Guinea's Captive Kings*, 149; *The Complete Works of Laurence Sterne*, ed. Wilbur L. Cross, 6 vols. (1904; New York: AMS, 1970), 3:xvi, xxii; Ignatius Sancho to Laurence Sterne, [July 21, 1766], in ibid., 4:117–19 (and also included in *Letters of the Late Ignatius Sancho*, 73–74); Sterne, *A Sentimental Journey*, 72–75; Peter Fryer, *Staying Power: The History of Black People in Britain* (London: Pluto Press, 1984), 75.

38. Betty Rizzo, introduction to Sarah Scott, *The History of Sir George Ellison* (1766; Lexington: University Press of Kentucky, 1996), ix–xlii, xii; Carreta, introduction, ix–xxxii, x–xiii; Arthur H. Cash, *Laurence Sterne, the Early and Middle Years* (London: Methuen, 1985), 84; Arthur H. Cash, *Laurence Sterne, the Later Years* (London: Methuen, 1986), 253–56; Laurence Sterne to Ignatius Sancho, [May 16, 1767], in *Complete Works of Laurence Sterne*, 4:147–48. Elizabeth Montagu, the famous bluestocking, had been a friend of Sterne's but broke with him over the clearly sexual sensibility of *Tristram Shandy*, in contrast to that of *Sir George Ellison*, which a reviewer suggested was derived from *Sir Charles Grandison*. Cash, *Laurence Sterne*, 200–209; reviewer cited in Rizzo, introduction, xii. See, too, Sypher, *Guinea's Captive Kings*, 150–51.

39. Scott, *Sir George Ellison*, 17, 3.

40. Rizzo, introduction, xxxvi–xxxvii; Sterne, *Sentimental Journey*, 177; Sypher, *Guinea's Captive Kings*, 268–87; Jordan, *White over Black*, 374; Soderlund, *Quakers and Slavery*, 4, 123, 150.

41. The editors of *AFC* remark on the popularity of Sterne among literate American colonists. See *AFC*, 3:xxiv. Thomas Jefferson to Peter Carr, August 10, 1787, in *Papers of Thomas Jefferson*, 12:15; "Lines Copied from Tristram Shandy by Martha and Thomas Jefferson," and note to same, both in *Papers of Thomas Jefferson*, 6:196–97; Linda Layne, "'He was a real baby with baby things': A Material Culture Analysis of Personhood, Parenthood and Pregnancy Loss," *Journal of Material Culture* 5, no. 3 (2000): 321–45, 332; Richardson, *Clarissa*, 4:421, 422; Jefferson, *Notes on Virginia*, 135.

42. Jefferson, *Notes on Virginia*, 135; Thomas Jefferson to Maria Cosway, October 12, 1786, *Papers of Thomas Jefferson*, 10:443–53.

43. Jefferson, *Notes on Virginia*, 134; Carreta, introduction, xii; Ignatius Sancho to Mr. S[tevenson], March 11, 1779, and October 24, 1777, in *Letters of the Late Ignatius Sancho*, 155, 103.

44. Jefferson, *Notes on Virginia*, 135, 137.

45. Ibid., 135–36; Ignatius Sancho to Mr. F[isher], January 1779, in *Letters of Ignatius Sancho*, 151–52.

46. Gouverneur Morris quoted in *The Records of the Federal Convention of 1787*, ed. Max Farrand, 3 vols. (New Haven, CT: Yale University Press, 1960), 2:222; Chase quoted in Garry Wills, *"Negro President": Jefferson and the Slave Power* (Boston: Houghton Mifflin, 2003), 51; Foner, *American Freedom*, 37. For context, see Jordan, *White over Black*, 322–25. Richard Brookhiser entitles his biography of Morris *Gentleman Revolutionary: Gouverneur Morris, the Rake Who Wrote the Constitution* (New York: Free Press, 2003).

47. Abigail Adams to John Adams, March 31, 1776, in *AFC*, 1:369; Abigail Adams to Ed-

ward Dilly, May 22, 17[75], in ibid., 202; Abigail Adams to William Stephens Smith, [September 18, 1785], in ibid., 6:366; *Letters of the Late Ignatius Sancho*, xi, xv, 180; Jordan, *White over Black*, 276.

48. Warren, *History of the American Revolution*, 1:110; other quotations from Jordan, *White over Black*, 378, 379.

49. *Journal and Correspondence of Miss Adams*, 2, pt. 2:163–84. The editors of the *Adams Family Correspondence* note that John Quincy Adams's remarks on *Othello* and Desdemona were "expressed in conversation with the actress, Fanny Kemble in 1833, recorded in 1835, and published in 1835 and 1836." *AFC*, 6:369 n. 9. Lawrence W. Levine, *Highbrow/Lowbrow: The Emergence of Cultural Hierarchy in America* (Cambridge, MA: Harvard University Press, 1988), 39. Gordon-Reed quotes and discusses both Abigail Adams's and John Quincy Adams's words on *Othello* at some length. See *Hemingses of Monticello*, 195–96.

50. Tocqueville, *Democracy in America*, vol. 2, bk. 3, chap. 1.

51. [Adams], "Report of a Constitution," 321; John Adams to Benjamin Waterhouse, August 7, 1805, in *AFC*, 3:226.

52. Abigail Adams to Lucy Cranch, April 2, 1786, in *AFC*, 7:126.

53. Ibid.; Barker-Benfield, "Sensibility in *The Federalist* and in Antifederalist Papers." See, too, Daniel W. Howe, "The Political Psychology of *The Federalist*," *William and Mary Quarterly*, 3rd ser., 44, no. 3 (July 1987): 485–509; Wood, *Radicalism of the American Revolution*, 215ff.; Waldstreicher, *In the Midst of Fetes*, 86–87; and Knott, *Sensibility and the American Revolution*, 113ff., 200, 238, 253.

54. Abigail Adams to John Thaxter, July 1, 1783, in *AFC*, 5:191–92; Abigail Adams to John Thaxter, October 20, 1783, in ibid., 262–63.

55. January 20, 1787, in ibid., 7:445–46. The quotations in the next paragraph are from this source as well. See, too, Abigail Adams to John Adams, December 30, 1786, in ibid., 413–45.

56. Barker-Benfield, *Culture of Sensibility*, 189–90; Abigail Adams to Mary Smith Cranch, July 28, 1784, in *AFC*, 5:402; Abigail Adams to Mary Smith Cranch, July 29, 1784, in ibid, 406. See, too, Abigail Adams to Mary Smith Cranch, August 2, 1784, in ibid., 417.

57. Abigail Adams 2nd to Elizabeth Cranch, September 4, 1784, in *AFC*, 5:428–29.

58. Abigail Adams to Mary Smith Cranch, February 20, 1785, in ibid., 6:67–69. The quotations in the next paragraph are from this source as well. A similar venturing out and then retreating to the deep-rooted, self-consciously American moralism that Abigail shared with her sisters can be seen in Lynne Withey's account of her "experiment" with sea bathing in England. Withey, *Dearest Friend*, 198–99.

59. Waldstreicher, *In the Midst of Fetes*, 74; Knott, *Sensibility and the American Revolution*, 195, 289–96.

60. Waldstreicher, *In the Midst of Fetes*, 76, 75; Knott, *Sensibility and the American Revolution*, chap. 5; Langford, *Polite and Commercial People*, 463–7.

61. Waldstreicher, *In the Midst of Fetes*, chap. 2.

62. Ibid., 143, 76, 77, 55, 83–84 (toasts quoted); Knott, *Sensibility and the American Revolution*, 231.

63. See chapter 5 above; Mary Beth Norton, "The Evolution of White Women's Experience in Early America," *American Historical Review* 89, no. 3 (1984): 593–619, 601–17; and Zagarri, *Revolutionary Backlasy*, 10, 156–57, 81, 7–8, 143. See, too, Lewis, "Of every age sex & condition," 132.

64. Waldstreicher, *In the Midst of Fetes*, 166, 82–84, 165–71; Zagarri, *Revolutionary Backlash*, 84–87, 125–29; Knott, *Sensibility and the American Revolution*, chap. 5 (Rush quoted 316).

65. Knott, *Sensibility and the American Revolution*, 138; Zagarri, *Revolutionary Backlash*, 79–

81 (for the "essentially" point, cf. 164–80). A contemporary of Knott's subjects was Elizabeth Fenimore Cooper, married to the entrepreneurial William. Neglected and alienated, she delighted in reading, "especially novels," while William's early efforts at upward mobility included voracious reading. Taylor writes that their daughter Hannah (1777–1800) seemed "the quintessential heroine of a sentimental novel," describing what he means in a section of his book entitled "Sensibility." See Taylor, *William Cooper's Town*, 21, 150, 22–26, 300–8.

66. Brackenridge quoted in Burstein, *Sentimental Democracy*, 176; John Quincy Adams to Abigail Adams Smith, March 17, 1794, in *Journal and Correspondence of Miss Adams*, 2, pt. 1:152. For a succinct account of the Jacobin/anti-Jacobin dimension of American politics in the 1790s, see Morton Borden, *Parties and Politics in the Early Republic* (Wheeling, IL: Harlan Davidson, 1967). For the politicization of sensibility, see Fliegelman, *Prodigals and Pilgrims*, 230–35.

67. Knott, *Sensibility and the American Revolution*, 262; Waldstreicher, *In the Midst of Fetes*, 99.

68. Furstenberg, *In the Name of the Father*, 8, 41, 36. Furstenberg here follows Waldstreicher in showing the identification of Washington with sensibility. See Waldstreicher, *In the Midst of Fetes*, 117–23.

69. Furstenberg, *In the Name of the Father*, 37; Kolchin, *American Slavery*, 59–62; Fliegelman, *Prodigals and Pilgrims*.

70. Furstenberg, *In the Name of the Father*, 37, 38, 42. See, too, Friedman, *Inventors of the Promised Land*, chap. 2.

71. Waldstreicher, *In the Midst of Fetes*, 161–63. Ladies attempted to cultivate sensibility in their Washington parlors (see Catherine Allgor, *Parlor Politics: In Which the Ladies of Washington Help Build a City and a Government* [Charlottesville: University Press of Virginia, 2000]), but they had done this in colonial parlors elsewhere since early in the century.

72. Friedman, *Inventors of the Promised Land*, 121–22, 126; Norton, *Liberty's Daughters*, 251–52; Kerber, *Women of the Republic*, 222–26, 282–83; Zagarri, *Revolutionary Backlash*, 40–43. See, too, Charles Michael Brown, "Mary Wollstonecraft; or, The Female Illuminati: The Campaign against Women and 'Modern Philosophy' in the New Republic," *Journal of the Early Republic* 15 (Fall 1995): 389–424; and Kelley, *Learning to Stand and Speak*, 238–42. Kerber notes that it was "likely" that Wollstonecraft "expressed what a larger public was already . . . willing to hear." *Women of the Republic*, 223–24.

73. A Lady, "On Pope's Characters of Women," *American Museum* 11 (1792), app. 1, pp. 13–15 (quotations in subsequent paragraphs are from this source); Wollstonecraft, *Vindication of the Rights of Woman*, 153.

74. Pope, "Epistle to a Lady," 44.

75. "Reflections on What Is Called Amiable Weakness in Woman," *Lady and Gentleman's Pocket Magazine* 1, no. 3 (1796): 174–79, 174, 175. Wollstonecraft pointed out that writers who argued on behalf of "the superiority of man," not simply in degree, but also in "essence," declared thereby that "the sexes ought not to be compared: man was made to reason, woman to feel: and that together, flesh and spirit, they make the most perfect whole, by blending happily reason and sensibility into one character." *Vindication of the Rights of Woman*, 154–55. For other references to Americans' citing Wollstonecraft, see n. 72 above; and Klinghoffer and Elkis, "'Petticoat Electors,'" 174, 177, 182.

76. *Only for the Eye of a Friend: The Poems of Annis Boudinot Stockton*, ed. Carla Mulford (Charlottesville: University Press of Virginia, 1995), 304–7. For Elias Stockton's support of women's rights, see Klinghoffer and Elkis, "'Petticoat Electors,'" 173–74.

77. John Adams to Abigail Adams, January 22, 1794, in *My Dearest Friend*, 351.

78. Barker-Benfield, *Culture of Sensibility*, 368–82.

79. Zagarri, *Revolutionary Backlash*, 170 (and see 107).

80. Ibid., 102–14; Knott, *Sensibility and the American Revolution*, 314–22.

81. Zagarri, *Revolutionary Backlash*, 77 and chap. 2 passim.

82. Klinghoffer and Elkis, "'Petticoat Electors,'" 191–92.

83. Lewis, "Of every age sex & condition," 129; Foner, *American Freedom*, 44, 74.

84. Rosemarie Zagarri, "Gender and the First Party System," in *Federalists Reconsidered*, ed. Doron Ben-Atar and Barbara B. Oberg (Charlottesville: University Press of Virginia, 1998), 118–34; Zagarri, *Revolutionary Backlash*, 6–7, 158; Catherine Allgor, *A Perfect Union: Dolley Madison and the Creation of the American Republic* (New York: Henry Holt, 2006), chap. 4.

85. Zagarri, *Revolutionary Backlash*, 157.

86. Waldstreicher, *In the Midst of Fetes*, 169; Gardner Child quoted in Zagarri, *Revolutionary Backlash*, 179.

87. "Sister Adelaide" quoted in Kelley, *Learning to Stand and Speak*, 18; Lewis, "The Republican Wife," 705.

88. Norton, *Liberty's Daughters*, 263–64; Foster quoted in Kerber, *Women of the Republic*, 241.

89. Withey, *Dearest Friend*, 190, 250, 266; Abigail Adams to Mary Smith Cranch, December 12, 1797, in *New Letters of Abigail Adams*, 117, 118; Bernard Fay, *The Two Franklins: Fathers of Democracy* (Boston: Little, Brown, 1933), 62–63, 98–99, 367, 368; Knott, *Sensibility and the American Revolution*, 286.

90. Abigail Adams to Mary Smith Cranch, December 12, 1797, in *New Letters of Abigail Adams*, 118–19, 119 n. 9. She wrote from Paris: "It may be in truth said, every man of this nation is an actor and every woman an actress." Abigail Adams to Hannah Quincy Lincoln Storer, January 20, 1785, in *AFC*, 6:65.

91. Quoted in Fay, *The Two Franklins*, 339. According to Fay, this unpublished letter is in the "family archives" of Franklin Bache, a descendant of the two Franklins. Ibid., 377. For John Quincy's and the young Bache's schooldays together, see Gelles, *Abigail and John*, 113.

92. For the popular reaction, see Waldstreicher, *In the Midst of Fetes*, 160ff.

93. Abigail Adams to Mary Smith Cranch, April 26, 1798, in *New Letters of Abigail Adams*, 164–66; Heather S. Nathans, *Early American Theater from the Revolution to Thomas Jefferson* (Cambridge: Cambridge University Press, 2003), 81, 79. See, too, Waldstreicher, *In the Midst of Fetes*, 130–31.

94. Nathans, *Early American Theater*, 81; Abigail Adams to Mary Smith Cranch, April 26, 1798, in *New Letters of Abigail Adams*, 164–65. For Abigail and the Alien and Sedition acts, see Gelles, *Abigail and John*, 247–50. Waldstreicher writes that the Alien and Sedition acts "represent a backlash against the rise of popular politics." Waldstreicher, "Founders Chic," 189.

95. Barker-Benfield, *Culture of Sensibility*, 262, 374; Sterne, *Sentimental Journey*, 96–100.

96. Abigail Adams to Mary Smith Cranch, April 26, 1798, in *New Letters of Abigail Adams*, 106.

97. Haraszti, *Adams and the Prophets of Progress*, 187.

98. Ibid., 187–88, 190, 234, 197, 198, 201, 208.

99. Ibid., 193–94, 211.

100. Abigail Adams to John Adams, December 15, 1798, in *My Dearest Friend*, 453; John Quincy Adams, "A Vision," in *Journal and Correspondence of Miss Adams*, 2, pt. 1:157–62; John Quincy Adams to Abigail Adams Smith, January 14, 1787, in *AFC*, 7:436.

101. Abigail Adams to John Adams, December 15, 1798, in *My Dearest Friend*, 413.

102. Kelley, *Learning to Stand and Speak*, 206–9, 77, 23; Heyrman, *Southern Cross*, 158–59.

103. Jack McLaughlin, *To His Excellency, Thomas Jefferson: Letters to a President* (New York:

Avon, 1991), 111, 129, and chap. 4 passim. In his first inaugural address, of March 4, 1861, Lincoln refers, e.g., to "civilized and humane jurisprudence," to "fraternal sympathies and affections," and to the well-known conclusion about "the mystic cords of memory," expressing a version of the nerve model, "our bonds of affection" transmitting "passion." One could similarly cite his October 16, 1854, speech "On the Kansas Nebraska Act," in which he asserted that "the great majority, south as well as north, have human sympathies, of which they can no more divest themselves than they can of their sensibility to physical pain." *Collected Works of Abraham Lincoln*, 4:271. For Lincoln's Kentucky idiom, see Rourke, *American Humor*, 152−55.

104. Kelley, *Learning to Stand and Speak*, 26; Bushman, *Refinement of America*, 81; *The Culture of Sentiment: Race, Gender and Sentimentality in Nineteenth-Century American*, ed. Shirley Samuels (New York: Oxford University Press, 1992), 4.

105. Caroll Smith-Rosenberg, "The Female World of Love and Ritual: Relations between Women in Nineteenth-Century America," *Signs* 1 (Autumn 1975): 1−29. Donald Meyer incorporates the insights of Smith Rosenberg and Rourke. See *Sex and Power*, xv, 256, and passim.

106. Samuel Langhorne Clemens [Mark Twain], *Adventures of Huckleberry Finn* (1885; New York: Norton, 1977), 84; "Sister Adelaide" quoted in Kelley, *Learning to Stand and Speak*, 157. Mark Twain's "satire of the towns along the banks" of the Mississippi includes a representation of "a residue of the eighteenth century cult of sensibility." Henry Nash Smith, *Mark Twain: The Development of a Writer* (Cambridge, MA: Belknap Press of Harvard University Press, 1962), 117. See, too, Lori Merish, *Sentimental Materialism: Gender, Commodity Culture and Nineteenth-Century American Literature* (Durham, NC: Duke University Press, 2000).

107. Mark Twain, *Adventures of Tom Sawyer* (1876; New York: Signet Classics, 1980), chap. 21; Clemens, *Huckleberry Finn*, 72. Rourke refers to "the sentimental strain" in Twain's work. See *American Humor*, 218.

# INDEX